62nd Yearbook of the Literacy Research Association

Edited by

Pamela J. Dunston
Susan King Fullerton
C. C. Bates
Pamela M. Stecker
Mikel W. Cole
Anna H. Hall
Danielle Herro
Kathy N. Headley
Clemson University

With the editorial assistance of

Heather McCrea-Andrews, Lead Assistant Editor
Clemson University

Tina Kautter, *Editor*
LRA Headquarters

Elaine York, *Graphic Designer*
LRA Headquarters

Lynn Hupp, *Executive Director*
LRA Headquarters

Published by
Literacy Research Association, Inc.
Altamonte Springs, Florida

2013

LRA Yearbook is published annually by the Literacy Research Association, 222 South Westmonte Drive, Suite 101, Altamonte Springs, FL 32714, Tel: (407) 774-7880.

POSTMASTER:

Send address changes to LRA Yearbook, 222 South Westmonte Drive, Suite 101, Altamonte Springs, FL 32714.

SUBSCRIPTIONS:

Institutions: $80 domestic or $90 foreign (surface), per year. Individuals who are LRA members in good standing as of October 1, 2013, will receive the *Yearbook* as part of their membership. Quantity discounts available for use in university or college courses. Write for information.

PERMISSION TO QUOTE OR REPRINT:

Quotations of 500 words or longer or reproductions of any portion of a table, figure, or graph, require written permission from the Literacy Research Association, and must include proper credit to the organization. A fee may be charged for use of the material, and permission of the first author will be secured.

PHOTOCOPIES:

Individuals may photocopy single articles without permission for nonprofit one-time classroom or library use. Other nonprofit educational copying, including repeated use of an individual article, must be registered with the Copyright Clearance Center, Academic Permission Service, 27 Congress Street, Salem, MA 01970, USA. *The fee is $1.25 USD per article, or any portion, or any portion thereof, to be paid through the Center. The fee is waived for individual members of the Literacy Research Association.* Consent to photocopy does not extend to items identified as reprinted by permission of other publishers, nor to copying for general distribution, for advertising or promotion, or for resale unless written permission is obtained from the Literacy Research Association.

Microfiche copy is available from ERIC Reproduction Service, 3900 Wheeler Avenue, Alexandria, VA 22304. The *Yearbook* is indexed in *Psychological Abstracts, Index to to Social Sciences & Humanities Proceedings and Educational Research Information Clearing House.* The LRA *Yearbook* is a refereed publication. Manuscripts must be original works that have been presented at the Annual Meeting of the Literacy Association, and that have not been published elsewhere.

ISSN
ISBN 1-893591-15-8
Printed in the United States of America

Literacy Research Association

Editorial Advisory Review Board

62nd Yearbook of the Literacy Research Association

Rhonda D. Goolsby
The University of Oklahoma

Michael F. Graves
University of Minnesota

AnnMarie Alberton Gunn
University of South Florida, St. Petersburg

Ying Guo
University of Cincinnati

Debra Gurvitz
National Louis University

Barbara Guzzetti
Arizona State University

Leslie Haas
Texas A & M University - Commerce

Juliet L. Halladay
University of Vermont

Lara J. Handsfield
Illinois State University

Rena M. Harris
Drexel University

Dawnelle Henretty
Oakland University

Jessica L. Hoffman
Miami University

Teri Holbrook
Georgia State University

Rosalind Horowitz
The University of Texas - San Antonio

SuHua Huang
Midwestern State University

Elizabeth M. Hughes
Duquesne University

Amy Hutchison
Iowa State University

Chinwe H. Ikpeze
St. John Fisher College, Rochester, NY

Ioney James
North Carolina Agricultural and Technical State University

Carole Janisch
Texas Tech University

Susan Kaye Jennings
University of Louisiana Monroe

Laura Jiminez
Boston University

Michelle Jordan
Arizona State University

Julie Justice
University of North Carolina at Chapel Hill

Catherine M. Kelly
St. Catherine University

Christopher Keyes
Shippensburg University

Debi Khasnabis
University of Michigan

Amy Suzanne Johnson Lachuk
University of South Carolina

Jayne C. Lammers
University of Rochester

Barbara Laster
Towson University

Judson Laughter
University of Tennessee, Knoxville

Georgette Lee
University of Illinois at Chicago

Christine M. Leighton
Emmanuel College

Kristin Lems
National-Louis University

Mellinee Lesley
Texas Tech University

Kimberly E. Lewinski
La Salle University

Tisha Y. Lewis
Georgia State University

Xiaoming Liu
Towson University

Minda Morren Lopez
Texas State University, San Marcos

Heather L. Lynch
Georgia State University

Judith T. Lysaker
Purdue University

Sara Mackiewicz
Clemson University

Jacquelynn Malloy
Anderson University

Erin E. Margarella
University of South Florida

Barbara Marinak
Mount St. Mary's University

Susan Marshall
Westminster College

Prisca Martens
Towson University

Nicole M. Martin
University of North Carolina at Greensboro

Pamela Mason
Harvard University

Laura May
Georgia State University

Sarah McCarthey
University of Illinois at Urbana-Champaign

DiAnn McDown
University of Central Oklahoma

Dot McElhone
Portland State University

Kathleen McGrath
Niagara University

Gae Lynn McInroe
McMurry University

Vicki McQuitty
Towson University

Carla K. Meyer
Appalachian State University

Gumiko Monobe
Kent State University

Nooreen Moore
The Pennsylvania State University Brandywine

Denise N. Morgan
Kent State University

Shadrack G. Msengi
Southern Illinois University Edwardsville

Charlotte Mundy
University of Alabama

Luz A. Murillo
The University of Texas Pan American

Kristina Najera
Temple University

Lori A. Norton-Meier
University of Louisville

William Ian O'Byrne
University of New Haven

Richard M. Oldreive
Bowling Green State University

Mary Ellen Oslick
University of Central Arkansas

Barbara Martin Palmer
Mount St. Mary's University

Jeanne R. Partore
Boston University

Seth Parsons
George Mason University

Patricia Paugh
University of Massachusetts at Boston

Kathryn S. Pegler
Eastern University

Julie L. Pennington
University of Nevada, Reno

Delores Perin
Teachers College, Columbia University

Monica Gordon Pershey
Cleveland State University

Ellen Pesko
Appalachian State University

Susan V. Piazza
Western Michigan University

Jodi Pilgrim
University of Mary Hardin-Baylor

Kelly Puzio
Washington State University

Margaret Lally Queenan
University of Bridgeport

Eric Rackley
Brigham Young University - Hawaii

Deborah K. Reed
The University of Texas at El Paso

Ray D. Reutzel
Utah State University

Kimberly A. Richard
Saint Joseph College

Leila Richey
George Mason University

Dana Robertson
University of Wyoming

Mary Roe
Arizona State University

Nancy L. Roser
University of Texas, Austin

Diane Santori
West Chester University

Roya Qualls Scales
Western Carolina University

Diane L. Schallert
University of Texas at Austin

Jenifer J. Schneider
University of South Florida, Tampa

Sarah E. Scott
University of Pittsburgh

Diane Carver Sekeres
University of Alabama

Peggy Semingson
The University of Texas at Arlington

Krishna Seunarinesingh
The University of the West Indies

Timothy Shanahan
University of Illinois at Chicago

Gerry Shiel
Educational Research Centre, St. Patrick's College, Dublin

Marjorie Siegel
Columbia University

Sunita Singh
Le Moyne College

Linda Smetana
California State University, East Bay

Patriann Smith
University of South Florida

Patrick H. Smith
The University of Texas at El Paso

Kristine Lynn Still
Cleveland State University

Mary E. Styslinger
University of South Carolina

Pamela Sullivan
James Madison University

Jeanne Swafford
University of North Carolina Wilmington

Sheelah Sweeny
Northeastern University

Anne Swenson Ticknor
East Carolina University

Guy Trainin
University of Nebraska Lincoln

Nancy Walker
University of La Verne

Allison E. Ward
George Mason University

Patricia A. Watson
Texas Women's University

Sarah Lohnes Watulak
Towson University

Sandra M. Webb
Georgia College & State University

Linda Wedwick
Illinois State University

Kimberly Welsh
Stephen F. Austin State University

Courtney West
Texas A & M

Joan A. Williams
Sam Houston State University

Amy M. Williamson
Angelo State University

Melissa B. Wilson
Tucson Unified School District

Angela M. Wiseman
North Carolina State University

Linda S. Wold
Loyola University Chicago

Rebecca Woodard
University of Illinois

Jo Worthy
University of Texas, Austin

Vivian Yenika-Agbaw
Pennsylvania State University, University Park

Bogum Yoon
State University of New York at Binghamton

Debby Zambo
Arizona State University

Katina Zammit
University of Western Sydney

Student Editorial Advisory Board

62nd Yearbook of the Literacy Research Association

James Nageldinger
Kent State University

Emily A. Nemeth
Ohio State University

Nicole Nesheim
North Carolina State University

Anita Nigam
Texas Tech University

SangHo Pang
Clemson University

Sohee Park
University of Delaware

Ashley N. Patterson
Ohio State University

Melissa Pendleton
North Carolina State University

Natasha Perez
Michigan State University

Nathan Phillips
Vanderbilt University

Grace Pigozzi
University of Illinois at Chicago

Jacquelynn S. Popp
University of Illinois at Chicago

Suzanne Porath
University of Wisconsin-Madison

Erin M. Ramirez
George Mason University

Lisa Reid
University of South Carolina

Audra K. Roach
University of Texas at Austin

Marla Robertson
Texas Woman's University

Aimee Rogers
University of Minnesota

Beth Rogowsky
Rutgers University

SangHee Ryu
Ohio State University

Leah K. Saal
Louisiana State University

Rachel Sanabria
Ohio State University

Lorien Chambers Schuldt
Stanford University

Ragina Shearer
University of North Texas

Stephanie A. Shelton
University of Georgia

Paulson Skerrit
University of Tennessee

Patriann Smith
University of South Florida

Caron St. Onge
University of Texas at Austin

Mary Pat Sullivan
University of Illinois at Chicago

Lina Sun
Saint Louis University

Laura Taylor
University of Texas at Austin

Andrea Tochelli
University of Buffalo, SUNY

Jamie Madison Vasquez
University of Illinois at Chicago

Tasha Anne Vice
Texas Tech University

Lorena Villarreal
University of Texas at San Antonio

Nora Vines
Appalachain State University

Aly Waibel
University of Arizona

Melanie Walski
University of Illinois at Chicago

Amber Warrington
University of Texas at Austin

Molly Trinh Wiebe
University of Texas at Austin

Ebony Wilkins
University of Illinois at Chicago

Becca Woodard
University of Illinois at Urbana-Champaign

Lindsay Woodward
Iowa State University

Student Editorial Assistants

62nd Yearbook of the Literacy Research Association

Jennifer Bostic
Clemson University

Tracy Butler
Clemson University

Lydia Callahan
Clemson University

Anastasia Homer
Clemson University

Emily Howell
Clemson University

Danielle Lavin
Clemson University

Jocelyn Long
Clemson University

Chris L. Massey
Clemson University

Heather J. McCrea-Andrews
Clemson University

Katelynn Monts
Clemson University

Sangho Pang
Clemson University

Julia Wilkins
Clemson University

62nd Yearbook of the Literacy Research Association

Section II: Adolescent, Disciplinary and Digital Literacies

Section III: Global Perspectives

Section IV: Teacher Development and Reflection

Section V: Writing

Preface

62nd Yearbook of the Literacy Research Association

Each year the LRA Conference includes an ever-widening range of topics presented in paper, roundtable, symposium, and alternative format sessions, as well as study groups. The 2012 conference was no exception. Attendees spent four days listening to, sharing, contemplating, critiquing, and discussing findings from cutting-edge research presented in stimulating sessions. The research presentations often stimulate our thinking and raise questions that lead us to design new research investigations to carry out at our own institutions in the coming year. This year, one question was posed by a well-known, long-time literacy researcher, to the *Yearbook* editor team following the conference that stimulated our thinking and left us with several questions. The researcher asked the editors if his/her manuscript stood a chance of being accepted for publication because, according to this individual, the current qualitative focus of our organization has made "publishing quantitative work nearly impossible in LRA venues." We were left with the following questions, which we pose for our members' consideration: Does LRA favor qualitative research over other research paradigms? If so, why? Do the proposals accepted for presentation at the annual meeting and papers published in the *Yearbook* provide evidence to support the researcher's claim? As editors, we assure LRA members, we work with the manuscripts that are submitted without regard to research paradigms represented. All submitted manuscripts are treated in the same manner and given the same consideration. We do wonder, however, why more quantitative research studies are not submitted for publication consideration in the *Yearbook*.

This year, Pamela Dunston, Susan Fullerton, C. C. Bates, Pamela Stecker, and Kathy Headley welcomed three new members to the Clemson editor team: Mikel Cole (language, literacy, and culture), Anna Hall (early childhood education and writing), and Danielle (Dani) Herro (digital media and learning). The team received 101 manuscripts for publication consideration. Three to five Editorial Advisory Review Board and Student-Editorial Advisory Review Board members reviewed each manuscript critically. Twenty manuscripts were accepted for publication for a 19.8% acceptance rate. Following procedures developed in previous years, accepted manuscripts were grouped by topic and leading scholars in the literacy field were invited to write introductions for individual sections. Each luminary wrote an introduction based on the manuscripts contained within his/her respective area. This year, the following luminaries honored us by introducing sections of the *Yearbook:* Judith Langer, Donna E. Alvermann, Patricia L. Anders, Kathleen A. Hinchman, and Douglas Fisher. As always, the luminaries' introductions offer thought-provoking insights that extend beyond the papers contained within each section of the *Yearbook*.

The 62nd *Yearbook* editors wish to thank our Dean, Dr. Lawrence Allen, and Interim Director of the Eugene T. Moore School of Education, Dr. Kathy N. Headley, for professional and financial support that made this work possible. Our doctoral student, Heather McCrea-Andrews, and her unflagging Master's degree student-assistant, Jocelyn Long, were the worker bees of the operation as they retrieved, printed, organized, and distributed manuscripts to the editor team. Heather and Jocelyn spent numerous hours working with manuscripts and editors throughout the review and editing process. We extend special thanks to Jenny Kasza from Technical Enterprises who offered guidance and support as responsibilities for LRA business and the *Yearbook* production were transferred to Kautter Management Group. We express sincere appreciation to Lynn Hupp, Executive Director (and Clemson University graduate, we might add!), and Elaine York, Graphic Designer, at KMG who collaborated with us throughout June and July to produce the *Yearbook*. Elaine worked tirelessly to maintain the consistency, integrity, and visual appeal of the *Yearbook*. We appreciate the thorough and timely work provided by members of the Editorial Advisory Review Board and Student Editorial Advisory Review Board in reviewing manuscripts on an especially tight schedule this year. Last but not least, we thank our student editorial assistants who conducted edits and APA checks on every manuscript printed on the pages herein.

Pamela J. Dunston
Susan King Fullerton
Lead Editors

The Literacy Research Association met November 28 to December 1, 2012, for the 62nd annual conference in San Diego, CA, at the Sheraton San Diego Hotel and Marina. The theme of this conference was *Investigating 21st Century Literacies: Exploring Uses of New Literacies,* a theme that reflects recent developments in new ways of learning literacy mediated by use of both print and digital tools, something that many conference presenters addressed in engaging ways, as reflected in the contributions to this year's 62nd *Yearbook* of the Literacy Research Association.

I was pleased that we set an all-time presentation and attendance record for this conference with 1,297 attendees and 258 sessions, making it the largest in LRA history. We received a record 871 proposals and accepted 623 of those proposals for an acceptance rate of 71.5%, resulting in 117 Paper Sessions with 345 individual papers, 42 Alternative Format Sessions, 85 Symposia, and 14 Roundtable Sessions with 138 Individual Roundtables. The overall response on the conference evaluation survey was positive with 90% of attendees rating the conference as exceeding or greatly exceeding expectations.

While our attendance record may be attributed to the allure of sunny San Diego in December, I also believe that it reflects the vibrancy of LRA as an organization whose members value attending the conference to share their research as well as maintain their close professional relationships with colleagues, relationships that, for many members, stretch back for decades. At the same time, we also had a lot of new first-time attendees, whom we hope will join the ranks of veteran conference attendees.

One new feature of this conference was the use of the All Academic online proposal system that served to streamline the proposal and review process, as well as the use of a SCHED app (http://lra2012.sched.org) for conference planning. Another change involved shifting the Study Groups from the previous early morning hour to the noon hour, a move that received a positive response on the conference evaluation survey. Thanks to all of the Study Group organizers for doing an excellent job selecting topics and speakers for these Study Groups, which continue to be a popular feature of the conference.

We also recorded about half of the conference sessions thanks to students from the Health Science High School (HSHS), San Diego, a project organized by Doug Fisher, San Diego State University, and Jeff Woods, from HSHS. These audio recordings are available for downloading from our Box.com site at http://tinyurl.com/kuh9yqy (to identify individual speakers and titles for these sessions, download the conference program at http://www.literacyresearchassociation.org/pdf/Final%20Program.pdf or use the SCHED app: http://lra2012.sched.org). LRA members are currently using these audio recordings as class assignments for their students.

We also had a number of inspiring plenary session presentations. Robert Jiménez delivered the Presidential Address describing the need for and value of culturally responsive instruction that builds on the rich, diverse experiences and knowledge of non-dominant groups for literacy learning. His focus on the value of diversity has become a major focus of literacy research, as well as an impetus for LRA itself to push for greater diversity as evident in the fine work of the Ethnicity, Race and Multilingualism Committee; the History, International, and Multilingual/Transcultural Literacies ICG; and the S.T.A.R. mentor program for new literacy research scholars of color.

In her address, Linda Gambrell, 2012 Oscar Causey Award winner, reviewed existing and needed research on motivation and engagement in reading as critical to improving reading instruction and fostering students' reading interests. Consistent with the conference theme, David Barton shared ways of conducting research on social aspects of local digital literacies in communities of practice such as Flickr image-sharing groups. Mimi Ito described ethnographic research on adolescents' uses of digital literacies to engage in creative media production, research supporting the value of adopting a Connected Learning (http://connectedlearning.tv) approach to literacy instruction that builds on students' outside-of-school uses of digital literacies for learning in schools. In his Saturday Integrative

Research Review, Kevin Leander analyzed examples of how innovative uses of physical and virtual spaces serve to promote learning through enhancing student engagement. (Videos of these plenary presentations are available on the LRA website https://literacyresearchassociation.org under 2012 Conference.)

We also had a number of inspiring presentations by Area Chairs Invited Speakers including Diane DeFord, University of South Carolina (Area 2); Pam Grossman, Stanford University (Area 4); Jonathan Osborne and Sam Wineburg, Stanford University; Jennifer J. Wimmer and Roni Jo Draper, Brigham Young University (Area 6); Olga A. Vásquez and Alison Wishard Guerra, University of California, San Diego; Belinda Flores and Ellen Riojas Clark, University of Texas, San Antonio Academy for Teaching Excellence (Area 8); and Roy Pea, Stanford University (Area 10). And, we had a successful Graduate Students'/Newcomers' Breakfast to inform graduate students and new attendees about ways to become involved in LRA activities and committees, including Field Council activities organized by Jennifer Jones, Field Council Chair.

We also honored LRA members for their research and contributions to the field and LRA. Leah Katherine Saal, Louisiana State University, received the J. Michael Parker Award for Contributions to Adult Literacy Research for her paper, "I'm Still a Slave: A Literacy Lesson from an Adult 'Burgeoning' Reader." Melody Zoch, University of North Carolina, Greensboro, received the Student Outstanding Research Award for "'Growing and Good Stuff,' Crafting Theoretically Defensible Literacy Teaching While Supporting Students With Text Preparation."

The Oscar S. Causey Award was given to Jerry Harste, Professor Emeritus, Indiana University, for his many contributions to literacy research; Jerry will deliver his Oscar S. Causey Award address at the 2013 conference in Dallas. Michael Halliday, Foundation Professor of Linguistics at the University of Sydney, Australia, received the Distinguished Scholar Lifetime Achievement Award. And, for her many years of service to LRA, including serving as Past President, the Albert J. Kingston Award was given to Patricia Edwards, Michigan State University.

The Early Career Achievement Award was awarded to Kristen H. Perry, University of Kentucky, for establishing an impressive research record early in her career, including articles in the Journal of Literacy Research, Reading Research Quarterly, and Research in the Teaching of English. Leigh Hall, University of North Carolina, Chapel Hill; Leslie Burns, University of Kentucky; and Elizabeth Carr Edwards, Georgia Southern University, received the Edward B. Fry Book Award for their book, *Empowering Struggling Readers: Practices for the Middle Grades.*

As conference chair, I want to thank all LRA members who worked on this conference — my co-chair, Arlette Willis; session chairs and discussants; Area Chairs who organized proposal reviews; members who served as reviewers; Award Committee members who vetted nominations for awards; Doug Fisher who arranged for school bus transportation to downtown restaurants; Tom Bean and Frank Serafini who provided musical entertainment on Thursday night; and the many members who prepared engaging presentations. All of you played a critical role in making the 2012 conference a success.

I would also like to thank the LRA *Yearbook* editors, Pamela Dunston, Susan King Fullerton, C. C. Bates, Kathy Headley, and Pamela Stecker, Clemson University, for their excellent work during their three-year tenure on the previous 60th and 61st *Yearbooks,* and on this 62nd *Yearbook.*

I'm very much looking forward to the 2013 conference co-chaired by Arlette Willis and Janice Almasi at the brand-new Omni Hotel in downtown Dallas. Arlette and Janice have put together an engaging group of plenary speakers for the 2013 conference. I do hope that members will continue to attend and support our conference given its centrality to LRA's work and mission. See you all in Dallas.

Richard Beach
President, Literacy Research Association
2012-2013

Dr. Patricia A. Edwards

Albert J. Kingston Award

The annual Albert J. Kingston Service Award honors an LRA member for distinguished contribution of service to the Literacy Research Association. Established in 1985, the award was designed to honor the work of NRC/LRA's 1965-1966 president, Albert J. Kingston. Professor Kingston, an educational psychologist and reading specialist, played a major role in the development of the National Reading Conference.

Dr. Patricia A. Edwards, Distinguished Professor of Teacher Education at Michigan State University, is the 2012 recipient of the Albert J. Kingston Award of the Literacy Research Association.

Dr. Edwards received her B.S. in Elementary Education from Albany State University (Albany, Georgia); M.S. in Elementary Education from North Carolina A&T University, Ed. Specialist in Reading Education from Duke University; and Ph.D. in Reading Education from the University of Wisconsin-Madison. Dr. Edwards has taught in public schools and universities for over 30 years. Her scholarship, which focuses on literacy issues for children and families, is prominent and extensive as evidenced in her voluminous publications of articles and books, as well as two highly acclaimed family literacy programs. In addition to her commitment to excellence in teaching and scholarship is Dr. Edwards' profound dedication to service, exemplified in a lifelong history of giving.

In 1983, Dr. Edwards attended her first LRA/ NRC in Austin, TX, during which she quickly observed that only three people of color attended the conference. From that first conference to the present, she has worked diligently in cultivating a more diverse LRA membership. Through her warm and welcoming spirit, Dr. Edwards has reached out to new members of color, as she does with all LRA members, graciously sharing her time and expertise as a mentor.

Dr. Edwards' service efforts within LRA are quite extensive. She has served on Field Council, the Student Outstanding Research Award Committee, the Oscar Causey Award Committee, and as an Area Chairperson for the conference. As a reviewer, she has reviewed hundreds of conference proposals and manuscripts for the LRA *Yearbook*.

Dr. Edwards' most visible service role to LRA was as President of the organization, with her accomplishments as president substantiated by their endurance. That is, Dr. Edwards created the *Manual* for Area Chairs, which streamlined the process of providing direction and guidelines to conference Area Chairs. And, under her presidency, Kathryn Au created the Multicultural Committee as a forum to officially welcome scholars of color. As a member, president, and past-president, Dr. Edwards has worked continuously to recruit and support members of color in LRA.

We extend our thanks and congratulations to Dr. Patricia A. Edwards, recipient of the 2012 Albert J. Kingston Award, in recognition of her service to the Literacy Research Association.

Marla H. Mallette, Recipient, Albert J. Kingston Award (2011)
Donna E. Alvermann, Chair,
Albert J. Kingston Award Committee (2011-2013)

Jerome C. Harste

Oscar S. Causey Award

The Oscar S. Causey Award is presented each year at the annual conference to honor outstanding contributions to literacy research. Dr. Oscar S. Causey, the founder of the National Reading Conference (now the Literacy Research Association), was the chair of the Executive Committee for several years, and served as President from 1952 to 1959. Individuals who are honored with this prestigious award have conducted and published research that generates new knowledge and is deemed substantial, significant, and original. The individual is also recognized as a leader in the conduct and promotion of literacy research.

Dr. Jerome C. Harste, the 2012 Oscar S. Causey Award honoree, is the Martha Lea and Bill Armstrong Chair Emeritus of Teacher Education at Indiana University. He earned his B.S. from St. Cloud State College and the M.A. and Ph.D. at the University of Minnesota. He was an elementary classroom teacher in Minnesota and then taught for the Peace Corp in Bolivia. Dr. Harste came to Indiana University in 1971, was awarded the Armstrong Chair in 1997, and retired from this same institution in 2006.

Dr. Harste has published significantly and substantially across varied topics such as teacher education, reading comprehension, early literacy, reading-writing relationships, semiotics, critical literacy, and socio-psycholinguistic processes in reading, writing, thinking, and learning. His ongoing work in classrooms with teachers has provided new and critical insights about literacy learning processes and environments. Out of his classroom work has emerged curricular processes and materials related to reading comprehension, the authoring cycle, literature circles, writing, inquiry, and multimodal learning.

At the same time, Dr. Harste has provided invaluable service to the profession. He has been president the National Reading Conference, the National Council of Teachers of English, the Whole Language Umbrella, and the National Conference on Research in Language and Literacy. He also served on the Board of Directors of the International Reading Association and chaired numerous committees within the aforementioned organizations. Dr. Harste has published numerous influential books, and his work has appeared in scholarly journals including *Reading Research Quarterly, The Elementary School Journal, Journal of Literacy Research, Research in the Teaching of English, Reading Research and Instruction, Yearbook of National Reading Conference,* and practitioner journals such as *Language Arts, Primary Voices, English Education,* and *The Reading Teacher.*

Dr. Harste has received professional honors and awards that attest to the breadth of his involvement and commitment to all matters of literacy. In 1997, he was elected to the Reading Hall of Fame. He was also awarded the Albert J. Kingston Award from the National Reading Conference, the David H. Russell Research Award for Outstanding Contributions to the Teaching of English from the National Council of Teachers of English (NCTE), a Special Service Award from the International Reading Association, the Lifetime Achievement Award from the Whole Language Umbrella Conference of NCTE, and in 2008 was named Outstanding Language Educator for lifetime achievements by the Elementary Section of NCTE. Professor Harste's legacy extends to his mentorship of many doctoral students; over two dozen have received dissertation awards from professional organizations. Jerome C. Harste's lifetime of impressive scholarship and service has made far-reaching contributions to his profession and to children's learning.

Susan King Fullerton, *LRA Yearbook* Editor

Bill Teale, Chair, Oscar S. Causey Award Committee

Optimal Outfitting: The Need for Culturally Responsive Instruction

Robert T. Jiménez
Vanderbilt University

Abstract: Culturally responsive pedagogy is an exciting innovation that has yet to transform the literacy learning of students from diverse backgrounds. Unresolved issues involve the identification of promising cultural and linguistic practices, their transformation into instruction, and convincing demonstration of effectiveness. In this presentation, I explore these issues and provide examples of the ways that CRP more fully engages students, involves them in disciplinary modes of reasoning, and empowers them as learners.

INTRODUCTION AND ORGANIZING PRINCIPLE

In 1967 when I was 12 years old, my uncle gave me a ride on a Yamaha motorcycle and I haven't stopped wanting to ride since. Anyone who knows me is aware of my obsession and my passion. I find motorcycles and everything related to them to be fascinating, compelling, and incredibly satisfying. As such I read about them, I write about them, and, of course, I ride them whenever I can. Right now, I will focus my comments on just one characteristic of motorcycles that I will use as my organizing principle and central metaphor. Although they move me in almost mystical ways without the limitations imposed by gravity, space and place, they do have certain limitations. One of the foremost is their lack of ability to carry much more besides the rider, and on occasion, a passenger. Because my primary use of motorcycles has always been to travel, that meant I had to figure out ways to carry necessary items. As you can see from my pictures of motorcycles, they almost never come equipped with the means to carry things.

This limitation means that motorcycles, even before you ever buy one, must be modified to accomplish their owner's purposes. If you go to any online listserv designed for motorcyclists and their machines, a great deal of the interaction involves how to modify the bikes. These exchanges involve everything from finding seats that are more comfortable to new suspension systems to handlebars. Almost always, though, people want to know where they can find high quality gear to carry things with them. This gear usually consists of saddlebags and often a kind of trunk that sits on the luggage carrier. These pieces are usually ridiculously expensive, typically costing between $200 for the most basic items, to $1500 or $2000 dollars for the more durable ones, and sometimes more depending on the manufacturer and the quality of the items.

The point is that if you ride a motorcycle and do any kind of traveling, you will eventually want luggage and that luggage can be difficult to find, pay for, and sometimes its utility will be an issue. For example, some luggage is watertight and some is not. Typically, one is

1

best served if the manufacturer of the motorcycle makes aftermarket pieces specific to the motorcycle in question. On the previous page is a picture of my latest and favorite motorcycle is built for long distance travel on both paved and unpaved roads. These are the panniers that I bought for this machine. They carry a lot and they even double as beer coolers!

If we think of teaching as a kind of vehicle that can take us where we want to go in terms of student learning, then I hope you'll understand that some modifications, additions, and possibly transformations are necessary for an optimal experience. Some outfitting is required to arrive at our destinations with everything that we want to take with us. This outfitting requires a good deal of specialized knowledge concerning teaching itself. At times, we need to radically redesign our instructional approaches or spend a good deal of time scouting out better alternatives. The kinds of choices that are available, the means to acquire them, the special tools that are required to make them a part of one's instructional repertoire, and the means to assess their usefulness are all part of the calculus. I like to think of culturally responsive instruction as a customized and effectively modified teaching approach.

The most important part of optimal outfitting, however, is that we need to talk to the most knowledgeable people who can help us achieve our goals. When it comes to teaching and learning, *those who are most knowledgeable and who have the most invested in the children that our instruction is designed to reach are students' families and the communities they live in.* These are the primary people who can help us to best optimize the experience. These are also the people whose insights, understandings, ways of thinking and living have the most to offer us with respect to the interactions, communication, and relationships that we hope to have with their children. In short, we need to heed Angela Valenzuela's directive in her amazing ethnography of a high school in Houston, TX, *Subtractive Schooling:* "We must become students of the history of subordination of the communities we wish to research or teach." Knowledge alone does not change things but without it, it is difficult to marshal the necessary energy, effort, and activity to bring about desired outcomes.

In my presentation today, some of my guiding questions included: What is culturally responsive pedagogy? Why is CRP needed? How did CRP emerge historically and what historical elements figure into how it might be conceptualized? How do we understand or support CRP through research? What issues, questions, and controversies does it address or inspire? And, what are its likely benefits and what will be lost if we fail to consider it?

BACKGROUND AND CONTEMPORARY DEVELOPMENTS

Serious students of the history of subordination of different groups understand that their primary goal is to disrupt said subordination. Culturally responsive pedagogy disrupts by rejecting deficit perspectives and embracing what Paris (2012) calls a resource orientation towards students' cultures and their communities. A resource orientation examines students' cultural and linguistic repertoires of practice and then uses these to modify existing curriculum and instruction for the purpose of promoting academic achievement. In a sense, CRP is about critically examining the existing curriculum and finding ways to supplement and expand it to promote equity. At times, CRP requires a complete re-think of the entire operation of schooling. Let me make what I believe is an important point. The curriculum ought never to be ossified. It needs to be constantly challenged, critiqued, and examined to determine whether it is achieving its intended purposes. More importantly, what gets taught is a field of struggle where multiple interested parties advocate for their own and others' interests. In other words, these struggles are not neutral; some interests are able to better advance their causes than others.

I have always found it pleasurable to learn how people in previous eras and places thought about and actually used written language to support their cultural and ideological beliefs, as well as their economic and political systems. Historical work has the power to show us alternative ways of organizing the world we live in. The way things are now isn't the way they must be and historical work provides us with alternatives. It also provides us with lots of bad examples that we should examine and avoid if at all possible. During our last winter break, I read a book called *Literacy and Power in the Ancient World*, that described schooling and literacy just before the end of the Roman Empire. What I found was that literacy played an incredibly important role in that society. In fact, it was literacy that held what was left of the empire together. Of course, it was a very specific set of literacy practices, and I would venture to guess that many of us would find these practices, at the same time, both familiar and quite alien.

Students of that time, the vast majority of them the children of the elites, were required to thoroughly master a small set of classics in either Latin or Greek. They spent 5 to 10 years in that pursuit, learning what was considered 'correct' Latin or Greek. Correct language meant learning all the rules of phonology, morphology and those involving parts of speech. They internalized these rules so that when they spoke and wrote, they would be recognized as members of the elite ruling classes. This type of education was required for any official position in the empire even though it provided little to no support for successfully performing these jobs. The writer of this history, Peter Heather, points out that "In late antiquity, absolutely correct language was everything; any linguistic failing made it clear that a person had socially dubious origins" (p. 193). Notice the links between schooling, inequity, and societal organization. I don't think it's an accident that today there is renewed emphasis on what we consider to be the literary canon. For many, the language used within canonical texts serves as the standard for correct language. The use of or deviance from literary language allows elites to recognize one another, and also provides a so-called 'neutral' mechanism to eliminate non-elites from consideration for any important position. Although I applaud efforts to strengthen the curriculum and to clarify instructional goals, we must make sure that movements such as the Common Core set of Standards do not exclude cultural and linguistic diversity from its purview.

History does not always repeat itself but history does offer us portraits of what different societal arrangements looked like and the outcomes produced from such arrangements. I think the parallels are painfully obvious. Rather than attempting to create or define an all-powerful curriculum to serve as a source of authority, CRP points us in a different direction back toward students and their communities as sources of information. By focusing our attention on students and their communities, we are much more likely to encounter more robust, current, and recent connections to economic, political, and social macro structures, which in turn are more likely to be relevant to the life worlds of the students we teach.

Basil Bernstein (1990) pointed out that the more rigid the boundaries between curricular subjects, the less access to learning on the part of minority or marginalized groups. Part of his reasoning involves what he calls recontextualization, or the process of taking information out of its original context and reformatting it for the purpose of instruction. Since dominant groups control this process young people from diverse backgrounds find both the content and the ways in which it is taught to be alienating. Recontextualization requires that the original context for information or practices is stripped away, and this results in obscuring the ideological and class-based origins of curricular information. This is what Bernstein calls the pedagogical device, and he claims that it shapes consciousness through its distributive, recontextualizing and evaluative rules. So then, a focus on what Gutierrez and Vossoughi (2011) call "students' histories of involvement in literacy practices in schools and elsewhere, rather than on their linguistic deficiencies…" (p. 103) provides a means to turn this process on its head and provide students a chance to acquire new information through the medium of practices that are more familiar, albeit recontextualized for use in school.

Many literacy scholars have recognized that a major shift in thinking was necessary to see useful and desirable information within the cultural and linguistic practices of children from minority backgrounds. For example, Carol Lee understood that such a move would subvert what Bourdieu (1998) called the "obviousness of ordinary experience." She recommends the identification of what she calls "cultural data sets," that are language practices familiar to students and that require similar higher order thinking skills as the "disciplinary modes of reasoning" used by experts in different content areas. She (2008) recommends privileging the "language resources that students bring from their everyday linguistic practices and repertoires outside school" (p. 275). Other scholars have recommended culturally responsive pedagogy (CRP) as a means to more *ethically, equitably, and effectively* teach students, particularly those from diverse backgrounds (Cummins, 2000; Gay, 2010; Ladson-Billings, 1995; Lee, 2007; Moll, 2010; Nieto, 2000). CRP is an approach that "teaches to and through [students'] personal and cultural strengths, their intellectual capabilities, and their prior accomplishments" (Gay, 2010, p. xxiii, p. 26). Moll (2010) claims that "the social, cultural, and linguistic processes of diverse communities [are] the most important resources for educational change" (pp. 451). Cummins (2000) argues that the difficulties many students experience in school are due to the fact that educators fail to "build on the wide variety of culturally specific literacy events (oral and written) that children experience in their homes" (p. 75). And he goes on to say that "the failure of the mainstream educational reform movement to acknowledge the sociopolitical roots of student failure is a major factor in the limited impact that this research has exerted to date on the process of reversing educational inequality" (p. 249). CRP then, involves changes to the curriculum, the methods of instruction, and the sociopolitical positioning of both students and teachers. Again, these insights beg the question as to whether the system can be modified and adapted to the extent necessary to achieve equity and excellence, or whether we need to revamp the entire system. These are open questions.

I should point out, however, that some have questioned whether the ways of thinking, being, and speaking found within working-class communities are, or could be, legitimate points of departure for thinking about both the content and form of instruction. Let me remind you that Lee (2007) recognized the radical nature of such a move. Keep in mind that many innovations in areas such as cognitive science built new understandings of how people comprehend written language on the routines, ways of interacting with text, and the thought patterns of primarily white, middle to upper middle class academics. Unless we believe that only one segment of the population has a monopoly on cognitive organization, it makes sense that other patterns might yield fruitful approaches. For example, one way to think about summarization is that it reflects mainstream desire to 'own' information. Ownership and acquisition are leading activities within mainstream culture. Within other cultural groups, much more value is given to learning and understanding the importance of how individuals are connected to one another through kinship ties, friendship ties, and work related relationships. It stands to reason that a reading comprehension instructional approach that showed students how to build spatial-graphic understandings of character relationships or those between events, might be equally useful.

A bit of caution is required, however. There are those who note that "informal learning leads people to form naïve and misconceived ideas at odds with disciplinary knowledge" (pp. 25-26) and also others who "view informal situations as characterized by a lack of thinking and the consumption of a degraded popular culture" (see Bransford, et al., 2006, p. 26). For example, many college graduates believe that the seasons occur because the earth gets closer to the sun at some points during its annual orbit. Obviously, there is need for caution when identifying and recruiting the linguistic and cultural practices for use in the classroom. Considerable thought is required every step of the way and empirical testing is needed to establish a practice's usefulness.

INFLUENCE OF DEMOGRAPHIC SHIFTS AND BACKLASH POLITICS: RETHINKING STUDENTS AND THEIR COMMUNITIES

While the curriculum has always been a contentious site of struggle, the question of who students are also has often been assumed and taken for granted. The academic achievement of students from diverse backgrounds has typically been seen as an anomaly that warrants concern but not often a rethinking of how the system as a whole operates. The real problem, of course, is that the U.S. has large numbers of students for whom equitable instruction has only rarely been provided, many of these are students learning English. In other words, the same resources in terms of funding, curriculum, and experienced and well-prepared teachers are not often available for students learning English. The only outcome reported, though, is that the academic achievement of students learning English is lower than that of mainstream students. For example, one only has to look at the funding disparities discussed by writers such as Jonathan Kozol (1991) in his book, *Savage Inequalities*, for evidence of this phenomenon. In addition, these students have been taught under conditions where they were viewed negatively, where little was known or understood concerning how they differed from mainstream students, and where they were often exposed to a curriculum that denied their existence. In other words, it is only recently that educators and schools have been held accountable for the academic achievement of students from non-mainstream backgrounds, one of the few celebrated outcomes of NCLB.

Evidence of the lower academic performance of students learning English has been produced for over a century now. For example, the Dillingham Commission in 1911 found that 43% of children whose parents were from a non-English speaking background were at least two years behind in school as compared to 28% of native white children. Other reports showed that no changes occurred between 1901 and 1933. Furthermore, the Dillingham Commission claimed that 51% of German origin children were a year or more behind, that 60% of Russian Jewish children were behind and that 77% of Italian children were behind. Later in 1926, 66% of the children of immigrants dropped out of high school while the rate was 36% for native white students. Joel Perlmann (2002) in a reexamination of earlier reports and census data showed that only 15 percent of Italian and 17 percent of Polish men graduated from high school during the decade 1911-1920, while 28 percent of NWNP males (native white of native parents) and 35 percent of NWNP females graduated. Whatever else one may think about the earlier waves of immigrants, they struggled mightily in US public schools.

At least as important, however, as the actual rates of immigrant student achievement is the context in which those numbers appear. For example, several scholars of U.S. immigration (Daniels, 2002; Higham, 1955) have pointed out that during times of optimism and confidence about the future, immigrants tend to be tolerated and mostly ignored whereas during difficult times, particularly difficult economic times, immigrants are the targets of punitive legislation. One of the goals of the Dillingham Commission was to provide a discursive justification for much more restrictive immigration policies and so it is not surprising that the intellectual and academic progress of the children of immigrants was called into question. The prevailing views of immigrants can often be determined from the legislation aimed at them. For example, an 1891 statute… barred the immigration of "all idiots, insane persons, paupers or persons likely to become a public charge, persons suffering from a contagious disease, persons who have been convicted of a felony or other infamous crime or misdemeanor involving moral turpitude," and "polygamists…" (Daniels, 2002, p. 274). The association between immigrants and criminality, deviance and disease are some of the more enduring stereotypes about immigrants in our culture.

Not only were these negative characterizations widespread, but the most important stereotype, for our purposes, was that of illiteracy. Higham (1955) argued that the demands for a literacy test, as a means of restricting the admission of undesirable persons from the nation was seen as a 'highly respectable cultural determinant.' Of interest is that in the popular mind, literacy and its absence was associated with specific racial and dominant groups, probably first established with respect to African Americans. Illiteracy was conflated with poverty and ethnic/racial background. It was simply assumed that a literacy requirement would bar the entrance of most immigrants. Unfortunately for the restrictionists, the courts interpreted literacy to mean the ability to read any language and since literacy rates had increased a great deal in much of Europe since the earlier peak periods of immigration, few were denied access to the U.S. because of its absence. Eventually, however, the restrictionists won the day in terms of closing the U.S. to most immigrants through the Johnson-Reed Act of 1924. This act limited the number legally allowed to enter the country to 2% of each sending nation's total in the U.S. at the time of the 1890 census. This had the effect of all but denying access to eastern Europeans, Jews, and many southern Europeans. Of course, the pattern for shutting the doors to future immigrants already had been set in 1882 with the Chinese Exclusion Act. Daniels (2002), claims that this act, once thought of as an aberration, was actually "the hinge on which American immigration policy turned" (p. 271). It provided the justification for barring entrance to entire groups, historically determined on the basis of racial/ethnic/linguistic background.

Even so, there was then, and now, cause for hope. Back then, there were a few who began to recognize the contributions made by immigrants to U.S. society. One of the most famous of these was Jane Adams who argued that the different groups made cultural contributions and that these contributions could be the basis for better integrating immigrants into U.S. society. The notion of cultural contributions presaged the idea of a need to learn about the different immigrant groups.

THE ROOTS OF CULTURALLY RESPONSIVE PEDAGOGY: RETHINKING THE CURRICULUM

At this point, I wish to discuss the work and ideas of only a small number of individuals who I believe have provided us with an important legacy dealing with culturally responsive pedagogy. I realize that I am selectively sampling only a very small number of those who produced important work in this area. In addition to asking several of my colleagues for feedback on this paper and presentation, I asked some of my closest colleagues for their feedback. I was fortunate to have Rich Milner as a colleague and to be able to ask him whose work he would consider as one of the earliest pioneers in this regard. He recommended the book, *The Souls of Black Folk* by W. E. B. Dubois, first published in 1903, and I read it this past summer. This book is a masterpiece and in it Dubois foreshadows many important themes that face our society in relation to race. Dubois recognized the distinctiveness of the African American community. He understood how the U.S. had profited from their presence. His insights into the economics of racism again, speak insightfully to those of us living today. He recognized the tremendous debt our nation owes to the African American community for its hard work and gifts of language, music, and understanding of the human spirit.

In his book, Dubois described his own teaching as a very young man while studying at Fisk University. He later taught in a tiny little country town about 40 miles east of Nashville, TN, called Watertown. He wrote: "We read and spelled together, wrote a little, picked flowers, sang, and listened to stories of the world beyond the hill" (p. 255). He cried out for an education that would teach White people about Black people. He wrote incredible stories of the South's heroes and villains. In short, he provided a wealth of material, a curriculum if you will, that if fully appreciated could serve as the basis for 'students of the history of subordination' of African Americans in the U.S. His focus was on trying to figure out how to make a quality education available to African American children. Of course, a great many of his insights are also relevant when thinking about poor White working class children in Appalachia, or students from immigrant backgrounds.

Another pioneer that comes to my mind is George Sánchez, for whom the College of Education at the University of Texas at Austin is named. In his book, *Forgotten People*, Sánchez pointed out back in 1940 that the problem of language differences was the fault of the schools, not the children. His argument was that the schools failed to teach English and they completely ignored the language that the children brought with them into the school. He noted that a wealth of literature in Spanish was widely available to educators, and he stated that generally accepted principles of instruction were applicable to the teaching and learning of Mexican-origin students. Strikingly, and very presciently, he added that these generally accepted principles of instruction needed to be adapted to the customs, traditions, language and historical backgrounds of these young people. He suggested that students' culture should inform the curriculum. While W. E. B. Dubois had a somewhat general sense of the value of African American language, culture, and its specific products, George Sanchéz, beginning in the 1930s and 1940s, more specifically identified Mexican music, folklore, architecture, foods, crafts and customs as topics worthy of study. Shades of 'funds of knowledge'! Sánchez recognized very early the need for educators to understand and become familiar with the linguistic and cultural backgrounds of their students. Both Sánchez and Dubois recognized the need for African American and Latino students to master the general curriculum, as it was then understood, but they also recognized that this could only be done through a kind of dialectic practice of examining the cultural and linguistic backgrounds of the children and then finding ways to adapt and modify both the content and the instructional methods used to teach that information.

For many of us, CRP made its debut in the 1970s. Ramírez and Castañeda wrote their very influential book, *Cultural democracy, bicognitive development, and education,* in 1974 where they called for cultural democracy and what they called bicognitive development and education. These scholars rejected what they called the 'damaging culture' perspective, or what we would call deficit theories, and argued forcefully that students have every right to be proud of and to identify with their ethnic group, language, and cultural values. Ramírez and Castañeda's work led the way in raising questions about the goals of teaching students from diverse backgrounds. In 1974, Larry Cuban wrote an article titled *Ethnic content and White instruction* in the Phi Delta Kappan where he advocated different instructional methods to accompany the new content of ethnic studies. James Banks wrote a piece in *Educational Leadership* in 1974 titled, *Cultural pluralism and the schools*, that is as fresh today as it was then. He told us to respect the cultural and linguistic backgrounds of students *so that* they might acquire the power they need to transform society. Of course, a good deal of work was also done on African American language and culture (Kochman, 1972; Piestrup, 1973; Smitherman, 1972), Hawaiian language and culture (Gallimore, Bogs & Jordan, 1974), Native American and Inuit language and culture (Kleinfeld, 1973, 1974, 1975) and Asian American language and culture (Chun-Hoon, 1973). Kleinfeld's work on Native Alaskan and Inuit students provided incredible insight into the specific ways that these young people became alienated from their teachers and their schoolwork, mostly because their socialization had taught them to think about relationships with teachers and their peers in distinctive, culturally shaped ways. She coined the term, 'warm demanders.' By this she referred to teachers who built caring relationships with their students but then demanded high levels of performance.

Many of these developments occurred during what has been called the 'ethnic revival' in the United States. This was groundbreaking work and it caught the attention of a great many who are now in senior positions within the academy. These projects were exciting; they broke new ground, and they offered insight into the academic achievement of students from diverse backgrounds that did more than find fault with them or their families. These understandings began to break free from the deficit thinking that was so popular then and that continues to dominate in too many arenas today.

Of course, there have been some bumps along the road. For instance, many are familiar with the "Bank Street readers," which may represent to some extent this approach, at least linguistically but which was opposed by many African-American parents who wanted their children to master the dominant dialect. As always, solutions need to be developed in consultation with the communities most affected. Top-down impositions of solutions, even when those solutions are well-intentioned and potentially quite effective, may be rejected by those they are meant to help.

Can CRP be integrated feasibly into instruction in ways that benefit students? But, it was the 1980s when researchers produced what I would consider the paradigmatic examples of CRP. Kathryn Au (1981; Au & Mason 1981) examined the linguistic interaction patterns of Hawaiian children during guided reading lessons. They looked carefully at the differences between two teachers, one who taught from a mainstream frame of reference and the other who was very familiar with Hawaiian culture. Their work is one of the classic lines of research that demonstrated increased student engagement during the ubiquitous practice of asking questions and engaging in post-reading discussions. Au and Mason also found that students taught using culturally responsive methods provided more reading and reading related responses to teacher prompts, more correct responses, and made more logical inferences than students taught using mainstream approaches. Luis Moll (1980) and his colleagues at the Laboratory for Comparative Cognition provided evidence that Spanish-speaking students could engage in much higher levels of thinking when they were encouraged to discuss English language text in their first language. Shirley

Brice Heath (1983) showed how something as taken for granted as the linguistic forms used to frame questions could vary along race and class lines. Keep in mind that Heath also recognized the plight of working class Whites in the South and Appalachia (see also, Finn, 1999). She also showed that modifying questions so that they resembled those used in the home could elicit more information from children. Susan Philips (1983) was able to document differences in the ways that Native American children in Oregon interacted verbally with others. Because the children she observed were much less willing to speak in public, particularly when required to do so, their teachers evaluated them poorly in terms of intelligence and learning. When they themselves were allowed to choose when to speak, they participated to a much greater extent. All of these studies, and a great many more, documented difficulties for students from diverse backgrounds because of the ways language was used in mainstream classrooms, found cultural and linguistic analogues in students' communities, and then demonstrated that with a little modification, students participated more, and at higher levels. In some cases, they made claims that the students learned more as a result and it was these claims concerning learning that are currently at the heart of controversy between those who advocate for CRP and those whose focus is solely on the efficiency of instruction.

ISSUES, QUESTIONS AND CONTROVERSIES WITHIN CRP

To my way of thinking, the history of CRP and the history of immigrant students is useful for understanding how we got to where we are now. For those seriously interested in implementing CRP, there are a good number of questions that need serious thought. In this section, I raise the issues, questions and controversies that I believe are related to CRP. My goal here is not to provide the definitive answer to each of these questions but rather to identify what the issues are, who some of the key players are with respect to these questions, and to lay out in as abbreviated form as possible what these key players think about each of them.

Perhaps the biggest question concerning CRP within the research community is whether or not it works. In other words, can it be demonstrated that students learn more and are more engaged in their learning when teachers employ CRP? Many of you are familiar with the report of the National Reading Panel, *Developing literacy in second language learners*, edited by Diane August and Tim Shanahan (2006). The authors of the chapter titled, Sociocultural influences on the literacy attainment of language-minority children and youth, Claude Goldenberg, Robert Rueda and Diane August, concluded that:

> Despite a belief among many in the field that instruction tailored to different cultural groups is superior to instruction based on general principles of teaching and learning, there is a paucity of data to support this claim. The best studies suggest that student engagement and participation, which are not the same as achievement, can be enhanced through the use of culturally compatible instruction, but even these studies are open to numerous alternative explanations (p. 266).

Table 1. Relevant Arizona and United States Demographics

Category	Arizona	USA
Persons under 18 years, 2010	26.6%	24.0%
Persons 65 years and over, 2012	13.8%	13.0%
Black persons, 2010	4.1%	12.6%
American Indian and Alaska Native persons, 2010	4.6%	0.9%
Persons of Hispanic or Latino origin, 2010	29.6%	16.3%
White persons not Hispanic, 2010	57.8%	63.7%
Language other than English spoken at home, age 5+, 2005-2009	27.9%	19.6%
English Language Learner, K-12 students	14%	
ELL's with Spanish as first language, K-12 students	81%	
High school graduates, persons 25+, 2005-2009	83.9%	84.6%
Median household income, 2009	$48,711	$50,221
Persons below poverty level, 2009	16.5%	14.3%

Keep in mind that the authors reviewed only research dealing with literacy and only looked at studies that focused on second language learners. In addition, their standard for instructional effectiveness included many of the parameters used in experimental research design. Even so, their conclusion is quite sobering and also entirely different from the conclusions reached by many advocates of CRP. For example, Geneva Gay writes in her book, *Culturally responsive teaching*, that: "When the instructional processes are congruent with the cultural orientations, experiences and learning styles of marginalized African, Latino, Native and Asian American students, their school achievement improves significantly," and also, "Students of color come to school having already mastered many cultural skills and ways of knowing. To the extent that teaching builds on these capabilities, academic success will result" (p. 213). Gay, of course, builds primarily from a literature and research base on African American students but she also includes work on students learning English. More importantly, she is one of the leading authorities on culturally responsive pedagogy. At any rate, these are two very different ways of thinking about CRP. And, even though the advocates and their critics arrive at very different conclusions, all sides agree that more, as well as somewhat different, research needs to be done in this area (Sleeter, 2012). I'll come back to this issue shortly.

A related question has to do with how is CRP distinct from 'jes plain ol' good teaching?' This is a question asked by researchers, pre-service teachers and practicing teachers. The answer given depends on who does the answering. However, the definition I gave earlier provides some of the necessary information. Culturally responsive pedagogy describes instructional approaches that value, identify, and implement aspects of students' culture and vernacular in ways that promote academic achievement. Ladson-Billings (1995) added that "a theory of culturally relevant pedagogy would necessarily propose to do three things—produce students who can achieve academically, produce students who demonstrate cultural competence, *and develop students who can both understand and critique the existing social order"* (p. 474). The latter two components are unique to CRP and not shared by those working from more mainstream conceptions of instructional effectiveness. Ladson-Billings points out that many earlier forms of multicultural education sought primarily to fit students into an existing order, an order that was unjust and inequitable. Her point is that without a critique of the current social order, the most we can hope for is a continuation of the status quo. So, while advocates of CRP recognize the need for achievement, they are also passionate about the need to create a more equitable society and they see their work in schools as one part of a much larger effort. Even so, it is important to point out that both are major concerns for those working in this area.

A difficult question for advocates of CRP is whether or not the approach makes unwarranted assumptions about the students being taught. This concern is often made in association with the term essentializing. Such thinking assumes the presence of innate characteristics that are associated with racial, ethnic, or cultural backgrounds. What would be problematic, for example, would be to assume that all students from an immigrant background prefer collaborative learning over more independent forms of achievement or that all students in the process of learning a second language prefer to read stories about immigrants over those that focus more generally on the process of becoming a contributing member of society. Gutierrez and Vossoughi (2010) recommend research designs that document both the regularity and variance of participants' behaviors across different contexts so as to avoid essentializing conclusions. Gay (2010) argues for a dynamic and fluid understanding of cultural characteristics and she proposes measuring students' degree of *ethnic affiliation* to determine their usefulness. She believes that cultural regularities provide "functional directions for modifying instructional techniques" (p. 174). There is little doubt that CRP theorists, researchers, and practitioners need to constantly monitor their assumptions and understandings of the students or learners in question. Such work can only be done through more substantive understanding of students and their local communities.

The next question is what are the cultural and linguistic practices that have the best fit with academic and school practices? A related question would be which of these practices has the most potential for improving the academic achievement of students learning English? Carol Lee's work is especially informative for thinking about these issues. She calls for field work that examines students' "routine practices outside of school." Note that her goal is to improve secondary students' reading and comprehension of literature. Norma González and Luis Moll (1995), expand the scope of potentially valuable information to the realm of economic activities. In that sense, a 'funds of knowledge' approach is more concerned with curriculum while 'cultural modeling' combines instructional practice with curriculum. The research on funds of knowledge provides a good deal of information on how to learn about the economic activities engaged in by the families of children in local schools, whereas the work on cultural modeling provides less information and relies more on insider knowledge about the language and cultural practices. Both approaches, however, see the need for first hand knowledge about the students and their communities. The question, however, is unsettled. Gay (2010) recommends that the features characteristic of African American communication patterns are good fits for culturally responsive teaching. She lists some of these characteristics as "prolific use of dramatics, body language, and gesturing; sermonic tone and techniques, cultural references; ethnolinguistic idioms and proverbs; conversational storytelling; and rhetorical devices such as rhythm, rhyme, rate, repetition, improvisation, lyricism, and histocultural contextualization" (p. 106). Without a doubt, before any of these broad categories could be translated into instruction, particularly the forms of instruction that researchers could hand off to teachers, a good deal of work would be necessary.

Orellana and her colleagues (Orellana & Reynolds, 2008; Orellana, Reynolds, Dorner & Mesa, 2003) provide one of the more in-depth discussions on how to identify practices within the linguistic and cultural repertoires of students from diverse backgrounds that have potential for improving their academic achievement. These scholars highlight the generative role of students' everyday practices and focus on ways to transform these practices for use in school contexts. They also declare that home and school practices should not be dichotomized but rather leveraged. In their words:

> The goal of leveraging is neither simply to celebrate students' everyday linguistic virtuosity nor to transfer those skills in a direct way to school tasks but rather to expand students' abilities to work with the various tools in their linguistic toolkits—the full range of practices that they use in both home and school contexts (2008, p. 50).

Drawing from the work of Carol Lee and her model of cultural modeling, they employ ethnographic techniques, both to describe students' out of school practices as well as to examine relevant school practices, or disciplinary modes of reasoning. The goal is to gain deep understandings of both before designing instructional innovations. This work is incredibly useful as a paradigmatic example of how to make productive connections between students' academic progress and their overall lives.

What can the literacy research community do to move the conversation forward? Know the literature in the area and cultivate relationships with teachers and members of the community to know what their concerns are for the academic achievement of the students in question. Probably no one emphasizes the need to show how culturally responsive pedagogy is connected to local communities better than does Sleeter (2012). She tells researchers to demonstrate how their work fits the context in which it is employed and she goes on to say that "researchers cannot skip over the task of grounding what it (CRP) means in the context being studied" (p. 576). Previous researchers have used their insider status, their time in the field, and their knowledge of related relevant research for this purpose. Sleeter does not specify exactly what would count but it is a good bet that she would privilege considerable time spent in the community as an important criterion for rigorous research.

Another important concern would be how does a teacher implement CRP when he or she faces students from multiple cultural and linguistic backgrounds? Lee (2008) states that the instructional practices that best characterize culturally responsive pedagogy are responsive to the cultural histories of the communities in which young people live. There is little doubt that Lee envisions informed, knowledgeable researchers who, if not insiders, have taken the time to really know and understand the communities that they wish to influence. For Lee, and probably many others who work in this area, this typically meant coming to know one cultural group. Other researchers, however, such as Django Paris (2011), are showing how researchers can come to know contexts that are characterized by much greater diversity. In his recent book, *Language across difference*, he shows how youths pick up on and incorporate language from various groups into their linguistic repertoires. For Paris, finding linguistic and cultural practices that can be mapped onto school practices would mean those practices that are picked up by multiple groups found in specific school contexts. In his case, these were African American, Latino, and Samoan influences. Paris' approach is one way to avoid ascribing characteristics based on ethnic or linguistic background.

Do the development work needed to transform cultural and linguistic practices into instruction. Test the resulting instructional approaches to be certain that they do indeed promote students' academic achievement. This last point might be the one that many of us find the most appealing. We like setting up research projects, designing them, carrying them out and then writing up the results. As many of us know, the majority of the research done in the area of CRP has consisted of small scale projects. Sleeter (2012) goes further than anyone else in this area to ask for more and better research on CRP. She states:

> First, there is a clear need for evidence-based research that documents connections between culturally responsive pedagogy and student outcomes that include, but are not necessarily limited to, academic achievement. Politically, it is difficult to build a case to change approaches to teaching without strong evidence. Small-scale case studies illustrate what is possible, but we also need research on the impact of scaled-up work in culturally responsive pedagogy, *including research showing how teachers can learn to use it in their classrooms* (see Sleeter, 2011) (p. 578).

Cummins argues for more practical implementation of the ideals embodied by CRP and calls for more specific identification of what CRP looks like:

> But critical perspectives must also move from a rhetoric and theoretical analysis to a more detailed focus on the specific forms of pedagogy that will develop the 'basic skills' assessed by most tests while at the same time expanding students' personal, intellectual, and academic horizons in transformative ways (p. 248).

Clearly, there is a need for more and better research on CRP.

POTENTIAL OF DESIGN RESEARCH

As we learned from David Reinking's presidential address, design research combines many of the strengths of both qualitative and quantitative research approaches. It also has the affordance of allowing researchers the time and the opportunity to investigate multiple instantiations of their ideas so that they can refine and reflect on them. For example, the research on CRP provides a lot of different ideas for what might work. These include the following that I found in Jim Cummins' (2000) and Geneva Gay's (2010) work:

- Compare and contrast the local variety of colloquial language vs. formal 'standard' language.
- Investigate the phenomenon of code-switching and how it functions in their lives.
- Analyze letters to the editor or online reader comments concerning bilingual education or other topics of interest such as immigration, minority student achievement, what it means to be American.
- Analyze the lyrics of popular songs and re-write them (new sentences, poems, lyrics).
- Write critical autobiographies from linguistic, cultural, political, economic, sociological, and psychological perspectives.
- Students write letters in L1 to their parents about their school program. They then translate their parents' letters into English.
- Students verbalize a story to showcase verbal creativity. This is recorded and transcribed. Technical writing skills are then taught using the transcriptions.
- Teach explicit contrasts between SAE and AAVE, compare grammatical patterns, translate from one dialect to another, edit one another's drafts.

While these are all undoubtedly wonderful ideas, they need a lot more thought and development before they could be reasonably implemented with any chance of success. Researchers would need to think through many more details before a reasonable research project could be put together and teachers would need to think through exactly how they plan to introduce these ideas, get students to engage in them, what counts as acceptable evidence of learning, and what the connections are to standards and assessments.

Design research requires the researcher to implement a number of iterative refinements characterized by what Collins, et al. (2004) referred to as progressive refinement (Cobb, McClain & Gravemeijer, 2003; Reinking & Bradley, 2008). This approach to research is particularly appropriate when there is little knowledge about the development of typical forms of student thinking, perhaps because the structure of the subject matter is being "radically reconceptualized, taught in a new way, or investigated with participants who do not usually learn it" (Lehrer & Schauble, 2004). Because few studies have explored how translation can support reading comprehension, we believed that design research was an ideal research method to explore and understand this instructional program. As a whole, a design experiment consists of cyclic processes of thought experiments and instructional experiments (Freudenthal, 1991); see Figure 3:

Figure 3.

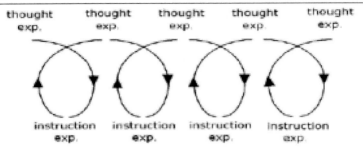

Using design research, my colleagues and I are currently working on a project called TRANSLATE (Teaching Reading and New Strategic Learning Approaches To English-learners). We have begun the work of determining the instructional conditions supporting students' participation and learning. We did this to address one of our research questions: What pedagogical moves lead to increased student strategy use, comprehension and engagement with curricular texts? Thus, iterative development is providing us with an understanding of not only "what works" but also "how, when, and why" it works (Cobb, et al., 2003, p. 13, Lehrer & Schauble, 2004). The goal of developing local instructional theories will facilitate answering another of our research questions: Does our intervention lead to enhanced strategy use, reading comprehension, and engagement with curricular texts for students learning English? If so, how and in what ways?

The findings from our project focused on three specific goals of CRP: increasing engagement, teaching disciplinary modes of reasoning, and empowering students to think about their cultural practices as resources for learning.

Engagement: Choosing Academic Excellence

We posited that by using translation, students became more engaged during reading because they appreciated school/teacher recognition of their first language. Translation provided opportunities for peer interaction about dual language processing, which validated students' bilingualism while promoting deeper understanding of both English and native languages.

Disciplinary Modes of Reasoning: Reading Like a Scholar

In terms of disciplinary modes of reasoning, translation required our participants the kind of close reading engaged in by experts in many fields, particularly those of authors who consider the needs of their audience. Close reading encouraged students to engage in a back and forth movement between the original text and their developing translation. They talked explicitly about vocabulary and the range of meanings of words, or the microstructure of text (Kintsch & Rawson, 2005) and they discussed central concepts, phrases, metaphors and idioms. This talk was optimal for discussing theme, plot, or character development within narratives, and relationships among details and central concepts in informational texts. One effect of translation included its ability to prompt students to make more connections to their prior knowledge.

Empowerment: Transforming Student Attitudes

While collaborative translation activities helped students understand more of the reading required by school, our underlying goal was for students to leverage their full linguistic resources for a variety of reading tasks in and out of school. This entailed a transformation in the way they thought about the practice of translation. As our student participants mastered the TRANSLATE approach they begin to think of translation not just as a way to render words in another language, but as a way to control their own learning. Lee argued that CRP can give students the tools to overcome obstacles created by hegemonic school practices (2008). Our position is that, for linguistically diverse students, this can happen when students feel empowered to use their first language resources.

CONCLUSION

I started off my presentation with a metaphor near and dear to my heart, that of how to best modify a motorcycle to achieve what I want to do. Many times, all that is needed is to add a bit here, replace a part there. However, there are times when an entirely different machine is necessary. My wife continually wants to know how many are enough. The old answer of 'just one more' is wearing thin. Most agree that more than 5 becomes unmanageable. Anyhow, even though upkeep, modifications and outright refurbishing can become tedious, the pleasures derived from riding make it all worthwhile. I think the ability to create new instructional approaches that more fully engage students from diverse backgrounds and that have as a consequence deeper understandings of written and oral language, are a similar kind of pleasure. The ultimate goal, of course, is to provide teachers with instructional resources that truly promote student learning.

In her most recent paper, Christine Sleeter tells us that CRP has not had the impact on student learning that it could have because many of its closest adherents do not fully understand that its primary goal is to help students achieve academically. She writes that there is a common notion that CRP is simply a means to celebrate students' cultural backgrounds. She adds that we need larger scale research studies grounded in CRP principles. Such studies must find a way not to lose the local as they attempt to uncover more general patterns. For the most part, I concur with Sleeter and I would add that CRP provides us with a means to escape the tyranny of a hidebound and ossified curriculum. As Moll makes clear, the greatest resource for teaching students from diverse backgrounds can be found within their own cultural and linguistic backgrounds.

Right now, we are at an interesting historical moment with respect to students learning English. Immigration has decreased dramatically from prior levels. Some claim that it is because of the harsh measures that many states have enacted to deny immigrants necessary services. Others point out that the levels have diminished because our economy is not currently demanding low-wage labor. What is very interesting is that immigration is a result of both factors within receiving nations as well as conditions found outside in the sending nations. Other sending nations, such as Ireland and Korea, have, for the most part, stopped sending their citizens to the western hemisphere looking for work. That is because their economies have developed to the point where it is no longer necessary to leave home. This same process is being repeated in places like Mexico and Latin America. In other words, the type of immigration that we are used to seeing will probably change in the next decade. The forms of CRP that we find useful now, while able to provide us with general principles for designing research and instruction, will need to be rethought, refreshed, and re-imagined as we move forward.

REFERENCES

Au, K. H. (1980). Participation structures in a reading lesson with Hawaiian children: Analysis of a culturally appropriate instructional event. *Anthropology and Education Quarterly, 11(2)*, 91-115.

Au, K. H., & Mason, J. (1981). Social organization factors in learning to read: The balance of rights hypothesis. *Reading Research Quarterly, 17(1)*, 115-152.

August, D., & Shanahan, T. (2006). *Developing literacy in second-language learners*. Mahwah, NJ: Lawrence Erlbaumn Associates.

Baker, L., & Brown, A. L. (1984). Metacognitive skills and reading. In P. D. Pearson (Ed.), *Handbook of reading research* (pp. 353-394). New York, NY: Longman.

Berliner, D. C., & Biddle, B. J. (1995). *The manufactured crisis : Myths, fraud, and the attack on America's public schools*. Reading, Mass: Addison-Wesley.

Bourdieu, P. (1998). *Practical Reason*. Stanford, CA: Stanford University Press.

Bransford, J. N. V., Stevens, R., Kuhl, P., Schwartz, D., Bell, P., Meltzoff, A., Barron, B., Pea, R., Reeves, B., Roschelle, J., & Sabelli, N. Learning Theories and Education: Toward a Decade of Synergy. In P. A. P. Winne (Ed.), *Handbook of Educational Psychology (2nd Edition)* (pp. 1-94). Mahwah, NJ: Erlbaum. Retrieved August 2, 2012 at: http://life-slc.org/docs/Bransford_etal-Learningtheories_2006.pdf

Brown, A. L. (1985). Metacognition: The development of selective attention strategies for learning from texts. In H. Singer & R. B. Ruddell (Eds.), *Theoretical models and processes of reading* (pp. 501-526). Newark, DE: International Reading Association.

Chun-Hoon, L. K. Y. (1973). Teaching the Asian American experience. In J. A. Banks (Ed.). Teaching ethnic studies: Concepts and strategies (pp. 118-146). Washington DC: National Council for the Social Studies.

Cobb, P., McClain, K., & Gravemeijer, K. (2003). Learning about statistical covariation. *Cognition and Instruction, 21*, 1-78.

Collins, A., Joseph, D., & Bielaczyc, K. (2004). Design research: Theoretical and methodological issues. *The Journal of the Instructional Sciences, 13*(1), 15-42.

Cuban, L. (1974). Ethnic content and "White" instruction. Phi Delta Kappan, 53(5), 270-273.

Cummins, J. (2000). *Language, power, and pedagogy*. Clevedon, Great Britain: Multilingual Matters.

Daniels, R. (2002). *Coming to America*. New York: Harper Perennial Dillingham Commission in 1911

Dubois, W. E. B. (1965). *The souls of Black folk*, in *Three Negro classics* (pp. 207-389). New York: Avon Books.

Finn, P. J. (1999). *Literacy with an attitude*. Albany: State University of New York Press.

Fischer, S. R. (2003). A history of reading. London, Reaktion.

Freudenthal, H. (1991). *Revisiting mathematics education*. Dordrecht: Kluwer Academic Publishers.

Gallimore, R. Bogs, J. W., & Jordan, C. (1974). Culture, behavior and education: A study of Hawaiian Americans. Beverly Hills, CA: Sage.

Gay, G. (2010). *Culturally responsive teaching*. New York, NY: Teachers College Press.

Gonzalez, N., Moll, L. C., Floyd-Tenery, M., Rivera, A., Rendon, P., Gonzales, R., et al. (1995). Funds of knowledge for teaching in Latino households. *Urban Education, 29*(4), 443-470.

Goldenberg, C., Rueda, R. S., & August, D. (2006). Synthesis: Sociocultural contexts and literacy development. In D. August & T. Shanahan (Eds.), *Developing literacy in second-language learners* (pp. 269-318). Mahwah, NJ: Erlbaum.

Gutierrez, K., & Vossoughi, S. (2011). Lifting off the ground to return anew: Mediated praxis, transformative learning, and social design experiments. *Journal of Teacher Education, 61*(1-2), 100-117.

Heath, S. B. (1983). *Ways with words: Language, life, and work in communities and classrooms*. Cambridge, MA: Cambridge University Press.

Heather, P. (1994). Literacy and power in the migration period. In A. K. Bowman & G. Woolf (Eds.), *Literacy and power* (pp. 177-197). Cambridge, UK: Cambridge University Press.

Higham, J. (1955). *Strangers in the land*. New Brunswick, NJ: Rutgers University Press.

Kleinfeld, J. (1975). Effective teachers of Eskimo and Indian students. School Review, 83(2), 301-344).

Kochman, T. (1972). Rappin and stylin' out: Communication in urban Black America. Urbana: University of Illinois Press.

Kozol, J. (1991). *Savage inequalities*. New York, NY: Crown.

Ladson-Billings, G. (1995). Toward a Theory of Culturally Relevant Pedagogy. American Educational Research Journal, 32(3), 465-491.

Lee, C. (2007). *Culture, literacy, and learning*. New York, NY: Teachers College Press.

Lee, C. (2008). The centrality of culture to the scientific study of learning and development: How an ecological framework in education research facilitates civic responsibility. *Educational Researcher, 37*(5), 267-279.

Lehrer, R., & Schauble, L. (2004). Modeling natural variation through distribution. *American Educational Research Journal, 41*(3), 635-679.

Moll, L. C., Estrada, E., Díaz, E., & Lopes, L. M. (1980). The organization of bilingual lessons: Implications for schooling. *The Quarterly Newsletter of the Laboratory of Comparative Human Cognition, 2*(3), 53-58.

Moll, L. C. (2010). Mobilizing culture, language, and educational practices: Fulfillng the promises of Mendez and Brown. *Educational Researcher, f39*(6), 451-460.

Nieto, S. (2000). Language, literacy, and culture: Intersections and implications. In T. Shanahan & F. Rodríguez-Brown (Eds.), *49th Yearbook of the National Reading Conference* (pp. 41-60). Chicago: National Reading Conference.

Orellana, M. F., Reynolds, J., Dorner, L., & Mesa, M. (2003). In other words: Translating or "para-phrasing" as a family literacy practice in immigrant households. *Reading Research Quarterly, 38*(1), 12-34.

Orellana, M. F., & Reynolds, J. F. (2008). Cultural modeling: Leveraging bilingual skills for school paraphrasing tasks. *Reading Research Quarterly, 43*(1), 48-65.

Paris, D. (2011). *Language across difference: Ethnicity, communication and youth identities in changing urban schools*. New York, NY: Cambridge University Press.

Perlmann, J. (2002). *Polish and Italian schooling then, Mexican schooling now? U.S. ethnic school attainments across the generations of the 20th century*: Levy Economics Institute of Bard College, Working Paper 350. Paper retrieved 7/28/2012: http://www.levyinstitute.org/pubs/wp350.pdf

Philips, S. U. (1983). *The invisible culture: Communication in classroom and community on the Warm Springs Indian Reservation*. New York, NY: Longman.

Ramírez, M., & Castañeda, A. (1974). *Cultural democracy, bicognitive development and education*. New York: Academic Press.

Reinking, D., & Bradley, B. (2008). *On formative and design experiments*. New York, NY: Teachers College Press/NCRLL.

Sánchez, G. I. (1940). *Forgotten people: A study of New Mexicans*. Albuquerque, NM: University of New Mexico.

Sleeter, C. (2012). Confronting the Marginalization of Culturally Responsive Pedagogy. *Urban Education, 47*(3), 562-584.

Smitherman, G. (1972). Black power is Black language. In G. M. Simmons, H.D. Hutchison, & H. E. Simmons (Eds.), Black culture: Reading and writing Black (pp. 85-91). New York: Holt, Rinehart & Winston.

How the Online World is Changing the Relationship Between Everyday Literacy Practices and Educational Possibilities

David Barton

Lancaster University

Taking account of the everyday, or 'out-of-school', or 'vernacular' reading and writing has been a key concern for literacy education at all levels since the beginning of literacy studies research. Exploring this relationship was fundamental to Shirley Brice Heath's work in the Appalachians in the early 1980s (Heath, 1983) and to Brian Street's work in Iran at that time (Street, 1984). It has been the central thread of (New) Literacy Studies or Literacy as social practice research up to the present, especially in the U.S. It remains a current concern which members of the Literacy Research Association are addressing.

In this paper I want to discuss and weave together three distinct topics. The paper begins with a general comparison between everyday literacy practices in the 1990s and now. It compares data collected 20 years ago as part of the 'Local Literacies' study (Barton & Hamilton, 1998/2012) with contemporary practices. It then examines a particular example of how people's everyday language practices have changed in the past 20 years. It provides an example from the online photo sharing site Flickr, based on the analysis of sites and interviews with users. This shows constant learning and an enthusiasm for learning in the reflective spaces of the internet. Here I drill down into the details of one example and then come out of it and discuss changes more generally. Thirdly, the main educational context I am thinking about concerns my undergraduate university students. As a way of helping them to understand the idea of literacy as social practice, for the past 20 years I have asked them to research everyday practices and they have carried out projects as diverse as buying a lottery ticket, celebrating Chinese New Year, sending a mother's day card, and much more. In recent years they have researched the online world. Taking the example of my students' investigations, the paper briefly explores how educational provision at all levels can take up the possibilities offered by researching everyday online language practices. Overall, the paper effectively examines what has happened to literacy studies and whether it is still relevant for making sense of reading and writing. It concludes that, yes, an orientation based on practices and a methodology of ethnographic approaches is particularly insightful in understanding the online world.

LOCAL LITERACIES THEN AND NOW

In all of this I take a particular approach, that of Literacy Studies, providing a detailed qualitative look at what people do and what literacy means to them and which emphasizes everyday or vernacular practices. Taking a literacy studies lens has shown things such as: the role of other people and the grouping people participate in, the networks of support and learning off each other which takes place, the constraints and possibilities, and the perceived affordances. The Local Literacies study, carried out more than 20 years ago, took a literacy studies approach. It examined everyday reading and writing practices in one town in England and identified a range of vernacular literacy practices which people drew upon (Barton & Hamilton, 1998/2012). We studied the role of reading and writing in the local community of the town in which we lived – the situated literacies

– using a multi-method approach. We interviewed the people over time; we followed them around in their everyday activities, and we collected documents and took photos.

The study identified key areas of everyday life where reading and writing were significant for people and it contrasted these vernacular literacies, which were often voluntary, self-generated and learned informally, with more dominant literacies which were more formalised and defined in terms of the needs of institutions. These vernacular practices are rooted in everyday experiences and serve everyday purposes; they are not particularly regulated or approved of by formal domains and are more common in private spheres with local circulation. They can be a source of creativity and innovation. Examples of vernacular literacy practices include the reading and writing around keeping a diary, ways of keeping in touch with family and friends, and pursuing hobbies and interests. They include the 'unnoticed' literacies of sports, cooking, and going on vacation. The research also demonstrated the importance of social networks and relationships in these practices, with literacy being used for social communication. People drew on these social networks to help them with particular literacy requirements.

We identified six areas of life where local literacies played a significant role. Literacy was used for *organizing life,* as in the keeping of diaries and appointment calendars. It was used in *personal communication,* as in the sending of notes and letters to each other, and it was used for *private leisure,* with leisure reading. We came across several examples of people writing poetry. And it was apparent that hobbies and pastimes like gardening and organizing sports involve a great deal of reading and writing. These three areas of life were expected and unsurprising, but others were less expected, at least to us when carrying out the research. There was a considerable amount of *documenting life,* where people kept family records or were interested in local history. Then there was a general area of *sense making,* where people used reading and writing to investigate such things as health problems, legal problems they encountered, and difficulties their children experienced at school. Finally, there was an area of *social participation,* where any local organizations people belonged to were held together with a web of notices, meetings and newsletters. It is worth pointing out that at this time we came across just two computers in the neighbourhood, one in the local community centre and the other in the house of a man who saw himself as a writer. Both were used by local people wanting to make simple adverts and print them off. There was no World Wide Web, no Google, no Facebook and no online shopping. Computers and computing were largely restricted to workplaces. Laptops were rare, heavy, and expensive. Mobile phones were just beginning to become common, and text messaging did not take off until the late 1990s after the project had finished. The study was carried out more than 20 years ago, so questions arise as to whether the significance of literacy has been changed by social developments and new technologies. Does the concept 'vernacular literacies' need a new definition in the context of Web 2.0? Are people still doing these activities and is literacy still important, or have they changed beyond recognition?

Comparing practices of 20 years ago with practices today involves revisiting. However, this is not a straightforward matter. Revisiting has several possibilities, each one slightly different. We could return to the same people, but 20 years older, and examine how their personal practices have changed. Inevitably some have moved, some may have died, and others will be uncontactable. We would be investigating the practices of a significantly older group of people. Alternatively, we could return to the same physical place. In this particular case, physically the neighbourhood is remarkably similar, with the same houses, the same fish and chip shop, and the same pub on the corner. However, the neighbourhood is very different in terms of the people and their relations to each other. Many of the families living there have relocated, and a significant proportion of the houses are now occupied by groups of students who live there for a year or two and then move on. House prices have increased considerably in the past 20 years. So revisiting the place would result in studying a very different group of people. Thirdly, we could attempt a comparison with a similar group of people studied 20 years ago in terms of age profile, occupations, and family structure. In fact, the approach taken here combines the first and third way of revisiting. Mary Hamilton has contacted and interviewed two of the people researched in the original study (Hamilton, 2012), and we have maintained informal links with the neighbourhood, but mainly we have turned to general published surveys to make a comparison with 20 years ago.

A comparison with contemporary practices points to significant changes in people's practices and a shift online in most areas of everyday life. This has happened across all age levels. Often families provide cross-age support. There is constant change, but most changes are quickly naturalized and assumed to be normal and taken for granted. In the six areas of vernacular activity, in a relatively short period of time, people's practices have changed significantly in terms of the impact of new technologies. All activities are affected; it is not just a question of going online. These changes were beginning to happen in the mid 1990s. People now extensively organize their lives with appointment diaries and address books which are on computers or mobile phones. Arrangements to meet and the micro-coordination of social interaction are mediated by technologies. Increasingly, relations with institutions like banks and tax offices are done online, and customers are required in many cases to move away from their previous print-based practices. The local council utilizes digital technology as well as print and face-to-face contact to represent itself and to communicate with citizens about diverse issues such as school entry, recycling, and adverse weather. Government policy itself may make new textual demands on people and assume access to up-to-date communication technologies.

Today, while people still reside in physical places, and government institutions still impact on them in those places, people increasingly interact with their virtual or digital city. Personal communication has been revolutionized by smart phones and social networking sites. As an example, the holiday postcard now exists alongside the holiday text message or the shared Facebook photographs. Postcards and an extensive variety of greetings cards still exist physically, but their meaning and significance is being renegotiated within the greater range of alternative possibilities. What was referred to as private leisure in the original study is increasingly done online, and as the boundaries between private and public are renegotiated, much activity is more social and public. In addition, although the online world is strikingly multimodal, it is nevertheless extensively mediated by literacy. Contemporary life is documented by the footprints left online through social participation on Facebook and elsewhere, even to the extent that it is seen as intrusive. Activities like documenting family and local history are supported by easily available online resources. In terms of sense making, the internet is a crucial part of researching health issues, problems with children's development, or legal grievances. Finally, social media are important for social participation obviously, but also political participation works through blogging and commenting.

THE CHANGING LITERACIES AROUND PHOTOGRAPHY

Having undertaken a broad overview of people's everyday literacy practices 20 years ago, I now turn to a specific example of language and literacy practices to examine how practices have changed in the past 20 years. The example is changes in language practices around photos and photo albums. I drill down into the details of this one example and then come out of it and discuss changes more generally. To understand photography as an everyday practice, first we need to briefly explore the history of everyday photography.

Since its early days, photography has been referred to by its proponents as 'the democratic art'. As a vernacular practice it has been relatively cheap, accessible, and easy to learn for at least a hundred years. Families have had cameras and have created photo albums. Twenty years ago, there was a set of practices with film cameras. You would have to buy a film which took 12, 24 or 36 photos. It might take several weeks to use up the film and get it developed. The camera could only be opened in the dark, and the camera had to be taken to a store to be developed and printed, maybe taking a couple of days before you could see your photos, and it cost money for every film developed. Families sometimes created albums, made to track the development of a child or to record events such as weddings and vacations. Photos would be stuck into pre-purchased albums. There was very little writing around these photos, maybe an overall title to the album and then for individual photos, usually just a name, a place, and a date. Writing was limited to the 'who', 'where' and 'when' of the photo and the writing was usually done by the creator of the album. As a vernacular practice, photo albums existed along similar books such as postcard albums and scrap books. Typically, such albums were kept on a shelf in the living room and might be shown to visiting family members or friends. An album would not leave the house, and it had limited circulation. To be shown a photo album by participants in the local literacies study was to be accepted as a friend. The practice has to do with documenting life and with passing memories on across generations.

Today photography is everywhere, and it seems as if everyone has a camera, or in fact several cameras. Everything is photographed and photographs are everywhere, and as a practice the taking and sharing of photos is ubiquitous. To explore the practices of today and how they are different from those of 20 years ago, we turn to online photo sharing sites, and in particular Flickr. We are interested in what has happened to the practice and what has happened to the language. With the so called Web 2.0 applications, people are creating, sharing and collaborating. On platforms such as blogs, wikis, and social networking sites like Facebook, writing activities play a central role as people create their own contents on these sites. We are interested in what is happening to vernacular literacy practices when people take up opportunities on Web 2.0. In choosing to study Flickr, a photo sharing site, we have in fact chosen a site where one is less likely to expect much writing, as its primary concern is images. We are interested in new spaces for writing and whether these are also new spaces for learning. We can also examine if vernacular writing practices change when they go online and whether we need to revise our definition of vernacular practices.

The link with family photo albums is that when people first use Flickr they often see it as a space which is similar to an album where they can share photos with their friends and family. Over time they may see new affordances and come across people they do not know and take up new practices, as discussed in Barton & Lee (2013). Flickr is not particularly associated with language.

However, if you look at a Flickr photo page, there are many opportunities for writing. These include a space for a title in bold letters, and underneath that a description space. Alongside the photo, people can list tags which relate to the photo and can be searched for. These spaces are available primarily to the user whose page and photo it is. Beneath all of this, there is a space for comments where anyone can write. Elsewhere there is a profile page where people can describe themselves. Some people do not take up any of these opportunities for writing, but there are many Flickr users who write extensively in these spaces. We regard a Flickr photo page as a complex assemblage of meaning making with distinct writing spaces with their own affordances.

In a study by Carmen Lee and myself, we studied the writing done by active Flickr users in these and other writing spaces, and we found it to be very rich linguistically. People write differently in these different spaces and create coherent patterned multimodal texts, pulling together the image and the writing. In the first study we carried out, we investigated multilingual users of Flickr, primarily Chinese-English speaking and Spanish-English speaking users. We examined their language choices, people's multilingual identities, and the role of English (Lee & Barton, 2010). The study had a mixed methods design. It began with an exploratory observation of 100 sites to examine the range of languages used. The second stage comprised an online survey which led to follow-up interviews. We invited Chinese and Spanish Flickr users to complete a general online survey. We then analysed the sites of 30 people who answered the survey, especially their 100 most recently uploaded photos. Based on this, they were then asked specific questions about their site and the photos. This was followed up, where appropriate, by further email exchanges. The study also partly grew out of our own interest in Flickr. Both of us are active Flickr users, and we regularly upload photos to our photostreams, give tags, and write about our photos; we also make contacts with other Flickr users, and comment on their photos. Auto-ethnographic reporting of our own activities on Flickr also contributed to the methodology. Subsequent to the study of multilingualism, other research has been concerned with global identities, language and image, and stance-taking. (See, for example, Barton & Lee, 2013.) Here we focus on issues of learning.

The original study was not about learning, and the survey and the interviews did not in any way mention learning. However, we continually noticed that people kept talking about learning as an important aspect of their participation in Flickr. For example, one of the Spanish speakers wrote in her profile, "this is a permanent learning for me and I have nothing to teach." This was written both in English and in Spanish. Another wrote, "I have learned so much on Flickr, from so many different people…" A Chinese speaker wrote, "still so many things need to learn."

In the interviews, these people also reflected on their learning, although this was not prompted by the questions they were asked – which were about details of their multilingual practices. These comments could reveal the different things they were learning about, as in, "I try to do research in ways of telling stories or expressing moods. Yes, I try to learn to make photographs too and Flickr members are very good at sharing knowledge." And "I learn about different places, people and cultures. It is not just a matter of improving, but it is also about learning and interacting with different people." One of the people we interviewed mentioned that he was part of a group called '365' where he undertook to take a photo a day for a year and to post it on Flickr. Further investigations revealed that many photographers have participated in this activity (which in fact has spread to other platforms). Studying a group of Flickr users in '365' groups, we found a great deal of writing surrounding this activity. People reflected on their participation, and others praised them and encouraged them to continue. In this writing, there was sometimes a particular focus on learning. When learning was mentioned, it was often linked up with the social, and other people were referred to, as in "learning some new tricks and making some new friends. Share a bit of this crazy life with super people." And it was seen as a challenge. These were deliberate acts of learning, of learning about photography, and about themselves and other aspects of their lives. People reflected spontaneously on what they hoped to learn from it at the beginning, how much they had learned, and at the end, the effect this had on their lives. As one person put it, "I'm a total newbie to all this photography malarky... started Project 365 at the end of January to hopefully be a better photographer and learn how to use Photoshop to its full potential." They also revealed their implicit theories of learning here, as for example when pointing to the importance of being able to make mistakes in order to learn, as in, "I've made more mistakes, learned from them, and opened my eyes a bit wider to the world around me." Learning was related to changes in one's life, and the metaphor of life as a journey was used. Some people reflected on how their whole lives had changed and as 'being better' as a result of participation in '365'. This was put dramatically by one person: "What a great experience this has been. I honestly feel that I am a better person because of it, not just a better photographer. ...Yes, I am better because of it." A set of '365' photos is a kind of album, but it has moved a long way from a physical family album. What we have seen is that the activity is strongly social. It involves extensive writing and that the internet affords reflexivity. It is a good place for writing. Flickr itself provides distinct spaces which afford different sorts of writing: the description of a photo, the personal profile, the short comments to others, and the tags are all distinct writing spaces. In this way, Flickr is a structured and supportive space for writing. Flickr also affords authentic writing: people can find it easy writing to do, and once again it is that 'unnoticed' vernacular writing as seen in the everyday lives of participants in the earlier local literacies study and elsewhere. Mimi Ito (Ito et al., 2010) divides young people's activities on the internet into people-oriented and interest-oriented activities. As we can see here with participation in '365', it is very powerful when sociality and content come together. In terms of learning, the '365' project reveals people's vernacular theories of learning. They are learning about different things; they are learning about photography, about life, about the self. There is constant learning in these reflective spaces; there are deliberate acts of learning, and a love of learning is expressed. It is a safe place for learning, where people can experiment and receive feedback. This is transformational life-changing learning, and there is a passion for learning. Finally whilst images are of growing importance, I would argue that this has not diminished the importance of language. Rather, language is essential to this image-based site. Language and image are used together strategically and powerfully by people to document, argue, express stance, assert identities, to learn, to make meanings, and to socialize. (For more on the '365' study, see Barton, 2012.)

With these new practices on Flickr in mind, we now return to the properties of vernacular literacies identified earlier. Like any vernacular literacy practices, the literacy practices on Flickr are voluntary and self-generated. What people do on this site has its roots in everyday experience. The people saw Flickr as providing many possibilities for them to discover new ways of using Flickr. They appreciated the freedom they had and did not refer to any perceived restrictions. Secondly, writing on Flickr can be very original and creative. This is evident in the participants' wide-ranging purposes for writing on Flickr, their creative deployment of language resources, as well as their specific ways of socializing there. In terms of learning, we can see that what people do on Flickr is learned informally. The role of teacher and learner is not clearly defined and users can slip back and forth between these roles. Such informal, self-generated learning not only helps generate new practices, but people also change and develop their practices as they learn to do things on Flickr. These changes are rapid, and practices are fluid, a point that has not been emphasized in earlier work on vernacular literacies. Writing practices on Flickr also challenge and extend earlier notions of vernacular practices. Firstly, vernacular practices are commonly thought of as less valued by society and are not supported or approved of by education and other dominant institutions. In the case of Flickr, however, these local practices are valued. Practices such as creative deployment of resources and using Flickr to socialize with others are all recognized ways of widening participation in Flickr. Through making comments on one another's photos, Flickr members have become reviewers and evaluators of their own and others' work, and these comments can be treated by members as valuable sources of learning, where they all draw upon and contribute to expanding global funds of knowledge. In addition to these aspects of vernacular practices, there is more writing being done online and such writing is more valued than it was. It can have a broader circulation as people participate in global dialogues.

There are many ways in which online platforms can be utilized in classroom-based teaching and learning of language and literacy. (See Barton & Lee, 2013, p.154-159 for some examples.) Photo sites such as Flickr provide a resource of photo images which can be the focus of literacy work. The distinct writing spaces surrounding a photo can support different kinds of language teaching and learning activities. The description text-box beneath the picture, for instance, can act as a powerful tool for story telling around images. Tagging allows students to make use of new words they have learned in class to describe an image. Not mentioned thus far, the notes function on Flickr, where one can write annotations on photos, has been found to be particularly useful, as a teacher can post a photo and get students to annotate what they see (as in Richardson, 2006). The commenting function can encourage further participation and discussion among students. (For further ideas on using Flickr in this way, see Davies & Merchant, 2009.)

Students Reflect on Their Own Practices

As I said at the beginning of this paper, I have been getting my university students to research everyday literacy practices and 20 years on, I am still doing it. There have been tremendous changes in their practices over this time. The approach of a detailed study of practices has been changing as well, and I now refer to it as researching their techno-biographies. This can work not just with university students, but also with kindergarten children, teenagers, pre-service teachers, and adult learners. The approach has a set of steps which will be covered one by one.

First, I get students to research their own current practices, the here and now. They do this by noting down and reflecting on what they do. They then discuss it with fellow students, and they get to see similarities and differences with their classmates: "I thought I was the only one with five email accounts," as one student commented when realising how similar his practices were to his fellow students. What the students say changes from year to year, and all such studies are reflecting practices in a certain place at a certain time. (It is important to note that this quote is taken from a group of undergraduates majoring in English Language or in Linguistics at a UK university in

November 2012. They were in a Language and Media course taught by Julia Gillen and myself.) The sorts of things they were mentioning included talk about integrating iPads with other technology, or getting into Twitter, and some were tiring of Facebook. They reflected on the different ways they watched TV programs, increasingly on a laptop, and watching programs at different times.

The second step, the next week in the course, is to interview other people who differ from them in age, gender or culture. In this way, they can explore differences across time and place. This is a moving outwards in both content and methodology. Students get beyond their own experiences and can compare themselves with others. They had age stereotypes: to them 'older people' meant anyone over 35 years, and as one of them put it "landlines are for grandparents." Some felt older people were out of touch, whilst others marvelled at the practices of grandparents researching family history online or being part of specialist networks. They also praised the online sophistication of their younger siblings, thus demonstrating that everyone, whatever their age, seems to regard anyone younger than themselves as being a digital native. Looking across cultures, we unravelled the different platforms used by students from China and how they used both Chinese and Western sites for social networking, micro-blogging, following news, searching, and buying.

The third step is to examine the results of large scale surveys like the PEW reports in the U.S. and the Ofcom reports and Oxford Internet studies in the U.K. In this way students get to locate their own experiences and those of their friends and families in broader patterns of national and international life. In all these steps, they are encouraged to find both similarities and differences which surprise them. The statistics of internet usage by age, for instance, can situate what they have discovered in earlier weeks. They also come across issues of access which they may not have thought about before, and they read statistics which challenge previous assumptions, such as that "Everyone has a smart phone." Each week they revisit their own practices, and over time they reveal more details which they had not thought of as being relevant earlier.

The students encounter and use different research methodologies. They start with mini auto-ethnographies or techno-biographies. In this way, they develop attention to ethnographic detail. They then carry out small surveys to get beyond their own experiences and, thirdly, they utilize the results of large surveys carried out by others. They are encouraged to see how different methodologies can complement each other and provide different ways of seeing the world. They learn the different sorts of generalizations they can make from different sorts of data. Throughout, they are encouraged to think in terms of practices and to locate 'skills' and 'habits' in this broader concept. Through examining practices they can see how uses of technology fit into people's lives.

Students also make a posting on the course website each week. They easily write 400 words a week, and it can be hard to keep them to the word limit. This is more 'unnoticed' writing and over the term, this can add up to more than 4000 words by each student. In these ways, students also become more reflexive about their practices and about their learning. This knowledge feeds into the course where they learn about language and media as well as about research methodology. That everyone's practices are constantly changing is precisely why we, as teachers, need to ask students about their practices, a topic where they are the experts. We need to learn about what they know and what they do. And, conversely, to stress the space for education, we need to understand what they do not know and do not do.

In conclusion, in this paper I have covered three distinct studies of how the online world is impacting on everyday literacy practices: revisiting local literacies, writing around photography, and students' techno-biographies. In all three there is an emphasis of focussing on practices to understand change and a demonstration that the approaches of literacy studies are particularly important for understanding language online, where so much of it consists of written language.

REFERENCES

Barton, D. (2012). Participation, deliberate learning and discourses of learning online. *Language & Education* *26*(2) 139-150.

Barton, D., & M. Hamilton (1998/2012). *Local literacies: reading and writing in one community*, London and New York, NY: Routledge.

Barton, D., & C. Lee (2013). *Language online: Investigating digital texts and practices.* London and New York: Routledge.

Davies, J., & Merchant, G. (2009). *Web 2.0 for schools*, New York, NY: Peter Lang.

Hamilton, M. (2012). Revisiting Local Literacies. Paper presented at workshop on *Revisiting learning lives – longitudinal perspectives on researching learning and literacy.* OISE, University of Toronto, Nov 7-9.

Heath, S.B. (1983). *Ways with words.* Cambridge and New York: Cambridge University Press.

Ito, M., Baumer, S., Bittanti, M., Boyd, D., Cody, R., Herr, B. et al. (2010). *Hanging Out, Messing Around, Geeking Out: Living and Learning with New Media*, Cambridge, MA: MIT Press.

Lee, C., & D. Barton (2011). Constructing global identities through multilingual writing practices on Flickr. com. *International Multilingualism Research Journal, 5*(1), 39-59.

Richardson, W. (2006). *Blogs, Wikis, Podcasts, and Other Powerful Web Tools for Classrooms.* CA: Corwin Press.

Street, B. (1984). *Literacy in theory and practice.* Cambridge and New York: Cambridge University Press.

Designing New Spaces for Literacy Learning

Kevin M. Leander
Ty Hollett
Vanderbilt University

Frontal attacks are even more wasteful in learning than in war. — Dewey, 1916

During this Literacy Research Association 2012 annual conference, we have been thinking and talking about how digital tools create new forms of literacy practice, about new social connections and identities forged with social media, about the development and assessment of new media practices in classrooms, and about researching multimodality as well as a host of other related issues. In this context of issues, it might seem strange to consider space and learning as a relevant topic, and perhaps especially strange as a concluding relevant topic. So, why space, or why space, technology, and learning?

Consider for a moment the structures and practices of space, technology, and learning that we have here, in this moment. On the surface, I stand up here and present, you listen, take notes, nod in agreement, and offer grant funding. You face me, I face you, my computer and the projector focus your attention on a single object—one to many communication. But, dig a little deeper, and it falls apart. Some of you are certainly using laptops to check into your flights, or upload graded papers, or check unwanted e-mails. Some of you are texting or tweeting sarcasms or props, some are posting to Vine GIFs of the person's head in front of you. Even in this moment, the bounded space of this platform event seems to fall apart, seems to be a patchwork of many events using and producing texts that extend into cyberspace within this physical space and well beyond it. As you digitally reach out to others—perhaps those who could not attend—you also grant them presence in this space as well. You are with me, but not entirely; and they are with me, but not entirely. There is a lot of production going on, and the material box of the room is somewhat unbounded, destabilized, vibrating with something new.

Still, all the same, something about this event holds together, conserves and preserves itself. As a social event, together we will still perform a large room lecture, a keynote. How is the structure of this event produced and maintained? Conversely, what would need to happen to produce a radical change in this platform event, or to nudge what is already starting here into keynote revolution?

THE PROBLEM OF TECHNOLOGY "INTEGRATION" IS POWERFULLY SPATIAL

These observations move toward a first general point to make: The problem of technology integration is powerfully spatial. In fact, the term "integration" is quite a misnomer, as it invites conceiving of technology as "outside" of something that can contain it and moving inside that thing (which largely doesn't change). Rather, to think spatially about technology and its relationship to learning environments such as classrooms requires a different discourse and perspective on the

29

relationship between technology and social space than terms such as "integration" provide. As a move in this direction, we start with several assertions:

- New media technology use involves changes in social relationships.

- Changes of the social world involve changes in space.

- Changing the spatial has power to change the social.

- Radical changes in the social world necessarily involve radical spatial changes.

- The spatial is not entirely produced or changed by structures, nor social practices, nor discourses. All of these are relevant and important.

- Virtual spaces (structures, practices, and discourses) have possibilities that are not the same as those of physical spaces.

- Virtual and physical spaces are inextricably linked.

- Virtual and physical spaces have both conserving and transforming effects on one another.

We will revisit these assertions in various ways throughout the course of this talk, but we lay them out in this way as a means of building toward alternate ways of spatially conceiving of designing learning environments for learning new literacies.

THE PROBLEM OF SPATIAL REFORM FOR EDUCATIONAL CHANGE IS AN OLD PROBLEM

Prior to considering new movements toward design, it seems worthwhile to step back in history to see education and education reform have always been spatial conceptions. The Boston Latin School, founded in 1635, is the oldest school founded in America, antedating Harvard College by more than a year (Boston Latin School). According to a history of the school (http://goo.gl/Vd6XtX), the school taught its scholars "dissent with responsibility and persistently encouraged such dissent" (Boston Latin School). This posture of dissent was conceived as an inner quality of the soul and mind. Following the Greeks, the only good things were the goods of the soul. Dissent or other qualities of mind and soul were not related to the material, embodied environment and practices of the school. The interior space of the school was, for the most part, a container for the learning of the humanities, including classics and Latin grammar. However, it appears that the outdoor space of the school was one in which the students exercised dissent in material fashion.

In winter it was not unusual for the boys to bring their sleds to school with them and, as soon as school was over, to coast down Beacon Street, across Tremont, and down School Street. During the winter of 1774-75 General Haldimand, a commander of British troops under General Gage, lived on School Street and had one of his servants ruin the coasting area by putting ashes on it. "The lads made a muster" – probably of the first class – "and chose a committee to wait upon the General, who admitted them, and heard their complaint, which was couched in very genteel terms, complaining that their fathers before 'em had improved it as a coast from time immemorial."

Apparently, the General ordered his servants to repair the damage to the coasting area, and conveyed the story to the Governor, who "observed that it was impossible to beat the notion of Liberty out of the people, as it was rooted in 'em FROM THEIR CHILDHOOD." This story is more than just a quaint or amusing bit of history—in it we see separations of inside and outside spaces, separations of spirit and beliefs from energetic bodies, and an early but enduring idea of the school as a form of inner cultivation and discipline.

In July of 1915, then General Education Board Secretary Abraham Flexner was charged with preparing a report "on the subject of a Modern School (Flexner, 1916). Flexner's primary arguments were that students should prepare for modern life and that recitation and drilling in classical subjects such as Latin were not relevant to most occupations. He advocated reading current literature, exploring outside the classroom (museums, zoos, libraries), and creating science activities that would bear some relationship to real life and would develop a child's powers of observation, reasoning, and imagination. Gone was the one room schoolhouse, and imagined were long corridors with rooms for separate disciplines. Envisioned was a multiple-use building for State "medical inspection and physical training," with vocational agriculture and domestic science classrooms and laboratories for children, special courses and field work for adults, and a community center. Newspaper headlines across the country reflected the ensuing controversy, and discourses around these plans, such as "John D. Would Banish Classics," "Are We Likely to Become Like Highly Trained Ants?", and "For Contentedly Ignorant (Adgent, 2012).

Eventually, and through a complicated set of political and pedagogical interactions, initiatives to develop a consolidated rural "modern school" were discarded. Why? As early as mid-1916, Flexner's correspondence reflected an emerging realization that educating rural students for modern life would not likely be achieved by erecting a building. *The real problem* was a lack of trained teachers and superintendents, exacerbated by incompetent teacher selection committees; the mandate that public school systems use teachers from state normal schools; and the deeply ingrained notion that Classical studies were necessary.

The example of the consolidated rural "modern school" underscores, first of all, the ways in which school reform and school building space have a long history of being dreamed up together, and secondly, the ways in which these dreams are often concluded with statements about "the real problem." Why does the redesign of school spaces not succeed? How are school architectures and building physical spaces discovered not to matter, in the end? Moreover, what does educational reform, including in literacy education, have to do with spatial reform?

Developments in educational philosophy at the time of Flexner's architectural designs were even further challenging beliefs about social space and learning. Dewey has been described elsewhere as a technologist; here we might also describe him as a key spatial thinker for educational reform. In drawing largely from *Democracy and Education* (1916/2004) and especially from David Hansen's (2006) treatment of Dewey's conception of a learning environment, we can tease out several principles of spatial design and learning environments from Dewey.

- Environment versus Surroundings
- Mixed Ontologies
- Emergence
- Transactional Theory and Environment
- Designed Environments and Chance Environments
- Indirectness of Teaching
- Teaching as Environment Regulation
- Teacher Development—Losing and Finding Oneself

First, Dewey makes a distinction between a learning environment and all of the physical or social surroundings, indicating that the environment pertains to the continuity between the surroundings and a person's "active tendencies" (1916/2004, p. 11). Hansen notes that for Dewey it is not with everything, but with things that we "vary" that forms our "active environment." This idea of co-variation is prescient and also appears in Deleuze and Guattari (1997) as does the idea of mixed ontologies. Dewey writes that "our desires, emotions, and affections are but various ways in which our doings are tied up with the doings of things and persons about us" (1916/2004, pp. 125-26). Boundaries between the subjective, personal, inner world and the objective, material, outer world are not maintained; self and world are engaged with each other fully in activity and development. Such views are of course resonant with those of us who cut our teeth on sociocultural theory and activity theories. But the consequences of taking seriously the non-separation of inner and outer worlds, of seeing not only mind, but also heart, desire, engagement, and affect as constructed through traversals of the inner and outer, have still to be seen. Such mixed ontologies are a basis for the emergence of networks of meanings as people and world enter into transactions—the environment itself is changed and developed in concert with the teacher and students.

In developing new social media technologies the ideas of mixed ontologies and emergence also ask us, in the intentionality of our designs for literacy learning, about how robust and immersive our virtual learning environments are, what kinds of objects they involve, and how they engage whole persons in affect, thinking, and ways of being. In literacy, we have tended to focus on the linguistic or literate aspects of online media. At the same time, we live in the world that moves us and compels us to action not through the separation of language and texts from objects and movements, but through their interweaving. Designed online environments for literacy will share these powerful characteristics.

Dewey makes a distinction between designed environments and chance environments, where designed environments are a major product of the work of the teacher, before and during interaction, and chance environments are those with no intention for education behind them, and "a school or classroom environment that is left up to chance is as likely as not to be mis-educative as educative" (Hansen, 2002, p. 270). Again, Dewey is incredibly prescient here, in considering mis-education by thoughtless environments, even if in his work we do not have a clear sense of the violence of institutional environments and their specific forms of mis-education.

Transactional theory has of course been an important construct in literacy education, from Dewey through Rosenblatt and others. But what we might tend to elide in these literacy-focused conversations about transactions with texts and teachers is that the organic relations and provocations of stimuli and responses that Dewey has in mind are not necessarily text-focused but involve all manner of subject-subject and subject-object relations. In fact, in speaking from a Deweyian perspective, and without departing to Latour (2007) or any other form of post-structural ontology, we might say that any transaction with a text is inextricably intertwined with all manner of other transaction. People "infuse intelligence, purpose, feeling, and hope into this transactive process" (Hansen, 2002, p. 271) that involves not just texts, but also furniture, book covers, the use of time, web links, the touch of a teacher, and physical and digital architectures for learning.

For Dewey, teaching with/through the environment is an indirect act. Direct teaching, is a "frontal attack" that is "wasteful." The image here is one of mis-education, education that isolates itself to subject-subject relations and is therefore ignorant of objective conditions. As an indirect act, teaching "includes what is done by the educator and the way in which it is done, not only words spoken but the tone of the voice in which they are spoken. It includes equipment, books, apparatus, toys, games played. It includes the materials with which an individual interacts, and, most important of all, the total social set-up of the situations in which a person is engaged." (p. 45)

According to Dewey, teachers "give the pupils something to do, not something to learn; and the doing is of such a nature as to demand thinking, or the intentional noting of connections; learning naturally results" (1997, p. 154). This is a particularly striking contrast to conceptions of teaching in an age of accountability, with teaching regulation focusing increasingly on the acts of teacher behaviors. Dewey has in mind something like the mirror opposite of this orientation—focus is not on the acts of the teacher herself, but on the teacher-student relations as constituted and as emergent in and with the environment. Teacher development in this conception does not involve the development of a finished teacher-subject who can be lifted out of an environment, but a series of transactions of teacher and world in which the teacher loses and finds herself in relation to the environment.

How many of our teacher education programs in literacy include courses in the design of learning environments? And if they do, how do these designs traverse and integrate physical and virtual realities? Of course, classroom literacy reforms can point to their own rich illustrations that involve transforming social spaces for literacy learning, including for example, environment print and writing workshop models. However, these transformations of the classroom are most often discussed as forms of pedagogy, and little as considerations of spatial design. Rather, as with the case of technology, designs are thought to be "integrated" into school social spaces, rather than fundamentally transforming them.

SPATIAL REFORM FAILS IN PREDICTABLE WAYS

Before considering innovations of literacy learning spaces, we turn now to a cautionary tale about spatial reform in schooling, considering the transformation of physical spaces first and the "integration" of digital space second. This cautionary tale is important not for subduing our expectations of reform—for decreasing our vision—but for seeing the ways in which spatial reforms are ultimately closed off, contained, and snapped back to traditional grids.

In the 1960s educators and architects engaged in a process to rethink the social organization and spatial configurations of schools (Cleveland, 2011). Driven by education and social reform and popularized by the Educational Facilities Laboratories (EFL) in the U.S., the open plan movement represented the first significant architectural departure from the traditional industrial model of the classroom (Cleveland, 2011). Open plan classrooms were spaces designed for a large number of students, active teaching/learning strategies, and aimed to be responsive in promoting flexible and individualized learning for students. The international open plan classroom movement was for a short period considered "best practice" in school design across westernized nations (Cleveland, 2011) including Australia, Britain, Canada, and the United States.

It's striking to think about how many of the following characteristics that were stated in the open plan movement remain characteristics of the call for new media and new technology integration—including flexible arrangements for learning, individualization, and the disruption of the classroom.

- Flexible arrangements for pedagogical innovation
- Disruption of classroom as unit
- Democratic education, experimentation
- Variable sized groups
- Highly responsive, low intention of design
- Individualized instruction
- New technologies: mobile dividers, acoustic screens, mobile chalkboards and tables, tote trays

By the 1980s however, the open plan school movement was deemed a "failure" and quickly faded into a return to the traditional industrial classroom and school structure.

Many schools erected walls, making them almost indistinguishable from egg crate schools. This history was born out in the brand new elementary school I (Kevin) went to in 4th-6th grades, Heatherwood Elementary School in Boulder, CO (Figure 1). While the outside of the building appears nearly just as it did in the early 70s (with the addition of an actual lawn) (Figure 2), the inside of the once open space building as been nearly entirely subdivided into corridors and traditional classrooms (Figure 2).

Figure 1. Heatherwood Elementary School

The failures of the open plan school movement are often cited as failures of schools (the familiar "space doesn't matter" argument). Recent international research, however, is challenging such a notion. Specifically, research has demonstrated that such failures exemplify how spatial reform must evolve from education reform (Newton & Fisher, 2009). Teachers have often been blamed in the failure—teacher conservatism—as if teachers should have learned from the environment itself how to change pedagogy. The built environment as physical space, classroom interactions, and pedagogy as the production of social space must co-evolve.

Figure 2. Heatherwood Elementary School Interior

In other ethnographic research work as part of the Synchrony study, I have reported on how a private school involved in a laptop program that involved extensive investment in technical tools and infrastructure, struggled to change teaching and learning practices in such a way that the new open digital architecture made sense with the traditional learning environment (Leander, 2007). For example, during classroom discussions, the students would also be online, and these online practices were seen as a disruption to a common, classroom-based focus. Laptops were thus closed. During testing, access to the Internet was seen as a disruption to a traditional understanding of learning as fixed in individual memory. Laptops were thus closed again. In this study, I reported how space was "pedagogized" in the school:

- Defined plans precede resources and activity.

- Sequential activity is dominant, and everyone follows the same sequential path.

- Asynchronous communication is primary (e.g., e-mail or web searching is more "schooled" than instant messaging).

- A single space is dominant (and under surveillance) for each task; "task" is mono-spatial and "off-task" is multi-spatial.

- Material print texts and print spaces (the built environment) are primary and authorized, while virtual texts are unauthorized and supplemental.

- The Internet is primarily a tool for information rather than a tool for communication.

These findings are consistent with those of others, such as Weiss (2007) who contended that educators had largely used new technologies in ways that conformed to the existing structures of space and time in traditional classrooms rather than integrating them into new practices based on "the inherent spatial and temporal logic of the resources themselves" (Weiss, p. 81). Cuban, Kirkpatrick, and Peck (2001) also conclude there is a paradox of high access and low use in schools.

In some ways, these closures of new technologies weren't complete—they had leaks in them, small openings, and there were sites of innovation. Still, in many ways, the closures remind me of the partitions dividing the open spaces of the classrooms in Heatherwood Elementary. They are not completely walls, but they are divided. Tensions and contradictions of different spatial ideologies and histories co-exist. And, the possibilities that were once imagined go unrealized, but for reasons we often do not understand when we do not think about reform through a multi-dimensional spatial lens.

HYBRID ARCHITECTURES FOR LITERACY LEARNING

While it is true that social spatial reform has always been connected in some way to school reform (that the problem of social space is not new), and that "openings" toward new ways of being in school get closed off in predictable ways, newly developing physical and virtual relationships pose very new ways of arranging "matter"—new ontologies. While these new ontologies are already all around us—while the virtual is in many ways fully domesticated into our everyday physical lives—we need ways of thinking about design that push our imaginations of how these relationships and hybridities already happen, and how they might happen. Such ways of thinking should account for the unique affordances of the physical and of the virtual.

Figure 3. Hybrid Spaces

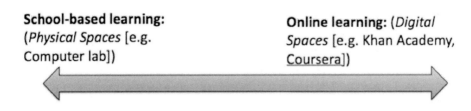

School-based learning: (*Physical Spaces* [e.g. Computer lab])

Online learning: (*Digital Spaces* [e.g. Khan Academy, Coursera])

Convergent Learning (Hybrid Spaces, mobile, permeable)

Formal, digitally-enhanced learning seems to take place on a spectrum. On the one end, we might have teachers taking students to a computer lab to complete a specific assignment, to write a paper, or participate in a web-quest. On the other end, we might have entire lectures in online settings such as are being rapidly developed in Massively Open Online Courses (MOOC) or other forms of resources in the Khan Academy.

[Insert Figure 3 about here] What if we thought about the middle of that spectrum, though, a hybrid space that depended upon both the digital and the physical, one that was permeable, that included interactions, communication, and forms of digital and physical production that flowed back-and-forth between the virtual and the physical, or rather, within an imbricated physical/virtual space?

In recent design work at the Nashville Public Library, where we have engaged youth in the architectural redesign of their own Learning Lab, we have developed several metaphors that we have found productive for re-thinking the relationships of the virtual and physical. Architecture is constantly informed by images and metaphors that come from nature, social life, and other arts. Educators and architects together have new possibilities to develop and design from new images and metaphors that re-imagine physical and virtual hybridities. Following are dominant metaphors guiding our design discussions:

1. Parallel World: In this metaphor, we imagine a virtual world that to some extent serves as a mirror of the physical—the world is doubled.

2. Windows and Doors: In this metaphor, we envision peering into the virtual from the physical (or vice versa), or moving from one to another through a portal.

3. Journeys: In this metaphor, we envision traversals that move across physical and virtual spaces, such as in designed learning activities that require movements across terrains made of digital bits on the one hand and dirt and dust on the other.

4. Affecting one world from the other: In this metaphor, which could build on the idea of a parallel world, we see transformations of the virtual that are automated from interacting with the physical (or vice versa). For instance, through RFID and tagging technologies, the re-arrangement of physical building blocks in activity would result in an automatic digital transformation of a model already existing online.

5. Augmented physical reality and augmented virtual reality: This metaphor can take many forms, and we will have more to say about augmentation in the following, but

the notion of the metaphor can be captured somewhat in the idea of "layering" forms of the virtual over the physical (or vice versa).

6. Identity kits composed across spaces. We borrow the notion of the "identity kit" from Gee (1989), and the working metaphor here is the way in which virtual and physical spaces both provide identity "equipment" or resources that can travel with the individual, and also combine in surprising ways.

Drawing on the windows and doors metaphor we have made initial designs for a physical/digital interface that would allow youth who are online and at distance from the learning lab to nevertheless peer into the activities of the lab, and perhaps also remotely move cameras to have some control over this type of peripheral participation. Conversely, youth in the physical learning lab space will be able to join in with their virtual counterparts in activities that are designed to draw on the unique affordances of the virtual. This metaphor is also present in the design of the physical space itself, for instance, in the design of a glass-walled enclosure of the physical gaming space. The enclosure will provide separation of activities and associated noise, while at the same time, gaming activities will be visible for those wanting to move from the periphery to more central participation (Lave & Wenger, 1991), or from hanging out to messing around with gaming. The identity kits metaphor has guided us in thinking about hybrid forms of embodied representation in the learning lab space. For instance, when initially entering the physical space, we envision youth being given the opportunity to construct an avatar of themselves that can indicate their presence with others in the physical space (through large monitors), and can also move into the digital learning lab spaces with others who are uniquely virtually accessible. Moreover, avatars could be used to represent the earned levels of participants in various activity types (e.g., music or maker space), through unique forms of coloring or badging.

Contemporary school and university architectural designs, for the most part, still reflect a container model or integrationist model with respect to the relationship of the physical and virtual, but designs are nevertheless changing and being increasingly influenced by virtuality and by digital culture. I (Kevin) recently toured the Academic Centre of the Ormond College of the University of Melbourne (http://www.ormond.unimelb.edu.au/support-ormond/impact-of-giving/academic-centre-1), with its stated design to "integrate academic, library, and IT functions." The building re-design, under the direction of Peter Jamieson (Director of the Design of Learning Spaces at the University of Melbourne), is beautifully done through metaphors and materials of nature, of Islamic art and geometries, and with explicit references to its own past. Relations to digital culture in the building include primarily the ways in which different types of learning spaces have been designed to support different forms of learning arrangements, including individual nooks for private study with wireless support (some even built directly into the book shelving), booths with restaurant-style comfortable seating for collaborative work in groups of 3-4, organized around shared monitors, and glassed-in tutorial rooms with smart board technology for teaching and project work in groups of 10-15. The building is also centered round a performance floor in the center, designed for large group lectures, artistic performances, etc. Of course, the idea of spaces for various sizes and types of groups has been around for some time and is not unique to digital culture, but at the same time, the social arrangements of new forms of peer-peer, inquiry-based, or "flipped classroom" learning as integrated with digital tools and practices seem to be pushing for the development of a differentiated range of learning spaces. A nice example of movement with influence beyond a mere "integrated" perspective at Ormond is the kitchen placed at the center of the building. This kitchen, while drawing on metaphors of home and warmth, has also been conceived of in relation to the maker movement—as a place where project work at the interface of physical/digital cultures might happen.

The Academic Centre at Ormond College is a nice example of what Cleveland (2011) terms "reflexive" learning environments, or learning environments that suggest to participants (teachers and students) how they might be used. The idea of reflexivity is posed in contrast to "flexible" learning environments, in which teachers and students have to constantly remake the relationship between structure (built environment) and practice (pedagogy), such as in the open space movement discussed earlier. The learning spaces at Ormond "speak" to participants within them about how to use them. The reflexivity of space—the power of space to produce social forms of learning, just as these social practices produce space—is evident also in designs by architect Trung Le, of Cannon Design in Chicago. Le and the design firm have coined the term the "third teacher" (OWP/P Cannon Design et al., 2010) to describe how learning environments participate in pedagogy (with educators and parents as first and second teachers). In the design of the Booker T. Washington STEM Academy at Champaign, IL (http://www.cannondesign.com/projects/project-catalog/booker-t-washington-stem-academy/#overview), the firm did not choose between supporting discipline-specific and interdisciplinary learning in STEM. Rather, the building has separate areas for different components of the curriculum (e.g., science, technology, math), all of which open into a large collaborative space for interdisciplinary project work.

Contemporary and innovative architectural design practices in education draw on a large and very mixed set of theories and visions concerning learning, some of which are separated from current debates among educators and learning scientists. For instance, new forms of embodied learning are little considered in architectural designs, and truly hybrid physical/virtual learning environment design is still in its infancy. Given the current status of this work, for literacy educators the time seems ripe for more and deeper engagement in the development of learning environments—a key time when theory, new literacy pedagogies, and the design of learning environments could energize one another. Another sign of hope for this type of work, and especially given current financial constraints, is that innovative learning environment design is occurring also in the re-design of extant buildings rather than only in new building projects. In fact, Ben Cleveland, a researcher of space and pedagogy, argues that the constraints of existing buildings create more energy for the imagination of new learning spaces than does the complete construction of new spaces (personal communication). The following few sites provide an opening exploration of innovative educational architectures:

Center for Transformative Learning, Walsh University (http://thethirdteacherplus.com/walsh-university-center-for-transformative-learning/)

Fuji Kindergarten in Tokyo, Japan
(http://www.architonic.com/aisht/fuji-kindergarten-tezuka-architects/5100019)

Northern Beaches Christian School, Sydney, Australia
(http://www.nbcs.nsw.edu.au/)

HYBRID SPATIAL PRACTICES FOR LITERACY LEARNING

Emerging, hybrid infrastructures can also be thought of as "networked localities" (Gordon and de Souza e Silva, 2011). Gordon and de Souza e Silva (2011) highlight the ways in which mobile technologies augment the experience of local, physical geographies. We no longer need to log on to the web, or go to a specific location—it is all around us. The web, the Internet, cyberspace—whatever label we want to affix to it—is welded to the real world. Pictures are geotagged with latitude and longitude coordinates, Google searches are delivered to us based upon our location (searching for something in Portland, ME, will uncover something quite different than when you're in Portland, OR). Friends gain virtual status by becoming the "mayor" of a physical location on Four Square, and an application like Yelp prioritizes nearby restaurants by location. As Gordon and de Souza write, "having access to a global network of information while situated within a local street, neighborhood, town, or city, potentially realigns how the individual deals with the scale of user experience" (Gordon and de Souza e Silva, 2011, p. 3).

Cyberspace is over. The "spatiality of the internet (i.e., the *space* of cyberspace)" has moved away from the desktop computer and out into the city streets (Farman, 2012, p. 17). Small towns, once thought isolated, are now potentially cosmopolitan as information and data flood its city streets. In a recent example of such net locality, the Austrian city of Klagenfurt—which does not have public library space—turned its entire city into a library. By scanning QR Code- and NFC (Near Field Communication) Chip-equipped stickers, users could locate books, freely available on Project Gutenberg, a public domain site, related to the physical location that they scanned. A mystery novel such as *The Killer*, for instance, could be found by scanning a sticker at the police station. You could imagine it looking something like this:

Figure 4. Hybrid Street Library

In many ways, this fusion of the digital and physical stems from an extended line of thought in spatial theory and research which has sought to avoid the creation of a digital/physical binary (Hine, 2000; Wakeford, 2000; Leander & McKim, 2003). Emerging in phrases like "digiplace" (Zook & Graham, 2007) and "code/space" (Dodge & Kitchin, 2005) the rise of pervasive, ubiquitous, mobile technologies has drawn further attention to action and interaction in these hybrid spaces.

In their earlier work on mobile technologies, Mimi Ito and Daisuke Okabe (2005), described the ways in which people used mobile devices within social situations. They argued that while mobile phones may, in fact, undermine traditional notions of social situations, they "also define new technosocial situations and new boundaries of identity and place" (p. 6). Mobile phones, to Ito and Okabe, "create new kinds of bounded places that merge the infrastructures of geography and technology, as well as technosocial practices that merge technical standards and social norms" (p. 6).

In building from Ito's work, we might be able to think of these hybrid actions and interactions as "techno*spatial* practices." Such technospatial practices, like their technosocial cousins, are facilitated not only by the ubiquity of mobile devices, but also by the data that flows all around us, that is pushed to our devices, stuck on our street poles, embedded in our neighborhoods.

Technospatial practices—especially those mediated by ubiquitous technologies—are not devoid of the physical environment. In *Digital Ground: Architecture, Pervasive Computing, and Environmental Knowing (2005)*, David McCullough emphasizes how "digital networks are no longer separate from architecture" (p. xiii). Pervasive computing, he asserts, continues to be "inscribed into the social and environmental complexity of the existing physical environment" (p xiii). Pervasive computing enables technology to be situated, to shape and be shaped by the people and things that make up a physical locale. While there was once the need to think about interface design, the pressing issue now is interaction design. With the rise of the Internet in the late 90s, architects feared that cyberspace would displace physical space, that it would make architecture moot; pervasive computing, however, "invites a defense of architecture" (p xiv). In short, McCullough argues that it is not the design of physical spaces that must be considered, rather the design of interactive spaces that play nicely with pervasive computing technologies.

McCullough unites pervasive computing and interaction design. As early as 2004, he notes, the paradigm had shifted from cyberspace to pervasive computing. Instead of "pulling us through the looking glass into some sterile, luminous world, digital technology now pours out beyond the screen, into our messy places...it is built into our rooms, embedded in our props and devices—everywhere" (p. 9). Pervasive computing partners with the built environment. This is "quiet architecture" (p. 63). The more the principles of "locality, embodiment, and environmental perception underlie pervasive computing, the more it all seems like architecture." (p. 63)

Informal learning environments, such as museums, have worked to bridge the physical space of their exhibits with digital information. The tiny Museum of Inuit Art (MIA) in Toronto recently sought to extend its reach to visitors by implementing both "online" and "onsite" digital experiences. Not only do they provide online opportunities like Skype conversations with artists and virtual tours of the museum, but they have also developed onsite, hybrid experiences for visitors, including using the game-based app SCVNGR to encourage users to take part in various challenges with their smartphones—ranging from interacting with other visitors, to taking pictures, to commenting on specific components of the exhibit. The MIA has also incorporated augmented reality into their exhibits, embedding videos of the artists working, audio clips, and images of other, related art pieces by the artist with which visitors can interact through their personal mobile devices.

SPATIAL DESIGN AS PEDAGOGY

Inspired by McCullough's emphasis of the ways in which the digital, especially once pervasive, or mobile, "pours out beyond the screen," two of my doctoral students, Ty Hollett and Christian Ehret, began to explore the ways in which students could layer the existing physical infrastructure of a school with digital material.

Equipped with an iPod Touch for each student, Hollet and Ehret first introduced this concept—this imbrication, or layering, of the digital and physical—through an app based on the popular *Flat Stanley* children's book (Brown, 1964). Their students created a multimodal composition by taking images in which the Flat Stanley avatar interacted with objects and people in the physical classroom.

Figure 5. Layering and Flat Stanley Activity

Hollett and Ehret then extended these technospatial activities, designing lessons in which students would further layer digital information over physical components of the classroom. In an ensuing project, students used an app, Audioboo, to record themselves making sense of the image-only graphic novel *The Arrival* (Tan, 2007). They then linked the audio file to QR codes affixed to pages within the book which, once scanned with the iPod touch's camera, enabled students to listen to their peers' own interpretation of the story as well as read peers' notes and comments about select pages.

These activities then built toward the students' creation of a digital brochure of the school using various apps on their mobile devices. Students recorded short videos, took pictures of and recorded themselves describing meaningful people, places, and things throughout the school. These digital creations were linked to QR codes affixed to those meaningful spots. Visitors could then tour the school, hearing about it through the videos, images, and recordings of its own students. Their initial findings report on the ways in which their students felt and sensed the school, reading it as a space simultaneously digital and physical as well as how their students experienced—and felt—time when moving and composing throughout such an environment.

SPATIAL REFORM AS MULTI-DIMENSIONAL

In this talk we have taken a critical perspective on integrationist discourse concerning technology and the development of new spaces for literacy learning. Borrowing from others (e.g., Lefebvre, 1991; Soja, 1996) we have argued that the production of space is multi-dimensional, including a transformation of our discourse around space itself. While we empathize with the intentions of integrating technology into schooled space and practice, the integrationist metaphor does not go far as a spatially transformative discourse for education. In its place, we have explored some initial ways through which a multi-dimensional, hybrid discourse around innovation and spatial transformation might guide design and development. As literacy educators invested in the shape of new literacies, our commitment to "shape" must also materialize in a commitment to the redesign of places and spaces where literacy learning happens. To make new literacies matter, we need to design learning with new "matter."

REFERENCES

Adgent, N. (2012). "More life and less Latin: The GEB, model schools, and vocational education. *New York History Review.* Retrieved from http://nyhrarticles.blogspot.com/2012/09/more-life-and-less-latin-geb-model.html

Bassett, C. (1997). Virtually gendered: life in an on-line world. In K. Gelder & S. Thornton(pp. 537-550). London: Routledge.

Boston Latin School. The Boston Latin School: History. Retrieved November 5, 2012, from http://goo.gl/Vd6XtX

Brown, Jeff. (1964) *Flat Stanley: his original adventure!* New York, NY: Harper Collins Publishers.

Cuban, L., Kirkpatrick, H., & Peck, C. (2001). High access and low use of technologies in high school classrooms: Explaining an apparent paradox. *American Educational Research Journal, 38*(4), 813-834.

Cleveland, B. (2011). *Engaging spaces: innovative learning environments pedagogies, and student engagemt in the middle years of school.* PhD Thesis. Faculty of Architecture, Building and Planning, The University of Melbourne.

Deleuze, G., & Guattari, F. (1987). *A thousand plateaus: Capitalism and schizophrenia.* U of Minnesota Press.

Dewey, J. (1916/2004). *Democracy and education.* Radford, VA: Wilder Publications.

Dodge, M., & Kitchin, R. (2005). Code and the transduction of space. *Annals of the Association of American Geographers, 95*(1), 162-180.

Farman, J. (2012). *Mobile interface theory.* New York, NY: Routledge.

Flexner, Abraham. (1916). Letter to General Education Board. General Education Board Archives, Rockefeller Archive Center, Sleepy Hollow, New York.

Gordon, E., & e Silva, A. d. S. (2011). *Net locality: Why location matters in a networked world.* Malden, MA: Wiley-Blackwell.

Gee, J. P. (1989). Literacy, discourse, and linguistics: Introduction. *Journal of Education, 171*(1), 5-17.

Hansen, D. T. (2006). *John Dewey and Our Educational Prospect: A Critical Engagement with Dewey's Democracy and Education.* SUNY Press.

Hansen, D. T. (2002). Dewey's conception of an environment for teaching and learning. *Curriculum Inquiry, 32*(3), 267-280.

Hine, C. (2000) *Virtual Ethnography.* London, Sage.

Ito, M., & Okabe, D. (2005). Technosocial situations: Emergent structurings of mobile email use. In M. Ito, D. Okabe, & M. Matsuda. *Personal, portable, pedestrian: mobile phones in Japanese life* (pp. 257-273). Cambridge: MIT Press.

Latour, B. (2007). *Reassembling the social.* Oxford, UK: Oxford University Press.

Lave, J., & Wenger, E. (1991). *Situated learning: Legitimate peripheral participation.* Cambridge, UK: Cambridge University Press.

Leander, K. M., & McKim, K. K. (2003). Tracing the everyday'sitings' of adolescents on the internet: A strategic adaptation of ethnography across online and offline spaces. *Education, Communication & Information, 3*(2), 211-240.

Leander, K. M. (2007). "You won't be needing your laptops today": Wired bodies in the wireless classroom. *A New literacies sampler.* In M. Knobel & C. Lankshear (pp. 25-48). New York, NY: Peter Lang.

Lefebvre, H. (1991). *The production of space.* Oxford: Blackwell.

McCullough, M. (2005). *Digital ground: Architecture, pervasive computing, and environmental knowing.* Cambridge: MIT Press.

Newton, C., & Fisher, K. (2009). *Take 8: Learning Spaces: the Tranformation of Educational Spaces for the 21st Century.* Manuka, ACT: Australian Institute of Architects.

OWP/P Architects, VS Furniture, & Bruce Mau Design. (2010). *The third teacher: 79 ways you can use design to transform teaching and learning.* New York, NY. Abrams.

Soja, E. W. (1996). *Thirdspace: Journeys to Los Angeles and other real-and-imagined places.* London: Blackwell.

Tan, S. (2007). *The Arrival.* New York, NY: Arthur A. Levine Books.

Wakeford, S. (2000). Gender and the landscape of community in an internet café. In M. Crang, P. Crang, & J. May (Eds.), *Virtual geographies: bodies, spaces, and relations* (pp. 178-201). London: Routledge.

Weiss, A. (2007). Creating the ubiquitous classroom: integrating physical and virtual learning spaces. *The International Journal of Learning, 14*(3), 77-84.

Zook, M. A., & Graham, M. (2007). Mapping DigiPlace: geocoded internet data and the representation of place. *Environment and Planning B: Planning and Design, 34*(3), 466.

Reading Motivation and Engagement: Research Trends and Future Directions

Linda B. Gambrell

Clemson University

For the past two decades, there has been increasing interest in the role of motivation and engagement in reading development. A position paper published in 2000 by the International Reading Association asserts that "the development and maintenance of a motivation to read" is one of the key prerequisites for fostering reading proficiency (International Reading Association, 2000). From the advent of the National Reading Research Center in 1992 to the recently appointed IRA Literacy Research Panel motivation and engagement have been central to the reading research agenda. It is clear that motivation to read should be a central goal of the reading curriculum because the amount and breadth of students' reading predicts reading achievement and general knowledge (Cox & Guthrie, 2001; Guthrie, Wigfield, Metsala, & Cox, 1999; Schiefele, Schaffner, Moller, & Wigfield, 2012).

The objectives of this paper are to explore the literature and research on motivation to read and to identify motivation terms and constructs, theories, influential scholars, and point to emerging research trends. First, I will focus on terminology and constructs used in the study of motivation. Second, I will provide a brief overview of the theoretical underpinnings of reading motivation research. Third, I will recognize three scholars whose work has had a dynamic influence on motivation research as it relates to classroom practice, and finally I will identify research trends that I view as emerging themes of importance.

In his recent book, *How Children Succeed,* Paul Tough (2012) addresses the perennial question of why some children succeed while others fail. He argues that while early adversity can affect development, we now have knowledge that can help children overcome the constraints of adversity and poverty. Tough acknowledges the important role of motivation in cognitive development and academic learning. With respect to the dilemma of how to motivate students to learn, he states, "This is the problem with trying to motivate people: No one really knows how to do it well . . . What motivates us is often hard to explain and hard to measure" (Tough, 2012, pp. 66-67). I think most of us would agree that reading motivation is complex, messy, and very complicated.

Much of the most meaningful research on reading motivation suggests that effective instruction is both pleasurable and empowering, and that such instruction supports students in becoming more proficient readers who read for enjoyment and enlightenment. A central goal of research on reading motivation is to identify reading instruction that is motivating and results in approach responses to reading and learning.

INFLUENTIAL THEORIES OF MOTIVATION

While there are literally dozens of theories and perspectives on motivation, self-determination theory is most often cited in the contemporary motivation literature. For the last two decades, self-determination theory (Deci & Ryan, 1985; Deci, 2009) has been the prevailing lens for the study of intrinsic reading motivation in relation to engagement in reading tasks. Self-determination is defined as an individual's capacity to choose and to behave according to those choices, rather than choices made based on reinforcement contingencies or other drives or pressures (Deci & Ryan, 1985). Research indicates that a high perception of self-determination leads to intrinsic motivation, while on the other hand, a low perception is related to the need for extrinsic motivation. Intrinsic motivation is associated with adaptive cognitive, affective, and behavioral outcomes such as choosing to read, becoming an avid reader, and engagement in reading tasks and activities. Other frequently cited and influential theories include expectancy-value theory, sociocognitive theory, and more recently, sociocultural theory. Expectancy-value theory (Eccles & Wigfield, 2002) focuses on the role of self-confidence and value in motivation.

Sociocognitive theory (Bandura, 1997; 2001) emphasizes the importance of learning from others and the role of modeling. Sociocultural theory (Vygotsky, 1978) highlights the role of interaction between people and the culture in which they live. In addition to these very influential theories of motivation that ground much of the research on motivation, there are other theories that have been critical to furthering our understanding of motivation to read. Prominent among them are goal theory (Pintrich, 2000), attribution theory (Weiner, 1986), and flow theory (Csikszentmihalyi. 1990).

INFLUENTIAL TERMS AND CONSTRUCTS

Terminology used to describe facets of motivation has been an area of study and investigation, due in large part to our increasing understanding of the construct. In 2000, Murphy and Alexander (2000) reviewed the motivation research from 1980-2000 to identify the terms used in the motivation literature associated with the study of academic achievement. Their search yielded 127 studies. More recently, Schiefele et al. (2012) published an extensive review of the research that examined the constructs of reading motivation and synthesized the qualitative and quantitative research findings over the past 20 years. These two research reviews are impressive and ambitious explorations of the conceptualization and dimensionality of reading motivation.

Several decades ago, Pintrich (1994) made note of the "fuzzy but powerful constructs" that populate the literature on motivation and argued for greater conceptual clarity (p. 139). In their survey of the literature on motivation terminology, Murphy and Alexander (2000) posit that what distinguishes particular groups as communities is not only their shared purposes or codes of conduct, but also their specialized lexicon. This lexicon develops as community members create labels for distinctive and valued constructs. This lexicon, in short, becomes the community's intellectual shorthand. In their review of 20 years of motivation research to identify motivation terminology associated with motivation, they looked at the broader literature on motivation to learn rather than motivation to read. Murphy and Alexander (2000) identified 15 motivation terms that were relevant to academic achievement. Seven of the 15 terms were related to goals: ego or ego-involved goals, learning goals, mastery goals, performance goals, task goals, work avoidance goals, and social goals. The remaining eight motivation terms were related to motivation and academic achievement: intrinsic motivation, extrinsic motivation, individual interest, situational interest, agency, attribution, self-competence, and self-efficacy.

In their 2012 review of the research on motivation to read, Schiefele et al. identified what they call "genuine" dimensions of reading motivation related to reading behavior and competence. They drew heavily from research by Guthrie and his colleagues (Guthrie, Klauda, & Ho, 2013; Guthrie, McRea, & Klauda, 2007; Guthrie et al., 1996) as well as the 1990 research review by Greaney and Neuman.

Schiefele et al. (2012) make a distinction between current and habitual motivation to read. Current motivation to read implies a particular instance of a person choosing to read, while habitual reading motivation denotes the relatively stable readiness of a person to initiate reading activities. I am particularly drawn to the conceptualization of habitual reading because of my strong belief that we need to address more seriously how, as teachers, educators, and researchers, we can help students develop the reading habit. I am concerned about the lack of current attention to pleasure reading—reading for enjoyment and enlightenment. I am convinced that more attention needs to focus on helping students read for pleasure and helping them develop the reading habit (see E. H. Hiebert's book, *Reading More, Reading Better,* 2009). If students do not choose to read, if they do not develop the habit of reading, it is unlikely that they will ever reach their full reading potential.

The major conclusions of Schiefele's et al. (2012) review of the research provide interesting insights about reading motivation as well as the effects of reading motivation on reading behavior and reading competence. But, their research review, as good research does, raises a number of questions. Their review of the research confirmed the findings of other researchers on the beneficial effects of intrinsic reading motivation and the small or negative impact of extrinsic motivation. Schiefele et al. (2012) subsume many constructs under the heading of intrinsic motivation including reading attitude, task value, and to some extent, goal orientation. They view these constructs as overlapping with intrinsic reading motivation and they do not view them as distinct constructs; instead they view these constructs as preconditions of reading motivation. The second finding of the Schiefele et al. (2012) research review was the identification of what they call seven "genuine" dimensions of reading motivation.

They suggest that the number of reading motivations, as currently assessed by questionnaires and surveys, can be reduced by eliminating those that are not genuine dimensions of reading motivation (e.g., importance, challenge and social goals are not considered as genuine dimensions). The first two genuine dimensions of motivation identified by Schiefele et al. (2012) are curiosity and involvement, both of which are associated with intrinsic reading motivation. The remaining five genuine dimensions of motivation they identified are associated with extrinsic reading motivation: competition, recognition, grades, compliance, and work avoidance.

One concern about the identification of these seven genuine dimensions is that they were derived primarily from research using self-reports. Future research conducted with students as they engage in reading tasks in the classroom context may provide a different perspective on what dimensions of motivation are most "genuine" or "critical" for promoting reading motivation.

Schiefele et al. (2012) concluded that reading motivation is more strongly related to reading for enjoyment than to reading for school. I suspect that this may be explained by the fact that school reading is primarily under the control of the teacher. This is an area that needs much greater attention and research. The very influential Common Core State Standards (CCSS; National Governors Association Center for Best Practices & Council of Chief School Officers, 2010) address the importance of instruction designed to help students become independent readers, but there is little attention devoted to supporting students in developing the reading habit.

Another finding from the Schiefele et al. (2012) literature review is that reading competence is positively related to intrinsic motivation and negatively related to extrinsic motivation. Schiefele et al. (2012) suggest that this finding has yet to be clarified and more research is needed to untangle the complex relationship between reading motivation and reading competence. They conclude that "...it should be a high priority for future research to reach a consensus on the definition of reading motivation (including its dimensions)" and instruments and tools for assessing motivation (p. 459). In addition, they urge researchers to consider alternative measurements of student motivation that go beyond self-reports such as parental reports, teacher reports, and student diaries. I agree with Shiefele et al. that future research on motivation to read needs to build on distinctions between recreational and academic reading and print and digital texts.

Influential Scholars

Since the 1990s, much of the motivation research has focused on motivation to read as distinct from motivation to learn. The research by Pressley (2006), Turner (1995), and Guthrie (2001) makes it amazingly clear that intrinsic motivation to read leads to reading engagement, persistence, and proficiency. These three researchers have influenced my research on reading motivation, and I believe their work has had a positive impact on classroom practice over the past two decades.

Michael Pressley: Research on Highly Effective Teachers, Classrooms, and Schools

Pressley's (2006) research focused on highly effective teachers and the classroom context they created. According to Pressley, "there is high academic engagement in these classrooms, in part because so much of teaching is aimed at motivating students" (p. 5). Pressley's contributions to our understanding of teachers and how they create motivating contexts is remarkable and has had a positive effect on teaching and learning in our classrooms. His work also extended to the importance of the climate of the school. He concluded that highly effective schools have

> ...an exceptionally positive environment, with many explicit attempts to motivate student literacy, from the many read-alouds in the library and classrooms...to enthusiastic discussions about books being read by students in a class. There is little failure, with students. A great deal of instruction in the context of substantial, authentic reading and writing occurs in great classrooms and in most of the classrooms of a great school. (p. 5)

Pressley was very interested in the complex relationship between literacy motivation and strategy instruction. His work on the role of motivation in effective teaching resulted in a number of books that translated research into best practices for literacy instruction. His work on transactional strategy instruction was firmly grounded in motivation.

Julianne Turner: The Influence of Classroom Contexts on Literacy Motivation

Julianne Turner's work has focused on the influence of classroom contexts on literacy motivation. According to Turner (1995), students demonstrate reading motivation by initiating, sustaining, and prolonging engagement in reading. Her early work had a great influence on my thinking about the role of the teacher in establishing a motivating context for literacy learning.

Turner's (1995) research revealed that the strongest predictor of motivation was the context of literacy tasks. She classified literacy tasks as open or closed, with open literacy tasks defined as those that reflected student specified processes/goals and required higher order thinking and closed literacy tasks defined as those that reflected other designated processes/goals and required recognition/memory skills. She found that during open tasks, students used more reading strategies, were more persistent, and more attentive to the literacy task. The factors in open tasks that were related to high motivation and engagement were opportunities for challenge, control, personal interest, and collaboration. Turner concluded that classroom tasks that establish literacy as a higher-level cognitive activity, with pleasurable goals, are more likely to succeed in melding literacy learning and engagement.

John Guthrie: Research on Concept-Oriented Reading Instruction (CORI) and the Characteristics of Motivating Literacy Instruction

According to John Guthrie (2001), "Engaged reading is a merger of motivation and thoughtfulness." In 1992, as co-director of the National Reading Research Center, Guthrie began to articulate the engagement perspective that posits engaged readers seek to understand, enjoy learning, and believe in their reading abilities. Furthermore, engaged readers are mastery oriented, intrinsically motivated, and have self-efficacy.

The linking of the terms "reading motivation and engagement" is fairly new in the literature, and just as there are different interpretations of motivation in our field, there are also different meanings ascribed to "reading engagement." While Guthrie and his colleagues (2007) describe engaged reading as a merger of motivation and thoughtfulness, others describe intrinsic motivation as being "internal," while "engagement" is described as external and observable behaviors.

Over the past two decades, Guthrie and his colleagues have conducted a number of studies that embedded motivational concepts in inquiry-based reading instruction. This approach is called Concept Oriented Reading Instruction (CORI). The studies on CORI have helped to identify motivational components of effective reading instruction and their relationship to increases in reading proficiency. In 2007, Guthrie, McRae, and Klauda conducted a meta-analysis of 11 CORI studies. They described CORI as instruction that emphasizes support for reading motivation, reading engagement, and cognitive strategies for reading informational text. The meta-analysis revealed that CORI increased both reading comprehension and motivation for reading. The instructional practices that were associated with increased comprehension and reading motivation were relevance, choice, success, collaboration, and thematic units.

The identification of thematic units is an important addition to the literature on reading motivation. We know that low motivation is associated with students who view schooling as a series of unrelated activities. Turner's (1995) work emphasized "construction of meaning," which compliments Guthrie's focus on thematic units (Guthrie, 2001; 2007). Thematic units are also complimentary to the goals of the CCSS because they focus on meaning construction as well as integration across the language arts.

In a recent CORI study, Guthrie, Klauda, and Ho (2013) investigated 7th graders informational text comprehension. One group participated in Reading/Language Arts instruction using CORI, while the other group participated in traditional Reading/Language Arts instruction. The purpose of the study was to explore whether motivation was associated with achievement directly or whether its connection to achievement occurred through engagement. Seven motivation constructs were explored, four positive and three negative. The four positive constructs were intrinsic motivation, self-efficacy, valuing, and prosocial goals. The three negative constructs were perceived difficulty, devaluing, and antisocial goals. In addition, reading engagement was represented by dedication to and avoidance of reading.

The major findings of this study were that CORI was associated with positive changes in motivation, engagement, and achievement. The most prominent connections of CORI to motivation for informational text comprehension were students' confidence in their capacity to succeed, and their perception that they were able to comprehend challenging text. The findings of this recent CORI study are important in light of the CCSS emphasis on reading informational text. CORI provides promising practices for improving informational text comprehension.

Interestingly, Guthrie et al. (2013) use the motivation constructs of self-efficacy, valuing, and prosocial goals. Schiefele et al. (2012) did not identify self-efficacy, valuing, and prosocial goals as genuine motivation constructs, instead viewing them as preconditions of intrinsic motivation. However, in the context of real reading instruction, I believe constructs such as self-efficacy, valuing, and prosocial goals are extremely important. While I think the recent review of motivation research by Schiefele et al. (2012) provides important insights about factors associated with reading motivation, I would argue that research on more specific dimensions of motivation, such as those identified by Guthrie, have greater potential for informing classroom practice related to increasing motivation to read.

While there are many other scholars who have made significant contributions to research on motivation to learn, Michael Pressley, Julianne Turner, and John Guthrie have led the way in designing research that focuses on motivation to read. Their research has played a major role in our thinking about reading motivation in the classroom context. Their work has been, and will continue to be, extremely influential, because their research provides insights about how to create motivating literacy contexts in the classroom.

Current Trends and Future Directions in Reading Motivation Research

In looking at current trends in literacy motivation research, it is clear that the CCSS and the IRA Literacy Research Panel are likely to influence the reading motivation research agenda over the next decade. The CCSS have the potential to improve classroom instruction, particularly with regard to literacy instruction. The overarching goal of the CCSS is to enable all students to become more knowledgeable through text. In keeping with this goal, the CCSS position *comprehension* as the centerpiece of *reading* and they position *reading* as the centerpiece of *learning*.

I have some concerns about the CCSS with regard to the lack of attention to the role of motivation in teaching and learning, as well as the lack of attention to helping students develop the reading habit. But, I acknowledge that the standards are focused on high-quality goals for instruction and that no set of standards could ever incorporate all the dimensions needed for effective reading instruction.

The recently appointed International Reading Association (IRA) Literacy Research Panel also has the potential to influence literacy research and practice over the next decade. The charge of this panel is to respond to critical literacy issues facing policymakers, school administrators, teacher educators, classroom teachers, parents and the general public. P. David Pearson is chair of the panel and many of the members of the panel are active members of the Literacy Research Association. The Panel is preparing documents for two initiatives. First, they are preparing a set of policy briefs, and second, they are preparing a collection of project-based integrated units for classroom instruction. It is particularly promising that motivation and engagement are at the center of the work of the panel because many students are not motivated or engaged in literacy learning in a way that will lead to success in academics or life.

With the backdrop of CCSS and the work of the IRA Literacy Panel, current research suggests some emerging trends and future directions for research on reading motivation. In the following section, I briefly discuss four emerging trends that I believe will provide direction for future research on reading motivation.

The first research trend focuses on the relationship between motivation and challenging text. This wave of research is clearly aligned with the CCSS emphasis on having students read increasingly challenging text. Fulmer and Frijters (2011) investigated students' reading motivation while reading excessively challenging text. They found that high-topic interest served a buffering role in that students were able to read and comprehend challenging text better when the text reflected a topic of high personal interest. In the adverse context of an excessively challenging reading task, interest in the topic supported students' motivation, attributions for difficulty, and persistence.

This finding is in keeping with flow theory (Csikszentmihali, 1991) and self-determination theory (Deci & Ryan, 1985), both of which suggest that moderate challenge supports motivation. We need to be mindful that there is research that indicates that excessive challenge can undermine motivation and persistence (Schweinle, Turner, & Meyer, 2006); however, the Fulmer and Frijters (2011) finding that text that reflects high-interest topics can serve to buffer the effects of excessively challenging texts has strong implications for practice. In the Fulmer and Frijters study, students who read a text they rated *as most personally interesting* reported higher interest and enjoyment, lower ratings of attributions of difficulty, and were almost twice as likely to persist with the reading tasks. This study lends support to the notion that challenging text may be less problematic if students are personally interested in the topic.

To date, there have been relatively few studies conducted on the reading of excessively challenging text. With the CCSS emphasis on supporting students in reading increasingly challenging texts, further research is needed to explore buffering effects that will support students in being more successful in reading and comprehending challenging text.

The second trend emerging in the literature is reading motivation research with international and cross-cultural populations. In 2000, when Murphy and Alexander surveyed the literature, they noted that the research on motivation was overwhelmingly conducted by American researchers studying American students. In the recently published review of reading motivation research by Schiefele and colleagues (2012), 64% of the research studies were conducted by non-North Americans, an indication that we are becoming a more international, global community and that socio-cultural theories may play a larger role in future motivation research.

The third trend on the reading motivation horizon is research on the role of relevant and authentic tasks. Turner (1995), almost 20 years ago, emphasized the relationship between motivation and construction of meaning. Guthrie (2007, 2013) in his recent work highlights the importance of relevance and authenticity in promoting reading motivation and achievement.

Purcell-Gates (2002) has also emphasized the concept of authentic literacy tasks in her work with both children and adults.

The work of these researchers inspired me, along with a number of colleagues (Gambrell, Hughes, Calvert, Malloy, & Igo, 2011), to do a year-long study in third-, fourth-, and fifth-grade classrooms using a pen pal intervention that engaged students in authentic reading, writing, and discussion tasks. The student and adult pen pal read the same high-quality books (fiction and non-fiction) and exchanged letters about the books across the school year. On a specific day, all students received a book and letter from the adult pen pal. The adult pen pal encouraged students to engage in close reading of the text by posing questions such as " let me know what you think about . . . " or "I'll be interested to know if you agree with . . . " The teachers supported students in reading the books and the letters from the pen pals, writing letters to the adult pen pal, and participating in small group discussions. Students participated in at least two small-group discussions for each book. The small-group discussions were purposeful because they helped students prepare their response letters to the adult pen pals. In this study, there was a statistically significant increase in motivation to read across all grade levels (third-, fourth-, and fifth-grades). This finding is particularly interesting in light of previous research indicating that motivation decreases across the school year (McKenna, Kear, & Ellsworth, 1995). Future research is warranted on the value of authentic literacy tasks and the potential for thematic units to increase students' literacy motivation (Guthrie, 2007).

The fourth trend is research on teacher characteristics associated with high-literacy motivation. Harkening back to Pressley's (2007) work, we still need more research on teacher characteristics associated with achievement and high-literacy motivation. A study conducted in Finland by Pakarinen et al. (2010), explored the roles of classroom organization and teacher stress in kindergarten children's motivation and literacy development. They examined the extent to which observed teaching practices and self-reported teacher stress predicted children's learning motivation and phonological awareness. The study revealed that low-teacher stress and high classroom organization predicted high learning motivation, which in turn contributed to students' level of phonological awareness. This study emphasizes the importance of teachers' pedagogical well-being and classroom organization skills in fostering children's motivation to read.

Also of interest in this study was the finding that children in the same kindergarten classes resembled each other in terms of learning motivation and phonological awareness, pointing to the importance of the teacher in creating a motivating context for learning. This line of research has strong implications for professional development and is particularly interesting because of the link among the factors of low teacher stress, high classroom organization, and students' motivation and literacy achievement. Clearly, we need future research that will continue to examine literacy instruction with a critical eye to determine how the contexts of instruction influence students' reading motivation and engagement.

I believe we will see these four research trends continue over the next decade, and I also believe that motivation research shows great promise for informing us about highly effective classroom instruction. Motivation is no longer a missing link in research about students' literacy development. While research on motivation to learn has a rich and long history, the research on motivation to read is still in many ways in its infancy. A clear focus on motivation to read began emerging only in the 1970s, but I think we can say that research on motivation to read truly blossomed in the decade of 2000. While there is still much to be learned about reading motivation, the research base is increasing at a rapid rate.

One of the reasons for the continuing interest in motivation is that teachers and researchers recognize it is at the heart of many of the pervasive problems we face in reading education. If students are not motivated to read, if they don't develop the reading habit, it is unlikely they will reach their full literacy potential. Adequate skills alone are not sufficient to guarantee that students will develop into motivated, independent, life-long readers. Clearly, motivation to read must be central to our research agenda. We need to know more about how teachers foster the love of reading and how they create classroom contexts that support students in becoming passionate, persistent, and proficient readers.

REFERENCES

Bandura, A. (1997). *Self-efficacy: The exercise of control.* New York, NY: Freeman

Bandura, A. (2001). Social cognitive theory: An agentic perspective. *Annual Review of Psychology, 52,* 1-26.

Cox, K. E., & Guthrie, J. T. (2001). Motivational and cognitive contributions to students' amount of reading. *Contemporary Educational Psychology, 26*(1), 116–131.

Csikszentmihalyi, M. (1990). *Flow: The psychology of optimal experience.* New York, NY: Harper & Row.

Deci, E. L. (2009). Large-scale school reform as viewed from the self-determination theory perspective. *Theory and Research in Education, 7,* 244-252.

Deci, E. L., & Ryan, R. M. (1985). Intrinsic motivation and self-determination in human behavior. NewYork, NY: Plenum.

Eccles, J. S., & Wigfield, A. (2002). Motivational beliefs, values, and goals. *Annual Review of Psychology, 53,* 109–132.

Fulmer, S. M. & Frijters, J. C. (2011). Motivation during an excessively challenging reading task: The buffering role of relative topic interest. *Journal of Experimental Education, 79,* 185-208.

Gambrell, L. B., Hughes, E., Calvert, W., Malloy, J., & Igo, B. (2011). Authentic reading, writing, and discussion: An exploratory study of a pen pal project. *Elementary School Journal, 112,* 234-258.

Greaney, V., & Neuman, S. B. (1990). The functions of reading: A cross-cultural perspective. *Reading Research Quarterly, 25,* 172–195.

Guthrie, J. T. (2001, March). Contexts for engagement and motivation in reading. *Reading Online, 4*(8). Retrieved from http://www.readingonline.org/articles/art_index.asp?HREF=/articles/handbook/guthrie/index.html

Guthrie, J. T., Klauda, S. L., & Ho, A. N. (2013). Modeling the relationships among reading instruction, motivation, engagement, and achievement for adolescents. *Reading Research Quarterly, 48,* 9-26..

Guthrie, J. T., McRae, A., & Klauda, S. L. (2007). Contributions of Concept-Oriented Reading Instruction to knowledge about interventions for motivations in reading. *Educational Psychologist, 42,* 237-250.

Guthrie, J. T., Van Meter, P., McCann, A. D., & Wigfield, A. (1996). Growth of literacy engagement: Changes in motivations and strategies during concept-oriented reading instruction. *Reading Research Quarterly, 31,* 306–332.

Guthrie, J. T., Wigfield, A., Metsala, J. L., & Cox, K. E. (1999). Motivational and cognitive predictors of text comprehension and reading amount. *Scientific Studies of Reading, 3,* 231-257.

Hiebert, E. H. (2009). *Reading more, reading better.* New York, NY: Guilford Press.

International Reading Association. (2000). Excellent reading teachers: A position statement of the International Reading Association. *Journal of Adolescent & Adult Literacy, 44,* 193-200.

McKenna, M. C., Kear, D. J., & Ellsworth, R. A. (1995). Children's attitudes toward reading: A national survey. *Reading Research Quarterly, 30,* 934–956.

Murphy, K., & Alexander, P. (2000) A motivated exploration of motivation terminology. *Contemporary Educational Psychology, 25,* 3–53.

National Governors Association Center for Best Practices & Council of Chief State School Officers (2010). *Common Core State Standards.* Washington, DC: Authors.

Pakarinen, E., Kiuru, N., Lerkkanen, M. K., Poikkeus, A. M., Siekkinen, M., & Nurmi, J. E. (2010). Classroom organization and teacher stress predict learning motivation in kindergarten children. *European Journal of Psychology of Education, 25,* 281-300.

Pintrich, P. R. (1994). Continuities and discontinuities: Future directions for research in educational psychology. *Educational Psychologist, 29,* 137–148.

Pintrich, P. R. (2000). An achievement goal theory perspective on issues in motivation terminology, theory, and research. *Contemporary Educational Psychology, 25,* 92-104.

Pressley, M. (2006). What the future of reading research could be. Paper presented at *The International Reading Association's Reading Research Conference,* Chicago, IL, USA.

Purcell-Gates, V. (2002). Authentic literacy in class yields increase in literacy practices. *Literacy Update, 11,* 7.

Schiefele, U., Schaffner, E., Moller, J., & Wigfield, A. (2012). Dimensions of reading motivation and their relation to reading behavior and competence, *Reading Research Quarterly, 47,* 427-464.

Schweinle, A., Turner, J. C., & Meyer, D. K. (2006). Striking the right balance: Students' motivation and affect in elementary mathematics. *Journal of Educational Research, 99,* 271–293.

Tough, P. (2012). How children succeed. Boston, MA: Houghton Mifflin Harcourt.

Turner, J. (1995). The influence of classroom contexts on young children's motivation for literacy. *Reading Research Quarterly, 50,* 410-441.

Vygotsky, L. S. (1978). *Mind in society: The development of higher psychological processes* (M. Cole, V. John-Steiner, S. Scribner, & E. Souberman, Eds. & Trans.) Cambridge, MA: Harvard University Press (Original work published 1934).

Weiner, B. (1986). *An attributional theory of motivation and emotion.* New York, NY: Springer-Verlag.

Crafting Theoretically Defensible Literacy Teaching While Supporting Students With Test Preparation

Melody Zoch

The University of North Carolina at Greensboro

Student achievement is increasingly "put to the test" as accountability pressures intensify from test-focused legislation and the enactment of federal education programs such as Reading First that require schools to use "scientifically-based" reading instruction (Yatvin, Weaver, & Garan, 2003). The question of how to promote change and literacy achievement in schools is highly debated and has been taken up in many different ways by literacy researchers, administrators, district personnel, and teachers. Schools that primarily serve students from low socioeconomic backgrounds face the biggest challenges in terms of interventions, takeovers, and prescribed curriculum (Anagnostopoulos, 2003; Smagorinsky, Lakly, & Johnson, 2002; Snow, Burns, & Griffin, 1998).

As a result, test preparation often dominates the instruction and culture of these schools. This reality is a source of great tension for teachers as their autonomy is encroached upon and their beliefs about teaching and learning are compromised. While much theorizing happens outside of schools about what should happen, it is inside of schools where teaching actually takes place on a daily basis. Teachers are ultimately the ones who make decisions about what to teach and how to teach (Pauly, 1991). The choices they make are guided by many decisions including professional identity (Rex & Nelson, 2004), the tested curriculum (Madaus, 1988), and accountability pressures (Spillane, 1999).

This study reports on teachers' literacy teaching practices in one urban elementary school as they negotiated the demands placed on them to prepare students for the state standardized tests. In particular, the focus of this study is on the ways in which a small group of teachers sought to make test preparation as theoretically compatible as possible with their own beliefs and theories about literacy teaching. Specifically this study asked, *how do teachers respond to expectations to prepare students for high-stakes literacy tests?* and *in what ways do teachers make agentive decisions about their literacy teaching in a high-stakes testing environment?*

LITERACY TEACHING AND HIGH-STAKES TESTING

In response to test-focused policies, in which states are expected to establish performance goals along with standardized tests for students beginning in the third grade, the business of high-stakes testing to promote accountability has become key to educational reform for policy makers. This movement towards "excellence" and "equity" reflects policy makers' concerns for achievement at the school level through the use of standards and high-stakes testing. These measurements of success highlight the political landscape of schooling where the quality of public schools is characterized by test scores rather than other indicators (Brandt, 2007).

Most educational researchers would argue that using test scores as a measurement of success is arbitrary and "an illusion that masks an intrusion of testing into good teaching" (Hoffman, Assaf, & Paris, 2001, p. 482). This intrusion often results in decontextualized test preparation, or teaching to the test, where teaching is reduced to an act of raising test scores through drill on practice items, and the curriculum is replaced with test preparation (McNeil & Valenzuela, 2001).

Studies that research the impact of high-stakes testing on teachers have found that although teachers have negative views of standardized tests (e.g., Haladyna, Nolen, & Haas, 1991; Moore, 1994; Urdan & Paris, 1994), they still spend a large amount of time and energy preparing students for the tests (Hoffman et al., 2001). Raising test scores is perceived as an immediate obligation of teaching because of the import placed on them (Smith, 1991), especially when test scores are made available as public knowledge. Such pressure has negative effects on teachers' affect (Barksdale-Ladd & Thomas, 2000; Johnston, Guice, Baker, Malone, & Michelson, 1995) and conflicts with teachers' understanding of excellent teaching, especially for students from diverse backgrounds (Achinstein & Ogawa, 2006). Such practices often create inequities in schooling (Camilli & Monfils, 2004) and raise concerns for the quality of instruction, especially whether or not teachers are able to teach in academically challenging, student-centered ways or take into account the sociocultural needs of their students (McNeil & Valenzuela, 2001).

Teachers construct varied responses to curricular mandates (e.g., Grant, 2001; Sloan, 2006). It is important to situate teaching within the social, historical, and political contexts created by high-stakes testing, and to consider the ways in which teachers are not only acted upon, but also act upon their situation in agentive ways. Agency is a central tool for teachers to strategically navigate structures of power, resist structural constraints, and produce self-authored actions (Holland, Lachicotte, Skinner, & Cain, 1998; Wertsch, Tulviste, & Hagstrom, 1993). Teachers do not just come into contact with a situation, but also create their surroundings as well as themselves through the actions they engage in (Wertsch, 1991). Lewis, Encisco, and Moje (2007) refer to this important act as agency, which they define as "the strategic making and remaking of selves within structures of power" (p. 4). They do not view agency as something that comes from the internal mind, but as a way of positioning oneself that allows for new ways of being or the creation of new identities.

Agency has important implications for practice as the pressure to teach to the test increases. In this study, the teachers' actions are examined in regard to the ways they demonstrated agency with consideration given to the context and cultural tools available to them (Tharp & Gallimore, 1988). In this way, it is possible to understand how these teachers crafted alternative responses to the restrictive conditions created by high-stakes testing.

RESEARCH DESIGN

The research design was qualitative and occurred during the 2010-2011 school year from August to April. Using ethnographic research methods (Emerson, Fretz, & Shaw, 1995; Glesne, 2006), I explored the literacy teaching practices of teachers at one elementary school. Data sources included field notes from classroom observations and observations of meetings between staff members (e. g., faculty meetings and grade level meetings); expanded field notes; video recordings; transcripts of semi-formal interviews; field notes from informal conversations with staff members; photographs of classrooms and materials; and documents such as photocopies of lesson plans and papers passed out during class. During classroom observations, I focused on literacy instruction and events. I defined these events as "observable episodes which arise from practices and are shaped by them. The notion of events stresses the situated nature of literacy, that it always exists in a social context" (Barton, Hamilton, & Ivanic, 2000). The kinds of events I focused on included whole-group lessons about reading such as word study; the teacher reading aloud to students; the teacher conferring with students about their independent reading; the teacher working with small reading groups; groups of students talking to each other about reading or writing; the teacher teaching a whole group lesson about writing; and the teacher conferring with individual students about their writing.

The participants were nine teachers in the same school with experience ranging from one to nine years. Initially the data set consisted of 18 staff members (including 15 classroom teachers, one literacy coach, and two reading specialists) who were involved with grades 3-5 (grades in which testing occurred) and consented to participate in interviews and be observed in their classrooms. There were four teachers who chose not to participate (two third grade teachers and two fourth grade teachers). The original focus of this study was on literacy teaching practices to answer the first research question: *how do teachers respond to expectations to prepare students for high-stakes literacy tests?* Through my initial analysis, I noticed that some teachers resisted curricular reduction by creating alternative practices to traditional test preparation, and thus the second research question arose: *in what ways do teachers make agentive decisions about their literacy teaching in a high-stakes testing environment?* Based on the addition of this second question, I purposefully selected nine teachers from the initial 18 based on their use of alternative literacy teaching practices that demonstrated agentive decision making about how to prepare students for the state test as evidenced through classroom observations and interviews. Table 1 provides information about the nine teachers who were selected along with information about the data collected. The amount of data for each teacher varied depending on their availability and scheduling.

Table 1: Information about the Nine Teachers

Teacher	Teaching Assignment	Years of Teaching Experience	Number of Classroom Observations	Number of Meeting Observations	Number of Interviews
Gina	Literacy Coach	9	5	21	4
Arturo	Third Grade (B)	5	10	4	3
Celestina	Third Grade (B)	6	4	4	2
Evelyn	Third Grade (E)	3	3	3	2
Sasha	Fourth Grade (B)	3	3	4	3
Leah	Fourth Grade (E)	6	4	4	2
June	Fourth Grade (B)	3	5	4	3
Rory	Fourth Grade (E)	2	9	4	4
Caitlyn	Fifth Grade (E)	1	3	2	2

(B)= Bilingual Spanish/English Classroom
(E)= English as a Second Language Classroom

The school where data were collected is located in a large metropolitan city in the Southwest where high-stakes testing was a priority among the school districts. This school was reflective of the pressures schools are placed under to increase test scores and appease school districts and state educational boards. Their ability to do so has historically been a struggle, especially with high teacher and administrative turnover.

The year data were collected, 1,000 students were enrolled in the school, one of the largest elementary schools in the city. Ninety-seven percent of the students were Latino, 2% were African American, and less than 1% were Anglo. Ninety-six percent of the students' parents indicated that Spanish was spoken at home on registration information. Ninety-seven percent of the students were eligible for free or reduced lunch based on household income. Seventy percent of the students were enrolled in a Bilingual or English as a Second Language classroom.

I used the constant-comparative method (Glaser & Strauss, 1967) to analyze data and develop themes that characterized the participants' literacy teaching practices, particularly those that existed in spite of the strong focus on test preparation. I began using open coding in August by reading and rereading my field notes and interview transcripts on a weekly basis to develop initial categories and theoretical hypotheses.

Through this highly reflexive process, I read line-by-line in order to name and categorize the phenomena. Initially I began by handwriting my notes and ideas directly on printouts of the field notes and transcripts. After a month of generating open codes in this way, I imported all of my data into ATLAS.ti, a computer software program designed for conducting qualitative research. At this time I recreated my handwritten notes in ATLAS.ti and then continued to code the rest of the data using the software program. At this level of coding, I chose language that explained what was occurring in the data, rather than impose a pre-established set of codes onto the data (Emerson, Fretz, & Shaw, 1995). Next, I grouped the initial codes into categories to create more meaningful units that I later refined and recoded to develop categories and themes. I developed these larger units by focusing on data that 1) were the most salient in terms of describing the data and answering my research questions, and/or 2) occurred with the most frequency.

Findings

In this study, I show teachers' alternative interpretations and responses to the unfavorable conditions created by high-stakes testing. The teachers represented here make important contributions to our understanding of what it means to teach under the umbrella of high-stakes testing. While we have considerable evidence about how teachers feel negatively towards the pressure to improve test scores (Moore, 1994), and the kinds of practices they adopt to support testing, such as limiting teaching to tested objectives (Shepard, 1990) and using materials that resemble the test (Darling-Hammond & Wise, 1985), we know less about how teachers counter the negative aspects of testing through their practices.

The interview data revealed the ways in which these teachers were aware of accountability pressure and disagreed with the use of high-stakes tests. They said things like "I don't think those tests really measure their intelligence, but it is part of the system and you can't change it right now" (Sasha, Final Interview) and "but then I remember that we're attempting to measure human beings against a generic, standardized measure" (June, Mid-year Interview). The purpose of this study, however, is not to contribute to the already large body of research that shows how teachers feel tension with high-stakes testing. Rather, this study focuses on how these teachers adapted their teaching to fit inside of the testing culture of the school despite their negative feelings towards testing. These teachers developed their own set of answers about teaching that reflected their beliefs about quality literacy teaching. They found a way to work within a system where test preparation was the norm by making choices that they believed supported their students' literacy learning and their own integrity as professionals. The alternative practices they developed were not as acquiescent to the testing culture as some of the oppressive practices created and intended for preparing students for high-stakes tests.

The narrowing of the curriculum and reduction of literacy practices to isolated skills not only creates unfair conditions for students, but also for teachers whose preparation and professional identities are challenged and hardly acknowledged. These teachers provide a look at how agentive decision-making can change one's experience of teaching in a high-stakes testing environment. An agentive stance is especially important as the teaching profession is continually encroached upon because of the demands created by test-dependent policies at the national and state levels (Cuban, 1998).

AUTHENTIC LITERATURE TO TEACH TESTING LANGUAGE AND STRATEGIES

With so much pressure to prepare students for high-stakes tests, teachers were expected to use materials that resembled the test—photocopied worksheets that contained reading passages and multiple-choice questions. Despite this expectation from the district, the teachers in this study continued to use children's literature during their language arts block, while others in the school only used test preparation materials. Gina, the literacy coach assigned to work with third through fifth grade teachers, supported and encouraged teachers to use "authentic literature," a term she used to describe high-quality children's literature. Her support for the use of authentic literature was apparent in the ways she spoke to teachers about their text choices, helped them in selecting texts, and even in helping two third grade teachers secure a $2,000 grant to buy culturally relevant children's literature for the campus.

Rather than use prepackaged test preparation materials to teach students tested skills, the teachers used children's literature to help students become familiar with the language used on the test and strategies to answer questions. By incorporating testing language into their read alouds, they were able to embed required skills and objectives into their lessons. These teachers familiarized themselves with the language used on the tests by reading past tests released by the state education agency. This familiarity allowed them to know the kinds of questions asked, the frequency of objectives tested, and the wording used to test specific objectives. In turn, they wrote their own test-like questions to accompany their read alouds. This helped them address the expectation to teach test-taking strategies. For example, Gina helped some of the third grade teachers write their own test-like questions while planning a unit on "people that make a difference" using a book about César Chavez. The following description from field notes shows how the teachers worked together to write these questions.

Gina asks, "What about cautioned?" She reads aloud the sentence from *Harvesting Hope* by Kathleen Krull (2003). She says that the word is well supported by contextual clues. "The definition isn't present but since it says he wasn't a fighter…it helps you to know that caution means warning them or telling them not to fight. Too hard or what do you think?" Gina says that she would read the book aloud, but when going back to teach word meaning, she would make copies for each kid. She suggests they make a copy, underline the word, and then make new copies because this way students will never have to search for the word they are supposed to define. (Field Notes, Third Grade Meeting, 01/25/11)

Being familiar with the test allowed teachers to develop their own teaching and assessment materials. Knowing the kinds of experiences they wanted their students to have with literature gave them the vision to be able to enact alternative practices that stepped away from test-preparation materials. Rather than resist or abandon test preparation, the teachers were able to find other ways of preparing students for testing without limiting their teaching to a narrow representation of literacy and texts created by the sole use of testing materials.

For Evelyn, a third grade teacher, using materials, such as children's literature, was freedom from only teaching to the test.

I think there's a lot of good things going on on our campus and I want people to see that what we are doing works for our kids and we care about what we are doing, and that we know that there's this looming test at the end of year but we aren't going to let that get to us. We can teach in other ways besides just teaching to the test…using meaningful literature and applying that and seeing it happen in classrooms. (Evelyn, Final Interview)

Evelyn strongly supported the use of materials that she viewed as related to good teaching and saw those materials as a bridge between quality teaching and the expectation to prepare students for the test.

One way teachers structured their use of authentic literature with test preparation was through the development of literature units. These were units of study that usually lasted between one and two weeks with literature selected around a common theme or topic. For example, the third grade teachers selected texts about heroes to simultaneously teach strategies for figuring out word meaning, one of the state's tested objectives. Some of the books they included were *Martin's Big Words* by Doreen Rappaport (2007), *When Marian Sang* by Pam Muñoz Ryan (2002), and *Amelia and Eleanor Go For a Ride* by Pam Muñoz Ryan (1999) (Field Notes, Third Grade Meeting, 01/25/11). In describing the decision to use units to guide instruction, one of the third grade teachers said,

What we decided to go off when doing literature units was things that we knew the kids are going to want to discuss because they are all into Martin Luther King, Jr., and these are topics they've known about. That's why we decided to do certain units. (Celestina, Final Interview)

By creating units based on students' interests, the teachers were responsive to their students while also creating their own curriculum that challenged the reduction of literacy teaching to test-based practice materials. Their careful selection of texts was their way of incorporating authentic reading material into their lessons that also covered the reading skills and objectives they were responsible for teaching based on the state standards.

Other examples of literature units included studies of strong women, the Civil Rights Movement, child labor, jazz appreciation, and the Civil War. When Caitlyn's fifth grade students asked her about the Olympic swimmer, Michael Phelps, she responded by creating a unit about him using information from the Internet and kids' magazines. The unit was in direct response to her students' interests and inquiries (Field Notes, 10/19/10).

Leah, a fourth grade teacher, described her decision-making based on her perception of what her students needed socially.

A lot of girls have self-issues and look at a normal girl, okay you are wearing this today. It helped with boys too, knowing where we came from. It was a way of saying, "You can speak your mind." Some of the girls who were quieter were able to speak out more and a lot of them wrote stories about being strong and I can do what I want, nobody has the right to tell me what I can and cannot do. With the Civil Rights Movement, it carried out the theme of being respectful and not judging people. I have kids say things like, "You don't know how that person is if you don't know that person." (Leah, Final Interview)

These units of study serve as a reminder that while preparing students for high-stakes testing can be limiting, teachers were able to broaden their literacy teaching through practices that connected to student interests and needs. Working in ways that did not mirror test preparation was one way teachers demonstrated the agency they had to teach in more desirable ways.

As a supplement to the literature units, the teachers used language charts as a way of capturing talk and thinking about each book. Language charts serve as an artifact of conversations students have about books in order to explore multiple and varied responses to literature (Roser, Hoffman, Labbo, & Farest, 1992). The teachers created hybrid language charts to not only record student talk, but also to introduce and reinforce the language of the test to provide students with practice. The language charts were mostly created using large sheets of paper that stretched across a bulletin board, as seen in Figures 1-2. Some teachers also created the language charts on letter-sized paper that they projected with a document camera. While these charts were organized around books

Figure 1. Language Charts

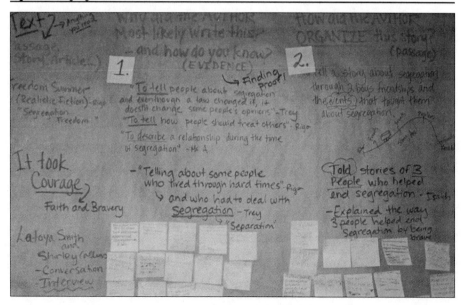

Figure 2. Language Charts

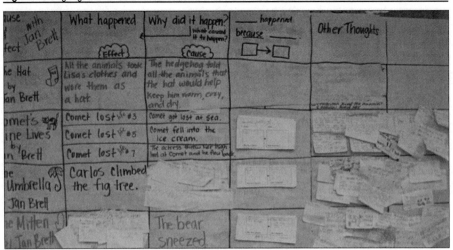

with guiding questions (e.g., "What is the author's message?"), they were graphically distinct from multiple-choice questions and worksheets. They allowed the teachers to focus on varied aspects of texts with a direct link to test preparation in an alternative format. Teachers wrote directly on the charts and also included student writing on sticky notes.

Some teachers used chapter books in place of picture books for read alouds. For Caitlyn, read alouds were "paramount when teaching the skills of reading" (First Interview). Rather than tie a collection of books together by theme or topic, the chapter books provided cohesion within one story.

I think chapter books went really well this year because I found how to incorporate all the reading habits and even the reading test-style strategies…and it felt a lot more connected because even though we were changing skills and strategies, that always feels choppy. We were still bound by this book and the same theme and the same idea of whatever we were reading. Like, *Becoming Naomi León* [by Pam Muñoz Ryan (2005)], we were trying main idea and summary, but it's still Naomi's life and her story and her struggles. I feel like that's a good way to, if you have to do the test stuff, you might as well do it in a way that's pleasant for you to teach. (June, Final Interview)

During this interview at the end of the school year, June, a fourth grade teacher, described how chapter books were a tool for her teaching, which she enjoyed and felt were valuable for her students. Rather than pulling from various picture books, she liked the consistency of reading one story to address reading skills and strategies. She also referred to this way of teaching as "pleasant," a reminder of the importance of enjoying how or what is taught.

In Sasha's case, using chapter books with her fourth grade students such as *The Lightning Thief* by Rick Riordan (2005), *Tuck Everlasting* by Natalie Babbit (1975), and *The Circuit* by Francisco Jiménez (1997) were ways to engage students in "real reading" where she could show them how readers do not use just one skill in one book, but they "use them all in one book." This move attempted to address the division of reading into individual skills in isolation by asking students to enact reading habits more aligned with how reading actually occurs. Incorporating chapter books into her language arts meant using "books that are more rich and have real issues that people really deal with. Picture books are good and all, but I want them to think beyond what they've normally been reading. Read outside what they are used to reading" (Sasha, Final Interview). By reading chapter books aloud, Sasha made them accessible to all of her students regardless of their independent reading level.

Other types of texts besides children's literature that teachers drew on included world news and articles from kids' magazines. Rory, a fourth grade teacher, in particular, drew on current events, local and international, to provide the content, such as reading about Libya and Qaddafi as well as dictatorships and protests. Although she was well aware of the expectation to prepare for the state test, she also saw the need to continue using "smart texts with good themes and topics" (Rory, Mid-year Interview) to engage her students in the content.

AUTHENTIC LITERATURE TO SUPPORT WRITING TO A PROMPT

For writing instruction, particularly for fourth grade teachers whose students took the state writing test, using authentic texts meant finding mentor texts to show how writers achieve certain effects. The writing portion of the fourth grade test consisted of having students compose a personal narrative in two pages or less that was in response to a prompt. The fourth grade teachers favored memoirs by Patricia Polacco and read them to students to show how they related to writing prompts (Field Notes, Fourth Grade Meeting, 01/03/11).

So I used a lot of Patricia Polacco. Not only because it was an author who we had already read prior to that, but also because I feel like the kids get the stories and they understand the meaning behind it. There's so many rich examples of what I would like for them to get as writers...so they could see a certain kind of author craft, like she does a lot of these things really well...And I feel like it was so much easier instead of trying to pull different things...They were able to read the whole thing and see how she used imagery or was able to "explode the moment." (Sasha, Final Interview)

Like Sasha, the other fourth grade teachers used children's literature to show students models of writing. They spent time reading these texts, discussing certain writing features, labeling those features, and showing students how one writing piece might be changed slightly to answer a variety of writing prompts (i.e., "write about a time you were surprised" or "write about a special person"). In opposition to providing formulaic ways to answer a prompt, such as writing a five paragraph essay, the fourth grade teachers saw children's literature as a way of making connections between having choice in writing, but still being able to answer a prompt.

Teaching writing in this way also involved helping students make connections across texts that were carefully chosen as model examples of good writing. Using document cameras to project pages from books was a popular method to allow all students to see the writing while discussing it. One day, Rory projected a picture book while reading it aloud. She stopped periodically to think aloud about the content of the story and how she connected to the text as a writer. As Rory stopped to talk about the writing and the kinds of reader thoughts she was having, she also invited students to contribute to the discussion. She introduced the book by saying, "The title of this book is called *On My Way to Buy Eggs* by Chih-Yuan Chen. And it sounds really plain, doesn't it? A lot of us, as we make our picture books that are going to be due next week, we have to think about our stories." Some of you may be thinking, "My story is kind of boring. All I ever do is go to Wal-Mart and pick out shoes, or I just babysit my sister." So *On My Way to Buy Eggs* reminded me of something that might sound boring but had a really neat, special adventure. (Video Transcript, 10/06/10)

Later Rory paused to draw attention to part of the story and how the author chose her words. She said, I love that sentence! [She rereads the sentence.] "Under the tree sits a pair of glasses that wants someone to wear them." I love it! Instead of saying there were glasses under the tree and I picked them up, but saying the glasses wanted someone to wear them.

A couple of pages later Rory paused to say, "This page especially reminded me of the part in Ralph Fletcher's book we read yesterday [*A Writer's Notebook* (1996)] about being fierce wonders and wondering. So she's just wondering in the middle of her story" (Video Transcript, 10/06/10). In this part, Rory connected the picture book to another book previously read aloud to show how both authors used their wondering as a way to compose. At the close of reading this book aloud, Rory asked her students to begin working on their picture book drafts and to think about the "treasures inside" that they wanted to share. She finished by reaffirming students' identities as writers when she said, "You have a lot of stuff going on, you're going to have to juggle it. You are going to be a writer, writers juggle lots of stories at lots of times. You already are a writer."

The picture books students were composing about a memory was one way Rory prepared her students for the writing test that increased their writing fluency while developing their sense of story and ease with the writing process. This provided a link to writing a personal narrative, the tested genre, without confining students to one prompt, and integrated the multiple modalities found in picture books. Rory also affirmed her students' identities as writers, rather than confirm their identities as test takers and without bringing the discourse of test taking into her lesson.

Teachers sometimes returned to books they had previously read with their classes to draw close attention to particular aspects of writing. For example, during her writing time, Rory projected the first pages of *Bud, Not Buddy* by Christopher Paul Curtis (2004), *Love as Strong as Ginger* by Lenore Look (1999), and *Charlotte's Web* by E.B. White (1952) to talk about how writers begin their stories with leads. After reading each page and asking students what they noticed, Rory said,

Today I am teaching you about leads. One thing I know about leads is they want to catch a reader. They are like someone going fishing. Whoop! And they throw out a line with a hook on the end. (Video Transcript, 10/07/10)

Rory then went on to record some of the words students used to describe leads on a chart and concluded her writing lesson by saying, "Today I want us to look at our leads and see if we can write a few more that might catch attention, catch some good words. We want to catch some good words and we want to catch our reader."

Rather than directly telling the students what a lead is accompanied by some sort of rubric for what a "good lead" looks like, Rory used mentor texts (Dorfman & Cappelli, 2007) for students to see effective examples with opportunities for students to notice and name what they read. Rory's take on teaching writing reflects philosophies shared by the National Writing Project, which Rory was connected to through professional development. Her increased knowledge and understanding of teaching writing seems to be a reflection of her professional development experiences and may have contributed to her sense of agency to teach in this way.

Incorporating new practices into their teaching, such as the use of literature studies to prepare students for the tests, demonstrates the agency these teachers had to develop alternative practices for test preparation. They never completely disregarded test preparation; in fact they did just the opposite and incorporated test preparation into their daily teaching, but they did so in a way that created their own set of answers to the problem of high-stakes testing. The practices they adopted came from their own teaching repertoires rather than reliance on test preparation materials. While there did come a time when these teachers did incorporate traditional test preparation materials into their teaching as the testing dates drew closer, they did so later in the school year than other teachers in the school and without completely replacing their language arts teaching with traditional test preparation.

The practices these teachers crafted took into consideration their own beliefs about quality literacy teaching and their students' interests and backgrounds. They constructed their own responses to accountability measures that showed how they acted as active agents in order to produce self-authored actions, actions that represented their own interests and reflected professional knowledge (Holland et al., 1998). Rather than passively assume the responsibilities placed on them to prepare students for high-stakes testing, the teachers positioned themselves in ways that allowed for a new way of being and making decisions in this context (Lewis et al., 2007). The agency teachers in this study exhibited allowed them to form an alternative response to their high-stakes testing environment (Datnow, Hubbard, & Mehen, 2002).

DISCUSSION

This study showed how teachers acted in agentive ways when their beliefs about literacy teaching were threatened by test preparation. The solutions the teachers came up with reflected the compromises they made to make their practices as theoretically compatible with their beliefs as possible when they understood the expectation to prepare their students for high-stakes testing. In this way, these teachers demonstrated how individuals with agency exhibit power to resist structural constraints and instead produce self-authored actions that reflect the ability to shape, and not just be shaped by, the context and situation (Holland et al., 1998; Wertsch et al., 1993). Despite their disagreement with high-stakes testing, they accepted it as a reality of teaching, and in turn responded strategically.

These findings are important in terms of expanding on what we know about how teachers respond to school reform and high-stakes testing. This study further illustrates how teachers can act with agency and develop adaptive practices in the restrictive contexts created by high-stakes testing. Their response provides a model of balancing test preparation with one's own beliefs about literacy teaching, and in ways that June termed "pleasant." Their ability to adapt their practices to account for both raises new questions about what it means to teach with agency and creativity in the age of high-stakes accountability. Even though the testing culture that results from such measures does little to promote the image of teacher-as-professional, the actions of these teachers offer a heartening example of what the teaching profession really needs—agentive, decision makers who are able to navigate the demands of working in a high-stakes testing culture while still promoting quality literacy instruction.

Through an analysis of teaching practices, I showed that the challenges teachers encountered in terms of teaching to the test did not necessarily mean they could only teach in the formulaic ways that often accompany test preparation. While the demands of preparing students for the state test were foreboding, teachers bridged the expectation to teach to the test with other supports for literacy learning—the use of authentic literature, reading for enjoyment, and choice about reading and writing—ways of teaching that are usually reduced or dropped as test-driven instruction takes over (Au & Raphael, 2000). Teachers found ways to act with agency in order to construct their own responses to accountability measures and enact their own beliefs about teaching literacy. For example, the use of hybrid language charts and literature studies to support test preparation serves as an example of how some teachers reacted to testing pressures by making their literacy teaching practices theoretically compatible with their beliefs about literacy teaching. This practice demonstrated their agency to respond to the context of standardized testing as they were able to shape and not just be shaped by the situation.

The findings from this study expand our understanding of how teachers respond to high-stakes testing to include a look at teacher agency. Previous research has shown the ways in which teacher autonomy is threatened by high-stakes testing and how practices as well as curriculum get altered in this environment. What is missing from the literature, however, is a look at how teachers work in agentive ways to combat the negative effects of testing in order to make their literacy teaching practices as theoretically sound as they can be. Although we know about and can see the ways in which teachers are affected negatively by testing, even to the point of feeling powerless (Barksdale-Ladd & Thomas, 2000; Smith, 1991), more research is needed that shows what teachers do when they feel empowered. This study begins to fill this need as it shows how some teachers constructed their own responses to high-stakes testing without having to work completely against their own beliefs.

The teachers in this study provide hope in terms of what can be done to contest the adverse consequences of accountability created in a high-stakes testing environment. Having agency and being able to "talk back" to limited literacy teaching practices made a difference for these teachers who did not have to completely compromise their own beliefs about literacy, teaching, and learning. Their efforts serve as an example of how teachers, while continually asked to teach in ways they may not agree with, can find ways to create leverage for the practices they value the most.

IMPLICATIONS FOR TEACHER EDUCATION

This study widens our understanding of what occurs as teachers go about the daily business of teaching literacy under the umbrella of high-stakes testing. As teacher educators, we do not just prepare teachers for best-case scenarios, but for all the contexts they might encounter. Part of the process of preparing teachers for the field must acknowledge the tensions new teachers will face with regard to testing and accountability systems. Rather than ignore or pretend these pressures are not a daily part of teaching, teacher educators need to address these issues head on so preservice teachers can enter the field with agency and confidence to enact the best practices they learned about, which may not have included what happens when asked to teach to a test.

In teacher preparation courses, preservice teachers continually build theories about what is best for students and what works or does not work. When preservice teachers enter the teaching field, the theories they have built get reshaped and reworked in response to the context of their classrooms and schools. The reality of teaching in high-stakes environments calls on teachers to develop theories and practices to teach literacy that may be very different from those we advocate in teacher education. The particularities of a school's context are important in how novice teachers take up the practices and theories we offer as part of teacher education. The re-theorizing and re-appropriating of practices is important work on the part of preservice teachers as they come to understand what it means to teach in a particular context and given situation. As teacher educators, we need to help them make connections across theory and practice so they have a broader understanding of what it means to teach in the present political environment. One way we can address this is by asking them to apply what they read about and discuss in class to a particular context where there may be challenges due to testing pressures, such as in their field placements. We need to help them not only notice and name when dissonance occurs between theory and practice, but to construct their own responses that demonstrate agentive ways of thinking and reacting. Another way we can help preservice teachers reimagine the possibilities of teaching in high-stakes testing environments is by showing them examples from the field, for example the teachers in this study.

Finally, understanding the role agency plays in learning to teach is important. Just as research examines teacher agency in in-service teachers, we also need to broaden our understanding of how agency might develop in preservice teacher-education programs. More research needs to examine experiences in teacher education that lead preservice teachers to develop agency and to be able to make sound decisions about their practices when their own beliefs are threatened.

REFERENCES

Achinstein, B., & Ogawa, R.T. (2006). (In)fidelity: What the resistance of new teachers reveals about professional principles and prescriptive educational policies. *Harvard Educational Review, 67*(1), 30-63

Anagnostopoulos, D. (2003). Testing and student engagement with literature in urban classrooms: A multi-layered perspective. *Research in the Teaching of English, 38*(2), 177-212.

Au, K.H., & Raphael, T.E. (2000). Equity and literacy in the new millennium. *Reading Research Quarterly, 35*, 170-188.

Babbit, N. (1975). *Tuck everlasting.* New York, NY: Scholastic.

Barksdale-Ladd, M.A., & Thomas, K.F. (2000). What's at stake in high-stakes testing: Teachers and parents speak out. *Journal of Teacher Education, 51*(5), 384-397.

Barton, D., Hamilton, M., & Ivanic, R. (2000). Situated literacies: Reading and writing in context. New York, NY: Routledge.

Brandt, R.S. (2007). High-stakes testing. In W.A. Owings, & L.S. Kaplan (Eds.), *Best practices, best thinking, and emerging issues in school leadership,* (pp. 195-200).

Camilli, G., & Monfils, L.F. (2004). Test scores and equity. In W.A. Firestone, R.Y. Schorr, & L.F. Monfils (Eds.), *The ambiguity of teaching to the test: Standards, assessment, and education reform.* Mahwah, NJ: Lawrence Erlbaum Associates, Inc., Publishers.

Chen, C. (2007). *On my way to buy eggs.* Tulsa, OK: Kane Miller EDC Publishing.

Cuban, L. (1998). How schools change reforms: Redefining reform success and failure. *Teachers College Record, 99*(3), 453-477.

Curtis, C.P. (2004). Bud, not Buddy. New York, NY: Random House, Inc.

Darling, Hammond, L., & Wise, A.E. (1985). Beyond standardization: State standards and school improvement. *The Elementary School Journal, 85,* 315-336.

Dorfman, L.R., & Cappelli, R. (2007). Mentor texts: Teaching writing through children's literature, K-6. Portland, ME: Stenhouse Publishers.

Emerson, R. M., Fretz, R. I., & Shaw, L. L. (1995). *Writing ethnographic field notes*. Chicago, IL: The University of Chicago Press.

Fletcher, R. (1996). The writer's notebook: Unlocking the writer within you. New York, NY: HarperCollins.

Glaser, B., & Strauss, A. (1967). *The discovery of grounded theory: Strategies for qualitative research*. Chicago, IL: Aldine.

Glesne, C. (2006). *Becoming qualitative researchers: an introduction*. New York, NY: Pearson Education, Inc.

Grant, S.G. (2001). An uncertain lever: Exploring the influence on state-level testing in New York state on teaching social studies. *Teachers College Record, 103*(3), 398-426.

Haladyna, T., Nolen, S.B., & Haas, N.S. (1991). Raising standardized achievement test scores and the origins of test score pollution. *Educational Researcher, 20,* 2-7.

Hoffman, J.V., Assaf, L.C., & Paris, S.G. (2001). High-stakes testing in reading: Today in Texas, tomorrow? *The Reading Teacher, 54*(5), 482-492.

Holland, D., Lachicotte, W., Skinner, D., & Cain, C. (1998) *Identity and agency in cultural worlds.* Cambridge, MA: Harvard University Press.

Jiménez, F. (1997). *The circuit: Stories from the life of a migrant child.* New York, NY: Houghton Mifflin.

Johnston, P., Guice, S., Baker, K., Malone, J., & Michelson, N. (1995). Assessment of teaching and learning in "literature based" classrooms. *Teaching and Teacher Education, 11,* 359-371.

Krull, K. (2003). *Harvesting hope: The story of César Chavez.* San Diego, CA: Harcourt, Inc.

Lewis, C., Enciso, P., & Moje, E.B. (2007). *Reframing sociocultural research on literacy.* New York: Routledge.

Look, L. (1999). *Love as strong as ginger.* New York, NY: Atheneum Books for Young Readers.

Madaus, G. (1988). The influence of testing on the curriculum. In L. Tanner (Ed.), *Critical issues in curriculum: 87th yearbook of the NSSE, Part 1.* Chicago, IL: University of Chicago Press.

McNeil, L. M., & Valenzuela, A. (2001). The harmful impact of the TAAS system of testing in Texas: Beneath the accountability rhetoric. In G. Orfield & M. L. Kornhaber (Eds.), *Raising standards or raising barriers? Inequality and high-stakes testing in public education* (pp. 127–150). New York, NY: Century Foundation Press.

Moore, W.P. (1994). The devaluation of standardized testing: One district's response to a mandated assessment. *Applied Measurement in Education, 7*(4), 343-367.

Pauly, E. (1991). *The classroom crucible: What really works, what doesn't, and why.* New York, NY: HarperCollins Publishers.

Rappaport, D. (2007). *Martin's big words: The life of Dr. Martin Luther King, Jr.* New York, NY: Hyperion Books for Children.

Rex, L. A., & Nelson, M.C. (2004). How teachers' professional identities position high-stakes test preparation in their classrooms. *Teachers College Record, 106*(6), 1288-1331.

Riordan, R. (2005). *The lightning thief.* New York, NY: First Hyperion Paperbacks.

Roser, N., Hoffman, J., Labbo, L.D., & Farest, C. (1992). Language charts: A record of story time talk. *Language Arts, 69*(1), 44-52.

Ryan, P.M. (1999). *Amelia and Eleanor go for a ride.* New York, NY: Scholastic Press.

Ryan, P.M. (2002). *When Marian sang: The true recital of Marian Anderson.* New York, NY: Scholastic Press.

Ryan, P.M. (2005). *Becoming Naomi León.* New York: Scholastic Press.

Shepard, L.A. (1990). Inflated test score gains: Is the problem old norms or teaching the test? *Educational Measurement: Issues and Practice, 9,* 15-22.

Sloan, K. (2006). Teacher identity and agency in school worlds: Beyond the all-good/all-bad discourse on accountability-explicit curriculum policies. *Curriculum Inquiry, 36*(2), 119-152.

Smagorinsky, P., Lakly, A., & Johnson, T.S. (2002). Acquiescence, accommodation, and resistance in learning to teach within a prescribed curriculum. *English Education, 34*(3), 187-213.

Smith, M.L. (1991). Put to the test: The effects of external testing on teachers. *Educational Researcher, 20*(5), 8-11.

Snow, C. E., Burns, M. S., & Griffin, P. (Eds.). (1998). *Preventing reading difficulties in young children.* Washington, DC: National Academy Press.

Spillane, J. (1999). External reform initiatives and teachers' efforts to reconstruct their practice: The mediating role of teachers' zones of enactment. *Journal of Curriculum Studies, 31,* 143-175.

Tharp, R., & & Gallimore, R. (1988). *Rousing minds to life.* Cambridge, New York: Cambridge University Press.

Urdan, T.C., & Paris, S.G. (1994). Teachers' perceptions of standardized achievement tests. *Educational Policy,* 8(2), 137-156.

Wertsch, J. V. (1991). A sociocultural approach to socially shared cognition. In L. B. Resnick, J. M. Levine & S. D. Teasley (Eds.), *Perspectives on socially shared cognition* (pp. 85-100). Washington DC: American Psychological Association.

Wertsch, J.V., Tulviste, P., & Hagstrom, F. (1993). A sociocultural approach to agency. In E.A. Forman, N. Minick, & C.A. Stone (Eds.), *Context for learning: Sociocultural dynamics in children's development* (pp. 336-356). New York, NY: Oxford University Press.

White, E.B. (1952). *Charlotte's Web.* New York, NY: HarperCollins.

Yatvin, J., Weaver, C., & Garan, E. (2003). Reading First: Cautions and recommendations. *Language Arts,* 81, 28–33.

Judith A. Langer
University of Albany
State University of New York

Section I:
Evolving Literacy Learners

The research reports included in this section focus on issues of central concern, as scholars and practitioners seek to develop research-based ways to align the CCSS with effective practice. The reports build from several different research traditions, exploring connections among them and applying them in new settings. The work contributes to the erosion of some long-standing dichotomies that have over-simplified issues in literacy development. Among them are the importance of group or universal patterns of development vs. individual differences, the understanding of engagement as a static vs. malleable process, and the approach to comprehension as a generic process vs. one that is deeply embedded in significant cultural contexts for literacy, such as the academic disciplines. While some years ago research treated these contrasts as alternative hypotheses about the nature of learning and development, the current studies create room to explore interrelationships in ways that are facilitative to evolving literacy learners. While the studies tackle very different problems, all assume that literacy development is a process in which culture, context, content, text, and purpose interact in the evolution of literacy, and that development is socially as well as individually situated. Brief comments about looking beyond each of the dichotomies follow.

Group vs. Individual Differences. Since the 19th century, fields as diverse as psychology, linguistics, anthropology and various other sciences that have informed educational theory sought to identify and then develop general constructs or rules to describe development. In an early effect of this focus on group (or universal development), in the early 20th century an influential group of researchers divided the curriculum in each of the subject areas into grade designations. Much work ensued to refine developmentally appropriate achievement, reflected in tests as well as grade-level designations. By the late 1960s, however, researchers were arguing that individual differences rather than general patterns of development were more important in understanding and supporting learning. These studies had in common the focus on the individual as learner. Yet for many years, despite the growing acceptance of sociocultural and socio-cognitive theories in learning and more recent approaches to differentiated instruction, the predominate approaches that students experience in curriculum development, instruction, policy, and assessment have been based primarily on average group development. The reports in this section look beyond these, to interesting and important ways in which such differences work together in effective instruction.

Engagement as Static vs. Contextually-based. While there is a long history of research on motivation in the field of psychology, it has often been conceptualized as based in individual differences. In the early 1980s, researchers made the connection between motivation and learning processes. It was then related to the concept of engagement and comprehension, and stimulated a large body of research in the field of literacy. In this work, engagement was seen to encompass affective, behavioral, social, and cognitive involvement, and was considered malleable in response to the various contextual and situational factors that are open to modification. Ensuing results have indicated a strong relationship between engagement, cognition, and learning in literacy tasks. Following from this work, engagement has become a topic that can be explored as fluid and evolving, varying even during the process of instruction. We will see this directly or indirectly considered in some of the reports to follow.

Comprehension as a Generic Process vs. One That is Deeply Embedded in Significant Cultural Contexts for Literacy. Another aspect of the research in this section is based in particular subject area content, as encountered in content area classes. It goes beyond broad genre-based distinctions such as informative and narrative, and is anchored within the disciplines themselves. In the field of literacy, as our definition of text as part of context has broadened to include a variety of oral, written and electronic texts, and has come to see writing as part of the literacy development process, the field is coming to view the particular academic disciplines as constituting differing textual contexts, and thus, somewhat different literacy experiences. From this perspective, each discipline can be seen as having its own ways of considering meaning that are based in the history and particularities of that discipline. In such contexts, a great deal differs, from the academic vocabulary, to the rules of argument and evidence, to expected syntax and rhetorical structure. From this perspective, subject-area and discipline-appropriate conventions are critical features of the literacy context for evolving literacy learners to experience and learn.

What is particularly interesting about the reports in this section is that the research upon which they are based approaches contested areas with open inquiry, in ways that highlight interesting interrelationships among previously established dichotomies. They remind us to ensure that the curriculum and instructional practices that are being developed in response to the CCSS will provide opportunity for the inherent complexity, variability, and needed flexibility underlying effective teaching, learning, and development. If we neglect to do so, we risk developing guideposts that will undercut the very literacy development that research indicates matters for evolving literacy learners.

Young Learners: An Exploration of the Notion "By Different Paths to Common Outcomes" in Early Literacy Assessment

Man Ching Esther Chan
The University of Melbourne, Australia

For more than 60 years, different literacy researchers have theorized about the sequence of literacy development in young children (e.g., Chall, 1996; Ferreiro & Teberosky, 1979/1982; Gates, 1947; Sulzby, Barnhart, & Hieshima, 1988). In recent times, literacy developmental sequences can be found in the form of curriculum standards in different parts of the world including Australia (Australian Curriculum Assessment and Reporting Authority, 2013), the United Kingdom (U.K. Department for Education, 2011), and the United States (National Governors Association Center for Best Practices & Council of Chief State School Officers, 2010). Consistent with a criterion-referenced or developmental assessment framework (see Glaser, 1994; Masters & Forster, 1996), student progress is generally evaluated according to the developmental sequence specified in these curriculum standards. The specification of a developmental sequence is seen as a way to match teaching with the developmental level of individual children in order to personalize teaching (Griffin, 2007). Despite the prevalence of these developmental frameworks, such a developmental approach to teaching and learning has been criticized by early literacy experts such as Clay (1998) for disregarding individual differences.

Even though Clay (1991, 1992, 1998) supported the rationale behind such developmental frameworks in terms of matching teaching with the learning needs of individual children, she believed the adoption of a common standard in education can be counterproductive for teaching and student learning. She asserted that any proposed developmental sequence in literacy is a generalized model and believed that such a model is not useful for predicting or describing how a particular child will develop or is developing. She considered many children to be flexible learners who can adapt to any particular teaching sequence laid out by the teacher or the curriculum. Problems arise when a teacher thinks that a particular child is not progressing or learning because the teacher overlooked other possible routes to literacy learning. Clay therefore emphasized the need to account for individual variability in standards-setting. However, the way individual variability can be accounted for within a standards-based or developmental assessment framework is not well understood.

This study explores Clay's notion of "by different paths to common outcomes," which is central to her 1998 book of the same title, by asking the question: "How can multiple pathways be operationalized within a developmental assessment framework?" This question is examined through the use of a mixed methods design to examine the structure and variability in early literacy. In this context, *structure* refers to general patterns in development such as a developmental hierarchy or sequence, while *variability* refers to diversity in how children develop.

REVIEW OF LITERATURE AND THEORETICAL PERSPECTIVE

This study evolved from the need to reconcile the structuralist and non-structuralist perspectives of early literacy development through engagement with the literature and the data collected to validate an early literacy assessment tool (Chan, 2012). In the study of human development, a structuralist approach can be seen as the attempt to search for structures in the development of thoughts and behaviors; a contrasting approach is an attempt to explain developmental differences through understanding the environmental context of individuals (Fischer & Silvern, 1985). In her review of the historical evolution of early literacy perspectives in the 20th century, Crawford (1995) considered an emergent theory of early literacy (e.g., Clay, 1966; Ferreiro & Teberosky, 1979/1982; Teale & Sulzby, 1986) to be in opposition to a social constructivist theory of early literacy (e.g., Harste, Woodward, & Burke, 1984). Even though Crawford considered that the two theories share many similarities, she believed the emergent literacy theory is underpinned by the assumption that "children's literacy learning is characterized by a progression through a series of developmental stages" (Crawford, 1995, p. 79), whereas the social constructivist theory "[rejects] the idea of universal developmental stages" (Crawford, 1995, p. 81). Based on this categorization, the former perspective can be seen as a structuralist approach to viewing early literacy, and the latter perspective can be seen as a non-structuralist approach. The distinction that was made in the review between emergent literacy and social constructivist theories seems to suggest that the two theories are incompatible with each other.

Although Crawford's (1995) review helps to distinguish between different early literacy theories, it did not appear to provide ways to reconcile the apparent contradictions within the work of different researchers based on her characterization. Even though Ferreiro and Teberosky (1979/1982) seem to lean towards a structuralist approach in their study of children's conceptual development in early literacy, the researchers clearly supported the idea that children's conceptual knowledge is socially constructed (pp. 285–286). In terms of Clay's (1991, 1998) work, her notion of "by different paths to common outcomes" can be interpreted as theoretically paradoxical when structure and variability are seen as opposing ideas. In order to explore different developmental pathways, a common standard is needed as a basis for comparing individual differences, which in turn appears to contradict the idea that a common standard can be established. The above examples suggest that a broader framework is needed in order to understand and resolve the tension between the structuralist and non-structuralist perspectives of early literacy development.

This study applied Overton's (2003) relational approach to reframe the concepts of structure and variability in early literacy development in light of the apparent contradictions found in the works of Ferreiro and Teberosky (1979/1982) and Clay (1991, 1998). When discussing the different philosophical debates in history regarding the nature of human development, Overton (2003) cautioned against splitting or dichotomizing terms such as stability–change, unity–diversity, universal–particular, and nature–nurture, which focuses only on their contradictions or opposing relationships. He proposed that the relationship between these seemingly opposing terms can be constructed as complementary, which can provide a more holistic understanding of the nature of the development of thought and behavior in humans.

According to Overton (2003), the first step to this relational construction is to force an understanding of the dichotomous terms as exclusive of each other (e.g., *stability* is exclusive of *change* and vice versa). This understanding allows a clearer boundary to be set between the concepts that are represented by the terms. The next step involves replacing the assumption about the exclusivity of the terms with the assumption that these terms are inclusive of each other. This apparently paradoxical task requires simultaneously establishing that two terms are dichotomous but also constitute one another, similar to the idea that *parts* and *wholes* define each other but at the same time are different from each other. A recursive process is then involved to switch back and forth between focusing on the inclusivity and the exclusivity of the concepts at different moments of analysis. When the moment of analysis is on the inclusivity of the concepts, the origin or character of any behavior of interest is seen as containing both concepts, which are intertwined and cannot be torn apart. When the moment of analysis is on the exclusivity, the focus on the individual identity of the concepts allows behaviors to be analyzed from the standpoint of each side of the dichotomy. A dialectic approach can be used to differentiate and integrate the findings from different standpoints, providing a more holistic understanding of human development.

Overton (2003) therefore has provided a way to construct seemingly opposing concepts as complementary to each other, which could be useful for reframing the supposed contradictions between the structuralist and non-structuralist perspectives of early literacy development. His approach appears to be particularly suited to the mixed methods research design, which this study has utilized to examine and contrast the concepts of structure, in the form of developmental hierarchy, and variability, in the form of individual differences.

RESEARCH DESIGN

In the last twenty years, the mixed methods approach in research has been increasingly seen as a way to interrogate multiple theoretical and methodological viewpoints within a single study (Greene & Caracelli, 1997; Tashakkori & Teddlie, 2010). According to Onwuegbuzie and Mallette (2011), although mixed methods studies in literacy have been conducted for several decades, research approaches that employ monomethods are more prevalent in literacy research. A mixed methods research design can be defined as a research design which "combines elements of qualitative and quantitative research approaches (e.g., use of qualitative and quantitative viewpoints, data collection, analysis, inference techniques) for the broad purposes of breadth and depth of understanding and corroboration" (Johnson, Onwuegbuzie, & Turner, 2007, p. 123). The research design is underpinned by a dialectic approach, which considers that assumptions and concepts from different philosophical traditions can be usefully and meaningfully used to inform the same study. The dialectic engagement of the assumptions and concepts within the same study allows these assumptions and concepts to be enhanced, reframed, or provide new understandings (Greene & Hall, 2010). The pluralistic stance of the mixed methods approach appears to be consistent with Overton's (2003) argument for the need to explore seemingly contradictory ideas and pose them as complementary partners.

The design of the current study is considered as mixed methods in the sense that it combines qualitative and quantitative viewpoints for interpreting the early literacy assessment responses of individual children. The study builds on the findings from a validation study (Chan, 2010), which analyzed cross-sectionally the responses of four- to six-year-old children to the Early Literacy Knowledge and Skills (ELKS) instrument (Barringer, Brown, Chan, & Care, 2009) using a developmental assessment approach. The developmental assessment approach involves applying item response modeling to identify a developmental progression within a learning domain based on the ordering of assessment task difficulty (Griffin, 2007; Meiers et al., 2006). The validation study included 293 children (145 males, 148 females) who lived in metropolitan Melbourne, Australia, with two-thirds of them (n = 183; 47 to 66 months old) in preschool and the rest in their first year of school (n = 110; 63 to 79 months old) at the time of assessment.

In terms of the differences between the validation study and the current study, the former study mainly focused on the group level statistics based on the 293 children's scored responses by examining model–data fit and item characteristics and to infer a developmental progression. The current study augments the validation study by analyzing the responses of two children who shared the same estimated ability level. The two children were strategically selected for this study to explore an alternative way to interpret the data within the developmental assessment framework. It should be noted that the purpose of this study is not to establish the prevalence of particular response patterns within the data.

METHODS

Procedures and Materials

In the validation study, all of the 293 children were assessed using the ELKS instrument in mid-2009, which was the middle of the school year in Australia. The ELKS instrument was developed as part of a larger research project (The Young Learners' Project [2007–2012]; http://www.education.unimelb.edu.au/younglearners/) and consists of a set of tasks based on studies carried out by Ferreiro and Teberosky (1979/1982) on preschool children's early literacy concepts. The instrument has three main components: an A4-size stimulus booklet, a response recording sheet which includes administration instructions, and a set of scoring criteria. The ten tasks in the instrument assess different early literacy knowledge and skills, including the concepts of silent reading behavior, writing, knowledge of print conventions, word reading, syntactic knowledge, and knowledge of the alphabet, letter–sounds, and words. The alpha coefficient of the ELKS instrument from the validation study was 0.95, indicating good reliability.

The ELKS instrument was individually administered. Most of the tasks involved giving children problem scenarios and asking them to select from a range of responses and explain their reasoning. The average administration time was around 20 minutes per child, ranging from 15 to 45 minutes. Table 1 provides a list and brief descriptions of the tasks.

Case Selection

Hilda and Hanson (pseudonyms) were selected from the sample from the validation study. They were chosen for case analysis on the basis that they shared the same ability estimate (0.38 logit; based on weighted likelihood estimates) while showing relatively distinct response patterns. The children's ability estimates had a small standard error (0.28 logit) compared to other children in the sample (between 0.28 and 1.49 logits). The two children were of similar age: Hilda was 6 years 0 months old, and Hanson was 5 years 11 months old at the time of assessment.

Table 1. A list of the Tasks in the Early Literacy Knowledge and Skills (ELKS) Instrument

Task	Description
1. Silent Reading Behavior	The test administrator holds a book and reads the book silently. The child is asked to name the behavior of the test administrator and provide explanations.
2a. Writing	The child is asked to draw a picture of a family member and label the person (e.g., *mummy*). The child is also asked to write his or her own name and other known words. The child is then asked to read out all the words that he or she has just written.
2b. Writing Re-reading	(Administered at the end after the Letter Identification task) The child is asked to re-read the words that he or she wrote earlier in the task.
3. Spacing Between Words	The child is presented with two sentences at the same time, one above the other on the same page. The two sentences are identical except one has spaces between the words, and the other has no spaces between the words, although the letters are spaced so that the length of the two sentences matches. The test administrator first reads out the sentence and asks the child to pick a sentence that represents what was read and provide explanations.
4. Differentiation Between Symbols	The child is presented with nine cards, each containing a symbol (three numbers, three letters, and three shapes). The cards are presented all at once, and the child is asked to point to the cards that display the given symbol category (i.e., numbers, letters, and shapes).
5. Word Structure	The child is given a list of letter combinations (*a, bbb, boat, h, cskp, fxt, salient, wn,* and *you*) and asked to categorize the items into words and nonwords according to his or her own criteria and provide explanations.
6. Reading With Pictures	The child is shown a picture with an associated word underneath it (e.g., a picture of a soccer player with the word *kick*). The child is asked to point to and read out the text.
7. Word Identification	The child is given four cards (e.g., *k, kt, ki tten,* and *kitten*) and asked to identify the target word (e.g., "Show me the word 'kitten'.") and provide explanations.
8. Word Reading	The child is asked to read out six nouns (*dog, mum, day, tree, water,* and *house*).
9. Swapping Terms	The child is shown a pair of matching sentences with the subject and object swapped around (e.g., *sam tickled mum* and *mum tickled sam*). The child is asked whether the sentences are different and to provide explanations.
10. Letter Identification	The child is presented with 10 capital letters all at once (*A, S, X, Z, C, T, M, H, B,* and *E*). The child is first asked to provide the verbal label of the set (e.g., "the alphabet" or "letters"). The child is then asked to provide the name and the sound, and a word that begins with each of the letters.

Data Formats and Analysis

An assessment that is conducted using the ELKS instrument can generate two types of data: qualitative and numerical. The qualitative data include the verbal and behavioral responses of the children hand-recorded by the test administrator. This qualitative data can be converted to numerical data using a scoring scheme, where the design of the scoring scheme is underpinned by the assumption of a hierarchy in early literacy development, as proposed by Ferreiro and Teberosky (1979/1982). Both the qualitative and numerical data were analyzed in this study for Hilda and Hanson. The developmental progression generated from the validation study was used as a framework for comparing and contrasting the scored responses of the children.

To explain how the developmental progression was inferred, Figure 1 presents the map of person ability and item step difficulty estimates (referred to as *item step difficulty map* hereafter) generated from the item response modeling based on the 293 children's responses to the ELKS instrument. The software ConQuest (Wu, Adams, Wilson, & Haldane, 2008) was used in the validation study to carry out the item response modeling and generate the item step difficulty map. The partial credit item response model (Masters, 1982; Masters & Wright, 1997) was used to order the assessment items according to difficulty at the individual score level and to infer a generalized developmental progression. The model allows items that have more than two item steps (i.e., score levels) to be analyzed, and assumes the difficulty of the item steps within an item to be of different intervals. For example, for a set of items each with three score levels (Levels 0, 1, and 2), the model allows the differences in difficulty between Levels 0 and 1, and Levels 1 and 2 to be different, and the difficulty interval between item steps can vary across the items. Compared to the Rasch model (Rasch, 1960/1980) for dichotomously scored items, the partial credit model allows greater differentiation between items and between the score levels within an item.

Similar to other item response models, the partial credit model orders scored responses and places them on a continuum of increasing difficulty. In Figure 1, the Xs in the middle of the map represent the 293 children in the validation study, while the ELKS items (i.e., questions in the ELKS instrument) are listed on the right. The numbers on the left of the map represent a scale for both person ability and item step difficulty in logits (log odds units). The ability of a child is determined by the number of item steps that the child can complete successfully. The difficulty of each item step is determined by the number of people who can successfully complete each step of an item. The fewer people able to achieve the particular item step within an item, the more difficult the item step is (Masters, 1982). Note that the origin of the scale is relative to the data in this analysis. That is, an item step of one logit difficulty in this analysis is not necessarily at the same difficulty level as another item or item step of one logit difficulty reported in a different study, where the origin of the scale could be different (Wu & Adams, 2007).

In the item step difficulty map, the suffixes *.1* and *.2* represent the second and third item steps of the particular item respectively. Three of the four Letter Identification (LID) task responses have only two item steps (0 and 1). Only one item step is shown on the map for each of those three items. A list with a brief description of the 30 items included in the item response analysis along with the item codes can be found in the appendix.

In terms of interpreting the map in Figure 1, the children in the validation study are positioned along the logit scale according to their ability level, while the item steps are placed according to their difficulty level. The more able children and more difficult item steps are located further up the scale,

Figure 1. Map of child ability and item step difficulty estimates.

Logit scale	Child ability*	Item step difficulty
	X|	
	X|	
	XX|	
	X|	
4	X|	
	XX|	
	XXX|	
	X|	SBW12.2
	XXXX|	WDR23.2
	XXX|	
	XXXX|	
3	XXX|	
	XXXX|	
	XXX|	WDS14.2
	XXX|	WDR22.2 WDR24.2
	XXX|	WDR21.2
	XXXX|	
	XXX|	
2	XXX|	
	XXX|	RWP16.2
	XXXXX|	WDR23.1 WDR24.1
	XXXX|	WDR21.1
	XXXX|	WDR22.1
	XXXXX|	
	XX|	RWP15.2 WDR19.2
	XXXX|	
1	XXXXXXX|	WRI02.2 WDR19.1 WDR20.2
	XXXXX|	
	XXXXXX|	
	XXXX|	SRB01.2 WRI08.2 WDR20.1 SWT25.2
	XXXXX|	
	XXXXX|	WRI02.1 WRI04.2 WRI08.1 WRI10.2
	XXXXX|	WRI04.1 WRI10.1 SWT26.2 LID29.1
0	XXXXX|	WRI03.2 WRI05.2 WRI09.2 WRI11.2
	XXXXXXXXX|	WRI09.1 WRI11.1
	XXXXXXXXX|	WRI05.1 WID17.2
	XXXXXXX|	WRI03.1 WID18.2 SWT25.1 LID27.2
	XXXXXXXXX|	SWT26.1 LID27.1
	XXXXXXXXXX|	SBW12.1
	XXXXXXXX|	WRI06.2
-1	XXXXXXXXXX|	WDS14.1
	XXXXXX|	
	XXXXXX|	DBS13.2 WID17.1 LID30.1
	XXX|	
	XXXX|	WID18.1
	XXX|	WRI07.2
	X|	
-2	X|	DBS13.1
	XX|	
	X|	SRB01.1 WRI06.1 WRI07.1
	X|	
	|	
	X|	LID28.1
	|	
	|	
-3	|	
	|	
	|	RWP15.1
	|	RWP16.1

* Each X = 1.4 children

and the less able children and easier item steps are located lower down the scale. The positioning of the children in relation to item step difficulty can be expressed in terms of the probability of achieving a certain item step. For example, a child who is located at -2 logits has a 50 percent chance of achieving Level 1 or Level 2 for the DBS13 item (differentiating between numbers, letters, and shapes). The child has greater than 50 percent chance of successfully completing the item steps that have an estimated difficulty level of less than -2 logits, for example, a Level 1 on the LID28 item (naming at least one letter).

At the group level, the 293 children's responses generally followed the developmental progression hypothesized by Ferreiro and Teberosky (1979/1982). When the item steps were ordered according to difficulty, they represented a progression of early literacy concepts. As seen in Figure 1, the lower end of the progression included responses that were relatively less sophisticated, such as relying on pictures when reading (RWP15.1 and RWP16.1). Responses in the middle section of the progression generally related to the application of simple rules such as the minimum quantity hypothesis or variation rules when differentiating words from nonwords (WDS14.1). The upper end of the progression included responses that demonstrated a more sophisticated understanding of rules of written language, such as the use of spacing (SBW12.2), reading direction (SBW12.1), subject–object position (SWT25.2 and SWT26.2), and letter–sound relationships (LID29.1). The progression supports a structuralist view of early literacy in terms of a developmental hierarchy (e.g., Chall, 1996; Meiers et al., 2006) and provides a means in this study for comparing the responses of Hilda and Hanson.

FINDINGS

An examination of Hilda's and Hanson's scored and raw responses suggests that although the children were estimated to share the same ability level according to item response modeling, there were variations in the ways the children responded to the ELKS tasks. Furthermore, their raw responses indicate that they tended to focus on different levels of text features when attempting the tasks.

Scored Responses

Figure 2 presents the same item step difficulty map presented in Figure 1 but denoting the scored responses of Hilda and Hanson. The responses of Hilda are denoted by a circle (●) and Hanson a square (□) to the right of an item step. As can be seen from the figure, Hilda's and Hanson's responses spread across more than four logits of the scale. Out of the 30 items, the children obtained the same scores or item steps on their responses for around a quarter of the items (8 items; 26.7%). From the item step difficulty map, Hanson appeared to have given more responses that are of a higher difficulty level than did Hilda. He appeared to have utilized more text features when reading, achieving Level 2 scores for the Reading With Picture (RWP) task, and Level 1 scores for most of the words in the Word Reading (WDR) task. Hilda, on the other hand, achieved Level 1 scores for the Reading With Picture task, which indicated that she inferred the meaning of a word from the accompanying picture. She read some of the easier words correctly (WDR19 *dog* and WDR20 *mum*), but did not attempt or gave irrelevant responses for the more difficult words. The item step difficulty map also indicated that Hanson was better at the Letter Identification (LID)

Figure 2. Map of child ability and item step difficulty estimates denoting Hilda's (●) and Hanson's (□) scored responses.

Logit scale	Child ability*	Item step difficulty
	X|	
	X|	
	XX|	
	X|	
4	X|	
	XX|	
	XXX|	
	X|	SBW12.2
	XXXX|	WDR23.2
	XXX|	
	XXXX|	
3	XXX|	
	XXXX|	
	XXX|	WDS14.2
	XXX|	WDR22.2 WDR24.2
	XXX|	WDR21.2
	XXXX|	
	XXX|	
2	XXX|	
	XXX|	RWP16.2 □
	XXXXX|	WDR23.1 □ WDR24.1 □
	XXXX|	WDR21.1
	XXXX|	WDR22.1 □
	XXXXX|	
	XX|	RWP15.2 □ WDR19.2 ●
	XXXX|	
1	XXXXXXX|	WRI02.2 ● WDR19.1 □ WDR20.2 ●
	XXXXX|	
	XXXXXXX|	
	XXXX|	SRB01.2 ● WRI08.2 WDR20.1 □ SWT25.2
Estimated ability level of Hilda and Hanson (0.38 logit) →	XXXXX|	
	XXXXX|	WRI02.1 □ WRI04.2 ● WRI08.1 ● WRI10.2 □
	XXXXX|	WRI04.1 WRI10.1 SWT26.2 LID29.1 □
0	XXXXX|	WRI03.2 ● WRI05.2 ● □ WRI09.2 ● WRI11.2 ●
	XXXXXXXXX|	WRI09.1 WRI11.1 □
	XXXXXXXXX|	WRI05.1 WID17.2 ● □
	XXXXXXX|	WRI03.1 □ WID18.2 ● SWT25.1 LID27.2 □
	XXXXXXXXX|	SWT26.1 □ LID27.1
	XXXXXXXXXX|	SBW12.1 □
	XXXXXXXX|	WRI06.2 ● □
-1	XXXXXXXXXXX|	WDS14.1 ●
	XXXXXX|	
	XXXXXX|	DBS13.2 ● □ WID17.1 LID30.1 □
	XXX|	
	XXXX|	WID18.1 □
	XXX|	WRI07.2 ● □
	X|	
-2	X|	DBS13.1
	XX|	
	X|	SRB01.1 □ WRI06.1 WRI07.1
	X|	
	X|	LID28.1 ● □
-3			
			RWP15.1 ●
			RWP16.1 ●

* Each X = 1.4 children

Note. Only item steps above zero are shown on this map. Hilda scored zero for items WRI10, SBW12, WDR21 to LID27, LID29, and LID30, and Hanson scored zero for items WRI04, WRI08, WRI09, WDS14, WDR21, and SWT25.

tasks whereas Hilda achieved Level 0 for most of those tasks. However, Hilda appeared to be better at some of the writing tasks, achieving a higher level than Hanson for her picture label (WRI02) and other word (WRI09) writing.

Raw Responses

Other than the scored responses, each child's raw responses were also examined. For Hilda, her responses indicated that she generally paid greater attention to the word level features of text when reading or writing. In contrast, Hanson's responses indicated that he generally paid more attention to the letter–sound level features of text. The following presents some of their responses as illustrations.

For example in the Writing task, which was administered at the beginning of the assessment session, the children were asked to draw a picture of their mother and label the picture as "mummy." They were also asked to write other known words on the page and read out all the words that they wrote. For the final ELKS task, the children were asked to re-read their writing. Figure 3 shows the drawing and writing by Hilda (figure a) and Hanson (figure b).

Figure 3. Drawing and writing by Hilda (figure a) and Hanson (figure b).

When asked to write the word *mummy*, Hilda wrote "MuM." When asked to write other words that she knew, Hilda chose to write some three letter words, but only provided two letters for each of the words. She wrote "DT" for *dad*, "dO" for *dog*, and "CA" for *cat*. At the end of the assessment session when Hilda was asked to re-read her writing, she read it in terms of what she had originally intended, that is, *dad*, *dog* and *cat*.

In comparison, when asked to write the word *mummy*, Hanson tried to sound out the word, saying to himself "/m/-/um/-/i/," but only wrote down the letter *M*. When asked to write other words that he knew, he only wrote the letter *B*, although the writing was not well formed. At the end of the assessment session when he was asked to re-read his writing, he read the letter *M* as "/m/," and the other letter as "G," although he initially said that the letter that he wrote was *B*.

Table 2: Hilda's and Hanson's responses to the Word Reading task

Target word	Hilda	Hanson
dog	"Dog."	"G."
mum	"Mum."	"/u/ and /m/."
day	"Cat... No, it doesn't have a C and an A."	"Don't know."
tree	"Don't know."	"Y for /e/."
water	"Don't know."	"/a/-/w/-/e/-/s/."
house	"Don't know."	"/m/-/u/-/o/-/s/."

Hilda and Hanson therefore showed distinct approaches in the way they attempted the writing task. What Hilda read out matched what she intended the writing to be and not what was on the page (e.g., *dO* as "dog"). Hanson, on the other hand, read his writing in terms of what was written on the page, rather than the letter or word that he intended to write. This was evident in the way that he said the last letter that he wrote was *G* even though he had originally intended to write *B*.

The difference in the ways the children responded to the early literacy tasks can also be observed in other ELKS tasks. For the Reading With Picture task, the children were shown a picture with an associated word underneath it (RWP15 shows a picture of a soccer player with the word *kick*, and RWP16 shows a picture of a red flag with the word *red*). The children were asked to point to and read out the text. For this task, Hilda said she didn't know what the text in the first item was, but read the text in the second item as "flag." Hanson, on the other hand, named the letters in the text ("K-I-C-K" and "R-E-F"). Hilda therefore inferred from the picture what the accompanying word was in the second item, and did not appear to refer to the grapho–phonic cues from the text. In contrast, when reading a word with an accompanying picture, Hanson appeared to disregard the picture and only referred to the letters in the word.

In the Word Reading task, the children were shown six words (*dog, mum, day, tree, water,* and *house*), and for each word, they were asked, "What does this [word] say?" The responses of Hilda and Hanson to the task are shown in Table 2. As can be seen from the table, Hilda read *dog* and *mum* correctly. She initially misread *day* as "cat", but self-corrected when she realized the word did not have the letters *C* and *A* like cat ("Cat... No, it doesn't have a *C* and an *A*."). She said "don't know" to the rest of the words in the task. Unlike Hilda, Hanson did not read any of the words correctly. He tried to name or sound out the letters in the words, but could not make out what the words were (e.g., "/u/ and /m/." for *mum* and "Y for /e/." for *tree*). Based on Hanson's responses to the above writing and reading tasks, he tended to segment words into smaller sound units when spelling and reading, albeit not always successfully.

Compared to Hilda, Hanson appeared to know the letter–sounds well from his performance in the Letter Identification task, as can be seen in Table 3. Hilda generally gave some words as her response when asked to provide the sounds to the letters.

Table 3: Hilda's and Hanson's responses to the Letter Identification task in response to the prompt "What sounds do they [these letters] make?"

Target letter	Hilda	Hanson
A	"And."	"/a/."
S	"Ant."	"/s/."
X	"Alex."	"/ks/."
Z	"Zoe."	"/z/."
C	"Cat."	"/k/."
T	"Don't know."	"/t/."
M	"Mum."	"/m/."
H	"Hilda [Own name]."	"/h/."
B	"Don't know."	"/b/."
E	"In."	(No response.)

Although most of the two children's responses appear to be distinguishable in terms of their focus on either words or letter–sounds, there was counter-evidence. For example, Hilda corrected herself when she misread the word *day* and compared the word to her knowledge of the spelling of the word *cat* ("Cat… No, it doesn't have a *C* and an *A*."). Her response showed that she did refer to letter level details when reading on this occasion. The counter-evidence suggests that although some overall patterns could be observed from the children's responses, not all of their responses could neatly fit into a particular approach or profile.

DISCUSSION

The purpose of this study was to explore the following question: "How can multiple pathways be operationalized within a developmental assessment framework?" This question is examined in this paper through juxtaposing the findings from the quantitative and qualitative analyses in this study, drawing upon the idea of conceptual dependency discussed by Overton (2003). As noted in the Research Design section, the focus of the data analysis was not to categorize the children's responses, as this would be another structuralist approach to create distinct groupings for understanding early literacy development. The focus of the analysis was to uncover information or viewpoints that may not be apparent from the usual focus within the developmental assessment framework, which is on identifying the developmental level that a child is at based on a generalized developmental progression.

The mapping of Hilda's and Hanson's scored responses on the item step difficulty map shows that the responses were not restricted to a single ability level, but instead covered a range of ability levels. Depending on the particular task, the children showed strengths in some areas, and weaknesses in others. Comparing the children's scored and raw responses also revealed that when individual children's responses were examined as a whole, certain patterns could be identified. As can be seen from the raw responses presented, Hilda tended to focus on the word level features of text, while Hanson tended to pay greater attention to the letter–sound features of text. These patterns were not apparent from the scored responses using the generalized developmental progression as a framework. Nevertheless, the individual variability found in this study should not be seen as contradicting the developmental progression identified in the larger validation study.

The comparison between Hilda's and Hanson's responses may help to illustrate the difference between group and individual level results. At the group level, the single developmental progression from the item response modeling appears to be theoretically coherent and empirically sound, supporting Ferreiro and Teberosky's (1979/1982) view of early literacy development as hierarchical and sequential. The scoring scheme used in the ELKS instrument and the item response modeling appear to have eliminated variations and inconsistencies in responses at the group level. This resulted in a clearer structure when the data were aggregated. When examined cross-sectionally, the children's responses generally followed a hierarchical order from low to high sophistication levels.

However, at the individual level, variations and inconsistencies remained, and the responses did not appear to neatly fit within a particular developmental stage or level. Hilda's and Hanson's scored responses appear to be diverse where their responses cover a large range on the developmental continuum. The variability in the children's responses supports Clay's (1991, 1998) idea that multiple pathways exist for children who achieve similar outcomes. Although Hilda and Hanson were estimated to be at the same ability level, they showed different strengths and weaknesses when responding to the ELKS tasks.

In response to the research question, multiple pathways can be operationalized within a developmental assessment framework as deviations from a particular developmental structure. In this sense, the developmental structure provides a "coarse ruler" (Fischer & Rose, 1999, p. 201) for identifying children who share similarities within a particular set of attributes. However, the structure may omit some aspects of development where children may differ from each other at the finer-grained level.

Drawing upon Overton's (2003) discussion of dichotomies and relational terms in developmental psychology, findings from this study suggest possible conceptual dependencies between structure and variability. Although the group level findings support the developmental structure postulated by a structuralist perspective of early literacy, at the individual level, the structure may be more varied and dynamic than it appears at the group level. On the other hand, the dynamic processes hypothesized by a non-structuralist perspective can be investigated more systematically if some structures are imposed so that comparisons can be made between different children.

This understanding of the relationship between structure and variability as interdependent is consistent with the recognition that Clay's (1991, 1998) notion of "different paths" is contingent upon the existence of "common outcomes." In the context of this study, multiple pathways may not be identifiable without a theorized structure or without setting a common goal for different children. Without the common tasks provided by the ELKS instrument or the generalized developmental progression generated using population statistics, the responses of different children would be difficult to compare. Findings from this study suggest the need to reconceptualize existing early literacy theories and analytical approaches to incorporate both structuralist and non-structuralist perspectives.

Through drawing out the similarities and differences in the children's responses, this study highlighted the complexity associated with investigating early literacy development, which has particular assessment and research implications. In terms of assessment reporting, the findings support Buly and Valencia's (2002) study, which showed that reading scores on standardized tests could hide individual differences in abilities. In their study, the researchers examined the profiles of 108 fourth-grade students in the United States who were found to be below the state benchmark using a range of measures (e.g., the Peabody Picture Vocabulary Test–Revised [Dunn & Dunn, 1981]; the revised Woodcock-Johnson Psycho-Educational Battery [Woodcock & Johnson, 1989]; and the Comprehensive Test of Phonological Processing [Wagner, Torgesen, & Rashotte, 1999]). Supporting their findings, the current study shows that differences in student profiles can also be identified within the same measure when the responses are examined at a finer-grained level.

Furthermore, this study shows that ability estimates or a generalized developmental progression may be limiting for describing the developmental status of individual children. Children can operate at multiple developmental levels at the same time depending on the nature of the tasks given. A single developmental level may not fully represent a child's knowledge and skills and variability in task performance (for example, see Yaden & Tsai, 2011). Nonetheless, a generalized developmental progression may still be useful to provide teachers with a general idea of how or where children could be heading. As endorsed by one of the reviewers of this paper, theories about developmental trajectories may provide a useful heuristic to help teacher trainees to organize information about individual students. Without such a structuralist framework, information about individual variability and cultural differences may appear too abstract and disconnected. Rather than using generalized developmental progressions as a "crystal ball" to provide an accurate prediction of how a child should develop, the progression may be used as a guide or as a reference. As illustrated in the comparison between Hilda's and Hanson's responses, the progression appears to be useful as a basis for comparing between children. A developmental progression can be used to examine how children may approach the same task differently but obtain identical or similar results.

In terms of research direction, this study underscored the need to examine both structure and variability within the developmental assessment framework. As demonstrated in this study, one research approach could be to identify a generalized developmental progression based on group results and then investigate variability using the progression as a reference point. This approach requires greater time and resources compared to traditional structuralist research approaches, as researchers need to fulfill both the goals of identifying a developmental structure and deviations from the structure. Nonetheless, this approach may help researchers to investigate developmental trajectories and patterns at a finer-grained level; at the same time, comparisons can be made between different cases through examining the levels of deviation from a particular developmental structure. Findings from this line of research may help teachers to deliver developmentally appropriate teaching that takes into account multiple routes to learning.

In terms of study limitations, for the purpose of answering the research question, this study mainly focused on describing rather than on explaining the differences in Hilda's and Hanson's responses. An investigation of the reasons that could explain the differences in the children's approaches to the ELKS tasks (e.g., in terms of their literacy experience or gender) would require a different research design and focus. In addition, although the case analysis in this study suggests that children may display different literacy approaches in assessment, more research is needed to understand its implication for teaching. Should the focus of teaching be on expanding students' repertoire of strategies, or should it be on accommodating the teaching to each student's literacy approach? If the answer is a combination of both, when would it be appropriate to place more focus on one area than the other? Rather than focusing on finding a teaching method that would benefit most children, more attention could be placed on identifying the characteristics of children and situations that would make a particular teaching method more suitable for them.

Researchers need to be to be aware that the variability in responses found in this study could be more pronounced because of the open-endedness of many of the ELKS tasks; the assessment procedures in the study, which involved noting down the verbal and behavioral responses of the children; and the difficulty of the assessment tasks relative to the children's ability. Past reviews (e.g., Meisels & Piker, 2001; Pearson, Sensale, Vyas, & Kim, 1999) have found that many formal and informal early literacy assessment tools tend to have more closed-ended questions, where children are asked to give a verbal response to a question which only has one correct answer. The use of closed-ended questions in assessment tasks limits the variability that can be found, especially if the data recorded are in dichotomous format (e.g., correct/incorrect). In addition, the ELKS tasks seem to be not so easy that Hilda and Hanson could answer most of the items correctly, nor were the tasks too difficult for the children, making them unwilling to attempt the tasks. The tasks therefore appear to be at the optimal level that maximizes the variability that could be found in the children's responses. Future studies that attempt to identify multiple developmental pathways adopting the theoretical and research approach in this study, therefore, need to take into consideration the constraints imposed by the assessment tool, data collection procedures, and task difficulty in relation to the participants' ability.

CONCLUSION

Clay's (1998) notion of "by different paths to common outcomes" provides thought provoking insights into the complexity of early literacy development. To broaden and deepen our understanding of the complexity of early literacy development may require juxtaposing seemingly contradictory ideas and research approaches. This juxtaposition may stimulate new theories of early literacy development and ways for teachers to assess the development of individual children.

Author Note: *The author is a recipient of the Australian Postgraduate Award (Industry) and this paper is based on the author's doctoral thesis titled* Standardised Assessment in Early Literacy: Reconciling Different Perspectives and Methods. *This research was funded by the Australian Research Council (Project Number: LP0883437) in conjunction with its partner organization the Australian Scholarships Group. The author wishes to acknowledge the parents, children, and teachers who participated in this research, and members of the Young Learners' Project. The helpful comments from Professor David Clarke of the University of Melbourne on a prior draft of this paper are greatly appreciated. Correspondence concerning this article should be addressed to Man Ching Esther Chan. E-mail: mcechan@gmail.com*

REFERENCES

Australian Curriculum Assessment and Reporting Authority. (2013). *The Australian curriculum* (Version 4. 2). Retrieved from http://www.australiancurriculum.edu.au

Barringer, E., Brown, P. M., Chan, M. C. E., & Care, E. (2009). *Early Literacy Knowledge and Skills Instrument.* Victoria, Australia: The University of Melbourne.

Buly, M. R., & Valencia, S. W. (2002). Below the bar: Profiles of students who fail state reading assessments. *Educational Evaluation and Policy Analysis,* 24, 219–239.

Chall, J. S. (1996). *Stages of reading development* (2nd ed.). Fort Worth, TX: Harcourt Brace.

Chan, M. C. E. (2010, August). *Young Learners: Using item response theory to examine early literacy development.* Paper presented at the biennial meeting of the Learning and Development in Early Childhood Special Interest Group, part of European Association for Research on Learning and Instruction, Lucerne, Switzerland.

Chan, M. C. E. (2012). *Standardised assessment in early literacy: Reconciling different perspectives and methods* (Unpublished doctoral thesis, The University of Melbourne, Victoria, Australia).

Clay, M. M. (1966). *Emergent reading behaviour* (Doctoral thesis, The University of Auckland, New Zealand).

Clay, M. M. (1991). *Becoming literate: The construction of inner control.* Portsmouth, NH: Heinemann.

Clay, M. M. (1992). It's time for a new standard in standard-setting. *Reading Today,* 10, 3.

Clay, M. M. (1998). *By different paths to common outcomes.* York, ME: Stenhouse Publishers.

Crawford, P. A. (1995). Early literacy: Emerging perspectives. *Journal of Research in Childhood Education,* 10, 71–86.

Dunn, L. M., & Dunn, L. M. (1981). *Peabody picture vocabulary test* (Rev. ed.). Circle Pines, MN: American Guidance Service.

Ferreiro, E., & Teberosky, A. (1979/1982). *Literacy before schooling* (K. Goodman Castro Trans.). Exeter, NH: Heinemann Educational Books.

Fischer, K. W., & Rose, S. P. (1999). Rulers, models, and nonlinear dynamics: Measurement and method in developmental research. In G. Savelsbergh, H. van der Maas, & P. van Geert (Eds.), *Nonlinear developmental processes* (pp. 197–212). Amsterdam: Royal Netherlands Academy of Arts and Sciences.

Fischer, K. W., & Silvern, L. (1985). Stages and individual differences in cognitive development. *Annual Review of Psychology,* 36, 613–648. doi:10.1146/annurev.ps.36.020185.003145

Gates, A. I. (1947). *The improvement of reading: A program of diagnostic and remedial methods* (3rd ed.). New York: The Macmillan Company.

Glaser, R. (1994). Instructional technology and the measurement of learning outcomes: Some questions. *Educational Measurement: Issues and Practice,* 13, 6–8.

Greene, J. C., & Caracelli, V. J. (Eds.). (1997). *Advances in mixed-method evaluation: The challenges and benefits of integrating diverse paradigms.* San Francisco, CA: Jossey-Bass.

Greene, J. C., & Hall, J. N. (2010). Dialectics and pragmatism. In A. Tashakkori & C. Teddlie (Eds.), *SAGE handbook of mixed methods in social and behavioral research* (2nd ed., pp. 119–143). Los Angeles: SAGE Publications.

Griffin, P. (2007). The comfort of competence and the uncertainty of assessment. *Studies in Educational Evaluation,* 33, 87–99.

Harste, J. C., Woodward, V. A., & Burke, C. L. (1984). *Language stories and literacy lessons.* Portsmouth, NH: Heinemann Educational Books.

Johnson, R. B., Onwuegbuzie, A. J., & Turner, L. A. (2007). Toward a definition of mixed methods research. *Journal of Mixed Methods Research,* 1, 112–133.

Masters, G. N. (1982). A Rasch model for partial credit scoring. *Psychometrika,* 47, 149–174. doi:10.1007/BF02296272

Masters, G. N., & Forster, M. (1996). *Developmental assessment: Assessment resource kit.* Camberwell, Victoria: Australian Council for Educational Research.

Masters, G. N., & Wright, B. D. (1997). The partial credit model. In W. J. van der Linden & R. K. Hambleton (Eds.), *Handbook of modern item response theory* (pp. 101–121). New York: Springer.

Meiers, M., Khoo, S. T., Rowe, K., Stephanou, A., Anderson, P., & Nolan, K. (2006). *Growth in literacy and numeracy in the first three years of school* (ACER Research Monograph No. 61). Melbourne, Victoria: Australian Council for Educational Research. Retrieved from http://research.acer.edu.au/acer_monographs/1/

Meisels, S. J., & Piker, R. A. (2001). *An analysis of early literacy assessments used for instruction* (CIERA Rep. No. 2-013). Ann Arbor: University of Michigan, Center for the Improvement of Early Reading Achievement. Retrieved from http://www.ciera.org/library/reports/inquiry-2/2-013/2-013.pdf

National Governors Association Center for Best Practices, & Council of Chief State School Officers. (2010). *Common Core State Standards for English language arts and literacy in history/social studies, science, and technical subjects.* Washington DC: Authors. Retrieved from http://www.corestandards.org

Onwuegbuzie, A. J., & Mallette, M. H. (2011). Mixed research techniques in literacy research. In N. K. Duke & M. H. Mallette (Eds.), *Literacy research methodologies* (pp. 301–330). New York: Guilford Press.

Overton, W. F. (2003). Development across the life span. In R. M. Lerner, M. A. Easterbrooks & J. Mistry (Eds.), *Handbook of psychology* (Vol. 6, pp. 13–42). New York: John Wiley and Sons, Inc.

Pearson, P. D., Sensale, L., Vyas, S., & Kim, Y. (1999). *Early literacy assessment: A marketplace analysis.* Paper presented at the National Conference on Large-Scale Assessment, Snowbird, UT.

Rasch, G. (1960/1980). *Probabilistic models for some intelligence and attainment tests.* Chicago: University of Chicago Press.

Sulzby, E., Barnhart, J., & Hieshima, J. (1988). *Forms of writing and rereading from writing: A preliminary report* (Tech. Rep. No. 437). Champaign, IL: University of Illinois, Center for the Study of Reading.

Tashakkori, A., & Teddlie, C. (Eds.). (2010). *SAGE handbook of mixed methods in social and behavioral research* (2nd ed.). Los Angeles: SAGE Publications.

Teale, W. H., & Sulzby, E. (Eds.). (1986). *Emergent literacy: Writing and reading.* Norwood, NJ: Ablex Publishing Corporation.

U.K. Department for Education. (2011). *Primary curriculum subjects: English.* Retrieved from http://www.education.gov.uk/schools/teachingandlearning/curriculum/primary/b00198874/english

Wagner, R. K., Torgesen, J. K., & Rashotte, C. A. (1999). *Comprehensive test of phonological processing.* Austin, TX: Pro-ed.

Woodcock, R. W., & Johnson, M. B. (1989). *Woodcock-Johnson psychoeducational test battery* (Rev. ed.). Allen, TX: DLM Teaching Resources.

Wu, M. L., & Adams, R. (2007). *Applying the Rasch model to psycho-social measurement: A practical approach.* Melbourne, Victoria, Australia: Educational Measurement Solutions.

Wu, M. L., Adams, R. J., Wilson, M. R., & Haldane, S. A. (2008). ConQuest: Generalised response modelling software (Version 2) [Computer program]. Camberwell, Victoria: Australian Council for Educational Research Ltd.

Yaden, D. B., Jr., & Tsai, T. (2011). Learning how to write in English and Chinese: Young bilingual kindergarten and first grade children explore the similarities and differences between writing systems. In M. Gort & E. B. Bauer (Eds.), *Early biliteracy development: Exploring young learners' use of their linguistic resources.* Florence, KY: Routledge.

APPENDIX

Code and Description of the ELKS Items

ELKS task	Item code	Description
1. Silent Reading Behavior	SRB01	Identification of silent reading behavior
2. Writing	WRI02	Picture label spelling
	WRI03	Direction of the writing referred to in Item WRI02
	WRI04	Reading of the writing referred to in Item WRI02
	WRI05	Re-reading of the writing referred to in Item WRI02
	WRI06	Own name spelling
	WRI07	Direction of name writing
	WRI08	Other words spelling
	WRI09	Direction of the writing referred to in Item WRI08
	WRI10	Reading of the writing referred to in Item WRI08
	WRI11	Re-reading of the writing referred to in Item WRI08
3. Spacing Between Words	SBW12	Concept of spacing between words
4. Differentiation Between Symbols	DBS13	Differentiating between symbols
5. Word Structure	WDS14	Concept of word structure
6. Reading With Pictures	RWP15	Item: *kick*
	RWP16	Item: *red*
7. Word Identification	WID17	Item: *kitten*
	WID18	Item: *spider*
8. Word Reading	WDR19	Word: *dog*
	WDR20	Word: *mum*
	WDR21	Word: *day*
	WDR22	Word: *tree*
	WDR23	Word: *water*
	WDR24	Word: *house*
9. Swapping Terms	SWT25	Item: *sam tickled mum*
	SWT26	Item: *the girl chased the boy*
10. Letter Identification	LID27	Labeling of the alphabet
	LID28	Letter name response
	LID29	Letter sound response
	LID30	Word response

"Books I Can Actually Read:" Kindergartners' Reading Choices and Reading Behaviors

Juliet L. Halladay

University of Vermont

In the primary grades, it is common practice to match young readers with texts by aligning levels of text difficulty with levels of student reading ability. There is considerable research to support the use of leveled texts in the early grades, particularly for building fluency (e.g., Hiebert, 2005). For example, some studies have shown that young readers can benefit from practicing conventional reading skills on texts they can decode independently (e.g., O'Connor, Bell, Harty, Larking, Sackor, & Zigmond, 2002).

However, there are also some unanswered questions about the use of leveled texts, particularly with emergent readers, who are still developing the skills needed to read texts conventionally. For instance, some researchers have described the benefits of having emergent readers practice "reading-like behavior" with more complex storybooks (e.g., Doake, 1985; Sulzby & Teale, 1991). Others (e.g., Neuman & Roskos, 2012) have emphasized the importance of exposing young students to complex concepts, rich vocabulary, and content knowledge – characteristics not often associated with many of the decodable texts used in primary classrooms.

This combination of research findings presents a dilemma for kindergarten teachers, whose students tend to be at the cusp of moving from emergent to conventional reading: emergent readers may benefit from opportunities to practice developing reading skills on decodable texts, but they might also benefit from spending time with texts that allow for less-conventional reading behaviors and provide exposure to more complex content. Sulzby and Teale (1991) hinted at this dilemma when they stated that, "For some children, reenactments become the primary avenue into conventional reading from print, thus raising questions for advocates of simplified texts for young children" (p. 736).

Research has also found that primary grade teachers tend to believe that it is important to give students experiences with a range of texts, including some they can read conventionally and others that present more of a challenge (e.g., Halladay, 2010). For example, Mesmer (2006) conducted a large survey of K-3 teachers and found that most respondents reported using both leveled texts and literature on a daily basis, with teachers' decisions about which texts to use strongly influenced by their instructional goals. In addition to reporting the use of multiple text types, corresponding to multiple instructional purposes, teachers have also expressed beliefs in the value of having young readers read in a variety of ways, ranging from using books as props for storytelling to reading conventionally by decoding individual words in sequence (Halladay, 2010). Studies such as these have examined teachers' beliefs and practices related to choosing appropriate texts for young readers; less is known about the ways experiences with different texts might influence the students' own beliefs about the nature and processes of reading.

The topic of early reading behaviors is not a new one, as numerous studies have examined emergent readers' interactions with texts (e.g., Pappas & Brown, 1988; Sulzby, 1985). Many of these studies have focused on preschool-aged children and on adult-child interactions, such as conversations during parent-child storybook reading. Less is known about the ways that kindergarten students interact with texts in classroom settings. In addition, although several studies have examined the ways that emergent readers use texts for various purposes (e.g., Dooley, 2010; Dooley & Matthews, 2009), few studies have also explored emergent readers' conceptions of reading itself. And finally, the existing research base pertaining to emergent reading behaviors would benefit from additional information about the ways that students' reading behaviors may be linked to characteristics of the texts they spend time with.

To address some of these remaining questions, this study explored kindergarten students' classroom-based independent reading experiences, focusing on the nature of the texts they read, the way they approached different texts, and their overall views of reading. The purpose of this study was to expand the research base on emergent literacy by exploring connections between text characteristics, reading behaviors, and beliefs about reading. The data used in this analysis come from a larger study of text matching practices across the elementary grades. This paper addresses the following research questions: 1) What texts do kindergarten students choose to read during independent reading time? 2) How do they interact with the different texts they read? and 3) How do students perceive the process and purpose of reading? Because much of the work for primary grade teachers involves using texts to help students become fluent readers, answers to these questions have important implications for classroom practice.

THEORETICAL PERSPECTIVES

In examining kindergarten students' interactions with texts during independent reading, this study draws on Doake's (1985, 1988) work on reading-like behaviors. Doake's rich depictions of children's early efforts to create meaningful stories offer useful language for describing reading behaviors. In particular, Doake's conceptions of fluent and arhythmic reading-like behavior provide a useful framework for thinking about the various ways that children imitate and create stories by drawing on multiple resources, including knowledge of story structure, pictures, and print cues. The data analysis in this study was also influenced by Sulzby's (1985) descriptions of emergent storybook reading as governed by print or governed by pictures, and as forming stories with characteristics of either oral or written language.

This paper also draws on the RAND Reading Study Group's (2002) model of reading comprehension, which considers factors related to readers, texts, and activities, all situated within a sociocultural context. The RAND model offers a structure for examining the complexity of students' reading experiences by looking at reader, text, and task not as unitary constructs but as complex, multi-faceted variables. The influence of the RAND model can be seen in the study's focus on multiple text variables, student perspectives, and relationships between text characteristics and reading behaviors.

Related ideas about comprehension come from Dooley and Matthews' (2009) ideas about emergent comprehension. Their extension of the RAND model for younger readers offers important insights about the ways that emergent readers construct meaning through their engagement with texts. Their work aligns well with Sulzby and Teale's (1991) description of an emergent literacy perspective, which "ascribes to the child the role of constructor of his or her own literacy" (p. 729).

Taken together, these various theoretical perspectives ground this study in the complex transitional area between emergent literacy and conventional reading practices.

METHODS

This small, descriptive study focused on kindergartners' experiences during independent reading time. As part of a larger study, researchers visited three kindergarten classrooms two to three times each week over a period of approximately four weeks toward the end of the school year, interacting with students during their independent reading time. The exact length of the data collection period varied somewhat across classrooms, depending largely on the weekly instructional schedule. Although this data collection period would be considered short for an in-depth, qualitative study, the amount of time spent in each classroom and with each student was sufficient for gathering the necessary data for this mixed methods analysis. Researchers interacted with each participating student on multiple occasions, gathering information about some of the texts they read and the ways they read them.

During these visits, researchers conducted a one-on-one, semi-structured interview with each participating student and collected multiple oral reading samples as students read aloud from texts they had chosen for independent reading. Depending on the schedule and the individual student, data collection for each student took place over the course of two to five visits. The researchers also copied text samples and gathered information about the texts students chose to read. The current analysis employs a mixed-methods design, including quantitative measures of lexical variety and qualitative data gathered through oral reading observations and semi-structured interviews. The combination of text data, oral reading samples, and student interviews provided sufficient information for addressing the three research questions described earlier. Each of the data sources is described in more detail in the sections that follow.

Participants

The sample for this analysis consists of 13 kindergarten students (7 boys, 6 girls), drawn from a larger set of 18 focal students. The 6 focal students from each classroom were chosen at random from the pool of consented students, and all 18 focal students completed either 2 or 3 oral readings of self-selected texts. The 13 students who completed 3 oral readings are the students who are included as participants in this analysis. The decision to include these 13 students and exclude the remaining 5 was made to provide the largest possible number of reading samples for each student and to ensure that all students had the same number of readings. Demographic and achievement data were not collected for individual students, a limitation that will be discussed further in the discussion section of this paper.

Data Sources

Chosen texts. For the three self-selected texts per student, researchers gathered information about each text's author and genre. Depending on the length of the text, either the entire text or a representative portion was used for some basic linguistic analysis. In particular, researchers calculated the Type Token Ratio for each text. Type Token Ratio (TTR) measures the diversity of words used in a text by comparing the number of total words in a text (tokens) with the number of individual words used (types). In other words, words that are used more than once in a passage count as a single type but as multiple tokens. Texts with large numbers of repeated words (e.g., predictable texts that follow a syntactic pattern) will therefore have a lower TTR than texts that use a broader range of words. For example, the popular children's book *Brown Bear, Brown Bear, What do You See?* (Martin, Jr., 1967), which follows a highly predictable structure, contains 196 total words but only 32 unique words, resulting in a TTR of .163. In contrast, an excerpt of similar length from the narrative picture book *Alexander and the Terrible, Horrible, No Good, Very Bad Day* (Viorst, 1972) had a TTR of .519, with 94 unique words in a sample of 181 total words. The rationale for using TTR as a means of text analysis is that it provides information beyond what can be gained from traditional readability formulae, offering an index of vocabulary diversity and a potential means for identifying the lexical predictability of texts (see Cunningham, Spadorcia, Erickson, Koppenhaver, Sturm, & Yoder, 2005; Hiebert, 1999).

Oral readings. Researchers asked students to read aloud from texts they had chosen to read during independent reading time, and each student chose three texts to bring to the researcher. Given that researchers' instructions could influence students' decisions about which texts to share, students were asked to provide three texts they had read during independent reading time. These instructions were intended to focus students' attention on texts they had chosen themselves and read independently at school, as opposed to texts they had read at home or during guided reading instruction. Following each of these oral readings, researchers used a guided retelling procedure to assess comprehension. All oral readings and retellings were recorded for later analysis. The purpose of the oral reading samples was to gather information about students' interactions with texts. In addition, researchers used the same oral reading and retelling procedures for a narrative leveled reading passage from the Analytical Reading Inventory (ARI; Woods & Moe, 2007). This leveled passage was designed to provide a point of comparison across students and classrooms; however, analysis of the ARI data is outside the scope of this particular paper.

Student interviews. The purpose of the student interviews was to learn more about students' perspectives on the instructional practices they experienced in their classroom. The interview protocol for the larger study consisted of a set of open-ended questions targeting issues such as reading preferences, enjoyment of reading, the role of the teacher in student reading choices, text selection processes, the nature and purpose of reading, and determinations of a text's appropriateness. This current analysis focused on a small subset of questions from the larger interview protocol, using students' responses to address the third research question (i.e., How do students perceive the process and purpose of reading?). Each interview took approximately ten minutes, with researchers asking questions from the protocol and adding probing questions as needed. All interviews were recorded for later transcription and analysis.

Data Analysis

After collecting text samples, recording oral readings, and conducting individual student interviews, all recordings were transcribed. The author individually coded all data, with coding categories checked, revised, and confirmed through an inter-rater reliability process involving a total of three coders.

Chosen texts. The lexical variety of each self-selected text was determined by using the software program AntConc (Anthony, 2011) to calculate TTR. Texts were also coded using a researcher-developed scale of linguistic predictability, as a means of describing the degree to which texts were predictable based on structural elements. This coding system was developed during the course of data analysis, as a means of making distinctions between texts in a way that corresponded to the level of support that a text's structure might provide to a young reader. This coding system was felt to be necessary because so many of the chosen texts were at least somewhat predictable, in ways that could support and influence students' reading behaviors. The predictability codes allowed for a richer exploration of possible connections between text characteristics and reading behaviors. Using this scale, texts were coded into one of four different categories: 1) highly predictable, with a single sentence pattern; 2) highly predictable, with a multiple sentence pattern; 3) somewhat predictable, with repeated syntactic elements and sentence structure; or 4) not predictable based on linguistic patterns.

Oral readings. Oral readings were transcribed and analyzed for evidence of both emergent and conventional reading behaviors. To allow for distinctions between various approaches to reading, readings were coded using a researcher-developed scale that draws heavily on the work of Doake (1985) and Sulzby (1985). Oral readings were coded as a) fluent reading-like behavior, which sounds like fluent reading but is not governed by print cues; b) arhythmic reading-like behavior, which shows some evidence of attention to print cues; c) conventional reading, with word-by-word decoding and consistent attention to print cues; or d) improvisational reading, which mostly consists of labeling and describing based on pictures. This last category corresponds closely to what Sulzby (1985) has described as picture-governed attempts at reading, without forming a story. During data analysis, the determination was made to also code oral readings as either having or lacking elaborative comments, which are unprompted side comments made by students and related to the meaning of the text. Examples of the oral reading categories and elaborative comments will be provided in the upcoming results section.

Student interviews. All interview responses were transcribed and coded, using an open coding procedure, in which coding categories arose from the data. As mentioned in the data sources section above, this analysis focuses on responses to a small subset of interview questions, targeted to find out more about students' perceptions of purposes and processes of reading: 1) Why do people read? 2) What do good readers do as they read? 3) What do you find hard about reading? and 3) How do you decide which books to read? These questions were chosen because they addressed the third research question, providing information about students' overall conceptions of reading – how it works, what it's for, and what it feels like for a young reader.

RESULTS

Again, this analysis addresses three related research questions about kindergartners' experiences with texts chosen for independent reading. Here, the results for each research question are presented in turn.

Reading Choices

The first research question focused on the texts that kindergartners chose to read during independent reading time. While all three classroom teachers provided some degree of advice and guidance about how to find a "just right" book, they also allowed students to choose freely from the books in the classroom. Students in all three classrooms had access to extensive classroom libraries as well as personal book boxes for storing texts. When researchers asked students to share three texts, students chose from a combination of these sources. The texts they chose represented a mix of genres and were characterized by varying degrees of lexical variety and linguistic predictability. In terms of genre, most of the selected texts were narrative texts (n = 33, or 84.6%), and a few were informational texts (n = 6, or 15.4%). Of the narrative texts, many followed a fairly predictable text structure, and several were rhyming books. All of the informational texts were about topics related to the natural world, such as frogs, snow, and rain forests. All of the texts contained high levels of picture support, with at least one image on every set of facing pages.

In terms of lexical variety, the TTR for the 39 texts ranged from a low of .251 to a high of .878, with a mean of .465 and a standard deviation of .163. Texts at the simpler end of the spectrum included *The Photo Book* (Randell, 1995), a fairly predictable text with a total of 55 words but only 14 individual words, resulting in a TTR of .255. Of the 14 individual words in the text, all but 2 were used at least twice. In contrast, the informational text *Frog* (Royston, 2001) contained a similar number of total words (57) but a much larger number of individual words (40), resulting in a TTR of .702. Of the 40 individual words in *Frog* (Royston, 2001), 8 were used at least twice, meaning that 32 of the words appeared only once in the text.

To analyze linguistic predictability, texts were categorized using the coding system described in the data analysis section. Nearly a third of the chosen texts (n=12, 30.8%) were highly predictable, with either single or multiple sentence patterns. Almost half (n=18, 46.2%) were somewhat predictable, with repeated structure and syntax. The remaining 9 texts (23.1%) were coded as not predictable based on linguistic patterns. As a rough test of the reliability of the researcher-developed predictability categories, the mean TTR for each group of texts was calculated (see Table 1). While statistical significance was not determined, the apparent differences in mean TTR between the categories of highly predictable (types 1 & 2), somewhat predictable (type 3), and not predictable (type 4) suggest a relationship between lexical variety and linguistic predictability. In other words, texts with higher degrees of repeated structure have larger numbers of repeated words, resulting in

Table 1: Text Predictability and Mean Type Token Ratio (TTR)

Type of predictability	n	Mean TTR
1) Highly predictable, single sentence pattern	6	.399
2) Highly predictable, multiple sentence pattern	6	.344
3) Somewhat predictable, with repeated structure or syntax	18	.430
4) Not predictable based on linguistic patterns	9	.691

lower TTR. This finding is not surprising, given the constructs under investigation; the objective TTR measure lends support to the reliability of the subjective predictability scale.

Reading Behaviors

The second research question focused on the ways that students interacted with the texts they read. To address this question, students' oral reading samples were examined closely for evidence of emergent and conventional reading behaviors. As described in the Methods section, each reading was coded as fluent reading-like behavior, arhythmic reading-like behavior, conventional reading, or improvisational reading. Examples of all four categories were found in the sample of 39 readings.

Fluent reading-like behavior. As described by Doake (1985), fluent reading-like behavior is characterized by fluent and expressive speaking, not governed by print cues but resembling competent reading. Of the 39 total readings, 6 (15.4%) were coded as belonging to this category. Students who read in this way used intonation and language appropriate to book reading, even when the words they said did not match the words in the text. Often, fluent reading-like behavior was seen when students read highly predictable texts with considerable accuracy, deviating in ways that suggested reliance on broad linguistic patterns and picture cues rather than print cues. For example, a young boy reading the book *Here, Kitty, Kitty* (Tovey, 2001) encountered the lines, "Kitty is in the keg. Kitty is in the kickoff" and read them as, "Kitty is in the bureau. Kitty is in the football field." For the closing sentence, "Kitty gets a kiss," the student read, "Kitty is coming at home." In terms of phrasing and structure, his reading sounded like fluent reading of an actual text; however, his lack of a one-to-one match between print and speech, combined with the presence of graphophonemically inconsistent errors (e.g., bureau for keg) suggests that his reading is governed by pictures and text structure rather than the print itself.

Arhythmic reading-like behavior. Arhythmic is the term Doake (1985) used to describe the process of reading with some initial attempts to match spoken words with the print in a text. As Doake explains, "Once children try to match what they are saying with what they are seeing, the problem of achieving an exact match appears" (1985, p. 91). In this study, 6 readings (15.4%) were coded as arhythmic. Students reading in this way spent some time reading in fluent-like ways, without attention to print cues, but with occasional efforts to match speech to text. For example, one girl read *Sam and Bingo* (Giles, 1999) with a combination of realistic (but not accurate) sentences and some corrections and comments clearly based on attention to print cues. Encountering the sentence, "Here is my farm, said Sam," she said "This is my farm, Sam," then commented, "I know how to say Sam, 'cause I can spell Sam's name. He's in the preschool down [the hall]." Her overall reading of the sentence lacks the one-to-one match that characterizes conventional reading, but her comments about the spelling of Sam's name show that she is not relying on pictures and memory alone.

Conventional reading. A majority of the readings (22 of 39, or 56.4%) fell into the category of conventional reading, with students showing evidence that they were approaching their texts in largely conventional ways – attempting to read page-by-page and word-by-word – with varying degrees of success. For example, a boy reading the book *Hot Sunny Days* (Smith, Giles, Randell, 2000) showed clear signs of conventional reading in making attempts at each word, following along with his finger, sounding out difficult words letter-by-letter, and making efforts to reconcile any mismatches. When he encountered the sentence, "You can put on a shirt," he initially read the word "put" as "putt," then paused. He commented, "Well, putt is a word, it's when you play golf, but I don't think that's it, 'cause I'm looking at the picture and they're not putting… You can something on a shirt. You can put on a shirt." Although he did use the picture as a resource for figuring out the word "put," his initial attempt was based on print cues.

Improvisational reading. A few readings (5 of 39, or 12.8%) were coded as improvisational because the students did not make attempts to read in ways that sounded like book reading, choosing instead to improvise based largely on illustrations and prior knowledge. For example, one student chose to read a fairly difficult informational text about rain forests. He prefaced his reading by saying, "Well, we don't really read it, but we just look at the pictures." As he flipped through the book, rather than reading the words on the page, he looked at photos and described his thinking: "I usually think that that's a volcano. M [a classmate] tells me it's a volcano, but I don't know if it is, because he says that he used to live here." Another student who read in a similar manner provided a somewhat stream-of-consciousness narration of the illustrations in her chosen text *If You Were My Bunny* (McMullan, 1996): "They're sleeping, and… they were running from the bees, and rain, and they got some honey…And thunder and lightning…The tiger cat wanted her baby because of the thunderstorm. And look it! [points to illustration]." These improvisational readings do not show the attention to print cues that characterizes conventional or arhythmic reading, but they also do not show the reading-like phrasing that characterizes fluent reading-like behavior. As Sulzby (1985) explained, this type of reading is governed by pictures and not in the form of a story.

After coding all readings as either fluent reading-like, arhythmic, conventional, or improvisational, additional analysis was conducted to look for relationships between the types of reading behaviors and the levels of text predictability (see Figure 1). For texts coded as highly predictable, students' reading behaviors were mostly coded as either fluent reading-like behavior or

Figure 1. Student reading behaviors, by level of text predictability.

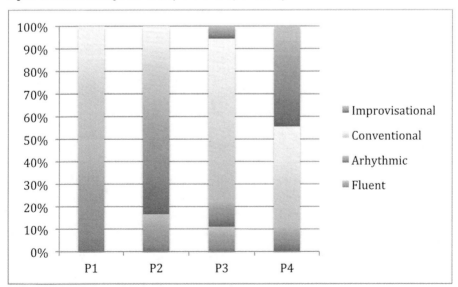

conventional reading, with some arhythmic reading behaviors noted in the highly predictable texts with multiple sentence patterns. Somewhat predictable texts were most likely to be read in ways coded as conventional, with less fluent and arhythmic reading-like behavior. The texts coded as not predictable based on linguistic patterns were associated with all but one instance of improvisational reading, and none of the students read these texts with fluent reading-like behavior.

As mentioned earlier, students' readings were also coded for the presence or absence of elaborative comments, which were side comments focused on making meaning. For example, when a student read the book *My Little Dog* (Smith, 1996), she correctly read, "My little dog goes," paused to look at the accompanying picture, and commented, "Where? Behind the trees?" After correctly finishing the sentence with "around the trees… and she comes back to us," she paused again and commented, "He's heading into the trees. It's like a secret passageway for him." These comments are connected to the reading and serve to elaborate on the meaning of the text. Of the 39 readings, students made elaborative comments on nearly half of them (18, or 46.2%).

In looking for possible connections between text characteristics and these elaborative comments, we find that students made these comments on only 2 out of 12 texts (16.7%) coded as highly predictable (types 1 and 2). Students made elaborative comments on 10 out of 18 texts (55.6%) coded as somewhat predictable and on 6 out of 9 texts (66.7%) coded as not predictable. Again, although no tests of significance were conducted with this small sample, there is an apparent pattern between the level of text predictability and the presence or absence of elaborative comments, with less predictable texts eliciting more meaning-related comments from young readers.

Perspectives on Reading

The third research question centered on students' perceptions of the process and purpose of reading, with data drawn from students' responses to a subset of the semi-structured interview questions. In describing purposes for reading, students frequently said that people read for academic or cognitive outcomes: to improve reading skills, to learn things, or to get smarter. For example, as one student explained, "We just keep on reading, so we get gooder and gooder, so we can all just read by ourselves." This comment suggests that the student understands the purpose of reading to be developing the ability to read independently. Several students also mentioned reading for enjoyment, "because stories are fun things to read."

In terms of the process of reading, the kindergarten students in this sample often referred to word-level skills; few students mentioned the construction of meaning. For example, when asked what good readers do when they read, common responses included behaviors like pointing to words as you read, sounding out words, and skipping difficult words. When asked what parts of reading were difficult, students again focused on word-level issues. For instance, one student said that chapter books are difficult "because they have lots of words that we don't know." Another student commented, "I find it, when you start reading, it's hard because you don't read that much. And the letters are, it just seems like a bunch of letters to you." In general, comments related to the reading process focused heavily on word-level skills.

In discussing their own reading process, a few students made clear distinctions between books they could read (i.e., use for storytelling) and books they could actually read (i.e., read conventionally). As one student explained:

I like to read *Hot Wheels Blast* (Landers, 2010), the shark book, and those over
there that I can actually read. Because some books that I can't read I just put
between the chairs and then when I'm done with my easy ones I'll try and do
those ones instead.

This comment shows the student's awareness of the different ways he might read different
texts, depending on his ability to read conventionally. It also shows his interest in spending time
with books that he "can't read," at least in conventional ways. For many of the students in this
sample, the shift toward conventional reading was facilitated in part by their efforts to memorize
predictable texts. For instance, one student described the process of moving toward being able
to read a book independently, saying that students read with a teacher first, then "you have to
re-memorize what they read."

DISCUSSION

Findings from this study provide additional information about the experiences of kindergarten
students as they interact with texts and progress from emergent to fluent reading. Given the
opportunity to choose freely from a broad range of classroom texts, the kindergarten readers in the
sample chose and shared a range of different texts, a finding that complements Mesmer's (2006)
finding that most primary grade teachers offer their students multiple types of texts over the course
of a school day. Many of the texts had some degree of predictable linguistic structure, in the form
of repeated sentences and phrases. The use of TTR offers a helpful metric for understanding how
the use of repeated words in a text can serve as a support for young readers who are still acquiring
and mastering basic skills in decoding and word recognition.

In terms of reading behaviors, the findings from this study support the frameworks developed
by emergent literacy researchers including Doake, Sulzby, and others. Students read in ways that
were governed by print, by pictures, or by some combination of the two. Students frequently read
in ways that mirrored the structure of actual texts, but not always. One important contribution
of this study is that it allows for not only a description of students' reading behaviors, but also an
analysis of relationships between reading behaviors and text characteristics. It makes intuitive sense
that the predictable structure of many primary grade texts could influence the ways students interact
with them, and this relationship was shown to exist. Students read the more predictable texts in
different ways than they read the less predictable texts, with more fluent reading-like behavior and
fewer elaborative comments. Students often improvised as they read texts that lacked a predictable
linguistic structure.

The findings related to different ways of approaching different texts were also confirmed
through students' interview comments about the purposes and processes of reading. Their comments
focused quite a bit on word-level processes, describing the difficulty of translating printed texts into
meaningful language. Students also made perceptive distinctions between the different types of
reading they sometimes do: reading as pronouncing printed text and reading as creative meaning-
making. Interestingly, despite the clear emphasis on word-level skills in their interview responses,
the kindergarten students in this sample also exhibited a good range of meaning-making skills as
they read. The presence of numerous elaborative comments, especially with less predictable texts,
shows that students were able to read for meaning even with slightly more complex texts.

Because of its small, descriptive nature, this study has some obvious limitations. First, because students were reading aloud to researchers, it is likely that their reading behaviors were altered somewhat by the nature of the reading situation. The results of this study are therefore not necessarily generalizable to other reading situations, such as true independent reading or even reading with a more familiar adult like a parent or teacher. Second, because data collection occurred over a relatively short period of time, this study does not provide any evidence of changes over time. A longer, more in-depth study of kindergarten reading behaviors in relation to text characteristics would provide additional insights into the ways students develop various reading strategies and behaviors over time. Third, the study relies on several measures that would benefit from additional reliability testing. Although inter-rater reliability was established for all coding procedures, and alignment between TTR and the linguistic predictability scale hints at its construct validity, conclusions based on these scales and coding categories should be drawn with some degree of caution. Despite these limitations, however, both the predictability scale and the categories of reading behaviors allow for important distinctions between types of texts and behaviors; additional research could prove useful in establishing their validity and reliability.

Another important limitation of this study also suggests some areas for future research. Although the RAND model of reading comprehension (2002) places roughly equal weight on readers, texts, and tasks, this study focused heavily on text characteristics in relation to reading behaviors and the context of independent reading. Other than the nature of their actual reading behaviors and their self-reported perspectives on reading, reader characteristics were not considered in this analysis. Future research should take additional student variables into consideration, providing a fuller description of the relationships between reader and text characteristics during the process of reading for different purposes. For example, it will be important to find out if the results from this study hold true with students of different demographic backgrounds and with students who have different levels of reading achievement. Another aspect of the RAND model that merits additional exploration is the sociocultural context that surrounds the reading choices and behaviors of individual students. For example, it would be useful to know more about the kinds of instruction and guidance that classroom teachers provide for independent reading. In other words, how do teachers' recommendations influence students' text selections? Although this study necessarily leaves behind some unanswered questions about kindergartners' reading behaviors, the findings provide an important foundation for future explorations of the nature of relationships between text characteristics and reading behaviors for primary grade students.

CONCLUSION

Text leveling and reader-text matching are important topics across the elementary grades, especially in light of the Common Core State Standards' emphasis on text complexity (National Governors Association Center for Best Practices and Council of Chief State School Officers, 2010). Teachers need to have good information about the ways that students interact with different types of texts, in different ways and for a variety of purposes. This study adds important information to our understanding of emergent readers' interactions with classroom texts, as well as their related beliefs about reading. This study has implications for researchers and practitioners who are interested in finding out more about emergent readers' interactions with texts in classroom settings. It builds on our understanding of emergent reading and emergent comprehension to describe the experiences of students who are progressing from emergent to conventional reading. Additional research will be needed to find out more about the nature of the pathways by which students move from emergent to conventional reading through their varied experiences with different types of texts.

REFERENCES

Anthony, L. (2011). AntConc (Version 3.2.4) [Software]. Available from http://www.antlab.sci.waseda.ac.jp/software.html.

Cunningham, J.W., Spadorcia, S.A., Erickson, K.A., Koppenhaver, D.A., Sturm, J.M., & Yoder, D.E. (2005). Investigating the instructional supportiveness of leveled texts. *Reading Research Quarterly, 40,* 410-427.

Doake, D. (1985). Reading-like behavior: Its role in learning to read. In A. Jaggar & T. Burke-Smith (Eds.), *Observing the language learner* (pp. 82-98). Newark, DE: International Reading Association.

Doake, D. (1988). *Reading begins at birth.* Ontario: Scholastic.

Dooley, C.M. (2010). Young children's approaches to books: The emergence of comprehension. *The Reading Teacher, 64,* 120-130.

Dooley, C.M., & Matthews, M.W. (2009). Emergent comprehension: Understanding comprehension development among young literacy learners. *Journal of Early Childhood Literacy, 9,* 269-294.

Giles, J. (1999). *Sam and Bingo.* Illustrated by Pat Reynolds. Crystal Lake, IL: Rigby.

Halladay, J. L. (2010). *Leveled reading in the elementary grades: Teacher beliefs, classroom practices, and student responses.* Paper presented at the annual meeting of the Literacy Research Association, Forth Worth, TX.

Hiebert, E.H. (1999). Text matters in learning to read. *The Reading Teacher, 52,* 552-566.

Hiebert, E. H. (2005). The effects of text difficulty on second graders' fluency development. *Reading Psychology, 26,* 183-209.

Landers, A. (2010). *Hot Wheels: Volcano blast!* Illustrated by Dave White. New York: Scholastic.

Martin, B. Jr. (1967). *Brown bear, brown bear, what do you see?* Illustrated by Eric Carle. New York, NY: Holt, Rinehart, & Winston.

McMullan, K. (1996). *If you were my bunny.* Illustrated by David McPhail. New York: Scholastic.

Mesmer, H. A. E. (2006). Beginning reading materials: A national survey of primary teachers' reported uses and beliefs. *Journal of Literacy Research, 38,* 389-425.

National Governors Association Center for Best Practices and Council of Chief State School Officers. (2010). *Common Core State Standards for English Language arts & literacy in history/social studies, science, and technical subjects.* Washington, DC: Author.

Neuman, S. B., & Roskos, K. (2012). Helping children become more knowledgeable through text. *The Reading Teacher, 66,* 207-210.

O'Connor, R. E., Bell, K. M., Harty, K. R., Larkin, L. K., Sackor, S. M., & Zigmond, N. (2002). Teaching reading to poor readers in the intermediate grades: A comparison of text difficulty. *Journal of Educational Psychology, 94,* 474-485.

Pappas, C.C., & Brown, E. (1988). The development of children's sense of the written story language register: An analysis of the texture of "pretend reading." *Linguistics and Education, 1,* 45-79.

RAND Reading Study Group. (2002). *Reading for understanding: Toward an R&D Program in Reading Comprehension.* Santa Monica, CA: RAND.

Randell, B. (1995). *The photo book.* Illustrated by Elspeth Lacey. Crystal Lake, IL: Rigby.

Royston, A. (2001). *Frog.* New York: Dorling Kindersley Publishing, Inc.

Smith, A., Gile, J., & Randell, B. (2000). *Hot sunny days.* Illustrated by John Pettitt. Crystal Lake, IL: Rigby.

Smith, A. (1996). *My little dog.* Illustrated by Julian Bruere. Crystal Lake, IL: Rigby.

Sulzby, E. (1985). Children's emergent reading of favorite storybooks: A developmental study. *Reading Research Quarterly, 20,* 458-481.

Sulzby, E., & Teale, W. (1991). Emergent literacy. In R. Barr, M. L. Kamil, P. B. Mosenthal & P. D. Pearson (Eds.), *Handbook of reading research* (Vol. 2, pp. 727-757). New York: Longman.

Tovey, M. (2001). *Here, Kitty, Kitty.* Illustrated by Suzanne Smith. Salt Lake City: Waterford Institute, Inc.

Viorst, J. (1972). *Alexander and the terrible, horrible, no good, very bad day.* New York: Atheneum.

Woods, M. L., & Moe, A. J. (2007). *Analytical reading inventory: Comprehensive standards-based assessment for all students, including gifted and remedial* (8th ed.). Upper Saddle River, NJ: Pearson.

Teaching Summarization Strategies to Intermediate-Grade Students in an Urban, Title 1 School

Diane Marie Braxton
Mariam Jean Dreher
University of Maryland, College Park

The achievement gap among certain groups of students in the United States is an issue of major concern to educators, policymakers, and researchers (Bell, 2009/2010; RAND Reading Study Group, 2002; United States Department of Education, 2002). In particular, despite longstanding concern (e.g., Coleman et al., 1966), family income and race/ethnicity continue to be associated with achievement. The 2011 National Assessment of Educational Progress (NAEP) indicates that, on average, students from more affluent families perform at a higher level than their less affluent peers and that White students perform at higher levels than Black and Hispanic students. (We have used NAEP's race/ethnicity terms.) For fourth-graders, NAEP documented a 29-point gap in reading performance between those who were eligible for free lunch (NAEP's proxy for family poverty) versus those who were not. Similarly, comparisons between White and Black fourth graders indicate a 25-point gap in reading, with a 24-point gap between White and Hispanic students (National Center for Education Statistics, 2011).

Thus, in urban, Title I schools, like the one in the current study, in which students are overwhelmingly from low-income, minority families, educators might rightly conclude that their students face great challenges if they are to meet the demands of the 21st century. We argue that educators need to focus on effective instruction to help narrow the gap, so urban learners are equipped to meet academic and societal expectations. With this student subpopulation rapidly increasing, it is critical to address the issue of improving their reading achievement (Block & Mangieri, 2004). To better prepare urban students for future success in school and the workplace, effective instructional approaches should be identified to help raise their reading achievement levels (Saenz & Fuchs, 2002).

Summarization is one of the most powerful strategies for improving comprehension (Graham & Hebert, 2010; Kamil, 2004; National Institute of Child Health and Human Development, 2000; Rosenshine, Meister, & Chapman, 1996; Shanahan et al., 2010). Summarization requires readers to think critically both during and after reading. Readers must analyze the text information to identify main ideas, involving such processes as reflecting on what has been read, making inferences, integrating ideas, and condensing information. Teaching students to summarize not only can improve the quality of their written summaries, but also their comprehension in content areas (Duke & Pearson, 2002; Taylor, 1982; Taylor & Beach, 1984). Moreover, engaging in summarization can improve long-term retention of information, which impacts students' learning in content areas (Rinehart, Stahl, & Erickson, 1986).

FOURTH AND FIFTH GRADERS IN URBAN SCHOOLS

In this study, we used social studies materials to teach summarization strategies to fourth- and fifth-grade urban, Title I students. We targeted fourth and fifth grades because it is at this level that many students experience what has been termed the fourth-grade slump. This slump has been attributed to a number of issues, most often to changing demands in the reading expectations. As Chall (1983, 1996) described in her work on the stages of reading development, it is at these grades that reading tasks increasingly involve "reading for learning the new" (1983, p. 20), with students expected to comprehend expository and other informational texts in the content areas. Many students face difficulty with informational texts because they present challenges including academic vocabulary and unfamiliar text structures (Chall, Jacobs, & Baldwin, 1990; Leach, Scarborough, & Rescorla, 2003; RAND Reading Study Group, 2002).

In fact, and particularly relevant to our study, Chall et al. (1990) found that low-income students may be at greater risk of a fourth-grade slump than their more affluent peers. Low income students, especially those attending schools with other low-income students, may be less likely to be exposed to a rich curriculum that affords them the opportunity to develop background knowledge, vocabulary, and familiarity with informational text structures. Although in recent years there has been a persistent call for instruction relevant to informational text even in the early grades (e.g., Dreher, 2000; Duke, 2004), evidence indicates that these texts are still typically not a focus in reading instruction (Duke, 2000; Jeong, Gaffney, & Choi, 2010; Moss, 2008; Ness, 2011). Hence, intermediate-grade urban, Title I students are likely to benefit from summarization strategy instruction aimed at helping them comprehend informational text.

Yet few summarization studies have been conducted involving students in urban, Title I schools. Moreover, studies that have done so have typically involved older students [e.g., low-income, urban minority high-school juniors (Hare & Borchardt, 1984); urban middle school students with learning disabilities (Jitendra, Hoppes, & Xin, 2000)]. But curricula and assessments in today's elementary schools indicate that summarization is an expectation (Dromsky & Dreher, 2012), underscoring the need for research on summarization instruction that works with urban elementary students.

RULE-BASED AND GIST SUMMARIZATION STRATEGIES

We identified two summarization strategies shown to be effective with students at or near our selected grade range: (a) rule-based, drawing on work by Kintsch and van Dijk (1978) and Brown and Day (1983), teaches students to summarize using a set of rules, and (b) Generating Interactions between Schemata and Text (GIST), developed by Cunningham (1982), uses an intuitive approach in which students have a word limit as they proceed through a paragraph incorporating each successive sentence until they have condensed the information. Research indicates that GIST is effective with fourth graders (Cunningham, 1982), rule-based with fifth graders (McNeil & Donant, 1982) and sixth graders (Rinehart et al., 1986), and both GIST and rule-based with sixth graders (Bean & Steenwyk, 1984). However, these studies did not deal with urban, Title I students (e.g., "suburban" students for Bean & Steenwyk, 1984; "middle class" for McNeil & Donant, 1982). Moreover, these studies typically used very short paragraphs, not related to the content area curriculum, for both the instruction and the outcome measures. For example, Bean and Steenwyk (1984) used single paragraphs (averaging 50 words) from a commercial skills series.

In the current study, we extended previous work by investigating these two strategies with urban, Title 1 students and with multi-paragraph social studies content from the school system's curriculum. We addressed two research questions about GIST or rule-based summarization: (1) Which approach is more effective in improving expository text reading comprehension with urban, Title I learners?, and (2) Which approach is more effective in improving the summary writing of urban, Title I learners?

METHOD

Using a quasi-experimental pretest-posttest design, we randomly assigned teachers to intervention condition. We examined students' performance in expository reading comprehension and summary writing.

Setting and Participants

We conducted the study in an urban, Title I school of 286 students spanning grades pre-kindergarten to five. The student population was 96% African-American, 3% Caucasian, and 1% Hispanic, with 90% eligible for free lunch and another 6% eligible for reduced-price lunch.

Both fourth grades were taught by experienced, effective teachers who had been at the school many years and had previously taught fifth grade. They delivered the summarization instruction for both grades (see *Procedure*) because neither fifth-grade class had a regular teacher. Both fifth-grade classes were taught by substitutes for most of the school year. One fifth-grade teacher had resigned early in the school year; the other was on long-term leave. Neither could be replaced due to budget cuts.

All fourth and fifth graders at the school—2 classes at each level—received either GIST or rule-based summarization instruction. However, data analysis included only the 64 students with parental consent and student assent. Table 1 summarizes participants' demographics. The higher

Table 1: Characteristics of Participants for Each Grade and Intervention

Class	4A GIST	4B Rule-based	5A GIST	5B Rule-based
Number of Participants (% of class)	17 (85%)	20 (100%)	13 (65%)	14 (70%)
Chronological Age Mean	10.48	10.18	11.15	11.18
Gender				
Male	10	11	9	6
Female	7	9	4	8
Free/Reduced Price Lunch Program	17	19	13	14
Special Education Services*	1	2	0	0
Number Scoring Basic on State Assessment (% of class)	13 (76%)	13 (65%)	7 (54%)	8 (57%)

* Students received services for attention deficit-hyperactivity disorder (ADHD)

percentage of participants in the fourth-grade classrooms is most likely due to the lack of regular fifth-grade teachers who could remind students to return their parent consent forms.

Pretest data from the Qualitative Reading Inventory-4 (see *Measures*) indicated that instructional reading levels in class 4A ranged from primer to fourth grade with the mode at first grade. Class 4B levels ranged from pre-primer to fifth with the mode at primer. Class 5A levels ranged from second to fifth with modes at both third grade and fifth grade. For class 5B, levels ranged from second to sixth with the mode at fourth grade. In the results, we report mean reading levels for each class using a continuous numeric scale (see *Measures*).

Measures

Qualitative Reading Inventory-4 (QRI-4). Both before and after the intervention, we assessed students' comprehension with the widely-used QRI-4 (Leslie & Caldwell, 2006). We chose this individually administered assessment for its potential sensitivity to change in a relatively short 15-lesson intervention (see *Procedure*) and because it provides expository passages at every level, matching our focus on expository text comprehension. The expository selections, ranging from pre-primer to high school levels, are representative of the structure and topics found in content area textbooks.

To address the reliability of the QRI-4, Leslie and Caldwell (2006) analyzed 122 readings for inter-scorer reliability on total miscues, acceptable miscues, and explicit and implicit comprehension. Data across all levels, including both narrative and expository text, indicated an extremely high degree of consistency between scorers with alpha reliability estimates of .99 for total miscues, .99 for acceptable miscues, and .98 for both implicit and explicit comprehension.

To address validity, Leslie and Caldwell (2006) examined the correlation between students' QRI instructional levels and standard scores on a group-administered standardized reading test (Terra Nova tests for grades three to eight). For grade five expository text, the correlation was .53 (n = 35, p < .01). Correlations were not listed for expository text below grade five; however, narrative text for grade four had a correlation of .66 (n = 31, p < .01).

Administering and scoring the QRI-4. A recently retired teacher, periodically observed in unannounced visits by the school principal, administered the QRI-4 to individual students in a vacant class. She began by flashing words in isolation from a graded word list, two grade levels below the current grade, as Leslie and Caldwell (2006) recommended. If the student did not know the word within a second, he/she was given an untimed opportunity to read it. The graded word list score (90% and above independent level, 70% - 89% instructional level, and below 70% frustration level) determined the appropriate starting level for the comprehension selection.

We used the QRI-4 specifically to assess expository reading comprehension. The student began reading the expository selection at his/her instructional level as determined by his/her graded word list score. As the student orally read a selection, the tester used the student's scoring sheet to make notations above words designating miscues, substitutions, insertions, or omissions. After the reading, the tester asked the student to retell the passage and then answer comprehension questions. For this study, we used the answers to the comprehension questions as our comprehension measure. To increase the construct validity of the QRI-4, the tester allowed for "look-backs" during questioning. Scoring of these questions followed Leslie and Caldwell's guidelines. Using total reading accuracy and comprehension score, the tester determined a student's overall reading level: independent 90% and above, instructional 67% to 89%, and frustration below 67%.

Continuous numeric scale. To facilitate statistical testing, each student's highest overall reading level was assigned a number on a continuous numeric scale (Appendix A) devised by Russell (2005), drawing upon the work of Paris and Paris (2003) in narrative comprehension. As Russell noted, the use of a continuous numeric scale for QRI levels for statistical analysis has precedent in other research (e.g., Leslie & Allen, 1999).

Summary Writing Assessment. Each student independently read an expository selection on social studies content and then wrote a summary. Students wrote a summary both before and after the intervention. At each grade, although the before and after intervention passages differed, they produced equivalent results in a pilot study (See *Materials* for more passage information.).

We scored the summaries using a 5-point rubric (Appendix B) developed during the pilot study. Two expert raters, both experienced teachers, scored the summaries, blind to condition, after being trained to use the rubric on pilot study summaries. Interrater reliability was 97%, with discrepancies resolved through consensus.

Materials

At both grades, we used 15 expository selections for instruction and 2 for assessing summary writing. Passages included description, problem/solution, sequence, cause/effect, and compare/ contrast text structures. We selected each passage based on its possible appeal to a diverse student population and its correspondence to topics in the social studies curriculum for each grade. The selections came from textbooks or resource books used in the school. In the pilot study, students at the school the prior year assessed each selection's appeal. All reading selections received favorable responses from students, as well as from two teachers who also evaluated them.

For both grades, we drew the topics from the social studies curriculum: Maryland history and geography for fourth grade and United States history and geography for fifth. Although students had not seen the instructional passages before, the passages dealt with topics that were somewhat familiar to students. However, the passages we used for testing were on aspects of the curriculum that students had not already studied.

At each grade, the 2 testing passages were equal on Flesch-Kincaid reading level (4.2 for fourth; 5.2 for fifth) and similar on length (approximately 140 words for fourth; 120 words for fifth). Instructional passages ranged from reading levels 3.4-5.0 and 99-176 words for fourth grade and from reading levels 4.4-6.0 and 99-165 words for fifth grade.

For some students, these materials were difficult. However, the school district expected all students to use the same material; during the instructional phase (see below), teachers supported lower level readers during independent practice and paired them during partner sessions with more able readers.

Summarization Instruction

In previous research, Bean and Steenwyk (1984) found that twelve, 25-30 minute lessons in either GIST and rule-based summarization enhanced the comprehension and summary writing of suburban sixth-graders. However, their research used single, short paragraphs, whereas the current study involved multi-paragraph passages as well as Title I students at lower grade levels. Based on pilot study results, we increased the time to 15 lessons of 45 (fifth grade) to 60 (fourth grade) minutes each for both the GIST and rule-based strategies. Each class had three lessons each week for five weeks.

Both approaches used teacher modeling during the first 3 lessons, guided practice during the next 3 lessons, partner work for 3 lessons, and finally independent practice for 6 lessons. In both groups, lessons used social studies materials relevant to the school curriculum.

Based on pilot study results, we added the identification of the text structure of each reading selection to both summarization approaches. Through teacher modeling and think-alouds, students learned how to identify the text structures of description, problem/solution, sequence, cause/effect, and compare/contrast. Teachers taught text structures as they were encountered in the

Table 2: Text Structures for Expository Text

Text Structure	Description	Signal Words
Description	Giving information about a topic, concept, event, object, person, idea, etc. by listing important features or characteristics	for example for instance to begin with most important in fact also
Sequence	Putting facts, events, or concepts into an order	first after second then third now previously later next finally before actual use of dates
Cause/effect	Showing how facts or events happen (effects) because of other facts or events (causes)	so that because of as a result since so in order to therefore this led to consequently nevertheless if.....then
Compare/contrast	Showing likeness and/or differences among facts, people, events, etc.	however but as well as yet while although unless in comparison on the other hand not only..... but also either.... or
Problem/solution	Showing a problem that develops and the solution or solutions	problem solution solve therefore

reading selections, modeling how to recognize signal words that helped with identification and comprehension of the structure. The students used a Text Structures for Expository Text chart (Table 2) to help them through all the phases of instruction.

GIST Instruction. Instead of using explicit rules, the GIST approach (Cunningham, 1982) leads students to induce how to summarize based on having a word limit. In this study, the teacher introduced the strategy by displaying the first paragraph of the first text on a transparency. Students read the text silently, followed by the teacher reading it aloud. Then modeling using thinking aloud, the teacher demonstrated how to summarize the text in a sentence or two of no more than 20 words.

When that single paragraph had been summarized, the teacher and students discussed what had been done. Then the teacher displayed the entire text. Students read the text, followed by the teacher reading it aloud. The teacher modeled identifying the text's structure and its main idea. Then the teacher modeled how to summarize the entire text in one or two sentences of up to 20 words. This modeling included thinking aloud about identifying and underlining key words and how doing so can help identify the gist. Based on the pilot study, we added underlining key words to the GIST approach. All lessons used a chart with 20 spaces.

During Lesson 2, the teacher reviewed the GIST strategy with selection 1 and then moved on to selection 2. Each subsequent lesson used one text selection. After the teacher modeling lessons, students practiced the GIST strategy collaboratively with the teacher. They then practiced the strategy with partners before practicing it

Figure 1. Chart for Writing a GIST Summary

Remember the Guidelines for Writing a GIST Summary

1. Read the selection several times if needed.
2. Identify its text structure.
3. Identify the gist of the selection with a partner or independently.
4. Identify the key words that helped you to identify the gist.
5. Follow the rules for writing a GIST summary:
   - One or two sentences
   - No more than 20 words
   - Summary captures the gist of the selection, and not all the details.

independently. The students had a chart (Figure 1) as a reminder of the guidelines.

Rule-based Instruction. Based on Kintsch and van Dijk's work (1978), Brown and her colleagues (Brown, Campione, & Day, 1981; Brown & Day, 1983) proposed an approach that uses a set of rules to teach summarization. In this study, students learned 5 rules: (1) delete information that is not important to the overall understanding of the selection; (2) delete redundant or repeated information; (3) identify a list of items or actions that can be replaced with a general term; (4) identify the topic sentence; and (5) invent a topic sentence, if one is not there.

During Lesson 1, the teacher displayed the first text on a transparency. Students read the text silently, followed by the teacher reading it aloud. Then the teacher modeled identifying the text's structure and its main idea. Next, the teacher modeled Rule 1, deleting unnecessary information, and Rule 2, deleting redundant information.

During Lesson 2, the teacher used the same text to teach Rules 3, 4, and 5. Rule 3 required them to identify lists of items or actions that could be replaced with a general term. Rule 4 guided the students to identify a topic sentence, and Rule 5 asked them to construct a topic sentence if necessary. Lesson 3 reviewed how to use all 5 rules with texts 2 and 3. Each subsequent lesson used

Figure 2. Chart for Rule-based Approach to Summarization

Rule 1:	Cross out information that is not important for your understanding.
Rule 2:	Cross out words that repeat information.
Rule 3:	Circle terms or actions that can be changed into a general term. (For example: red, yellow, orange can be changed to"colors": pine, maple, oak can be changed to "trees.")
Rule 4:	Find a topic or main idea sentence. Highlight it in yellow.
Rule 5:	If a topic sentence is not there, invent one.

Now you're ready to write a great summary with your topic sentence and remaining important details.

a single text. Students used yellow highlighters to mark topic sentences, circled words that could be combined into general terms, and learned to cross out unnecessary information.

After teacher modeling lessons, students engaged in guided practice with the teacher. In the remaining lessons, students practiced the rule-based strategy collaboratively with partners and then independently. For all lessons, students had a chart (Figure 2) as a reminder of the rules.

Procedure

Prior to the intervention, students completed the QRI-4 and the Summary Writing Assessment. After the intervention, these measures were used again.

We randomly assigned the two teachers to one of the summarization strategies. Each teacher received four one-hour training sessions on the assigned approach, as well as a daily lesson plan which indicated the purpose, materials needed, and instructional practices to be addressed. Each plan was in the form of a checklist.

As noted, the two teachers were the fourth-grade teachers at the school. Each teacher taught the assigned approach to one fourth grade and one fifth grade. They instructed all classes in their own rooms, and all instruction took place in the morning during the language arts block using social studies materials. For the fourth graders, the language arts block was broken up by a resource class (e.g., art). The fourth graders received their summarization instruction at the beginning of that block before they went to their resource classes. While their own students were in a resource class, the teachers taught the fifth graders.

To ensure that the two types of instruction were kept separate, teachers taught only one summarization approach. In each group, student folders for storing notebooks and other materials were distributed at the beginning and collected at the end of each lesson. These were stored in containers in the teachers' classrooms. In addition, all charts and other materials were taken down and stored after each lesson.

Treatment Fidelity

As an estimate of treatment fidelity, both teachers checked each step for each of the 15 lessons as it was completed. They recorded beginning and ending times and student attendance for each lesson. In addition, an administrator observed each class twice and an instructional support teacher observed each class once. These unannounced observations occurred once each during modeling, guided practice, and partner sessions. The observers checked off the steps listed on the lesson plan as they were completed.

We also used audiotapes to provide treatment fidelity information. Because only some children had permission to be audiotaped, we could not record the entire intervention. However, during partner sessions, we paired and audiotaped students with permission. We recorded three pairs for each of the three partner sessions in each class, totaling nine recordings per class.

RESULTS

Treatment Fidelity

Checklists and observations. The teacher checklists indicated that the instruction took place as intended, with all steps for each lesson checked. The observers' checklists matched the teachers' lesson plans with all steps checked off. Attendance rates during lessons in the four classes ranged from 92% to 94% and the average lesson length in all classes matched the intended time.

Interaction during partner summary writing. We transcribed all recordings of partner sessions, then analyzed each comment to see if it related to steps taught during the teacher modeling and guided practice. These recordings showed that partners were able to write a summary using the procedure and terms that were taught by the teachers.

We present two examples of students' dialogue, one from each summarization approach, showing how the readers worked together to construct meaning from the text. We selected these examples in two steps: First, we randomly selected a pair of students from each approach for whom we had permission to audiotape. Second, for that pair of students, we randomly selected one of their three partner sessions.

Fourth-grade rule-based partner session

Table 3 is an excerpt from the second partner session of fourth-graders who scored below grade level on the district reading benchmark test. This excerpt shows that they had internalized the process the teacher had taught. Before they started to use the rules for summarization, they read the selection twice and then discussed its text structure. Because Student 1 wasn't sure if the text structure was description, both students referred back to the chart (Table 2) that listed all the text structures with definitions and key words/phrases. Student 1 assured himself that it was description by giving supporting evidence from the selection - describing the walls, what the houses were made of, what was inside.

During guided practice lessons, students quickly discovered that going to Rule 4 first was very important because it helped them to identify the text's main idea. They verbalized that you have to know the main idea so you know what information is important or unimportant. In this excerpt, after the students identified the text structure, they immediately proceeded to Rule 4. After they highlighted the topic sentence, they knew one didn't have to be created, so they skipped Rule 5. They then started at the beginning of the text, read each sentence, and discussed whether to keep it or cross it out, employing Rule 1. If the partners weren't sure about information, they kept it and revisited it at a later time, as was modeled for them. After completing Rule 1, the students then proceeded to use Rules 2 and 3. They also reminded each other that a summary should be short, and sentences should not be copied directly from the text. The students wrote a draft copy of their summary and revised it twice to produce the finished product, as was modeled by the teacher.

Table 3: Fourth-Grade Rule-based Students' Dialogue

Reading Selection: The Woodland Indians' Shelter
After students read the text twice, the partners proceeded to go through the process of summarizing using the rules.

Student 1:	Okay, let's think what the text structure is.
Student 2:	Description.
Student 1:	I don't know. Read the definitions from our text chart. (Student 2 read all the definitions for the different text structures).
Student 2:	I still think description.
Student 1:	Okay, it describes the walls, what the houses were made of, what was inside.
Student 2:	Okay, so let's go to rule 4 and see if a topic sentence is there.
Student 1:	I think Woodland Indians needed shelter like all of us to survive.
Student 2:	I think it's they lived in wigwams or longhouses. Wait, no, that's a detail because that describes a shelter. Okay, we found the topic sentence so highlight it in yellow.
Student 1:	The story had a topic sentence so we can skip rule 5. So let's go to rule 1 and cross out information that's not important. (They read each sentence to decide what to delete).
Student 2:	I think we should keep what they made their homes of.
Student 1:	Cross out the chief's house was the largest.
Student 2:	Not important not much furniture. We don't want to know what is inside.
Student 1:	I'm not sure about covering the hole in the roof so let's keep it for now.
Student 2:	They sat on the platforms. Oh, that's why they built platforms. They were like chairs.
Student 1:	Fire should go.
Student 2:	They used if for heat and cooking. Oh, so keep the fire because that talks about surviving.
Student 1:	Now rule 2. Do we have anything that is repeated? Let's cross out some of the words.
Student 2:	Now let's do rule 3. Look for lists. Wood, bark, and other natural materials. Circle that and we'll just put natural materials.
Student 1:	We found our topic sentence and highlighted it in yellow. Let's see if we can write the summary in two or three sentences. Don't we have to put the topic sentence or main idea first?
Student 2:	Woodland Indians needed shelter like all of us to survive. They used natural materials they found nearby to build their houses.
Student 1:	We can't copy from the story remember.
Student 2:	We changed wood, bark, and grasses to things in nature or natural materials.

Their finished summary was: The Woodland Indians needed shelter to survive. They used the natural materials found nearby to make the shelter. They also made platforms to sit and sleep on, and they built fires for warmth and cooking.

Table 4: Fifth-Grade GIST Students' Dialogue

Reading Selection 7: The Star-Spangled Banner

After students read the text twice, the partners proceeded to go through the process of summarizing in 20 or fewer words.

Student 1:	Let's underline the key words first. In the first sentence, I think we should underline Baltimore and national anthem because that's going to be part of our main idea, or gist.
Student 2:	We need to underline Great Britain and the year 1814.
Student 1:	I don't think we need to keep the ship attacked the fort, but we need to keep Francis Scott Key because he wrote the national anthem. Do you think we need the year 1814?
Student 2:	I think we need important dates because they're related to our main idea, or gist.
Student 1:	Maybe U.S. Army and 1895.
Student 2:	I'm not sure about that. Keep it for now.
Student 1:	1931, and the Star-Spangled Banner became the national anthem.
Student 2:	Let's start to write the summary and we'll use process of elimination to take out words we don't need. We have to get down to 20 words.
Student 1:	In 1814 a ship from Great Britain had attacked the United States. Francis Scott Key then wrote the Star-Spangled Banner. In 1931 the Star-Spangled Banner was the national anthem.
Student 2:	We have to eliminate because we're over 20 words. In the first sentence we don't need ship or had so cross it out. Should we cross out Great Britain?
Student 1:	I don't think so because that's important.
Student 2:	I got it! Let's change Great Britain to British and say the British attacked. Okay, let's write this down.
Student 1:	Do we need Francis Scott Key?
Student 2:	Of course, he wrote it. But I don't think we need all three names. Let's just put Key. The national anthem was written in.... Wait a minute, we can use a comma instead of and.

Their finished summary was Star-Spangled Banner, written in Baltimore in 1814 by Key when the British attacked, became the national anthem in 1931.

The students' dialogue also showed how meaning was gained from the text. Student 1 stated that the information about a fire in the middle of the wigwam should be deleted. Student 2 read the next sentence, which stated the fire was used for heat and cooking, then immediately said that the fire information had to stay because it referred to survival. On the first reading, Student 2 was confused about platforms in the wigwams. With rereading, he then compared their platforms to our chairs in that they provided a place to sit.

Fifth-grade GIST partner session

Table 4 is an excerpt from the third partner session of fifth graders who scored on grade level on the district reading benchmark test. It shows that they had internalized the process that the teacher had taught. In order to help the students focus on important information, the teacher taught them to underline key words in the selection after reading it. As noted, this step was not included in previous studies using the GIST method but was added based on pilot study results to help the students focus on important information.

After reading the selection twice, the partners began to identify and underline key words. If they were not sure, they underlined it and revisited it later, as was modeled. Even though this summarization strategy did not include rules, students began to eliminate unimportant information (as in Rule 1) and words that were repeated (as in Rule 2). They also began to collapse lists into general terms (as in Rule 3) in order to reach the 20-word goal. Although there was no explicit instruction in rules, students deduced the same types of processes as in the rule-based strategy. The students learned quickly that every word in their summaries had to be important, as stressed by the teacher during the initial lessons.

During the modeling and guided practice lessons, the teacher allowed students to dictate as much information as they thought necessary for a summary. The students then counted the number of words and realized that they had far more than 20 words. The teacher then emphasized that they had to use the process of elimination to get down to the 20 most important words. The students in this excerpt clearly learned not only the term, but also the process.

As shown in Table 4, the students decided that some dates were important and had to be included in their summary. Student 2 used his prior knowledge to change "Great Britain" to "British," and "had attacked" to just "attacked." He also knew that Francis Scott Key was an important fact from the selection, but knew it could be revised to the last name, Key. In order to reach the 20-word mark, Student 2 also realized that a comma could replace the word "and" and not be counted as a word, as modeled by the teacher. Therefore, these students were able to write a summary with only 20 words after three revisions.

Table 5: Comprehension Scale Score Means (Standard Deviations) on the QRI- 4

Instructional Group	Pretest Mean (SD)	Posttest Mean (SD)
Grade 4		
GIST (N = 17)	2.21 (1.93)	4.62 (2.57)
Rule-based (N = 20)	2.26 (2.75)	4.96 (3.85)
Grade 5		
GIST (N = 13)	5.46 (2.50)	8.15 (2.41)
Rule-based (N = 14)	5.38 (2.93)	8.50 (2.35)

Expository Text Reading Comprehension

Grade 4. The upper part of Table 5 shows the fourth-grade QRI-4 pretest and posttest mean reading comprehension scale scores. At pretest, the mean reading level was just above level 2 instructional (see Appendix A) for both fourth grades. At posttest, both classes' means were approaching level 3 independent.

Because of its small scale, this study lacked sufficient power for a nested analysis, such as hierarchical linear modeling. Thus, we analyzed scores using a mixed analysis of variance (ANOVA) with time (pretest vs. posttest) as the within-subjects factor and instructional group (GIST vs. rule-based) as the between-subjects factor. We analyzed the grades separately because our goal was not to compare the grades but to, in effect, replicate the study at two grades.

In all analyses in the study, the Box's Test of Equality of Covariance Matrices was not statistically significant, indicating that homogeneity of variance was not violated. For fourth grade, there was a statistically significant main effect for time, Wilks' Lambda = .308, $F (1, 35) = 78.633$, $p < .001$, partial eta squared = .692. According to guidelines proposed by Cohen (1988), this partial eta squared value suggests a very large effect size (.01 = small effect, .06 = moderate effect, .14 = large effect). Neither the main effect for instructional group, $F (1, 35) = .046$, $p = .832$, partial eta squared = .001, nor the time by group interaction was statistically significant, Wilks' Lambda = .993, $F (1, 35) = .242$, $p = .626$, partial eta squared = .007. Thus, fourth graders' scores increased from pretest to posttest regardless of the type of summarization instruction they received.

Grade 5. The lower part of Table 5 shows the fifth-grade QRI-4 comprehension scale score means. At pretest, both classes had means between level 3 independent and level 4 instructional (Appendix A). At posttest, both classes' means were above level 5 instructional.

A mixed ANOVA with time as the within-subjects factor and instructional group as the between-subjects factor indicated a statistically significant main effect for time, Wilks' Lambda = .296, $F (1, 25) = 59.470$, $p = .000$, with a very large partial eta squared of .704. Neither the main effect for group, $F (1, 25) = .018$, $p = .895$, partial eta squared = .001, nor the time by group interaction was statistically significant, Wilks' Lambda = .986, $F (1, 25) = .355$, $p = .557$, partial eta squared = .014. These results parallel the fourth-grade findings, indicating that fifth graders' comprehension scores also increased from pretest to posttest regardless of the type of summarization instruction they received.

Table 6: Summary Writing Assessment Means

Instructional Group	Pretest Mean (SD)	Posttest Mean (SD)
Grade 4		
GIST (N = 17)	2.06 (.24)	3.06 (.89)
Rule-based (N = 20)	1.85 (.37)	3.80 (.83)
Grade 5		
GIST (N = 13)	2.54 (.66)	3.77 (.59)
Rule-based (N = 14)	2.14 (.36)	3.86 (.54)

Summary Writing

Grade 4. The top portion of Table 6 shows fourth-grade pretest and posttest summary writing means. A mixed ANOVA with time as the within-subjects factor and instructional group as the between-subjects factor indicated that the main effect for group was not statistically significant, $F_{(1, 35)} = 3.007$, $p = .092$, partial eta squared = .079. However, the main effect for time was statistically significant, Wilks' Lambda = .266, $F_{(1, 35)} = 96.681$, $p = .000$, with a very large partial eta squared of .734, as was the time by group interaction, Wilks' Lambda = .777, $F_{(1, 35)} = 10.026$, $p = .003$ with a very large partial eta squared of .223. The interaction indicates that the change in

Figure 3: Summary Writing Grade 4: Time by Instructional Group Interaction

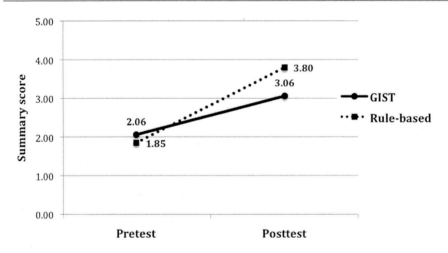

summary writing over time was different for the 2 groups. As Figure 3 shows, the rule-based group made a greater gain from pretest to posttest than the GIST group.

Grade 5. For fifth-grade summary writing scores (lower part of Table 6), the main effect for group was not statistically significant, $F_{(1, 25)} = .701$, $p = .410$, partial eta squared = .027. However, the main effect for time was statistically significant, Wilks' Lambda = .109, $F_{(1, 25)} = 2.040$, $p = .000$, with a very large partial eta squared of .891, and the time by group interaction was also statistically significant, Wilks' Lambda = .820, $F_{(1, 25)} = 5.499$, $p = .027$, with a very large partial eta squared of .180. As in fourth grade, the interaction for fifth grade indicated that the change in summary writing over time differed for the two groups. The pretest to posttest change lines are not parallel (Figure 4), with the rule-based group showing a greater gain in summary writing than the GIST group.

DISCUSSION

Previous research indicates that both GIST and rule-based summarization strategies can be effective with intermediate-grade students. However, these prior studies involved student populations quite different from the students with whom we worked. Moreover, these studies

Figure 4: Summary Writing Grade 5: Time by Instructional Group Interaction

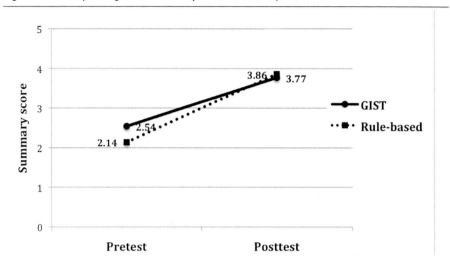

typically involved single paragraphs from skills series isolated from the curriculum (e.g., Bean & Steenwyk, 1984; Cunningham, 1982), and, in one case, used stories rather than content area texts (McNeil & Donant, 1982).

In this study, we compared the effects of GIST and rule-based summarization strategies on fourth and fifth graders in a high poverty, virtually all minority school. Using multi-paragraph expository texts situated in the school curriculum, we found that both strategies improved the quality of the students' written summaries and their expository text comprehension. Although there was some advantage on summary writing for the rule-based approach, both summarization strategies improved summary writing. Thus, teachers could use either approach depending on their preferences.

Our results extend previous findings on these two strategies to younger students in an urban, Title 1 school. Fourth and fifth graders in a school where many students did not read at grade level can successfully learn to summarize and improve their comprehension of expository text. Moreover, our study demonstrates that multi-paragraph social studies material drawn from resources available in a school can be effectively used by teachers in summarization instruction.

A limitation of this study is that we lacked a no summarization instruction comparison group due to the small number of students at the participating school. Although it is unlikely that students would have improved on summarization without summarization instruction, it is possible that students could have improved in reading comprehension, even with no summarization instruction. However, the relatively short intervention (15 lessons spanning five weeks) makes that less likely.

Another limitation is that we could not randomly assign students, instead using a quasi-experimental design with random assignment of teachers. But given the small number of classes at fourth and fifth grades, we lacked power for a nested statistical analysis. Therefore, our statistical analyses and effect sizes should be interpreted with caution. Nevertheless, the same pattern of results was evident at both grades, and treatment fidelity data collected during partner work documented that students learned and used what was taught. Taken together, the analyses and the partner work information provide evidence to encourage the teaching of summarization strategies to promote reading achievement.

These results are especially important because they show that summarization strategies can be effective even with students who lag behind their peers in reading. Teachers were able to use these approaches with texts from the school's social studies curriculum even though the materials, in keeping with district policy, were difficult for some students, given the average reading levels in these classes. Modeling, guided practice, and partner sessions appeared to support students at a range of levels, including below grade level readers, as in Table 3. Providing an intense focus on the comprehension via summarization instruction proved to be beneficial to these urban, Title I students.

Indeed, the results are important to consider in terms of real world context of an urban, Title I school (e.g., Noguera, 2003). As noted, fourth graders were taught by experienced teachers who delivered the instruction for both grades, whereas fifth graders had substitute teachers most of the year. Despite difficult circumstances, the fifth graders were extremely receptive to the summarization instruction. They were eager to receive the instruction, most likely because the fourth-grade teachers were effective and well-respected in the school and community (Turner, 2005), and these students were very aware of not having "real" teachers. Like their fourth-grade counterparts, fifth graders improved in both summary writing and reading comprehension when they had the opportunity to learn how to summarize.

With the No Child Left Behind Act in 2001, closing the achievement gap has been a major goal in U.S. schools. Achievement trend analyses suggest some progress, with a narrowing of the gap in reading achievement in many states between various subgroups of students; however, in 23% of states, gaps in reading achievement have widened (Chudowsky, Chudowsky, & Kober, 2009). Unfortunately, even where narrowing has occurred, the achievement gaps remain substantial (Schugar & Dreher, 2013), making attention to powerful strategies like summarization particularly important in schools where students need to accelerate their progress in reading.

Summarization is a sophisticated undertaking that involves learning to identify essential information, as readers make decisions and actively reflect on what they read. Readers who are able to summarize show better comprehension and retention of information. In this study, we showed that both the GIST and rule-based summarization strategies can be successfully implemented with urban, Title I fourth and fifth graders. Both approaches led to improved comprehension of expository text and summary writing. By demonstrating that urban, Title I elementary school students can benefit from summarization instruction, this study contributes to the body of work that may help narrow the achievement gap between students from minority and low-income families and their more affluent peers.

REFERENCES

Bean, T., & Steenwyk, F. (1984). The effect of three forms of summarization instruction on sixth graders' summary writing and comprehension. *Journal of Reading Behavior, 16*, 297 – 306.

Bell, M. (2009/2010). Major new literacy initiative proposed in US Congress. *Reading Today, 27*, 1-4.

Block, C., & Mangieri, J. (2004). What are the implications of recent policy initiatives for the classroom? Innovations for instruction in urban settings. In D. Lapp, C. Block, E. Cooper, J. Flood, N. Rose, & J. Tinajero (Eds.). *Teaching all the children* (pp. 103-121). New York: Guilford Press.

Brown, A., Campione, J., & Day, J. (1981). Learning to learn: On training students to learn from texts. *Educational Researcher,* 10, 14-21.

Brown, A., & Day, J. (1983). Macrorules for summarizing texts: The development of expertise. *Journal of Verbal Learning and Verbal Behavior,* 22, 1 – 14.

Chall, J. S. (1983). *Stages of reading development.* New York: McGraw-Hill.

Chall, J. S. (1996). *Stages of reading development* (2nd ed.). Fort Worth, TX: Harcourt Brace College Publishers.

Chall, J. S., Jacobs, V. A., & Baldwin, L. E. (1990). *The reading crisis: Why poor children fall behind.* Cambridge, MA: Harvard University Press.

Chudowsky, N., Chudowsky, V., & Kober, N. (2009). *State test score trends through 2007-08, Part 3: Are all achievement gaps closing and is achievement rising for all?* Washington, DC: Center on Education Policy.

Cohen, J. W. (1988). *Statistical power analysis for the behavioral sciences (2nd ed.).* Hillsdale, NJ: Erlbaum.

Coleman, J. S., Campbell, E. Q., Hobson, C. J., McPartland, J., Mood, A. M., Weinfeld, F. D., et al. (1966). *Equality of educational opportunity.* Washington, DC: Department of Health, Education, and Welfare, U.S. Government Printing Office.

Cunningham, J. W. (1982). Generating interactions between schemata and text. In J. A. Niles & L. A. Harris (Eds.), *New inquiries in reading research and instruction* (pp. 42-47). Rochester, NY: National Reading Conference.

Dreher, M. J. (2000). Fostering reading for learning. In L. Baker, M. J. Dreher, & J. T. Guthrie (Eds.), *Engaging young readers: Promoting achievement and motivation* (pp. 68-93). New York: Guilford Press.

Dromsky, A., & Dreher, M. J. (2012, December). *A comparison of two strategies for teaching third graders to summarize information text.* Paper presented at the meeting of the Literacy Research Association, San Diego, CA.

Duke, N. K. (2000). 3.6 minutes per day: The scarcity of informational texts in first grade. *Reading Research Quarterly,* 35, 202-224.

Duke, N. K. (2004). The case for informational text. *Educational Leadership,* 61, 40.

Duke, N. K., & Pearson, P. D. (2002). Effective practices for developing reading comprehension. In A. E. Farstrup & S. J. Samuels (Eds.), *What research has to say about reading instruction* (3rd ed., pp. 205-242). Newark, DE: International Reading Association.

Graham, S., & Hebert, M. (2010). *Writing to read: Evidence for how writing can improve reading: A Carnegie Corporation Time to Act Report.* Washington, DC: Alliance for Excellent Education.

Hare, V., & Borchardt, K. (1984). Direct instruction of summarization skills. *Reading Research Quarterly,* 20, 62-78.

Jeong, J., Gaffney, J. S., & Choi, J. O. (2010). Availability and use of informational texts in second-, third-, and fourth-grade classrooms. *Research in the Teaching of English,* 44, 435-456.

Jitendra, A., Hoppes, M., & Xin, Y. (2000). Enhancing main idea comprehension for students with learning problems: The role of a summarization strategy and self-monitoring instruction. *Journal of Special Education,* 34, 127-139.

Kamil, M. (2004). Vocabulary and comprehension instruction: Summary and implications of the National Reading Panel findings. In P. McCardle & Chhabra (Eds.). *The voice of evidence in reading research* (pp. 213-234). Baltimore: Brookes.

Kintsch, W., & van Dijk, T. A. (1978). Toward a model of text comprehension and production. *Psychological Review,* 85, 363-394.

Leach, J., Scarborough, H., & Rescorla, L. (2003). Late emerging reading disabilities. *Journal of Educational Psychology,* 95, 211-224.

Leslie, L., & Allen, L. (1999). Factors that predict success in an early literacy intervention project. *Reading Research Quarterly,* 34, 404-424.

Leslie, L., & Caldwell, J. (2006). *Qualitative Reading Inventory - 4.* Boston: Pearson.

McNeil, J., & Donant, L. (1982). Summarization strategy for improving reading comprehension. In J. A. Niles & L. A. Harris (Eds.), *New inquiries in reading research and instruction* (pp. 215-219). Rochester, NY: National Reading Conference.

Moss, B. (2008). The information text gap: The mismatch between non-narrative text types in basal readers and 2009 NAEP recommended guidelines. *Journal of Literacy Research,* 40, 201-219.

National Center for Education Statistics. (2011). *The Nation's report card: Reading 2011: Assessment of student performance in grades 4 and 8.* Washington, DC: United States Department of Education.

National Institute of Child Health and Human Development. (2000). *Report of the National Reading Panel. Teaching children to read: An evidence-based assessment of the scientific research literature on reading and its implications for reading instruction: Reports of the subgroup*s. (NIH Publication No. 00-4769). Washington, DC: U.S. Government Printing Office.

Ness, M. (2011). Teachers' use of and attitudes toward informational text in K-5 classrooms. *Reading Psychology, 32*, 28-53.

Noguera, P. (2003). *City schools and the American dream: Reclaiming the promise of public education.* New York, NY: Teachers College Press.

Paris, A. H., & Paris, S. G. (2003). Assessing narrative comprehension in young children. *Reading Research Quarterly, 38*, 36-76.

RAND Reading Study Group. (2002). *Reading for understanding: Toward and R & D program on reading comprehension.* Washington, DC: RAND Corporation.

Rinehart, S., Stahl, S., & Erickson, L. (1986). Some effects of summarization training on reading and studying. *Reading Research Quarterly, 21*, 422-438.

Rosenshine, B., Meister, C., & Chapman, S. (1996). Teaching students to generate questions: A review of the intervention studies. *Review of Educational Research, 66*, 181-221.

Russell, S. (2005). *Challenging task in appropriate text: Designing discourse communities to increase the literacy growth of adolescent struggling readers* (Doctoral Dissertation. University of Maryland, College Park).

Saenz, L., & Fuchs, L. (2002). Examining the reading difficulties of secondary students with learning disabilities: Expository versus narrative text. *Remedial and Special Education, 23*, 31-41.

Schugar, H. R., & Dreher, M. J. (2013). *Fourth graders' informational text comprehension: Indicators from NAEP.* Manuscript submitted for publication.

Shanahan, T., Callison, K., Carriere, C., Duke, N. K., Pearson, P. D., Schatschneider, C., Torgeson, J. (2010). *Improving reading comprehension in kindergarten through 3rd grade: A practice guide (NCEE 2010-4038).* Washington, DC: National Center for Education Evaluation and Regional Assistance, Institute of Education Sciences, U.S. Department of Education. Retrieved from whatworks.ed.gov/publications/practiceguides

Taylor, B. (1982). Text structure and children's comprehension and memory for expository material. *Journal of Educational Psychology, 74*, 323-340.

Taylor, B., & Beach, R. (1984). The effects of text structure instruction on middle grade students' comprehension and production of expository text. *Reading Research Quarterly, 19*, 134-146.

Turner, J. D. (2005). Orchestrating success for African American readers: The case of an effective third-grade teacher. *Reading Research and Instruction, 44*, 27-48.

United States Department of Education (2002). *Public law 107-110: The No Child Left Behind Act of 2001.* Washington, DC: Department of Education.

Appendix A: QRI-4 Continuous Numeric Scale

QRI-4 Selection Level	Assigned Numeric Score
Pre-Primer – Instructional	.1
Pre-Primer – Independent	.1
Primer – Instructional	.1
Primer – Independent	.1
Level 1 – Instructional	.5
Level 1 – Independent	1.0
Level 2 – Instructional	2.0
Level 2 – Independent	3.0
Level 3 – Instructional	4.0
Level 3 – Independent	5.0
Level 4 – Instructional	6.0

Level 4 – Independent	7.0
Level 5– Instructional	8.0
Level 5 – Independent	9.0
Level 6 – Instructional	10.0
Level 6 – Independent	11.0
Upper Middle School – Instructional	12.0
Upper Middle School – Independent	13.0

Note. From Russell (2005, page 153). The first 4 levels -- Pre-Primer and Primer – are assigned scores approaching zero because they represent non-reading.

Appendix B: Summary Writing Rubric

Score	Descriptors
5	Clearly identifies main idea Uses relevant details to support main idea Does not include irrelevant information Briefly stated in own words All ideas are in a logical order
4	Clearly identifies main idea Uses relevant details to support main idea Does not include irrelevant information Most of ideas are in a logical order
3	Main idea is unclear or partially identified Does not use relevant details to support main idea Includes irrelevant information Copies some sentences from the text Ideas are not in a logical order
2	Does not identify the main idea Includes irrelevant information Copies almost all sentences directly from text Ideas are not in logical order
1	No response or response does not correlate with the text

Methods for Evaluating Literacy Engagement as a Fluid Construct

Jacquelynn A. Malloy
Clemson University

Seth A. Parsons
Allison Ward Parsons
George Mason University

We would like to acknowledge Sarah Cohen Burrowbridge for working with us on this project, allowing us to observe her excellent instruction. We would also like to acknowledge Lauren Serpati for calculating the inter-rater reliability presented in this paper.

METHODS FOR EVALUATING LITERACY ENGAGEMENT AS A FLUID CONSTRUCT

The study of literacy motivation builds upon earlier research on achievement motivation and was the focus of a five-year investigation by the National Reading Research Center (1992-1997). From this U.S. Department of Education funded research initiative emerged an *engagement perspective* of reading motivation that served as a guide to developing "motivated and strategic readers who use literacy for pleasure and learning" (Baumann & Duffy, 1997, p. 5). Most notably, the subsequent research using the engagement perspective included the work of Guthrie and colleagues (Guthrie, Anderson, Alao, & Rinehart, 1999; Guthrie et al., 1996, 1998, 2004; Wigfield et al., 2008). These researchers explored Concept-Oriented Reading Instruction (CORI) as a method of integrating content area learning with engaging classroom practices.

During the decade of this investigative agenda, the conceptualization of engagement evolved from an individually localized construct to that of a contextually influenced one (Lutz, Guthrie, & Davis, 2006; Urdan & Schoenfelder, 2006). However, engagement has typically been measured as a fairly stable trait that reflects the engagement of students who attend a certain school or participate in a specific intervention, for example (Fredricks & McColskey, 2011). As classroom context and situational interest are now understood to influence engagement at a more fine-grained level (Lutz, Guthrie, & Davis, 2006; Schraw, Flowerday, & Lehman, 2001; Urdan & Schoenfelder, 2006), measuring engagement as a malleable construct becomes imperative. As opposed to viewing students as either wholly engaged or disengaged in a lesson or a task, there is much to learn from understanding how engagement varies, or flows, across an instructional segment; that is, how engagement is fluid rather than static. Therefore, the purpose of this paper is to discuss the efficacy of methods developed to evaluate literacy engagement as a multidimensional, construct across a yearlong study in a sixth grade classroom that explicitly integrated Social Studies and Language Arts instruction.

RESEARCH CONTEXT

Developing research methods to guide teachers in improving their instruction is a focus of literacy researchers who are aligned with Professional Development Schools (PDSs) through their university affiliations (Barksdale-Ladd, 1994). In this study, research methods were developed to support a PDS affiliated teacher who was interested in improving the engagement of her students during integrated content instruction. This research was conducted in a suburban school district just outside a major metropolitan area in the Mid-Atlantic region of the United States. The school was in its third year of a PDS partnership with a local university. This sixth grade classroom included 22 students: one Caucasian student, two African-American students, three Asian-American students, and 16 Hispanic students. Nineteen students in the class (86%) were eligible for free or reduced lunch prices and 11 were classified as having limited English proficiency. The variety of ability levels in the classroom, particularly with regard to their reading ability and background knowledge for Social Studies content, and of American history in particular, presented pedagogical challenges for the teacher.

The researchers, who were university faculty associated with the PDS and active in the school, helped the teacher develop instructional methods that would engage students and support their learning growth in the integrated Social Studies-Language Arts instruction. To study the efficacy of this instruction, a yearlong study was developed to explore the influence of various instructional tasks on the engagement of students of high, average, and low academic performance. Research methods were piloted and refined during the remainder of one academic year (January-April) and then used to explore the relationship between teaching and engagement in the next academic year. These methods were developed with an eye to being both comprehensive and informative and are the focus of this report.

UNDERSTANDING ENGAGEMENT AND TASKS

The literature suggests three theoretically grounded sub-constructs of engagement: affective engagement, behavioral engagement, and cognitive engagement (Fredricks, Blumenfeld, & Paris, 2004; Fredricks & McColskey, 2011). For the purpose of this study, *affective engagement* is operationally defined as a student's interest, curiosity, or preference for the topic or task, as is suggested by theories of intrinsic motivation (Deci & Ryan, 1985). With a basis in theories of self-regulation (Zimmerman, 2008) and self-efficacy (Bandura, 1993), *behavioral engagement* is defined as the observable actions of the student during the activities that indicate levels of attentiveness and interaction with others (Fredricks, 2013). *Cognitive engagement*, based on an understanding of information processing theory (Baddeley & Hitch, 1974), is operationalized as changes in learning due to strategic involvement with the task that represent attempts to encode new information. Taken together, these sub-constructs embody the current view of engagement as a multidimensional construct (Appleton, Christenson, & Furlong, 2008; Reschly & Christenson, 2012; Skinner & Pitzer, 2012).

As we sought to investigate engagement as a fluid construct, we examined students' engagement in academic tasks. The literature supports the operationalization of instructional tasks as *open* or *closed* (Turner & Paris, 1995) based on the presence or absence of the following six elements: choice, challenge, control, collaboration, constructive comprehension, and consequences. Parsons (2008) adapted this research to develop a framework for rating task openness. This framework incorporates the elements of choice, challenge, and collaboration with additional attention to the authenticity of the task (Gambrell, Hughes, Calvert, Malloy, & Igo, 2011; Purcell-Gates, Duke, & Martineau, 2007; Teale & Gambrell, 2007) as well as opportunities to sustain instruction across more than one lesson (Guthrie & Humenick, 2004; Miller & Meece, 1999).

Engagement as a Critical Issue

Researchers have demonstrated the relationship between engagement and achievement, and specific ties to reading achievement exist (Guthrie, 2004; Ivey & Broaddus, 2007; Reschly & Chistenson, 2012; Skinner & Pitzer, 2012). Similarly, researchers who reviewed the Programme for International Student Assessment (PISA) results report a strong correlational tie between engagement and reading achievement (Ackerman, 2013; Brozo, Shiel, & Topping, 2008; Kirsch et al., 2002).

Researchers investigating what distinguishes high-performing classrooms from low-performing classrooms have found that teachers who involve their students in engaging instruction guide their students toward higher levels of achievement (Bogner, Raphael, & Pressley, 2002; Dolezal, Welsh, Pressley, & Vincent, 2003; Taylor, Pearson, Clark, & Walpole, 2000). However, other researchers indicate that highly engaging instruction occurs infrequently in classrooms (Brophy, 2010; Guthrie, 2004; Guthrie, Wigfield & You, 2012; O'Brien, Beach, & Scharber, 2007) and developing teachers who engage their students at a high level is of great importance to the field.

Measuring Engagement in the Classroom Context

In the past decade, the view of engagement has undergone a change from that of a static and somewhat one-dimensional construct to that of being multidimensional, fluid, and contextualized. Current research posits that engagement is a malleable construct that is highly influenced by the context of the classroom where the instruction occurs (Fredricks et al., 2004; Reschly & Christenson, 2012; Skinner & Pitzer, 2012). The focus at present, then, is to determine ways to explore engagement in the classroom in a manner that can effectively and positively influence instructional practices.

In a report to the Institute of Education Sciences (IES) addressing instruments for measuring student engagement, Fredricks and her colleagues (2011) reviewed 21 measures of engagement for upper elementary through high school learners. The authors found that three aspects of engagement were noted as important in identifying engagement measures. These included behavioral engagement (participation and involvement), affective engagement (emotional response), and cognitive engagement (thoughtful, purposeful approach). Five of the 21 instruments measured all three aspects of engagement. However, the authors noted that these terms were used inconsistently when looking across reports. For example, some measures classified participation as cognitive engagement. The measures were culled from a targeted review of the literature and categorized by domain of study (i.e., general academic engagement or content related). These measures were further classified into three categories: student self-report, teacher report, and observation.

Of these studies, only one emerged as a measure of engagement during literacy instruction: the Reading Engagement Index (REI) (Wigfield et al., 2008). The REI is an eight-item teacher report scale, with items intended to address all three aspects of engagement (behavioral, affective, and cognitive). The total score derived from ratings on the eight items represents the teacher's perception of student engagement in their particular classroom context and addresses all three sub-constructs. This retrospective view on the part of teachers is informative for classifying more and less engaged students as a formative means of designing instruction. However, the current view of engagement as a malleable and dynamic construct requires a more fine-grained view. How does engagement change for students of varying levels of academic proficiency within a single lesson? As Fredricks and McColskey (2011) observed:

> Unfortunately, many of the current measures make it difficult to test questions of malleability. The majority of engagement measures tend to be general (i.e., I like school). Furthermore, measures are rarely worded to reflect specific situations or tasks, making it difficult to examine the extent to which engagement varies across contexts (p. 778).

A study by Lutz and colleagues (2006) sought to determine the effects of student engagement on reading comprehension in three fourth-grade integrated science-literacy classrooms. Besides engagement and reading comprehension, they also focused on text complexity and teacher scaffolding. Their methods involved assessing four dimensions of engagement: affective, behavioral, cognitive, and social. The researchers developed rubrics for evaluating the engagement of four focal students (two high- and two low-achieving) per classroom during one instructional period in 30-second intervals. The scores for each aspect of engagement that were derived via observation were added to determine a variable total engagement score for each interval of observation.

Rating all four aspects of engagement through observation with well-established rubrics permits a single-source view of engagement—that of the researcher conducting the observation. Behavioral engagement, described as participation and attention to task, is particularly open to observational methods. However, affective and cognitive engagement may also be determined through student report. Student interviews occurring immediately following a task may be more illuminative in shaping an understanding of the perceptions of interest and strategic thinking during a task when compared to a researcher's observation of the student. Using student interviews to make determinations regarding affective and cognitive engagement would provide an additional data source to the study of engagement in the classroom—that of the student who participated in the lesson. Therefore, the research reported here integrated observational methods to determine ratings of behavioral engagement with student interviews such that ratings of affective and cognitive engagement could be derived from student report of their participation during various instructional tasks.

METHODS

Six focal students and their teacher from a sixth-grade Title I classroom in a suburban Mid-Atlantic elementary school participated in this descriptive yearlong study. The teacher recommended the focal students, who represent three levels of academic performance: above grade level (AGL), on grade level (OGL), and below grade level (BGL). Each performance level includes

Table 1: Focal Student Characteristics

Teacher Designation	Gender	Ethnicity
Above Grade Level	Male Female	Hispanic African-American
On Grade Level	Male Female	Hispanic Hispanic
Below Grade Level	Male Female	Hispanic Hispanic

one male and one female. The four OGL and BGL students were receiving services as English language learners. The student demographics are presented in Table 1.

The following research question guided this study: *What is students' affective, behavioral, and cognitive engagement in different types of tasks?* To answer this question, researchers visited the classroom during the Social Studies-Language Arts class period once each week for 26 weeks. One researcher observed the teacher and wrote field notes regarding the types of tasks the teacher presented. Task type served as the independent variable.

The other researcher observed three of the six focal students: one AGL, one OGL, and one BGL to evaluate levels of behavioral engagement. These focal student triads were alternated each week. Additionally, the researchers interviewed the three observed focal students at the end of the class to evaluate affective and cognitive engagement using a semi-structured interview protocol. These evaluations of engagement (behavioral, affective, and cognitive) served as the dependent variables. The researchers piloted and refined the three rating scales in the year previous to the full study.

Data Collection and Analysis

Student observations. A researcher observed three focal students during the entirety of the lesson in a series of one-minute intervals. The researcher observed and wrote notes on the behavior of the first student for one minute and then assigned a rating on a scale of 1-4 before moving to the next student. In this manner, the researcher observed each student approximately 15 times during the class period for the length of one minute at three-minute intervals. The four-point scale used for rating behavioral engagement was adapted from one used by Lutz and colleagues (2006) and refined during the pilot year. For this study, behavioral engagement is defined as the degree to which students are observably attending to and participating in the instructional activities. The behavioral rating scale is displayed in Table 2.

Using a document template, the researcher entered the description of student behavior in a time-designated box for each student and then entered a rating of engagement in the corresponding box before moving on to the next student observation. An excerpt of one three-minute section of the observation protocol is provided in Table 3. At the beginning of the year, two researchers simultaneously observed students' behavioral engagement in five lessons. After each observation, the researchers discussed their ratings and notes. Differences were mutually resolved. With each subsequent observation, observer agreement increased. By the final combined observation,

Table 2: Behavioral Engagement Rating Scale (adapted from Lutz et al., 2006)

Rating	Description	Behavior
1	Clearly not engaged	Sighs, looks bored; yawns, head down; distracted by something unrelated to task; not participating; not paying attention, off task.
2	Difficult to tell	Bland expression; monotone; not off task but not particularly involved; wavering attention to teacher/classmates/task; flipping pages without looking at any. Attention but partial.
3	Engaged	Maintains attention; appears interested; clearly on task; posture toward speaker (does this for entire minute); other evidence: writing, speaking, clearly listening; brief response.
4	Highly engaged	Posture or tone reflects enthusiasm or excitement; eagerness to participate; response reveals deep or critical thinking; makes connection, response is extensive; elaborates.

Table 3: Behavioral Rating Template Excerpt

AGL Student	Rating	OGL Student	Rating	BGL Student	Rating
2:18 I. Sitting on floor as students chatter to teacher – teacher begins instruction – attention on teacher – raises hand – is not called on looks at student who is called on- raises hand	3	2:19 G. looks toward teacher as she talks – looks around; turns back to teacher	2	2:20 O. moves up to table so can see film; writes John Locke in notes at top (teacher said was important) -writes Philosopher beside it	3

disagreements were rare, indicating that observers had achieved an acceptable level of inter-rater reliability.

Focal student interviews. At the end of the observed class period, each of the three focal students met with a researcher in an adjoining classroom to respond to a semi-structured interview designed to probe their affective and cognitive engagement with the tasks just completed. The interview was structured such that the researcher would briefly describe each task in the order that it occurred, and then ask "Did you like that activity? Why or why not?" (affective engagement) and "What were you thinking as you completed that activity?" (cognitive engagement). Researchers asked follow-up questions as needed to encourage clarity and completeness of responses. The researchers recorded and then transcribed the interviews for later analysis.

The researchers developed rating scales to evaluate affective and cognitive engagement (see Tables 4 and 5). To create these scales, researchers followed an inductive analysis of similarly structured interviews from the pilot study and based them on operational definitions of the sub-constructs developed from the literature. Affective engagement was operationally defined as the degree to which the students report interest, efficacy, or enthusiasm in the task. Reports of interest,

Table 4: Affective Engagement Rating Scale

1	Not interested in topic or task and/or low efficacy
2	Some interest in topic or task, few details regarding interest
3	Reports efficacy in topic or task and/or many details regarding interest
4	Enthusiastic or curious about topic or task

Table 5: Cognitive Engagement Rating Scale

1	No awareness of thinking
2	Surface level thinking or aware of challenge
3	Focusing on the content or the task
4	Thinking beyond the content or the task (comparing it to something - e.g., their own life or making connections) and/or using strategies to complete the task

enjoyment, or boredom with the tasks were used to determine the rating. Cognitive engagement was defined as the degree to which students make connections or use strategies within instructional activities. Reports of strategic or critical thinking were rated for this category. Each researcher read the transcripts several times before meeting to rate the level of engagement for each sub-construct. Where differences occurred, discussion continued until agreement was reached.

Task type. Using the field notes of the types of tasks implemented by the teacher during the observed lesson, researchers assigned a rating of task openness by designating a rating of 1 to 3 for each of the following elements: authenticity, collaboration, challenge, choice, and sustained learning as indicated by the scale provided in Table 6. Based on the rating totals for each of the five areas, researchers determined task openness using the following score ranges: closed = 5-8; moderately open = 9-11; and open = 12-15. To establish inter-rater reliability for the task rubric, two researchers independently rated half (33) of the documented tasks. Krippendorff's alpha was calculated as an indicator of inter-rater reliability (Hayes & Krippendorff, 2007). Inter-rater reliability of the task openness score was acceptable ($a_K = .73$).

FINDINGS

Overall Findings

Behavioral engagement. Looking across all student data, student ratings of behavioral engagement in tasks was 2.84 for open tasks, 2.73 for moderately open tasks, and 2.58 for closed tasks. All ratings were on a 4-point scale. When disaggregating by student performance level, focal students who were AGL and those who were OGL evidenced higher behavioral engagement on average for open tasks than for closed tasks, as displayed in Table 7. However, students who were BGL revealed higher behavioral engagement in moderately open tasks and least engagement with closed tasks. Across all task types, AGL students were more engaged than OGL and BGL students.

Table 6: Instructional Task Rating Scale

Authenticity (adapted from Duke, Purcell-Gates, Hall, & Tower, 2007)

1 – The task is limited to tasks that are completed primarily in school.

2 – The task mimics outside-of-school tasks, but has features of school-based activities.

3 – The task closely replicates tasks completed in day-to-day lives outside of school.

Collaboration

1 – Students work alone on the task.

2 – Students collaborate minimally in the task.

3 – Students collaborate throughout the task.

Challenge (adapted from Miller & Meece, 1999)

1 – The task requires letter- or word-level reading or writing.

2 – The task requires sentence-level reading writing.

3 – The task requires passage-level reading or paragraph-level writing.

Student Directed / Choice

1 – The students have no input on the task.

2 – The students have input, but the choices have minimal influence on the task.

3 – Students have input into many substantial aspects of the task.

Sustained (adapted from Miller & Meece, 1999)

1 – The task takes place within one sitting.

2 – The task takes place within one or two days.

3 – The task spans over three or more days.

(adapted from Parsons, 2008)

Table 7: Focal Student Behavioral Engagement

	AGL	OGL	BGL	All Students
Open Tasks	3.04	2.79	2.69	2.84
Moderately Open	2.70	2.69	2.81	2.73
Closed Tasks	2.64	2.50	2.59	2.58
	2.79	2.66	2.70	2.72

Table 8: Focal Student Affective Engagement

	AGL	OGL	BGL	All Students
Open Tasks	3.09	2.50	2.90	2.84
Moderately Open	3.21	2.29	2.71	2.74
Closed Tasks	2.52	2.30	2.40	2.41
	2.94	2.36	2.67	2.66

Additionally, students of all levels were, on average, more behaviorally engaged in open tasks than in moderately open and closed tasks.

Affective engagement. Table 8 reveals that open tasks were on average more affectively engaging to students across all ability levels than moderately open tasks, and these were more engaging than closed tasks. When looking within ability levels, students who were OGL and BGL were more interested in open tasks than the others, while AGL students were more affectively engaged in moderately open tasks. Again, AGL students received higher ratings of affective engagement across tasks than the students who were OGL and BGL.

Cognitive engagement. Interestingly, students received fairly uniform ratings on cognitive engagement with relation to task type. Students of all ability levels received higher ratings for cognitive engagement on moderately open tasks when averaged across all lessons observed. Students

Table 9: Focal Student Cognitive Engagement

	AGL	OGL	BGL	All Students
Open Tasks	3.20	2.44	2.20	2.62
Moderately Open	3.64	2.79	2.71	3.05
Closed Tasks	2.82	2.23	2.43	2.49
	3.22	2.49	2.45	2.72

presenting AGL ability were rated as more cognitively engaged than students who were OGL and BGL. Table 9 displays the data for cognitive engagement.

Lesson Level Findings

In order to more comprehensively demonstrate what the research methods reveal about the interaction between task types and student engagement at a more fine-grained level, an in-depth analysis of a single lesson is presented. The 15th observation, which occurred in the second semester of the academic year, was selected as it offered a variety of tasks—closed, moderately open, and open—and occurred at a point in the study where students were accustomed to the researchers being present in the classroom to observe and conduct interviews and may, therefore, have been more natural in their behavior and responses.

In this particular lesson, the teacher sought to guide students in developing a more detailed understanding of the significant figures in the American Revolution. This lesson served as an introduction to a series of lessons with a culminating product of working with a partner to present a visual and written presentation of a historical figure from the American Revolution.

Task descriptions and ratings. In this particular lesson, there were three tasks. The first task required students to write down every person they could think of who was famous for their involvement in the American Revolution. This task segment lasted five minutes and students were allowed to use their notes. At the end of the segment, students were instructed to compare their lists with their group mates. The first task was rated as closed with a total rating of 5 (receiving a rating of 1 for each of the five task components).

The second task involved a guided discussion of a PowerPoint presentation that reviewed various historical figures associated with the American Revolution. The teacher presented images of the historical figures and a detailed description of what made them famous while guiding students to understand the context of the historical period and to make connections between that period of time and the lives of her students. This task lasted almost 24 minutes and was rated as moderately open, as indicated in Table 10.

Table 10: Rating of Task 2 of Observation 15

Authenticity	Collaboration	Challenge	Choice	Sustained	Total
1	2	2	2	2	9 – mod. open

The third task lasted about three minutes and was designed to prepare students for the next day's lesson. Students were instructed to find a partner and agree on a historical figure to study. The product, to be created in subsequent days, was a 'mask,' where students drew the face of their selected historical person on a face shape and attached it to a craft stick. Also, students conducted research and wrote a description of what made this person a prominent figure in the American Revolution, attaching it to the back of the mask. Students presented their masks orally to the class in a culminating lesson. For this lesson, as the end of the period coincided with the end of the school day, students were just to find a partner and agree on a historical figure. As an exit ticket, students received the following instruction: "When you choose the person, you have to give me a really good reason *why* you selected this person." This task was determined to be open with a score of 14 as indicated in Table 11.

Table 11: Rating of Task 3 of Observation 15

Authenticity	Collaboration	Challenge	Choice	Sustained	Total
2	3	3	3	3	14 – open

Students' responses to tasks. Inez, an AGL student, opened her notes and began writing immediately when given the first task: to write down everyone you can think of who is famous from the American Revolution. She continued to write, with brief pauses, for the entire segment. When asked how interested she was in this task (affective engagement), she remarked that she was curious to see how many names she could remember "because there's a lot of people and if I would remember any of them or at least maybe one because there's so much we're learning I forget, but I remembered a lot." In this, Inez also reported a cognitive challenge of distinguishing historical figures. She stated, "I was trying to remember if did they even go with the Revolutionary War because there were a lot of people because I get, sometimes I mix up some of the history stuff… so it was kind of confusing." During the guided PowerPoint discussion, Inez demonstrated a high degree of behavioral engagement by attending to the images and the teacher and raising her hand frequently to be called upon. She wrote in her notes often and appeared to working quickly to write notes before the teacher moved to the next slide.

Inez indicated in her interview that she was affectively engaged in the teacher's discussion of how official portraits were highly symbolic, framing the subject of the portrait in certain ways. She stated, "Now I know paintings are a lie because, especially when you paint people, because people can be very demanding in what they want [to show] and not to show." She also remarked on the teacher's discussion of how some people were left out of the historical record, such as women, African Americans, and how a woman rang a warning bell for the colonists, while Paul Revere received the credit for alerting them. She pointed to this part of the discussion as the impetus for her decision to report on Paul Revere in her culminating product, observing that "…it wasn't actually fair that people got left out of what had, could have been their credit, could have became famous in history and people have known that for a long time." Inez's engagement scores for this lesson are reported in Figure 1.

During the first task, Geraldo, the OGL student in this focal group, wrote consistently in his notes once he was settled at his table. He paused at the end to compare notes with another student in his group and to copy a name to his list from her suggestion. He expressed affective engagement in the task: "Because all those people had different reasons to be remembered." However, he did not expand on his cognitive engagement beyond stating, "I was thinking a lot of stuff." When the lesson moved to the guided PowerPoint discussion, Geraldo attended to the discussion for the most part, writing in his notes, but was also distracted by classmates who joked about the images, such as when one remarked, "Thomas Paine is a real pain!" He did not participate in the discussion, but found the topic of who was left out of the historical narrative to be affectively engaging. He noted that the discussion was "Good because, like, I didn't even know about Phyllis Wheatley." He chose George Washington for his culminating product because, "He was a general of the Revolutionary War." He explained that he liked the last activity because, "It was our choice." However, he stated that he had a difficult time thinking of reasons for choosing Washington and that the justification was difficult for him. Geraldo's engagement scores for this lesson are presented in Figure 1.

Ophelia, a BGL student, divided her time in the first task between writing names and leafing through her notes. She frequently paused to look around the room and then returned to her writing. Ophelia reported that the task of thinking of names of famous persons in the American Revolution was initially confusing until she requested the help of a group mate. She stated, "It was, like, kind of confusing and then, like, I asked my friend for one and she helped me out and then I started to remember all of them." When the task changed to the discussion of the PowerPoint images, Ophelia was observed to take the cue of the teacher to know what to add to her notes. When the teacher said that something was important to remember, she would write in her notebook, checking the text on the PowerPoint as she wrote. She did not raise her hand or add to the discussion while she was being observed. She found it interesting that Phyllis Wheatley was the only woman presented in the PowerPoint presentation. She was observed to find a partner and to quickly write up an exit ticket selecting Wheatley to make sure that she got to research her. When asked about this task, she stated, "I don't know, like, when she started doing her own poems and studying—because slaves did not used to go to school. You have to do work." Ophelia's engagement scores for this lesson are presented in Figure 1.

Figure 1: Student engagement for observation 15 by dimension and ability.

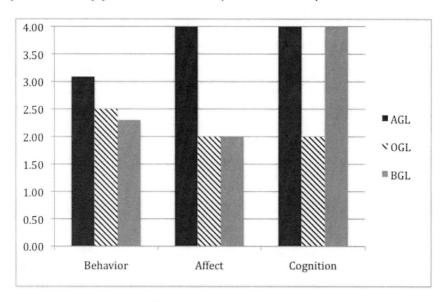

WHAT THESE METHODS REVEAL

Designing methods for studying student engagement as it occurs during classroom teaching is a challenging venture. First, engagement is multidimensional (Appleton et al., 2008; Fredricks et al., 2004; Fredricks & McColskey, 2011; Reschly & Christenson, 2012; Skinner & Pitzer, 2012), and operationally defining these constructs requires a careful culling of previous research to isolate distinguishing characteristics of the three sub-constructs that are strongly supported by the research on engagement. Once the research team agreed upon these definitions and characteristics, they developed scales to measure these characteristics as observed in the classroom (behavioral engagement), or noted in the students' responses to the interview questions (affective and cognitive engagement). The researchers designed the interview questions to provide opportunities for students to report on their affective and cognitive engagement. Thus, the team hoped to elicit multiple measures of engagement from both observed and reported data.

The second challenge is to understand the nature of engagement as a malleable construct. Observing students in one-minute segments provided a fine-grained view of behavioral engagement that can be more fully understood when integrated with student reports of what they found to be interesting and cognitively challenging during the tasks. The methods employed in this study reveal that across a lesson, engagement varies by task as well as by task supports such as background knowledge of topics of study. As demonstrated through their interview responses, students were variably engaged in writing names of famous historical figures depending upon how well supported they were by their background knowledge and notes. The AGL student seemed to find this task more cognitively engaging because she was working through the disequilibrium of keeping the names of persons associated with various points in American history aligned. The guided discussion engaged students when certain topics were discussed, such as how figures were portrayed in their

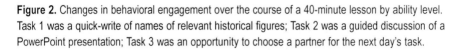

Figure 2. Changes in behavioral engagement over the course of a 40-minute lesson by ability level. Task 1 was a quick-write of names of relevant historical figures; Task 2 was a guided discussion of a PowerPoint presentation; Task 3 was an opportunity to choose a partner for the next day's task.

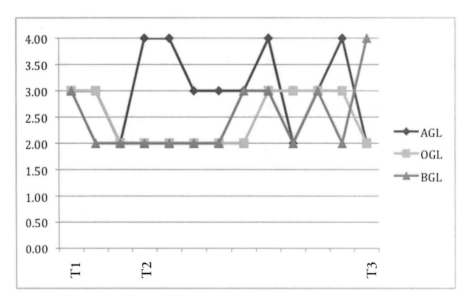

official portraits and who was left out of the historical narrative. These points where there was an affective connection or point of controversy were more engaging, as indicated by the rising trends in behavioral engagement during the mid to latter portions of the lesson displayed in Figure 2.

The indication in the findings that AGL students are more engaged in all task types than their OGL and BGL counterparts is not surprising; the ties between achievement and engagement are well supported in the literature as they are in this investigation. Ackerman (2013) demonstrated that positive traits (e.g., engagement and achievement) tend to be positively correlated. Therefore, he suggested, researchers should focus on interventions that support at-risk students who are both disengaged and underachieving.

The support offered to all students when moderately open tasks are presented is also an important finding. Teachers engage students when they present new content with supplementary discussions of interesting or provocative asides, such as how people were portrayed in paintings or who was left out of the history. All three students mentioned these topics in their interviews, noting that they were interested in the discussion and sometimes moved to make choices in their culminating products based on these discussions. These methods were, therefore, illuminating in providing an understanding of what engages students of differing ability levels when presented with tasks of various types.

These measures were instrumental in demonstrating the ebb and flow of engagement across tasks as evidenced in graphical representations such as Figure 2, providing visual support for the conceptualization of engagement as a fluid construct. Further, the integration of student reports of affective and cognitive engagement at the task level permits a closer view of what engages students as they participate in various instructional tasks. In all, the methods employed in this study provide a toehold for understanding engagement as fluid and multidimensional in pedagogically meaningful ways.

LIMITATIONS

A main limitation in this study was that the integrated Social Studies-Language Arts instructional period came at the end of the school day and it was sometimes difficult to find the time to elicit elaborated responses from students. Students were interviewed in a prioritized order according to when they needed to leave the classroom for dismissal, but despite these measures, there was, on occasion, limited time to fully explore the students' perceptions of their engagement with the tasks. It was also difficult to determine the significance of differences between ratings as there were only six students and the rating scales were ordinal. As with all classroom research, the results are difficult to generalize as the context was specific to the region, district, school, and the particular focal students selected for this study.

IMPLICATIONS FOR PRACTICE AND RESEARCH

The measures employed in this study suggest that support offered during moderately open tasks may be particularly influential in student engagement. In this sense, engagement is not only multidimensional and malleable, but it is transformative. The way that topics are presented and the connections that are provided may influence affective and cognitive engagement in positive ways. Providing interesting asides can spur students to exploration and research, particularly when they are provided choice when preparing culminating products. What these measures may help educators understand is that a careful balance of closed, moderately open, and open tasks for students may support learning and engagement in meaningful ways. Future research should further explore the optimum balance of tasks to improve engagement for students of varying levels of ability.

In evaluating the available paradigms for conducting literacy research, Dillon, O'Brien and Heilman (2000) concluded that:

> A pragmatic stance values communities engaged in literacy research who focus on solving problems; the selection of the theoretical frameworks and methodologies are tailored to the complexity of the problem and the promise of useful findings rather than discrete technical standards (pp. 23-24).

In this investigation, the research methods provided an opportunity to explore the ways that tasks influence engagement in a manner that may be extended to improve pedagogies for content and literacy learning. The methods supported the teacher and researchers in addressing an authentic pedagogical dilemma in a specified classroom context, exemplifying this pragmatic lens to conducting classroom research. In this case, the methods succeeded in meeting the challenge of exploring engagement as a multidimensional, malleable, and transactional construct in situ and over time.

REFERENCES

Ackerman, P. L. (2013). Engagement and opportunity to learn. In J. Hattie, & E. M. Anderman (Eds.), *International guide to student achievement* (pp. 39-41). New York, NY: Routledge.

Appleton, J. J., Christenson, S. L., & Furlong, M. J. (2008). Student engagement with school: Critical conceptual and methodological issues of the construct. *Psychology in the Schools, 45,* 369-386. doi:10.1002/pits.20303

Baddeley, A. D., & Hitch, G. (1974). Working memory. In G. H. Bower (Ed.), *The psychology of learning and motivation: Advances in research and theory* (Vol. 8, pp. 47–89). New York, NY: Academic Press.

Bandura, A. (1993). Perceived self-efficacy in cognitive development and functioning. *Educational Psychologist, 28,* 117–148. doi:10.1207/s15326985ep2802_3

Barksdale-Ladd, M. A. (1994). Teacher empowerment and literacy instruction in three professional development schools. *Journal of Teacher Education, 45,* 104-111. doi:10.1177/0022487194045002004

Baumann, J. F., & Duffy, A. M. (1997). *Engaged reading for pleasure and learning: A report from the National Reading Research Center.* Athens, GA: National Reading Research Center.

Bogner, K., Raphael, L. M., & Pressley, M. (2002). How grade-1 teachers motivate literate activity by their students. *Scientific Studies of Reading, 6,* 135-165. doi:10.1207/S1532799XSSR0602_02

Brophy, J. E. (2010). *Motivating students to learn* (3rd ed.). New York, NY: Routledge.

Brozo, W. G., Shiel, G., & Topping, K. (2008). Engagement in reading: Lessons learned from three PISA countries. *Journal of Adolescent and Adult Literacy, 51,* 304-315. doi:10.1598/JAAL.51.4.2

Deci, E. L., & Ryan, R. M. (1985). *Intrinsic motivation and self-determination in human behavior.* New York, NY: Plenum Press.

Dillon, D. R., O'Brien, D. G., & Heilman, E. E. (2000). Literacy research in the next millennium: From paradigms to pragmatism and practicality. *Reading Research Quarterly, 35,* 10-26. doi:10.1598/RRQ.35.1.2

Dolezal, S. E., Welsh, L. M., Pressley, M., & Vincent, M. M. (2003). How nine third-grade teachers motivate student academic engagement. *Elementary School Journal, 103,* 239-267.

Duke, N. K., Purcell-Gates, V., Hall, L. A., & Tower, C. (2007). Authentic literacy activities for developing comprehension and writing. *The Reading Teacher, 60,* 344-355.

Fredricks, J. (2013). Behavioral engagement in learning. In J. Hattie, & E. M. Anderman (eds.), *International guide to student achievement* (pp. 42-44). New York, NY: Routledge.

Fredricks, J. A., Blumenfeld, P. C., & Paris, A. H. (2004). School engagement: Potential of the concept, state of the evidence. *Review of Educational Research, 74,* 59-109. doi:10.3102/00346543074001059

Fredricks, J. A., & McColskey, W. (2011). The measurement of student engagement: A comparative analysis of various methods and student self-report instruments. In S. L. Christenson, A. L. Reschly, & C. Wylie (Eds.), *Handbook of research on student engagement* (pp. 763-782). New York, NY: Springer.

Fredricks, J., McColskey, W., Meli, J., Mordica, J., Montrosse, B., Mooney, K. (2011). *Measuring student engagement in upper elementary through high school: A description of 21 instruments.* (Issues & Answers Report, REL 2011–No. 098). Washington, DC: U.S. Department of Education, Institute of Education Sciences, National Center for Education Evaluation and Regional Assistance, Regional Educational Laboratory Southeast. Retrieved from http://ies.ed.gov/ncee/edlabs

Gambrell, L. B, Hughes, E. M., Calvert, L., Malloy, J. A., & Igo, B. (2011). Authentic reading, writing, and discussion: An exploratory study of a pen pal project. *Elementary School Journal, 112,* 234-258. doi:10.1086/661523

Guthrie, J. T. (2004). Teaching for literacy engagement. *Journal of Literacy Research, 36,* 1-29. doi:10.1207/s15548430jlr3601_2

Guthrie, J. T., Anderson, E., Alao, S., & Rinehart, J. (1999). Influences of Concept-Oriented Reading Instruction on strategy use and conceptual learning from text. *Elementary School Journal, 99,* 343-366. doi:10.1086/461929

Guthrie, J. T., & Humenick, N. M. (2004). Motivating students to read: Evidence for classroom practices that increase reading motivation and achievement. In P. McCardle & V. Chhabra (Eds.), *The voice of evidence in reading research* (pp. 329-354). Baltimore: Paul H. Brookes.

Guthrie, J. T., Van Meter, P., Hancock, G. R., Alao, S., Anderson, E., & McCann, A. (1998). Does concept-oriented reading instruction increase strategy use and conceptual learning from text? *Journal of Educational Psychology, 90,* 261-278. doi:10.1037/0022-0663.90.2.261

Guthrie, J. T., Van Meter, P., McCann, A. D., Wigfield, A., Bennett, L., Poundstone, C. C., et al. (1996). Growth in literacy engagement: Changes in motivations and strategies during concept-oriented reading instruction. *Reading Research Quarterly,* 31, 306-332. doi:10.1598/RRQ.31.3.5

Guthrie, J. T., Wigfield, A., Barbosa, P., Perencevich, K. C., Taboada, A., Davis, M. H.,...Tonks, S. (2004). Increasing reading comprehension and engagement through concept-oriented reading instruction. *Journal of Educational Psychology,* 96, 403-423. doi: 10.1037/0022-0663.96.3.403

Guthrie, J. T., Wigfield, A., & You, W. (2012). Instructional contexts for engagement and achievement in reading. In S. L. Christenson, A. L. Reschly, & C. Wylie (Eds.), *Handbook of research on student engagement* (pp. 601-634). New York, NY: Springer.

Hayes, A. F., & Krippendorff, K. (2007). Answering the call for a standard reliability measure for coding data. *Communication Methods and Measures,* 1, 77-89.

Ivey, G., & Broaddus, K. (2007). A formative experiment investigating literacy engagement among adolescent Latina/o students just beginning to read, write, and speak English. *Reading Research Quarterly,* 42, 512-545. doi:10.1958/RRQ.42.4.4

Kirsch, I., de Jong, J., Lafontaine, D., McQueen, J., Mendelovits, J., & Monseur, C. (2002). *Reading for change: Performance and engagement across countries.* Paris: Organisation for Economic Co-operation and Development.

Lutz, S. L., Guthrie, J. T., & Davis, M. H. (2006). Scaffolding for engagement in elementary school reading instruction. *The Journal of Educational Research,* 100, 3-20. doi:10.3200/JOER.100.1.3-20

Miller, S. D., & Meece, J. L. (1999). Third-graders' motivational preferences for reading and writing tasks. *Elementary School Journal,* 100, 19-35. doi:10.1086/461941

O'Brien, D., Beach, R., & Scharber, C. (2007). "Struggling" middle schoolers: Engagement and literate competence in a reading writing intervention class. *Reading Psychology,* 28, 51-73. doi:10.1080/02702710601115463

Parsons, S. A. (2008). Providing all students ACCESS to self-regulated literacy learning. *The Reading Teacher,* 61, 628-635. doi:10.1598/RT.61.8.4

Purcell-Gates, V., Duke, N. K., & Martineau, J. A. (2007). Learning to read and write genre-specific text: Roles of authentic experience and explicit teaching. *Reading Research Quarterly,* 42, 8-35. doi:10.1598/RRQ.42.1.1

Reschly, A. L., & Christenson, S. L. (2012). Jingle, jangle, and conceptual haziness: Evolution and future directions of the engagement construct. In S. L. Christenson, A. L. Reschly, & C. Wylie (Eds.), *Handbook of research on student engagement* (pp. 1-19). New York, NY: Springer.

Schraw, G., Flowerday, T., & Lehman, S. (2001). Increasing situational interest in the classroom. *Educational Psychology Review,* 13, 211-224.

Skinner, E. A., & Pitzer, J. R. (2012). Developmental dynamics of student engagement, coping, and everyday resilience. In S. L. Christenson, A. L. Reschly, & C. Wylie (Eds.), *Handbook of research on student engagement* (pp. 21-44). New York, NY: Springer.

Taylor, B. M., Pearson, P. D., Clark, K., & Walpole, S. (2000). Effective schools and accomplished teachers: Lessons about primary-grade reading instruction in low-income schools. *Elementary School Journal,* 101, 121-165.

Teale, W. H., & Gambrell, L. B. (2007). Raising urban students' literacy achievement by engaging in authentic, challenging work. *The Reading Teacher,* 60, 728-739. doi:10.1598/RT.60.8.3

Turner, J. C., & Paris, S. G. (1995). How literacy tasks influence children's motivation for literacy. *The Reading Teacher,* 48, 662-675.

Urdan, T. & Schoenfelder, E. (2006). Classroom effects on student motivation: Goal structures, social relationships, and competence beliefs. *Journal of School Psychology,* 44, 331-349. doi:10.1016/j.jsp.2006.04.003

Wigfield, A., Guthrie, J. T., Perencevith, K. C., Taboada, A., Klauda, S. L., McRae, A., & Barbosa, P. (2008). Role of reading engagement in mediating effects of reading comprehension instruction on reading outcomes. *Psychology in the Schools,* 45, 432-445. doi:10.1002/pits

Zimmerman, B. J. (2008). Investigating self-regulation and motivation: Historical background, methodological developments, and future prospects. *American Educational Research Journal,* 45, 166–183. doi:10.3102/0002831207312909

Donna E. Alvermann
University of Georgia

Section II:
Adolescent, Disciplinary and Digital Literacies

The five articles in this section individually and collectively address a pet peeve of mine, and maybe that's why I found them instantly insightful and appealingly useful. Granted, I thought twice about bringing a personal pet peeve into a scholarly publication such as the *62nd LRA Yearbook*; in fact, I wrote and rewrote this brief introduction to Section 2 several times. In the end, however, it was a concept that stuck and here's why. Whether as a classroom teacher, teacher educator, or researcher, I find it extremely annoying—in fact, downright arrogant—to have to act on some curricular or social issue without knowing how the young people I'll be teaching or researching identify (or not) with that issue. And more pointedly, how their lives may feel the impact of my actions. Teaching or researching in even a partial vacuum is uncomfortable, and yet I've fallen prey to this phenomenon all too often: sometimes the result of my own doing and at other times the consequence of having no choice but to heed an unexamined policy or procedure.

The authors in Section 2 were clearly motivated to ask the difficult question: Will our research matter for adolescents, and if so, how? Their work is part of a growing literature that points to how young people's ways of perceiving, reading, viewing, and communicating are rapidly changing and affecting their self-understandings of who they are as literate beings (Brader & Luke, 2013; Christenbury, Bomer, & Smagorinsky, 2009). Although this literature has implications for classroom practice, it remains relatively untapped by teachers and teacher educators, perhaps because the lives of students who self-identify as users and producers of digital texts are rarely visible to their teachers (Alvermann, 2011). However, if the authors' work previewed here is any indication of future scholarship in adolescent, disciplinary, and digital literacies, the invisibility factor may be on the wane. For instance, in their study of a digital partnership involving middle class preservice teachers interacting with youth from a predominantly lower socioeconomic class background half a continent away. Garcia and Seglem (this volume) showed how digital space provided high school youth a safe context in which "to more powerfully voice their frustrations and thoughts."

Teacher beliefs about digital literacies and student beliefs about mathematics as a discipline complicate any one-size-fits-all model of adolescent literacy instruction. According to Ito and her colleagues (2008), when youth turn to their peers for assistance in using digital media rather than to teachers or other adults, notions of expertise and authority get turned on their heads. This was demonstrated clearly in Ruday, Conradi, Heny, and Lovette's exploratory study (this volume) in which middle and high school English Language Arts teachers said that they valued digital literacy instruction but felt underprepared and lacking agency in making decisions about how to integrate such instruction into their regular routine. Moreover, some of what we presently know from research on young people's online activities is that "contrary to adult perceptions, while hanging out online, youth are picking up basic social and technological skills they need to fully participate in contemporary society" (Ito et al., 2008, p. 2). They are acquiring these skills, however, in ways that vary greatly from traditional instruction, a point not lost in Davis and Brown's interpretation (this volume) of data gathered from a quantitative literacy survey administered to non-math majors enrolled in a regional campus of a large university system. Their follow-up classroom observations and interviews with a select number of participants revealed that students preferred "step-by-step" methods (e.g., teacher think-alouds and teacher questioning strategies) when learning content in their discipline. Although arguably trite, it is the old proverb of French origin—the more things change, the more they stay the same—that comes instantly to mind.

A paradigm shift did occur in the early- to mid-1990s, however, that influenced greatly what researchers have learned about adolescents' literate identities. Basically, this shift entailed a social turn—one in which literacy was understood to be a social practice and thus implicated in social reasons for getting things done. It is the same paradigm in which Skerrett, Bomer, Fowler-Amato, and Jansky (this volume) situated their study of youth literacies in and out of school. And while practically speaking it is nearly impossible to eliminate overlapping literacy practices and learning in these two contexts (Leander & Lovvorn, 2006), Skerrett and her colleagues examined connections between the two in a way that contributed to an important methodological finding: namely, that "students' ways of participating in the research were themselves performances of literate identities" that needed to be studied as such. But, it took Beach and her international team of co-researchers' large-scale study of early adolescents' literate identities (this volume) to drive home the point that categorizations by geographic locale rarely hold; instead, it is the nuanced processes involved in talking with students directly that produce the greatest insights about young people's literate identities.

REFERENCES

Alvermann, D. E. (2011). Moving on, keeping pace: Youth's literate identities and multimodal digital texts. In S. Abrams & J. Rowsell (Eds.), *Rethinking identity and literacy education in the 21st century. National Society for the Study of Education Yearbook* (vol. 110, part I, pp. 109-128). New York, NY: Columbia University, Teachers College.

Brader, A., & Luke, A. (2013). Re-engaging marginalized youth through digital music production: Performance, audience and evaluation. *Pedagogies: An International Journal, 8*(3), 197-214.

Christenbury, L., Bomer, R., & Smagorinsky, P. (Eds.). (2009). *Handbook of adolescent literacy research*. New York, NY: Guilford.

Ito, M., Horst, H., Bittanti, M., Boyd, D., Herr-Stephenson, B., Lange, P. G., et al. (2008, November). *Living and learning with new media: Summary of findings from the Digital Youth Project.* (Funded by The John D. and Catherine T. MacArthur Foundation). Boston, MA: The MIT Press.

Leander, K. M., & Lovvorn, J. F. (2006). Literacy networks: Following the circulation of texts, bodies, and objects in the schooling and online gaming of one youth. *Cognition and Instruction, 24*(3), 291–340.

Meeting Them Where They Are: Researching Youth Literacies In and Out of School

Allison Skerrett
Randy Bomer
Michelle Fowler-Amato
Katrina Jansky
The University of Texas at Austin

In this chapter, we report on the methodological successes and challenges of a study in which educational researchers worked alongside a reading teacher and her students as they drew upon adolescent literacy research to identify and connect their out-of-school literacy skills to those required by the official curriculum.

THEORETICAL FRAMEWORK AND RELATED LITERATURE

Researchers have documented young people's engagement in purposeful, complex literacy practices at home, in after-school activities, in unofficial worlds, and on the Internet (Christenbury, Bomer, & Smagorinsky, 2009; Vadeboncoeur & Stevens, 2005). Typical methods used for discovering such knowledge include observations of youth during self-sponsored literacy practices, interviewing them about their literate lives, and analyzing literacy artifacts they produce and consume (Christenbury, Bomer, & Smagorinski, 2009). Another important, but less utilized, method is engaging youth as ethnographic partners, asking them to document their own activities with literacy (Farrell, 1990; Zenkov, 2009). Farrell (1990) and Zenkov (2009) noted the surprising and rich data that youth, as research partners, collected on their own literate lives. Such knowledge may have otherwise remained invisible to the adult scholars had they employed more traditional approaches that position youth as research subjects, rather than agentive collaborators, in research. Yet youth as research partners can pose unique challenges. Some of Zenkov's adolescent research partners, for instance, sometimes proved hard to reach, or were slow or inconsistent in supplying data on their literate activities. He resorted to frequent text messaging and other rapid digital communications to keep the research agenda and roles on the youths' minds.

Based on growing knowledge about the sophistication of youths' outside-school literate lives, literacy scholars propose that productive links may exist between students' out-of-school literacy practices and the literacy work required by the school (e.g., Weinstein, 2007). This proposition is undergirded by theories of borderzones as productive spaces for learning and development (Bhabha, 1994; Gutiérrez, 2008). Calls for attending to the potential links among adolescents' outside-school literacies and school-based literacies have been especially urgent for culturally and linguistically diverse youth whose language and literacy repertoires have been historically dismissed or marginalized by schools (Hull & Shultz, 2001; Martínez-Roldán & Fránquiz, 2009). Limited studies exist, however, that examine such connections.

Fisher (2005) inquired into how using spoken word poetry, a literacy practice in the African American community, in two language arts classrooms, expanded the writing practices of teachers and students beyond writing into speaking and performing. In an alternative school context,

145

Weinstein (2007) stopped fighting her students' writing and performance of rap lyrics in her English classroom and turned it into official curriculum study. She found that writing, performing, and critiquing rap lyrics mirrors much of the traditional poetry work done in school. Hong Xu (2008) studied a teacher who created a hybrid space that drew on in- and-out-of-school literacies (mainly popular culture texts with a heavy emphasis on television shows) in her English classroom. And West (2008) used weblogs with her students and found their engagement, comprehension, and responses to literature enhanced in this digital writing mode. In terms of research design, these studies involved curriculum units of short duration focused on a specific type of literacy practice. And although the researchers studied how students' outside-school literacies found their way into school through these curricular innovations, they neither concomitantly nor longitudinally studied youth engaging in outside-school literacies. Consequently, these studies could not uncover the connections youth and their teachers may have been making among a range of in- and outside-school literacies over time.

In one longitudinal effort, Kalantzis and Cope (2005) developed and implemented with teachers a theory they called "Learning by Design" in which teachers and students drew on the knowledge and skills students developed in informal learning contexts to scaffold in-school learning. However, students' outside-school literacies were brought in through students' reports. The researchers did not study youth in outside-school literate activities, neither were the youth positioned as researchers of their own literate lives. In implementing the "Learning by Design" method, Kalantzis and Cope noted a challenge for teachers of working from the learner's subjectivity while maintaining disciplinary rigor and meeting broader intellectual goals. They identified benefits in that teachers and students are at the core of this collaborative curriculum development and are co-constructors of knowledge. The researchers further noted the importance of teacher-colleagues working together in such curriculum projects and involving educational researchers as resources for teachers. Our study emulated how, in Kalantzis and Cope's project, teachers were positioned as co-researchers and they and their students jointly designed curricula that bridged in- and outside-school literate lives.

Additionally, we sought to fill the gaps in the aforementioned literature in two key ways. First, to address the dearth of research on the out-of-school literate lives of culturally and linguistically diverse students, we studied the literate lives of diverse youth. Second, to address the need for longitudinal and substantive inquiry into potential links among in- and out-of-school literacies, we studied how two groups of youth and their literacy teacher, over the course of an entire school year, made connections among in- and out-of-school literacies to support students' development of academic literacies.

METHODS

Case study methods (Dyson & Genishi, 2007) were used over a period of two years to explore the literate lives of diverse adolescents in school and out-of-school contexts and how knowledge about those lives might inform the teaching and learning of literacy.

Setting

In both years, the study took place in one of the ninth grade reading classrooms of the same reading teacher in a diverse urban high school, "Southwest High School," and in the surrounding community in a southwestern U.S. state. The community was culturally, linguistically, and socioeconomically diverse and located about twelve miles from one of the state's major metropolises. Students who were placed in this reading class were identified as reading below their grade level and had failed, or were thought to be in jeopardy of failing (for example, if they were English language learners), the state's standardized test in reading. This class was offered as an opportunity to improve students' reading skills; completing the class was required, but did not count toward students' high school graduation credits. Because of how the class was positioned within the official curriculum, there was no prescribed curriculum for the teacher to follow. This curricular freedom enabled the teacher to design and implement a reading and writing curriculum that connected to her students' out-of-school literacy practices. The site was thus an appropriate one for conducting the research because it allowed inquiry into how the broad range of diverse youths' literacy practices might productively inform literacy education.

Participants

Students. In year one of the study, 11 of the 13 students in the class participated in the study. In year two, 13 of the class's 16 students participated. In both years, the students came from primarily Latina/o backgrounds with a smaller number of African American and Caucasian students. For example, in year two, students self-identified as Latina/o (Mexican or Mexican American and one boy from Colombia), with a smaller number of students identifying as African American (one girl and two boys). Students were between 14 and 17 years of age.

The teacher. "Molly," was a White, middle class woman who had been teaching for 17 years, three of those at Southwest High. Molly was trained and certified as a reading teacher and also held master reading teacher and English language arts certification from an alternative teacher certification program. She had taught reading almost exclusively for all of her career except for an occasional English language arts or writing course. At Southwest High, Molly only taught reading. Additionally, Molly had recently completed a master's degree and, for her thesis, had conducted an extensive literature review of adolescent literacy practices. Consequently, she was unusually informed about multiliteracies practices and understood their value in the research community, though she had not previously attempted to build official curriculum upon them.

Researchers. Two university faculty whose teaching and research focus on literacy education in diverse settings led the study and graduate students assisted with data collection and analysis. Our team represented racial and cultural diversity: the university faculty were Allison Skerrett, a Black woman who identifies as an Afro-Caribbean immigrant in the U.S.; and Randy Bomer, a White male. Graduate students included an African American male, an Asian American woman, and Caucasian female graduate students who had taught in culturally and linguistically diverse schools. Two of those students, Michelle Fowler-Amato and Katrina Jansky, are co-authors on this paper. Although none of the researchers held strong affiliation with Spanish, some spoke some Spanish and one was fluent in the language.

DATA COLLECTION AND ANALYSIS

In year one, academic year 2008-2009, we collected data only through classroom observations and interactions with the teacher and students, taking detailed fieldnotes. Classes met for 75 or 90 minutes two or three times a week depending on the school's block schedule. We attempted to observe every class meeting in order to collect as much rich data as possible; thus, different members of the research team observed classes across a given week. Molly took primary responsibility for curriculum planning. Each week, she would share with Allison and Randy her curriculum plans, explaining how she intended to draw on students' outside-school literacy practices in achieving her curriculum goals and invite our feedback. Debriefings after classroom observations and email correspondence throughout the week provided a space for Molly, Allison, and Randy to assess the successes and challenges of lessons and discuss revisions for future lessons. Allison and Randy also participated in classroom conversations about connections among in- and out-of-school literacy practices. They also interacted one-on-one with students during independent work periods to learn what connections students themselves might be making among their in- and out-of-school literacies. In one instance, Randy co-taught a class with Molly in which students explored their literacy practices.

In year two of the study, academic year 2009-2010, the team continued to study the teacher's enactment of a literacy curriculum that bridged in- and outside-school literacies. To do so, we conducted classroom observations and interactions with the teacher and students once to twice each week, this time, audiorecording the classroom, as well as taking detailed fieldnotes. In addition, with the assistance of graduate students, we studied in-depth the literate lives of seven focal students in the class. To do so, each focal student participated in three semi-structured interviews with either Allison or a graduate student researcher with whom they were paired. Interviewers collected biographical data, information on the youths' reading and writing histories and current reading and writing practices and identities, and other self-sponsored multiliteracies practices. Each interview lasted an average of one hour and all interviews were audiorecorded and transcribed.

Focal students were also asked to allow one of the adult researchers to accompany them to at least one outside-school or extracurricular activity that was an important site of literacy practice for them and to talk with us about their literate thinking and work in these venues. These spaces ranged from the soccer field, to dance and theatre performances, to public libraries where they participated in virtual social worlds. The numbers of out-of-school observations varied across the seven focal youth, ranging from zero (in the cases of Horatio, Kandace, Tomas, and Nina) to three (two each with Lydia and Angelica, and three with Vanesa). Videorecordings were taken of one of Angelica's two-hour long soccer games and two of Vanesa's dance performances (45 minutes per videorecording). Fieldnotes were taken on all outside-school observations. Following the work of Gonzalez, Moll, and Amanti (2005), we asked focal students, and they agreed, to allow us to visit them at home to learn more about their and their families' ways of using language and literacy in that space. We conducted home visits with all but one (Kandace) of the focal youth. Home visits ranged in length from one to two hours and detailed fieldnotes were taken in all cases.

Additionally, focal students, serving as ethnographic partners (Farrell, 1990), collected data on their literacy practices using videos, photographs, and audio-recorders. Vanesa showed Allison segments of two of several videorecordings of her dance practices and performances. Each recording averaged 50 minutes. Horatio, Lydia, Tomas, and Vanesa each took 27 photographs of their literate life (using disposable cameras we provided). The youth also provided and described a variety of artifacts that represented their diverse literacy practices. These included their composition notebooks and folders for their literacy class, stories they composed for two class magazines, and, in the case of Vanesa, two drawings and a collage. Other artifacts we examined that remained in the youths' possession included their cell phones, iPods, jewelry and art they made, content of their MySpace pages, libraries of books and movies at home, and scrapbooks and photo albums.

Analysis

Data analysis involved iterative reading of data and progressive focusing (Glaser & Strauss, 2006) to identify portions of the data related to the study's design and implementation. We then conducted a thematic analysis to establish recurrent and substantive concepts within that data (Miles & Huberman, 1994). For instance, reading across classroom and out-of-school observation fieldnotes brought out the theme of building student trust. We conducted member checks (Lofland & Lofland, 1995) with the teacher via email and in face-to-face or phone conversations to gain feedback and additional insights about emerging themes. Five members of the team who collected substantial amounts of data then wrote memos, which served both reflective and analytic purposes (Charmaz, 2000), to think further through data collection experiences with focal students and the teacher. This analytic and reflective work included our identification of specific elements of research design and implementation: significant events, or smaller but noteworthy recurring events, behaviors, interaction patterns, and the like that emphasized particular successes or challenges in our research efforts. Each writer then developed tentative explanations or initial assertions related to the main issues raised in his or her narrative.

The entire research team then read across and discussed these five memos. We conducted member checking among ourselves and with the teacher and students as needed and when possible (Lofland & Lofland, 1995), and, through this process identified significant and recurring themes across the memos. We then returned to the initial themes we developed from our analysis of the original data portions related to research design and implementation. Keeping in mind the themes raised in our initial analysis, as well as those that emerged during the memo-writing stage of analysis, we sought to triangulate themes and finalize our findings. Allison wrote a final round of three analytic memos to consider whether recurring themes were adequately substantiated by the data, what available theories might help explain them, and how they related to the findings of pertinent existing research.

FINDINGS

Successful elements of our research design included the teacher's knowledge of adolescent literacy research and her collaboration as a co-researcher with university researchers. Challenges included building student trust, enlisting their participation in the study, and youths' data collection on their own literate lives.

The Teacher's Knowledge of Adolescent Literacy Research and Teacher-Researcher Collaboration

Molly's professional knowledge and experience, including her knowledge of adolescent literacy research, enabled her to work as a teacher-researcher on the team and make complex decisions about how to draw on educational research to suit the particularities of her classroom context, students, and curriculum goals. The university researchers' weekly conversations with Molly about curriculum and instructional design helped them jointly identify and devise responses to the theoretical and practical issues associated with activating adolescent literacy research in the classroom. For example, in one of Molly's emails to Allison and Randy, she wrote:

> Because all this is so new to me, my major concern is keeping my eye on the big picture. I could use some help with this too. I've told the kids that we are constructing our identities as readers and writers so they can begin to see how much they really do with reading and writing, that it's not separate. They get this. I get this. But eventually, I want to focus on the thinking they do with these literacies… and arching toward this part of the lesson planning has me good and stumped. What will we do with all this information we've collected? How can I go back and get them to think about what skills they are using, and how we can apply these skills to SSR [Sustained Silent Reading]?

The following excerpt from our field notes depicts a typical after-class conversation between Molly and Allison about these curricular and pedagogical dilemmas. This particular conversation took place after a class session in which students constructed a heart map in which they placed treasured people, things, and events from their lives that might contain literacy:

> We talk about her uncertainty about where the activity is going, how to wrap it up and have it segue into SSR. We talk about how to get kids who write about things like jewelry and photos to see literacy in there. I (Allison) suggest thinking about it in terms of symbols of identity—the jewelry—the meaning they hold, the messages we intend to send by wearing certain types of clothing, etc. Photos that hold memories and can be "read" in that sense. She agrees that it would be helpful to expand the notion of literacy beyond printed form to help kids see literacy. We talk about how in SSR… if students are reading different genres we can connect those forms to other literacy practices they have or look for connections in the kinds of thinking they do with their outside-school literacies and the kinds of thinking they are doing when they are reading and writing in school. She wants to focus on visualization when reading and says she has some ideas here. I tell her I'm happy to work with kids during SSR and other class activities… [field notes, September 9, 2008]

This kind of emergent curriculum design in the midst of complex interactions with students is too rarely highlighted in research on secondary school literacy educators.

Building Student Trust and Enlisting their Participation

We, the university-based researchers, built relationships with students early in the school year by being a constant presence in the classroom and engaging in authentic, caring, and respectful interactions with them. As noted in the methods section, in the first year of the study, we used multiple classroom observers. This design, students told us, made them feel uncomfortable and under surveillance—like they were being "watched," "stalked," and "judged," "to see if we are smart." In the second year of the study, we modified our design to using just one researcher, Allison, as the classroom observer who also worked "like a teacher" with students, as they requested. This was a labor intensive undertaking, but critical to build relationships that would allow the study to continue.

In that second year, we exercised caution with turning the researcher's gaze onto students. For the first month of observations, Allison handwrote notes in a notebook, focusing on her general impressions of the classroom—the physical environment, participants and their interactions, and instructional activities; and summarized key classroom conversations and events. In Dyson and Genishi's (2007) words, she "situated [herself] on the edge of local action…slowly but deliberately amass[ing] information about the configuration of time and space, of people, and of activity in their physical sites" (p. 19). For that first month, Allison purposefully used just a notebook, rather than a laptop and audio recorder, to give students time to get used to her presence and to "attune [herself] to the rhythms of daily activity" (Dyson & Genishi, p. 29) in that space.

Thereafter, Allison switched to taking notes on a laptop and using an audio recorder in an attempt to capture as much classroom conversation as possible and to describe events more fully. She typically spent about one hour of each class observing and taking notes. For the remaining 15 to 30 minutes, she interacted with students, talking with them about the reading or writing they were doing. In these instances, she took her digital recorder with her to students' desks, and when she returned to hers, typed in notes summarizing the interactions. Beyond these interactions with students, Allison participated in class when the teacher or a student invited her into a whole class discussion by asking her a question or soliciting her opinion on a topic being discussed. Because she arrived in the classroom a few minutes before each class began, and remained for up to 45 minutes after class talking with Molly, Allison regularly enjoyed informal social interactions with students and observed them interacting informally with peers and with Molly.

These formal and more informal social interactions helped build student trust and encouraged their participation in the research. Our student participants, who had been marginalized by school, questioned the value or motives of educational research. They needed frequent opportunities to ask questions about the researchers' intentions, the purposes of the study, and the requirements of their voluntary participation. Additionally, we learned that offering students multiple and fluid levels of participation (for instance, involvement in the classroom study but not the out-of-school portion, the ability to change level of participation at any point) helped secure the participation of some students who might otherwise have not participated at all.

Nonetheless, we felt frustrated with our failure to recruit some youth who we sensed could be key informants to the research. There was the young man who claimed a biracial (African American and Latino) identity and who offered compelling insights about race, gender, culture, and language in class discussions. He declined to participate at any level in the study despite Molly's additional efforts to recruit him by telling him how interested we were in his perspectives. We wondered whether gender or cultural differences between him and Allison, and/or power differentials between them, influenced his decision to not participate. For many of our potential participants who had been positioned under the authority of adults in school, the research was a rare opportunity to say no to an adult, without repercussion, in an official context. There was also a young man who was an avid poet, a new father and who expressed interest in participating in the study. But he had serious attendance issues, was eventually transferred into another of Molly's classes, and, ultimately, left the school, preventing us from building a relationship.

Adolescents' Data Collection on Their Literate Lives

Despite our relationship-building efforts in the first year of the study, so few students agreed to participate in the out-of-school portion of the study that this component was delayed until the second year. As detailed in the methods section, in the second year, seven students agreed to be focal students and study with us, in-depth, their literacy practices. Students working as ethnographic partners (Farrell, 1990) proved both fruitful and frustrating. Some participants, like Vanesa and Angelica, eagerly invited us to their homes and outside-school activities and promptly took their photographs and turned in artifacts from their literate lives. Other youth—like Lydia and Kandace—were dealing with family mobility and other personal challenges resulting in frequent and sudden cancellations of, or no-shows to, prescheduled interviews and observations. Changed or disconnected phone numbers, cell phones that were shared among family members, and academic schedule changes that moved some focal students out of the focal classroom posed constant challenges to the continuity and quality of data collection.

One young man, Tomas, lost camera after camera we supplied, and declared voluminous reading and journaling practices, but never showed us any related artifacts. During a home visit and across interviews, Katrina, the graduate student paired with him, asked Tomas to show her these journals and other literacy artifacts but he never produced them. Allison also knew from observing and speaking with Tomas during classes, and from his teacher's reports, that he struggled with literacy in school. In Tomas' narration of his reading and writing life, however, we recognized much of the talk about literate lives in which he had participated in Molly's class. In describing his literate life, then, we wondered whether Tomas was trying on a literate identity that he wished to mature more fully in the future (Gee, 1990, 1994). We came to realize that students' ways of participating in the research were themselves performances of literate identities and we needed to analyze them as such. Below, we present two extended vignettes that show the diversity of ways in which our out-of-school data collection unfolded with focal students.

Vanesa: A case of when things go well. Vanesa, who was 15 years old at the time of the study, immigrated to the U.S. at 12 years of age with her mother, Luce, and younger sister, Isa. They migrated from a town about a 30-minute drive from Mexico City to the suburban community in which the study took place. In the year prior to the study, the family had received their newest family member, a baby boy, who was born in the U.S., thus deepening the family's transnational identity. The children's father had stayed behind in Mexico to run a family-owned business but he visited them regularly—at least every few months. During school vacations and for important events in Mexico, Vanesa's mother and the children crossed the U.S.-Mexico border to participate in the lives they still had there. The family relocated permanently to Mexico at the end of the 2009-2010 academic school year. The pull back toward Mexico was strong as Vanesa's father wanted to maintain the family's profitable business there. Additionally, because they did not have many relatives in the U.S. in comparison with Mexico, her mother felt isolated. Vanesa was conflicted about this decision. She looked forward to reuniting with family and friends in Mexico, but as she had been enjoying her school and social life in the U.S., cried over the prospect of leaving. She hoped to return to the U.S. someday to attend college, a goal her mother supported.

Allison, who collected classroom data, was paired with Vanesa as her focal student. The first interview occurred in mid-December as a pullout session from Molly's class. Vanesa's mother and two siblings accompanied her to the second and third interviews, occurring in mid-March and mid-May, respectively, and her mother participated in these formal conversations. Allison got the sense that mom wanted to understand firsthand the nature of the conversations her daughter was having with this university researcher. Allison and Vanesa's mother grew to have a friendly relationship. With a shared background as immigrants to the U.S., over the year, they talked about differences in the children's educational experiences across Mexico and the U.S., assimilation challenges in the U.S., and college opportunities for Vanesa in the States.

Vanesa invited Allison to observe her in three school-sponsored dance events and a school play. Allison also visited Vanesa at home to learn more about Vanesa and her family's uses of language, reading, writing, and other literacy practices at home. This visit occurred at an opportune time, when Vanesa's father was visiting, and when an uncle and aunt had also stopped by. Allison spent two and a half hours with Vanesa and her family on that day, observing their interactions with each other in English, Spanish, and Spanglish, and examining and discussing with Vanesa numerous literacy artifacts she kept in her bedroom. As an ethnographic partner, Vanesa took photographs of herself making art and pictures of different art pieces she had composed such as decorative masks and religious artifacts. She also provided two drawings, a collage, a composition notebook and folder from her reading class, and two stories she composed for her reading class's magazines.

Additionally, during the home visit and in interviews, Vanesa showed off other artifacts that remained in her possession such as a bracelet she made; a jacket she decorated; a scrapbook she created containing photographs, signatures, and notes from her friends and teachers; a collage she created for her mother as a Mother's Day gift; several videos, saved on her laptop, of her dance group practices and performances; and a video recorded by her mother of one of these performances. To address the purposes for which she created particular products, and the meanings she ascribed to them, Allison invited Vanesa to discuss these artifacts in detail. Vanesa represented a case of when things go well with research with young people. We learned much about this young woman's literate life that assisted our thinking about how teachers' curricula and instructional practices might recruit out-of-school literacies for building students' academic literacies.

Lydia: A case of when the going gets tough. Lydia, another 15-year old youth, also taught us much about the literate lives of diverse youth and about ways of doing research with them. Lydia was born in the U.S. and identified as Mexican American. Upon meeting her for the first time in the school's cafeteria, it was clear to Michelle, her assigned researcher, that Lydia was a storyteller. Although she was quick to claim that literacy did not serve much purpose in her life outside the classroom, as she began to open up to Michelle, Lydia shared stories about the important people and events in her life, using her phone to illustrate these stories with the pictures she had collected over time. This multimodal storytelling was a practice Lydia demonstrated throughout the research process, not unlike the way she told the story of who she was while participating in the virtual world of MySpace. Although Lydia had struggled to find relevance in her middle school literacy curriculum, her time in Molly's ninth grade reading class provided her with opportunities to read young adult literature with which she connected and to tell the stories of her own life through writing. Lydia continued to grow in Molly's classroom but, unfortunately, a schedule change required her to join a new reading class halfway through the school year. This transition, along with numerous others affecting her personal life, likely led to Lydia's resistance in the literacy classroom as well as in her role as a participant in the research.

Over the course of the study, Lydia visited with Michelle on five different occasions and communicated with her through telephone conversations, text messages, emails, and once through MySpace. Because the first interview was conducted by Allison as a pull-out conversation during Molly's class, Michelle first scheduled an informal meeting with Lydia to start building their relationship and answer any questions Lydia had prior to beginning the formal research. At this meeting, a date was set for the first formal interview focusing on Lydia's reading life. The reading interview, and the subsequent one on writing, took place at a restaurant in Lydia's community. This setting allowed Michelle to spend time in Lydia's neighborhood and provided Lydia and her an opportunity to continue building a relationship through sharing a meal while discussing Lydia's reading and writing practices. The interview focusing on Lydia's reading practices was conducted in mid-January. Lydia was eager to participate in the first interview on reading, and, at that time, had many positive experiences to share about her time spent in Molly's classroom. In addition, she seemed proud to claim the identity of reader and writer, both inside and outside the classroom, despite her claim that she did not often practice literacy outside school.

It proved more difficult to contact Lydia for the second interview. It was during this time that Lydia's academic schedule was changed and she was moved out of the focal reading class into another reading class Molly taught. This change put Lydia out of the reach of Allison who conducted classroom observations; we no longer saw her inside school and could not continue to study firsthand how she was experiencing Molly's pedagogy. Furthermore, the research team no longer had an official space where we knew we would find Lydia and encourage her to continue participating in the outside-school portion of the research with Michelle. From Molly's reports, we learned that upon being moved to this new class, Lydia resisted participation and often cut class, as well as failed to turn in work. In that class, Molly struggled with creating the supportive and safe literacy community that she had in the focal reading class. As such, Molly also struggled with encouraging Lydia to continue participating productively in literacy learning in school. Molly relayed messages from the researchers to Lydia whenever Lydia came to class, but with spotty attendance and a changed attitude, that strategy was of limited success.

Adding to our difficulties in finding Lydia, her phone was regularly cut off. In addition, her living situation was fairly unstable. Michelle made frequent efforts to track Lydia down, calling the numbers of various friends and family members. These were numbers from which Lydia had contacted her at different times throughout the study. Michelle's perseverance paid off; she finally got in touch with Lydia and Lydia agreed to meet for the second interview. Lydia cancelled that meeting, however; and yet another after that. Still, after a couple of cancellations, in mid-April, Lydia did finally participate in the second interview focused on her writing practices. However, she was far less engaged in the second interview than in the first, perhaps because of the tumult in her personal life and the changed academic schedule.

Maintaining contact with Lydia remained difficult. Yet, every once in a while, Lydia contacted Michelle and voiced interest in getting together again to talk more about her literate life. In their personal communication, Molly mentioned to Michelle how important the relationship she had formed with Lydia was to the young woman. In discussing a phone call Lydia made to Michelle during Molly's class, Molly wrote, "Her face LIT UP when you answered. Things are not easy now for her, but you are definitely a bright spot in her day." She added, "Seriously, you have made an impression on that lonely little girl." We offer this example as one of many that taught us the importance of building authentic and caring relationships with youth when engaging with them in research.

In June, Lydia invited Michelle to meet her at the public library to observe and discuss her online social networking. This appointment, too, was difficult to schedule. However, upon visiting with Lydia, she shared with Michelle her thinking as she navigated MySpace and her purposes for participating in that world. This conversation allowed Michelle to ask questions in order to better understand the literacy practices and processes in which Lydia engaged through MySpace. A couple of weeks later, Michelle was finally able to visit Lydia at home. Lydia and her family had recently moved. Upon moving to their new house, four additional family members had moved back in with Lydia and her mother, leaving Lydia without a bedroom. Despite the seeming transitional state of the home, Michelle was able to gain insight about the ways Lydia and her family engaged with literacy. During this visit, Michelle noticed only two examples of print-based literacy in the house, one of which was a class magazine that Molly and her students had compiled. For that publication, Lydia had composed a story about the special relationship she shared with her older brother.

During the move, Lydia had lost the camera she was given to capture the different ways she engaged in literacy throughout her daily life. In the home visit, Michelle provided Lydia with a new camera, promising to come by in two weeks to pick it up. However, Lydia did not follow through with several planned appointments with Michelle to return the camera. On Michelle's final attempt to pick up the camera, she learned Lydia's family had, once again, relocated. Her efforts to contact Lydia at school were unsuccessful as well. Upon speaking to an administrator the following school year, she learned that Lydia continued to struggle, both academically and behaviorally, during her tenth grade year, and was often absent from school.

DISCUSSION AND IMPLICATIONS

This study was specifically designed to respond to a call to the literacy research community to hear from culturally and linguistically diverse students who had been labeled as underperforming in school, many of whom had successful out-of-school literate lives (Hull & Shultz, 2001).

Several commitments seemed to be helpful in facilitating youths' voicing of their literate lives: authentic relationships steeped in an ethic of care (Noddings, 2005); seeing and accepting students as they are, both culturally and linguistically (Wickstrom, Araujo, & Patterson, 2011); shared and flexible roles and responsibilities among researchers, teachers, and youth; and responsiveness in research design. For literacy scholars working within theories of literacy as social practice, our analysis and experience suggest the need to educate and work alongside literacy teachers and their students as they recycle through theorizing, designing, implementing, critiquing and revising their practices of multiliteracies (New London Group, 1996). Taking literacy practices themselves as objects of classroom investigation and inquiry, we think, avoids the co-optation of youths' language and literacy practices for school purposes (Gustavson, 2007) as students and teachers take on roles of curriculum designers in multiliteracies pedagogy.

Our experience also speaks to some of the difficulties of conducting research with vulnerable populations about whom the profession needs to develop more emic understandings. Adolescents placed in this ninth grade reading classroom had been identified as not meeting expectations, as being at risk of school failure, as being a problem in an accountability system and culture. They arrive in this place with a history of being identified in that way across multiple grades, and their identities, confidence, and sense of affiliation with schooling and literacy have been bruised. In that social, political, and emotional setting, an invitation to be participants in a research study is not always welcomed open-heartedly. Our desire as researchers to understand, to represent, and even to re-figure and re-story may sometimes be at odds with these young people's intent to refuse, to protect themselves, to guard against further hassle from the school. One way to claim control and power, an unusual opportunity, was to say no to us. This was of course understandable, but it also frustrated our attempt to excavate the details of competence, intelligence, and purpose in their literacies, which we saw as potentially emancipatory.

Moreover, our analysis argues convincingly that such research agendas must be carried outside classrooms and school doors. Across the out-of-school data collection experiences with focal students, we found that the youth granted Allison, the primary classroom researcher, most access to their outside-school literate lives. This suggested to us the need to meet youth regularly in official as well as unofficial social contexts in which they participate. Furthermore, our graduate students' persistence, flexibility, availability, and genuine caring for students—many of whom were dealing with significant personal challenges—were eventually rewarded with students' sharing with us their literate lives. Pairing each focal student with one researcher proved critical to making each youth feel known and cared for. Knowledge about youth and their literate lives is best attained by taking the long and un-chartable journey with the young people who inform us. Only then can literacy researchers approach seeing and knowing them more fully, thus enabling us to consider, along with them and their teachers, how school environments may better support their literacy development.

REFERENCES

Bhabha, H. K. (1994). *The location of culture*. London, England: Routledge.

Charmaz, K. (2000). Grounded theory: Objectivist and constructivist methods. In N. Denzin and Y. Lincoln (Eds.), *Handbook of Qualitative Research* (2nd ed., pp. 509-535). Thousand Oaks, CA: Sage Publications.

Christenbury, L., Bomer, R., & Smagorinsky, P. (Eds.). (2009). *Handbook of adolescent literacy research*. New York, NY: Guilford.

Dyson, A. H., & Genishi, C. (2007). *On the case: Approaches to language and literacy research*. New York, NY: Teachers College Press.

Farrell, E. (1990). *Hanging in and dropping out: Voices of at-risk high school students*. New York, NY: Teachers College Press.

Fisher, M. T. (2005). From the coffeehouse to the schoolhouse: The promise and potential of spoken word poetry in schools. *English Education, 37*, 115-131.

Gee, J. P. (1990). *Social linguistics and literacies. Ideology in discourses*. London, England: Falmer Press.

Gee, J. P. (1994). Discourses. Reflections on M. A. K. Halliday's "toward a language-based theory of learning". *Linguistics and Education, 6*, 33-40.

Glaser, B. G., & Strauss, A. L. (2006). *The discovery of grounded theory: Strategies for qualitative research*. Chicago, IL: Aldine Publishing Co.

Gonzalez, N., Moll, L. C., & Amanti, C. (2005). *Funds of knowledge: Theorizing practices in households and classrooms*. Mahwah, NJ: Lawrence Erlbaum Associates.

Gustavson, L. (2007). *Youth learning on their own terms: Creative practices and classroom teaching*. New York, NY: Routledge.

Gutiérrez, K. D. (2008). Developing a sociocritical literacy in the Third Space. *Reading Research Quarterly,* 43, 148-164.

Hong Xu, S. (2008). Rethinking literacy learning and teaching: Intersections of adolescents' in-school and out-of-school literacy practices. In K. A. Hinchman & H. K. Sheridan-Thomas (Eds.), *Best practices in adolescent literacy instruction* (pp. 39-56). New York, NY: Guilford.

Hull, G., & Schultz, K. (2001). Literacy and learning out of school: A review of theory and research. *Review of Education Research,* 71, 575-611.

Kalantzis, M., Cope, B., & The Learning by Design Project Group (Eds.). (2005). *Learning by design.* Alton, Canada: Common Ground.

Lofland, J., & Lofland, L. H. (1995). *Analyzing social settings: A guide to qualitative observation and analysis* (3rd ed.). Belmont, CA: Wadsworth.

Martínez-Roldán, C., & Fránquiz, M. E. (2009). Latina/o youth literacies: Hidden funds of knowledge. In L. Christenbury, R. Bomer, & P. Smagorinksy (Eds.), *Handbook of adolescent literacy research* (pp. 323-342). New York, NY: Guilford Press.

Miles, M. B., & Huberman, M. (1994). *Qualitative data analysis: An expanded sourcebook.* Thousand Oaks, CA: Sage Publications.

New London Group. (1996). A pedagogy of multiliteracies: Designing social futures. *Harvard Educational Review,* 66, 60-92.

Noddings, N. (2005). *The challenge to care in schools: An alternative approach to education.* New York, NY: Teachers College Press.

Vadeboncoeur, J. A., & Stevens, L. P. (Eds.). (2005). *Re/Constructing "the adolescent": Sign, symbol, and body.* New York, NY: Peter Lang.

Weinstein, S. (2007). A love for the thing: The pleasures of rap as a literate practice. *Journal of Adolescent & Adult Literacy,* 50, 270–281.

West, K. C. (2008). Weblogs and literary response: Socially situated identities and hybrid social languages in English class blogs, *Journal of Adolescent and Adult Literacy,* 51, 588-598.

Wickstrom, C., Araujo, J., & Patterson, L. (2011). Teachers prepare students for career and college: "I see you," therefore I can teach you. In P. J. Dunston, L. B. Gambrell, K. Headley, S. K. Fullerton, P. M. Stecker, V. R. Gilles & C. C. Bates (Eds.), *60th Yearbook of the Literacy Research Association* (pp. 113-125). Oak Creek, WI: Literacy Research Association.

Zenkov, K. (2009). The teachers and schools they deserve: Seeing the pedagogies, practices, and programs urban students want. *Theory Into Practice,* 48, 168-175.

Early Adolescents' Views of Good Readers and Writers in School and Their Literate Identities: An International Exploration

Sara Ann Beach
University of Oklahoma

Angela Ward
Unversity of Saskatchewan

Jennifer Dorsey
University of Oklahoma

Libby Limbrick
University of Auckland

Jill Paris
University of Otago

Klaudia Lorinczova
Keuka College

Marcela Maslova
The Orava Association for Democratic Education

Sapargul Mirseitova
Kazakhstan Reading Association

In these new times, what counts as literacy in a global society is in a constant state of flux, tailored to and situated within a time and place, and as such cannot be decontextualized or universal (Rex et al., 2010). Thus, a view of what counts as competence in literacy is also historically, politically, and socially constructed. For this study, we are defining literacy proficiency as grounded in participation in social practices around written, visual, and digital texts, each of which require four sets of practices, with the reader performing as: code breaker, text participant, text user, and text questioner (Luke & Freebody, 1999). Literacy proficiency, then, can be defined as the ability to use linguistic, cognitive, social and cultural resources to interpret and critique the various types of texts that are part of the learner's discourse community. In this view, language and literacy are learned within communities of practice, as discourses associated with a profession, discipline, or institutional context such as schools.

This view of proficiency, however, cannot be confounded with the view of literacy achievement promulgated in the national and international assessments. While the National Assessment of Educational Progress (NAEP) still advocates primarily a cognitive and linguistic view of literacy, the Programme for International Student Assessment (PISA) and Progress in International Reading Literacy Study (PIRLS) have added a social dimension to literacy achievement. They have expanded the view of what counts as text to include interactive digital texts, and have added the effective interpretation and use of such texts to their definitions of achievement (Mullis, Martin, Foy, & Drucker, 2012). Achievement in these assessments is viewed as the ability to respond correctly to questions about different types of texts without regard to the social or cultural contexts of the reader or the literacy practices that occur around those texts in non-schooled contexts. Within this view of achievement, engagement in literacy activities, both in- and outside-of-school settings leads to higher achievement and proficiency regardless of the type of instruction (OECD, 2010; Wigfield et al., 2008).

THEORETICAL FRAMEWORK

Engaged literacy learning, as described by Guthrie and colleagues (Guthrie & Wigfield, 2000; Wigfield et al., 2008), is internally motivated, strategic, social, and goal directed. Recent theories of engagement assert that engagement is composed of multiple dimensions including the behavioral, cognitive, and emotional aspects, which can be discerned through student participation in classroom practices; use of self-regulation strategies during learning; and identification with and valuing of the learning events offered in the classroom community (Wang & Holcombe, 2010). This view has begun to emphasize the importance of school and classroom environments to engagement and has led to the formulation of socio-culturally based theories. Hickey (2003) defines engagement as meaningful participation in a context where what is to be learned is valued, and one is negotiating an identity as a member of a community of practice stating, "engagement is a function of the degree to which participants in an activity are attuned to the constraints and affordances of the social practices defining those activities" (Hickey & Zuiker, 2005, p. 283). McCaslin (2009) and McCaslin and Burross (2011) have proposed that engagement and motivation are the result of co-regulation between the cultural, social, and personal sources of influence that shape a person's view of him or her self in a particular context. Thus, learners differentially recognize and respond to resources, activities, and relationships dependent upon how they see themselves as valued or competent within the classroom setting. Gresalfi, Barnes, and Cross (2012) assert that engagement is situational, based on the task offered and the context in which it is offered to particular students, making engagement in learning possible but not obligatory. Accordingly, learners' identities within the context of a discipline and their recognition of affordances for participation in literacy practices leads to engagement in those practices.

Literate Identity

Learners develop tacit understanding of what it means to be knowledgeable about literacy, what behaviors are valued, and what it means to be competent in a particular setting. This sense of being literate (Heath, 1991; Young & Beach, 1997) leads learners to interpret literacy events in a particular context, to participate in those events in particular ways, and to develop a literate identity in that context consistent with their interpretation (Beach & Ward, 2013; Young & Beach, 1997). A person's literate identity is a personal view of one's set of literate attributes. These attributes include a sense of one's competence as a literate person in a specific context, a sense of one's role as a literate individual in one's personal and professional world, and one's relationships with others in a literate society (Young & Beach, 1997). Literate identities develop and are manifested in different ways as part of membership in different social groups (Gee, 1996). Literacies "are positioned in relation to the social institutions and power relations which sustain them" (Barton & Hamilton, 2000, p. 1); they develop as individuals participate in literacy events and practices throughout their lives and as a part of participation in multiple communities of practice (Wenger, 1998). Therefore, literate identities are neither static nor stagnant, but dynamic and changing with the changing circumstances of life, and the ways in which they develop provide powerful insights into the practices and values of the social setting in which they occur. There is no easy separation of the identity and the literacy practices in which a learner participates, according to Vasudeven, Schultz, and Bateman (2010), because literate identity is seen as "not intrinsic or separate from social contexts and interactions; rather…embodied and enacted in practice" (p. 447).

Each person has multiple literate identities that are outcomes of living in, through, and around the cultural practices of literacy (Holland, Lachicotte, Skinner, & Cain, 1998). These literate identities enable people to interpret the multiple signs and messages that surround them on a daily basis and to develop a portfolio of literacy practices they can draw from in different contexts. Learners bring to school literate identities developed through participation in literacy practices valued at home. These vernacular literacy practices, as Gee (2008) notes, are the basis for learning new literacy practices and the basis for evaluating oneself in relationship to those practices. Gee (2008) asserts that if new forms of literacy resonate with and bridge vernacular literacies, engagement with the new practices can enhance learning. Gee further states: "These children come to associate school and school-based ways with their home and community based identities, thanks to the initial overlap between home and school practices. This is a powerful form of affiliation" (p. 102). If there is not a bridge between vernacular and school literacies, an affective filter can be raised so the learner does not engage. Without affiliation, learners see themselves as not competent and view literacy practices as merely for 'doing school' better now or in the future.

Engagement and Identity

Engagement in school activities has been described through descriptions of activities, individual behaviors, and dispositions. Activity theorists suggest, "physical and psychological mediational tools are used to build cultures" (Ellis, Edwards, & Smagorinsky, 2010, p. 3), including subcultures such as the classroom. So the ways in which texts are used and valued, how tasks and invitations are offered, and how teachers respond to students' writing, all provide insight into learning and dynamically create both school culture and individual literate identities. In this view, students and their teachers both transform, and are transformed by, the relational engagements of the classroom (Ivey & Johnston, 2010). The emphasis of activity theory on the agency concomitant with participation in social practices is helpful in understanding students' range of identities in and out of school. A sense of agency "provides others and self with resources for making attributions about the kind of person one is" (Roth & Lee, 2007, p. 215).

A sociocultural view of literacy suggests students' active engagement in school and home literacy activities is mediated by both cognitive and social experiences in reading and writing. As a result, the concept of literate identity is pivotal in understanding student engagement in classroom literacy practices. Engaging literacy experiences are those that go beyond superficial engagement in school social life to intellectual engagement with others in learning about and through literacy activities. According to Dunleavy, Willms, Milton, and Friesen (2012), intellectual engagement in school literacy activities is too rare. In fact, students may "do well" in school without being intellectually engaged. In our view, positive literate identities developed in and out of school are both the result of engaging literacy experiences and also predictors of continuing deep engagement in schooled and community literacy activities. Beach and Ward (2013) note "[students'] feelings of competence and confidence in joining communities of literacy practice constitute and are constituted by their literate identities" (p. 242).

The purpose of this study was to explore early adolescents' sense of being literate at school in five countries. Specifically, our research questions were: How do early adolescents (ages 9-13) from different cultures, languages, and educational systems describe good readers and writers? How do they perceive themselves in comparison to that description? Are there differences by the number of years in school, gender, or country? Students tell stories of their own literate competences to themselves and to others, and hear stories told about themselves (Sfard & Prusak, 2005). This study enabled adolescent students to share perceptions of their own and their classmates' literate identities, and more tellingly, to reveal their understandings of how teachers and educational institutions value particular literate activities.

METHODOLOGY

This study is a mixed methods study using a concurrent nested strategy. Quantitative and qualitative data were collected concurrently to answer different research questions and then integrated during data analysis. In this study, qualitative data were gathered to determine how the children described good readers and writers, and quantitative data were gathered to find out about children's literate identities in relation to that standard.

Participants

Participants were 1,021 children from the United States (n = 152), Canada (n = 115), New Zealand (n = 256), Slovakia (n = 232), and Kazakhstan (n = 258) who were in each country's equivalent of grades 4, 5, and 6. The countries outside of North America were chosen for the following reasons: Slovakia and Kazakhstan had taken part in a sustained professional development program supporting critical thinking and democratic practices. The Slovak language uses the Roman alphabet and has a one-to-one correspondence between letters and sounds. In Kazakhstan, both Kazakh and Russian use the Cyrillic alphabet, and students have the opportunity to attend school in either language. New Zealand was chosen because of its consistently strong showing in international comparisons of literacy. Table 1 shows the demographic information for participants in each country. Demographic information was solicited differently in each country depending on whether ethnicity was determined by race or nationality. Parental education, specifically father's educational level was used as a proxy for the family's socioeconomic level in each country.

Educational contexts. Children were recruited from two or more schools in each country, often in different geographic locations in the country and from different sized towns or cities. Schools were recruited to participate by one of the researchers who resided in that country or geographic area. All of the researchers were active in either or both in-service or preservice teacher preparation in their geographic region and were familiar with both the national school context and the schools where they recruited participants.

Table 1: Participant Demographic Information

US (n = 152)	Canada (n = 115)	New Zealand (n = 265)	Kazakhstan (n = 258)	Slovakia (n = 232)
61% girls 39% boys	47% girls 53% boys	57% girls 43% boys	60% girls 40% boys	55% girls 45% boys
57% White 14% N.A. 22% Biracial 2% Hispanic 4% Black	81% White 10% Immigrant 7% Metis 2% other	52% White 10% NZ Maori 7% Chinese 7% Asian Pacific 7% Biracial 17% other	39% Kazakh 35% Russian 26% Other ethnicities (Korean, Tatar, German, etc.)	99% Slovak 1% Roma
57% fathers HS grad, or some college	46% fathers at least college degree	18% fathers at least college degree	77% fathers at least college degree	66% fathers HS grad (regular, vocational, prep)
34% grades 4 & 5 66% grade 6	33% grade 4 45% grade 5 22% grade 6	28% year 5 (gr.4) 33% year 6 (gr.5) 33% year 7 (gr.6)	31% grade 4 38% grade 5 31% grade 6	32% grade 4 30% grade 5 38% grade 6

In the United States, participants came from three schools in a southwestern state, two located in a rural area close to a suburban city near one of the largest cities in the state, and one located in a small city in the eastern part of the state. The rural schools, part of the same school district, had a significant Native American and Hispanic population, although most of the students were Caucasian. The majority of the students at both schools qualified for free or reduced lunch. The classrooms at the elementary school (600 students in PreK to 5th grade) were self-contained with one teacher for all subjects and three to four classes per grade level. The middle school (250 students in grades 6-8) was departmentalized with teachers teaching one subject to all grade levels. The sixth graders at this school had both an English language arts teacher and a reading teacher. The English class focused on grammar and writing while the reading class included activities focusing on vocabulary and reading skills using novels. The middle school in the small city (800 students in grades 6-8) had similar demographics and was similarly organized for instruction. Students attended a language arts class daily that focused on both reading and writing. This was the sole middle school in the city so students came from all the elementary schools in the area. All teachers in all schools were considered highly qualified by the state department of education, indicating the teachers had university degrees and were teaching in the subjects for which they were qualified.

In Canada, education is a provincial responsibility. A number of provinces participate in a national assessment, where students are randomly selected for testing. Students also participate in international assessments. The two Canadian schools that participated in this study are from one province where students could be educated in French, Cree, or Ukrainian, or participate in a publicly-funded Catholic school system. Schools in the study were in an expanding "bedroom community" outside the fastest-growing city in Canada. They were originally in what was considered a rural area, but rapid local growth has led to an increasing student population, including immigrant and refugee families. The majority of students still come from European backgrounds (mostly German and Ukrainian farm families). The elementary school included students from kindergarten through grade 5 and enrolled close to 700. Most classrooms had a homeroom teacher to teach core subjects, with some specialists for music and physical education in grades four and five. The middle/high school in the study was nearby, had 750 students in grades 6 to 12, and typically used specialist teachers for most subjects. All teachers had university degrees, and most were experienced. Class sizes were between 25 and 30, with multiple classes at the same grade level.

In New Zealand, four schools from the North Island, and two schools from the South Island participated. The schools in this study used English as the medium of instruction for the national curriculum, and had different demographic profiles as designated by the Ministry of Education. Most children in New Zealand start school on their fifth birthday, and continue through Primary, Intermediate, Middle and High schools. In most schools up to Year 6 (Grade 5 equivalent) there is one classroom teacher per class who teaches all subjects. In Years 7 and 8 specialist teachers may teach some classes. Typical class size is between 20 and 30 students. The North Island schools were from an urban area and ranged in size from 300 to 585 students: one school had mainly Maori and Pasifik students, another had a balance between European and Maori/Pasifik students, another fairly equally included European and Asian students, while the fourth enrolled similar numbers of students from European and Asian backgrounds. In the South Island the schools were from rural towns in a farming region (one school enrolled 150 students and the other 220). Both schools had predominantly New Zealand European students. The teachers of the New Zealand students in the study were experienced and actively involved in professional development. Teachers in New Zealand have a three or four year qualification, or a graduate diploma.

In Kazakhstan, education is free for all citizens, and the Ministry of Education directs the curriculum for primary and secondary schools. School begins in kindergarten at the age of five, and instruction is given in Kazakh or Russian in most schools. Students attend primary school (grades 1-4), lower secondary school (grades 5 – 9), and one of three tracks offered for higher secondary education: a general track, an initial vocational track that trains students in a profession, or a secondary vocational track given through colleges. Four schools participated in the study: an ordinary public school from a small town in the central part of Kazakhstan with instruction in Russian, a boarding school from a large city in the central part of Kazakhstan dedicated to talented children from rural places with instruction in Kazakh, an academic college preparatory school from a large city in the central part of Kazakhstan with instruction in Russian, and an academic college preparatory school from a high socio-economic region of the biggest city in southern Kazakhstan with instruction in Kazakh. The average school size was between 800 – 900 children with 25-30 children in a class. All teachers hold university diplomas, and had several years of experience teaching.

In Slovakia, the two schools that participated included both primary and lower secondary grades (grades 1-9). Both schools had principals who had participated in a large-scale professional development effort over the last 15 years that focused on the development of critical thinking and democratic practices. They used the national curriculum prescribed for mother tongue instruction (the equivalent of language arts instruction in North American schools). One school was situated in a small town in the mountains (total number of children in the school was 405 with 32 teachers) while the other was in a small city located more in an agricultural area (730 children with 49 teachers). Both schools served families that were primarily middle class (less that 6% were considered disadvantaged in each school). In the primary grades, teachers taught core subjects to the same group of children, and the rest of the subjects were taught by different teachers. In the lower secondary (grades 5-9), teachers taught one or two subjects to different grades and classes of children. All teachers had at least a Magister degree (three years of bachelor's level course work and two years of master's level coursework and practice).

Data sources

Data were collected using two data sources: a literate identity survey completed either online in situations where the students were used to using computers or going to a computer lab or by paper and pencil where computer access was limited, and focus group discussions. Data were collected in each country by the in-country researchers and were collected in the mother tongue of the country, except in Kazakhstan where data were collected in two languages: Russian and Kazakh. All data sources had been translated by native speakers into Slovak, Kazakh and Russian, with wording modified to fit the cultural context.

The construct of literate identity was operationalized using a survey adapted from the Reader Self-Perception Scale (Henk & Melnick, 1995) and the Writer Self-Perception Scale (Bottomley, Henk, & Melnick, 1997). Henk and Melnick (1995) identified four factors in how readers and writers feel about themselves: how they feel about the progress they are making in their reading or writing performance (e.g., I read/write better than I could before; Progress subscales), how they feel their reading or writing compares with that of their peers (e.g., I read/write more than other kids; Observational Comparison subscales), what they perceive others think about their reading or writing (e.g., My teacher thinks I'm a good reader/writer; Social Feedback subscales), and how they feel internally when they read or write (e.g., I enjoy reading/writing; Physiological States subscales). A group of items that tapped into specific writing progress were not included as they tapped into explicit writing ability, not general progress, and had no analog in reading. The remaining items from the two scales were put in random order. Directions at the top of the sheet mirrored those on the original scales. Children were asked to respond to each statement by circling one of the following responses: strongly agree, agree, disagree, strongly disagree. There were two general statements (I think I am a good reader; I think I am a good writer) and 54 other statements. Items were scored on a scale from 0 (strongly disagree) to 3 (strongly agree). Because the subscales contained different numbers of items, mean item scores were computed for each subscale so comparisons between subscales could be made. The entire survey for the whole sample had an internal consistency reliability coefficient of a= .96. Internal consistency reliability for the scale for each country ranged from .92-.96.

The purpose of the focus group discussions was to find out children's perceptions of the classroom literacy activities they were offered and their view of what good readers and writers looked like. At each school within a country, children were randomly chosen at each grade level to participate in the focus groups. There were two focus groups of 5-6 children at each grade level at each site. Either one of the researchers, or a research assistant trained by the researcher, conducted the discussion. Using a semi-structured set of questions, each group discussed the activities that occurred during their literacy time (e.g., Tell me about some of things you regularly do in reading or language arts class.), and what they thought a good reader and good writer looked like (e.g. Think about a good reader/writer in your classroom. How do you know that person is a good reader/writer?). While every group began with the same set of questions to organize the discussion, the discussion leader followed up with a variety of probes based on how the children responded. The discussions were recorded, then transcribed, and translated by a native speaker if necessary.

Data analysis

The literate identity survey was analyzed quantitatively by country. In each country, multivariate analysis of variance was used to look for differences by gender and grade level on the subscales. Once differences, if any, were examined in each country, K-means cluster analysis was used to categorize groups of participants who were the most similar to each other. Using previous research as a guide (Collins & Beach, 2012), the entire sample was analyzed into both three and four cluster solutions to determine which more clearly defined unique groups. If there was a main effect by grade on three or more subscales, the cluster analysis was completed on each grade level. If there was a main effect of gender on three or more subscales, the cluster analysis was completed on each gender separately. The clusters were then summarized narratively to describe how each group of children perceived themselves as literate people within the classroom setting and were compared across countries.

The focus group discussion was analyzed qualitatively. The transcriptions were read and re-read by at least two of the authors and key words and phrases were recorded for each group. Emerging themes were discussed and elaborated. Narratives were composed of the characteristics of good readers and writers for each context. These narratives were compared across countries.

FINDINGS

The early adolescents in each country could describe what good and readers and writers looked like in their classrooms, and exhibited both similarities and differences in those narratives. Additionally, children's literate identities across the different countries were similarly diverse and very nuanced, particularly in the ways they compared themselves to others and felt their teachers, parents, and peers evaluated their competence.

Good Readers and Writers

Across all five countries, good readers were identified by their use of decoding, vocabulary and strategies, their disposition towards and engagement in reading, through various social aspects such as talking about books and helping, and through schooled aspects of reading such as grades and reading speed. Good writers were identified through their use of good mechanics, style, disposition toward writing and engagement with it, their ability to share their writing and get feedback from others, and schooled aspects such as grades, use of multiple genres, and correctness. We did, in fact, ask participants in the focus groups to "think of someone you know who is a good reader and writer" and describe such a student to us. The next section will present in narrative form how our respondents conceptualized "good readers" and "good writers" in their own classrooms. Descriptions from each country were more similar than different, although there were some aspects that stood out: (a) southwestern state (U.S.) students talked more about grades than did those in the other countries; and (b) the social aspects of literacy were important in the English speaking countries but were barely mentioned by students in Kazakhstan or Slovakia.

In Kazakhstan, students in the focus groups were less voluble than in other countries, perhaps because discussing teaching and learning was an unfamiliar activity. Students valued oral performance as evidenced in comments like: "A good reader reads with feeling, like an actor, and is good to listen to." As in other countries, Kazakhstani students who are good readers read a lot at home, including a range of materials not assigned by school. A good writer "writes like an adult," writes a lot (even when not asked), and loves to write poems and songs.

Slovak students were specific about the strategies good readers use and thought of their expert colleagues as rereading to recall details, and remembering what they read "even in long books." Like Kazakhstani students, students in Slovakia thought that good readers "recite poems with expression" and also have a good vocabulary. Good writers in Slovak classrooms do not make mistakes and have a lot to write about; they also practice at home.

Good readers in the U.S. southwestern state "can read big words alone" and use a variety of cues to decode. The social aspects of being a good reader show in "helping others figure out words" and in recommending books. Reading with a "loud voice and sound effects" is valued as supporting "how to express the story." And, of course, good readers read thick books. Good writers' "hands never get tired" and they can correct their own mistakes. Imaginative writers capture their readers' interests without pictures as they write using powerful adjectives from their "vast vocabulary." Good readers are often the ones who have "creative minds" shown through their writing, which "sucks you in." Southwest students appreciate their classroom fellows who help others publish written work when they have finished their own writing.

Being a good reader in Saskatchewan classrooms means reading "humungous books" as well as reading with expression and being able to communicate articulately about literature. Indeed, a good reader may choose to read the book before watching a movie. For Saskatchewan students, good writing involves checking over your own writing and "taking it seriously" as well as using rich vocabulary. It helps to be a good reader and writer if you "come from a culture that loves to learn and read and write" and would "rather read than draw."

New Zealand students (from both the North and South Islands) were especially insightful about the good readers and writers in their midst. As readers they "summarize the whole story so you know what the whole thing's about." Good readers use many strategies; they reread, use context to figure out word meanings, and "understand what's happening through think-alouds." Not only does a good reader read confidently and with expression, but "doesn't get distracted, concentrates and does not worry about anyone else in the room." In their enthusiasm, good readers like to share and are "excited to talk about their reading," although they may be tempted to "show off" a little as well. Like good readers in other countries, good readers in New Zealand can answer questions easily and usually get "good scores on assessments." Our participants in New Zealand described a good writer who "looks like she's a grownup," and noted "you have to be a good reader to write well." Great stories have a "good hook," include "cool words," and engaging stories "flow and don't blabber on," keeping up suspense. Good writers in New Zealand classrooms are recognizable because they take more books from the library (including the public library), "don't complain about not having good ideas" and are "really keen" about writing and working with others. The social aspects of literacy were salient in discussions with all of the New Zealand focus groups.

Profiles of Literate Identity

There were likewise similarities in the profiles of literate identity identified by the cluster analysis but also some marked differences. The MANOVA showed a significant difference between the grade levels on the different subscales of the literate identity survey in Kazakhstan but not in any other country while differences by gender were significant in the United States and Slovakia. The differences by grade or gender in Canada and New Zealand were minimal, occurring on only one subscale in each country. Consequently, the profiles of literate identity were constructed by grade level in Kazakhstan, by gender in Slovakia and the United States, and as a whole for Canada and New Zealand.

Table 2. MANOVA by Country

Country	Overall	Grade	Gender	Grade x Gender
US	Main effect by Gender (p = .000)	None	WP, WOC, WSF, WPS Girls > boys (p <. 003)	None
Canada	None	RSF 4 > 6 (p = .01)	WSF, WOC Girls > boys (p <. 003)	None
New Zealand	Main effect by Grade (p = .005)	RSF 4>5 (p = .03)	WPS Girls > boys (p = .005)	None
Kazakhstan	Main effect by Grade (p = .001)	RP 4,5 > 6 ROC, RSF, RPS 5 > 6 (p < .01) WOC 5 > 4 WSF, PS 5 > 4,6 (p < .02)	WOC, WSF Girls > boys (p < .02)	None
Slovakia	Gender x grade interaction (p = .007)	None	RPS, WSF, WPS Girls > Boys (p < .03)	ROC, WOC Girls > Boys 4,6 Boys > Girls 5 (p < .03)

Note. RP = Reading Progress; ROC = Reading Observational Comparison; RSF = Reading Social Feedback; RPS = Reading Physiological State; WP = Writing Progress; WOC = Writing Observational Comparison; WSF = Writing Social Feedback; WPS = Writing Physiological State.

A common profile across all of the countries was a large group of children who considered themselves great readers and writers, although there were subtle nuances in the way in which they compared themselves to others, interpreted social feedback they received, and described whether they liked to read or write. While they all believed they were continuing to make excellent progress in becoming better readers and writers, some of these students felt they were at least as good, if not better than, their peers, and others saw them as proficient, and really enjoyed reading and/or writing. Others felt more equivocal about how they compared with their peers, or how they felt others saw them, or even if they really liked to either read or write.

In Kazakhstan, New Zealand, and Slovakia, another common profile was a small group of children who did not believe that they were good at either reading or writing. While they felt they were making at least some progress in becoming better readers and writers (except the Slovak girls who did not feel they were making progress in writing), they did not think they compared well to peers nor did they think others thought they were proficient in either reading or writing. Not surprisingly, they either did not like to read or write or were equivocal about their feelings. Interestingly, children in Canada and the United States did not describe themselves as "not good" at both reading and writing. They instead were more equivocal about their reading proficiency while offering a similar view of their progress, comparison with their peers, and feedback from others as the children with the entirely negative literate identity.

The remaining two profiles of literate identity in each country included a profile where the children felt more positive than negative about their reading and more negative than positive about their writing or vice versa. While this pattern was evident across the countries, the strength of the positive or negative literate identity varied as did how they compared themselves to others, how they thought others saw them, and if they liked to either read or write.

Adolescents' Perceptions of Literate Identity: Discussion of Stories Students Tell

Students demonstrated engagement by enthusiastic participation in this study in a number of ways. They took the task of completing the survey seriously, and were anxious to fill it out 'correctly' (as evidenced by children asking for help with questions), especially in countries where testing is a frequent occurrence. The focus group discussions were lively and open. Students were especially interested in passing on "advice to teachers" and thoughts on in-school activities that engaged or discouraged them from participation (These data are not specifically reported on here.). Responses to questions about "good readers and writers" became easier for students to consider when focus group facilitators reinforced the suggestion that participants hold in their mind's eye particular peers who embodied expert characteristics. Students were most able to describe the behavioral and dispositional/emotional aspects of good readers' and writers' literate behaviors in their classrooms (Wang & Holcombe, 2010), but intellectual engagement (Dunleavy et al., 2012) was more difficult to gauge in a snapshot study.

In all countries, the focus group participants were very specific about expert readers' and writers' command of the forms and structures of literacy as valued by their teachers (and probably parents). Their first responses described peers who could decode and spell without difficulty; several participants visualized classmates who were 'like grownups' in their ease with schooled literacy. But all groups went beyond the surface to value evidence of peers' positive literacy dispositions, in fact, students especially admired their expert peers' strong sense of competence and positive literate identity, as shown in lively oral readings and poetry presentations, powerful story lines and skill in supporting other readers and writers. Participants described class members who had invested fully in the classroom community (McCaslin & Burross, 2011) because they were competent to engage in the literacy activities available to them. This ability to characterize themselves and others as readers and writers (Roth & Lee, 2007) provides students with the agency to decide to engage in literacy practices in and out of school, joining in those communities of practice where they feel valued and competent (Beach & Ward, 2013).

The profiles created from the cluster analysis indicate that literate identity in school is very nuanced. Although many of the participants saw themselves as either competent or very competent in either or both reading and writing overall, when asked specifically to compare themselves to their peers or to speculate about how others saw them, there were differences in the responses. One potential explanation is that they may see themselves as more competent in reading or writing specific genres of texts. Another potential explanation is the questions in the subscales targeted literacy at school, and their overall view of themselves as literate people encompasses both schooled and vernacular literacies. Additionally, cultural or social expectations of the different countries almost certainly mediated how participants presented themselves to others, especially adults.

The power of teachers within the classroom context is evident throughout the data, as students appropriated not only particular ways to value literacy but also echoed the language and terminology of their teachers. Many students' understanding of literate practice is situated around a literate person's mastery of the surface layers of literacy (In one focus group, Canadian students spent five minutes discussing the importance of excellent handwriting.). There were deeper instances, especially in New Zealand, where teachers gave students the language to discuss complex literary and metacognitive understandings (how to think about themes in literature, for example). It was clear from students' discussions when teachers had set up communities of practice that supported diverse literate identities in their classrooms. Sometimes students nostalgically referred to past experiences in classes where they had more opportunities to read at higher levels, for example. There were frequent examples of "ventriloquation" (Bakhtin, 1981) where students' comments demonstrated how they had internalized literacy strategies and concepts from their interactions with a responsive teacher. This appropriation of language underlines the importance of teachers' awareness of the impact of their own language and literacy practices on student understanding of what counts as literacy.

Reflections: Stories Across Cultures

We have the expected concerns about interpreting data from international perspectives; even though we have collegial connections with researchers in each country, it is difficult to ensure that the variations between educational contexts and curricula have been sufficiently considered. Since we have bilingual researchers in each country, we are confident that the translations are trustworthy. However, the similarities in the findings from the focus groups were initially surprising to us, especially considering the diverse cultural contexts of Kazakhstan and Slovakia. As we reflected on our academic and professional connections with these countries, the similarities became less remarkable, but remained of great interest. In both Kazakhstan and Slovakia, students who were in our study were part of a post-communist professional development initiative to support teachers in those countries in developing active learning approaches, especially in literacy teaching. Although we had not worked directly with all the teachers of students in our study, we had certainly given workshops to many current teacher leaders in both countries. Whether we regard this as an example of hegemonic western power changing educational practices, or evidence of positive growth in teaching strategies influenced by international cooperation, there are shared understandings of classroom literacy across the five participating countries. Since we have no comparable data from the communist era, the data present us with a question that we cannot answer.

We plan on further conversations with students from highly successful educational systems in Scandinavia and Asia as well as Australasia. This could be greatly enriched by classroom observations as well as individual interviews to tease out more fully the role of intellectual engagement within an individual student's sense of being literate at school and at home.

It would be valuable to collect longitudinal data as well, to revisit the students with whom we spoke as they near school-leaving age.

Perhaps the deepest insight for us as researchers and teacher educators is that there is much to be learned from talking with students. Other studies have focused on student motivation and engagement through large scale surveys (Gambrell, Palmer, Codling, & Mazzoni, 1996; Guthrie & Wigfield, 2000), and quantitative data such as that provided by PISA is useful in understanding patterns of engagement in school and at home. The nuanced richness of focused conversations with adolescents about their literacy experiences, sense of competence, and literate identities speaks directly to teachers about what it is like to be in their classrooms, and how their students are engaged in learning.

REFERENCES

Bakhtin, M. M. (1981). *The dialogic imagination: Four essays.* (C. Emerson & M. Holquist, Trans.). Austin: University of Texas Press.

Barton, D., & Hamilton, M. (2000). Introduction. In D. Barton, M. Hamilton & R. Ivanic (Eds.), *Situated literacies: Reading and writing in context* (pp. 1-6). London, England: Routledge.

Beach, S. A., & Ward, A. (2013). Insights into engaged literacy learning: Stories of literate identity. *Journal of Research in Childhood Education, 27,* 239-255. *doi:10.1080/02568543.2013.767290*

Bottomley, D. M., Henk, W. A., & Melnick, S. A. (1997/1998). Assessing children's views about themselves as writers using the Writer Self-Perception Scale. *Reading Teacher, 51,* 286-296.

Collins, J., & Beach, S. A. (2012). Profiles of literate identity. *Literacy and Diversity: Proceedings of the 17th European Conference on Reading,* Mons, Belgium, July 31-August 3, 2011.

Dunleavy, J., Willms, D., Milton, P., & Friesen S. (2012). *What did you do in school today? Report number one: The relationship between student engagement and academic outcomes.* Toronto, Canada: Canadian Education Association.

Ellis, V., Edwards, A., & Smagorinsky, P. (Eds.). (2010). Introduction. *Cultural-historical perspectives on teacher education and development.* London, England: Routledge.

Gambrell, L. B., Palmer, B. M., Codling, R. M., & Mazzoni, S. A. (1996). Assessing motivation to read. *The Reading Teacher, 49,* 518-533.

Gee. J. P. (1996) Identity as an analytic lens for research in education. In W. G. Secada (Ed.) *Review of research in education* (pp. 99-125). Washington, DC: American Educational Research Association.

Gee, J. P. (2008). A sociocultural perspective on opportunity to learn. In P. A. Moss, D. C. Pullan, J. P. Gee, E. H. Haertel, & L. J. Young (Eds.), *Assessment, equity, and opportunity to learn* (76-108). Cambridge, MA: Cambridge University Press.

Gresalfi, M. S., Barnes, J., & Cross, D. (2012). When does an opportunity become an opportunity? Unpacking classroom practice through the lens of ecological psychology. *Educational Studies in Mathematics, 80,* 249-267.

Guthrie, J. T., & Wigfield, A. (2000). Engagement and motivation in reading. In M. Kamil, P. D. Pearson, & R. Barr (Eds.), *Handbook of reading research*, (Vol. 3, pp. 403-422). Mahwah, NJ: Erlbaum.

Heath, S. B. (1991). The sense of being literate: Historical and cross-cultural features. In R. Barr, M. L. Kamil, P. B., Mosenthal, & P. D. Pearson (Eds.), *Handbook of reading research*. (Vol. 2, pp. 3-25). New York, NY: Longman.

Henk, W. A., & Melnick, S.A. (1995). The Reader Self-Perception Scale (RSPS): A new tool for measuring how children feel about themselves as readers. *Reading Teacher*, 48, 470-482.

Hickey, D. T., & Zuiker, S. J. (2005). Engaged participation: A sociocultural model of motivation with implications for educational assessment. *Educational Assessment*, 10, 277-305.

Hickey, D. T. (2003). Engaged participation versus marginal nonparticipation: A stridently sociocultural approach to achievement motivation. *The Elementary School Journal*, 103, 401-429.

Holland, D., Lachicotte, Jr. W., Skinner, D., & Cain, C. (1998). *Identity and agency in cultural worlds*. Cambridge, MA & London, England: Harvard University Press.

Ivey, G., & Johnston, P. (2010, December). *Reading engagement, achievement, and moral development in adolescence*. Paper presented at the annual meeting of the Literacy Research Association, Fort Worth, TX.

Luke, A., & Freebody, P. (1999). Further notes on the four resources model. *Reading Online*. Retrieved from http://www.readingonline.org/past/past_index.asp?HREF=/research/ lukefreebody.html

McCaslin, M. (2009). Co-regulation of student motivation and emergent identity. *Educational Psychologist*, 44, 137-146.

McCaslin, M., & Burross, H. L. (2011). Research on individual differences within a sociocultural perspective: Coregulation and adaptive learning. *Teachers College Record*, 113, 325-349.

Mullis, I. V. S., Martin, M. O., Foy, P., & Drucker, K. T. (2012). *PIRLS 2011 International Results in Reading*. Chestnut, MA: TIMSS & PIRLS International Study Center.

OECD. (Organisation for Economic Co-operation and Development). (2010). *PISA 2009 Results: What Students Know and Can Do—Student Performance in Reading, Mathematics, and Science* (Vol. 1). Retrieved from http://dx.doi.org/10.1787/978264091450-en.

Rex, L. A., Bunn, M., Davila, B. A., Dickinson, H. A., Ford, A. C., Gerben, C., … Carter, S. (2010). A review of discourse analysis in literacy research: equitable access. *Reading Research Quarterly*, 45, 94-115.

Roth, W-M, Lee, Y-J. (2007). "Vygotsky's neglected legacy": Cultural-historical activity theory. *Review of Educational Research*, 77, 186-232.

Sfard, A., & Prusak, A. (2005). Telling identities: In search of an analytic tool for investigating learning as a culturally shaped activity. *Educational Researcher*, 34, 14-22.

Vasudevan, L., Schultz, K., & Bateman, J. (2010). Rethinking composing in a digital age: Authoring literate identities through multimodal storytelling. *Written Communication*, 27, 442-468.

Wang, M. T., & Holcombe, R. (2010). Adolescents' perceptions of school environment, engagement, and academic achievement in middle school. *American Educational Research Journal*, 47, 633–662.

Wenger, E. (1998). *Communities of practice: Learning, meaning, and identity*. Cambridge, UK: Cambridge University Press.

Wigfield, A., Guthrie, J. T., Perencevich, K. C., Toboada, A., Klauda, S. L., McRae, A., & Barbosa, P. (2008). Role of reading engagement in mediating effects of reading comprehension instruction on reading outcomes. *Psychology in the Schools*, 45, 432-445.

Young, J. R., & Beach, S. A. (1997). Young children's sense of being literate at school: What's it all about? In C. K. Kinzer, K. A. Hinchman, & D. J. Leu (Eds.), *Inquiries in literacy theory and practice. Forty-sixth yearbook of the National Reading Conference* (pp. 297-307). Chicago, IL: National Reading Conference.

The Quantitative Literacy Connection: Is Literacy Instruction the Key to Teaching Mathematical Habits of the Mind?

Hope Smith Davis
Anne E. Brown
Indiana University South Bend

Recent research in the field of literacy has supported a shift from content-area literacy instruction to instruction focused on disciplinary literacy (Shanahan & Shanahan, 2010). The contrast indicates a change from generalizable strategies for reading and writing designed to enhance comprehension of text regardless of content area, to the development and use of instructional methods derived from strategies and approaches used for communication, thought, and comprehension by experts in correspondent disciplinary fields (Shanahan, Shanahan, & Misischia, 2011). If a goal for literacy researchers and instructors in literacy education courses is to aid in the development of teacher candidates' tools for and knowledge of literacy instruction in relation to disciplinary practice, the evolution of the concept implies a greater understanding of the ways of knowing and methods of interpretation embodied in the individual academic disciplines. In other words, literacy strategies promoted as tools for improved comprehension, especially with regard to reading and text, may need to be re-examined in relation to the ways of knowing as enacted in specific disciplinary contexts. Disciplinary literacy research suggests that educational researchers may need to take a closer look at the literacy practices present in different fields, and, as a result of their findings, identify and develop instructional practices specifically geared toward fostering literacy expectations for those fields.

In the field of mathematics, Siebert and Draper (2008) noted that the traditional focus on content-area literacy instruction in pre-service education courses presents multiple problems for mathematics educators. Characterized as a "communication problem" (p. 235) between literacy and mathematics educators, Siebert and Draper's (2008) content analysis of documents and texts commonly used in literacy education courses indicated that literacy methods identified as content area reading strategies are often contrary to the literacy practices of the discipline of mathematics. Their analysis "suggest[ed] that many literacy messages fail to resonate with mathematics educators because they neglect, deemphasize, or misrepresent the nature and content of the discipline of mathematics" (Siebert & Draper, 2008, p. 231). According to the authors, should content-area literacy instruction be a goal for teacher educators, and, ultimately for classroom teachers, literacy researchers should expand their definitions of text, reading, and writing, in order to more fully account for the ways of knowing in the disciplinary fields. They also suggested that literacy researchers work to become more familiar with the expectations and practices of the discipline, rather than prescribing generalized methods for literacy instruction. This is a suggestion with which we fully concur. Acknowledging differing expectations for literacy across fields, however, should not imply that there are no commonalities in relation to literacy across fields or disciplines, but research designed to identify those differences, as well as common practice, is necessary.

The exploratory study described in the following sections was designed to establish a foundation for future research about the disciplinary literacy practices in the field of mathematics. The purpose was to examine the instructional practices already in place in an undergraduate mathematics course designed to increase quantitative literacy for non-math majors. Using a disciplinary-literacy lens, our goal was to discover: (1) what types of instructional practices related to literacy were present, and (2) if present, could the literacy practices used be linked to students' increased quantitative literacy?

LITERACY METHODS IN MATHEMATICS INSTRUCTION

In recent years, the National Council of Teachers of Mathematics (NCTM) has called for a greater emphasis on instructional methods that support *reasoning* and *sensemaking* (NCTM, 2009), which aligns with many of the instructional practices supported by an educational focus on disciplinary literacy. Although some mathematics teacher-educators have promoted the use of literacy strategies specifically calibrated for use in mathematics classrooms (Kenney, Hancewicz, Heuer, Metsisto, & Tuttle, 2005), Siebert and Draper (2008) have noted that mathematics teachers tend to resist adopting literacy strategies because they are often presented in ways that seem unrelated or contrary to mathematical ways of knowing – especially when presented in content-area literacy coursework. Even when specific literacy strategies are observed in mathematics courses, research supporting a connection between the use of those strategies and the development of quantitative literacy is rare. Generally, such support is implied through studies focusing on other aspects of the use of literacy strategies, including performance of mathematical tasks, rather than as the result of a dedicated investigation of the use of the strategies to promote students' ability to adopt mathematical "habits of mind"(Wilkins, 2010).

For example, Friedland, McMillan, and del Prado Hill (2010-11) studied middle school teachers' use of literacy strategies, but no analysis of the impact of the methods on student learning or quantitative literacy was provided. Pape, Bell, and Yetkin (2003) suggested the use of metacognitive strategies in mathematics courses would aid student performance on mathematical tasks; however, the impact on students' overall quantitative literacy was not discussed. Similarly, teachers' attendance to meaning-making in algebra classes has been studied (Harel, Fuller, & Rabin, 2008), but the overall focus was on aspects of the teacher's mathematical explanations that might affect students' non-attendance to meaning in mathematical learning, and not directly on student learning.

THE QUANTITATIVE LITERACY MODEL

Grounded in the work of the literacy theorists presented in the previous section, the exploratory study described here used Wilkins' (2010) Quantitative Literacy (QL) Model as the basis for assessing the use of literacy instruction in a mathematics course designed to bolster students' quantitative literacy. The model was developed through data derived from the Second International Mathematics Study (SIMS) Student Background Questionnaire (Westbury, 1991) and is comprised of three components: students' beliefs about mathematics, their mathematics cognition, and their mathematical dispositions (Wilkins, 2010). The intent of this study was to examine only student beliefs and dispositions about mathematics and to identify classroom events and practices consistent with disciplinary literacy instruction. Our intent was not to examine mathematical achievement or knowledge (eg., students' ability to solve problems or perform procedures), and we acknowledge that this research can make no claims about the relationship between literacy instruction and this very important domain. As a result, we leave questions about implications for mathematical reasoning and skill for future studies.

METHODS AND DATA COLLECTION

The study was conducted by two researchers, one with a background in mathematics, and the other with a background in literacy, over the course of an academic year at a regional campus of a large mid-western university system. A pre/post quantitative literacy survey based on the original SIMS survey (Westbury, 1991; Wilkins, 2010), was administered to all students in nine sections of a 100-level mathematics course designed for non-math majors (see Appendix A). The course, titled *Mathematics in the World*, was designed to convey the essence of mathematical applications across mathematical disciplines in real-world contexts. Pre- and post-survey data from a total of 103 students were analyzed. In addition, three separate sections of the course were observed twice, once by each researcher focusing on observations relating to her area of knowledge (literacy or mathematics). Following preliminary analysis of the data, invitations were sent to participant volunteers whose pre/post survey data showed positive or negative movement in relation to quantitative literacy. Questions from the semi-structured interviews were loosely based on the Burke Interview Modified for Older Readers (BIMOR; Goodman, Watson, & Burke, 2005). Four students agreed to participate in the interviews, which lasted approximately 45 minutes each. The interviews contained general questions for all participants and additional questions relating to their specific responses on the survey. (See Appendix B for the protocol and sample questions.) Quantitative data were analyzed in aggregate using McNemar's Test for Correlated Proportions for movement toward or away from QL over the course of the semester. Observational and interview data were coded for classroom events, literacy practices, and QL episodes, based on Spradley's (1980) methods for thematic analysis.

Quantitative Analysis

In order to use survey data to determine movement toward or away from QL, we first independently examined the survey statements to categorize each as positive or negative in relation to QL. Following a discussion of our individual categorizations for norming purposes, we then sent a brief query to the mathematics faculty at our university for their input on statements for which we disagreed. Based on our analysis we determined that four of the questions (18, 24, 26, and 30) were worded in a way that could not easily be interpreted as either positive or negative; thus, we did not include data from these questions in our findings.

After the surveys were administered, data were examined only from students who participated in both the pre- and post-assessments. Analysis looked for movement toward or away from QL over the course of the semester during which the students were enrolled in the mathematics course. For example, Statement 2 "I think mathematics is fun" was categorized as a positive statement, thus responses of agree or strongly agree on the survey were interpreted as positive in relation to QL. Statements of disagree or strongly disagree were interpreted as negative in relation to QL. Alternatively, Statement 5 "If I had my choice, I would not learn any more mathematics" was determined to be a negative statement, and responses of disagree or strongly disagree were interpreted as positive evidence in relation to the Dispositions/ Motivation domain of the QL model, while agree or strongly agree would have indicated negative QL. As a result of the analysis significant $(p=.05)$ movement was seen in a positive direction on some survey questions in the Motivation area of the Mathematical Dispositions Domain. Movement toward or away from QL in the Beliefs Domain did not appear to be significant.

Table 1: Analysis of Pre-/Post-Survey Data

Question	Significance of change between 1st & 2nd Administrations
Q.2: I think mathematics is fun.	Agreement rose significantly (p-value = .008); Disagreement fell significantly (p-value = .0262)
Q.5: If I had my choice, I would not learn any more mathematics.	Disagreement rose significantly (p-value = .0353)
Q.6: I refuse to spend a lot of my own time doing mathematics.	Disagreement rose significantly (p-value = .0447)
Q.11: I would like to work at a job that lets me use mathematics.	Agreement rose significantly (p-value = .015)
Q.15: I could never be a good mathematician.	Agreement fell significantly (p-value = .010); Disagreement rose significantly (p-value = .0004)
Q.19: Mathematics is useful in solving everyday problems.	Agreement rose significantly (p-value = .021); Disagreement fell significantly (p-value = .0245)

As is shown in Table 1, movement toward QL was statistically significant only on questions 2, 5, 6, 11, 15, and 19. In this case positive movement was determined when agreement with a positive statement rose between survey administrations, and/or disagreement decreased; conversely, for statements identified as negative, movement toward QL was determined if agreement with the statement decreased and/or disagreement increased between administrations.

Additionally, the aggregate movement toward QL that was statistically significant in the questions analyzed was not consistent across individual students. In other words, a student showing movement toward QL in the area of dispositions toward mathematics may have shown no movement or movement away from QL in one or more of the other facets of the model.

Qualitative Analysis

Analysis of the observational data indicates that some constructivist literacy strategies, including metacognitive practices, questioning, teacher modeling, and think-aloud, were present in the classes, but most interactions were limited to traditional lecture or question-and-answer recitation (Nystrand, Wu, Gamoran, Zeiser, & Long, 2003). During interviews, students indicated a preference for "step-by-step" instruction that, upon further analysis of the classroom observational data, seemed to coincide with teacher modeling and think-aloud (TA). TA episodes were subsequently analyzed based on Boaler and Greeno's (2000) learner stance and Ciardiello's (1998) question levels.

The Observations. Data from the observations and field notes were coded thematically, following Spradley's (1980) model. Initially, events were coded based on classroom instructional events, including specific literacy practices observed. For example, the following excerpt from observation of Mr. Blane's class (all names are pseudonyms) was coded as an example of *guided practice*. During the event, Mr. Blane demonstrated the process for graphing linear equations, presenting the steps using a transparent overhead that contained graphing lines.

Mr. Blane: If x and y were both 0, would this be true?" [Indicates shaded area]

Student: Yeah

Mr. Blane: All of that would be shaded in and that would be the graph of the linear equality. [Explains that shading indicates all of the parts where $2x+y < 20$] (Observation 1, November 21, 2011)

Coded data were then examined for instructional practices that were seen across all four classrooms and in observations by both researchers. Literacy practices that were observed included references to metacognition or how students know what they know, or in some cases do not know; explicit vocabulary instruction; the use of questioning strategies; and teacher modeling through thinking aloud.

The Interviews. Interviews from each student were also transcribed and coded, specifically looking for evidence of or references to QL, based on Wilkins' (2010) model. For example, the following excerpt from Taylor, a sophomore majoring in education, was coded under *mathematical dispositions/attitudes toward math and self*.

Taylor: I love math

HSD: And what do you enjoy about it?

Taylor: I love that it is black and white, typically. Um, there's always an, there's always an answer, you know, and there might be 7,000 different ways to get to that answer, but, typically, it's black and white. You know, it's not like with English where "well, in my opinion" you know. It's very logical and I like that. And that it's universal, that's a big thing too. You know, it's pretty much the same everywhere in the world that you go, you know, dependent; it's not dependent on language or anything like that. I really like it. (Interview, March 27, 2012)

During coding of the interview data, a theme that emerged was the students' preference for what they identified as "step-by-step" instruction. In fact all four of the students participating in the interviews used the exact phrase "step-by-step" spontaneously during the discussions. Upon further examination of the data, it became possible to note fine distinctions between how the students understood or interpreted "step-by-step." For example in Table 2 we display statements made by Taylor, Kim, and Ronnie, each discussing "step-by-step" as a method for solving mathematical problems that provided consistency and security. Provided one follows the appropriate steps, one will end with the correct result.

In another instance Ronnie again used the term "step-by-step" however the meaning of the phrase changed this time to indicate an effective method of instruction used by teachers to explicitly guide students through mathematical tasks.

Table 2: Sample Participant Interview Responses Indicating Preference for Step-by-Step Problem Solving

Participant	Interview Statement
Taylor	If you can, if you can analyze something, a formula, then you can pick out directions and then you can follow it step, by step, by step, by step. And it helps you feel like you have kind of a guide of getting through the mathematical equation as opposed to just looking at it and trying to have a bunch of guesswork. Which I feel like a lot of the other disciplines you end up doing is a lot of guesswork because there is no foundation set down. With math, for the most part, unless you're going to get into the discovery of dark matter and all that kind of stuff, there's pretty much, you know, there's foundation already laid for you.
Kim	I have to go step-by-step [to solve a math problem]. . . I follow, like, [a] certain path to get there. . .I'm good at math because, like, I like to follow directions, and that's what math is to me. You know, you have to follow this, like, certain steps. You can't just do it however you want, 'cause then [you're] not going to get the right answer . . .[In math] you have to follow rules. Like, you have to follow the steps to find the answer.
Ronnie	In order to solve a problem correctly there are certain steps you gotta take. You have to do everything in a certain order. It's usually always do things in the right order to get the right answers.

Ronnie: I like being taught, step-by-step. I know that's. . .the way everybody does it, but some teachers do it more than others. (Laughs). (Interview, April 4, 2012)

Similarly, Chris, referred to the importance of "step-by-step" in relation to instruction.

Chris: I like it when the math teacher goes step-by-step to make sure that everybody's on the same page . . . Just working through the problem with you helps, and then giving you homework to work on your own to make sure you get the concept . . . I would ask [the instructor] how to do [a difficult problem], and, when he'd go step-by-step, he didn't just write the answer, he would ask, like me or someone else in the class, if they could figure out what the answer was for each step. (Interview, April 9, 2012)

Following preliminary analysis of the interviews, noting the students' references to step-by-step in both problem solving and instruction, we re-examined the observational data for events during which processes seemed to be taught in a step-by-step fashion. Commonly throughout the observational data, we saw this through teacher *think alouds*.

Thinking Aloud. *Thinking Aloud* is an instructional process supported by literacy researchers as a method that allows teachers to explicitly demonstrate ways of knowing and thinking within their academic disciplines (Zwiers, 2008). The technique involves the verbalization of the thoughts and processes that are typical of the teachers' internal processing of discipline-related material in a way that allows students to observe the methods of thinking and knowing within a particular field.

During our site visits we noted that instructors in each of the three classes we observed often talked through the methods for solving mathematical tasks in a manner similar to Thinking Aloud. Often these visual and verbal demonstrations highlighted procedures which generally, though not always, included specific steps.

Table 3: Field Note Excerpt: Mr. Blane, Teacher Think Aloud

Speaker	Notes
Mr. Blane	Remember, we spent some time [previously] graphing linear equations. [Reminds students of the steps for graphing linear equations.]This time, it's just a little bit more difficult. I'm going to do [a] problem on the board and really break it down" [Writes an inequality on board] How do you say that symbol? [Symbol is $\geq$]
Students	Greater than or equal to [Multiple Responses]
Mr. Blane	First I'm going to look at the equal part . . .We know that. . .if x is 0, y would be 20. [Writes where 20 would be on the y axis of the grid.] If x is 0, y would be?
Student	10
Mr. Blane	10. Then we would connect [20 and 10] with a line [on the grid] [Draws connection between two points]

For example in the excerpt from the field notes displayed in Table 3, Mr. Blane shows the students how to graph a linear inequality. During this instructional event, the instructor uses what appears to be a Think Aloud process to walk students through the process for graphing a linear equation in a step-by-step manner reflective of the descriptions made by the interview participants; thus, this event was coded as a Think-Aloud.

In a second example, displayed in Table 4, Mr. Giles shows the students how to use an algorithm to schedule multiple concurrent events. During this event Mr. Giles also provides step-by-step instruction for completing the mathematical task, but this variation includes examples of mistakes and misdirection during the process. Students participating in the exchange supply responses (both correct and incorrect) when directed to do so, but also volunteer questions as they arise, indicating participation in construction of their own knowledge for completion of the task.

Question Levels. Analysis of the classroom episodes coded as Think Aloud and the variations among those episodes, as indicated in Tables 3 and 4, led us to consider both levels and quality of student participation during the Think Aloud events. In the example from Mr. Blane, though seemingly engaged in the demonstration based on the responses supplied by some of the students, the interaction is reflective of recitation (Nystrand et al., 2003), in which the teacher is the authority and the students are asked to provide responses to questions for which there is an expected answer. In the example from Mr. Giles, however, students initiated questions and attempted to provide

Table 4: Field Note Excerpt: Mr. Giles, Teacher Think Aloud

Speaker	Notes
Mr. Giles	[Responds to student question about a homework problem by noting that the language in the textbook is confusing. Explains the problem in his own words]. Apply this processing algorithm . . . which basically means [explains meaning of the word algorithm, draws diagram on board; uses ELMO to show diagram from book. Writes on board. Uses fingers to trace "Critical Path" in problem. Task is to create a list of tasks in order, to be completed in the shortest amount of time using an algorithm.] There's a lot of ways to do this. . . just make it neat so that you can understand or keep track of what you're doing. [Thinks aloud as he is working through the problem. Uses statements like "I'll tell you the biggest trouble I have" "This is where I have trouble sometimes. . . I do this,. . .then I have to do this" Shows process of elimination to determine which steps to take next.] "Whoops! This can happen sometimes" [Indicating consequence of an incorrect selection of paths. Demonstrates trying another approach.] What does this task tell me? . . Can I do this? That's what I want to do. Yes, I can . . .[Asks class] "Who's gonna get it?" [Which processer will be assigned to the next task on the chart?]
Student X	Processor 1 [Incorrect]
Mr. Giles	Task 3? [A different student supplies the correct response]. What happens to this guy? [Indicates a different processor on the chart]
Student X	Idle [Meaning that that processor has no task during that period of time]
Mr. Giles	Yes
Student X	Idle time, is that where you say you mess up?
Mr. Giles	Yes. [Explains how mistakes can be made, and provides example.] The key to doing well [with this mathematical task] is taking your time.

responses, even if they were not sure they were correct. Some of these questions also demonstrated curiosity about approaches to mathematical tasks by mathematics experts, or the ways of knowing in the field. As a result, we determined more analysis was needed to explain the variations in student-teacher interaction during the Think Aloud events.

Drawing from Ciardiello's (1998) levels of questions, the observations were again re-visited, this time with coding questions asked by both instructors and students during Think Aloud episodes. The question levels used were *memory*, based on basic recall of content-based information; *convergent*, questions that required students to use mathematical knowledge to construct responses;

divergent, questions that required students to use their knowledge of mathematics content, structures, and ways of thinking to predict or infer; and *evaluating,* questions that required students to use their mathematical knowledge to judge, defend, or evaluate.

For example, during the session on critical path scheduling shown in Table 4, Mr. Giles asked students to indicate which processor should receive the next task according to the algorithm used. The event was coded as a *convergent question* as students were required to demonstrate mathematical understanding through their responses.

Mr. Giles: I didn't hear the right number yet. [Two separate students provide incorrect answers]. Two shots and 0 for 2. Who do I give it to? (Observation 2, November 17, 2011)

In a separate example, also from Mr. Giles' critical path scheduling lesson, the instructor himself models asking and responding to *evaluating* questions commensurate with expectations from the field:

Mr. Giles: [Continues explanation of Number 11. Thinks aloud. Asks himself about the consequences of his choices.] Will this [option] work? No. This one? No. . .I finally get to this one [Processor Number 4, and that one is correct]. Use your head here. I did not use mine. [Points out an error he made during his example, using the diagram on board] (Observation 2, November 17, 2011)

FINDINGS AND DISCUSSION

The student preference for "step-by-step" methods in mathematical teaching and learning contexts that emerged during interviews, and the variations we noted in the classroom events coded as Think Alouds, seemed reflective of the four types of *learner stance* defined by Boaler and Greeno (2000). For our study, we interpreted these types of knowledge in the following ways: *Received knowing* views knowledge as something to be provided by an external authority, typically the teacher, believing that the responsibility for evaluating one's current knowledge and for creating new knowledge lies mainly with the teacher rather than the student. *Separate knowing* sees the aim of learning as primarily to align one's content knowledge to the parameters set by the discipline. Separate knowers are cognizant of the rules of the discipline and seek to refine their knowledge to meet disciplinary standards. *Connected knowing* views learning as being constructed socially through texts, conversations, and other representations of disciplinary content. Connected knowers seek others' perspectives on the content in order to enrich their understandings, and they attempt to reconcile those perspectives with their own. Finally, *constructed knowing* combines both separate and connected knowing in constructing, refining, and validating the learner's own knowledge.

The goal to improve instruction for quantitative literacy, which includes students' beliefs about and dispositions toward math (Wilkins, 2010), seems consonant with moving learners toward more empowered stances. The participants' preference for step-by-step instruction in mathematics classes, as well as their references to the step-by-step nature of mathematics initially seemed to connect to *received knowledge,* but evidence from Think Alouds similar to and including the Mr. Giles' excerpts in the previous sections, seems to indicate that this method may provide a tool for more fully apprenticing students into the ways of thinking and knowing in mathematics, especially when particular attention is paid to *convergent, divergent,* and *evaluating* questions (Ciardiello, 1998) during the exchange. Furthermore, because variations of Thinking Aloud may already be common in mathematics instruction and because Thinking Aloud is supported by disciplinary literacy researchers, this instructional technique may provide a link between mathematics and literacy instruction that can be further explored for the development of students' quantitative literacy.

WHAT TYPES OF INSTRUCTIONAL PRACTICES RELATED TO LITERACY WERE PRESENT?

Through analysis of the observations and interviews, we found evidence of the following strategies consistent with methods discussed in content-area literacy and disciplinary literacy coursework: metacognition and self-regulation of learning, vocabulary acquisition, classroom discussion, the use of questioning strategies, and teacher think-alouds. Metacognition was especially prevalent during student interviews when students shared how they independently recognized or navigated difficult or confusing material, often taking a step-by-step approach for solving. During classroom observations, metacognitive efforts were noted most often when students asked instructors clarifying questions about material presented in class or in class-based texts. Vocabulary was explicitly taught by instructors as they introduced new terms during think aloud demonstrations. Classroom discussion, though present, most often occurred between students just before class regarding homework or impending test material. Some classroom discussion occurred during teacher think alouds/demonstration, but the amount of participation by students tended to correspond with the levels and types of questions asked by the instructor and their peers. Finally, the most prevalent of all of the literacy activities observed was modeling through teacher Think Aloud.

Could the Literacy Practices Identified be Linked to Students' Increased Quantitative Literacy?

As the study was not developed to determine causality, this research question remains unanswered; however, based on the quantitative literacy (QL) survey administered at the beginning and end of the semester, it does appear that some students enrolled in the course did show improved QL in the dispositions domain, meaning that, in aggregate, the students ended the semester with more positive feelings toward mathematics than when they began. There are a variety of factors that may have contributed to this, including the real-world content of the course, the specific group of students who were enrolled during the semester when the study was conducted, or the instructional methods used, and further research with larger sets of participants over several semesters would be necessary to confirm these findings.

IMPLICATIONS AND FUTURE DIRECTIONS

An important point brought up by some educational researchers, especially with regard to literacy instruction in mathematics, is that often instructional recommendations for literacy appear to be divided from the ways of thinking and knowing in the discipline (Siebert & Draper, 2008). Research in disciplinary literacy supports disconnection as the emerging literature has begun to focus on specific differences between the ways that experts in disciplinary fields participate in and interact with various types of texts prevalent within their academic contexts (Shanahan, Shanahan,

& Misischia, 2011). The purpose of this exploratory study was to examine students' movement in relation to the mathematical beliefs and dispositions domains of quantitative literacy as they were enrolled in an undergraduate mathematics course for non-math majors and to observe instructional practices and student preferences for instruction within that context in order to better understand where literacy methods and mathematics content instruction converge. Based on the findings from this study, we believe that it may be possible to build on what is already present in mathematics instruction to create more opportunities for QL development within the context of the curriculum. Further investigation of the strategies already in place in mathematics classrooms and connections to students' development of quantitative literacy, especially in relation to the opportunities provided through teacher Think Alouds, is necessary. We also believe that it may be beneficial to work specifically with pre-service mathematics teachers to increase their awareness of QL and to expose them to different types of Think Aloud structures, formats, and levels of questions during their literacy-based coursework, for use in their future classrooms.

LIMITATIONS

This study was conducted on a single campus, with a relatively small number of student and faculty participants. As such, the data and findings are not generalizable to any larger contexts. Furthermore, during the interview portion of data collection, we became aware that the survey instrument, initially designed for secondary-level, and not university-level students, did not sufficiently account for the experiences and dispositions of older learners. The tool provided a useful starting place for our investigation of QL, but modification to address the needs and interests of adult learners for future research may prove beneficial. Finally, only two domains of Wilkin's (2010) model (mathematical beliefs and dispositions) were addressed in this study. The third domain, mathematical knowledge, was not studied. Conclusions about a connection between the data from this study and student mathematical performance or achievement are not possible.

REFERENCES

Boaler, J., & Greeno, J. G. (2000). Identity, agency, and knowing in mathematics worlds. In J. Boaler (Ed.), *Multiple perspectives on mathematics teaching and learning* (pp. 171-200). Westport, CT: Ablex Publishing.

Ciardiello, A. V. (1998). Did you ask a good question today? Alternative cognitive and metacognitive strategies. *Journal of Adolescent & Adult Literacy*, 42, 210-219.

Friedland, E. S., McMillen, S. E., & del Prado Hill, P. (2010-11, Fall/Winter). Moving beyond the word wall: How middle school mathematics teachers use literacy strategies. *NCSM Journal*.

Goodman, Y. M., Watson, D. J., & Burke, C. L. (2005). *Reading miscue inventory: From evaluation to instruction* (2nd ed.). Katonah, NY: Richard C. Owen Publishers.

Harel, G., Fuller, E., & Rabin, J. M. (2008). Attention to meaning by algebra teachers. *The Journal of Mathematical Behavior*, 27, 116-127.

Kenney, J. M., Hancewicz, E., Heuer, L., Metsisto, D., & Tuttle, C. L. (2005). *Literacy strategies for improving mathematics instruction*. Alexandria, VA: Association for Supervision and Curriculum Development.

Lave, J., & Wenger, E. (1998). *Situated learning: Legitimate peripheral participation*. New York, NY: Cambridge University.

Lee, C. D., & Spratley, A. (2010). Reading in the disciplines: The challenges of adolescent literacy. *Final Report from Carnegie Corporation of New York's Council on Advancing Adolescent Literacy*. Retrieved from: http://carnegie.org/fileadmin/Media/Publications/PDF/tta_Lee.pdf

National Council of Teachers of Mathematics. (2009). *Focus in high school mathematics: Reasoning and sensemaking* (Executive summary). Retrieved from: http://www.nctm.org/uploadedFiles/Math_Standards/FHSM_Executive_Summay.pdf

Nystrand, M., Wu, L. L., Gamoran, A., Zeiser, S., & Long, D.A. (2003). Questions in time: Investigating the structure and dynamics of unfolding classroom discourse. *Discourse Processes, 35*, 135-198.

Pape, S. J., Bell, C. V., & Yetkin, I. E. (2003). Developing mathematical thinking and self- regulated learning: A teaching experiment in a seventh-grade mathematics classroom. *Educational Studies in Mathematics, 53*, 179-202.

Rosenblatt, L. M. (1994). The transactional theory of reading and writing. In R.B. Ruddell, M.H. Ruddell, & H. Singer (Eds.), *Theoretical models and processes of reading* (4th ed., pp. 1057-1092). Newark, DE: International Reading Association.

Siebert, D., & Draper, R. J. (2008). Why content-area literacy messages do not speak to mathematics teachers: A critical content analysis. *Literacy Research and Instruction, 47*, 229-245. doi: 10.1080/19388070802300314

Shanahan, C., Shanahan, T., & Misischia, C. (2011). Analysis of expert readers in three disciplines: History, mathematics, and chemistry. *Journal of Literacy Research, 43*, 393-429. doi: 10.1177/1086296X11424071

Shanahan, T., & Shanahan, C. (2010). Teaching disciplinary literacy to adolescents: Rethinking content-area literacy. *Harvard Educational Review, 78*, 40-59.

Spradley, J. P. (1980). *Participant observation*. Toronto, ON: Thompson Learning, Inc. Westbury, I., & Thalathoti, V. V. (1989). *United States: Population B*. Urbana, IL: Board of Trustees of the University of Illinois.

Westbury, I. (1991). *IEA Second International Mathematics Study: Population B Data Sets*. Urbana, IL: University of Illinois at Urbana-Champaign.

Wilkins, J. L. (2010). Modeling quantitative literacy. *Educational and Psychological Measurement, 70*, 267-290. doi: 10.1177/0013164409344506

Zwiers, J. (2008). *Building academic language: Essential practices for content classrooms*. San Francisco, CA: Jossey-Bass.

Appendix A: Quantitative Literacy Survey (based on Wilkins, 2010 and Westbury, 1991)

SA: Strongly Agree; A: Agree; N: Neutral; D:Disagree; SD: Strongly Disagree

1	Working with numbers makes me happy.	SA	A	N	D	SD
2	I think mathematics is fun.	SA	A	N	D	SD
3	I am looking forward to taking more mathematics classes.	SA	A	N	D	SD
4	I like to help others with mathematics problems.	SA	A	N	D	SD
5	If I had my choice, I would not learn any more mathematics.	SA	A	N	D	SD
6	I refuse to spend a lot of my own time doing mathematics.	SA	A	N	D	SD
7	I will work a long time in order to understand a new idea in mathematics.	SA	A	N	D	SD
8	I really want to do well in mathematics.	SA	A	N	D	SD
9	I feel good when I solve a mathematics problem by myself.	SA	A	N	D	SD
10	I feel challenged when I am given a difficult mathematics problem to solve.	SA	A	N	D	SD
11	I would like to work at a job that lets me use mathematics.	SA	A	N	D	SD
12	I usually understand what we are talking about in mathematics class.	SA	A	N	D	SD
13	I am not very good at mathematics.	SA	A	N	D	SD
14	Mathematics is harder for me than for most people.	SA	A	N	D	SD
15	I could never be a good mathematician.	SA	A	N	D	SD
16	No matter how hard I try, I still do not do well in mathematics.	SA	A	N	D	SD
17	It is important to know mathematics to get a good job.	SA	A	N	D	SD
18	Most people do not use mathematics in their jobs.	SA	A	N	D	SD
19	Mathematics is useful in solving everyday problems.	SA	A	N	D	SD
20	I can get along well in everyday life without using mathematics.	SA	A	N	D	SD
21	Most applications of mathematics have practical use on the job.	SA	A	N	D	SD
22	Mathematics is not needed in everyday living.	SA	A	N	D	SD
23	A knowledge of mathematics is not necessary in most occupations.	SA	A	N	D	SD
24	Mathematics helps one think according to strict rules.	SA	A	N	D	SD
25	Learning mathematics involves mostly memorization.	SA	A	N	D	SD
26	There is always a rule to follow in solving a mathematics problem.	SA	A	N	D	SD
27	Mathematics is a set of rules.	SA	A	N	D	SD
28	There is little place for originality in solving mathematics problems.	SA	A	N	D	SD
29	There are many different ways to solve most mathematic problems.	SA	A	N	D	SD
30	A mathematics problem can always be solved in different ways.	SA	A	N	D	SD
31	Mathematics will change rapidly in the future.	SA	A	N	D	SD
32	New discoveries in mathematics are constantly being made.	SA	A	N	D	SD
33	There have probably not been any new discoveries in mathematics for a long time.	SA	A	N	D	SD

Appendix B: Semi-Structured Interview Protocol

Questions asked of all participants:

1. What was the purpose of this math course?
2. Do you believe this class was necessary for your education?

    a. How do you see yourself using mathematics in your future?
3. What concepts in the class interested you most, and why?
4. Describe the most effective math teacher you've ever had, and explain why this teacher was effective.
5. What do you do when you don't "get" a mathematical task?
6. What does it take to be good at math?
7. Who is a person that you know who is good at mathematics?

    i. What makes _____ good at mathematics?

    ii. Do you think _____ ever comes to something that gives him/her trouble when he/she is working on math?

    iii. When _____does come to something that gives him/her trouble, what do you think he/she does about it?
8. How would you help someone who was having difficulty with mathematics?

    a. What would a teacher do to help that person?
9. Do you enjoy mathematics?

    a. If yes - what do you enjoy about it?

    b. If no - what do you not enjoy about it?

    c. Can you give an example of when this type of thinking might be beneficial outside of mathematics?

Sample questions for individual participants, based on individual survey responses:

1. At the beginning of the semester you said you neither agreed nor disagreed with the statement "There is little place for originality in solving mathematics problems," but at the end, you said you strongly disagreed. Can you please explain how you see originality in approaches for solving mathematics problems?
2. We noticed that you agreed with the statement "Mathematics helps one think according to strict rules" on the written survey.

    a. What does that statement mean to you?
3. We noticed that your opinion on the statements "I will work a long time in order to understand a new idea in mathematics" and "I really want to do well in mathematics" both moved from Agree/Strongly Agree at the beginning of the semester to disagree at the end of the semester. Can you tell me a little about this change?

"That is dope no lie": Supporting Adolescent Literacy Practices Through Digital Partnerships

Antero Garcia
Illinois State University

Robyn Seglem
Colorado State University

Luke: how are you going to make your introduction for your paper, are you going to give your arguments right away?

Camila: yeah i think so cuz it says in the first paragraph i should state my three claims

Luke: it sounds like you know how you want to write it then, if you have your claims it should be pretty easy to start.

Camila: yepp i guess so, im gonna start it later though cuz i need to finish the essay outline paper

After two months of conversation, Luke, a preservice teacher, has assumed the role of mentor for Camila, a high school sophomore. During this time, he has learned to balance informal language practices with the language of school, enabling Luke to develop an appreciation of Camila's informal language use while guiding her through academic endeavors such as the persuasive writing process. Despite the hundreds of miles separating Luke, who lives in central Illinois, and Camila, a resident of Los Angeles, the pair spent an hour a week throughout the fall of 2011 sharing their expertise with each other through the online forum TodaysMeet.com. For Luke, this was a time to learn about the culture and language of students with very different experiences from his own, as well as a time to gain insights into how youth perceive teachers and teaching practices. For Camila, this experience provided her with more individualized instruction where she could practice using the academic terms taught to her by her English teacher and discuss readings assigned in class. And Luke and Camila were not alone in their experiences. Around them, similar conversations occurred every Monday, building a community in both the university and high school classrooms that impacted learning beyond that one hour each week.

With technology ushering in new learning challenges for the first "always-connected generation" (Lenhart, 2009), teachers grapple with the digital world's role in the classroom. Should there be a paradigm shift in the educational system that reflects the changing literacy demands required by technology? Though the New London Group (1996) described the changing nature of literacy more than 15 years ago, researchers and educators still struggle to account for the ways that texts are produced, consumed, and understood across physical and virtual boundaries and forms. Clearly, the digital dimension created by new technologies possesses attributes that physical classrooms do not (Alvermann, 2008; Lewis & Fabos, 2005). Evidence shows youth have embraced this dimension, defying the limitations imposed by physical space and reaching out to each other to share their lives, talents, and ideas (Alvermann, 2008; Kirkland, 2009; Knobel & Lankshear, 2007).

Thus, students find themselves participating in multiliteracies, composing written texts, creating videos, and inferring meaning from written language and visual images.

Despite burgeoning research around the role of multiliteracies, educators are identifying challenges toward implementation. Limited teacher skill and belief in their students' abilities yield consistently, "unstimulating, rote-oriented teaching" (Darling-Hammond, 2010). Conversely, tech-savvy teachers can be lured by the social appeal digital tools hold for youth, creating classroom experiences that embrace the social nature of digital technologies without a firm educational purpose for its use (O'Brien & Scharber, 2008). Neither extreme adequately prepares students for a world that has been "flattened" by mobile media, social networking, and virtual environments (Friedman, 2005). Interrelated changes in society, media, and education mean that new modes of shared learning spaces for teachers and students to work collaboratively and equitably are no longer novel; they are a necessity in the context of 21st century education reform if schools are to meet new global demands.

This study was designed to examine what happens when the two communities most inculcated in the United States' "educational debt" (Ladson-Billings, 2006) share learning experiences focused around multiliteracies that expand notions of text to include a "multiplicity of discourses" (New London Group, 1996); it places middle class preservice teachers in a shared virtual space with urban high school youth. Although the larger study explored the growth of both the preservice teachers and high school students involved in the study, the emphasis of this article rests on the experiences of the urban youth. We examine how in-class collaboration using digital tools such as chatrooms and video conferencing introduced multiple texts and literacies into the students' English classroom, and how the resulting relationships influenced their academic experiences through new media literacy practice. Our findings demonstrate how the urban youth accepted opportunities to practice and hone language practices while sharing their own expertise pertaining to youth culture, practices, and dispositions toward formal school learning.

THIRD SPACE AND THE CONTEXT OF LEARNING

An influx of digital tools has resulted in an increase in multiliteracies practices, as creators and consumers of text experiment with the impact of combining audio, video, images, and printed words in new ways. Thus, as we began our study, we were interested in how youth multiliteracies practices outside of school could impact in-school literacy practices and learning. During the course of the study, it struck us that the influx of technology has also pushed the notion of space. Space became increasingly important as we began to consider the experiences of the urban youth in our study. There was an obvious difference in spaces when we looked at the surface of our study. The two groups involved came from very different spaces both geographically and culturally. It was the virtual, online spaces we created, however, that made it possible for high school students and preservice teachers in different time zones to collaborate. As we began examining the relationships developed via these online spaces, we became increasingly convinced that this virtual space resulted in relationships between the high school students and preservice teachers that looked very different than they would have if conducted in a shared physical space. To help us explore this concept, we tapped into what a growing body of research names the third space (Gutierrez, 2004; Moje, 2004; Soja, 2006).

While the definition of this space shifts as technologies advance and our understanding of how participants use the third space deepens, third space is generally accepted as a place where formal and informal learning environments intersect, providing students and teachers with a space to explore learning in a more authentic way (Gutiérrez et al., 1995). As Gutiérrez (2008) has more recently stated, "it is a transformative space where the potential for an expanded form of learning and the development of new knowledge are heightened" (p. 152). Through the third space, teachers can tap into the funds of knowledge (Moll, Veléz-Ibañéz, & Greenberg, 1989) students acquire through their experiences with their families, peer groups, and other important relationships. Gutiérrez (2008) argues that we can see within third spaces a movement from everyday knowledge to academic concepts, tapping into Vygotsky's (1978) Zones of Proximal Development.

Much of the value of this project stems from our intent to create a "productive hybrid cultural space" (Moje et al., 2004, p. 43). By bringing together two very different populations, we hoped to help both groups of learners "see connections, as well as contradictions, between the ways they know the world and the ways others know the world" (Moje et al., 2004, p. 44). Both groups, urban youth and future teachers, face educational challenges imposed upon them by others in power. They are often told how to learn and how to teach, creating environments that do not cater to effective learning. Third spaces have the potential to reallocate the power relationships in the classroom by giving students and teachers a voice in teaching and learning (Benson, 2010). As argued by Castek, Coiro, Guzniczak, & Bradshaw (2012), "Teaching students creative problem-solving, collaboration, and fluency with technology is not only difficult, but it also represents a significant shift for most classroom teachers who are tentative about using technology to support and extend learning." This research utilizes technology in ways that support not only classroom learning but youth interest. Though digital tools cannot replace actual content, the fact that youth are engaged in online discussions and communication help reflect existing trends in youth attitudes toward technology. For example, Coiro (2012) looked at the ways young people perceive the Internet as creating more interesting learning opportunities and claims that educators can "support personal reading dispositions" online (p. 647). Further, recent research suggests that online mentoring can lead to significant academic gains (Liu, Macintyre, & Ferguson, 2012; Sinclair, 2003). However, while the online space developed for this study also offers powerful academic opportunities, our research focused less on academic gains as measured by tests and more on student attitudes toward language, and their relationship with adults.

Gutiérrez, Baquedano-López, Alvarez, and Chiu (1999) help make clear the *purpose* of online engagement in a third space. Instead of merely talking with and gaining mentorship from adults who are further away, the blurred space allowed the youth to better understand the classroom content and cultural knowledge of the surrounding world. Further, building off Gee's (1996) discussion of big "D" discourses, Moje et al. (2004) note that, "teachers and students bring different instructional, home, and community knowledge bases and Discourses to bear on classroom texts. The potential for competing Discourses and knowledges is especially high in classrooms where students come from backgrounds and experiences different from those of their peers or their teachers" (pp. 5-6). In bridging the varied experiences of high school youth and preservice teachers, the online *space* helped move beyond the constraints of physical classroom space in ways that allowed varied literacy and language practices to foment.

METHODOLOGY

We approached this study qualitatively to better understand the attitudes, experiences and challenges students faced throughout their interaction in a digital third space. We felt qualitative research was the best approach because it allows the researcher to dig deeper into the questions of interest and is "not constrained by predetermined categories of analysis" (Patton, 1990, p. 165). Utilizing field notes, focus group interviews, coded analysis of student work, and online chat transcripts, the data were collected over 3 months of interaction between the preservice university students and the 10th grade high school students. There were two sites for this research project; preservice teachers communicated from Midwest University, and 10th grade students interacted from South Central High School (SCHS) in Los Angeles. These sites were selected based upon access. Robyn worked with the preservice teachers at Midwest University, and Antero worked with the teacher of the high school students. For the 16 White preservice teachers at Midwest University, their clinical teaching assignments largely matched their middle-class backgrounds: 15 taught in schools that were more than 70% White, and only one taught at a school with a student body comprised of 61% White, 23% Black, and 7% Latino students. The physical buildings that housed the high schools they were placed in, as well as the classes they attended, were well-tended and equipped with technology.

Compared to Midwest University, the Los Angeles high school in this study looked significantly different in racial and class make up. South Central High School is located south of downtown Los Angeles. The school faces steep achievement challenges with a student body made up of 83% Latino and 17% Black students, 89% classified by the district as "economically disadvantaged," and a graduation rate of 48% (Los Angeles Unified School District [LAUSD], 2012). Twenty-six 10th grade students who mirrored the school's demographics participated in this study. For most of these students, their day-to-day experience with White adults is primarily through their teachers. Overcrowded conditions, with more than 30 students in a classroom, as well as the constant demands placed on teachers, often lead to less than positive relationships, as both the students and teachers cope with the stressors of their realities. To help create a third space, the chatroom TodaysMeet.com was selected because it was easily accessible to all students and not blocked by school filters. Skype was used to communicate with whole classes, and Dropbox allowed students to share videos. We maintained 13 online meeting spaces, ensuring 10th grade students in groups of two and three were paired with one or two university students. To ensure the high school students felt an ownership in the project, after the initial class Skype meeting and viewing of introductory videos, the high school English teacher, Ned Snow, allowed his students to partner with their friends and then request their preservice teacher.

During the course of our study, we met weekly with the high school English teacher, Ned Snow, to align the interaction to his school's mandated pacing plans. In coplanning this study with Mr. Snow, he made it clear he hoped the digital space would provide his students with a voice in responding to the mounting pressures and mandates faced at the high school. The third space allowed these students to address the school's learning goals while exploring their own interests.

This study draws qualitative data from literacy events (Hymes, 1974) by examining specific language events and the way students *talk* and participate in discussion both within virtual environments and in the offline dialogue of whole class debriefings, focus group interviews, and coursework. This study relied on inductive coding, and in analyzing the hundreds of pages of conversation, student writing, and video products, we attempted to identify salient data samples that depict the ways students in both spaces interacted, engaged, and learned. For the purpose of this article, we focused on data derived from the high school students. The codes were developed directly from the data in the transcripts and student work. We independently coded the data to identify themes and then used grounded theory to categorize our findings (Strauss & Corbin, 1990). After analyzing four or five transcripts and further examination of each of the codes, we met virtually to discuss our initial findings. We began seeing overlap between ideas. In particular, we coded for instances when students moved between formal and informal English language practices; for example, we noted times when students utilized emoticons and slang like "lol" [laughing out loud] when discussing essay writing or other forms of academic content. In looking at the varied instances of language practice that emerged online, we were able to better identify specific ways online relationships fostered in-class writing and vocabulary development. Once we had developed our themes, we continued to code the data, looking for the emergence of more themes. We began to see we had reached a saturation point and began to actively look for the occurrence of the themes in the remaining transcripts (Strauss & Corbin, 1990). We also contemplated the disconfirming evidence that challenged our conceptions of literacy development and community interaction through a digital medium.

STUDENT LEARNING OUTCOMES

Increased Awareness of Language

Though initially construed as an opportunity to share youth cultural knowledge with preservice teachers, sustained engagement and communication with preservice teachers contributed to the academic learning experiences of the high-school students. In coordination with the school's required pacing plans, Mr. Snow encouraged the initial conversations to focus on vocabulary development. Preservice teachers supported this emphasis by including discussions of words' connotations and their multiple forms. At the same time, this vocabulary exercise incited an exchange of cultural vocabulary; using Skype during the second week of class, the 10th grade students identified key slang words from their daily lives, defined these words, and used them in sample sentences. The college students took notes and asked clarifying questions, then completed an assessment of their understanding of student language. Words like shawty (a girlfriend), lagger ("saying you're going to do something and you end up not doing it"), and moska ("Spanish for 'fly': "You look like a moska") were playfully taught to teachers largely unfamiliar with the code-switching these students engage in as they switch linguistic repertoires from class to social context and back throughout the day. The purpose was not to shift students' vocabulary and enforce

Standard English, but to encourage students to be intentional about their grammar and vocabulary choices.

For example, after sharing informal vocabulary with the college students, Ned's class focused on understanding the words' formal structures: students practiced their understanding of denotation and connotation by analyzing the words they shared with their partners. Explaining the denotation of "that's cold" is "it's freezing" and the connotation is "very mean," Maria's connotation and denotation worksheet completed after her conversation with her mentor reinforces the ways these informal language practices supported academic language development. Furthermore, the activity demonstrated an interest and value in students' informal English practices. Mr. Snow's goal of incorporating student voice about the curriculum reflected much of our decision to shift away from a purely academic mentorship and to, instead, focus on facilitating a space of familiarity and mutual inquiry. In doing so, Ned's students were able to engage in district-mandated curricula in a manner that was meaningful to them, allowing them to embrace the possibilities the third space provided.

This exchange also encouraged a dialogue about why students tend to rely on various vocabulary choices. In one chatroom, high-school student Ramiro asked his college partner if he thinks he might use profanity while teaching students. The teacher confessed he might slip up accidentally. For Ramiro, such a statement allowed him to consider the ramifications of different language practices within various social contexts and to consider how such a slip up can impact his view of his teacher. Appreciating his mentor's candor, Ramiro wrote, "that is dope no lie." The duo's conversation over the remaining weeks was filled with slang, emoticons, and mutual statements of support for each others' academic and professional trajectories. Mr. Snow connected the online discussions of language and slang to the class' first debate. Reflecting on this, he said, "because of that [the debate], that gave us a great foundation for whenever we were learning new vocabularies. Because before I introduced them to any new vocabularies to learn, they already had to teach someone else vocabulary: using it in sentences, giving multiple examples."

Evidence the high school students were thinking about the impact of language choices could be found throughout chat transcripts. This was particularly apparent when Luis was discussing the use of slang with Jane, who was visiting his chatroom because her group was absent. When she asked how students benefited from using slang in classrooms, Luis replied, "Well, I know using slang in English class helps show the student that there are multiple types of ways to speak. Who knows, they might also stop using their current language and switch over." Jane then asked him whether switching was a "good thing," and Luis demonstrated an awareness of the function of language within contexts in his response, "I wouldn't say bad, but I wouldn't say good either. It depends on what tthe student wants, actually."

In later discussions, the preservice teachers continued to help distinguish between different language practices by modeling academic terms such as arguments, thesis statements, and counterarguments as seen in the exchange that begins this article. When Luke offers the semistructured comment in the opening vignette, "how are you going to make your introduction for your paper, are you going to give your arguments right away?" he was careful to use the language of persuasion to reinforce the ideas the students were learning in their English class. His academic mentoring is mediated by informal language practices: Camila's responses include "yeah i think so cuz […]" and "yepp i guess so, im gonna […]." Camila accepts the advice and guidance Luke provides and expresses her understanding of academic writing even when writing back in non-Standard English. Within this non-Standard English, however, there are times Camila responds using academic terms, such as when she tells Luke she still needs to complete her "counterclaim and response to it." This demonstrates her ability to effectively code-switch throughout the conversation.

Developing Meaningful Relationships

Directly related to improved academic learning outcomes is the way meaningful relationships between adults and high school students were mediated through digital technology. Though they only "talked" with each other on a weekly basis–and this was usually through the deliberate pacing of chat discussion–students slowly learned about each other's interests, goals, and concerns. Their closeness to each other was the most telling in an exchange between high school student Cathy and preservice teacher Jane. While discussing the homemade tamales Cathy enjoyed over Thanksgiving, she offered to have her mother bring some to Jane, forgetting the miles between them. In another room, the 10th graders said they like shuffling, "a type of dance where you mostly use your feet. Everybody has their own style but it's rare when a girl really does know how to do it." The teens then asked Alice what she liked to do outside of school.

Alice: I love to read, I play ice hockey, running (in good weather), cooking, hanging out with friends

Maria & Cindy: woould you like to cook for us ? :DD just kidding aha !

Because she had established a relationship with Maria and Cindy, she then steered the conversation toward a more serious topic.

Alice: We have heard of some of the issues happening at your school. Can you tell us about it has affected the mood of students?

Alice: And - to answer your question: I cook for people all the time. But it is an awful long drive for a meal

Maria & Cindy: well its harder for us to learn since we dont get alot of attention like before since the rooms are really packed, and its harder to pay attention since some students are hard headed and dont let the teacher teach.

Maria & Cindy: you could cyber cook for us :DD

For Maria, Cindy, and Alice, the chatroom mediated critical inquiry into school equity with a space to share interests and online socialization practices. The chatroom demonstrated youth engagement through digital media that mirrors out-of-school participation. Ito et al.'s ethnographic study of youth's social use of digital media, points to the prevalence of youth "hanging out" in virtual spaces. However, within the digital third space of the classroom-mediated chatroom, Maria and Cindy are able to critically reflect on their schooling experience and get external validation in the process. The not-quite peer relationship between the adult and adolescent students meant "hanging out" each Monday involved receiving feedback on schoolwork and socializing with individuals who had significantly different cultural experiences. The affordances of this chatroom as a tool for learning and engagement are ones that could not have been easily replicated outside of a digital space. The high school youth were able to speak using language practices they were comfortable with while discussing content that was still often academic in nature.

Likewise, the high school students' expertise in communicating online and socializing in digital spaces often surpassed the college students' knowledge. This, too, validated youth in school practices as in this brief exchange about emoticons between Luis, Michael, and Jill:

Luis and Michael: o.o

Jill: ok whats o.o??

Luis and Michael: o.o is another "smiley" for surprised.

Jill: Great, I'm glad we're getting these symbols down!

Luis and Michael are able to offer language expertise, share their practices and inform their adult partner about youth language repertoires. The high school students were able to reflect on their language practices, encouraging stronger intentionality about how they communicate and code-switch.

In the culminating focus groups, nearly all of the high school students described how the informal space provided space to better understand their partners. For instance, Cathy said, "I never knew how much Jane cared about being a teacher. She's worked hard because she cared and I didn't know teachers cared like that." Ramiro, another student, noted, "[My partner] was really easy to talk to. She would ask what we're doing in school, gives us advice and try to get in depth with me." Though the students focused much of their interactions on academic work, the time invested at the beginning of this study to allow students to get to know each other within the digital space acted as a crucial means for opening up academic conversation and youth agency.

Though many youth experienced powerful online support in the study, there was a notable counterexample. In particular was one chatroom where three students increasingly resisted the project as the weeks progressed. According to Mr. Snow, "What happened was some of [the students] didn't look forward to the chatting but it wasn't because of the project or what we were doing but because of individuals. They weren't resisting against the actual activity. It was very personal." Because this group did not develop as strong mentoring relationships as others, the time spent discussing academic work felt less engaging. By the fifth week of the study, other groups comfortably balanced talk about out-of-school activities and academic work. However, the transcript of the chatroom that "resisted" clearly shows that all of the talk was focused entirely on student writing. While other students shared how their Thanksgiving break went, the college student in this chatroom asked for students' persuasive essay arguments and provided direct feedback like "in your papers you both need to go into detail about your facts." Though useful feedback, they could not relate to their mentor so they resisted the work because the students–according to a later focus group–"felt frustrated." These students sought out other chatrooms in order to meet their personal needs in the class. As with other schoolwork, the students who did not buy into the activities shifted from enthusiastic participants to passively resisting the efforts of their college partner. Our finding here is significant in highlighting the necessity to invest in student interest. Without seeing the students on the other end of a chat exchange as interesting and interested individuals, this preservice teacher inadvertently made them feel like they were an assignment required for their class.

While the majority of communication occurred on TodaysMeet.com, the classes also sent emails and videos to each other throughout the study and engaged in several whole-class Skype sessions. The first time each class met, in fact, was via Skype. Noting this probably allowed the high school students to better acclimate to the unique learning environment, Mr. Snow stated, "That was probably the way to do it. It was low risk for our kids because they got to sit in a group and see a collective group of possible teachers in a classroom. Those outgoing gregarious personalities, like Ramiro and Michael, really jumped at it and allowed the other students to kind of just take in the personalities and the human qualities of the teachers. I think [the class] could kind of look forward to individual conversations."

Discussing the differences between the class that participated in this project and his four other 10th grade classes, Mr. Snow noted this class was "the most consistent in terms of attendance and participation." Specifically pointing to feeling there was more trust developed amongst the students as a result of communicating and sharing with outsiders, Mr. Snow felt the project helped foster a stronger community that lasted throughout the year.

Pushing Back and Speaking Up

Similar to being able to academically grow through "hanging out," this digital space allowed the high school youth in this activity to be able to more powerfully voice their frustrations and thoughts. Within the traditional power structures of their urban schooling experience, the students were not shy about reflecting on the challenges they face at their Title I school, as Maria and Cindy's excerpt above notes. Other topics of discontent, such as disgusting cafeteria food, math teachers who cannot control their classes, and substitutes who "always act like if we're going to steal from them" were reflected upon within the groups of students. These discussions functioned as much more than mediated venting; the SCHS students drew upon their frustrating experiences to offer advice to the preservice teachers and to explore ways both teachers and students can "push back" on existing inequitable urban school conditions. Discussing the importance of respect, high school student Sarah advised her partner, "The respecting part that is going to be like a mission if it does happen. You got to bust a mission and try to earn their respect." For Sarah, the importance of undertaking the mission of getting student respect cannot be overstated. Telling a future teacher to "bust a mission" allows Sarah to express the value of respect in her schooling context and to do so in a way that validates her own language practices. In this instance, students powerfully voiced their ideas both in content and form. Sarah's and other similar comments find the SCHS students pushing back on assumptions of the use of formal academic language when speaking with adults and on how student knowledge can be incorporated into a teacher's professional development.

Students also pushed back through leading the discussions within their chatrooms. In the beginning, most of the high school students chose a more passive role: they would respond to the college students' questions or draw out the information Mr. Snow required of them. However, as students became more comfortable within this space, many took on much more active roles. Two months into the sustained discussion, both classes read the short Sherman Alexie essay, "The Joy of Reading and Writing: Superman and Me." In discussing this text, Luis and Michael (sitting side by side at SCHS but working from two different computers) guide their college partner through a discussion of the text. They lead this conversation and, ultimately, turn it toward a group reflection on social norms, aspirations, and concerns:

Luis:	Hello. Good Morning. Today we are going to talk about the Biographical essay of Sherman Alexie."Superman and Me."
Jill:	Very good, do you have thoughts to start our conversation about the essay?
Michael:	cool..
Michael:	"at the same time i was seeing the world in paragraphs"
Luis:	What do You think or feel about that quote, Jill?
Jill:	Could I ask which paragraph this quote came from?
Michael:	the start of the fourth paragraph
Jill:	I can see both sides... sometimes things come to us in a single thought, or paragraph and other times I feel like I see the world as a bunch of random words... what do you think of my thought?

The trio then delves into personal reflections related to this passage. It is important to recognize how Michael and Luis drive this conversation. They do this not simply through picking the quote that starts the lengthy conversation that follows; the two high school students offer a question about the quote for Jill and are validated throughout the discussion as the "experts" in this discussion: Jill asks them where the quote can be found and solicits feedback about her initial reflection. Youth leadership emerges here through the facilitation of this conversation in a natural and unforced manner. It is also important to see this youth-driven leadership is collaborative in nature. Luis and Michael both take turns in the discussion and later, as the conversation moves towards more personal reflections, both students weigh in with their thoughts:

Jill:	I think the sentences of the paragraph speak about the individuals decisions, attitudes, and actions...
Michael:	yes they all have their own unique attributes and thus are paragraphs
Jill:	What kind of actions or decisions in our lives make for a solid, flowing paragraph?
Luis:	Decisions that affect our life's outcomes. School is one of them. College. Work. Stuff like that.

Perhaps most novel about this exchange is that the critical consciousness that emerged from the chatrooms of Luis, Michael, Jill and their peers was done so through youth-driven discussion around academic texts. Through being given a conduit to voice and receive feedback and a space to practice leadership skills by directing the academic conversation, the digital third space of this study invoked simultaneous academic reflection and critical consciousness.

LIMITATIONS

While this collaborative experience helped guide student growth, the project was also hampered by a few looming constraints. In particular, the high school's focus on standardized test preparation felt like a conflict for Mr. Snow as he attempted to balance the enthusiasm many of his students expressed with his obligations to keep them on pace with the preparation the rest of his classes were engaged in. Noting "how much of the curriculum was going to be hamstrung by mandates," Mr. Snow was frustrated with the instructional shifts he was required to make during the 3 days of the week his class was not in dialogue with the preservice teachers. Because much of the class time was dedicated to standardized instruction, little additional time was spent by the students discussing or reflecting on this project.

Further, as noted in the counterexample above, the relational nature of the online space was not always sufficient to support the work that was to be done between the two groups in the study. Without support on both ends of seeing connections online as more than "work," the possibilities of the online space will falter. As such, it is important to recognize that the technology is neither the possibility nor the limitation in this study as much as the medium to better connect the youth and preservice audiences.

CONCLUSION

Through an exploration of the possibilities of Third Space as mediated through technology, this study provides a clear direction for empowering students and utilizing cultural and social contexts of students' lives to help engage them in academic work. High school students had the opportunity to turn the tables on traditional classroom interaction and to teach their preservice teachers through media similar to the tools they were comfortable using outside of school. This led to more engagement, trusting relationships, and increased participation in this class that was not seen prior. Additionally, the possibilities of new media to engender teachers and students into communities of sentiment are significant contributions to the field of teacher research. Even when the original partnerships fell short, students in this study were empowered to seek out new spaces of engagement in the digital Third Space. Throughout this study, the relational possibilities of the online space fomented youth identity in ways that face-to-face interactions would not have allowed. The high school students were able to look beyond the traditional teacher-student power structures that occur within classrooms. They could engage, discuss, and learn in ways a digital third space can foster that cannot be garnered through traditional teacher-student or preservice teacher-student relationships.

Further, the online space established went beyond simply conveying information across physical space; it transcended the cultural barriers that separate urban youth Discourses from those of the preservice teachers. As Moje et al. (2004) found, educators must help youth "in learning how to navigate and cross the sets of assumptions they encounter and the identities they construct in those different spaces." The project in this study expanded the *spaces* for such learning opportunities in order to better situate the practical experience of preservice educators and for the context of learning to shift beyond traditional classroom environments.

As the language practices demonstrated by urban youth in this project often differed significantly from Standard English, these students highlighted the fluidity of language practices by young people, how these practices are engaged to communicate with non-youth community members, and the danger of ignoring the methods students typically utilize in communicating with each other. In particular, the trust and validation supported through accepting youth literacy practices online pushed toward enriched academic discussion. "Since she was friendly, it was easy to open up to her," Cathy said about working with her college partner Jane. "I felt more comfortable going over my writing and debate topics since we knew each other." The digital Third Space of the online chatrooms allowed students to be "hanging out" while still developing persuasive essay outlines, analyzing academic texts, and building critical consciousness. This project helped us recognize the ways youth literacies on and offline can foster academic growth, as well as give youth a voice against the inequities that can occur in schools. Lewis and Fabos (2005) note that often educators "disregard the vitality of their [students'] literate lives and the needs they will have for their literate and social futures at home, at work, and in their communities" (p. 498). By partnering youth with the teachers of tomorrow, this project helps illuminate potential avenues for merging the needs of students in and out of school.

REFERENCES

Alvermann, D. E. (2008). Why bother theorizing adolescents' online literacies for classroom practice and research? *Journal of Adolescent & Adult Literacy,* 52, 8-19.

Benson, S. (2010). "I don't know if that'd be English or not": Third space theory and literacy instruction. *Journal of Adolescent & Adult Literacy,* 53, 555-563.

Castek, J., Coiro, J., Guzniczak, L., & Bradshaw, C. (2012). Examining peer collaboration in online inquiry. *The Educational Forum,* 76, 479-496.

Coiro, J. (2012). Digital Literacies: Understanding dispositions toward reading on the Internet. *Journal of Adolescent & Adult Literacy,* 55, 645-648.

Darling-Hammond, L. (2010). *The flat world and education: How America's commitment to equity will determine our future.* New York, NY: Teachers College Press.

Friedman, T. (2005). *The world is flat: A brief history of the twenty-first century.* New York, NY: Farrar, Straus and Giroux.

Gee, J. P. (1996). *Social linguistics and literacies: Ideology in Discourses* (2nd ed.). London, England: Taylor & Francis.

Gutiérrez, K. (2004). Literacy as laminated activity: Rethinking literacy for English learners. In J. Worthy, B. Maloch, J. V. Hoffman, D. L. Schallert, & C.M. Fairbanks (Eds.), 53rd yearbook of the National Reading Conference (pp. 101–114). Oak Creek, WI: National Reading Conference.

Gutierrez, K. (2008). Developing a sociocritical literacy in the Third Space. *Reading Research Quarterly,* 43, 148-164.

Gutiérrez, K. D., Baquedano-López, P., Alvarez, H. H., & Chiu, M. M. (1999). Building a culture of collaboration through hybrid language practices. *Theory into Practice,* 38, 87-92.

Gutierrez, K., Rymes, B., & Larson, J. (1995). Script, counterscript, and underlife in the classroom: James Brown versus Brown v. Board of Education. *Harvard Educational Review,* 65, 445-471.

Hymes, D. (1974). Models of the interaction of language and social life. In C. B. Paulston & G. R. Tucker (Eds.), *Sociolinguistics: The essential readings.* Malden, MA: Blackwell.

Ito, M., Baumer, S., Bittanti, M., Boyd, D., Cody, R., & Herr-Stephenson, B. (2009). *Hanging out, messing around, and geeking out: Kids living and learning with new media.* Cambridge, MA: MIT Press.

Kirkland, D. E. (2009). Researching and teaching English in the digital dimension. *Research in the Teaching of English,* 44, 8-22.

Knobel, M., & Lankshear, C. (Eds.). (2007). *A new literacies sampler.* New York, NY: Peter Lang.

Ladson-Billings, G. (2006). From the achievement gap to the education debt: Understanding achievement in U.S. schools. *Educational Researcher,* 35, 3-12.

Lenhart, A. (2009). Teens and mobile phones over the past five years: Pew Internet looks back. Pew Internet & American Life Project. Retrieved from http://www.pewinternet.org/~/media/Files/Reports/2009/PIP%20Teens%20and%20Mobile%20Phones%20Data%20Memo.pdf

Lewis, C., & Fabos, B. (2005). Instant messaging, literacies, and social identities. *Reading Research Quarterly,* 40, 470–501.

Liu, H., Macintyre, R., & Ferguson, R. (2012). Exploring qualitative analytics for e-mentoring relationships building in an online social learning environment. *Second International Conference on Learning Analytics and Knowledge* (LAK12), 2012, Vancouver, Canada.

Los Angeles Unified School District (2012). School report card. Retrieved from http://getreportcard.lausd.net/reportcards/reports.jsp

Moje, E. (2004). Powerful spaces: Tracing the out-of-school literacy spaces of Latino/a youth. In K. M. Leander & M. Sheehy, (Eds.), *Spatializing literacy research and practice* (pp. 15-38). New York, NY: Peter Lang.

Moje, E. B., Ciechanowski, K. M., Kramer, K., Ellis, L., Carrillo, R., & Collazo, T. (2004). Working toward Third Space in content literacy: An examination of everyday funds of knowledge and Discourse. *Reading Research Quarterly,* 39, 38-70.

Moll, L. C., Veléz-Ibañéz, C., & Greenberg, J. (1989). *Year one progress report: Community knowledge and classroom practice: Combining resources for literacy instruction* (IARP Subcontract L-10, Development Associates). Tucson, AZ: University of Arizona.

New London Group. (1996). A pedagogy of multiliteracies: Designing social futures. *Harvard Education Review,* 66, 60-92.

O'Brien, D., & Scharber, C. (2008). Digital literacies go to school: Potholes and possibilities. *Journal of Adolescent & Adult Literacy,* 52, 66-68.

Patton, M. Q. (1990). *Qualitative evaluation and research methods.* Newbury Park, CA: Sage Publications.

Sinclair, C. (2003). Mentoring online about mentoring: possibilities and practice. *Mentoring and Tutoring,* 11, 79-94.

Soja, E. (1996). *Thirdspace: Journeys to Los Angeles and other real-and-imagined places.* Malden, MA: Blackwell.

Strauss, A., & Corbin, J. (1990). *Basics of qualitative research: Grounded theory procedures and techniques.* Newbury Park, CA: Sage.

Vygotsky, L. S. (1978). *Mind in society: The development of higher psychological processes.* Cambridge, MA: Harvard University Press.

"You Can't Put the Genie Back into the Bottle": English Teachers' Beliefs and Attitudes Regarding Digital Literacies in the Classroom

Sean Ruday
Longwood University

Kristin Conradi
North Carolina State University

Natasha Heny
Gail E. Lovette
University of Virginia

The ubiquity of technologies in today's classrooms is undeniable. According to Gray and Lewis (2009), 100% of American public schools have at least one instructional computer with Internet access and the average ratio of students to computers has been measured at 1:3.1. Additionally, 97 % of schools have access to projectors, 73% contain an interactive whiteboard, and 93% have a digital camera (Gray & Lewis, 2009). Digital methods of communication are also prevalent in adolescents' out-of-school lives: 85% of teens aged 12-17 engage in some form of electronic personal communication (Lenhart, Arafeh, Smith, & Macgill, 2008), creating a social environment in which adolescents' access to each other is increased, while the time they spend communicating in person is decreased (Lenhart, Madden, & Hitlin, 2005).

Given the prevalence of technologies, both in and out of school, calls to engage our students with digital literacies have come from both the National Council of the Teachers of English (NCTE) and the International Reading Association (IRA). In addition, although the Common Core State Standards (CCSS) do not specifically delineate a separate strand for technology, the CCSS actually integrate expectations that students be proficient in both the consumption and production of digital literacies throughout the English Language Arts standards (McKenna, Conradi, Young, & Jang, 2013; see CCSS.ELA-Literacy.CCRA.R.7).

Despite both the presence of these literacies inside and outside the classroom and the wide-ranging expectations that students engage with diverse literacies, little is known about English teachers' beliefs and attitudes towards digital literacies. Specifically, what do English teachers believe about their role as teachers of digital literacies? How and why do they make the decisions they do regarding the inclusion of digital literacies in their instruction? An investigation of this topic can both provide insight into teachers' decision-making processes and reveal influential factors related to their technology use.

BACKGROUND AND PREVIOUS RESEARCH

In this section, we define what we mean about digital literacies and then we examine why teacher beliefs matter. We focus specifically on beliefs regarding technology integration and digital literacies.

Digital literacies. Several terms (including *digital media, new technologies, new literacies,* and *New Literacy Studies*) are associated with digital literacies, leading to some confusion about what digital literacies actually comprise (see O'Brien & Scharber, 2008, for a discussion). For the present study, we join others (e.g., Beach, Hull, & O'Brien, 2011; O'Brien & Scharber, 2008) in adopting the position that digital literacies involve both the understanding and representation of ideas using multiple modes and employing digital tools. In other words, digital literacies involve communication mediated by digital technologies. We feel the combination of technology and communication encompassed by digital literacies make this term especially relevant to English instruction, as English teachers are tasked with equipping their students with communication skills that are constantly evolving in our increasingly digital world (IRA, 2012).

Lankshear & Knobel (2011) suggest that the mere presence of technology in classrooms hardly indicates that students are meaningfully engaging with new literacies. Consequently, we must understand not only what teachers believe about technology integration, but also how they see this in light of teaching English. The use of digital literacies in classrooms has been framed by many in terms of dichotomies, including: "potholes and possibilities" (O'Brien & Scharber, 2008, p. 67), "affordances and limitations" (Swenson, Rozema, Young, McGrail, & Whitin, 2005, p. 211), and "risks" and "rewards" (Hagood, 2012, p. 10). These dichotomies provide insight into factors that influence the decisions that teachers make about including digital literacies in their instruction, making them relevant to a study of teacher beliefs on this topic.

Teacher beliefs. Although several studies have examined teachers' integration of technology within their literacy practices, few have focused on teachers' beliefs regarding this integration (Ertmer, 2005; Ertmer & Ottenbreit-Leftwich, 2010; Fisher, 2006) and regarding digital literacies, specifically. It is widely accepted that one's beliefs influence one's actions (e.g., Ajzen & Fishbein, 2005; Bandura, 1986; Rokeach, 1968), and Pajares (1992) argues "that the investigation of teachers' beliefs is a necessary and valuable avenue of educational inquiry" (p. 326). Ertmer (2005) suggests that teacher beliefs regarding technology integration have been ignored in part because "knowing how to facilitate and support these types of [belief] changes is much less familiar to staff developers who typically have been concerned with facilitating first-order change" (p. 26). But until teacher beliefs are studied, she maintains, technology integration will remain somewhat shallow.

Beliefs about technology integration in the English classroom. One of the first studies to explore the intersection of the Internet and teachers' understanding of literacy instruction was published over a dozen years ago. Karchmer (2001) examined 13 teachers' understandings of the role of the Internet as it interacted with literacy instruction. These teachers—who had been identified as technology experts—highlighted concerns regarding the appropriateness, safety, and accuracy of Internet materials, but also shared how the Internet provides an audience with the potential to motivate writing. What the participants did not express was how technologies were changing the very nature of literacy. In fact, Karchmer noted that teachers kept coming back to how the new skills were simply "extensions of what they taught students while reading print-based text" (p. 461).

Turbill and Murray (2006) describe the reluctance of primary-grade Australian literacy teachers to embrace information communication technologies (ICT), noting that a major challenge associated with integrating technology into literacy instruction is helping teachers "understand that ICT is indeed a critical component of the literacy curriculum" (p.105). McGrail (2006) studied secondary English teachers, examining their perspectives regarding a schoolwide laptop initiative, and described the incorporation of technologies in schools as occurring in a "top-down fashion" (p. 1056). The study found that the "top-down" nature of this initiative was problematic, as "teachers found themselves on the receiving end of a technology they did not initiate" (p. 1074) and were frustrated by their lack of agency.

Teacher-researchers Curwood and Cowell (2011), a secondary English teacher and a library media specialist, respectively, collaborated on a multimedia poetry project to address how technologies can change the nature of literacy instruction. Their objective was to "allow students to create presentations using digital tools to infuse additional meaning into their previously constructed poetry" (p. 113). This type of collaboration, they maintain, "constitutes a progressive form of professional development" (p. 117) and provides an alternative to existing instructional models that present new literacies as decontextualized skills. Curwood and Cowell's work speaks to the importance of teaching practices that integrate media and literacy into the curriculum in purposeful ways.

Results from a recent U.S. survey of teachers' perceptions of integrating technology into literacy instruction (Hutchison & Reinking, 2011) indicate that virtually all literacy teachers believe technology should be integrated into literacy instruction, with two-thirds of the respondents indicating that technology should be supplemental to instruction. Hutchison and Reinking describe their study as "a broad backdrop to inform more narrowly focused studies in the future" (p. 331) on literacy teachers' beliefs about teaching with technology, such as how specific contexts, goals, and demographics can shape teachers' attitudes toward incorporating digital literacies. They found that teachers for the most part fail to see the integration of technologies as a curricular enhancement, but rather as an obligation taken on for the sake of technology. Further, they identified several obstacles to incorporating technology, primarily in the areas of teacher knowledge and training.

Beliefs about digital literacy. Despite the importance of teachers understanding both the affordances and limitations of technologies as they relate to literacy (Swenson et al., 2005), we lack a rich knowledge base regarding teachers' beliefs about digital literacies.

At the primary level, McDougall (2009) interviewed 26 teachers from preschool through seventh grade and found that teachers' beliefs about digital literacy varied widely. Many adopted what McDougall called a "traditionalist approach" (p. 683) and were frustrated by expectations to include technologies. One sixth-grade teacher, for example, prioritized traditional literacy noting that her first priority was to teach "the basics" (p. 684), with any attention to technologies possible only after the basic competencies had been achieved. McDougall described other teachers as being in "survival mode" (p. 684), and though they accepted a growing importance of other media, they conceded that a lack of time, confidence, or know-how was to blame for ignoring technologies in their instruction. Finally, McDougall found that some teachers adopted a "futures-oriented approach" (p. 684). These teachers described the potential value of technologies in enhancing the learning process, but fell short of fully embracing the importance of digital literacies.

McDougall's findings are consistent with what Leander (2009) suggests are the four different stances that teachers hold toward digital literacies. If a teacher holds a *resistant* stance, he/she hesitates to use digital literacies, preferring traditional, print-based literacy. By contrast, if teachers hold a *replacement stance*, they think digital literacies are more important than traditional literacies and that we should effectively replace old literacies with the new. Teachers holding a *return* stance believe that digital literacies are important in helping students become better readers, with the end goal of returning to traditional literacy. And finally, if teachers hold a *remediation* stance, they place equal emphasis on both traditional and digital literacies, and adopt a "parallel pedagogy" (p. 149) in their instruction. Our study seeks to contribute to the professional conversation about the uses of digital literacies in the English classroom and the reasons behind those uses.

THE PRESENT STUDY

In this exploratory study, we investigated secondary English teachers' beliefs about digital literacy. We approached this study from a sociocultural perspective, viewing literacy as a practice in which multiple cultural factors are involved (Lankshear & Knobel, 2011). Lankshear and Knobel (2011) explain that literacy, when viewed from a sociocultural perspective, is a social act and that literacy practices must be situated in their specific contexts to fully make sense. In addition, literacy, when viewed from a sociocultural perspective, is a practice occurring at the point where social, cultural, political, historical, mental, and physical factors meet and form the meaning that transpires around texts (Lewis, Enciso, & Moje, 2007). This theoretical lens is especially relevant to our study, as we explored the specific contexts, values, and influences that contributed to the participants' decisions regarding the use of digital literacies within their classrooms.

In order to ascertain and better understand teachers' present beliefs, we invited them to participate in a focus group. At this session, we engaged in a conversation about the changing nature of literacy and the relationship of technologies to literacy. We ended with a discussion of the challenges these teachers face with the integration of technology into their secondary English instruction. Our study addressed the following questions:

(1)   What do teachers say they are doing regarding the integration of digital literacies into their English instruction?

(2)   What do they say (standards, administrative pushes, values, efficacy, convenience, desire to please) informs these decisions?

We chose these questions based on our belief that they could provide important insight into both *how* teachers incorporate digital literacies into their classes and *why* they choose to incorporate them in the ways they do. This conversation, in turn, might provide insight into teachers' beliefs about and attitudes toward digital literacies as well as the external forces that may contribute to their decision-making processes. These questions also stem from the existing literature, discussed above (such as Leander, 2009; McDougall, 2009; and McGrail, 2006), concerning English teachers' beliefs about technology integration and digital literacy.

METHODOLOGY

Participants. All public and private middle and high school teachers in a medium-sized city in a South Atlantic state received personalized e-mails from one of the four authors inviting them to participate in the study. In order to be included, teachers had to teach at least one section of English Language Arts in grades 6 through 12 at the time of the focus group.

Seven teachers agreed to participate in a focus group and signed consent forms. The teachers, six female and one male, averaged 10.4 years of experience with a range of three through nineteen years. Two of the teachers taught at the middle school level and the remaining five taught high school. Additionally, two taught at private schools, and five taught at public schools. Five of the teachers held state certifications to teach English in grades 6 through 12, one had a state middle school certification, and another, who taught at a private school, was not certified to teach.

Researchers. We came to this investigation with keen interest in the topic. With a combined 34 years of experience in classrooms (ranging from elementary through high school), each of us has substantial teaching experience. Moreover, our teaching careers span an important shift in pedagogical practice. We began teaching just as technology substantively infiltrated the classroom (in 1997, 1999, 2000, and 2002, respectively). What a classroom looked like in 2000, for example, was markedly different from what it looked like when we each left the classroom to pursue doctoral degrees (2007 or later). Having experienced these shifts ourselves, we were motivated to further explore how teachers were currently making sense of them.

Focus group procedures. Our focus group meeting took place after the end of the school day in early June at a local educational resource center. The discussion was facilitated by one of this study's researchers: a doctoral student who also was a former high school English teacher in the area. When the teachers first arrived, they completed an open-ended survey designed to provide background into their experiences teaching with technology, the kinds of technology-related professional development available in their schools, and the types of technology that they use in their classroom as well as in their personal lives.

Table 1 summarizes the participants' uses of technology in their school settings. Table 2 summarizes the participants' uses of technology in their personal lives.

After the participants completed this survey, the facilitator opened the discussion by reiterating the purpose of our study and the reasons why we were especially interested in learning about their

Table 1: School Technology Use

Technology	Daily	Often	Occasionally	Rarely	Never
Email	6				1
Twitter			2	1	4
Other Social Media				1	6 (1 said: no access)
Presentations	1	4	2		
Digital Camera		1	2	4	
Video Camera		1	1	4	1
Other	smartboard	word processing/ ELMO	Blogger, audiobooks Googlevoice		

Table 2: Personal Technology Use

Technology	Daily	Often	Occasionally	Rarely	Never
Email	7				
Twitter			1	3	3
Other Social Media	5	1		1	
Presentations		2	3	1	1
Digital Camera		4	3		
Video Camera		2	3	2	
Other	iPad apps iPhone	Kindle			

beliefs about digital literacies. The focus group topic guide, found in Appendix A, provides specific details about the major aspects of the focus group discussion.

Data sources. The data sources used for analysis were the teachers' responses to an open-ended questionnaire (see Appendix B) and a transcript of the focus group conversation. In order to encourage candid, forthcoming participation, this conversation was not recorded. Rather, the transcript was constructed by two of the researchers, who sat in the back of the room during the focus group, writing down what was said and by whom. After independently transcribing the conversation, the researchers combined their information, resolving any inconsistencies.

Data analysis. We analyzed the data through the three-pronged process of data reduction, data display, and conclusion drawing and verification (Miles & Huberman, 1994). To begin the data reduction process, we developed a list of 30 "start codes" (Miles & Huberman, 1994) from an analysis of digital-literacy standards identified in three documents: a) IRA Standards 2010: Middle and High School Content Classroom Teacher, b) International Society for Technology in Education (ISTE) Standards for Students, and c) ISTE Standards for Teachers (see Appendix C). Using those codes, the four of us individually conducted initial reviews of the data with the goal of identifying the start codes most relevant to the data we had collected. We found nine of the original 30 codes useful to our data set: Instructional Tool, Legitimacy, Students' Out-of-School Experiences, Authenticity, Relevance, Student Access, Equity, Digital Fluency: Research, and Digital Fluency: General. This narrowing of codes represented the initial stage of our analysis, as it allowed us to focus on especially significant comments from the participants in our focus group and organize these data chunks in ways that informed our continuing analysis.

Following the reduction of our data, we identified four emergent themes and used them to construct data displays. We initially constructed these displays independently and then checked one another's work, confirming that we were all in agreement that specific excerpts from the data aligned with the key themes and discussing any disagreements until a consensus was reached. These emerging themes were intentionally general, as we sought to identify major ideas we could use to display the data, knowing that we would refine these themes as analysis continued. As we created displays of data based on initial emerging themes, we revised these themes and created sub-themes. Table 3 illustrates the evolution of our analysis from initial codes to sub-themes.

Table 3: Developing Sub-Themes

Codes from Data Reduction Process	Themes from Initial Analysis	Sub-themes
Instructional Tool	Technology over Content	Technology as a means of "Keeping up with the Joneses"
		Technology's role in creating an environment of suspicion
		Teacher need for control of learning process & environment
Legitimacy Authenticity Relevance	Relevance	Opportunity for students to see themselves as readers (especially struggling students)
		Opportunity to validate out-of-school literacies/popular literacies
Students' Out-of-School Experiences Student Access Equity	Access Concerns	The Digital Divide

As we created and revised these displays, we continued to return to the data to remind ourselves of the context in which the participants' comments were initially said and to determine if any other sections of text could be displayed in the categories we were continually refining.

We completed our analysis by drawing and verifying our conclusions. Although we had already constructed working themes, we drew "final" conclusions by revisiting our data displays, the themes and sub-themes we constructed, and the participants' comments used to construct these themes. However, we did not truly finalize our conclusions until we sought to verify them by looking for disconfirming evidence (Creswell & Miller, 2000): evidence that is either consistent with or disconfirms previously established themes. Our search for disconfirming evidence allowed us to be even more confident in our findings; it confirmed some of our existing conclusions and helped us to revise some of our other findings to make them as clear and representative of our interpretations of the data as possible.

FINDINGS

In this section, we first share what we found about the specific technology integrations teachers were practicing within their classrooms at the time of the focus group. Next, we share four themes that emerged regarding teachers' beliefs about technology integration and digital literacy.

Teacher Background and Current Use of Technology

At the start of the focus group discussion, teachers filled out an open-ended questionnaire detailing their experiences with technology, how they defined digital literacy, and the technology they had available in their classrooms and that they utilized in their personal lives. From this information, we derived findings related to the participants' knowledge of technology and their definitions for digital literacy.

Knowledge about technology. Of the seven teachers, six had received some form of technology instruction during either their undergraduate or graduate coursework. This coursework varied in content, with most saying it was limited to basic word-processing and instruction in the use of PowerPoint. All had had some level of school-wide professional development regarding technology, but some expressed frustrations that these were mostly confined to school-wide technology systems related to grading or communication. Teachers were enthusiastic about occasional opportunities for training in instructional practices such as "digital storytelling," "using ebooks in the classroom," and working with interactive whiteboards. We next asked participants to share what resources they use when they need to learn more about a specific tool or technology. Overwhelmingly, participants referred to technology coordinators, other colleagues they perceived as "expert," spouses, or friends as resources. When asked to rate their own skills with technology, answers varied from "okay" (n=1) to "very competent" (n=2), with the majority of participants (n=4) noting that they felt moderately proficient but suggested they had more to learn.

Defining digital literacy. We asked teachers to define "digital literacy" and were given diverse responses, some of which are listed in Table 4.

Table 4: Definitions of Digital Literacy

"Digital literacy means both the evolving sense of reading in a media/technology environment as well as the ability to evaluate those online sources"

"An ability to navigate websites, be critical of sources, work through technical issues, and enhance presentations"

"Use of digital tools for literacy, literacy development, and exploration"

"The ability to use digital resources (computers, Internet, etc), to read, write, and produce new products"

"Facility with technology use for a required purpose"

TEACHER BELIEFS

Teachers believe it is their responsibility to teach digital literacy. When we asked teachers to identify their stance towards digital literacies, most of our teachers resonated with a "remediate stance" (Leander, 2009), acknowledging the necessity of focusing on both types of literacies. Without dismissing the role of traditional literacy, all teachers acknowledged that for students to be literate in the 21st century, they must also be fluent with digital literacies. One teacher shared, "I feel like this is the world we are going to live in...it's more and more going to be like this. You can't punt on the responsibility to teach digital literacies."

A particular concern of teachers regarding digital literacies involved the consequences of easy access to information. For example, they believe students have a hard time understanding that the information found on the Internet originated from and belonged to a person. One teacher shared, "I used the example of a friend in graduate school driving to Princeton to get to the library and it's clear, then, that when he finds a book in the library, that information belongs to someone. But now you just type in a catchphrase and thousands of things pop up. It's harder for the idea of the information belonging to someone to sink in." While acknowledging a responsibility to teach digital literacies, teachers were very much concerned with students' abilities to think critically and evaluate information. One teacher shared that she felt that her students write papers based on the "first five hits off of Google" and explained that "having it readily available to them means they're not making assessments of it."

Teachers believe digital literacies increase the relevance of the English curriculum, allowing all students to view themselves as readers and writers. The participants explained that digital literacies help to increase the relevance of their curriculum by validating students' existing online literacy practices and allowing even those who struggle with in-school literacies to see themselves as readers and writers. One teacher explained that the use of digital literacies provided her with instructional opportunities to validate students who do not usually view themselves as readers. She commented on how the self-perceptions and literacy practices of struggling readers shaped her beliefs about teaching them: struggling readers "don't see themselves as readers at all. But they do a lot of reading through digital literacy and I want to value that for them." This teacher articulated a desire to cite the use of digital literacies to show some of her students that the title of a "real reader" is not reserved just for students who read print texts: "I want to show them that they are readers and I want to validate the reading they do online as 'real reading' for them. I want to say to them, 'You're reading a sports article [online]—you ARE a reader.'"

This teacher described both the challenges and benefits associated with validating students' online reading practices, explaining that valuing digital literacies is like "trying to switch [her] brain" because it involves her utilizing unfamiliar instructional practices. Although she described using digital literacies as "a hard thing" for her to do as a teacher, she also clearly articulated the possible benefits of this kind of instruction: "I feel like [students] gain confidence as readers when you, as a teacher, validate that kind of reading." This increased student confidence, made possible through her validation of students' digital literacy practices, subsequently led to increased student engagement: "They are more interested when I give them a book or article because I've validated them."

Teachers believe technology integration allows for them to appeal to students' differences. The teachers who participated in our focus group identified a number of differences between students, such as their distinct ability levels, comfort levels with verbal participation, and desires to be active and manipulate information, and they described situations in which digital literacies can be effective in designing lessons and learning activities that appeal to these student differences. The remainder of this section is divided into two categories, each addressing a way participants felt digital literacies can be used to maximize the learning of students with specific characteristics: digital literacies can help teachers (1) facilitate the participation of students who are reluctant to share in class, and (2) create activities that appeal to active students.

Digital literacies facilitate the participation of students who are reluctant to share in class. Multiple teachers in our focus group asserted that digital literacies can facilitate the participation of students who are reluctant to verbally share their ideas. One explained that the act of posting to a class blog enabled the in-class participation of some of her quieter students; after students read each others' comments in the electronic forum, they found it easy to continue that conversation in a face-to-face format: "The blog posts are good because [the students will] read what the others have to say and then say things like, 'Hey man, I really like what you posted' and bring that conversation back into the classroom…Those who wouldn't speak up do now."

Another teacher found digital literacies to be especially helpful in aiding the participation of English Language Learners (ELLs), explaining that many of her ELL students feared making mistakes when speaking and describing how online communication helped ease their fears: "I don't know how many people here work in ELL classes, but they're great with [digital literacies]. [ELLs] are usually so reserved in class and afraid of making a mistake." Another teacher contrasted his ELL students' fears with their observed ease using digital communication, and he noted a subsequent increase in their class participation: "They've really done well with the online back and forth. They participate more." He described the increased comfort and confidence of his ELL students as an "unanticipated upside" of his incorporation of digital literacies into his instruction.

Digital literacies can help teachers create activities that appeal to active students. Participants depicted the use of digital literacies as especially effective for designing activities that appeal to active students. One described how, in a unit on persuasion and the media, the students made video public service announcements that were ultimately shared with a wider audience: "We talked about how they would get their persuasive points across and they had to storyboard and plan for them. It culminated with a film festival." This teacher explained that her students appreciated the way this assignment provided them with opportunities to take ownership of their work and integrate some humor into it: "They got really into that project. They're all boys, so being able to direct and being active and comedic was a big draw for them."

Another teacher explained that many of her students enjoy the opportunities that technological innovations such as interactive whiteboards offer, both to manipulate information and appeal to more active students. She described how the boards can be used to highlight examples of literary terms in specific colors: "We can highlight in green the good examples of elaboration, similes in red, et cetera." This teacher addressed the benefits of other features to literacy instruction, stating, "You can do lots of things with the Smartboard with reading and writing."

Teachers believe they lack agency in technology integration. Although our teachers expressed a great deal of enthusiasm for technology integration and digital literacies, they also shared frustrations, revealing their lack of agency in their local district's and/or school's policies and processes for the adoption and required implementation of new technology. One teacher commented, "The reality is these policies are made by people who aren't us, that aren't in the classrooms. And they're saying we have to go with this [new technology]." Several teachers expressed concern that though they often feel pressure to include technology in their instructional practices, the push for technology often comes without the appropriate training. These reservations dealt mostly with the idea of integrating technology in the classroom purely for the sake of having the new technology. One teacher shared a story about her school's disastrous foray into iPod Touches a few years prior. She pointed out, "Nobody thought about how to use it. It was a means to an end. We just had it as an end. The technology can't be the end. It has to be the means."

Forces that bring technology into the classroom often feel beyond teachers' control. Several teachers questioned the rationale behind the implementation of new technologies, sometimes required by school leadership, intimating that often technology was used a means of "keeping up with the Joneses." In fact, the majority of the teachers felt that the "seductive" marketing of the latest technology often led to its swift installation into the classroom without a plan for training the teachers to use it effectively. Below is one teacher's experience with this type of shortsightedness:

> Our school put Smartboards in every classroom. It was like that's what they thought they were supposed to do. They were put over our whiteboards. I come in one day and a Smartboard is completely covering my white board. I was like, "Can I write on this?" I mean we didn't have any training. I didn't know how to write on it or anything. Either take it down or show us how to use it. That's the story too often with technology.

Many of the teachers felt unprepared to effectively integrate the new technology into their instructional practices and they would often utilize it on a limited basis; one explained the contrast between her perception of her school leadership's attitude toward technology integration and her use of these resources: "Someone in charge says, 'You need these technologies. I'll give them to you.' I didn't use the laptops. They're spending all this money and they don't ask the teacher if they want it." This comment reveals the distinction between purposefully selected technological resources for classroom use and purchasing technology simply for the sake of having it.

These forces sometimes seem irrational and at great costs, leading to teacher frustrations and even resentment, and ultimately making some teachers feel like they've lost control. Although our teachers were generally enthusiastic about technology, some felt as if they had lost control over parts of their instructional decision-making due to the infusion of new technologies. In addition to the lack of timely and adequate training in the use of the technology, a few of the teachers expressed that the technology could sometimes overshadow the content they were teaching. Further, several of the teachers made note of the economic impact involved with the wide implementation of new, state-of-the-art technologies. One teacher pointedly asked, "When the cost [is] raising class sizes and dismissing teachers, is it worth it?" Moreover, every teacher in the group expressed some frustration with the technology they used in the classroom, ranging from power issues to resistance to policies that require technology use to become an integral part of their instruction.

DISCUSSION

We feel this exploratory study provides a useful point of entry into the conversation about the beliefs and attitudes teachers hold toward digital literacies. Two aspects of this study's findings stand out as especially significant. Although teachers believe digital literacies can be beneficial to their students, teachers believe they lack agency in making choices about how to integrate technology into their instruction. These ideas reveal a key issue associated with teachers' beliefs about the incorporation of digital literacies in the English classroom: the challenge of maximizing potential benefits for students while providing agency for teachers. Although teachers believe these technological innovations can enhance the relevance of their instructional practices and curriculum and make it easier for students of different ability levels and attributes (such as those who are shy or especially active) to learn, they also feel pressured to use forms of technology without appropriate training and a thorough understanding of the benefits.

The fact that teachers believe digital literacies are important is consonant with previous research (Hutchison & Reinking, 2011; McDougall, 2009) and is in line with national and state standards (e.g., IRA, NCTE, ISTE, CCSS). But also in line with previous research (e.g., Hutchison & Reinking, 2011), our teachers expressed dissatisfaction with the lack of professional development they were receiving. Although our participants acknowledged excitement about the potential of digital literacies, they did express concerns regarding the use of tools that they are sometimes unprepared to use. The fact that some of the teachers involved in our focus group felt that they were often compelled to use technology simply for the sake of using technology departs from recommendations that technology be used strategically and with an understanding of its benefits in classrooms (e.g., Pasternak 2007; Young & Bush, 2004).

This idea of being forced to use certain technologies further represents the lack of agency our teachers expressed. Given the extensive body of literature pointing to the importance of teacher beliefs in changing teacher behaviors and instruction (e.g., Ertmer, 2005; Pajares, 1992), this issue becomes especially important.

Our findings relate to the sociocultural perspective with which we viewed this study. The key ideas that emerged – that teachers believe digital literacies can be beneficial to their students and that they feel they lack agency in making choices about how to integrate technology – connect to the sociocultural belief that literacy practices incorporate social, cultural, political, historical, mental, and physical factors (Lewis, Enciso, & Moje, 2007). The finding that teachers believe digital literacies can benefit their students reflects an openness to new forms of literacy and the new social and cultural ideas that these literacy practices represent. When viewed from a sociocultural perspective, the benefits that teachers associate with digital literacies represent effective teaching methods that align with and are embedded in significant cultural movements. Similarly, the idea that teachers feel they lack agency when making choices about technology integration reflects cultural and political factors related to the uses of technology in the classroom. These findings and the corresponding beliefs of our focus group participants address the issues of social, cultural, and political factors essential to a sociocultural perspective on literacy instruction. Our findings further support Moje and Lewis' (2007) contention that sociocultural theory be renamed Critical Sociocultural Literacy theory to address and reflect ideas related to identity, power, and agency in literacy learning. The ideas addressed by Moje and Lewis certainly emerged in our findings.

IMPLICATIONS AND FUTURE DIRECTIONS

On the one hand, findings from this study prove promising: English teachers acknowledge the immense benefits of technology integration and want to incorporate value-added technology practices into their instruction. In order to maximize the potential of these tools, participants did express a need for professional development. This holds important implications for teacher educators.

Teacher educators need to move beyond discussing the importance of digital literacies and instead provide preservice teachers with meaningful (and value added) activities that incorporate digital literacies. Our findings that teachers already believe digital literacies are beneficial for students but that teachers feel they lack agency when implementing these tools in the classroom support the argument that technology should be adopted and used with a clear understanding of the particular pedagogical goals to be achieved (e.g., Pasternak 2007; Young & Bush, 2004). Teacher educators should promote the skillful integration of content, pedagogy, and technology—perhaps drawing on the principles of the Technological Pedagogical Content Knowledge framework (TPACK; Mishra & Koehler, 2006) and should emphasize the value of thinking critically about technology use (Richards, 2000).

Preservice teachers who are trained to use forms of digital literacy with specific learning goals in mind will maximize their effectiveness of their instructional methods and will be well-positioned to advocate for agency in the kinds of technology used in their classes. As new teachers enter the profession with strong understandings of purposeful technology use, they will be able to articulate needs for specific technology tools and ideally to avoid the use of technology "for the sake of using technology," a concern voiced by our focus group participants.

In addition to these implications for teacher education programs, this study can also inform future related research. Such research can inquire further into teachers' beliefs that they lack agency in technology integration, with a focus on how technology initiatives can be crafted in a way that promotes purposeful technology use.

REFERENCES

Ajzen, I., & Fishbein, M. (2005). The influence of attitudes on behavior. In D. Albarracín, B. T. Johnson, & M. P. Zanna (Eds.), *The handbook of attitudes* (pp. 173-221). Mahwah, NJ: Erlbaum.

Bandura, A. (1986). *Social foundations of thought and action: A social cognitive theory.* Englewood Cliffs, NJ: Prentice-Hall.

Beach, R., Hull, G., & O'Brien, D. (2011). Transforming English language arts in a web 2.0 world. In D. Lapp & D. Fisher (Eds.), *Handbook of research on teaching the English Language Arts* (3rd ed., pp. 161-167). New York, NY: Routledge.

Common Core State Standards Initiative. (2011). *English language arts standards.* Retrieved from http://www.corestandards.org/ELA-Literacy

Creswell, J. W., & Miller, D. L. (2000). Determining validity in qualitative inquiry. *Theory into Practice, 39,* 124-130.

Curwood, J. S., & Cowell, L. L. (2011). iPoetry: Creating space for new literacies in the English curriculum. *Journal of Adolescent and Adult Literacy, 55,* 110-120.

Ertmer, P. A. (2005). Teacher pedagogical beliefs: The final frontier in our quest for technology integration. *Educational Technology Research and Development, 53,* 25-39.

Ertmer, P. A., & Ottenbreit-Leftwich, A. T. (2010). Teacher technology change: How knowledge, confidence, beliefs, and culture intersect. *Journal of Research in Technology Education, 42,* 255-284.

Fisher, T. (2006). Educational transformation: Is it like "beauty" in the eye of the beholder, or will we know it when we see it? *Education and Information Technologies, 11,* 293-303.

Gray, L., & Lewis, L. (2009). *Educational technology in public school districts: Fall 2008* (NCES 2010-003). Washington, DC: National Center for Education Statistics, Institute of Education Sciences, U.S. Department of Education.

Hagood, M. C. (2012). Risks, rewards, and responsibilities of using new literacies in middle grades. *Voices from the Middle, 19,* 10-16.

Hutchison, A., & Reinking, D. (2011). Teachers' perceptions of integrating information and communication technologies into literacy instruction: A national survey in the United States. *Reading Research Quarterly, 46,* 312-333.

International Reading Association. (2012). *Adolescent literacy* (Position statement, Rev. 2012 ed.). Newark, DE: IRA.

Karchmer, R. (2001). The journey ahead: Thirteen teachers report how the Internet influences literacy and literacy instruction in their K-12 classrooms. *Reading Research Quarterly, 36,* 442-466.

Lankshear, C., & Knobel, M. (2011). *New literacies: Everyday practices and classroom learning.* Buckingham: Open University Press.

Leander, K. (2009). Composing with old and new media: Toward a parallel pedagogy. In V. Carrington & M. Robinson (Eds.), *Digital literacies: Social learning and classroom practices* (pp. 147-164). London, UK: SAGE Publishing, Ltd.

Lenhart, A., Arafeh, S., Smith, A., & Macgill, A. R. (2008). *Writing, technology and teens.* Washington, DC: Pew Internet & American Life Project.

Lenhart, A., Madden, M., & Hitlin, P. (2005). *Teens and technology: Youth are leading the transition to a fully wired and mobile nation.* Washington, DC: PEW Internet and Family Life.

Lewis, C., Enciso, P., & Moje, E. B. (2007). Introduction: Reframing sociocultural research on literacy. In C. Lewis, P. Enciso, & E. B. Moje (Eds.), *Reframing sociocultural research on literacy: Identity, agency, and power* (pp. 1- 11). Mahwah, NJ: Lawrence Erlbaum.

McDougall, J. (2009). A crisis of professional identity: How primary teachers are coming to terms with changing views of literacy. *Teaching and Teacher Education, 26,* 679–687.

McGrail, E. (2006). "It's a double-edged sword, this technology business": Secondary English teachers' perspectives on a schoolwide laptop technology initiative. *Teachers College Record, 108,* 1055-1079.

McKenna, M. C., Conradi, K., Young, C. A., & Jang, B. G. (2013). Technology and the Common Core Standards. In L. M. Morrow, T. Shanahan, & K. K. Wixson (Eds.), *Teaching with the Common Core Standards for English Language Arts* (pp. 152-169). New York, NY: Guilford Press.

Miles, M. B., & Huberman, A. M. (1994). *Qualitative data analysis.* Thousand Oaks, CA: Sage.

Mishra, P., & Koehler, M. J. (2006). Technological pedagogical content knowledge: A new framework for teacher knowledge. *Teachers College Record, 108,* 1017-1054.

Moje, E. B., & Lewis, C. (2007). Examining opportunities to learn literacy: The role of critical sociocultural literacy research. In C. Lewis, P. Enciso, & E. B. Moje (Eds.), *Reframing sociocultural research on literacy: Identity, agency, and power* (pp. 15- 48). Mahwah, NJ: Lawrence Erlbaum.

O'Brien, D., & Scharber, C. (2008). Digital literacies go to school: Potholes and possibilities. *Journal of Adolescent and Adult Literacy, 52,* 66-68.

Pajares, M. F. (1992). Teachers' beliefs and educational research: Cleaning up a messy construct. *Review of Educational Research, 62,* 307-332.

Pasternak, D. L. (2007). Is technology used as practice? A survey analysis of preservice English teachers' perceptions and classroom practices. *Contemporary Issues in Technology and Teacher Education, 7,* 140-157.

Richards, G. (2000). Why use computer technology? *English Journal, 90* (2), 38-41.

Rokeach, M. (1968). *Beliefs, attitudes, and values: A theory of organization and change.* San Francisco, CA: Jossey Bass.

Swenson, J., Rozema, R., Young, C. A., McGrail, E., & Whitin, P. (2005). Beliefs about technology and the preparation of English teachers: Beginning the conversation. *Contemporary Issues in Technology and Teacher Education, 5,* 210-236.

Turbill, J., & Murray, J. (2006). Early literacy and new technologies in Australian schools: Policy, research, and practice. In M. C. McKenna, L. D. Labbo, R. Kieffer, & D. Reinking (Eds.), *International handbook of literacy and technology* (Vol. 2, pp. 93-108). Mahwah, NJ: Lawrence Erlbaum.

Young, C. A., & Bush, J. (2004). Teaching the English language arts with technology: A critical approach and pedagogical framework. *Contemporary Issues in Technology and Teacher Education, 4,* 1-22.

APPENDIX A

Topic Guide for Focus Group
- What we hope to gain from the discussion:
- Teacher perspective on the relationship of technology to literacy
- How you incorporate technology into your classroom
- Challenges you face incorporating (or trying to) technology in the classroom

Common definitions/understanding of digital literacies (DL)
Explain that we've asked for their own perception of digital literacy, but we need to have an in-common understanding for the purpose of this discussion. When we speak here about digital literacy, we mean communication mediated by digital technologies.

Prompts:
- How does this understanding compare to what you identified as your own?
- What do you think the relationship is between technology and literacy?
  - literacy instruction
- (Shift) What media do you incorporate into your instruction? Why?
  - What technology do you use?
  - standards — ELA/technology?
  - activities
  - types of text
  - audience
  - purpose of your incorporation of DL in the classroom
  - Challenges you face
    - Access?
      - Websites/social networking
      - Technology
      - Email
    - Administration? Colleagues?
- Kevin Leander, a professor at Vanderbilt interested in digital literacies, identified 4 different stances teachers can have towards digital literacy. Look at the slide and see if you see yourself holding one of these stances.
  - Show slide with stances
- Which are you? Why?

Stance-Related Talking Points
- Teachers' beliefs about importance of literacy (e.g., What does being literate mean? What do you want your students to be able to do by the time they graduate? Are there new literacy demands that did not exist 50 years ago?).
- Perceived literacy differences in digital versus print settings (e.g., What are some differences between reading online versus reading in print settings?).

- Role of the teacher in light of these differences (e.g., Whose job is it to teach students strategies for success in digital literacy? If it is your job, what are perceived threats/challenges?).

Practices
- Identification of all technology used in Language Arts/English classrooms.
- Identification of all web applications used
- Perceived advantages and challenges of these technologies and applications

APPENDIX B

Teacher Questionnaire
- How many years have you been a teacher?
- What is your certification subject and grade area(s)?
- Have you had any instructional technology courses in your undergraduate or graduate schooling? If so, please describe content.
- Have you participated in any professional development related to incorporating technology into your English classroom? If so, did your school provide the development or did you seek it out? Please describe.
- What resources do you use if you are interested in incorporating a new technology into your classroom? (A technology coordinator, a website, a book, a friend, etc.)
- How would you define digital literacy?
- How often do you use email for personal use?
- How often do you use twitter for personal use?
- How often do you use social media (like Facebook and MySpace) for personal use?
- How often do you create electronic presentations (such as PowerPoint, Keynote, Prezi, etc.) for personal use?
- How often do you use a digital camera for personal use?
- How often do you use a video camera for personal use?
- Are there any other technologies you regularly use for personal use?
- How often do you use email for instructional use?
- Please list any of your favorite websites that you use in teaching English content.
- Overall, how would you rate your own skills with technology

APPENDIX C

"Start Codes" for Data Reduction Process

The following codes emerged from an analysis of the standards identified in three documents: a) IRA Standards 2010: Middle and High School Content Classroom Teacher, b) ISTE Standards for Students, and c) ISTE Standards for Teachers.

1. MOTIVATION
2. DIFFERENTIATION
3. PERSPECTIVE
4. STUDENT ACCESS
5. INSTRUCTIONAL TOOL
6. STUDENTS' OUT-OF-SCHOOL EXPERIENCES
7. EQUITY
8. STUDENTS' DIVERSE LITERACIES
9. STUDENT ACCESS
10. LEARNING ENVIRONMENT
11. LEGITIMACY
12. HIGHER-ORDER THINKING
13. AUTHENTICITY
14. REFLECTION/META-COGNITION
15. RELEVANCE
16. DIFFERENTIATION
17. TEACHER DIGITAL FLUENCY
18. COLLABORATION
19. COMMUNICATION
20. TEACHER MODELING
21. ETHICAL USE OF TECHNOLOGY
22. CULTURAL UNDERSTANDING/GLOBAL AWARENESS
23. LEARNING COMMUNITIES
24. CREATIVITY
25. TEACHER USE
26. PERSONAL EXPRESSION
27. INNOVATION
28. MULTIMODALITY
29. DIGITAL FLUENCY—RESEARCH
30. DIGITAL FLUENCY--GENERAL

Patricia L. Anders
University of Arizona

Section III:
Global Perspectives

Scholarly attention to literacy around the globe falls into one of three broad types: comparative studies, studies of a particular geographic region, usually conducted in the ethnographic tradition, and studies investigating "scapes," spaces created to describe "dimensions of global cultural flows that are fluid and irregular, rather than fixed and finite" (Maira & Soep, 2005, p. xvi) .

Comparative studies are typically designed to investigate the similarities and differences in literacy performance and achievement between different regions or countries with other regions and countries. Much of this scholarship has been funded by UNESCO; memorably by Gray's (1956) ground breaking study comparing the teaching of reading and writing around the world. Another seminal publication (Downing, 1973), compared literacy in 13 countries, first describing the research methods, then framing the reports in terms of linguistics, teachers, and cultural expectations, and finally reporting on the literacy status and practices of the countries. More recently, the best known international comparisons of student literacy achievement are the reports of the Programme for International Student Assessment (PISA). A recent report, which departs from the tradition of comparing literacy achievement, is by Goodman and colleagues (2011) describing reading across Asian languages.

Ethnographic-type studies are not designed to make comparisons; rather, these studies closely describe literacy in a bounded community. Purcell-Gates (2007) claims, "In the postmodernist world, grand theories no longer hold, and local contexts are seen as wholes, providing ground for 'little theories' that reflect local cultural contexts" (p. 3). Brian Street (1984) is credited for articulating this line of inquiry, arguing persuasively that literacy is ideological and that for literacy to be understood in all of its complexity, close studies of particular contexts are needed. The article in this section, authored by Sailors and colleagues, is an example of this type of scholarship. Although a theoretical frame based on "beating the odds" in United States schools is used, the study's methods and interpretations are particularized to a South African school and community.

Whereas comparative studies are likely to be organized according to national boundaries and ethnographies designed to richly describe a particular community, the third type of studies is considered "transnational" or "transcultural;" that is, investigations "that includes a space for participants whose life experiences place the negotiation of multiple national cultural identities at the center of how people engage in literacy events" (Medina, 2010). These are studies that investigate particular practices and contexts that represent participants from diverse linguistic and national experiences and backgrounds. Three studies in the following section represent this line of inquiry, demonstrating the relationship of national and cultural experiences on reading and writing practices.

Denise Davila investigated "Cultural Boundaries or Geographic Borders" describing how future teachers narrate "American" in response to a bilingual book, Garza's *In My Family/En Mi Familia.*" This close examination of the responses of future teachers within this literacy event reveals the powerful ways personal cultural identities privilege some groups and disenfranchise other groups.

In a similar vein, Erika Mein and Luciene Wandermurem investigated ". . . the Multiliterate Identities of Pre-Service Teachers on the U.S.-Mexico Border," exploring pre-service teachers' conceptions of future (multi-)literate practice when teaching culturally and linguistically diverse students. Like the teachers in the Davila study, tensions and contradictions among preservice teachers' cultural models were found. Her study establishes a need to focus on border-centered pedagogies in teacher education programs so as to better understand future literacy teachers who have their feet planted in two cultures.

Susan Hopewell, author of another article in this section, examined ways in which Spanish-English emerging bilingual students participate in classes when their linguistic resources are used to process English language text. She links her findings to how classroom language policy can limit students' use of translanguaging, narrowing their options for constructing text meaning.

The contributions in this section are evidence that what is trending in global perspectives in literacy research is to investigate closely questions of language and literacy as informed and influenced by multiple transcultural and transnational considerations. These chapters challenge us to examine assumptions about both language and literacy processes and practices as we transverse the globe.

REFERENCES

Downing, J. (1973). *Comparative reading: Cross-national studies of behavior and processes in reading and writing.* New York, NY: The Macmillan Company.

Goodman, K. S., Wang, S., Iventosh, M., & Goodman, Y.M. (2011). *Reading in Asian languages.* New York, NY: Routledge.

Maira, S. & Soep, E. (2005). *Youthscapes: The popular, the national, the global.* Philadelpha, PA: University of Pennsylvania Press.

Medina, C. (2010). "Reading across Communities" in biliteracy practices: Examining translocal discourses and cultural flows in literature discussions. *Reading Research Quarterly, 45,* 1, 40-60.

Purcell-Gates, V. (2007). *Cultural practices of literacy: Case studies of language, literacy, social practice, and power.* Mahwah, New Jersey: Lawrence Erlbaum Associates, Publishers.

Street, B. (1984). *Literacy in theory and practice.* New York, NY: Cambridge University Press.

Implementing a School-Wide Reading Program in Malawi: A Case Study of Change

Misty Sailors*
James Hoffman**
Troy Wilson*
Lorena Villarreal*
Katie Peterson**
Henri Chilora***
Liviness Phiri***
Tionge Saka***

The University of Texas at San Antonio

**The University of Texas at Austin*

***Malawi Institute of Education, Zomba, Malawi*

Although Malawi is one of the most peaceful countries on the Sub-Sahara African continent, it faces many challenges. With adult literacy rates of only 70%, the government is aggressively working to raise educational standards. Recognizing the need for greater change, the Malawi Ministry of Education, Science and Technology (MOEST), with the Malawi Institute of Education (MIE) and support of donor partners designed and instituted the National Primary Curriculum (NPC). Following the curriculum design, the MIE disseminated textbooks for each core subject area in grades 1-8, both Chichewa (national) and English (official).

This attempt to reform education in Malawi was challenging. In a system where schooling became free under Free Primary Education Policy, Malawi supports almost three million learners in primary schools, made up of grades 1-8. The government currently employs over 50,000 teachers, providing for a described student to teacher ratio of 76:1 and a student to trained teacher ratio of 92:1 (DOEP, 2011). Malawi faces a lack of qualified teachers. Teacher attrition is a serious issue (Macro International, 2008) as is teacher turnover, which has been called "profound and overwhelming even by Sub-Saharan Africa standards" (Kayuni & Tambulan, 2007, p. 89). Finally, teachers were asked to implement the national primary curriculum but were given very little training, an "orientation," on how best to do that.

As a result, we partnered with the MOEST, the MIE, and the United States Agency for International Development (USAID), along with various local international partners, to design, develop, and implement a reading program known locally as Read Malawi. This program was inclusive of (a) complementary reading books and teacher's guides for learners in grades 1-3, (b) teacher training on how to incorporate the reading program into their existing school day, (c) school leader training on how best to support teachers as they implemented the program, and (d) community sensitization on the program and training on how to support schools as the reading program was implemented. This two-year program demonstrated successes: Teachers learned to improve their practices and student reading achievement improved as measured through a pre-, post-test, quasi-experimental design (Sailors et al., 2012).

As part of the program, each participating school received over 4,100 complementary reading books (guided reading and read alouds) with accompanying teachers' guides. The guided reading books were designed for students to read with teacher support and were much shorter in word density than read alouds. Guided reading books utilized patterns of vocabulary control, word repetition, and picture support to insure students could be successful. Each guided reading book was linked to a read aloud book topically or thematically.

The vast majority of both types of books were fiction; approximately 10% were expository and the remainder included fantasy stories drawing on oral folklore traditions in Malawi. Each book was focused on support for reading strategies, including word identification and fluency strategies (in guided reading books) and ongoing, active comprehension strategies (in read alouds) following Almasi's (2003) outline of these reading strategies. Because the accessibility of texts is essential to successful reading encounters with young and beginning readers (Heibert & Sailors, 2008; Hoffman, Roser, Salas, Patterson, & Pennington, 2001), the books were carefully leveled for learners in ways that balanced decoding demands of the text (e.g., word difficulty, regularity) and support features of the text (e.g., repeated phrases, picture support).

Because teachers' guides assist teachers in knowing what to do with learning materials in developing countries (Craig, Kraft & du Plessis, 1998), we created a teachers' guide for each of the paired sets of books. The teachers' guides were designed using a patterned approach; while they were not scripted, they each contained 12 recommended steps to be implemented over a two-day period and were linked directly to national curriculum. Since language policy in Malawi called for attention to the home language (Chichewa) and the second national language (English), therefore, materials, books and teachers' guides were provided in each language. The teachers were asked to implement the program two days per week for approximately 90-120 minutes each day. Freedom was given to select from grade appropriate book sets to use with classes based on matching the set to core textbooks and curriculum.

As we examined our evaluation results (Sailors et al., 2012), we noticed some schools in the intervention group seemed to be implementing at higher and more complete levels than other participating schools; this observed variability in implementation became the focus of this study. We conducted an intensive case study of one of these schools. Our study was guided by the following research question, "What are the characteristics and qualities of a high implementing school that might explain the school's success at program adoption?"

BACKGROUND

We situate this study within the "Beating the Odds" framework embedded inside the larger body of work known as the "effective schools" literature. From an historical perspective, the effective schools literature began in response to findings of the Coleman report (Coleman et al., 1966), which established that family and community characteristics in combination with innate intelligence were sufficient to predict achievement in schools. Based on analyses in the Coleman report, school factors such as resources available and teacher quality, made no significant contribution to student achievement. Many policy makers interpreted the report, as "schools don't make a difference." Weber (1971) challenged this report, claiming the data set did not allow for the few schools, "outliers", that did exist under these conditions and where student achievement was high. Weber found those schools and described the qualities that may have contributed to their success. Others followed their example, thus beginning the effective schools literature (Hoffman & Rutherford, 1984).

There has been a renewed interest in this body of literature in light of the high stakes testing movement in the United States (Hoffman, Assaf, & Paris, 2001). Operating under the label, beating the odds research, several have re-focused their attention on the instructional practices of classroom teachers as a way of understanding the achievement of schools that "should" not normally be achieving (see the work of Taylor, Pearson, Clark, & Walpole, 2000). While many of these studies have been conducted in the US, the interest in using the framework for international contexts is growing. For example, Sailors, Hoffman & Matthee (2007) used the frame to study high performing schools in rural South Africa. Their cross-case analysis revealed six themes associated with high-performing schools that served students from low-income communities, including safe, orderly, and positive learning climates with strong leaders, effective teachers, and a significant partnership with the local community. Additionally, these schools had a positive identity and focused on literacy outcomes.

Methodologically, studies in this paradigm employ various tools for data collection and analysis. But the thoughtful use of qualitative examination of all aspects of the school's operation, including teacher practices, student actions, and community involvement appear to be the most widely used method for capturing and analyzing these types of studies. It was under these circumstances and conditions that we engaged in this study. Specifically, we sought to explore those aspects of one high implementing/performing school in rural Malawi that appeared to be successful at implementing a primary-based, school-wide literacy program.

METHODOLOGY

This study is interpretivistic in nature and follows a case-study approach (Merriam, 1997). We were interested in uncovering the perspective of stakeholders in these schools; we elected to use inductive research strategies as a way of obtaining those goals (Merriam, 1997). The approach allowed us to investigate the nature of the school "within its real-life context" (Yin, 1994, p.13). Because case studies are both the process and the product of such investigations, we held the school as the unit of study to help us gain "insight, discovery, and interpretation" and meaning for our "case" (Merriam, 1997, p. 27).

PARTICIPANTS

Our case includes one school, drawn from 21 schools that participated in a feasibility trial of the Read Malawi program. During the feasibility trial, we randomly assigned 14 zones (organizational structure of Malawi schools) to one of the two groups (intervention and wait list control). We then randomly selected three schools from each zone to participate in the feasibility trial. Thandiza Primary School (PS), the focus of this report, was one of three schools that demonstrated higher degrees of implementation than others in the feasibility trial (as measured through our pilot feasibility implementation checklists, student achievement scores on posttest measures, observations of teaching practices and classroom print environment ratings, and anecdotal evidence from the monitoring team).

Thandiza PS is located in a rural village in the southern area of Malawi. It is situated approximately 30 minutes from the former colonial administrative capital city. Traveling to the school is not as much of a challenge as is the case with other schools in Malawi—the main road to the school is tarred with an adjoining dirt road that leads directly to the school. Thandiza is surrounded by small privately owned farms; the vast majority of the students draw from 10 of the 17 surrounding villages that are rural and primarily farming communities.

The school consists of three buildings used for teaching, with each building containing two classrooms. At the time of this study, there were eight teachers assigned to the school, including the head teacher who also teaches in addition to his administrative duties. The school served 1,052 learners across grades, or "standards", 1-6. Primary grades 1-3 were the vast majority of the student population as there is a significant drop in enrollment in upper grades 4-6, which is an ongoing challenge for schools in Malawi (World Bank, 2010).

DATA COLLECTION

We collected a variety of data for this study, including observational data in the form of field notes, audio taped interviews, which were later transcribed, and other artifacts of the print environment of school and classroom environments. We collected data with a team of Malawian researchers from the MIE across five consecutive school days. Our team was international and included the authors of this paper, four of whom are Chichewa speakers. Each non-Chichewa speaker on our team was paired with at least one Chichewa speaker for purposes of lesson observations in Chichewa and for some interviews. The school knew the majority of the team; we were introduced to the community on the first day of data collection. Our data collection in classrooms spanned the entire school day. After school, we conducted our interviews with school personnel, children and community members. At the end of every day, team members met for debriefing. The debriefing sessions centered on key observations, salient points, identification of preliminary themes, and tentative scheduling of the next day's observations. We describe each data source in the sections that follow.

Observations. We collected observational data each day of our school visits. Our field notes were taken during literacy instruction and in other subject areas. Our team used paper and a writing utensil to capture the observations so that we would not disturb the children with laptops. We found ourselves "writing like crazy" (Wolcott, 1995) as a way of keeping up with various activities in the classrooms. We noted how the teacher and students were interacting with texts in their environment, as well as what forms of interaction were taking place between various groups, whether teacher to student, or student to student. We also noted whether or not teachers were following the prescribed nature of the reading program and noted modifications when observed. We followed the same pattern of observations during content lessons, observing closely to see if teachers used, or modified, any instructional practices from the literacy lessons as part of their content practices. We audio recorded one guided reading and one read aloud lesson for each of the three classrooms in which we were observing, in both English and Chichewa.

Interviews. Over the course of the data collection time frame, we conducted 27 interviews with various stakeholders. In total, we interviewed the head teacher five times and each of the three classroom teachers, grades 1-3, twice. We also interviewed 12 students across the three classrooms. We conducted a focus group interview with the mother group, the Parent Teacher Association, and the School Management Committee. We also interviewed one member of the traditional governance system, the village head. We conducted interviews with school personnel in English; our colleagues conducted all other interviews in Chichewa and translated them to English. We began semi-structured interviews with a set of guiding questions (see Appendix A) and asked follow up questions accordingly. Interviews with students centered about their favorite books, why they liked the books and what books they took home. All interviews were transcribed using a denaturalized method (Oliver, Serovich & Mason, 2005).

Other artifacts. We collected 123 digital images of the physical environment related to the school. We centered this digital documentation on the print environment of the head teacher's office. We documented school enrollment, passing rates, and other school information related to demographics. We also collected digital images of classroom texts.

DATA ANALYSIS

Data analysis occurred in three phases. Phase I occurred at the end of each site visit during our team debriefing sessions. These meetings lasted approximately one and one half hours. It was at these meetings that team members compared notes from the school and began to interpret the data. During these discussions, one member was designated as the "note taker" and recorded conversations including discussions of emerging themes. These discussions were followed by plans for follow-up data collection on subsequent days, based on our emerging understanding of the phenomenon.

Phase II took place after full data collection had been completed and we left the site. During this phase, our team read the observational field notes, read the transcribed interviews, and examined the artifacts as a way of developing an open coding scheme, using constant comparative methods (Glaser & Strauss, 2012). We discussed all codes until consensus was built; disagreements were handled through discussions and turning back to the original sources of data. Through this process, we generated themes, revisiting codes during the process and always turning back to the data.

During Phase III, which occurred approximately three months later, we revisited schools and engaged various stakeholders in member checking. During these member-checking sessions, we presented the case to various stakeholders at Thandiza. We read the case to them with translation assistance when necessary and asked them to correct any misrepresentations. We sought clarification and elaboration on outstanding issues. We also identified and asked them to describe any updates or changes to their implementation since our last visit. Finally, we probed to determine if the themes were representative of their perspective. We used data collected during member checking as part of our data set, finalizing our themes as a result of this member checking.

FINDINGS

Five themes emerged from our analysis. We found (a) the school and community worked in unison with each other and, (b) as a result of training, saw an increased capacity (c) while holding each other accountable for the implementation of the program. Additionally, (d) books appeared to be at the center of innovation in the school even though the school (e) faced ongoing challenges. Each theme is presented below.

Unity Among Stakeholders

Across our participants, the theme of "unity" was commonly mentioned and discussed. This unity was forged through factors including interaction of all stakeholders, increased capacity of stakeholders, entry of the books into the community, and the fact that stakeholders held each other accountable. A first grade teacher alluded to this unity when she stated that successful implementation was due to "cooperation between teachers, community, and learners." Also, a second grade teacher was very specific about the role of unity in program implementation,

> Teachers are united. We assist each other: when one teacher is not around we take over his/her class and make sure that teaching and learning is going on well all the time. Teachers also assist one another during continuing professional development. This strengthens teachers' weak areas. The head teacher has also been instrumental. He observes lessons and provides advice to teachers.

The village head, as well as members of the Parent Teacher Association (PTA) and the School Management Committee (SMC), also believed unity to be a contributing factor. Members of the SMC mentioned they "all do development activities together." The Primary Education Advisor (PEA) also noticed the school's united commitment to success of the program, stating,

> It does not surprise me, because the teachers and the head teacher at this school showed determination in implementing the program, and I was there just to support them. This school is different from the other schools in that, at this school, there is cooperation among teachers. The community is friendly compared to the other communities…

In separate interviews with various stakeholders, it was clear that each group within the community was well aware of the program. There was evidence the program had become a priority for the community. For example, the teacher volunteers (community members who volunteered to help children read books that were brought home each evening) took great pride in working with students outside of school. The twice per week, two-hour tutoring sessions were a major part of the community's connection with the program. This connection appeared to be directly fostered by and linked this theme of unity.

The Role of Training and Increased Capacity

Training directly related to the implementation of the program appeared to play a prominent role in increasing the capacity of all stakeholders. The PEA, the head teacher, teachers, students, and participating community members all felt a positive increase in their ability to perform tasks asked of them, based on our interviews. This, in turn, seemed to foster further investment in the program. For example, the PEA noted that proper training played a primary role in the success of the program, beginning with his initial training in 2010. He believed, because of the training, he was able to grasp the program as a whole. He felt it helped him understand the new concepts and how they "can be implemented in different situations." He attributed his role as a trainer of teachers at his school, on the core national training team, and his participation in development of the training manuals to successful implementation of the program. It was clear through our interviews that successful implementation of the program was due in part to the head teacher having a clear and systematic understanding of the program, including the goals and implementation of the program.

Teachers also believed training was a major factor in success of the program. For example, the second grade teacher was very direct in attributing training to success of other teachers, when he stated, "This strengthens teachers' weak areas." The first grade teacher believed that training and interactions with other teachers assisted her in "perfecting" her practices and that she could "deliver a Read Malawi lesson completely even without arranging one in advance." "Teachers helping teachers" was prevalent throughout many interviews and is consistent with the theme of unity as it relates to improving capacity across the campus. Although the initial program training was only provided to three teachers, other teachers on the campus were exposed to the program through intentional interaction with the three trained teachers.

Also in keeping with the connections between the theme of unity and capacity building were references to working with the community. For example, the first grade teacher told us that she and other teachers "sensitized the community about the program," and asked the community "to get involved in implementing the program." The capacity of the community appeared to increase due to general awareness, goals, and expected outcomes of the program. All major groups were reported to be at the initial sensitization meeting, including the village head, the SMC, and the PTA.

We documented evidence of students' increased capacity in a variety of ways, including our observations and in interviews with participants. For example, members of the SMC credited the program for teaching first grade children writing skills. Additionally, we observed children eagerly interacting with and successfully reading books during literacy lessons. Our interviews with teachers and the head teacher suggested that learners were equipped with the ability to listen and summarize word problems in numeracy because of the program. The second grade teacher told us, "Read Malawi materials have equipped learners with skills on how to search for information, and deal with issues." In all, the program seemed to have built capacity for all major stakeholders, based on the data we collected.

Accountability

It was clear that all stakeholders were holding each other accountable through direct and indirect monitoring of each other's actions and this accountability drew on existing structures of hierarchy within the system. For example, monitoring appeared to draw on the vertical structure of Malawian education, beginning with the PEA, to the head teacher, to the teachers. Not stopped there, accountability flowed in and through the community. Throughout the interview process, it was apparent that each group of stakeholders was quite aware of roles, responsibilities, and impact of other stakeholders involved in the program. For example, the PEA told us his role was to,

Monitor teachers, learners, the SMC, and the activities of the mother group in the implementation of (the) Read Malawi program. I have been encouraging the stakeholders to implement Read Malawi activities.

He also stated that he changed the way he monitored the program based on the school, "I visited the school at least once a week and upon being convinced there was good progress, I started visiting the school at least once every fortnight." The volunteer teachers explicitly noted his direct monitoring as a positive influencing factor in their role as tutors for students.

The head teacher also played an important role in monitoring implementation of the program through ongoing assessment and feedback of teachers' lessons. The head teacher felt committed to the program and described a sense of ownership because he was one of the three head teachers chosen to participate in the original training program. He felt that because of his participation in the training, he was committed to keeping the program going "even after the Read Malawi people are gone."

Accountability was apparent in monitoring responsibilities of other stakeholders, most notably the village head, the SMC and the PTA. The village head stated that his main role was "encouraging parents to send their children to school" and he did this in village meetings he led. Members of the SMC and the PTA monitored attendance; they stopped at the school and checked on classes to make sure students were present and lessons were taking place. They felt they were to "ensure that there is no unjustified learner's absence from school" and their responsibility was to also "monitor teaching and learning going on within the school." To that end, community members visited often and were proud that they saw "learners reading during some of our visits." These findings indicated that the school drew upon their existing structures as they implemented the program.

Books at the Center of Change

It was very clear through observations and multiple interviews that students were taking books home, for both tutoring with teacher volunteers and to share with their families. This is unusual. Historically and traditionally, our participants told us, Thandiza did not have books for children to take home and when they first heard children were to take books home, everyone was concerned. However, because of their training, they felt they were unified in their approach toward caring for and accountability of the books; they appeared to be in agreement: Taking books home by young children was a good idea. This sharing of books appeared at all grades, 1-6, in the school, even though the program was only implemented in grades 1- 3. Although the first grade children were initially thought to be too young to take books home, stakeholders decided to modify the program. They assigned older siblings to carry the books to and from school for younger children.

Based on our interviews and observations, the vast majority of students in grades 1-3 did check out books to take home. At the time of our visit, Chichewa titles had been checked out more frequently than English titles. According to the third grade teacher, this was because many learners did not have relatives at home to support them in reading English titles. The village head reported that his daughter, who was in grade 1, brought home many books to read. He also reported that the family spent time together with these books to support her literacy development.

Book check out was handled by the teacher in the classroom and was a rather simple process. Logbooks were used to keep track of which books were checked out to which students. Because of this modified system, the head teacher reported that all books were accounted for, and not a single book had been lost or misplaced at the time of this report. This seems to demonstrate the community's support of the program and its effort to ensure the caring of the books. The teachers valued books going home. One teacher reported, "We thought we could build a reading culture among learners. This is also done to keep learners busy even when they are at home."

We confirmed through interviews with both students and community members that the books were used at home; all were able to list titles they read and describe their favorite book. In addition, several participants reported that they saw the books as a mechanism for resurrecting oral story telling traditions in the villages. The introduction of these books in the community fostered a reconnection with the tradition, which had largely been abandoned, according to our participants. Because many stories found in the books were similar to stories told to the older generation, the books were given credit for fostering a connection between generations, which indicated that the program fit well within the cultural context of the school and community.

Ongoing Challenges

While these themes appeared to play a role in the successful implementation of the program, the school faced lingering challenges. For example, there was a shortage of teachers and materials in this school and on average more than 120 learners per grade level, which created an ongoing challenge for teachers. In an attempt to cope with the situation, teachers modified ways in which they grouped students for lessons. As an example, there are 157 children in the grade 1 classroom—the teacher and her assistant created three large groups, and provided a literacy activity for each. While most of us who visited the classroom stood in awe of this teacher and her assistant, there was never a time that we did not witness all first grade children in that classroom with a book or a literacy activity in their hands.

According to the head teacher, the shortage of teachers was directly attributed to the lack of teacher homes on the school's grounds as government teachers are provided housing as part of their contract. Most teachers made a daily commute, with some traveling as many as four to five kilometers each way. The head teacher believed it was difficult to keep teachers at the school because, "When they get here and see that there is not a house provided for them, they do not stay." The village head also made clear that this is an issue for the school, stating, "Teachers have to move long distances to the school." He specifically stated a need for more teacher houses to keep teachers here after their initial assignment.

In addition, the school and the community were adamant that the books provided were not enough. While they appreciated the fact that books were available to their children, they were very vocal that 4,000 books were not enough. In large classrooms like the ones in which we observed, on average, children were sharing one book across groups of 10 and 20 children, there were simply not enough books to go around. Additionally, the community was insistent that books, and training for teachers, should be provided for the fourth through sixth grade classrooms that were not resourced. Recognizing the value of the books and the ways in which books brought community and school together, the school and the community continuously asked the research team to assist in making this possible. Clearly, books were valued in this community and challenges that surrounded providing books to all students still existed.

In summary, it is important to note that although we presented each theme separately, each theme was related to and dependent upon other themes. The interactive nature of the themes formed a greater whole, in that the presence of each element recursively and positively impacted the other. Accountability was fostered through capacity building activities, which helped define and outline stakeholders' roles within the intervention. This increased both capacity and accountability and seemed to encourage and foster a deeper sense of unity among the stakeholders, which created a desire for even more training capacity building. This across the board capacity building appeared to continue to increase accountability, as all stakeholders seemed to have gained a greater understanding of their role and others within the intervention. In the next section, we disentangle out ways in which our findings align and contribute to the body of literature on effective schools and beating the odds literature.

DISCUSSION

We elected to study Thandiza Primary School because it seemed to be implementing the Read Malawi program at high and successful levels. In response to our research question, our findings indicated there were five themes that assisted this school in its successful implementation, including (a) the school and community worked in unison with each other and, (b) as a result of training, saw an increased capacity (c) while holding each other accountable for the implementation of the program. Additionally, (d) the books appeared to be at the center of the innovation in the school even though the school (e) faced ongoing challenges. Our findings are not unlike those of previous studies. In the sections that follow, we summarize the ways in which our findings both align and contribute to those bodies of literature.

Of note is the role of working together toward a common goal, the successful implementation of the program. Although referred to in other studies as "shared decision making," "collaboration," and "collectiveness: equal partnership" (Sailors et al., 2007, p. 376), the notion of teachers and principals working together to achieve an end is required for reform efforts to be successful (Allington & Cunningham, 2007). Other studies have noted the importance of those same kinds of connections between homes and schools. Referred to in the literature as positive home-school connections (Hoffman & Rutherford, 1984), reform efforts also require attention from parents.

Our study also indicates that communities should be considered an important part of reform. Previous research documented the critical role that schools play in communities (Sailors et al., 2007). Our findings indicate it is equally important for community stakeholders especially the more traditional stakeholders such as the mother groups and village heads) to be just as involved in reform efforts as the school. Our findings demonstrated that these stakeholders were as invested in the success of the program as were the teachers and head teacher at the school. When communities are involved in decisions concerning school resources, curriculum, and support, schools succeed (Allington & Cunningham, 2007). Our data substantiates these claims.

Other studies have also looked at the role of social resources in the efforts to reform schools. For example, in one large-scale reform effort aimed at a process of decentralization in the Chicago public school system, Bryk and his colleagues (Bryk, Sebring, Allensworth, Luppescu & Easton, 2010), were interested in why reform was difficult to advance in some communities when compared to similar communities as measured by socioeconomic status. Turning to the "enhanced ability of communities to mobilize for local problems" (Bryk et al., 2010, p. 169), Bryk and his colleagues explored the role of social capital in school improvement. Specifically, they found that bonding social capital, or the supportive social ties within a neighborhood or community, which afford group solidarity making the achievement of collective goals much more likely, played a significant role in the capacity of a school to improve student outcomes. While our study did not collect data that would quantify and measure the bonding social capital in the community that surrounded Thandiza, our data does reaffirm Bryk's findings and illustrates in a more narrative sense the ways in which community members of Thandiza utilized social bonding capital for successful implementation of the program.

With respect to our second question, we discovered numerous challenges faced in the school setting that were never "overcome" but rather managed. Class size, insufficient quantities of learner materials, and the absence of on-site support for change were present throughout the study. However, teachers, school leaders, and community leaders never saw these challenges as impossible. Through sheer effort, ingenuity, and modest program modifications they were able to move on the path to success.

IMPLICATIONS

Our study offers several implications for literacy reform efforts in developing countries such as Malawi as well as in the U.S. The role of community is very clear in this study—significant participation that draws on strengths of the community appears to be an essential to success. While unity, capacity, and accountability are also important components to establish and build the rethinking and restructuring process, the community feature also sets these findings apart from prior research in this area of school reform. This study moves literature in developing countries beyond the formula of providing books and adds significant teacher training and support (as in Elley, 2000) to include community mobilization as a significant contributor to change. We cannot help but observe that findings from this case study, as with early effective schools studies, not only disprove the claim that SES controls student learning outcomes in ways that cannot be overcome by instruction, but also turn the Coleman report findings around to suggest that community is the point of intervention for change that is essential.

This study has several limitations worth mentioning. First, we were only in this school for what would appear to be a short amount of time. While we wish we could have spent more time, budgetary limitations restricted our engagement with the school. Second, while most of our English speaking team members had spent extended amounts of time in Malawi working with teachers prior to this study, our linguistic limitations may have been a limitation in the richness of data we were able to gather in classrooms. While many of the lessons we observed were in English, many of the interviews were in Chichewa. At least half of our team members were more than likely missing the nuances of those interviews because of our linguistic limitations. Finally, while we believe our previous relationship with this school positively influenced our ability to gather large amounts of data in only five days, we also believe that same relationship may have limited the way participants talked about the program.

Having said that, our findings point to the need for further study of the relationship of community mobilization on implementation of programs and student learning. Is the effect we observed particular to this community and the context of Malawi? Can this relationship become an important key in leveraging change in other contexts including the U.S.? Moreover, if so, what changes must be made to the way schools in the U.S. typically think about interacting with their communities? A shift of this sort might require a counter post-colonial practice—one that turns "westernized expertise" that is typically imported into countries in Africa into an "African expertise" that influences the western world.

REFERENCES

Allington, R. L. & Cunningham, P. M. (2007). *Schools that work: Where all children read and write.* Boston, MA: Pearson Education, Inc.

Almasi, J. F. (2003). *Teaching strategic processes in reading.* New York: Guildford Press.

Bryk, A. S., Sebring, P. B., Allensworth, E., Luppescu, S., & Easton, J. Q. (2010). *Organizing schools for improvement: Lessons from Chicago.* Chicago: University of Chicago Press.

Craig, H. J., Kraft, R. J., & du Plessis, J. (1998). *Teacher Development: Making an Impact.* Washington, DC: Academy of Educational Development.

Coleman, J. S., Campbell, E. Q., Hobson, C. J., Mcpartland, J., Mood, A. M., Weinfield. A. D., & York, R. L. (1966). *Equality of educational opportunity.* Washington, DC, U. S. Department of Health, Education, & Welfare, Office of Education. (No FS 5.238:38001). Retrieved from: http://www.scribd.com/doc/89990298/Coleman Report-Equality-of-Educational-Opportunity-1966

Department of Education Planning, Ministry of Education Science and Technology (DOEP) (2011). *Education statistics 2011.* Lilongwe, Malawi: Author.

Elley, W. B. (2000). The potential of book floods for raising literacy levels. *International Journal of Educational Research, 46,* 233-255.

Glaser, B. G., & Strauss, A. L. (2012). *The discovery of grounded theory: Strategies for qualitative research.* New Brunswick, N.J: Aldine Transaction.

Heibert, E. H., & Sailors, M. (Eds.). (2008). *Finding the right texts for beginning and struggling readers: Researched-based solutions.* New York, NY: Guilford.

Hoffman, J. V., Assaf, L. C., & Paris, S. G. (2001). High stakes testing in reading: Today in Texas, tomorrow? *Reading Teachers, 54,* 482-492.

Hoffman, J. V., Roser, N., Salas, R., Patterson, E., & Pennington, J. (2001). Text leveling and "little books" in first-grade reading. *Journal of Literacy Research, 33,* 507-528.

Hoffman, J. V., & Rutherford, W. (1984). Effective reading programs: A critical review of outlier studies. *Reading Research Quarterly,* 79-92.

Kayuni, H. & Tambulan, R. (2007). Teacher turnover in Malawi's Ministry of Education: Realities and challenges. *International Education Journal,* 8, 89-99.

Macro International. (2008). *Malawi education assessment report.* Calverton, Maryland, USA: Author.

Merriam, S. B. (1997). *Qualitative research and case study applications in education.* San Francisco: Jossey-Bass.

Oliver, D. G., Serovich, J. M., & Mason, T. L. (2005). Constraints and opportunities with Interview transcription: Towards reflection in qualitative research. *Social Forces,* 84, 1273-1289.

Sailors, M., Hoffman, J. V., Matthee, B. (2007). South African schools that promote literacy learning with students from low-income communities. *Reading Research Quarterly,* 42, 364-387.

Sailors, M., Hoffman, J. V., Pearson, P. D., Shin, J., McClung, N. & Chilora, H. (2012). Improving reading practices and student outcomes through "Read Malawi": Challenges, opportunities and outcomes," Paper presented at the sixty second annual meeting of the Literacy Research Association, San Diego, CA.

Taylor, B. M., Pearson, P. D., Clark, K., & Walpole, S. (2000). Effective schools and accomplished teachers: Lessons about primary-grade reading instruction in low-income schools. *Elementary School Journal,* 101, 121-165.

Weber, G. (1971) *Inner city children can be taught to read: Four successful schools.* Washington, DC: Council for Basic Education.

Wolcott, H. F. (1995) *The art of fieldwork.* Walnut Creek, CA: AltaMira Press.

World Bank. (2010). *The education system in Malawi.* Washington, DC: The International Bank for Reconstruction and Development/ The World Bank.

Yin, R. K. (1994). *Case study research: Design and methods.* (Second Ed.). Thousand Oaks, CA: Sage.

APPENDIX A. GUIDING QUESTIONS FOR INTERVIEWS

Teacher and Head Teacher Interviews

1. Why has your school been so successful in implementing the Read Malawi program?
2. What modifications/changes have you made to the Read Malawi program that may be different from the training you received? How/ why did you make these changes?
3. What influence has the training you received as part of the Read Malawi program had on your language instruction? On other content areas?
4. What else would you like to tell us?

Parent Teacher Association/ School Management Committee/ Mother Group Questions

1. What is your role in the implementation of Read Malawi? What support does your committee/do you offer to the school in implementing the program?
2. This school has been identified as a high performing school. What factors do you think have contributed to this high implementation?
3. What do you think is the influence of the program has been in the community?
4. Are the books traveling home? What do the learners do with the books at home?
5. What changes would you like to see in the program in the future? Changes centered on positive aspects or negative aspects you have seen . . .
6. What else would you like to tell us?

Primary Education Advisor Interview

1. Is this label of "high performing/implementing" consistent with your observations of this school or does it surprise you?
2. What is your role in the implementation of Read Malawi? What support do you offer to the school in implementing the program?
3. This school has been identified as a high performing school. What factors do you think have contributed to this high implementation?
4. Have you observed any modifications or changes in the way the program has been implemented so that it is fully implemented? If so, what are they?
5. What else would you like to tell us?

Strengthening Bi-Literacy Through Translanguaging Pedagogies

Susan Hopewell

The University of Colorado at Boulder

Scholars and researchers in the field of bilingual education have often promoted the importance of maintaining linguistically 'pure' language environments in which only one language is used at a time. This traditional approach suggests that restricting the instructional environment to a pedagogy grounded in strictly separating languages, especially to promote language and literacy development, will result in superior language acquisition (Gaarder, 1978; Lessow-Hurley, 2000). Theoretically, requiring students to maintain the language of the learning environment provides students with sufficient time to engage in and practice each language purposefully (Cloud, Genesee, & Hamayan, 2000). These arguments use the same logic that those who argue for time-on-task use when arguing for English-only education (Imhoff, 1990; Porter, 1990). In other words, the more time spent comprehending and producing the target language, the more likely one is to learn it. Importantly, time-on-task has been proven repeatedly to be a faulty argument when one examines the research comparing the language acquisition of emerging bilinguals educated in English-only learning environments to emerging bilinguals educated in bilingual learning environments (Greene, 1997; Rolstad, Mahoney & Glass, 2005; Slavin & Cheung, 2005; Willig, 1985).

Transfer theory tells us that what is known and understood in one language contributes to what is known and understood in the other (Olivares, 2002). This is, after all, a mainstay in the justification for bilingual education. Theories that call for strict language separation are referred to as theories of *two solitudes* (Cummins, 2005) or *parallel monolingualism* (Fitts, 2006; Heller, 2001). Despite the fact that bilingual educators have borrowed liberally from research done in monolingual English-speaking communities that require de facto adherence to one language only, Cummins reminds us that there is *no empirical evidence* to support monolingual orientations to instruction that call for language separation or for the prohibition of translation and the use of bilingual dictionaries within bilingual communities (Cummins, 2005). He further argues that separating languages has the potential to limit students' opportunities to develop powerful literacy competencies (2000). Although evaluation studies like those conducted by researchers such as Collier and Thomas demonstrate that students of dual language education outperform those enrolled in other models, and a fundamental characteristic of dual language education is the non-negotiable or inviolable separation of languages, the extant research does not actually test alternatives in which spaces for bilingualism are created within dual language models (2009). Further, many of the researchers who initially insisted on strict language separation (e.g., Cloud, Genesee, & Hamayan, 2000; Collier & Thomas, 2009; Howard, Sugarman, Christian, Lindholm-Leary, & Rogers, 2007), have more recently modified this position to allow for some exceptions including the exploration of cross-lingual and metacognitive patterns (Hamayan, 2010; D. Rogers, personal communication, April 5, 2013; Thomas & Collier, 2012). Given this, it is imperative that we scrutinize and explore more nuanced and holistic paradigms and pedagogies to teach and assess bilingual students (Grosjean, 1989). If we accept that students draw from, and contribute to, a common conceptual reservoir (Commins & Miramontes, 2005), it stands to reason that bilingual teachers and students are capable of using languages in strategic and choreographed ways to enhance and convey learning (Escamilla & Hopewell, 2010; Hopewell, 2011; Moll & Diaz, 1985). Promising practices stemming from pedagogies of translanguaging are in need of greater empirical study.

Translanguaging refers to the flexibility with which bilingual human beings use their linguistic resources to communicate and make sense of their worlds (García, 2012). It is purposeful, adroit, and effective alternation among languages. Contrary to the often-maligned behavior of code-switching, translanguaging practices are evidence that in order to activate a single multilingual linguistic repertoire strategically and effectively, bilinguals must understand in a profound way how their languages support and reference each other (Canagarajah, 2011). By studying the ways in which bilingual learners rely upon and use their languages in social and academic situations, we can, perhaps, develop pedagogies that not only capitalize and build upon these practices and ways of interpreting and understanding the world, but also expand our ability to influence the cognitive domain of metacognitive awareness. Canagarajah has argued that although translanguaging is a natural way for bilinguals to exist and communicate in the world, it should not be romanticized to the extent that we ignore the importance of teaching students explicitly to increase their translanguaging abilities (2011). The practice of translanguaging begins from the assumption that bilinguals have an expanded repertoire with which to amplify communication and express comprehension. These resources have the potential to be both communicative tools and pedagogical tools. By exploring students engaged in translanguaging, we may be able to better research it as a viable pedagogy that rejects the reductionist assumption that restrictive monolingual pedagogies should undergird bilingual instruction (Creese & Blackledge, 2010). Instead, the dynamic and intersecting relationship of languages is optimized via context-sensitive teaching and learning through spaces that have been referred to as hybrid (Gutiérrez, Baquedano-López, and Tejada, 1999; Hornberger & Link, 2012). These environments are hypothesized to increase the likelihood that the totality of a student's background knowledge will be activated in service to language and literacy acquisition. Translanguaging pedagogies increase the possibility that students can be taught to consciously detect, understand, and talk about how their languages are similar and dissimilar through developing their metalinguistic awareness. Further, the theory implies that opening up spaces for bilingualism will increase our ability to understand and diagnose students' comprehension while simultaneously augmenting teachers' ability to expand educational opportunity (Hopewell, 2011). A caution, however, is that a pedagogy of translanguaging differs in fundamental ways from concurrent translation, a technique that has been soundly rejected through research that shows that students learn not to attend in one language if they can rely on a consistent translation of the primary learning objectives (Faltis, 1996; Ulanoff & Pucci, 1993).

PURPOSE STATEMENT

The purpose of this study was to examine the ways in which Spanish–English emerging bilingual students participated differently when using all of their linguistic resources to process English language text, and to explore how classroom language policy limited or enhanced students' engagement and ability to negotiate text meaning. Data will be shared indicating that students are purposeful and strategic in their translanguaging, and that these practices expand their ability to negotiate the meaning of English-language texts.

RESEARCH QUESTIONS

Data will be presented to answer the following research questions:

1. Is there evidence in student discourse patterns that they draw upon more than one language when negotiating the meaning of an English language text within small groups?

2. How do fourth grade Spanish-English speaking bilingual students participate differently and make meaning in English-as-a-second-language (ESL) literature groups when they are invited to use all of their linguistic resources versus when they are restricted to communicating in English only?

In other words, I wanted to understand whether students engage in translanguaging practices when negotiating text meaning, and, if so, whether or not there was a difference in the types and purposes of this practice when bilingual interactions were welcomed versus when they were explicitly prohibited.

METHODOLOGY

The study reported herein is an analysis of a subset of data obtained during a larger study conducted in 2009. While the larger study was mixed-methods in design, the subset of data informing these research questions was qualitative in nature. The purpose of this qualitative study was to examine how fourth grade Spanish-English speaking bilingual students participated differently in English-as-a-second-language (ESL) literature groups when they were invited to use all of their linguistic resources versus when they were restricted to communicating in English only.

The outcome of interest was the use and purpose of Spanish language in conversations designed to increase comprehension of English language texts. All students participated in groups in which they were asked to read, recall and discuss texts written in English. The design required each student to participate in four literacy events. A literacy event was defined as a researcher-led small group experience reading a two-page English language passage. Each student read and responded to four passages. Two of the passages were about inventions, while two were about math in the garden. Although the paired passages addressed the same broad topics, the information contained within each passage differed. The choice of four passages on two topics ensured that each student had the opportunity to read, recall, and discuss each topic once in English-only and once bilingually. Following the reading, each child produced a written recall of the passage. Half of the written recalls were restricted to English-only, and half invited the use of Spanish in addition to, or instead of, English. Following the individual written recall activity, students participated in a group dialogue in which talking structures were either restricted to English-only or sanctioned the use of Spanish in conjunction with English. The language of the discussion mirrored the language(s) of the written retell. It is these discussions, and the languages used within them, that are the subject of this analysis. All 64 student dialogues were audio- and/or video-recorded, logged, and transcribed.

Because repeated measure designs are subject to carryover effects related to practice, it was important to counterbalance this by controlling the testing order such that each treatment was equally likely to occur at each stage of the experiment (Wendorf, 2004). Using a Latin Square framework in which each possible occurrence represented a different testing order, and keeping in mind that the topics needed to alternate, there were eight possible sequencing orders (See Table 1) Students were randomly assigned to groups, and each group was randomly assigned to a sequence.

Table 1: Sequence of Reading Events by Topic and Language Condition

Sequence 1:	Bilingual T1	English-only T2	English-only T1	Bilingual T2
Sequence 2:	Bilingual T1	Bilingual T2	English-only T1	English-only T2
Sequence 3:	Bilingual T2	Bilingual T1	English-only T2	English-only T1
Sequence 4:	Bilingual T2	English-only T1	English-only T2	Bilingual T1
Sequence 5:	English-only T1	Bilingual T2	Bilingual T1	English-only T2
Sequence 6:	English-only T1	English-only T2	Bilingual T1	Bilingual T2
Sequence 7:	English-only T2	Bilingual T1	Bilingual T2	English-only T1

T1 = Topic 1 (Inventions)   T2 = Topic 2 (Math in the Garden)

Participants. The participants were 49 fourth-grade students enrolled in two biliteracy classrooms in a large urban school district. All were Latino and shared Spanish and English in their linguistic repertoires. All students' families qualified for free and reduced price lunch.

Data Analysis. This inquiry was meant to investigate whether and how students engaged with the text and the members of their reading groups differently when they were asked to negotiate and construct meaning by consciously and publicly using two languages versus one. Further, it was an opportunity to explore how student discourse illuminates the ways in which students use their knowledge of two languages to make sense of an English language text. Data were coded and analyzed using a deductive framework to annotate and understand when, how, and for what purpose students used Spanish while discussing the English language text (LeCompte and Schensul, 1999). Beginning broadly, I noted all instances of Spanish interjections and subdivided these by whether or not the research condition sanctioned or prohibited the use of Spanish. I further noted which passage was being discussed to understand whether or not the use of Spanish was topic- or passage-specific. These were low-level inference codes in that students either did or did not interject Spanish, and the testing condition was either English-only or bilingual. The passages were clearly delineated by Topic 1-Passage 1, Topic 1-Passage 2, Topic 2-Passage 1, and Topic 2-Passage 2. I further analyzed these interjections to note the length of the utterance, whether or not the corresponding response was in Spanish or English, and what the communicative purpose of the utterance was. The length of utterance was tallied by utterances of 1-3 words, 4-6 words, and 7+words. Further, these language utterances were categorized as all English in an English condition, all Spanish in an English condition, mixed language utterance in an English condition, and mixed language utterance in a bilingual condition. There were no instances of students using all English or all Spanish in the bilingual condition. The corresponding responses were then noted to attempt to discern receptive comprehension patterns. Higher levels of inference were required to analyze the receptive comprehension and to assign communicative purpose to the utterances.

An additional layer of analyses was required when a closer examination of language use indicated that Spanish was used more often and for different purposes in the bilingual condition. These data, therefore, were interpreted and categorized to better understand what linguistic and academic purposes Spanish served in the bilingual condition which were unique from those in the English-only condition. Particular attention was given to cross-language connections and Spanish used in service to extending opportunity to learn and comprehend.

FINDINGS

There were two major findings from this study:
1. Bilingual students use all of their linguistic resources when processing text regardless of the external regulations imposed to limit language use, and that these translanguaging processes aid in increased ability to communicate and negotiate comprehension of an English language text.
2. Students' use of Spanish differed in substantive ways when employed in the bilingual condition as compared to the English-only.

Language and Text Processing. First research question: Is there evidence in student discourse patterns that they draw upon more than one language when negotiating the meaning of an English language text? Evidence from student discourse reveals that bilingual students use all of their linguistic resources when processing text regardless of the external regulations imposed to limit language use, and that these translanguaging processes aid in increased ability to comprehend English language text. Substantial evidence for these claims will be shared to demonstrate that students' productive language use and receptive language comprehension during passage discussions, both in the English-only condition and in the bilingual condition, confirm the hypothesis that bilingual students negotiate meaning while thinking and accessing more than one language (translanguaging). All corroborative evidence comes from a careful examination of when and how students used Spanish while discussing the English language passages.

Initial evidence regarding translanguaging as an indication of bilingual processing includes the fact that group members always included Spanish language exchanges in the bilingual condition. In other words, of the 32 instances in which students participated in the bilingual condition, they never chose to limit the discussion to English-only. More definitive data surfaced during an examination of how these same students participated when in the English-only condition. When in English-only groups, students were asked to maintain English as the sole language of communication. All writing and verbalizations were to occur in English.

Students used substantially more English in the English-only condition than they did in the bilingual condition; however, the groups rarely used English exclusively for the entirety of the discussion. In other words, it was challenging for groups of students to restrict themselves to English only. Students in class one interjected at least one word of Spanish in 14 out of 16 English-only groups. Stated differently, 88% of the time, either consciously or unconsciously, students used, or were exposed to, Spanish while discussing the English language texts in an English-only condition. This figure, however, may be inflated and should not be used to generalize this disposition. By way of comparison, I offer the corresponding analysis of the class two data. The students in the second classroom were a bit more likely to restrain from interjecting Spanish. They used Spanish in the English-only condition 66% of the time. When considered in their entirety, these data indicate that despite students' conscious attempts to suppress the Spanish language, it surfaced in their group dialogues three-quarters of the time. These aggregated data provide strong evidence that bilingual children access and use two languages when processing text regardless of the language of the text, or of the prohibition from using one language or the other.

Vocalizations were not the sole source of data that contributed to the finding that bilingual students use all of their linguistic resources when processing and discussing text. Although theories of parallel monolingualism would have us believe that it is possible to maintain monolingual social spaces in which one consciously employs only one language at a time, it appears from this examination of comprehension patterns that bilinguals do not activate one language while deactivating the other. Even when successful in maintaining English as the language of communication, students' responses to others' use of Spanish indicated that there were no barriers to comprehending utterances in languages other than the one dominating the verbal exchange. This ability to flow in and out of languages allowed students to remain focused on making sense of the text. In other words, their receptive capacities were equally adept at interpreting a word uttered in English as in Spanish. Individual words did not appear to be dependent on the language base of the words surrounding them. Despite the conscious attempt to modify language use and to activate and use only English, students' responses indicated that they successfully comprehended others when Spanish was infused into the dialogue. These exchanges provided windows into how students were thinking and processing across languages, and bolstered support for the finding that students were unable to deactivate Spanish when required to use only English. By way of example, consider the following sentence that was uttered by a student when discussing *Math in the Garden* during a discussion supposedly restricted to English-only: "We were planting *elotes* [corn]." If an individual were to employ only one language, in this case English, while processing discourse, and given no other scaffolds, visual or otherwise, it would be impossible to understand this sentence. Yet, after its utterance, the students' responses indicated not only that all group members had correctly interpreted the phrase, but that the student who uttered it also knew, and could have chosen to use, the word 'corn.' Both the employment of, and the comprehension of, translanguaging indicate that bilinguals have constant access to their entire linguistic repertoire. Further, because languages are not activated and deactivated in response to artificial frameworks, words and concepts expressed in English are often heard and interpreted through a Spanish language lens. The following example illustrates this tendency. After being asked to define B.C. (i.e., 1900-1600 B.C.), I began, "B.C. means…," but was immediately cut off by a student who interjected "*bicicleta*! [bicycle!]" (e.g., *bici* [bike]). The oral pronunciation in English of the acronym B.C. sounded exactly like the commonly used shortened version of the Spanish word *bicicleta* [bicycle]. Had this child's Spanish linguistic system been suppressed, this interpretation would have been impossible.

That it is unnatural and difficult to suppress a language does not mean that students are incapable of restricting themselves. It is well documented that emerging bilingual children consider their audience when choosing a language for communication (Wei & Martin, 2009; Willoughby, 2009). They adjust their language use to ensure communicative success. When in the company of monolingual speakers of either language, they maintain the language of their audience. When in the company of other bilinguals, they are more likely to participate in forms of code-switching (García, 2009; Kenner, 2004; Zentella, 1997). Had anyone in our reading groups been a monolingual speaker of Spanish or English, the group utterances may have been substantively different. It is clear, in fact, from my data, that the overall amount of English spoken in the English-only group was much greater than that in the bilingual condition. Further, 42% of the students were able to remain in English throughout the English-only condition indicating that approximately 2/3 of the students were responsible for all of the Spanish language utterances during the English-only condition. Contrast this with the fact that 100% of the students used at least some Spanish during the bilingual condition.

A critical caveat to this finding is that because students activate their entire linguistic system to make sense of the literacy environment, the oral prompts that teachers use during reading instruction may not always be interpreted by the student in the ways that the teacher anticipates. The following example, taken from an English-only condition reading of a passage about the invention of the wheels, demonstrates how the generic nature of teaching prompts resulted in students automatically thinking across languages:

S: What does ancient mean? "This ancient clay model." Any ideas? No? Does it look like any other word you know?

I :   You add the "o" and it's *anciento* [seat] (The student wanted to say *asiento*, the Spanish language word for 'seat'. The addition of the letter n simply reflects her linguistic variation. At this point in the dialogue, I had not yet discerned her intent.)

S: And what does that mean? That's a really good strategy adding an "o" and seeing if it looks like anything in Spanish. That's a really good strategy.

I: *anciento* is like when you go in the car, is like the chair in, the chariots inside the car.

S: Hmmmm

I: where you sit (she means *asiento*! [seat])

This excerpt demonstrates how a simple teacher prompt such as "Does it look like any other word you know?" is interpreted as an invitation to scan and utilize all words in the child's lexicon, not simply those that match the language of the text. The student in this passage noticed the similarities between the words ancient and *asiento* [seat] and chariot and chair to formulate a hypothesis regarding the relationships among the words. Despite the mandate to think, act, speak, and read in English-only, this child responded to the teacher prompt by articulating how she could use Spanish strategically to problem-solve an English language reading challenge.

Use of Spanish by Language Condition. Second research question: How do fourth-grade Spanish-English speaking bilingual students participate differently and make meaning in English-as-a-second-language (ESL) literature groups when they are invited to use all of their linguistic resources versus when they are restricted to communicating in English-only? A close analyses of students' language to discuss English language texts under varying conditions, reveals that students' use of Spanish differed in substantive ways when employed in the English-only condition as compared to the bilingual condition. In English, students were likely to interject quick 1-3 word phrases, there were no multi-turn exchanges, and longer utterances in Spanish were to clarify a concept only after an attempt had been made in English. Spanish use was often rushed and quiet. In the bilingual condition, on the other hand, the exchanges were longer and more detailed. Students often included an analogy or an example that expanded their peers' opportunities to deepen comprehension. The exchanges involved multi-turn exchanges in which students often summarized the primary themes of the English language text by reverting to Spanish. Students made cross-language connections in both conditions; however, the prohibition from using two languages in the English-only condition, kept the facilitator and students from taking up some ideas that may have developed an explicit self-extending metalinguistic system that capitalized on students' bilingual resources. The following paragraphs will offer evidence to warrant these claims, and will be used to develop theories about ways in which translanguaging pedagogies can build upon what we know children do naturally.

The use of Spanish in the English-only condition was often limited to a one to three word interjection and never included a multi-turn exchange. Spanish was summoned to encourage others (e.g., "*ándale* [come on], come on, you can do it"), to initiate a thought or phrase using tag words that would subsequently shift to English (e.g., "*Como* [like] fifteen centimeters" or "yeah, *cuando* [when], when it's not too wet and not too hot…"), to define and extend understanding (e.g., Question: "What does wet mean?" Answer: "*Mojado* [wet]. Like the ground is, like it rained, and it's like muddy"), to assist a peer in finding information within the text (e.g., *allí está* [it's right there]), to clarify instructions (e.g., *no más hasta aquí* [just read to here]), to admonish a peer (e.g., *en inglés* [in English] or *levanta la mano* [raise your hand]), and to note a cross-language connection (e.g., "It's almost saying *velocidad* [velocity/speed]"). Additionally, when students were reading numerals aloud, they would often default to Spanish. For example, the sentence "Dig down at least 12 inches" was articulated as "Dig down at least *doce* [twelve] inches." The longest single Spanish language utterance during an English-only condition was an 18-word statement that a student expressed after an English language attempt to explain a concept to a peer in English was unsuccessful. The following is the exchange:

G: I need 'get help if you can.'

S: Ah. Okay, let's see. "Find a helper if you can." What does that mean? L?

L: Um, that um, maybe, um if you need help you can go to your neighbor's and sometimes they're too busy, so you can't.

S: That's true, sometimes they're too busy and you can't, but the idea is you go find a friend. Does that make sense, G?

G: No.

S: No? Not yet? It's ok.

L: *Como, como buscar un amigo, pero a veces no puede. Dice, sí puedes buscar*
            un amigo, sí puedes. [Like, like, look for a friend, but sometimes they aren't
            able to help. It says you can look for a friend. You can.]

G: Yes.

The students in this exchange attempted to stay in the target language, but when the student
asking for clarification expressed that she did not understand the English language explanation, her
friend quickly offered a rephrasing in Spanish. Spanish was another tool to navigate the meaning-
making process. The longer the utterance in Spanish during the English-only condition, the more
likely it was that a student was using it to help a peer grasp a concept. Students risked being
admonished by peers or the group facilitator to remain in English to ensure a peer's comprehension.
These exchanges often involved students lowering their voices and speaking quickly, almost as if to
acknowledge that the communicative act was subversive within the artificial language boundaries
established by the teacher. The communication was generally completed and the message received
before anyone could step in and cut off the exchange with a reminder to speak English.

In the bilingual condition, on the other hand, students' dialogues were rich mosaics of Spanish
and English intricately intertwined and variegated. The students consistently demonstrated a
sophisticated ability to flow in and out of Spanish and English to accomplish a variety of linguistic
and cognitive tasks. The following dialogue represents a typical group exchange in the bilingual
condition:

S: Ok. What else do you need to have clarified, G.?

G: Drown.

S: Drown. Look at that last sentence. It says, "You could drown your plants!"
            What do you think drown means?

L: *Como ahogar. Porque, echar mucha agua y se ahogan las plantas. Como*
            cuando vas nadando, párate de nadar y ahogas, y puedes ahogar las plantas.
            [Like drown. If you over-water the plants, they will drown. It's like when
            you go swimming. If you stop swimming, you drown. Plants can drown,
            too.]

S: *Exacto. Esta, sí, es buena explicación.* [Exactly. This is a good explanation.]
            Ok, what else?

L: When it says "never let the soil dry out" . . .

This discussion continues in English as students negotiate the meaning of "dry out" and
"moist," but returns to Spanish to clarify "weeds." These data demonstrate the fluidity with which
groups were able to move from one language to another while maintaining a coherently focused
discussion that increased overall text comprehension. This fluidity provides evidence that the
natural flow from one language to another does not require a mechanism that turns off or blocks
one language while accessing the other, and demonstrates how bilingual students easily converse and
expand meaning through translanguaging. Further, the student who engages in the act of clarifying
the concept suggests an analogy (a person drowning) in order to help a peer comprehend. In another

example, a student referred to tying one's shoes when explaining the concept of staking a plant. The use of examples and extension by analogy happened only in the bilingual condition.

Students in both conditions were likely to make cross-language connections; however, the English-only restrictions limited the ability to build upon or clarify these cross-language opportunities. In the English-only condition students made a comparison at the graphophonemic level [e.g., "*Listen* is funny because we don't say the 't.' It's like the *h muda* (silent h) in Spanish."]. They also indicated an awareness of cognates and their importance in making sense of unknown vocabulary (e.g., In reference to the word velocity, "It's almost saying *velocidad*."). They were also able to articulate strategies to each other such as "add an o" as a way to see if there were a Spanish language equivalent that might be useful (e.g., ranch/*rancho*). The bilingual condition, too, provided an opportunity for students to demonstrate their metalinguistic analysis, but because it could be taken up as a pedagogical tool, the comparisons were richer and more likely to create a self-extending system. For instance, the observance of morphological cognates (e.g., constitución/constitution; activity/actividad) prompted the creation of an anchor poster that explicitly examined the relationship of lists of words in Spanish and English. Further, when an English language text used phonetic spelling and capitalization to indicate pronunciation [e.g., transmissions (trans-MISH-unz)], the facilitator was able to compare the use of the accent in Spanish as a guide for where to place phonological emphasis. In other words, students made cross-language connections in both environments, but the ability to use these connections as the foundations for developing and strengthening students' comprehension strategies was stifled when the language policy insisted on English-only.

DISCUSSION AND IMPLICATIONS

These findings call into question the common, but questionable, practice of signaling to students that they are to think, speak, and act in one language or another, and that under no circumstances should they refer to, or produce knowledge that cannot be communicated in the target language. Translanguaging, or the "*multiple discursive practices* in which bilinguals engage in order to *make sense of their bilingual worlds*" (García, 2009, p. 45), provides an alternative pedagogy that affords students the opportunity to strengthen their multilingual identities through flexible pedagogical practices that encourage the use of multiple languages to make sense of their experiences and the texts they read and produce (Cummins, 2008; Creese & Blackledge, 2010).

When we refrain from inviting students to use the knowledge and skills that they associate with one of their languages, we deny them access to their funds of knowledge and to potential linguistic and cognitive resources (González, Moll, & Amanti, 2005). Separation of languages and literacies is problematic when it results in the suppression of students' strengths and prior knowledge, thereby denying them access to a full foundational basis for learning. Learning endeavors that integrate reading, writing, speaking, listening, viewing, processing, creating, and analyzing across languages capitalize on these abilities and broaden the scope of prior experiences that inform new learning. These structures expand the range of patterns, possibilities, and connections that students can use to negotiate meaning and incorporate new learning into their expanding repertoire of strategies and approaches to learning. As was illuminated by my data, encouraging students to think, learn, and communicate across languages resulted in differential participation patterns with the text, with each other, and with the facilitator. Explicit policies of translanguaging expand our opportunities to teach for transfer.

There is a dearth of studies that have examined when, why, and how often students use Spanish in service to English-language text comprehension. Being bilingual adds a layer of complexity to reading comprehension that has not been widely explored. It expands a person's meaning-making, or comprehension, repertoire. In as much as comprehension strategies are presented in the English language based literature as a definitive laundry list that is representative of all reading comprehension strategies, it is an inadequate framework for developing biliteracy. Those who advocate and market the potential advantage of emphasizing the teaching of top-down comprehension strategies over an inordinate focus on the teaching of bottom-up decoding strategies would probably argue that nothing in the popular list of comprehension strategies (e.g., making connections, questioning, visualizing, inferring, determining importance, synthesizing, monitoring & fixing up) precludes doing so across languages, however; their guidelines abstain from distinguishing how biliterate children utilize these strategies differently, and their exemplars are exclusively in English (Harvey & Goudvis, 2000; Keene & Zimmerman, 1997; Zimmerman & Hutchins, 2003). The development of a pedagogy that embraces the potential of bilingualism and translanguaging requires recognition of the need to teach, and explicitly employ, uniquely bilingual comprehension strategies including cognate recognition, cross-language word and morphology analogy, judicial use of translation, alternative explanations, explicit comparison of convention functions, etc., and to understand and demonstrate how traditionally celebrated monolingual comprehension strategies can be modified to recognize a broader cognitive and linguistic base such as that embodied by bilingual students.

By analyzing fourth grade student discourse patterns in a carefully controlled language environment, I was able to add to our knowledge about this subject by confirming that young bilingual students always have access to both languages, and that they play significant roles in the processing and comprehending of second language texts. The fact that it is neither easy nor natural to suppress a linguistic resource calls into question whether or not the potential language and literacy gains projected from monolingual environments outweigh those to be nurtured in a bilingual/biliterate environment in which students are encouraged to access and use all linguistic and cognitive resources as part of an integrated foundation for learning. Findings from the analyses of the qualitative data collected in this study suggest that there is much to be gained from rich bilingual discussions.

This is important as it has implications for how instructional practices can be organized to support students in their quest to negotiate meaning. Even the message we send when we ask students to deactivate one language in service to the acquisition of another may be counterproductive. After all, if students are incapable of turning off one of their languages, our requests to do so may inadvertently signal to the learners that they are innately deficient.

Translanguaging pedagogies, however, cannot be developed or included unless we hire and support bilingual educators to work with bilingual children. Not only are these teachers better able to provide explicit and direct guidance about the relationship of the two languages, they are also better positioned to analyze students' productive language in ways that consider how the two languages inform students' approximations. Like their students, they have a larger linguistic pool from which to draw examples and from which to provide clarifications. Using two languages to process text expands opportunities to teach and learn, but only if the educator is able to analyze and synthesize these connections.

It is not enough, however, to hire bilingual educators and assume that they will have the foresight to consider language and literacy in holistic ways. Most literacy methods courses at the higher education level focus exclusively on monolingual theories of literacy instruction, with precious little emphasis on how complex and fundamentally different the process is for bilingual children. Teachers need professional development opportunities that emphasize when they draw on their training as monolingual educators, they may fail to recognize and embrace students' full learning potential. They need explicit instruction to understand that the questions they ask in order to help students develop a self-extending system may not elicit the responses they sought because the students' language and literacy repertoires are greater than those available to monolingual children. They need assurance that these responses are not indications of linguistic interference or confusion, but rather are evidence of children's ability to generalize across languages and to utilize the entire linguistic system to make sense of the language-based task that they face. Students will use and access their entire linguistic system to respond to teacher questions and prompts. Prompts that may invite bilingual responses include: (a) Does that look like another word you know? (b) Are there any little words within that big word that you recognize? (c) Do you know another word like that? (d) Do you know another word that ends with those letters? (e) What do you know that might help? (f) Get your mouth ready to say that word. (g) What sounds can you hear in that word? etc. Teachers need preparation that encourages them to use a bilingual lens when examining student behaviors.

Knowing that there is a body of research that affirms that concurrent translation is a bad idea, however, reminds us that it is important to define carefully what is meant by strategic use of language and to explore how translanguaging practices that foster explicit cross-language connection provide both teaching and learning opportunities. They are not the spontaneous or continuous translation of instruction and concepts. Further, these practices are not meant to undermine the importance of having time to learn in and about individual languages. Rather, providing a time and a space to capitalize on students' natural tendencies to translanguage should be strategic and planned as a means to optimize biliterate learning.

In sum, purposeful translanguaging has the potential to tap into powerful learning opportunities for bilingual learners. It recognizes that bilingual learners are not two monolinguals in one and that their languages provide unique opportunities to deepen comprehension and to strengthen language and literacy practices.

REFERENCES

Canagarajah, S. (2011). Codemeshing in academic writing: Identifying teachable strategies of translanguaging. *The Modern Language Journal*, 95, 401- 417.

Cloud, N., Genesee, F., & Hamayan, E. (2000). *Dual language instruction: A handbook for enriched education.* Boston, MA: Heinle.

Collier, V. P. & Thomas, W. P. (2009). *Educating English learners for a transformed world.* Albuquerque, NM: Fuente Press.

Commins, N. L. & Miramontes, O. B. (2005). *Linguistic Diversity and Teaching.* Mahwah, N.J.: Lawrence Erlbaum.

Creese, A. & Blackledge, A. (2010). Translanguaging in the bilingual classroom: A pedagogy for learning and teaching? *The Modern Language Journal*, 94, 103-115.

Cummins, J. (2000). *Language, power, and pedagogy.* Clevedon, UK: Multilingual Matters.

Cummins, J. (2005, September). *Teaching for cross-language transfer in dual language education: Possibilities and pitfalls.* TESOL Symposium of Dual Language Education: Teaching and Learning Two Languages in the EFL Setting. Istanbul, Turkey. Sept. 23.

Cummins, J. (2008). [Forward]. *AILA Review*, 21, 1-3.

Escamilla, K. & Hopewell, S. (2010). Transitions to biliteracy: Creating positive academic trajectories for emerging bilinguals in the United States. In J. Petrovic (Ed.) *International Perspectives on Bilingual Education: Policy, Practice, Controversy.* Charlotte, NC: Information Age Publishing.

Faltis, C. (1996). Learning to teach content bilingually in a middle school bilingual classroom. *Bilingual Research Journal*, 20, 29–44.

Fitts, S. (2006). Reconstructing the status quo: Linguistic interaction in a dual-language school. *Bilingual Research Journal*, 30, 337-366.

Gaarder, B. (1978). The golden rules of second language acquisition by young children. *NABE Journal*, 2, 58-59.

García, O. (2009). *Bilingual education in the 21st century: A global perspective.* West Sussex, UK: Wiley-Blackwell.

García, O. (2012). Theorizing translanguaging for educators. In Celic, C. and Seltzer, K. (Eds.). *Translanguaging: A CUNY-NYSIEB Guide for Educators.* NY: CUNY_NYSIEB, The Graduate Center, The City University of NY. Retrieved on 11/04/2012 from http://www.nysieb.ws.gc.cuny.edu/files/2012/06/FINAL-Translanguaging-Guide-With-Cover-1.pdf

González, N., Moll, L.C., & Amanti, C. (2005). *Funds of knowledge: Theorizing practices in households, communities, and classrooms.* Mahwah, NJ: Lawrence Erlbaum Associates.

Greene, J. (1997). A meta-analysis of the Rossell and Baker review of bilingual research. *Bilingual Research Journal*, 21, 103-122.

Grosjean, F. (1989). Neurolinguists beware! The bilingual is not two monolinguals in one. *Brain and Language*, 36, 3-15.

Gutiérrez, K. D., Baquedano-López, P., & Tejada, C. (1999). Rethinking diversity: Hybridity and hybrid language practices in the third space. *Mind, Culture, and Activity: An International Journal*, 6, 286-303.

Hamayan, Else. (2010). Separado o together? Reflecting on the separation of languages of instruction. *Soleado*, Albuquerque: Dual Language Education of New Mexico.

Harvey, S. & Goudvis, A. (2000). *Strategies that work: Teaching comprehension to enhance understanding.* York, ME: Stenhouse.

Heller, M. (2001). Undoing the macro/micro dichotomy: Ideology and categorization in a linguistic minority school. In N. Coupland (Ed.), *Sociolinguistics and social theory* (pp. 261-296). Harlow, England: Pearson.

Hopewell, S. (2011). Leveraging bilingualism to accelerate English reading comprehension. *International Journal of Bilingual Education and Bilingualism*, 14, 603-620.

Hornberger, N. H. & Link, H. (2012). Translanguaging and transnational literacies in multilingual classrooms: A biliteracy lens. *International Journal of Bilingual Education and Bilingualism*, 15, 261-278.

Howard, E. R., Sugarman, J., Christian, D., Lindholm-Leary, K. J., & Rogers, D. (2007). *Guiding principles for dual language education* (2nd ed.). Washington, DC: Center for Applied Linguistics.

Imhoff, G. (1990). The position of U.S. English on bilingual education. In CB. Cazden & C.E. Snow (Eds.) *English Plus. Issues in bilingual education*, (pp. 48-61). The Annals of the American Academy of Political and Social Science.

Keene, E. O. & Zimmerman, S. (1997). *Mosaic of thought: Teaching comprehension in a reader's workshop.* Portsmouth, NH: Heinemann.

Kenner, C. (2004). Living in simultaneous worlds: Difference and integration in bilingual script-learning. *Bilingual Education and Bilingualism, 7,* 43-61.

LeCompte, M. D. & Schensul, J. J. (1999). *Analyzing & interpreting ethnographic data.* Walnut Creek, CA: AltaMira Press.

Lessow-Hurley, J. (2000). *The foundations of dual-language instruction.* New York: Longman.

Moll, L. C. & Díaz, S. (1985). Ethnographic pedagogy: Promoting effective bilingual instruction. In E.E. García and R.V. Padilla (Eds.), *Advances in bilingual education research.* Tucson: University of Arizona Press.

Olivares, R. A. (2002). Communication, constructivism and transfer of knowledge in the education of bilingual learners. *International Journal of Bilingual Education and Bilingualism* 5, 4-19.

Porter, R. (1990). *Forked tongue. The politics of bilingual education.* New York: Basic Books.

Rolstad, K., Mahoney, K., & Glass, G. (2005). The big picture: A meta-analysis of program effectiveness research on English language learners. *Educational Policy,* 19, 572-594.

Slavin, R., & Cheung, A. (2005). A synthesis of research on language of reading instruction for English language learners. *Review of Educational Research,* 75, 247-284.

Thomas, W. P. & Collier, V. P. (2012). *Dual language education for a transformed world.* Albuequerque, NM: Fuente Press.

Ulanoff, S. & Pucci, S. (1993). *Is concurrent-translation or preview-review more effective in promoting second language vocabulary acquisition?* Paper presented at American Educational Research Association, Atlanta, GA, April 12-16.

Wei, L. & Martin, P. (2009). Conflicts and tensions in classroom code-switching: an introduction. *International Journal of Bilingual Education and Bilingualism,* 12, 117-122.

Wendorf, C. A. (2004). Manuals for univariate and multivariate statistics. Retrieved from http://www.uwsp.edu/psych/cw/statsmanual/index.html

Willig, A. (1985). A meta-analysis of selected studies of the effectiveness of bilingual education. *Review of Educational Research,* 55, 269-317.

Willoughby, L. (2009). Language choice in multilingual peer groups: Insights from an Australian high school. *Journal of Multilingual and Multicultural Development,* 30, 421-435.

Zentella, A. C. (1997). *Growing up bilingual.* Oxford, UK: Blackwell Publishers.

Zimmerman, S. & Hutchins, C. (2003). *7 keys to comprehension: How to help your kids read it and get it!* New York: Three Rivers Press.

Tracing the Multiliterate Identities of Pre-service Teachers in the U.S.-Mexico Border

Erika Mein
Luciene Wandermurem
The University of Texas at El Paso

The increasingly diverse and multilingual character of U.S. schools, combined with the increasingly digital nature of communication in U.S. society, necessitate a re-envisioning of teachers' pedagogical – as well as epistemological and ontological – stances towards teaching and learning in the 21st century. At the heart of this re-envisioning is teachers' (multi-)literate practice, that is, the ways in which teachers understand and engage in reading and writing pedagogy across multiple languages, literacies, and modalities. One site to explore teachers' conceptions of future (multi-)literate practice is in teacher education programs, particularly those that are focused on working with culturally and linguistically diverse students.

This qualitative study is based in one such context: a teacher education program located in the bilingual/bicultural context of the US-Mexico border. Drawing on sociocultural theories of literacy/biliteracy (Barton, 1994; Hornberger, 2003; Street, 1984), transnational literacies (Jiménez, Smith, & Teague, 2009; Warriner, 2007), and multiliteracies (Cope &Kalantzis, 2000; New London Group, 1996), as well as situated perspectives on identity (Holland, Skinner, Lachicotte, and Cain, 1998), we explore the literacy practices and multi-literate identities of *transfronterizo* pre-service teachers who cross the U.S.-Mexico border on a regular basis and whose social interactions straddle two nations. In keeping with Gloria Anzaldúa (1987), we see the border as a space of contestation, where symbols, meanings, and ultimately identities sometimes co-exist, but often collide with one another. The experiences of border-crossing pre-service teachers can provide a valuable glimpse into these "cultural collisions" (Anzaldúa, 1987, p.100) within and across educational contexts.

The questions that formed the basis of this study included:

1. What are the literacy practices of transfronterizo pre-service secondary teachers in the U.S.-Mexico borderlands?

2. What are the (multi-)literate identities of transfronterizo pre-service teachers in the borderlands, and how do they construct and enact these identities within a teacher education setting?

3. How do transfronterizo pre-service teachers envision the incorporation of multiple literacies into their future teaching?

In this paper, we focus on the multiliterate identities and practices of six border-crossing pre-service teachers, drawing primarily on interviews and written reflections produced as part of a Content Area Literacy course that we taught. In our analysis we highlight some of the tensions and contradictions present in these pre-service teachers' representations of their own literate engagement with digital tools and technologies, and with their ideas about the use of technologies as future teachers. In particular, we show how all six of the pre-service teachers used digital technologies as a resource for their own academic learning but how, at the same time, they expressed ambivalence toward the use of technology in their own classrooms. This ambivalence, we argue, is tied to conflicting cultural models of literacy, teaching, and learning that could stem in part from the participants' social locations as border-crossers.

TRANSFRONTERIZO IDENTITIES AND LITERACY PRACTICES

This study focuses on the literacies and identities of pre-service teachers who cross the US-Mexico border on a regular basis, in this case to pursue undergraduate studies. In her book, *Borderlands/La Frontera*, Chicana feminist scholar Gloria Anzaldúa (1987) draws attention to the ambiguous, contradictory, and contentious material and symbolic space of the "borderlands," which represents an intersection of linguistic, ethnic, racial, gender, and sexual identities. Such ambiguities, contradictions, and hybridities make up the space of "entremundos, between and among worlds" (Anzaldúa, 2002, p. 3), a space that defies strict categorization of race, ethnicity, nationality, language, and gender.

In referring to the pre-service teachers in this study as "transfronterizo," we draw on the work of sociolinguists Zentella (2009) and Relaño-Pastor (2007). Relaño-Pastor's (2007) study of border-crossing youth in Tijuana/San Diego draws attention to "the continuous linguistic and cultural contact that border youth maintain as part of the multiple daily transactions across both sides," which in turn "blur...the boundaries between nationality, citizenship, language, and social class" (p. 264). In recent years, several ethnographic studies focusing specifically on the literacy practices of transfronterizo youth have emerged, opening the way to understanding how border-crossing students navigate the material, linguistic, and social complexities of two worlds, particularly in relation to schooling (See de la Piedra & Guerra, 2012). De la Piedra and Araujo (2012), for example, uncovered the ways in which transfronterizo upper elementary school students in a dual language program on the Ciudad Juárez/El Paso border "recontextualized" print and digital literacies across different borders (U.S. and Mexico, home and community) in order to make sense of academic literacy tasks at school.

That the pre-service teachers in this study can be labeled transfronterizo means that they are transnational: their everyday lives span two nations, and their educational experiences are interwoven into two educational systems, that of Mexico and the U.S. Embedded in the transnational-ness of their daily lives are digitally- and sometimes print-mediated social practices around texts that cross national boundaries – what has been referred to as "transnational literacies" (Jiménez et al., 2009; Warriner, 2007;).

The work on digitally-mediated transnational literacies is part of a larger body of sociocultural research on multi-modal literacies, "new" literacies, and multiliteracies (Kress, 2003; Lankshear & Knobel, 2003; New London Group, 1996). This body of work has drawn attention to the ways in which technology has transformed print-based communication across time and space. Kress (2003) argues that the present "age of the screen" has broken down the traditional distinction between writers and readers as producers and consumers of printed text, as "the new technologies of information and communication...bring together the resources for representation and their potential with the resources of production and the resources of dissemination" (p. 23). Similarly, Lankshear & Knobel (2008) define digital literacies as "the myriad social practices and conceptions of engaging in meaning making by texts that are produced, received, distributed, exchanged, etc., via digital codification" (p. 5). These approaches to digital and multimodal literacies stem from a broader sociocultural perspective that sees literacy as a social practice, implicated in and shaped by particular social contexts and relations of power (Barton, 1994; Gee, 1996; Street, 1984).

In order to make sense of transfronteriza pre-service teachers' identities, we rely on Holland et al.'s (1998) notion of "figured worlds" as a way of understanding how social actors construct and enact identities within particular contexts. Holland et al. (1998) define figured worlds as "collectively realized as-if realms" (p. 49) where "particular characters and actors are recognized, significance is assigned to certain acts, and particular outcomes are valued over others" (p. 52). Figured worlds, in this view, invoke conceptual models or representations of how-things-are or how-things-should-be, implicating social actors in these shared meanings. Figured worlds are mediated via cultural artifacts, that is, "objects or symbols inscribed by a collective attribution of meaning in relation to figured worlds" (Bartlett, 2007, p. 217). Two examples of cultural artifacts given by Holland et al. include the poker chip denoting sobriety in the figured world of Alcoholics Anonymous and husbands' use of the informal "you" with their wives in one Nepali village; both signal "a conception of the tasks to which they are put, and a conception of the person(s) who will use them and be the object(s) of them" (p. 62). In this way, cultural artifacts draw attention to the simultaneous material and ideational aspects of figured worlds, which are fluid and dynamic rather than static; it is in the constant "flux" of the figured world that identities are shaped and enacted, within what Holland et al. (1998), drawing on Bakhtin, call "the space of authoring" (p. 63).

This study thus uses these multiple lenses to explore the ways in which pre-service teachers on the U.S.-Mexico border understand and enact multiple literacies and multiliterate identities. While there have been several studies of pre-service teachers' literacies across multiple modalities (Love, 2004; Sheridan-Thomas, 2007; Skerrett, 2010), there has been little exploration of pre-service teachers' literacies across multiple modalities as well as multiple languages and contexts. The present study seeks to fill that gap by looking at the ways in which pre-service teachers in one undergraduate literacy course, many of whom are bilingual (Spanish/English), understand and take up the notion of multiple literacies, and how they view themselves as readers and writers in the multilingual, multimodal context of a university situated on the U.S.-Mexico border.

RESEARCH CONTEXT: METHODS OF DATA COLLECTION AND ANALYSIS

The site of this study was a Content Area Literacy course for undergraduate pre-service teachers at a southwestern university located on the U.S.-Mexico border. In order to explore students' understandings and enactments of literacy across languages, contexts, and modalities, we utilized qualitative methods for data collection and analysis (Denzin & Lincoln, 2005), placing particular focus on participants' narrative accounts about their experiences with literacies and technologies. Initial data were collected in fall 2011 in four sections of the course taught by the authors, each of whom taught two sections but invited students from opposite sections to participate in the study in order to avoid potential conflicts of interest; interviews with selected students were conducted in spring 2012.

The key sources of data included participants' written reflections submitted through Blackboard; their autobiographical writings/productions (including PowerPoint presentations and videos), where they represented their own literacy histories; surveys of participants' language histories, which asked primarily about their use of Spanish and English across different settings; and in-depth interviews with select participants, which took place after the course ended. Eleven students participated in the in-depth interviews, which generally lasted one hour and included questions about participants' educational and language histories, experiences with reading and writing, approaches to handling academic reading/writing at the college level, and views on digital technology. This paper focuses on the experiences of six of the eleven participants, all female, who we identified as transfronteriza because they crossed the border on a daily or regular basis, and because they did much, if not all, of their K-12 schooling in Mexico.

All of the interviews were transcribed by the co-author of this paper, who is currently a doctoral student at the same institution. Our data analysis relied heavily on thematic coding approaches, starting first with "open coding" and then moving on to more "focused coding" (Emerson, Fretz, and Shaw, 2011) of the data. The process involved two rounds of coding, combined with two data analysis sessions where we compared and contrasted notes, as a form of triangulation. The first round of coding, which was conducted by Wandermurem, involved looking for general themes related to our research questions, that is, themes connected to the multiliterate practices and identities of pre-service teachers and to the ways in which pre-service teachers envision the use of multiple literacies in their future classrooms. Initial codes that emerged in this first round of analysis included: "reading practices," "writing practices," "math literacy practices," "digital literacy practices," and "technology and teaching."

After this preliminary analysis, we held an intensive data analysis session where we discussed the preliminary codes and developed a strategy for the second round of coding, which was conducted by both of the authors on an individual basis. The categories and codes that emerged in the second round of coding included: (1) Views of literacy/biliteracy (codes: in-betweenness; positioning by teachers; and bilingualism as a resource); (2) Strategic knowledge of educational systems of both Mexico and U.S.; and (3) Digital literacies and multiliterate identities (codes: strategic use of technology for academic purposes; Internet/Facebook as the main means of communication across borders; and ambivalence about technology). For the code of "ambivalence about technology" under the third category of "digital literacies and multiliterate identities," there were two examples that did not fit with the code; in other words, there were two students, one a math major and the other a Spanish major, who expressed no ambivalence about the use of technology in their future classrooms. We acknowledged these counter-examples by clearly attributing the finding of "ambivalence" to only three of the six focal participants in the write-up of this study.

While several themes emerged related to students' views of bilingualism/biliteracy and of themselves as readers and writers, we chose to focus this paper on three themes that emerged regarding participants' identities and practices related to digital technologies: (1) the use of digital technology to sustain transborder social relationships; (2) the strategic use of digital technology for academic purposes; and (3) ambivalence toward the use of technology in future teaching. Each of these will be explored in detail in the next section.

PARTICIPANTS

This study relied on data from six participants who were selected from the larger pool of participating students based on their *transfronterizo* (border-crossing) status. Lorena, Maria, Ana and Nadia (all pseudonyms) were mathematics pre-service teachers, while Lucia and Juana were pursuing undergraduate degrees in Spanish. All of the participants except Maria were in their early or mid-twenties; Maria was in her forties. All women were *transfonterizas* in the sense of having crossed the international border throughout their lives. Their first language was Spanish and that was the language that they spoke at home.

Lorena, a math major, was born in Mexico and, despite having always lived there, her experiences as a border-crosser started at the age of seven when she was enrolled in English classes in the United States. Also a math major, Nadia was born in the US and moved to Mexico a few years later. She moved back to the U.S. with her family at the age of ten; she reported physically crossing the border every weekend to visit family and friends in Mexico. Maria, another mathematics student, was born in Mexico and lived there until she completed high school. She then moved to the U.S., where she attended community college for two years. She returned to Mexico to complete a bachelor's degree in civil engineering. Three years prior to this study, Maria returned to the U.S. to live but continues to work in a *maquila* (manufacturing plant) in Mexico. The fourth mathematics pre-service teacher in this study, Ana, was born in Mexico and moved to the U.S. when she was 13 years old. When describing her experiences moving to the U.S., Ana shared some of the frustration and embarrassment she went through as a teenager who did not speak English. Lucia, a Spanish major, was born in Mexico. She moved to the U.S. in 2002 at the age of 16. As a high school student in the U.S., she was placed in ESL classes. Like Lucia, Juana was a Spanish major who spent most of her childhood in the U.S. but moved back to Mexico three years prior. Of these six students, three crossed the international border on a daily basis (Lorena, Maria, and Juana), and three others (Nadia, Ana, and Lucia) did a significant amount of their schooling in Mexico and maintain close social ties there although they reside in the U.S. The following table summarizes the focal participants:

Table 1: Summary of Focal Participants

Name	Major	Daily/Regular Border Crosser
Lorena	Math	Daily
Maria	Math	Daily
Juana	Spanish	Daily
Nadia	Math	Regular
Ana	Math	Regular
Lucia	Spanish	Regular

DIGITAL LITERACIES AND THE ENACTMENT OF MULTILITERATE IDENTITIES

Use of Social Media to Sustain Transborder Social Relationships

Active engagement with digital technologies was one clear facet of transfonteriza pre-service teachers' repertoire of multiliterate practices. Facebook, Twitter, websites, text messaging, YouTube, and Google emerged as the most important tools used both for social and academic purposes. One social use of technology was that described by Lorena, who provided an account of how social media played a key role in her personal relationships. Lorena lived in Mexico and crossed the border on a daily basis to study at the university, where she was pursuing a degree in mathematics. Lorena said that she sometimes returned to Mexico from the U.S. at 11:30 pm, while needing to be on the bridge again the next day by 4:15 am to make the two-hour crossing back to the U.S. Lacking the time for face-to-face interactions with community members in her home country during the week, Lorena explained how Facebook was particularly useful for sustaining these relationships:

> I have my Facebook because I am a volunteer in a church in [border city in Mexico] and we are in a group, so every week we do activities and that's the way we communicate. So I have to be constantly checking Facebook and that's the only way that I can contact them sometimes. Sometimes they haven't paid their phones or something like that but they always check Facebook. I know that if I post something there they are going to see it. This is like having their phone number. If they didn't have Facebook, I think I couldn't contact them (Interview, 7 May 2012).

In this quote, Lorena highlights the role of online social media in maintaining relationships and facilitating activities connected to her church in Mexico; she describes a reliance on this digital medium in part because of her busy schedule as a student, which involves up to two hours of wait time daily at the international border. In this sense, Lorena's transborder social network was digitally-mediated, and her literate engagement via Facebook in Spanish was the means by which she was able to sustain participation in meaningful extracurricular activities, in this case, with her church. Previous research has shown how online media have supported transnational networks among Chinese migrant youth (Lam, 2009) and transfronterizo upper elementary students in the El Paso-Juarez region (de la Piedra & Araujo, 2012). Through technology-mediated interactions, children and youth not only are able to maintain group membership across countries but also develop their literate repertoire through a combination of several semiotic channels including different languages and linguistic codes (de la Piedra & Araujo, 2012; Lam, 2009).

Use of Digital Technology for Academic Purposes

In addition to the use of digital literacies to maintain cross-border social relationships, this study also pointed to the use of such tools for academic purposes. Two students, Maria and Lucia, mentioned that they lacked confidence in their English language proficiency and emphasized the use of certain technology-based strategies to meet the requirements of academic language conventions. In one interview, Lucia mentioned the use of technology to assist her in academic writing in English: "I don't know if I should use *was, were* or *will* so I put the sentence in the Google translator and see how it looks in Spanish. I see if it makes sense in Spanish. That's my strategy" (Interview, 9 May 2012). Maria, on the other hand, was more concerned about expanding vocabulary. In her words:

> My daughter subscribed to a webpage. It says SAT or S-A-T and she enrolled me in that website, so every day they send me a question. It is a paragraph like a story and then 'we showed these words, now explain this paragraph'. And every day we need to answer the question and that's why I am more or less learning one word per day (Interview, 28 February 2012).

Maria's concern about English vocabulary acquisition was evident throughout the interview and in written reflections. Describing herself as a "literate person who masters the Spanish language," Maria sought to position herself and be positioned as "proficient in the English language," as part of the mathematics educator identity she envisions herself enacting in the U.S. context. From a figured worlds perspective, the SAT website represented a cultural artifact that invoked the figured world of academic success, which for Maria equated to being a "proficient English speaker/writer." This finding is consistent with Bartlett's (2007) ethnographic study on social relations and identity construction among transnational high school students in New York City. Examining one transnational Spanish-speaker student's educational trajectory, Bartlett (2007) found that recognition as "a good student" in a Spanish class functioned as a cultural artifact that motivated the student to work harder in other classes (i.e., math and English) where she was perceived as a struggling student.

In addition to engagement with digital literacies for English language development, transfonteriza pre-service teachers relied on Internet tools to deepen disciplinary knowledge as well. Instructional videos accessed through YouTube or specific websites were often cited as strategies to reinforce knowledge constructed in classroom settings. In her interview, Lorena mentioned, "if I don't remember how to solve an equation or a process, I look at an explanation on YouTube. It is usually very helpful"(Interview, 7 May 2012). Likewise, Lucia accessed YouTube videos to learn how to develop a thematic unit in her specialization area, Spanish. The same strategy was also used by Spanish major Juana with the purpose of exploring ideas on how to design creative lesson plans in Spanish. Similarly, Ana, a math major, described some websites she found useful to expand her knowledge on certain topic or to clarify concepts she did not understand through classroom lectures:

> There is a website called *wolframalpha.com* and I use that website whenever I have to understand a topic deeper. Sometimes it has animations like a little graph so we can understand what they are talking about. So an animation like a little video... and there is also another website called *khanacademy.com* and it is has a lot of topics in math and they have videos (Interview, 3 May 2012).

Ana explained that the features of those two particular websites were helpful for her to understand concepts taught in a differential equations class. She complained about the mode of instruction in that class, saying, "The professor wasn't very helpful because he would only put the book like that in the projector and he would read it like that and then we would be like oh, how are we supposed to learn?"(Interview, 3 May 2012). Rather than rely on the teacher to explain the concepts, however, she became an active participant in her own learning via forms of multiliterate engagement that crossed contexts and media: she used various math-related websites and videos to make sense of content included in the textbook. Similar to the other two participants, Ana's multiliterate engagement – in this case, with instructional videos – became a resource for understanding difficult concepts in order to better navigate academic tasks in her discipline.

Ambivalence Toward Use of Technology in Future Teaching

As demonstrated previously, digital literacies were not only practices that implicated and helped shape transfonteriza pre-service teachers' multiliterate identities, but they were also a way for the participants to author new identities, such as "proficient reader/writer" and "good student" in their disciplines. Even though all of the participants highlighted the strategic use of digital technology as a resource for their own learning, three math major pre-service teachers, Nadia, Lorena, and Maria, expressed ambivalence about the usefulness of technology tools for their own future teaching. As future mathematics educators, these students expressed concern about the negative effects of using calculators in their classrooms, concerns that signaled particular conceptions about, or figured worlds of, mathematics teaching and learning. Two comments by Lorena and Nadia were particularly revealing:

> Lorena: Calculators are making students lazy. They rely so much on the calculator. They don't want to do the processes if they know that the calculator is going to give them the answer in three seconds. So they don't want to do it by hand. I think it is helpful if the students are engaged and interested in the class but if they are not interested, they are only going to rely on the calculator and aren't going to know what happens behind using the calculator (Interview, 7 May 2012).

> Nadia: Oh well, I don't really like the calculators. They [students] can't add one plus one. They really can't. Maybe it would be like half of the semester without a calculator and the second half with a calculator. Because once you give them the calculator, they stop analyzing it (Interview, 12 April 2012).

In these quotes, the students evoke "calculators" as a cultural artifact that positions students who are learning mathematics in the U.S. as "lazy." This positioning of students who use calculators as lazy signals a conflict with these pre-service teachers' cultural models of mathematics teaching and learning, which involve "doing problems by hand" and "analyzing" rather than relying on technology.

In addition to common calculators, the participants were also critical of other types of technology such as iPads, smart boards, and graphing calculators. Lorena spoke negatively about the overuse of digital technology devices in U.S. classrooms. She went on to say that "in some districts instead of math books they are giving students iPads. I think that's not a good idea because they are high school kids." While Lorena's perspective highlighted the overuse of technology in schools, Maria was more focused on the misuse of it. In her words:

> I went to observe a class and the teacher was using the smart board and he closed all the windows so the classroom was dark and all students were sleeping instead of paying attention to the class. So I don't believe it is a good idea. They were sleeping or playing with their cell phones. I don't think it is good idea (Interview, 28 February 2012).

In this quote, Maria creates an image of a technology-infused classroom with "sleeping" and distracted students. In her representation, the teacher, the smart board, the dark classroom, and the sleeping and disengaged students together point to the pitfalls of technology use in the classroom; this positioning of teachers, students, and technology suggests a sense of violation of her own conceptions of what constitutes valid mathematics teaching and learning. For Maria, as well as the others, the use of technology was equated with "bad teaching," while solving problems by hand and analyzing was equated to "good teaching."

While in some instances the participants maintained binary (good/bad) conceptions of math teaching and learning, these conceptions were also complicated in other instances by their understanding of their location on the border and the different demands involved in teaching in the U.S. and in Mexico. In the case of Lorena, when asked if she saw herself using technology as a teaching resource, she argued:

> I know if I am working here in the United States I will have to use technology because I am a math teacher and math teachers are required to use a lot of technology. They want the kids to be interested in the STEM areas so they want them to have graphing calculators and use the smart boards and things like that. But if I teach in [border city in Mexico], it is very difficult to have those types of technology. For example, I don't own a graphing calculator of my own. Now that I am a math major I don't even have one because I am used to do my graphs on the paper. I know how to do those. And in [border city in Mexico] they teach how to do it by hand because they don't have so many resources to provide students with a graphing calculator, with smart board. If I teach in Mexico, I don't think I will be able to use these technologies. It depends on where I work (Interview, 7 May 2012).

Here, Lorena presents a more complex scenario about the use of technology in a future math classroom. The figured world of mathematics teaching is no longer comprised of good pedagogy ("doing things by hand") versus bad pedagogy (signaled by the use of calculators). Instead, for Lorena, models of mathematics teaching were now tied to their location in either the U.S. or Mexico. In this quote, the figured world of teaching in the U.S. is evoked via teachers' complying with rules, in this case, the requirement to use technology, as well as schools' use of technology to lure students to study in STEM areas ("They want the kids to be interested in the STEM areas so they want them to have graphing calculators and use the smart boards and things like that").

This representation of mathematics teaching in the U.S. stands in stark contrast to the figured world of mathematics teaching in Mexico, where students and teachers have to "rough it" because of fewer technological resources in the classroom. Lorena clearly aligns herself as both student and teacher with that world, stating that she still does not own a graphing calculator (in spite of being a math major) because she is accustomed to doing her own graphs on paper. Lorena's competing and conflicting discourses about mathematics teaching can be seen to reflect a state of *in-betweenness* described by Anzaldúa (1987): "Like others having or living in more than one culture, we get multiple, often opposing messages. The coming together of two self-consistent but habitually incompatible frames of reference causes *un choque*, a cultural collision" (p. 100).

DISCUSSION AND IMPLICATIONS

This study explored how the identities of pre-service teachers in the U.S.-Mexico borderlands were constructed through active engagement with multiliterate practices. Additionally, it examined pre-service teachers' perspectives on the incorporation of multiple literacies into their future teaching. Data analysis pointed to three recurrent themes: Use of social media to sustain transborder social relationships; the strategic use of digital technology for academic purposes; and ambivalence toward the use of technology in future teaching.

The first theme, use of social media to sustain transborder social relationships, illustrated how social networks were sustained across countries through the use of digital media. The second, strategic use of digital technology for academic purposes, showed how pre-service teachers made use of digital tools such as an SAT website to develop the identity of "proficient English speaker/writer" and "good student." These two first findings show the potential for digital tools to shape identities through practices involving the manipulation of various semiotic channels (New London Group, 1996; Hull & Nelson, 2005). In other words, by actively engaging with technology-mediated literacy practices, individuals can author new meanings while at the same time transforming their identities.

The third theme found in this study was ambivalence toward technology use in future teaching, where conflicts emerged in pre-service teachers' cultural models of what counts as "good" mathematics teaching and learning. On the one hand, three of the pre-service teachers equated the use of calculators and digital technologies in the math classroom with "bad" teaching and learning. On the other hand, at least one teacher demonstrated an understanding of the different demands and constraints upon teachers in the US and Mexico, and articulated a more nuanced stance toward her use of technology as a teacher, one contingent on the context in which she will work.

Challenging traditional pedagogies, several scholars have called for multiliteracies (New London Group, 1996; Street 2003; Street, 2011) or pluriliteracies (García, Bartlett & Kleifgen, 2007) approaches that take into account the diversity of languages and linguistic codes that characterize student populations as well as the various modes of communication channels available to them. For Hull and Nelson (2005), multimodality – that is, the movement across different modalities such as speech, writing, image, gesture, and sound - represents "a democratizing force, an opening up of what counts as valued communication, and a welcoming of varied channels of expression" (p. 253). From this perspective, the multimodal nature of digital technologies can open up opportunities for students from diverse cultural backgrounds and characterized by different learning styles to design new meanings connected to their academic learning (Hull & Nelson, 2005; New London Group, 1996). The urgency for multimodal approaches to teaching and learning is perhaps even more pressing in the hybrid context of the borderlands, where histories, languages, and cultures mesh with one another within defined material and political boundaries.

The tensions and contractions that pre-service teachers manifested with respect to competing cultural models (Gee, 1999) of teaching and learning in Mexico and the U.S. speaks to the need for a greater focus on border-centered pedagogies, particularly in teacher education programs located in borderlands contexts. Cline and Necochea (2002) explain that a border pedagogy must draw on students' rich literacy practices in order to form bilingual and bicultural citizens. They argue that it is critical for U.S. and Mexican teachers in the borderlands to work in collaboration to analyze and compare instructional methods in both countries in order to design curriculum that caters to the needs of transfronterizo students whose lives are rooted in both places (Cline & Necochea, 2006). A border pedagogy would not only benefit *transfonterizo* students but also *transfonterizo* pre-service teachers. As found in this study, future math teachers expressed different views on the use of technology in math classes. Those views and concerns could be fruitful ground for an analysis of educational practices in both countries and an examination of the ways U.S. and Mexican teachers could learn from each other, with the goal of designing and re-designing border pedagogy. Drawing on Anzaldúa (1987), a border pedagogy could be seen as artifact of amestiza consciousness whose "energy comes from continual creative motion that keeps breaking down the unitary aspect of each new paradigm" (p. 102).

REFERENCES

Anzaldúa, G. (1987). *Borderlands/La frontera, the new mestiza.* San Francisco, CA: Aunt Lute Books.

Anzaldúa, G. (2002). Preface: (Un)natural bridges, (un)safe spaces. In G. Anzaldúa & A. Keating (Eds.), *This bridge we call home: Radical visions for transformation* (pp. 1-5). New York, NY: Routledge.

Bartlett, L. (2007). Bilingual literacies, social identification, and educational trajectories. *Linguistics in Education,* 18, 215-231.

Barton, D. (1994). *Literacy: An introduction to the ecology of written language.* Oxford, England: Blackwell.

Cline, Z., & Necochea, J. (2002). Education in the borderlands: A border pedagogy conceptual model. *El Bordo: Retos de Frontera,* 6, 43-58.

Cline, Z., & Necochea, J. (2006). Teachers dispositions for effective education in the borderlands. *The Educational Forum,* 70, 268-281.

Cope, B., & Kalantzis, M. (Eds.) (2000). *Multiliteracies: Literacy learning and the design of social futures.* London, England: Routledge.

De la Piedra, M.T., & Guerra, J.C. (2012). The literacy practices of transfronterizos in a multilingual world. *International Journal of Bilingual Education and Bilingualism (Special Issue: Literacies Crossing Borders),* 15, 627-634.

De la Piedra, M. T., & Araujo, B. E. (2012). Literacies crossing borders: Transfronterizo literacy practices of students in a dual language program on the USA-Mexico border. *Language and Intercultural Communication,* 12, 214-229.

Denzin, N. K., & Lincoln, Y. S. (2005). Introduction: The discipline and practice of qualitative research. In N. K. Denzin and Y. S. Lincoln (Eds.), *The SAGE handbook of qualitative research* (pp. 1-42). Thousand Oaks, CA: Sage.

Emerson, R. M., Fretz, R. I., & Shaw, L. L. (2011). *Writing ethnographic field notes* (2nd ed.), Chicago, IL: University of Chicago Press.

García, O., Bartlett, L., & Kleifgen, J. (2007). From biliteracy to plural literacies. In L. Wei & P. Auer (Eds.), *Handbook on multilingualism and multilingual communication* (pp. 207-228). New York, NY: Mouton.

Gee, J. P. (1996). *Social linguistics and literacies: Ideology in discourses* (2nd ed.), London, England: Taylor & Francis.

Gee, J. P. (1999). *An introduction to discourse analysis: Theory and method.* London: Routledge.

Holland, D., Skinner, D., Lachicotte, W., Jr., & Cain, C. (1998). *Identity and agency cultural worlds.* Cambridge, MA: Harvard University Press.

Hornberger, N. H. (Ed.). (2003). *Continua of biliteracy: An ecological framework for educational policy, research, and practice in multilingual settings.* Clevedon, UK: Multilingual Matters.

Hull, G. A., & Nelson, M. E. (2005). Locating the semiotic power of multimodality. *Written Communication,* 22, 224-259.

Jiménez, R. T., Smith, P. H., & Teague, B. L. (2009). Transnational and community literacies for teachers. *Journal of Adolescent and Adult Literacy,* 53, 16-26.

Kress, G. (2003). *Literacy in the new media age.* London, England: Routledge.

Lam, W. S. E. (2009). Multiliteracies on instant messaging in negotiating local, translocal, and transnational affiliations: A case of an adolescent immigrant. *Reading Research Quarterly,* 44, 377-397.

Lankshear, C., & Knobel, M. (2003). *New literacies: Changing knowledge and classroom learning.* Philadelphia, PA: Open University Press.

Lankshear, C. & Knobel, M. (2008). *Digital literacies: Concepts, policies, and practices.* New York, NY: Peter Lang.

Love, M. S. (2004). Multimodality of learning through anchored instruction. *Journal of Adolescent and Adult Literacy,* 48, 300-310.

New London Group. (1996). A pedagogy of multiliteracies: Designing social futures. *Harvard Educational Review,* 66, 60-92.

Relaño-Pastor, A. (2007). On border identities: Tranfronterizo students in San Diego. *Diskurs Kindheits- und Jugendforschung Heft,* 3, 263-277.

Sheridan-Thomas, H. K. (2007). Making sense of multiple literacies: Exploring pre-service content area teachers' understandings and applications. *Reading Research and Instruction,* 46, 121-150.

Skerrett, A. (2010). Lolita, Facebook, and the third space of literacy teacher education. *Educational Studies,* 46, 67-84.

Street, B. (1984). *Literacy in theory and practice.* Cambridge, UK: Cambridge University Press. Street, B. (2003). What's "new" in New Literacy Studies? Critical approaches to literacy in theory and practice. *Current Issues in Comparative Education,* 5, 77-91.

Street, B. (2011). Literacy inequalities in theory and practice: The power to name and define. *International Journal of Educational Development,* 31, 580-586.

Warriner, D. (2007). Transnational literacies: Immigration, language learning, and identity. *Linguistics and Education,* 18, 201-214.

Zentella, A. (2009). Transfronterizo talk: Conflicting constructions of bilingualism on the US-Mexico border. Retrieved from http://www.swarthmore.edu/transfronterizo-talk-conflicting-constructions-of-bilingual. xml.

Cultural Boundaries or Geographic Borders? Future Teachers Define "American" in Response to *In My Family/En mi familia*

Denise Davila
The University of Georgia

Like many people, some undergraduate students who enter university teacher licensure programs embrace different social narratives about who is/isn't American. Sometimes these narratives or taken-for-granted assumptions are aligned with the anti-immigration/anti-Latino rhetoric that has long been promoted by some news agencies and politicians (Begala, 2012; Media Matters For America, 2012; National Hispanic Media Coalition, 2012). Unrecognized and unexamined, such assumptions could shape the kinds of perspectives some future public school teachers might intentionally and unintentionally reinforce among learners (Gee, 2011). They could likewise influence some teachers' conscious and unconscious decisions around the selection, censorship, and discussion of multicultural children's literature (Beach, 1997).

This Yearbook entry tells the tale of one group of future teachers' (FTs') responses to the real-life childhood experiences of Chicana narrative artist Carmen Lomas Garza as depicted in Garza's acclaimed picturebook memoir *In My Family/En mi familia* (1996). The story is an excerpt from a larger research project I conducted with multiple works of Latino children's literature (Davila, 2012). This Yearbook telling begins with an overview of Garza's work and a critical context for considering the multicultural education agenda in dominant American society. It continues with a theoretical framework that connects dominant social Discourses and notions of "typical" American and non-American identities with teachers' curricular and pedagogical decisions. The methodology section describes the study design and approach to data collection and analysis. The subsequent discussion and implications sections examine the relevance of the FTs' response to Garza's childhood memoir to teacher education and licensure programs.

Garza (2012) says that since 1969, her life's goal has been to create art that instills pride in Mexican American history and culture. Her work depicts "special and everyday events in the lives of Mexican Americans… [that] elicit recognition and appreciation among Mexican Americans, both adults and children, while at the same time serve as a source of education for others not familiar with our culture" (para. 1). As a result, Garza's picturebooks are accessible and appealing to a wide audience of readers. *In My Family/En mi familia*, for example, won the Tomás Rivera Mexican American Children's Book Award (1996), the Américas Book Award for Children and Young Adult Literature (1996), and was honored by the Pura Belpré book award committee (1998). It is the companion to *Family Pictures/Cuadros de familia* (1990), Garza's first collection of paintings and narratives about her childhood growing up in Kingsville, TX.

Both titles are recognized in the contemporary cannon of children's literature and included on top children's reading lists (e.g., American Library Association, Library of Congress, and School Library Journal). In 2005, a *quinceañera*/15th anniversary edition of *Family Pictures/Cuadros de familia* was published with a special introduction by Sandra Cisneros and afterword by Pat Mora. These renowned Chicana authors honor Garza for sharing her family and community with others. Children's literature textbooks advocate for the inclusion of Garza's picturebooks in a multicultural education curriculum (Kiefer & Tyson, 2013; Norton, 2012) and curriculum guides about Garza's work have been professionally developed for educators (Denver Public Schools, 2002; San Jose Museum of Art, 2001).

Memoirs for children like *In My Family/En mi familia*, are especially relevant given that nearly one in four (24.7%) public elementary school students identified as Hispanic/Latino in 2011 (Fry & Lopez, 2012). While approximately 84% of U.S. teachers identify as White, non-Hispanic women (National Center for Education Information, 2011), the multicultural education agenda calls on these teachers to affirm "the pluralism (ethnic, racial, linguistic, religious, economic, and gender, among others) that students, their communities, and teachers reflect" (Nieto & Bode, 2008, p. 44). In contrast to this agenda, teachers' lack of preparedness to serve diverse populations is one of the primary reasons there is a crisis in the education of Latino students (Gándara, 2008). Moreover, many Latinos are concerned that the predominantly White teaching pool is neither culturally competent nor responsive to Latino students (Pew Hispanic Center/Kaiser Family Foundation, 2004). Thus, analyzing FTs' responses to Garza's memoir provides one window into the kinds of perspectives about children of Hispanic/Latino heritage that some teachers might consciously or unconsciously bring to school.

THEORETICAL FRAMEWORK

The study presented here is grounded in sociocultural theory. First, it is framed by Gee's (2008) theory that social Discourses with a capital "D" are unconscious and uncritical socially accepted ways of speaking/listening and writing/reading that are "*coupled* with distinctive ways of acting, interacting, valuing, feeling, dressing, thinking, believing, with other people and with various objects, tools, and technologies, so as to enact specific socially recognizable identities engaged in specific socially recognizable activities…" (p. 155, emphasis in original). Discourses are ideological in nature and advance the values and viewpoints of the social group they represent. They define who is an insider and who is an outsider to the social or cultural groups and oftentimes who or what is "normal" and who or what isn't (Gee, 2008). Moreover, Gee (2008) suggests that the dominant Discourses in society are relevant to the distribution and acquisition of social goods such as money, power, and status. Persons who are member of the dominant social group are usually fluent in the dominant Discourse.

Second, the study is informed by the concepts of cultural models (Holland & Quinn, 1987) and figured worlds (Gee, 2011), which are personal theories, notions, or taken-for-granted assumptions about what is "normal" or "typical" of people and the world around them. To illustrate the pervasiveness of such take-for-granted assumptions, Shannon (1994) asked the preservice and practicing teachers in his children's literature courses, the majority of whom were women, to identify the default (prototype) values and characteristics of a "typical American." The group generally described an educated, able-bodied, White, male, heterosexual, Protestant from a family with two parents. When Shannon invited the teachers to compare this prototype of a normal American with their personal sense of identity, some were surprised and sobered by considering who benefits from being a "typical" American.

With regard to defining a "typical" person of Latino heritage, Chavez (2008) observes that in U.S. dominant Discourse, Latinos are construed to be outside the realm of U.S. citizenry. Chavez

(2008) suggests that a Latino Threat Narrative (LTN) fuels anti-Latino rhetoric. In the LTN, persons of Hispanic/Latino heritage pose a threat to the well-being of "average" Americans. As described by Chomsky (2007), the LTN is perpetuated by myths that all persons of Hispanic/Latino heritage are immigrants who undermine American identity, procure American jobs, drain the economy and social services, and increase crime and poverty. Moreover, the LTN essentializes all persons of Hispanic/Latino heritage as monolingual Spanish speakers who live in their own communities, marry fellow Latinos, and ultimately resist integration into dominant American society and culture (Chavez, 2008). In short, the LTN disenfranchises Hispanics/Latinos from the American populous and feeds anti-Latino/anti-Immigration rhetoric.

Similar to the LTN, Santa Ana (2002) argues that there is a pervasive Anglo-American Narrative (AAN), which likewise casts immigrants and U.S.-born persons of Hispanic/Latino heritage as non-English speaking foreigners. The AAN additionally establishes a set of criteria for Hispanics/Latinos to be recognized as members of the American populous. Santa Ana (2002) suggests that the only way persons of Hispanic/Latino heritage can demonstrate their allegiance to the dominant Anglo-American culture is by embracing the AAN in at least three ways. They must (a) present themselves as monolingual English speakers; (b) present themselves as White-identified by rejecting all "foreign" qualities associated with being from Latin America; and (c) try to become White in as many ways as possible, which includes accepting the racial hierarchy that ranks White Americans superior to Americans of darker skin tone (Santa Ana, 2002).

Persons of Hispanic/Latino heritage who do not adopt the AAN or sufficiently integrate themselves into the dominant sociocultural group are cast as "foreigners," "non-Americans," and/or "invaders" in the dominant Discourse (Chavez, 2008; Chomsky, 2007; Santa Ana, 2002). These and other dehumanizing labels have been reinforced by elected officials, spewed across public radio airways, and reinforced by news media outlets (Begala, 2012; Media Matters For America, 2012; National Hispanic Media Coalition, 2012). In short, the Latino Threat Narrative and Anglo-American Narrative illustrate that dominant social groups' simplified assumptions of "normal," on which their cultural models or figured worlds are based, can perpetuate harmful, dismissive, and unjust notions about other people (Gee, 2011).

Such assumptions about the identity of "typical" Americans and foreigners could be sustained from one generation to the next. Within the institution of public education, for example, some teachers rely on their own educational experiences, personal histories (Britzman, 1986), and/or apprenticeships of observation (Lortie, 1975) to inform their performance as teachers. As many teachers attended U.S. public schools and experienced an Anglo-American approach to education, dominant middle-class perspectives could be reinforced in school (Seidl, 2007). Moreover, in conceiving of Discourse as subject matter knowledge, which sometimes informs the content teachers will take up with students (Grossman, 1990; Shulman, 1987), teachers might cyclically privilege certain kinds of knowledge and narratives over others. Thus, some teachers' reliance on their personal histories and figured worlds about curriculum and instruction could reify dominant perspectives of "normal," at the detriment of students who are not members of the same sociocultural groups as the teachers (Gee, 2008).

Teachers mediate children's reading in various ways that can impact what children bring to and think about a text (Apol, 1998). Hence, this study is also framed by Rosenblatt's (1995) theory that a reader will "bring to his reading the moral and religious code and social philosophy primarily assimilated from [his] family and community background" (p. 89). This notion is consistent with Gee's (2011) concept of figured worlds and serves as a foundation for Beach's (1997) reader response theory of subject positioning, which considers the connections between readers' ideological orientations and their acceptance or rejection of multicultural literature. Beach (1997) argues that readers, including teachers, are socialized to assume reading stances that validate their membership or status in certain groups. These stances are constructed and influenced by the ideological discourse of the group to which the reader belongs. As readers, teachers' notions of "normal" representations of gender, class, culture, and nationality may be reflected in their stances toward certain works of children's literature. Collectively readers' stances and/or responses provide data points that could serve as a springboard for critical conversations about multicultural children's books with teachers (Cai, 2008). Albers, Harste, and Vasquez (2011) add that this is difficult work. Their research illustrates that teachers, "must have opportunities to analyze issues critically through both language and art in order to identify the implicit and explicit issues, stereotypes, and underlying messages in picturebooks with difficult social issues" (p. 193).

The ability to recognize and thereby discuss one's reading stance toward a work of children's literature could be cultivated through the development of one's critical consciousness (Friere, 1970) and/or meta-knowledge (Gee, 2008). Gee (2008) argues that schools and educators have an ethical responsibility to foster meta-knowledge about the perspectives that underpin dominant Discourses, particularly when members of the dominant group are privileged over members of other groups.

METHODS

I addressed the following research questions in the study: (a) Do future teachers (FTs) see themselves including *In My Family* in their future classroom? Why or why not? and (b) What kinds of social Discourses and figured worlds do FTs construe about Mexican American families in response to reading *In My Family*?

Participants

As part of a larger study, I collected data from a pool of 83 education students who were enrolled in three sections of the undergraduate course Introduction to Children's Literature that I taught at a major midwestern university in the fall of 2011. This course was a prerequisite for several postbaccalaureate teacher licensure programs in the Midwest, thus all of the participants identified themselves as future educators. Following the structure of the 2010 U.S. Census survey, 89% of the participants self-identified as White, 81% identified as female, and 88% were 23 years old or younger. (See Table 1.) The demographics of this sample are consistent with the demographic make-up of teachers nationwide in which 84% identify as White/Non-Hispanic women (National Center for Education Information, 2011). The 16 men in the study also identified as White.

The participants' background knowledge was solicited through an in-class writing prompt about the FTs' relationship to the content of Garza's childhood memories in *In My Family/En mi familia*. This was key to the critical reading strategy the FTs practiced in class during Week 8 of the course (McLaughlin and DeVoogd, 2004). Almost 22% of the respondents stated that they did not

Table 1: Respondents' Race and Gender

Race	Female	Male	Total
White	58	16	74
Asian	2	0	2
Black	1	0	1
Chinese	1	0	1
Hispanic	1	0	1
Korean	1	0	1
South African	1	0	1
White/Latin American	1	0	1
White/Puerto Rican	1	0	1
Total	67	16	83

have any previous knowledge of Mexican and Mexican-Americans. One FT specified that she did not have any background knowledge because "I am an American and I am not related to anyone and do not know much about the culture." Approximately 13% of the FTs referenced Spanish language classes as a source of information. Nearly 12% stated that they had prior knowledge, but did not provide any descriptors. Ten percent referenced "school" experiences, and 5% mentioned friends. Another 5% highlighted Mexican food. The remaining responses (less than 5% each) included tourism, Day of the Dead, various media resources, and independent research. Only one person stated that she was of Hispanic heritage. The variety of sources that informed FTs' background knowledge is noteworthy given that only 5% identified actual relationships with people/friends.

Data Collection

The initial data set was generated by nonrandom electronic surveys, which included several open- and closed-ended questions. Via an impartial and rigorous approach, well-structured surveys allow researchers to draw conclusions about communities of people (Rea & Parker, 2005). One of the benefits of using electronic surveys is that data can be systematically collected from large pools of participants. A significant limitation to electronic surveys is that it is not possible to ask clarifying or follow-up questions of individuals at the time the data are solicited. Hence, additional data sources were gathered from field notes and in-class activities such as the writing prompt described in the previous section.

The FTs completed electronic surveys during the first and eighth weeks of the children's literature course via SurveyMonkey. During Week 1, the FTs provided demographic information and responded to questions about their future book selections. In preparation for the Week 8 in-class discussion, the FTs independently read *In My Family/En mi familia* and responded to a survey about the book via SurveyMonkey. Prompts included: (a) "In a paragraph or two, please describe your general response to *In My Family*"; (b) "Was there anything that surprised you about Garza's depiction of her life in Kingsville, TX, from the late 1950s through the 1970s? If so, what?"; and (c) "Would you use *In My Family* in your future classroom? Why or why not? Please be specific." The complete survey tool is included in my doctoral dissertation (Davila, 2012).

Data Analysis

This study employs Gee's (2011) concepts of figured worlds and Discourses, which "are tools of inquiry in the sense that they lead us as discourse analysts to ask specific sorts of questions about our data" (p. 214). As tools, they act as "thinking devices" (Gee, 2011, p. 60) that guide the analysis of pieces of written and oral language, such as the written response and class discussions of the FTs in this study.

The study also employs thematic network analysis (Attride-Sterling, 2001). Although similar to Strauss and Corbin's (1990) grounded theory methodology, thematic network analysis organizes the data set as a web-like network. Attride-Stirling's (2001) strategy represents a three-stage process of thematic analysis: a) the reduction of the text; b) the exploration of the text; and c) the amalgamation of the exploration. To ensure the validity of the data reduction and to safeguard against cognitive bias, I worked with a European quantitative social scientist peer-debriefer who studies human rights issues, but who wasn't at the time aware of anti-Latino narratives in U.S. discourse. Our analysis began with the identification of "Basic Themes" in the data. In this study, the lowest-order themes of the data codes reflect ideas such as: Persons of Mexican heritage are family oriented and/or have close-knit families (see Figure 1). We then sorted the Basic Themes into categories according to common qualities. Each category reflects an "Organizing Theme" that describes the quality of the grouping. The Organizing Themes that emerged from our analysis include the categories: Family Composition of people of Mexican heritage; Profile of people of Mexican heritage; Milieu of people of Mexican heritage; and Ordinariness of people of Mexican heritage. Finally, we synthesized the Organizing Themes into a macro "Global Theme" to interpret the codes and reveal the collective tenets of the data. The notion, "People of Mexican heritage may be like us Americans, but are not us," surfaced as the Global Theme of the data. A detailed description of the codes that were employed in the data analysis is included in my dissertation (Davila, 2012).

Figure 1: Thematic Network Analysis

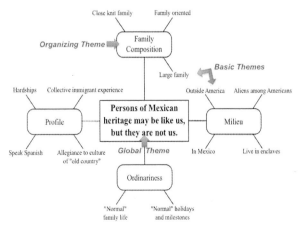

FINDINGS AND DISCUSSION

General Response to In My Family

In writing their general first responses to *In My Family/En mi familia,* 45% of the FTs specified personal connections they made to Garza's (1996) childhood memories. In addition, 12% stated that the book was "relatable." For example, one FT suggested, "Our cultures are relatable, even if we aren't doing the same things." Another wrote, "I too have a very large family. We have many family get-togethers with lots of people and more food than anyone can eat." A third person offered, "Spanish families [like Garza's] get together to eat and celebrate and so do we."

Nearly half (46%) of the FTs also suggested that *In My Family* provides a window into a different culture. For 12% of the FTs, Garza's childhood memories were so different that they could not relate to the picturebook. One FT wrote, "The experiences of children growing up Mexican are so different than the ones I had." Another reflected, "This book led me to think about the differences between our culture and Mexican culture. I realized that there were a great deal of differences." Another person proposed, "I would use this book because of all the different ways it ... show[s] different cultures." Overall, the FTs' general responses most frequently regarded the similarities and differences between their assumptions about "typical" families and Garza's family.

In My Family in Future Classrooms

The FTs were asked whether they would use *In My Family* in their future classroom. The majority of respondents (74%) said that they would be willing to use this book. Thirteen percent of the respondents answered negatively, while the remaining 13% of the FTs said that they would use the book under certain conditions (e.g., "I would be more willing to use this if I have students from Mexico or who celebrate these traditions.").

Arguments for using book in the classroom. Among the 74% who saw themselves using *In My Family* in their future classrooms, most would employ the book to discuss family life, traditions, relationships, and/or familial childhood experiences (48%), and to foster cultural awareness among their students (40%). In terms of using the book to discuss families, one FT stated, "I would use *In My Family* in my future classroom because I think it provides readers with the importance of spending time with family." Another shared, "I feel this book does a great job of illustrating a close knit family and explaining the importance of family to students." In terms of using the book to foster cultural awareness, a respondent suggested, "It [*In My Family*] is a great way to teach about Mexican culture. The students would be able to relate well many of the main events that were discussed in the story." Another added, "I think it would be a good book to talk about different cultures of families such as Hispanic."

The preceding examples of FTs' objectives for fostering cultural awareness are representative of several responses in the data set. These responses indicate a possible assumption that Garza's family life in Texas represents Mexican or Hispanic culture. Only one of the FTs identified Garza's family as being of Mexican-American culture (i.e., "I would use the book because I think it is an excellent representation of the Mexican American culture and all of its similarities to mainstream American culture"). Nonetheless, this response positions Mexican American culture outside of "mainstream" American culture.

Arguments against using book in the classroom. Thirteen percent of the FTs assumed stances of resistance (Beach, 1997) to using *In My Family/En mi familia* in their future classrooms. For them, the book does not include content they would like to teach; students might not relate to the characters; and/or the format of the book is not appealing. "I believe my class could lose interest in the text," one person argued. "[T]eachers should be as excited about a book as they want their students to be. . . . I just couldn't really get into this," offered another. These stances/responses point to a possible assumption among some FTs: Their future students will share their very same perspectives toward Garza's paintings and stories. Such an assumption could lead FTs to privilege narratives and Discourses that are consistent with their personal educational experiences (Britzman, 1986; Lortie, 1975; Seidl, 2007) and dismissive of others' experiences (Gee, 2008).

Conditions for using book in the classroom. In the remaining 13% of the group, respondents said that they would use the book under certain conditions including studying different cultures, satisfying curriculum/content standard requirements, and/or working with students of Mexican heritage (e.g., "If I had students from Mexico"). This latter condition suggests that some FTs could be interested in providing literature that serves as a "mirror" (Sims-Bishop, 1997) for their students. This condition alternately indicates that some FTs might be less inclined to select "window" books (Sims-Bishop, 1997), which give readers access to stories and experiences of people who are not members of their same social and cultural groups. Collectively, the FTs' conditions are as much criteria for the inclusion as they are justifications for the exclusion of certain literature from the classroom.

Discourse and Figured Worlds

The final analysis of the FTs' independent responses to the text considers the data set through Gee's (2011) lens of Discourses and figured worlds. In thinking about this analysis, it may be helpful to recall that the participants were in their early twenties with varied sources of background knowledge to inform their readings of *In My Family/En mi familia*. Another key consideration is that the FTs' responses to *In My Family/En mi familia* were constructed as part of their children's literature coursework. Therefore, many of the responses could have been expressed in a manner that the FTs deemed consistent with the Discourse of school. The exemplars presented in this analysis cut across participants' responses. In some instances, the racial identities of the future teachers are intentionally noted. This notation is to reinforce that while 89% of participants identified themselves as "White," being White is not an exclusive indicator of certain perspectives.

Establishing who is "Normal." Thematic network analysis of the data reveals some of the FTs' assumptions about the qualities of "normal" or "typical" Americans. For example, one respondent suggested that the characters of *In My Family/En mi familia* "were easy to relate to as they were just a *normal* family" (emphasis added). It seems that for this White female future-teacher, a "normal" family is a family that engages in activities that are familiar to her. Another FT proposed that Garza's memoir paintings "seemed to try to depict how 'Americanized' the family was. The brother had a baseball mitt and gloves, the family celebrated the same holidays *as most Americans*, and the father was even in WWII" (emphasis added). This woman's response describes the familial qualities of "most Americans." It also suggests that Garza's family members adopted "American" patriotism, pastimes, and holidays. In other words, they embraced the AAN, the Anglo-American

Narrative (Santa Ana, 2002). The respondent's use of the label "Americanized" to describe Garza's family implies acculturation. At the same time, it excludes Garza's family from "typical" American families.

Some FTs also highlighted similarities and differences between "typical" ways of celebrating events and holidays and Garza's traditions. For example, in considering Garza's narrative-painting *Birthday Barbecue/Barbacoa para Cumpleaños*, a man remarked, "The family BBQ part was close to being as accurate as could be, besides having a piñata." In other words, the way Garza's family celebrated birthdays is consistent with the ways a typical birthday party is celebrated—except for the nonconforming piñata.

This same type of sentiment was reflected by several FTs whose notions about "typical" Easter holiday traditions were generally satisfied by Garza's narrative-painting *Easter Eggs/Cascarones*. "I also gather around with my family on Easter Sunday for a big meal, and then work together to paint Easter eggs," one respondent reflected. "They, as well, dye eggs and celebrate with family," another reported. Indicating the existence of a dominant social group, another White woman mused that *Easter Eggs/Cascarones* "showed interesting variations to mainstream culture. For example, the way the characters in the story fill their Easter eggs with confetti rather than candy." Here, this FT accounts for what is "typical" in the dominant group and suggests that the use of confetti is a deviation from the mainstream use of candy. Collectively, such responses reflect a Global Theme (Attride-Sterling, 2001) that persons of Mexican heritage (e.g., the members of Garza's family) might be "like Americans," but they are not "Americans."

Furthermore, some FTs drew a line of separation between Garza's family and "typical" American families. For example, one person suggested that as a classroom activity her future students might "talk [about] the similarities and differences about how they—Americans—celebrate Easter and weddings compared to how the Mexicans celebrate it." It appears that this FT assumes that her future students will be typical Americans. Her response also suggests that Garza's family is not American. The subtext of this proposed classroom activity is consistent with the AAN (Santa Ana, 2002) as well as the LTN, the Latino Threat Narrative (Chavez, 2008), by which U.S.-born Americans and immigrants of Mexican/Hispanic heritage are collectively regarded as foreigners in American society.

Allegiance to culture of "old country." Some FTs argued that Garza's family was allegiant to Mexican social customs. For example, an FT who identifies as a Hispanic woman was "surprised" by "all of the Mexican traditions that her [Garza's] family carried throughout that time and how proud they were of them." Her surprise suggests that embracing one's cultural traditions is not a typical norm. Similarly, a White man reported, "the biggest thing that surprised me was the fact of how much of Hispanic tradition was still part of her life even though they lived in the States." A Chinese American woman likewise proposed that Garza's family members were "able to uphold their traditions and culture even when they weren't in their own country." Reflecting on the way Garza's family grew and harvested food from the garden, the only African American person in the study shared, "it was strange that they [Garza's family] relied so heavily on food that they harvested because they are in America….They still rely on the customs of their Mexican culture." Like other responses, this response seems to reflect an assumption that Garza's family elected to maintain the "old ways." It might also reflect a present-day perspective that "typical" Americans do not grow and harvest their own food. Taken together, the aforementioned exemplars are consistent with the AAN, which suggests that Hispanics/Latinos who maintain the cultures of their homelands cannot be fully "American" (Santa Ana, 2002).

Collective immigrant experience. Congruent with the notion that families like Garza's sustain Mexican customs is the assumption that persons of Mexican heritage share a common immigrant experience. This perspective does not accommodate Mexican American families who have lived in the U.S. for generations. Nonetheless, the idea that persons of Mexican heritage are immigrants has been reinforced in prominent anti-Latino rhetoric (Begala, 2012; Media Matters For America, 2012; National Hispanic Media Coalition, 2012). For example, a male FT presumed that Garza's family was an immigrant family: "When I think of immigrant families living in Texas, large family atmospheres come to mind." Congruently, other FTs reported that *In My Family* "does a good job depicting the lives of Latino immigrants as they carry on with their day" and reflects the notion that "Texas was having a lot of Mexicans coming up to live" at the time the story was set (1950s – 1970s). One FT even claimed, "I was surprised at how easily life seemed for this...Mexican family. Texas isn't exactly the best place to be especially when it comes to border control, but the family seemed to be living carefree." For this respondent, the notion that Garza's family might have been unconcerned by the presence of border police in the region could imply that in this FT's figured world, (a) families of Mexican heritage are, in fact, undocumented immigrants who would normally be anxious and fearful of deportation; and/or (b) American citizens of Mexican heritage can be adversely affected by anti-immigrant laws and practices too. In short, these responses illustrate the pervasive nature of the Latino Threat Narrative (LTN) and Anglo American Narrative (AAN) in the Discourse.

Subject to hardship. Following up on the immigrant status that some FTs assigned to Garza's family, this next section addresses another common assumption: people of Mexican heritage are subject to hardship. It might be for this reason that some FTs expressed surprise in responding to *In My Family*, such as, "I was surprised the story didn't focus more on the hardships that the Mexicans faced— especially when living so close to the border;" or "I was shocked that this aspect [of hardship] was not mentioned." Congruently, another White woman argued, "I actually thought that it was surprising that this family lived a pretty normal, happy life in Texas even though they are of a different culture. I thought they would have harder times back then." These responses suggest that for some FTs, Garza's memories of a happy life are inconsistent with their views on the "typical" life of a family of Mexican heritage. From their perspective, Garza's family would have suffered harder times.

Live outside of America. This last section examines the phenomenon by which some FTs assumed that people of Mexican heritage do not live in Texas or America proper. Despite Garza's introduction that *In My Family* is set in her hometown of Kingsville, TX, several FTs agreed, "*In My Family* was a good representation of family life in Mexico. It was full of traditions of the Mexican people." In this particular response, the FT assumed that Garza's family did not live in the U.S. Making the same assumption, another respondent remarked, "Obviously, being from the Americas, I don't really know much of Hispanic culture, so I found this to be a very fun and informational picture book." As an inhabitant of the "Americas" this FT stated that she did not have knowledge about Hispanics/Latinos because they do not reside in her country.

While some respondents acknowledged that *In My Family/En mi familia* was set in Texas, their comments suggested otherwise. For example, an FT remarked: "The book seemed as though it was based in Mexico rather than Texas. Everything reminded me of Mexico." Another FT who identifies as a Pacific Islander American remarked, "I forgot that the setting was in Texas because the pictures were made so much to reflect the Mexican culture." Similarly, an FT who identifies as White/Latin American reported, "It looked more like a scene in Mexico than Texas." Yet another FT reflected, "When I was reading I forgot this was set in Texas. It felt like it was set in Mexico because of all the Spanish traditions." The popular assumption that *In My Family/En mi familia* is either set outside of the United States in Mexico, or in a Mexican enclave resonates with the LTN and AAN. These pervasive narratives suggest that persons of Hispanic/Latino heritage are outsiders who cannot integrate with the dominant group until they denounce their ethnic, cultural, and linguistic lineage.

Going further, some FTs' responses appear to cast persons of Mexican heritage as outsiders to the human species. As if clarification was necessary, one respondent suggested that Garza's family members were "shown to be human just like the rest of us despite the cultural barrier." Congruently, two other FTs remarked that the children in Garza's family "have brothers and sisters" and "can get hurt by a fire ant" just like humans. Inadvertently positioning Garza's family members as alien-foreigners is consistent with the way Hispanics/Latinos have been portrayed on the national stage by some news agencies and politicians (Begala, 2012; Media Matters For America, 2012; National Hispanic Media Coalition, 2012) as a means to promote public policies that exclude immigrants from the distribution of social goods and services including access to education and medical care (Chavez, 2008; Chomsky, 2007; Santa Ana, 2002).

CONCLUSION AND IMPLICATIONS

In examining future teachers' responses to Garza's renowned picturebook *In My Family/En mi familia*, this paper has revealed the kinds of assumptions that some FTs hold about persons of Mexican heritage. The story of this research began in querying FTs about their inclusion of Garza's *In My Family* in their future classrooms. Collectively, most of the FTs would use the book to foster cultural awareness and appreciation for diversity among their future students. The sequence of study culminated in applying Gee's (2011) concept of figured worlds as a tool of inquiry and employing Attride-Sterling's (2001) strategy for thematic network analysis.

The results point to a Global Theme that some future teachers assume that persons of Mexican heritage might be *like* Americans but they are *not* Americans. Uncritical, unconscious, and unreflective, this "like us but not us" perspective is consistent with the LTN and AAN narratives that permeate dominant American Discourses. Since Discourses are "resistant to internal criticism and self-scrutiny... uttering viewpoints that seriously undermine them defines one as being outside them" (Gee, 2008, pp. 161-162). Thus, it is not surprising that some FTs may be inherently socialized to sustain both positive and harmful elements of the dominant Discourse. The results of this analysis imply that the LTN and AAN could be unconsciously reinforced among children via teachers' comments about works of children's literature like *In My Family/En mi familia*.

The data also show that racial identity does not appear to be an indicator of FTs' resistance to anti-Latino narratives of the dominant Discourse. This finding is consistent with the work of

Murillo (2010) who found anti-Spanish ideologies among prospective teachers of color. Regardless of racial identity, the data show that some future teachers, whose own K – 12/College educations were theoretically informed by the multicultural education agenda of the last 20 years, might not have the meta-knowledge to recognize that the Discourses in which they participate could privilege some groups and disenfranchise other groups (Gee, 2008). As a result, teacher educators cannot assume that prospective teachers who enthusiastically support diversity are immune to social Discourse and narratives that cast persons belonging to non-dominant religious, social, or cultural groups as outsiders. Rather, it is imperative that teacher education programs actively support FTs in developing the meta-awareness needed to recognize oppressive narratives.

Diverse texts and works of children's literature could serve as tools in this endeavor. However, these tools are only as effective as the craftsperson. In the hands of inattentive users, they could damage as much as they could build students' and future teachers' understanding of fairness and equality. In addition to the critical work of exploring with FTs the underlying messages, stereotypes, and complicated issues in picturebooks (Albers, Harste, & Vasquez, 2011), teacher educators might also consider the exploration of other readers' responses to certain picturebooks as texts analysis. The data set here could provide one venue for cultivating future teachers' critical consciousness such that they might recognize and attempt to disrupt destructive narratives like the LTN and AAN, which undermine the call for cultural pluralism through public education.

REFERENCES

Albers, P., Harste, J., & Vasquez, V. (2011). Interrupting certainty and making trouble: Teachers' written and visual responses to picturebooks. *60ᵗʰ Yearbook of the Literacy Research Association, 179-194.*

Apol, L. (1998). "But what does this have to do with kids?" Literary theory and children's literature in the teacher education classroom. *Journal of Children's Literature, 24,* 32-46.

Attride-Stirling, J. (2001). Thematic networks: An analytic tool for qualitative research. *Qualitative Research,* 1, 385-405.

Beach, R. (1997). Students' resistance to engagement with multicultural literature. In T. Rogers & A. Soter (Eds.), *Reading across cultures* (pp. 13-41). New York, NY: Teachers College Press.

Begala, P. (2012, March). Romney's attack on Latinos sends the Right off a cliff. *The Daily Beast.* Retrieved from http://www.thedailybeast.com/newsweek/2012/03/11/romney-s-attack-on-latinos-sends-the-right-off-a-cliff.html

Britzman, D. (1986). Cultural myths in the making of a teacher: Biography and social structure in teacher education. *Harvard Educational Review,* 56, 442-456.

Cai, M. (2008). Transactional theory and the study of multicultural literature. *Language Arts,* 85, 212-220.

Chavez, L. (2008). *The Latino threat: Constructing immigrants, citizens, and the nation.* Stanford, CA: Stanford University Press.

Chomsky, A. (2007). *"They take our jobs!": and 20 other myths about immigration.* Boston, MA: Beacon Press.

Davila, D. (2012). *In the figured worlds of culture and religion: Prospective teachers' discourse around Latino literature for children.* (Unpublished doctoral dissertation). Ohio State University, Columbus, OH.

Denver Public Schools. (2002). *Carmen Lomas Garza: Chicana author and illustrator.* Denver, CO: Denver Public Schools.

Friere, P. (1970). *Pedagogy of the oppressed.* New York, NY: Bloomsbury Academic.

Fry, R. & Lopez, M. (2012). *Now largest minority group on four-year college campuses: Hispanic student enrollments reach new highs in 2011.* Washington, D.C.: Pew Hispanic Center.

Gándara, P. (2008). *The crisis in the education of Latino students. NEA research visiting scholars series, 1a.* Retrieved from http://www.nea.org/home/17404.htm

Garza, C.L. (1990/2005). *Family Pictures / Cuadros de familia.* San Francisco, CA: Children's Book Press.

Garza, C.L. (1996). *In My Family/En mi familia.* San Francisco, CA: Children's Book Press.

Garza, C.L. (2012, April 15). Artist statement. Retrieved from http://www.carmenlomasgarza.com/ artiststatement.html.

Gee, J. (2011). *An introduction to discourse analysis: Theory and method* (3rd ed.). New York, NY: Routledge.

Gee, J. (2008). *Social linguistics and literacies: Ideology in discourses* (3rd ed.). New York, NY: Routledge.

Grossman, P. L. (1990). *The making of a teacher: Teacher knowledge and teacher education.* New York, NY: Teachers' College Press.

Holland, D., & Quinn, N. (1987). *Cultural models in language and thought.* Boston, MA: Cambridge Press.

Kiefer, B., & Tyson, C. (2013). *Charlotte Huck's children's literature: A brief guide* (2nd ed.). New York, NY: McGraw Hill.

Lortie, D. (1975/2002). *Schoolteacher.* Chicago, IL: The University of Chicago Press.

Media Matters for America. (2012, December 4). Fox interrupts its anti-immigration rhetoric. Retrieved from http://mediamatters.org/blog/2012/12/04/fox-interrupts-its-anti-immigrant-rhetoric-to-p/191671

McLaughlin, M., & DeVoogd, G. (2004). Critical literacy as comprehension: Expanding reader response. *Journal of Adolescent & Adult Literacy,* 48, 52-62.

Murillo, L. A. (2010). Local literacies as counter-hegemonic practices: Deconstructing anti-Spanish ideologies in the Rio Grande Valle. *59 Annual Yearbook of the National Reading Conference,* 276-287.

National Center for Education Information. (2011). *Profile of teachers in the U.S. 2011.* Washington, DC: National Center for Education Information.

National Hispanic Media Coalition. (2012). *American hate radio: How a powerful outlet for democratic discourse has deteriorated into hate, racism and extremism.* Pasadena, CA: National Hispanic Media Coalition. Retrieved from http://nhmc.org/american_hate_radio_nhmc.pdf

Nieto, S., & Bode, P. (2008). *Affirming diversity: The sociopolitical context of multicultural education* (5th ed.). Boston, MA: Allyn & Bacon.

Norton, D. (2012). *Multicultural children's literature.* (4th ed.). New York, NY: Allyn & Bacon.

Pew Hispanic Center & Kaiser Family Foundation (2004). *National survey of Latinos: Education, summary & chartpack* (Publication No.3031). Menlo Park, CA: The Henry J. Kaiser Family Foundation.

Rea, M. L., & Parker, A. R. (2005). *Designing and conducting survey research.* San Francisco, CA: Jossey-Bass.

Rosenblatt, L. M. (1995). *Literature as exploration.* (5th ed.). N1ew York, NY: The Modern Language Association.

San Jose Museum of Art. (2001). *Carmen Lomas Garza: A retrospect.* San Jose, CA: San Jose Museum of Art.

Santa Ana, O. (2002). *Brown tide rising: Metaphors of Latinos in contemporary American public discourse.* Austin, TX: University of Texas Press.

Seidl, B. (2007). Working with communities to explore and personalize culturally relevant pedagogies: Push, double images, and race talk. *Journal of Teacher Education,* 20(10), 1-16.

Shannon, P. (1994). I am the canon. *Journal of Children's Literature,* 20(1), 1-5.

Shulman, L. S. (1987). Knowledge and teaching: Foundations of a new reform. *Harvard Educational Review,* 57(1), 1-22.

Sims Bishop, R. (1997). Selecting literature for a multicultural curriculum. In V. Harris (Ed.), *Using multiethnic literature in the K-8 classroom* (pp. 1-19). Urbana, IL: National Council of Teachers of English.

Strauss, A., & Corbin, J. (1990). *Basics of qualitative research: Grounded theory procedures and techniques.* London, England: Sage.

U.S. Census Bureau. (2010). *2010 census demographic profile summary file* Retrieved from: http://www.census. gov/prod/cen2010/doc/dpsf.pdf

U.S. Department of Education. (2008). *Schools and Staffing Survey.* Retrieved from: http://nces.ed.gov/

Kathleen A. Hinchman
Syracuse University

Section IV:
Teacher Development and Reflection

A group known as the National Council on Teacher Quality recently released a controversial review of U.S. teacher preparation programs. Notable for its lack of attention to outcomes, the widely publicized review concluded that, "Three out of four elementary teacher preparation programs are still not teaching the methods of reading instruction that could substantially lower the number of children who never became proficient readers, from 30 percent to 10 percent (Greenberg, McKee, & Walsh, 2013, p. 2). In her critique of this report, Darling-Hammond (2013) explained that more credible research focused "attention on developing accurate and reliable data about program outcomes and useful evidence of program quality."

Reviews of topics or texts on syllabi do not begin to explain what might be gleaned from a methods course or program. Several recent reviews of the literature explain in more detail the kind of teacher education research that's needed. Cochran-Smith and Zeicher (2005) argued for teacher education research which "helps to identify and explain what the active ingredients are in teacher preparation programs whose graduates have positive impact on students' learning and other important educational outcomes" (p. 4). Ball and Tyson (2011) recommended paying particular attention to the roles language, generativity, and globalization play as active ingredients in teaching and learning.

Risko and her colleagues (2008) noted a lack of wide scale funding for literacy teacher education research in particular, reporting that extant work suggests the importance of combining explanations, demonstrations, and guided practice and calling for more work into the histories and cultural influences of participants and teaching approaches being used in classrooms. The studies reported in this section of the Literacy Research Association's annual *Yearbook* should be applauded for heeding Risko and her colleagues' calls for credible research. The studies in this volume looked at the active ingredients of preservice and inservice teachers' day-to-day decision-making, along with the impact of their practice, drawing on an exciting array of theoretical perspectives and qualitative and mixed-method approaches.

For instance, Hayden and Chiu's mixed-method study, "Lessons Learned: Supporting the Development of Reflective Practice and Adaptive Expertise," explores how novice literacy teachers developed the ability to reflect on their practice to orchestrate responsive literacy instructional interactions. In the paper, "Creating Praxis: Determining Teacher Perceptions of Struggling Readers and Their Impact on Instruction," Liebfreund and Mattingly used Q-methodology to discover that three main sets of teachers' beliefs about students drove literacy instruction provided to struggling readers, noting that professional development could be seen as ineffective if it failed to address these factors.

In Hunt-Barron, Kaminski, and Tracy's mixed-method study, "Professional Development in Writing Instruction: Common Factors Among High-Adopting Teachers," researchers demonstrated how student writing can improve when teachers are highly engaged in writing professional development. MacPhee's qualitative study, "Professional Development as the Study of Self: Using Self-Knowledge to Mediate the Act of Teaching," explored how three practicing elementary literacy teachers came to understand themselves in collaboration with a literacy coach, including their beliefs, identities, conflicts, and practices, in hopes of initiating new, more effective ways of teaching.

The lack of a unified agenda for literacy teacher education research may seem frustrating to those looking for straightforward descriptions. Yet the delightful complexity of the studies in this section of the *Yearbook* suggests that, ultimately, the effectiveness of literacy teacher education has much to do with understanding the complex nature of higher education, schools, and other constituent communities, individuals within these communities, and the evolving nature of literacy itself. Each new theory and method for studying how people situate literacy in relation to one another benefits us in important ways. Taken together, nuanced insights about this complexity will yield increasingly more equitable literacy teacher education and help to undercut over-simplified attempts to diminish the importance of such work.

REFERENCES

Ball, A.F., & Tyson, C.A. (Eds). (2011). *Studying diversity in teacher education.* Lanham, MD: Rowman & Littlefield Publishers for the American Educational Research Association.

Cochran-Smith, M., & Zeichner, K.M. (2005). *Studying teacher education: The report of the AERA panel on research and teacher education.* New York, NY: Lawrence Erlbaum Associates for the American Educational Research Association.

Darling-Hammond, L. (2013). Why the NCTQ teacher prep ratings are nonsense. In V. Strauss', "The Answer Sheet." *The Washington Post,* retrieved from http://www.washingtonpost.com/blogs/answer-sheet/wp/2013/06/18/why-the-nctq-teacher-prep-ratings-are-nonsense/

Greenberg, J., McKee, A., & Walsh, K. (2013). *Teacher preparation review: A review of the nation's teacher preparation program 2013.* Washington, DC: National Council on Teacher Quality. Retrieved from http://www.nctq.org/dmsView/Teacher_Prep_Review_2013_Report

Risko, V. J., Roller, C. M., Cummins, C., Bean, R. M., Block, C. C., Anders, P. L., & Flood, J. (2008). A critical analysis of research on reading teacher education. *Reading Research Quarterly, 43*(3), 252-288.

Lessons Learned: Supporting the Development of Reflective Practice and Adaptive Expertise

H. Emily Hayden
Ming Ming Chiu
SUNY University at Buffalo

Teachers are continually required to "solve ill-defined problems...[and] make decisions quickly...on the basis of incomplete information" (Le Maistre & Pare, 2010, p. 561), and they must develop reflective patterns of thought and habits of mind to meet these demands. A fundamental task for novice teachers is to develop these reflective practices, the combination of thought and analysis with action in practice (Schon, 1983) that enables teachers to ask and answer critical questions about their teaching. Such inquiry practices ultimately lead toward adaptive expertise and the real-time enactment of pedagogical content knowledge (Shulman, 1986; Bransford, Darling-Hammond, & LePage, 2005).

Reflective thought provides a space for thinking deeply about the events of teaching interactions, analyzing student feedback, identifying needs, and considering adaptations, all with the goal of improved student learning (Dewey, 1933). Teachers who are reflective can balance efficiency with innovation (Parsons, 2012), first by identifying instructional roadblocks, and then by generating and enacting targeted responses (Hammerness et al., 2005). But how do novices learn reflective practices that guide them to "think like a teacher" (Hammerness et. al., 2005, p. 382) when faced with instructional challenges? What can teacher educators do to provide early access to this elemental part of effective teaching?

We analyzed structured reflections written by 23 novices after weekly teaching in a reading clinic to explore their enactment of reflective practices in a supportive, scaffolded setting. Our questions were:

1. What problems of teaching practice did novices write about in their reflections?
2. How did novices' use reflection writing to develop patterns of reflective practice? Specifically, what relationships, if any, were present between writing about problems in their teaching practice, enactment of instructional adaptations, and resolution of problems?

RELEVANT LITERATURE

Theoretical Frameworks

Dewey's (1916) view of knowledge as 1) connected inseparably to action and 2) resulting in the combination of action with reflection on that action provided the framework for our analysis. Reflecting on the connections between what one knows (knowledge) and what one does (action) allows for a "systematic inspection of the situation...to identify and state the problem [and] develop suggestions for addressing [it], for finding a way to act, and hence finding out what the meaning of the situation actually is." (Biesta, 2010, p. 109) Kinsella (2007) called this embodied reflection since it "arises through the bodily lived experience [and is] revealed through action" (p. 396). Knowledge gained through active, embodied reflection becomes freely available for use in other experiences helping us to "plan intelligently and direct our actions" (Biesta, 2010, p. 107).

Exploration of ideas through language shapes and drives the development of knowledge (Vygotsky, 1978). In preservice experiences knowledge development is first socially mediated when novices learn theory in their college experiences, and then becomes intrapersonal as novices build pedagogical skill and reconstruct theory for application through instructional action. Reiman (1999) linked intrapersonal language to reflection and argued that "a pedagogy of action/reflection and journaling can frame language in new ways, promoting deeper understanding" (p. 599). Writing to reflect "focuses attention and permits the symbolizing of meaningful experience" (p. 604). Hacker, Keener, and Kircher (2009) declared "[p]roduction of thought is the core of writing" (p. 155) and Wells (2003) asserted that writing allows "complex structures of meaning to be articulated more precisely than … in everyday conversation" (p. 55). Perhaps these views explain why Roskos, Vukelich, and Risko (2001) noted the prevalence of studies on teacher reflection that used written reflections as units of analysis. Most emphasized the intellectual demands of writing that require "explicitness and integration of ideas, [and] create fertile conditions for reflective thinking" (p. 611).

Expertise

Reflections of novice teachers are often highly personalized, focused on delivery of lesson elements (Hayden, Moore-Russo, & Marino, 2013). Novice teachers function in survival mode (Geursen, de Heer, Korthagen, Lunenberg, & Zwart, 2010), so absorbed in mastering the routines for managing the classroom day, or "commonplaces" (Berliner, 1988, p. 2) that they have difficulty interpreting student responses, drawing conclusions, evaluating, and adapting their teaching. With time novices acquire and assimilate more practical knowledge, notice and take responsibility for student responses, learn timing and targeting of instruction, and make goal-directed plans (Berliner, 1988). Responses become more fluid and teachers may "seem to sense the appropriate response to make" (p. 5). This is the result, in part, of many hours of experience and embodied reflection. The knowledge of more expert teachers can be applied in the moment, smoothly and seamlessly (Ball & Cohen, 1999) precisely because it has become intrapersonalized through reflection.

Developing Reflective Practices

Reflective practice involves integrating specific thinking activities with analysis to develop new habits of mind (Risko et al., 2008) and novice teachers may recognize their need for focused guidance and models to develop such practices (Loughran, 2006; Lunenberg & Korthagen, 2005; Nilsson, 2009). Many researchers have described models (Jay & Johnson, 2002; Korthagen & Vasalos, 2005; Nelson & Harper, 2006) including Rodgers (2002, 2006) whose re-visioning of Dewey outlined a four-part reflective process of "1) Presence in experience … 2) Description of experience … 3) Analysis of experience … [and] 4) Experimentation: learning to take intelligent action" (2006, p. 215). Active presence in the moment of teaching, and learning to see by description allows teachers to notice and explore what *is* (Rodgers, 2006). Focused analysis then leads to intelligent action through generation of adaptive instructional responses.

While written reflections often provide a descriptive outlet for the strong emotions that can occur around one's teaching, this must be deliberately balanced with concurrent analysis and action

(Brookfield, 1995; Fendler, 2003). Doing so develops agency (Lizzio & Wilson, 2007) because it helps novices become aware of "spaces where [they] can take initiatives" (Greene, M., 1988, p. 17) and bridge theory and practice by "perceiving more in a particular situation and finding a helpful course of action [based on] strengthened awareness" (Korthagen & Kessels, 1999, p. 7). Reiman (1999) identified the need for scaffolds or guided formats to provide such connections between reflection and teaching action, and promoted dialogic reflection where teachers write for an audience (e.g. a teacher educator) and can expect a response. This method is especially useful for supporting pre-service teachers (Farrell, 2007; Lam, 2011) and helping novices negotiate their first years of practice (Tillman, 2003). By deliberately scaffolding with guiding questions, frameworks, and prompting to solidify learning, teacher educators can emphasize the differences between reflection leading to evaluation, meaning-making, and responsive action, and reflection that describes but never moves to analysis and action (Amobi, 2006).

Connecting to Action

Noticing and describing experiences of uncertainty (Jay & Johnson, 2002), and "puzzling, troubling or interesting phenomenon" (Schon, 1983, p. 50) can lead to some highly efficacious reflection experiences. Exploration of cases can provide opportunities to explore such puzzles, but cases explored apart from the real action may have more well-defined edges, encouraging discrete solutions that don't reflect the reality of classroom teaching and don't provide opportunities for thinking and adapting in the moment (Le Maistre & Pare, 2010). If instead reflection is focused on challenges encountered during real-time teaching, teacher educators have more weighty opportunities for scaffolding. In practical teaching experiences such as reading clinics teacher educators can encourage novices to label and describe events shortly after they are experienced, interrogate current methods and their potential for student learning, and evaluate new insights that arise from teaching interactions. This scaffolded analysis can result in the development of new understandings that enhance and deepen teaching practice (Hayden, Moore-Russo, & Marino, 2013).

However, asking teachers to reflect deeply about all events in the day is unrealistic. For this research Cuban's (1992) distinction of problems from dilemmas in teaching provided a sorting mechanism. While dilemmas are messy, requiring teachers to choose among "competing highly prized values" (Cuban, 1992, p. 6) and interrupting the flow of teaching, even for experts, problems are the more routine, structured situations that produce conflict because a goal is blocked. Problems have an element of predictability. Learning when to re-teach and when to move on is a problem of timing and targeting that will be resolved as novices become better able to assess student learning. Experience provides solutions to this and other pedagogical issues, so teachers at later stages of development spend minimal time reflecting on problems.

Possessing a repertoire of responses to problems of teaching practice that can be accessed in the moment of teaching is a marker of development. It requires the ability to filter problems by reflecting in ways that generate adaptations and lead to resolution. This frees up time and space for reflection on deeper dilemmas of practice, improves self-efficacy for teaching, and decreases burnout (Haverback & Parault, 2008). Developing such routines is a crucial milestone, and an indicator of growth through the novice stage. When novice teachers notice and describe problems (Jay & Johnson, 2002; Pui-lan et al., 2005), and they feel "empowered and perplexed enough to pose questions" (Miller, 2007, p. 312) and then reflect and generate solutions, they move toward adaptive expertise.

METHOD

The purpose of this exploratory mixed methods study was to discover problems of teaching practice novices described, and examine how the novices used reflection writing to develop patterns of reflective practice. Consent to gather and analyze written reflections was obtained from 23 novice teachers, all female, enrolled in an elementary reading assessment and evaluation course with a teaching component at a public Midwestern university. Six were graduate students uncertified in teaching who were adding teaching credentials, and 17 were undergraduates in their junior year. Eighteen novices provided information on previous teaching experiences. Four of the graduate students had worked as para-educators in public schools for less than four years, one was an English Language instructor overseas for two years but uncertified to teach in the U.S., and one had a degree and two years' experience in school counseling. Undergraduate novices reported two-six semesters of practicum.

Context

The course in which novices were enrolled focused on developing reflective inquiry and theoretical frameworks to link assessment, instruction, and student performance. Instruction focused on reading/writing/spelling assessment and analysis, and research-based elements of instruction. Teaching in the reading clinic coincided with the class, but there was no accompanying seminar for dedicated discussion of teaching. The only regular time this discourse occurred was during novices' writing of their reflections.

Each novice taught one child in one-hour afterschool sessions twice a week. Children were predominantly Caucasian, attended public or private schools in a Midwestern metropolitan area, and ranged from first to sixth grade. Fourteen of the 23 children were boys, and nine of the 23 children attended schools where 40% or more of the population qualified for free/reduced lunch. Novices used the first three teaching sessions to administer assessments and set four instructional goals. Each lesson plan included one objective for each goal. Each novice was assigned a supervisor. Supervisors were all experienced reading teachers with masters degrees or higher in reading. Supervisors observed lessons, provided written feedback on lesson plans and reflections, and sometimes met with students outside of lessons.

Data

Novices submitted written reflections at the end of each teaching week. Reflections were structured via an acronym (SOAR) and included: a Subjective retelling of lesson events, progress toward lesson Objectives, self Analysis of the lesson, and Reflection. Each reflection was one- to two-pages long. Since recognizing and describing problems is a first step in reflective practices (Jay & Johnson, 2002; Pui-lan et al., 2005; Rodgers, 2002, 2006), novices were encouraged to describe teaching challenges they encountered, plan instructional responses, and develop questions to explore during further teaching. Focusing the reflections this way addressed course goals of linking assessment, instruction, and student learning through goal-directed teaching and systematic intentional inquiry into practice (Cochran-Smith & Lytle, 1993).

Novices began writing reflections the second week of teaching, and reflections were collected from the confidential class web log for eight weeks of teaching. Five novices submitted fewer reflections due to absences, for a total of 175 collected. These reflections made up the entire data set.

Establishing Quality and Rigor

Validity and reliability are treated differently within qualitative and quantitative traditions, and in mixed method studies integrity must be maintained for both types of analysis (Calfee & Sperling, 2010; Creswell & Plano Clark, 2007; Greene, J. C., 2007; Morse & Niehaus, 2009). We used an integrative framework (Teddlie & Tashakkori, 2009) to guide our methods of establishing rigor and quality in all phases of this study, including inter-rater reliability. The integrative framework is presented in Table 1.

Table 1: Establishing Quality and Rigor in this Study

Quality: Design suitability	Writing makes internal reflective process partially visible; organization and structure writing brings to thought processes strengthen data quality. Descriptions grounded in first-person accounts.
Quality: Within-design consistency, analytic adequacy	Logical progression: qualitative analysis identified critical incidents of reflection, supportive axial codes exploration-adaptation-resolution cycle; quantitative analysis confirmed significant occurrence of cycle.
Rigor: Interpretive consistency, distinctiveness	Inter-rater reliability established 1) for coding scheme: comparison to second coder's ratings for 100 quotations from data set: problem exploration $\alpha = .71$, adaptation $\alpha = .74$, resolution $\alpha = .70$. 2) for problem/dilemma names: comparison to experienced teachers' ratings of examples as either problem/dilemma: $\alpha = .67$ and 3) by second coders' dual-coding of one case (second coder was research partner for pilot study).
Rigor: Theoretical consistency, interpretive agreement	Identification of themes, axial codes reviewed by external reviewer (Research 1 tenured professor of education). Review of literature specifically focused on novice teachers.
Rigor: Integrative efficacy of design	Inferences made in qualitative analysis subjected to quantitative confirmatory analysis. Inferences from each strand of sequential analysis compared to research questions. Conclusions considered findings from both sets of data and types of analysis.

Initial Coding and Review of Cases

The two authors of this study shared analysis duties. Analysis began with author one reviewing all novice cases using as guideposts six broad themes that had emerged during open coding (Strauss & Corbin, 1990) of a pilot sample of experienced teachers in the same reading clinic: description, confidence, locus of control, discourse, teaching adaptations, and transfer of learning to students (Hayden & Pasman, 2008). Prior to this review author one searched literature on teacher development to ensure these themes were relevant for novice teachers as well. Table 2 presents theoretical evidence supporting these themes for teachers at all levels of development. Evidence of each pilot theme in novices' reflections was highlighted and each reflection read multiple times in the constant comparative manner (Glaser & Strauss, 1967). Problem description and problem resolution emerged as axial codes of the discourse theme, representing types of discourse that appeared regularly within the sample of novice teachers' written reflections. Analysis of these two axial codes is reported here as well as teaching adaptation codes that are described below.

During this recursive analysis author one observed the co-occurrence of discourse on problems with generation of teaching adaptations. Axial codes that emerged from the teaching adaptations theme described adaptations the novices either planned for future lessons, implemented in the present moment of teaching, or those that represented simple scope-and-sequence types of teacher planning. To explore any outcomes of adaptations, author one also looked for co-occurring statements of problem resolution. This process involved searching across each of the 23 novice cases to view problem exploration, adaptation and resolution over the series of lessons, and this search caused both authors to wonder: once novices identified a problem, how likely were they to generate and apply instructional adaptations, and how likely were they to perceive that the problem was resolved? Recognizing the connection between actions and consequences then taking instructional action aimed at resolving problems would be a critical marker of development, demonstrating the enactment of reflective practices.

Table 2: Theoretical Framework for Themes and Axial Codes

Theme	Supportive Theory
Description	Content knowledge, pedagogical knowledge (Shulman, 1986); descriptive reflection (Jay & Johnson, 2002); learning to see by description (Rodgers, 2006)
Confidence	Disequilibria (Shulman & Shulman, 2004; English, 2008)
Locus of Control	Responsibility, connection to events/results (Berliner, 1988)
Adaptations	Reactive responses vs. thoughtful adaptations, (Duffy, et al. 2008); strategic processing (Alexander & Fives, 2000); connecting thought to action (Schon, 1983; Risko et al., 2008; Rodgers, 2002, 2006)
Discourse	Expert pedagogy (Berliner, 1986): Strategic processing (Alexander & Fives, 2000)
Transfer	Strategic processing (Alexander & Fives, 2000)

Further Qualitative Analysis.

After initial coding and review of cases, author one read all reflective notes again (n = 175), first to identify instances when novices used detail and more than one sentence to reflect on a problem. These critical incidents were coded as problem explorations. A colleague's assertion that novices would be unlikely to reflect deeply on any aspect of their teaching challenged both authors to apply close analysis to novices' problem explorations, and author one re-read each to code the type of problem the novice described. Problem names were drawn from Berliner (1986, 1988) and Cuban (1992). Ten problem types emerged as axial codes within problem exploration (see Table 3). Author

Table 3: Problems of Practice in Novices' Reflections

Problem	Frequency
Teacher skill development	236
Identifying student skill deficits	166
Timing and Targeting	101
Identifying student strengths	62
Time management	48
Identifying new needs	37
Strategy implementation	19
Implementing teaching plan	15
Monitoring learning	15
Challenging behaviors	14

one then read the problem exploration again to code any adaptations the novice generated and any resolution the novice described for problems.

Quantitative Analysis

The problem exploration-adaptation-resolution cycle that emerged from qualitative analysis suggested important patterns in novices' reflections and provided pictures of individual teachers' responses. Both authors wanted to gain a picture of the responses of the entire novice teacher sample to this reading clinic experience. Did the structured reflection process indeed give this sample of novices early access to recognizing the connection between actions and consequences and then planning responsive action? The quantitative, confirmatory strand of analysis performed by author two allowed us to explore this question for the entire sample by providing an additional view of the co-occurrences in novices' reflections. To begin, author one quantitized axial codes for problem exploration, adaptation, and resolution by performing a frequency count, assigning a score (1) to each code each time it appeared in a reflection (Caracelli & Greene, 1993; Tashakkori & Teddlie, 1998; Teddlie & Tashakkori, 2009).

Because this data was longitudinal, cross-section panel data (multiple phenomena, multiple time periods for the same individuals) author two's analysis modeled for nestedness (multiple observations per novice, within the same setting), and adjusted for missing data and differences across novices, students, types of schools students attended, and time. Missing data, nestedness, time series data, serial correlation, and false positives were addressed with Markov Chain Monte Carlo multiple imputation (MCMC-MI), multilevel regressions (teacher level, reflective note level) and vector autoregression (VAR) that attempts to predict an outcome based on previous outputs and explores interdependencies between multiple time series data (Goldstein, 1995; Kennedy, 2004). Since testing multiple hypotheses might yield false positive results, this analysis used the two-stage linear step-up procedure, which controls the false discovery rate and increases statistical power (Benjamini, Krieger & Yekutieli, 2006).

After imputing the missing data (6%) with MCMC-MI, author two modeled problem resolution with a multilevel VAR (Goldstein, 1995) entering the variables into the analysis according to possible causal relationships, likely importance, and time.

$$Problem\ Resolution_{ij} = \beta_{00} + \mathbf{e}_{ij} + \mathbf{f}_{0j} \tag{1}$$

β_{00} is the grand mean intercept of Problem Resolution$_{ij}$, for each note (*i*) of each novice (*j*). The note- and novice-level residuals are $\mathbf{e}_{ij}$ and $\mathbf{f}_{0j}$. To see if novices' characteristics significantly influenced problem resolution, author two entered teaching experience, experience in schools, graduate or undergraduate in Model 1 (**Teacher**$_t$). Next, to see if child characteristics influenced problem resolution author two added child ethnicity, gender, teaching grade, reading level and qualification for free/reduced school lunch for Model 2 (**Pupil**$_p$). Author two also added school variables (private school, low income) for the school that each child attended (**School**$_s$).

$$Problem\ Resolution_{ij} = \beta_{00} + \mathbf{e}_{ij} + \mathbf{f}_{0j} + \beta_{0t}\mathbf{Teacher}_{0j} + \beta_{0p}\mathbf{Pupil}_{0j} + \beta_{0s}\mathbf{School}_{0j}$$

Finally, for Model 3 author two entered reflective note characteristics from the current week (weeks one-eight) …

Problem Exploration, Teaching Adaptation. (**Current_Note**$_c$)

… and characteristics of the reflective note written the previous week, specifically, whether or not the novice wrote about *Problem Exploration* or *Adaptation.*

Problem Exploration (-1), *Teaching Adaptation* (-1) (**Previous_Note**$_n$)

$$+ \beta_{cj}\mathbf{Current\_Note}_{ij} + \beta_{nj}\mathbf{Previous\_Note}_{ij} \tag{2}$$

To test whether each set of these explanatory variables was significant, a nested hypothesis test was used (Kennedy, 2004) and an alpha of .05.

RESULTS

Question 1: What problems did novices describe?

Three types of problems were reflected in more than half of the total problem explorations. Problems of teacher skill development, when novices identified an area of recognized need for development, occurred most frequently. Identifying skill deficits of students also occurred frequently, since the focus of the course was on diagnosing needs and individualizing instruction. Timing and targeting was the third most frequently occurring problem, when novices reflected on their students' success with objectives, need for review, or readiness for new learning. Table 4

Table 4: Illustrations of the Three Most Frequent Problem Types Novices Explored

Teacher Skill Development	Identifying Skill Deficit	Timing and Targeting
Teacher 12: As much as I want to make observations of her reading, in the moment I'm too consumed with what's going on with the lesson to do much of anything other than the lesson itself. Plus, I feel my lack of experience in knowing when to move on to another [book] level and what to push her on.	Teacher 4: Jim is showing me that he is capable of reading but there are aspects [that are slowing him down]. His reading is choppy because he is spending considerable … time to decode. This week I am seeing that he has a problem with long vowels and endings.	Teacher 11: I am struggling with planning word work activities. He really liked the initial word work with the Elkonin sound boxes, but it was way too easy for him. Word building has been more of a struggle. The first activity I implemented with him seemed too easy and he became bored … So, the next lesson I tried something more difficult, and although it held his attention better, he didn't perform as well as I thought he would. It's all just really kind of confusing to me and I think I am definitely struggling to find the right balance for him.

Table 5: Illustrations of the Types of Adaptations Novices Described

Teaching: Plan Future	Adaptations: Present	Adaptations: Future
Teacher 2: Tim is doing so well with QuickReads. His correct words/minute continue to increase. We are going up a level.	Teacher 1: I tried to be cognizant of how many times I was correcting Donny during his reading.	Teacher 18: by having Howard fill out the story map I recognized his inability to make inferences. As a result …I [will focus] more on implicit questions than explicit.
Teacher 3: After having him do this for the short i sound I will have him do word sort for short a, e, and i sounds.	Teacher 16: He had trouble reading the word "we" and became frustrated. I didn't want to start off on a bad note, so we stopped. I reassured him. He was not interested in trying to solve the word or what would make sense. We moved to finding smaller words hidden inside larger words. I sneakily put the word "be" and "me" together on the magnet tray which he read just fine, then I switched beginning sound to 'w' to see if he'd read the word "we" which he did. I said, "You know it! Let's finish our book because we solved that tricky word".	Teacher 23: after discovering during the previous session that Sam consistently put the 'r' first in many r-controlled vowel words I created a word sort.

provides quotations from across the sample of 23 novices that illustrate each of the three problem axial codes appearing most frequently in novices' reflections. Table 5 provides quotations from across the sample illustrating types of adaptations novices made in response to identification of problems in their teaching practices.

Carol's case is excerpted below because she wrote about the three most frequent types of problems novices in the sample reflected on, and because she utilized the exploration-adaptation-resolution cycle in a way that is representative of the sample. Carol explored a small number of problems in depth and generated many adaptations. She returned to explore these problems frequently, reflecting on outcomes and continually refining her adaptations, eventually finding resolution. The quantitative analysis showed that this was a significant pattern in the sample data as well.

Carol was an undergraduate in her last semester prior to student teaching. Her reflections provided a picture of persistence in problem exploration, with recursive reflection and adaptation. Her trial and refinement approach exemplifies that of a significant number of the novices, an approach that Roskos, Risko, and Vukelich (1998) have characterized as "no magical, linear line from novice to expert, but rather many false starts, recursive thinking, reflective moments, and problem solving episodes" (p. 234). In her first weekly reflection Carol described her student Kady's strengths and needs. Codes assigned during qualitative analysis are bracketed after each quotation.

> Kady really enjoyed reading aloud together versus reading aloud to me. I saw her taking time to incorporate the pictures after she finished reading. [*Problem: Identifying Student Strengths*]

> When I had the game board for working with long vowel sounds I found there were certain combinations Kady especially was having trouble with, such as the o-e, u-e, and oa patterns. [*Problem: Identifying Student Skill Deficits*]

Carol used problem exploration to describe "puzzles of practice" (Jay & Johnson, 2002, p. 77) and documented adaptations she made in the moment and planned for the future:

> Kady still was quiet and wouldn't really [respond] when I talked with her about making connections with what she was reading [*Problem: Identifying Student Skill Deficits*] I gave her examples [*Adaptation: Present*] talking about how I love playing with my dog thinking it would get her to talk also. I know that she loves dogs, so therefore picked a book about a little girl and her dog, thinking it would encourage easy connections, yet I failed. For [week 2] I have chosen a real-life book about a dog, thinking maybe the real pictures will help trigger connections. [*Adaptation: Future*]

To respond to this puzzle Carol applied thoughtful adaptation, defined by Duffy et al. (2008) as the actions teachers take to "modify professional information and/or practices ... to meet the needs of particular students or instructional situations within the framework of the lesson plan" (p. 161).

In week two Carol explored an unsuccessful adaptation and made strategic decisions to adapt her comprehension instruction.

> I thought it wouldn't be that hard to understand, yet I overlooked that she might not get it by just hearing 'make a connection'. I gave examples that would fit me and her both, yet she was still hesitant. I think I will try to stay away from making connections, for now anyways ... focus on predicting and choose another strategy to try. [*Adaptation: Future*]

After noting Kady's responses for a few more lessons, Carol wrote, "[Kady] really responds well to the questioning strategy, therefore I may shift between strategies, to point out ways that specific strategies can help us understand what we read." [*Adaptation: Future*] The recursive problem exploration-adaptation cycle helped Carol guide Kady to develop flexibility with varied comprehension tactics, an approach that researchers (Almasi & Fullerton, 2012; Clay, 1991) have affirmed as vital for student confidence and success.

For vocabulary instruction, Carol used a strategy that combined conversation about words with drawings and application to text. She first collected data that informed her adaptation: "I wrote down the words she had troubles with so I could shape lessons and choose books that would help with those words" [*Adaptation: Future*] then used problem exploration in her reflection to analyze the outcomes of her instruction and adapt.

> I need to put limits on (her) picture, since she is really into detail. [*Problem: Time Management*] Maybe that is something I could send home for her mom to help with. I could have Kady write the vocabulary word on the card, with a sentence she makes up, and she could take the cards home and finish the picture. [*Adaptation: Future*]

Carol used adaptions in the moment of teaching to scaffold for difficulties in early lessons:

> Kady found it hard, yet still was able to come up with three sentences that included our vocabulary words. For a couple I said she could look through the book to get an idea from the pictures, [*Adaptation: Present*] because she absolutely had no idea.

By week three Carol began to find resolution in Kady's decoding strategy acquisition:

> Kady struggled at first, but once I talked with her about how to pick which vowel
> to say within the word, how to decide fast, and not stop on a word, [*Adaptation*]
> Kady had no problem, spelling a word, saying it, and identifying the vowel sound
> [*Problem Resolution*].

Moving Kady from building words with letter cards to reading complete words required another adaptation, illustrating the persistence essential to adaptive expertise (Roskos, et al., 1998; Shulman & Shulman, 2004):

> Objective: Kady will automatically (decode) words as she draws cards with new
> words on them. We did this differently than planned. I took a word, wrote it on
> the dry-erase board, and had her identify it. [*Adaptation: Present*]

Using the dry-erase board proved very effective, and Carol described how she ramped-up this adaptation:

> I had words picked from the new text that had a common feature and I predicted
> Kady would get stuck on. I wrote the word on the dry-erase board and asked
> Kady to say [it]. I then asked Kady to write the word and asked what the vowel
> sound was. She was able to see "moaned" and just sound it out as 'm-o-n-e-d'.
> I believe it helped her see that even though the word had the 'a' in it, it wasn't
> sounded out. It really was a last minute change [*Adaptation: Present*] yet I do think
> it helped Kady see how the two vowels make one sound if they're sitting right next
> to each other. [*Problem Resolution*]

Carol capitalized on this success by applying this innovation (Parsons, 2012) in vocabulary instruction:

> Again, I changed the original plan and incorporated the dry-erase board to keep
> Kady engaged. [*Adaptation: Present*] I had a stack of words from the story. I drew
> a card, wrote it on the dry-erase board, had her write it down below, then we
> talked about what it was verbally and literally and how it could be a part of the
> story. This strategy really worked for Kady. We kept all five words on the board,
> referring back to them as we read. [*Problem Resolution*]

Later in the same reflection Carol explored her own skill development:

> My confidence really decreases if I don't see a purpose or a place where I want
> the children to end. By simply doing word study on words from a given text, it
> really wasn't connecting to the reading. Tuesday Kady built the words, yet I didn't
> have enough tiles to keep the words built, so she used the letters from the previous
> word to build the second word and so on. [*Problem: Teacher Skill Development*] If
> I'd had more copies of the letters, I could have had Kady build the words and stick
> them on a cookie sheet in the groups I said. We could have stopped and reflected
> on the words while reading if she got stuck. [*Adaptation: Future*] It's something as
> easy as that I need to keep in mind. [*Problem Resolution*]

These and other opportunities to practice adaptations in the moment of teaching supported the development of reflective practice: the ability to combine thought and analysis with action in

Table 6: Summary Statistics (N = 175)

Variable	Mean	SD	Min	Median	Max
Problem Resolution	0.19	0.57	0	0	4
Teacher characteristics					
Teaching experience	0.05	0.21	0	0	1
Total years in schools	2.74	1.89	0	2.44	6
Graduate student	0.17	0.38	0	0	1
Student characteristics					
Black	0.17	0.37	0	0	1
Hispanic	0.08	0.28	0	0	1
White	0.75	0.43	0	1	1
Female	0.40	0.49	0	0	1
Grade	2.81	1.37	1	3	6
Reading level	2.22	1.71	0	1.75	6.75
Free/reduced lunch	0.34	0.48	0	0	1
School characteristics					
Private school	0.32	0.47	0	0	1
Low income	1.05	3.69	0	0.24	19.50
Reflection Note Characteristics					
Problem exploration	0.19	0.51	0	0	3
Present adaptations	0.49	0.82	0	0	4

practice (Schon, 1983). At the same time, identifying instructional roadblocks and generating and enacting responses paved the way for development of adaptive expertise (Hammerness et al., 2005).

Question 2: How did novices use reflection writing to develop patterns of reflective practice? What relationships, if any, were present between their writing about problems in their practice, their enactment of instructional adaptations, and resolution of problems?

Carol's reflections excerpted above represent the recurring patterns of problem exploration-adaptation-resolution that emerged during qualitative analysis. Subsequent quantitative analysis revealed statistically significant relationships among these three variables across the sample, supporting our belief that written reflections provide a powerful framework for novices' developing reflective practices and adaptive expertise.

Novices made an average of 0.19 problem explorations, 0.49 adaptations, and 0.19 resolutions per reflection (see Table 6 for summary statistics, and Table A for correlation-variance-covariance). Of the differences in resolutions 79% was due to differences across reflections and 21% was due to novice characteristics such as teaching experience, experience in schools, and graduate or undergraduate status (See Table 7). Model 2 added student and school characteristics to the analysis. Novices who worked with a female student, in a higher grade, or not receiving free/reduced

Table 7: Summary of Multilevel Regression Models: Predicting Problem Resolutions With Unstandardized Regression Coefficients (Standard Errors in Parentheses)

Explanatory variable	3 Multilevel regression models of Problem Resolutions								
	Model 1			Model 2			Model 3		
Teacher characteristics									
Some teaching experience	0.289	(0.236)							
Total years in school	0.057	(0.059)							
Graduate student	-0.269	(0.135)	*	-0.191	(0.091)	*	-0.206	(0.101)	*
Student characteristics									
African American student	-0.266	(0.454)							
White student	-0.221	(0.390)							
Female	0.262	(0.093)	**	0.147	(0.067)	*	0.163	(0.082)	*
Free/reduced lunch	-0.186	(0.084)	*	-0.192	(0.083)	*	-0.178	(0.090)	*
Grade	0.077	(0.032)	*	0.061	(0.030)	*	0.073	(0.034)	*
Reading level	-0.010	(0.037)							
School characteristics									
Private school	0.091	(0.177)							
Low income	0.006	(0.018)							
Current Reflection Note									
Problem exploration	0.000	(0.055)							
Thoughtful adaptation	0.151	(0.049)	**	0.152	(0.047)	**	0.177	(0.050)	***
Previous Reflection Note (-1)									
Problem exploration (-1)							0.143	(0.054)	**
Thoughtful adaptation (-1)							0.147	(0.048)	**
Variance at each level	Explained variance at each level								
Teacher (21%)	0.321			0.307			0.305		
Note (79%)	0.057			0.054			0.176		
Total variance explained	0.112			0.107			0.203		

Note. Each regression model included a constant term

*p<.05, **p<.01, ***p<.001

lunch documented more resolutions. In Model 3, reflective note characteristics were analyzed. Novices who described more adaptations in a reflection identified significantly more resolutions in that same reflection. Furthermore, novices who had more problem explorations or adaptations in the previous week's reflection had significantly more resolutions the following week. No other variable was significant. This explanatory model accounted for over 20% of the differences in problem resolution across reflections.

While novice characteristics provided relatively little information about the occurrence of resolution, graduate novices were significantly less likely to document resolution than undergraduate novices. This echoes the results of research with experienced teachers in the same reading clinic (Hayden & Pasman, 2008). It may be that more seasoned novices, such as the graduate students in this sample, reserve judgment, waiting for additional evidence before stating that a problem is resolved. Many challenges in teaching are recurring (Cuban, 1992), and teachers become more keenly aware of their successes and failures as they amass experiences (Berliner, 1986, 1988). Shulman (1987) asserted that teacher development progresses "from expertise as learners through a novitiate as teachers [and] exposes and highlights the complex bodies of knowledge and skill needed to function effectively as a teacher. The neophyte's stumble becomes the scholar's window" (p. 4). Perhaps the graduate novices in this study were more likely to view problem exploration-adaptation as a process of refinement, not yet reaching resolution but opening "the scholar's window" for more consideration.

DISCUSSION

If "the central issue teacher education must confront is how to foster learning about and from practice *in* practice" (Darling-Hammond, 2010, p. 42), then this analysis is an important step in understanding what problems of practice concern novices and how novices use written reflections to *do* teaching practice. Novices across the sample used detailed exploration of breakdowns in student learning during instruction to generate targeted, responsive adaptations. Carol revisited the problems she identified to engage in extensive adaptations and refinement of instruction. The result of her "systematic inspection" (Biesta, 2010, p. 109) of several key problems was that she was able to try on different pedagogical and instructional interventions, find meaning, and apply that meaning to develop an approach that fit her student's needs and habits of learning more closely.

Practicing this recursive inquiry approach in a supportive setting helped prepare Carol and the other novices for classroom teaching by learning ways to observe closely, over extended time, and continue to adapt to address challenges. While the in-depth individual observation novices engaged in for this study is not directly transferable to classroom teaching, in classrooms there will often be opportunities to observe, collect, and analyze student data that can be used to refine instruction. Indeed, we expect classroom teachers to use just such methods and data to make instructional decisions. By practicing these habits of mind in the reading clinic novices prepared for application in broader contexts.

Novices in this sample noticed student responses, documented them in written reflections, and took action. Noticing, or presence, is the first step in developing reflective practice that leads to adaptive expertise (Rodgers, 2006). When novices are present in the moment, noticing and adapting, they are "learning to take intelligent action" (Rodgers, 2006, p. 215). Even if the adaptation is not a perfect match for the student's needs, practicing this reflective cycle in a supportive setting such as a reading clinic affords the opportunity to take advantage of the counsel of more experienced mentor/supervisors.

It is reasonable to assume that supervisor/novice interactions (which were not accounted for in this analysis) and the reflection writing structure mediated novices' reflective writing while they taught in the reading clinic. Indeed, that was a goal of the class and of the requirement to write reflections. While supervisors could intervene during lessons, and read all lesson plans and reflections, one supervisor responded consistently in writing to the reflections of her supervisees while the others preferred to intervene during novices' lessons or respond to questions face-to-face. Specific evidence of all supportive moves by supervisors was not collected and thus supervisor impact on the development of novices' reflective practices was not analyzed. This impact needs to be studied more closely in future research, perhaps in the manner of Collet's (2012) studies of the gradual increase of responsibility utilized by reading clinic coaches.

Reflective practices support perceptions of agency for novice teachers, helping them develop instructional responses that can successfully impact the learning of their students, even when presented with challenges, and reinforcing the qualities of teacher persistence and tolerance for ambiguity and disequilibria that are critical to student success (Shulman & Shulman, 2004). Additionally, the significant relationships we found between problem exploration, adaptation, and resolution reinforce Dewey's (1916) theories of discovery learning while specifically describing problems of practice that novices are labeling and learning (Berliner, 1988). Puzzlement and perplexity caused these novices to pause and reflect (Dewey, 1933). If teacher educators can learn what problems cause novices to pause and reflect we can design real time teaching experiences that provide opportunities to actively and reflectively engage with these during training, when novices have easy access to experienced mentors who can mediate this learning (Alexander & Fives, 2000; Vygotsky, 1978). The requirement to write structured written reflections prompted these novices to engage with habits of mind that helped them to "think like a teacher" (Hammerness et. al., 2005, p. 382). As a result, they gained early access to resolving some commonplace problems of practice, thinking and planning reflectively and adapting instruction to teach responsively.

REFERENCES

Alexander, P., & Fives, H. (2000). Achieving expertise in teaching reading. In L. Baker, M. Dreher, & J. Guthrie, (Eds.), *Engaging young readers: Promoting achievement and motivation* (pp. 285-308). New York, NY: Guilford Press.

Almasi, J. F., & Fullerton, S. K. (2012). *Teaching strategic processes in reading*, 2nd edition. New York, NY: Guilford Press.

Amobi, F. (2006). Beyond the call: Preserving reflection in the preparation of "highly qualified" teachers. *Teacher Education Quarterly*, 33, 23-35.

Ball, D., & Cohen, D. (1999). Developing practice, developing practitioners: Toward a practice-based theory of professional education. In L. Darling-Hammond & G.Sykes, (Eds.), *Teaching as the learning profession: Handbook of policy and practice* (pp. 3-32). San Francisco, CA: Jossey-Bass.

Benjamini, Y., Krieger, A. M., & Yekutieli, D. (2006). Adaptive linear step-up procedures that control the false discovery rate. *Biometrika*, 93, 491–507.

Berliner, D. C. (1986). In pursuit of the expert pedagogue. *Educational Researcher*, 15, 5-13. doi:10.2307/117505

Berliner, D. C. (1988, February). *The development of expertise in pedagogy*. Charles W. Hunt Memorial Lecture, presented at the annual meeting of the American Association of Colleges for Teacher Education, New Orleans, LA.

Biesta, G. (2010). Pragmatism and the philosophical foundations of mixed methods research. In A. Tashakkori & C. Teddlie, (Eds.), *SAGE Handbook of Mixed Methods in Social and Behavioral Research*, 2nd Edition, (pp. 95-118). Washington, DC: Sage Publications.

Bransford, J., Darling-Hammond, L., & LePage, P. (2005). Introduction. In L. Darling-Hammond & J. Bransford, (Eds.), *Preparing teachers for a changing world: What teachers should learn and be able to do* (pp. 1-39). San Francisco, CA: Jossey-Bass.

Brookfield, S. D. (1995). *Becoming a critically reflective teacher*. San Francisco: Jossey-Bass.

Calfee, R., & Sperling, M. (2010). *On mixed methods: Approaches to language and literacy research*. New York, NY: Teachers College Press.

Caracelli, V. & Greene, J. (1993). Data analysis strategies for mixed method evaluation designs. *Educational Evaluation and Policy Analysis*, 15, 195-207.

Clay, M. M. (1991). *Becoming literate: The construction of inner control*. Portsmouth, NH: Heinemann.

Cochran-Smith, M., & Lytle, S. (1993). *Inside/Outside: Teacher research and knowledge*. Columbia University: Teachers College Press.

Collet, V. (2012). The Gradual Increase of Responsibility Model: Coaching for Teacher Change. *Literacy Research and Instruction*, 51, 27-47.

Creswell, J., & Plano Clark, V. (2007). *Designing and conducting mixed methods research*. Thousand Oaks, CA: Sage Publications.

Cuban, L. (1992). Managing dilemmas while building professional communities. *Educational Researcher*, 2, 4-11. doi:10.2307/1176344

Darling-Hammond, L., (2010). Teacher education and the American future. *Journal of Teacher Education*, 61, 35-47.

Dewey, J. (1916). *Democracy and education: An introduction to the philosophy of education*. New York, NY: The Free Press.

Dewey, J. (1933). *How we think: A restatement of the relation of reflective thinking to the educative process*. Boston, MA: D.C. Heath and Company.

Duffy, G., Miller, S., Kear, K., Parsons, S., Davis, S. & Williams, B. (2008). Teachers' instructional adaptations during literacy instruction. In Y. Kim, V. J. Risko, D. L. Compton, D. K. Dickinson, M. K. Hundley, R. T. Jimenez, K. M. Leander & D. Wells Rowe, (Eds.), *57th Yearbook of the National Reading Conference* (pp. 160-171). Oak Creek, Wisconsin: National Reading Conference, Inc.

English, A. (2008, March). *Teachers as listeners: Learning to listen to interruptions as a guide to reflective practice*. Paper presented at the American Educational Research Association Annual Meeting, New York, NY.

Farrell, T. S. C. (2007). Failing the practicum: Narrowing the gap between expectations and reality with reflective practice. *TESOL Quarterly*, 40, 193-201.

Fendler, L. (2003). Teacher reflection in a hall of mirrors: Historical influence and political reverberations. *Educational Researcher*, 32, 16-25. doi: 10.3102/0013189X032003016

Geursen, J., de Heer, A., Korthagen, F. A. J., Lunenberg, M., & Zwart, R. (2010). The importance of being aware: Developing professional identities in educators and researchers. *Studying Teacher Education*, 6, 291-302.

Glaser, B., & Strauss, A. (1967). *The discovery of grounded theory*. Chicago, IL: Aldine.

Goldstein, H. (1995). *Multilevel statistical models*. Sydney, Australia: Edward Arnold.

Greene, J. C. (2007). *Mixed methods in social inquiry*. San Francisco, CA: Wiley and Sons, Incorporated.

Greene, M., (1988). *The dialectic of freedom*. New York, NY: Teachers College, Columbia University.

Hacker, D. J., Keener, M. C., & Kircher, J. C. (2009). Writing is applied metacognition. In D. J. Hacker, J. Dunlosky & C. A. Graesser, (Eds.), *Handbook of metacognition in education* (pp. 154-172). New York, NY: Routledge.

Hammerness, K., Darling-Hammond, L., Bransford, J., Berliner, D., Cochran-Smith, M., McDonald, M., & Zeichner, K. (2005). How teachers learn and develop. In L. Darling-Hammond & J. Bransford, (Eds.), *Preparing teachers for a changing world: What teachers should learn and be able to do* (pp. 358-389). San Francisco, CA: Jossey-Bass.

Haverback, H. & Parault, S. (2008). Pre-service reading teacher efficacy and tutoring: A review. *Educational Psychology Review*, 20, 237-255. doi:10.1007/s10648-008-9077-4

Hayden, H. E., Moore-Russo, D., & Marino, M. (2013). One teacher's reflective journey and the evolution of a lesson: Systematic reflection as a catalyst for adaptive expertise. *Reflective Practice: International and Multidisciplinary Perspectives*, 14, 144-156.

Hayden, H. E. & Pasman, T. D. (December, 2008). Developing reflective practice: Just a matter of time? Paper presented at the annual meeting of the National Reading Conference, Orlando, FL.

Jay, J. K., & Johnson, K. L. (2002). Capturing complexity: A typology of reflective practice for teacher education. *Teaching and Teacher Education*, 18, 73-85. doi: 10.1016/S0742-051X(01)00051-8

Kennedy, P. (2004). *Guide to econometrics*. Cambridge, MA: Blackwell.

Kinsella, E. A. (2007). Embodied reflection and the epistemology of reflective practice. *Journal of Philosophy of Education*, 41, 395-409. doi:10.1111/j.1467-9752.2007.00574.x

Korthagen, F. A. J. & Kessels, J. P. A. M. (1999). Linking theory and practice: Changing the pedagogy of teacher education. *Educational Researcher, 28,* 4-17. doi: 10.2307/1176444

Korthagen, F., & Vasalos, A. (2005). Levels in reflection: Core reflection as a means to enhance professional growth. *Teachers and Teaching: Theory and Practice,* 11, 47-71. doi:10.1080/1354060042000337093

Lam, B. H. (2011). A reflective account of a pre-service teacher's effort to implement a progressive curriculum in field practice. *Schools: Studies in Education,* 8, 22-39.

Le Maistre, C. & Pare, A. (2010). Whatever it takes: How beginning teachers learn to survive. *Teaching and Teacher Education,* 26, 559-564.

Lizzio, A., & Wilson, K. (2007). Developing critical professional judgement: The efficacy of a self-managed reflective process. *Studies in Continuing Education,* 29, 277-293.

Loughran, J. J. (2006). *Developing a pedagogy of teacher education: Understanding teaching and learning about teaching.* New York, NY: Routledge.

Lunenberg, M. & Korthagen, F. A. J. (2005). Breaking the didactic circle: A study on some aspects of the promotion of student-directed learning by teachers and teacher educators. *European Journal of Teacher Education,* 28, 1-22.

Miller, S. M. (2007). How literature discussion shapes thinking: ZPDs for teaching/learning habits of the heart and mind. In A. Kozulin, B. Gindis, V. S. Ageyev & S. M. Miller, (Eds.), *Vygotsky's educational theory in cultural context* (pp. 289-316). New York, NY: Cambridge University Press.

Morse, J., & Niehaus, L. (2009). *Mixed method design: Principles and procedures.* Walnut Creek, CA: Left Coast Press, Inc.

Nelson, C., & Harper, V. (2006). A pedagogy of difficulty: Preparing teachers to understand and integrate complexity in teaching and learning. *Teacher Education Quarterly,* 33, 7-21.

Nilsson, P. (2009). From lesson plan to new comprehension: Exploring student teachers' pedagogical reasoning in learning about teaching. *European Journal of Teacher Education,* 32, 239-258. doi:10.1080/02619760802553048

Parsons, S. (2012). Adaptive teaching in literacy instruction: Case studies of two teachers. *Journal of Literacy Research,* 44, 149-170.

Pui-lan, K., Brown, W. P., Delamarter, S., Frank, T. E., Marshall, J. L., Menn, E., & Riggs, M. Y. (2005). Taken with surprise: Critical incidents in teaching. *Teaching Theology and Religion,* 8, 35-46.

Reiman, A. J. (1999). The evolution of the social roletaking and guided reflection framework in teacher education: Recent theory and quantitative synthesis of research. *Teaching and Teacher Education,* 15, 597-612. doi:10.1016/S0742-051X(99)00016-5

Risko, V. J., Roller, C. M., Cummins, C., Bean, R. M., Block, C. C., Anders, P. L., & Flood, J. (2008). A critical analysis of research on reading teacher education. *Reading Research Quarterly,* 43, 252-288. doi:10.1598/RRQ.43.3.3

Rodgers, C. R. (2002). Seeing student learning: Teacher change and the role of reflection. *Harvard Educational Review,* 72, 230-253.

Rodgers, C. R. (2006). Attending to student voice: The impact of descriptive feedback on learning and teaching. *Curriculum Inquiry,* 36, 209-237.

Roskos, K., Risko, V. J., & Vukelich, C. (1998). Conversations: Head, heart, and the practice of literacy pedagogy. *Reading Research Quarterly,* 33, 228–239. doi: 10.1598/RRQ.33.2.4

Roskos, K., Vukelich, C., & Risko, V. (2001). Reflection and learning to teach reading: A critical review of literacy and general teacher education studies. *Journal of Literacy Research,* 33, 595-635. doi: 10.1080/10862960109548127

Schon, D. (1983). *The reflective practitioner: How professionals think in action.* New York: Basic Books.

Shulman, L. (1986). Those who understand: Knowledge growth in teaching. *Educational Researcher,* 15, 4-14. doi:10.2307/1175860

Shulman, L. (1987). Knowledge and teaching: Foundations of the new reform. *Harvard Educational Review,* 57, 1-22.

Shulman, L. S. & Shulman, J. H. (2004). How and what teachers learn: A shifting perspective. *Journal of Curriculum Studies,* 36, 257-271. doi:10.1080/0022027032000148298

Strauss, A., & Corbin, J. (1990). *Basics of qualitative research: Grounded theory procedures and techniques.* Newbury Park, CA: Sage Publications.

Tashakkori, A. & Teddlie, C. (1998). *Mixed methodology: Combining qualitative and quantitative approaches. Applied social research methods series, Vol. 46.* Thousand Oaks, CA: Sage Publications.

Teddlie, C., & Tashakkori, A. (2009). *Foundations of mixed methods research: Integrating quantitative and qualitative approaches in the social and behavioral sciences*. Thousand Oaks, CA: Sage.

Tillman, L. C. (2003). Mentoring, reflection, and reciprocal journaling. *Theory into Practice*, 42, 226-233. doi:10.1253/tip.2003.0038

Vygotsky, L. S. (1978). *Mind in society: The development of higher psychological processes*. Cambridge, MA: Harvard University Press.

Wells, G. (2003). Los ninos se alfabetizan hablando. (Children talk their way into literacy.) In J.R. Garcia (Ed.), *Ensenar a escribir sin prisas ... pero con sentido* (pp. 54-76). Sevilla, Sapin: Publicaciaones del M.C.E.P.

APPENDIX

Correlation, Variance, Covariance of Key Variables

Table A: Correlation-Variance-Covariance Matrix of Outcome and Explanatory Variables

	Variable	1	2	3	4	5	6	7	8	9	10	11	12	13	14	15	16
1	Problem Resolution	**0.28**	0.01	0.05	-0.04	-0.01	0.02	0.04	-0.03	0.04	0.05	-0.01	-0.15	0.03	0.11	0.09	0.10
2	Some teaching experience	0.05	**0.04**	-0.03	0.03	-0.01	0.01	0.03	-0.02	0.06	0.12	-0.01	-0.04	-0.01	-0.01	-0.01	-0.02
3	Total years in school	0.05	-0.09	**3.53**	-0.05	0.17	0.04	-0.26	0.07	-0.39	0.33	-0.19	-0.52	0.05	0.16	-0.03	0.20
4	Graduate student	-0.11	0.37	-0.07	**0.19**	0.00	-0.03	0.03	-0.04	0.28	0.39	-0.04	0.55	-0.03	0.01	-0.06	0.02
5	African American student	-0.04	-0.10	0.25	0.02	**0.14**	-0.12	0.06	0.11	0.13	0.09	-0.05	-0.06	-0.02	-0.03	-0.03	-0.03
6	White student	0.09	0.12	0.06	-0.16	-0.78	**0.18**	-0.03	-0.12	-0.23	-0.22	0.08	0.13	0.03	0.03	0.05	0.05
7	Female	0.16	0.27	-0.28	0.13	0.32	-0.13	**0.24**	0.04	0.03	0.09	-0.08	-0.27	-0.03	0.00	-0.04	0.01
8	Free/reduced lunch	-0.12	-0.16	0.08	-0.19	0.62	-0.57	0.16	**0.22**	0.06	-0.09	-0.06	-0.19	-0.04	0.01	-0.05	-0.01
9	Grade	0.11	0.19	-0.15	0.47	0.26	-0.38	0.05	0.09	**1.87**	1.33	-0.12	0.93	-0.05	-0.07	-0.04	-0.11
10	Reading level	0.06	0.32	0.10	0.52	0.14	-0.30	0.11	-0.11	0.56	**2.99**	-0.28	1.15	-0.05	-0.06	-0.11	-0.07
11	Private school	-0.02	-0.15	-0.22	-0.20	-0.30	0.39	-0.35	-0.27	-0.19	-0.35	**0.22**	-0.31	0.03	-0.01	0.08	-0.01
12	Low income school	-0.07	-0.05	-0.07	0.33	-0.05	0.08	-0.14	-0.11	0.18	0.18	-0.18	**14.02**	-0.14	-0.11	-0.24	-0.03
13	Problem exploration	0.13	-0.08	0.05	-0.14	-0.12	0.13	-0.11	-0.16	-0.08	-0.07	0.15	-0.08	**0.23**	0.07	0.02	-0.02
14	Adaptation	0.25	-0.08	0.10	0.04	-0.09	0.10	0.01	0.02	-0.06	-0.05	-0.03	-0.04	0.19	**0.63**	-0.03	0.05
15	Problem exploration (-1)	0.23	-0.08	-0.02	-0.18	-0.12	0.15	-0.10	-0.15	-0.04	-0.09	0.22	-0.09	0.06	-0.05	**0.57**	0.03
16	Adaptation (-1)	0.23	-0.13	0.13	0.07	-0.09	0.13	0.03	-0.02	-0.10	-0.05	-0.03	-0.01	-0.06	0.07	0.05	**0.68**

Professional Development in Writing Instruction: Common Factors Among High-Adopting Teachers

Sarah Hunt-Barron
Converse College

Rebecca Kaminski
Clemson University

Kelly Tracy
Western Carolina University

Measures of writing proficiency continue to indicate many students lack the skills they need as writers. For example, the 2011 National Assessment of Educational Progress data on writing indicates only 27% of high school seniors achieved the level of proficient or higher. Whether these sorts of tests are accurate measurements of students' abilities is arguable, but this trend is costly. Corporations in the United States spend an estimated $3.1 billion annually to remediate employees' writing skills; state governments spend an estimated $221 million on remediation (National Commission on Writing, 2005). Statistics such as these bring public scrutiny, as well as calls for improved teacher preparation and more effective teaching practices that lead to improved student achievement in writing.

This push for higher student writing achievement is only increasing with the adoption of the Common Core State Standards (National Governors Association Center for Best Practices and Council of Chief State School Offices, 2010), which elevate expectations for the amount and quality of writing that students are doing (Calkins, Ehrenworth, & Lehman, 2012). Districts are re-evaluating their English language arts (ELA) curricula and looking for ways to further prepare their ELA teachers to meet these new standards, including through professional development (PD) in writing instruction. These attempts raise questions about the effects of such PD on improving teacher practice, as well as students' writing. The present study aims to address some of these questions: specifically, why do some educators more readily adopt writing instructional practices presented in PD, which practices are adopted at higher rates, and how do higher adoption rates affect students' writing achievement?

These questions arose from a larger two-year study supported by the resources of the National Writing Project (NWP) and undertaken in an effort to understand the effects of PD in writing instruction in grades 3-5. An NWP site conducted PD at two separate elementary schools in the southeastern United States, using the NWP's "teachers teaching teachers" model for PD (NWP, 2010). The PD focused on using explicit and consistent writing strategy instruction within a writer's workshop, defined in this study as a mode of instruction in which teachers and students write together in a community of practice (Rogoff, 1990). Through strategy instruction, teachers explicitly teach the steps needed to plan, revise and edit texts with the goal of students using these strategies independently (Graham, 2006). Components of a typical workshop include mini-lessons, independent writing time with teacher and peer conferencing, and share time (Ellis & Marsh, 2007). Students are given extended class time to compose and/or revise and student choice is essential to this approach. Writing workshop has a joint focus on development of the craft of writing and building students' ability to self-assess their competence (Atwell, 1987; Calkins, 1994). Upstate Writing Project (UWP) Teacher Consultants (TCs) modeled explicit writing instructional strategies and taught demonstration lessons in teachers' classrooms in an effort to share research-based instructional practices.

Although previous research has examined qualities of effective PD (e.g., Flint, Zisook, & Fisher, 2011; Scott & Sutton, 2009; Troia, Lin, Cohen, & Monroe, 2011) and has indicated that student writing improves when teachers are part of a National Writing Project (NWP) PD program (Blau, Cabe, & Whitney, 2006; Campos & Peach, 2006; Singer & Scollay, 2006; Swain, Graves, & Morse, 2006), few studies have specifically analyzed *why* some educators more readily adopt writing instructional practices presented in PD and how this higher adoption rate affects students' writing achievement. The present study sought to deepen our understanding of the relationship between PD in writing, teacher change, and student achievement.

THEORETICAL FRAMEWORK

Professional Development

Research suggests that effective PD emphasizes active learning and engagement through discussions, planning, and practice (Lieberman, 1996), incorporating elements such as active teaching, observation, assessment, and reflection rather than abstract discussions (Darling-Hammond & McLaughlin, 1995). PD is more effective when it occurs over a period of time, is integrated into a school's improvement efforts, and involves the entire faculty in a collaborative and collegial environment (Darling-Hammond & Richardson, 2009). These findings are in concert with Garet, Porter, DeSimone, Birman, and Yoon's (2001) five core features of effective PD: a focus on content knowledge, opportunity for active learning, coherence with other learning activities, collective participation, and duration.

To determine if our PD model was effective, we used Desimone's (2009, 2011) proposed core conceptual framework for studying the effects of PD. Desimone's (2009) theory of action for effective PD summarizes the interactive relationships we envisioned for our own study of PD. According to Desimone (2009),

> a core theory of action for PD would likely follow these steps: a) teachers experience PD; b) PD increases teachers' knowledge and skills and /or changes their attitudes and beliefs; c) teachers use their new knowledge and skills, attitudes and beliefs, to improve the content of their instruction or their approach to pedagogy, or both; d) the instructional changes foster increased student learning (p. 184).

If our PD was successful, we theorized we should see this core conceptual framework enacted by the teachers who experienced professional development, as well as through improved student outcomes in writing.

Communities of Practice

In communities of practice (COPs), learning is situated, embedded authentically within a culture, activity, and context (Lave & Wenger, 1991). Individuals grow, change, and learn through engagement in social interactions, sustained practice, and situated activity within the community (Lave & Wenger, 1991). The PD sought to develop a community of practice among teachers. Using

Figure 1: Embedded case study model

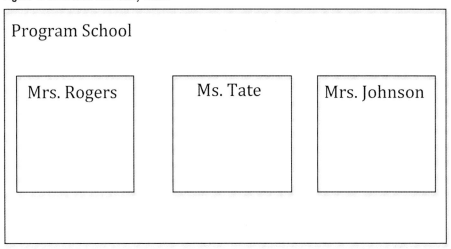

the NWP's model of "teachers teaching teachers," teachers with expertise in writing instruction facilitated activities focused on writing instruction and sought to uncover and share understandings about writing instruction, as well as develop new shared understandings among participating teachers.

DESIGN OF THE STUDY

As noted previously, this case study emerged from a larger study using a concurrent mixed model design (Tashakkori and Teddlie, 2003) conducted over two school years. Data was collected to compare teacher practice and philosophy, as well as student outcomes. Using Yin's (2009) embedded case study methods, we framed our analysis by looking at each school as a case and each high-adopting teacher as a sub-unit of analysis (Figure 1). For the purpose of this paper, we will focus on three participants of interest who demonstrated the highest implementation levels of classroom practices modeled in the PD over the course of a single school year. The three teachers were part of a voluntary pool of 27 teachers in grades 3- 5 at a school with a year-long contractual agreement with the NWP site for PD. After an initial viewing and analysis of videotaped lessons from all 27 teachers, we identified nine teachers for further analysis. We then added two additional teachers to this group based on feedback from school administrators, giving us 11 teachers of interest. These teachers represented all levels of implementation of modeled practices (low, mid, and high). We selected the three highest adopting teachers from this group for a case study. Our goal was to identify any common dispositions among these high-adopting teachers that may have led them to try new instructional strategies in the teaching of writing. We sought to explore which practices were adopted and furthermore, examine if higher implementation levels led to improved student outcomes.

Table 1: Data Sources

Data source	Time of collection
Qualitative Data	
Teaching practice survey	Fall and spring
Writing lesson tapes	Fall and spring
Interview	Spring
Quantitative Data	
Student writing samples	Fall and spring

Data Collection

Measures of teacher practice and philosophy. Multiple pre/post qualitative and quantitative indicators were collected to determine how the PD impacted third, fourth and fifth-grade teachers' practice and philosophy at the school (Table 1).

Teaching practice surveys. All teachers completed surveys centered on their instructional writing practices at the beginning of the year (prior to any PD) and at the end of the year. The surveys used open-ended questions requiring short responses and Likert scale statements. The fall survey focused on writing practices employed the prior year; the spring survey focused on writing practices in the current school year. These surveys also provided information about teacher experience and participation in outside writing PD (e.g., conferences, courses).

Writing lesson tapes. All teachers taped two typical writing lessons, one in fall and again in spring. Researchers supplied videocassettes and cameras and teachers received guidelines on how to tape the lesson. Teachers self-taped, using a tripod, or selected a videographer from within the school community to reduce the possibility of observer effect.

Interviews. The research team conducted semi-structured onsite interviews with teachers at the end of the academic year. The interview protocol included questions related to each teacher's writing instruction and attitudes toward writing.

MEASURES OF STUDENT WRITING PERFORMANCE.

Prompt writing samples. Although the PD emphasized student choice during writing instruction, teachers were asked to administer pre/post-writing prompts using common directions in an effort to provide writing samples that responded to a writing task with equivalent demands. The prompts were judged to be of equivalent levels of difficulty and prompted students to write in similar genres.

QUALITATIVE DATA ANALYSIS

Qualitative data were analyzed using both an *a priori* coding scheme and emergent coding using the constant comparative method of analysis (Strauss & Corbin, 1990). As new themes emerged, researchers revisited data sources, confirming and disconfirming themes throughout the process.

Videotape analysis. To describe variations in the degree to which teachers were implementing strategies presented in PD, the research team constructed an extensive checklist of teacher and student behaviors associated with teaching writing and writing workshop. The checklist included elements typically found in a workshop classroom such as mini-lessons, conferencing (teacher and peer), time to write, students at various places in the writing process, and author's chair. The checklist also included a list of strategies modeled over the course of the year, as well as space for the viewer to note evidence of the behaviors observed.

Researchers viewed all tapes, with 30% of the tapes viewed twice. Inter-rater reliability was established at 90% within one point for this initial level of descriptive analysis. These results were evaluated, computing a difference score for each teacher using the raw counts as indicators of possible changes in practice from fall to spring. Teachers who showed the highest difference scores were selected for the case study.

The research team viewed the selected participants' taped lessons a minimum of three times, examining specific practices teachers exhibited during their initial and final taped lessons. This data was examined for common and unique practices and charts were developed (using NVivo 8) to aid in the understanding of patterns across participants.

Interviews and surveys. Researchers transcribed and analyzed interviews and surveys. Researchers read each interview transcript and survey to develop an initial impression of the data. The transcripts were re-read and revisited as new themes emerged, confirming and disconfirming themes throughout the process. After completing the coding for all of the interviews and surveys, researchers examined the codes, grouping them into logical categories.

Quantitative data analysis. All student writing samples were scored independently of the researchers at the NWP Annual Scoring Conference using the NWP's Analytic Writing Continuum. Inter-rater reliability across all scores was 89.3%. Quantitative data in the form of six analytic scores (content development, structure, stance, fluency, diction, and conventions) and one holistic score on each pre- and post-writing sample were used to compare the writing growth of students on papers written to a prompt. Scores were analyzed using paired samples t-tests.

RESULTS

Teacher Change

An introduction to the high-adopting teachers.

Initially, the high-adopting teachers in this study appeared to have little in common. Mrs. Rogers, Mrs. Johnson, and Ms. Tate (pseudonyms) had different levels of experience, education, and exposure to professional development in writing (Table 2). The following descriptions are intended

Table 2: Participant Demographic Information

	Mrs. Rogers	Ms. Tate	Mrs. Johnson
Age (at time of study)	53	32	35
Years Taught	9	10	10
Grade Level	3	5	5
Highest Level of Education	B.A., Elementary Education	M.A., Reading	B.A., Education
National Board Certified Teacher	No	Yes	No
Prior PD Experiences in Writing	None	Write From the Beginning	4 Blocks, Working with Words

to offer a snapshot of each teacher as she presented herself at the start of the year through surveys and taped lessons.

Mrs. Rogers. Mrs. Rogers began the year apprehensive about teaching writing. In a year-end interview, she reflected, "I didn't know how to teach writing. I just kept hoping for the best." Her initial writing goals for her students, "...to increase [their] awareness of the types of writing and become comfortable using each type," seem based primarily on district- and state-mandated writing goals and standards. This focus on meeting requirements might also be a reflection of her apprehension. Mrs. Rogers' fall writing lesson on memoirs seemed to demonstrate a lack of confidence in writing instruction. Mrs. Rogers began with a read-aloud, Cynthia Rylant's *When the Relatives Came.* After reading the entire book, she asked students if they had similar experiences to the one described. She shared a story from her childhood about relatives coming to visit and periodically asked for a show of hands as she asked students questions related to her story. After the story, students returned to their desks and began working on memoirs. Researchers noted that while Mrs. Rogers used a text that modeled the type of writing she wanted students to complete, she did not explicitly connect her instruction and student writing, nor did the instruction specifically address strategies for writing.

Mrs. Johnson. An analysis of Mrs. Johnson's initial data shows a teacher attempting to implement a process approach to writing, but the process is linear rather than the recursive process described by Flower and Hayes (1981). Furthermore, she seems focused on editing over other aspects of writing. Mrs. Johnson's goals for her students as writers included "... fully develop[ing] a piece from pre-write to final" and "improv[ing] their editing" (beginning of year survey). Her attention to editing and to a "lock step" version of writing is evident in her fall video, which focused on conferencing with a student writer (John). Only Mrs. Johnson and John are heard speaking, while the other students work quietly at their desks. She began the conference asking John to read his work to her and stopped him several times to ask a question about his conventions: "Do you think you need a comma there, where you paused?"; "Remember how we talked about paragraphs. What do you need to do when you start a paragraph?" She also asked John questions about his piece, focusing on elements of his story that could confuse the reader. After a brief discussion, she and John agreed he might return to this piece later if he would like and he returned to his desk. As he walked across the room, John moved his stick on the writing process chart on the board from conferencing to revision, despite the fact that he was still not finished writing the first draft of his story.

Ms. Tate. Unlike Mrs. Rogers, Ms. Tate was confident in her ability to teach writing, noting on her beginning of the year survey that she saw herself as a writing teacher. Her goals for her students demonstrate a long-term view of students as writers: "….to enjoy writing and be motivated to expand their writing," as well as "read for enjoyment," "explore new ideas," and "share their writing." In Ms. Tate's fall lesson, it was evident that writing instruction was a part of the regular classroom routine. At the start of the lesson, which focused on identifying parts of speech, students took notes in their "writer's notebooks," copying definitions from the whiteboard for the parts of speech. The directions for this note taking were specific.

> In your table of contents, on the line below page 51, where it says 52, write parts of speech. Once you have written that, turn to page 52. It should be right past the writing rubrics we put in there. On the top of the page, I would like for you to write part of speech. That's going to be your heading for the top of this page, parts of speech. So the first thing I want you to write down is nouns. Nouns are your people, places, and things.

Students were encouraged to offer examples, with each part of speech discussed by the group. For practice, students completed an activity similar to Mad Libs as a group, with students providing nouns, verbs, adverbs, and adjectives at random and laughing at the resultant paragraph. Ms. Tate ended her lesson by offering students books with lists of examples of parts of speech to consult when writing. While it was obvious from the students' "writers notebooks" that they regularly engaged in this sort of instruction, it was not clear how much students actually wrote and if the teacher explicitly tied her instruction to what students were writing.

Shared practices.

Although these three teachers started the year with different styles of instruction, by year-end they shared many practices modeled through the PD sessions.

Traits as common vocabulary. Each high-adopter incorporated the language of the traits of writing into her everyday instruction and discussions of writing. These traits (ideas, organization, sentence fluency, voice, word choice, conventions, and presentation) were a cornerstone of the PD offered. Specific writing strategies (improving sentence variety, for example, to improve sentence fluency) and literature models were shared. The teachers referred repeatedly to the language of the traits in the spring lesson tapes, the interviews, and on the surveys. For example, Mrs. Johnson's spring lesson focused on developing voice in writing through the use of dialogue.

Mrs. Rogers expressed strong feelings about the effectiveness of a common vocabulary for students and teachers alike in her year-end interview:

> Having a set vocabulary for the various writing traits has been the most powerful thing for the whole PD. I was thinking about my own child. He will hear the same terminology used throughout each grade level…That's probably us, coming together as a unit to understand those traits more thoroughly, being able to empower the children to listen for a particular trait in a particular piece of writing, that was fabulous.

Focused instruction explicitly connected to student writing. Just as a common vocabulary emerged for discussing writing, mini-lessons became more focused for each of the high-adopters. In the fall tapes, the connection between instruction and writing was not always evident. For example, Ms. Tate worked with her students on the definitions and examples of parts of speech for 17 minutes, but there was no explicit connection made between this information and their own writing.

By spring, mini-lessons were short, focused, and had a clear connection to student writing in the classroom. Ms. Tate's spring lesson offers an example of this change. She began with reading excerpts aloud from a novel the class had been reading together. Students wrote down phrases they thought demonstrated effective word choice by the author. After each short excerpt was read aloud, students shared their phrases, explaining how the phrase they chose demonstrated effective word choice. The class then discussed the overall impact of word choice on the book. Ms. Tate put a piece of her own writing on the overhead and the class helped her revise it, focusing on choosing the right words for that text, particularly strong verbs. The mini-lesson again lasted 17 minutes. Students chose a piece from their writing folders and focused on word choice as they revised and/or composed. Ms. Tate conferenced with individual students, focusing her comments on strengthening their pieces through effective word choice, again using strong verbs. This continuity and focus is markedly different from the lesson at the start of the year.

Focused mini-lessons left students more time for writing in each classroom, as well as offered students concrete strategies for improving their writing. Students were consistently asked to immediately use what they learned in the lesson in their own writing.

Use of authentic models. Studying models of good writing can be effective in improving student writing (Graham & Perin, 2007) and mentor texts, defined as published texts used as models to a teach specific writing skills, were used each time TCs modeled strategies. The high-adopters used mentor texts extensively in their lessons and talked about the value of the book suggestions offered through the PD in their end-of-year interviews. In the spring tapes, all three high-adopting teachers started the mini-lesson with a mentor text and led students through a brief analysis of the mentor text as part of the lesson. For example, Mrs. Johnson read a picture book aloud to her students, specifically asking them to pay attention to the author's voice and the techniques used to develop that voice. She remarked in her interview that students needed to see "…examples, examples…so they were learning from each other, and the best way to do it is with published work, you know? Things that other people have done."

Evidence of workshop approach to writing instruction. Each high-adopting teacher demonstrated a clear shift to a workshop approach to instruction. In spring lesson tapes, we see components of writers workshop in place: focused mini-lessons, students at different places in the writing process, student-teacher conferencing, peer conferencing, revision, writing instruction based on student needs, students sharing their work, and writing as a recursive process. Seating was re-arranged in all the high-adopters rooms to facilitate student collaboration, which has been shown to have a strong effect on student writing (Graham & Perin, 2007). These shifts provided evidence that high-adopting teachers embraced a workshop approach.

Shared dispositions. Given their differences, what led these teachers to adopt the PD practices so readily? Several themes emerged in our analysis of the data regarding the shared dispositions of the high-adopting teachers.

Positive attitude toward PD. Each of the high-adopters expressed a positive attitude toward PD, which ultimately translated to positive attitudes about writing by both teachers and students. In her year-end interview, Ms. Tate remarked, "All the PD we had at Piper Elementary (pseudonym) was great. They [sic] helped me in having ideas for students who had writer's block. There were a lot of good ideas for books to use." Mrs. Johnson attached a list to her spring survey, highlighting all the sessions she had attended for the PD program, and wrote, "I used a lot of the ideas presented in my classroom (toys, drawing) and found new read-alouds to share with my students." Mrs. Rogers, describing what led her students to write, noted, "I didn't do anything…it was the culmination of all this (referring to the PD)" (year-end interview). Each teacher seemed to feel she gained useful practices from the PD that she incorporated into her daily practices.

Value student engagement. Prior to the PD, all three teachers expressed a belief in the importance of student engagement in writing instruction. For example, Ms. Tate noted she wanted her students to enjoy writing, be motivated to write independently, and share their writing. Mrs. Johnson reported that she used a combination of student interests and needs to determine the direction of her instruction and encouraged students to be active in tracking their own progress through an interactive writing process chart on the wall. Mrs. Rogers noted she wanted to set up a writing center for her students in the coming year and allow students to work as individuals and groups on pieces of writing. Although these teachers were at different places in the implementation of a writer's workshop at the start of the year, they all valued student engagement.

Thoughtful practitioners. Each of the high-adopting teachers was able to think about her own practices with a critical eye and make changes as needed in her classroom. Mrs. Rogers started the year with an intensely structured classroom and little time for students to write in class. She noted in her year-end interview:

> I was like everybody else, being convention-driven, with a little bit of the ideas and organization… It was hard, you know, from a time standpoint. I kept thinking, 'I'm never going to get his done…how will I ever fit it in?' Now I can't imagine not taking the time [to write].

She remarked that the change in her instruction this year meant a change in student learning:

> But now, they all know what makes a great piece. It takes time, but that's the other thing helping them to see that this isn't something that I need you to sit down and do in thirty minutes and be done with it. That was the approach I had taken before.

High-adopters were able to look at their own practices, make decisions about their classroom instruction, and develop ideas for improving instruction in the future.

Willingness to change. Finally, the high-adopters in this study were willing to change their classroom practices. Of the three high-adopters, Mrs. Rogers provided the most dramatic example of shift in practice. At the beginning of the year, Mrs. Rogers started with the least background in writing instruction and seemed the most uncomfortable with teaching writing. Her instructional coach described the changes she saw:

> Mrs. Rogers was the teacher I saw the most change in. "You've got standards… you've got all this you've got to cover. I don't know how I'm going to do that." At the beginning of the year, [the principal] kept shaking her head and saying, "She's not getting it. She won't be able to do it." And then she was the one that we saw the biggest shift—from over here to way over here….huge, just huge attitude changes, changes in how [she] manages her classroom, changes in what you see in the classroom.

In her year-end interview, Mrs. Rogers described incorporating ideas she had seen in the PD into her classroom practice and her new philosophy for instructional planning: "It won't be me going, 'Well, how I am going to do that?' It will be all about using what I've learned and what works with my students."

This willingness by high-adopters to try new instructional approaches in their classrooms may have led to the shifts in practice captured in the spring taped lessons and also witnessed by their instructional coach and principal.

STUDENT OUTCOMES

Instructional Changes Foster Increased Student Learning

For each of the three teachers selected for this case study, we examined student growth in writing, as measured by a pre-post sample. Table 3 illustrates the range of student outcomes demonstrated by students in these teachers' classrooms and Table 4 shows the scores of these teachers as compared to three low-adopting teachers in the study. The students in the three high-adopters' classrooms demonstrated the highest mean improvement rates in their school. Mrs. Rogers' students showed the highest mean improvement rate for the entire study, with one section of Mrs. Johnson's classes representing the second highest mean improvement and Ms. Tate's students demonstrating the third highest mean improvement rate. The second section of Mrs. Johnson's class had an average mean improvement, when compared with the rest of the school. For clarity, the mean improvement scores for teachers teaching multiple sections have been combined in Table 5.

DISCUSSION AND IMPLICATIONS

In an era of accountability, where empirical evidence of student outcomes is seen as the gold standard, the lack of studies linking writing instruction and student outcomes leaves teachers without compelling evidence to support their practices or little evidence to suggest change could be beneficial for their students. Within this environment, this study sought to examine if teachers who chose to implement new teaching practices in their writing classrooms, including those typically seen in a workshop approach to instruction, had common dispositions. Furthermore, we sought to examine which practices were adopted and if their adoption related to improvement in student writing performance.

Table 3: Mean Scores for All Criteria, by Teacher

	Mean Scores								
	Rogers n=20			Tate n=18			Johnson n=16		
Criterion	Pre	Post	Mean Improvement	Pre	Post	Mean Improvement	Pre	Post	Mean Improvement
Holistic	2.45	3.85	1.400	3.222	4.25	.917	3.133	4.414	1.281
Content	2.475	3.975	1.600	3.069	4.208	1.028	3.361	4.611	1.250
Structure	2.275	3.825	1.550	2.875	4.056	1.139	2.900	4.181	1.281
Stance	2.4	3.875	1.475	3.208	4.319	1.118	3.233	4.389	1.156
Sentence Fluency	2.475	3.65	1.175	3.208	4.278	.941	3.173	4.323	1.150
Diction	2.475	3.925	1.450	3.264	4.417	1.278	3.200	4.325	1.125
Conventions	2.55	3.825	1.275	3.181	4.111	.889	3.167	4.386	1.219

Table 4: Mean Scores for All Criteria, Low Adopters vs. High Adopters

	Low Adopters Mean Improvement Scores			High Adopters Mean Improvement Scores			
	Teacher 1 n=15	Teacher 2 n=20	Teacher 3 n=19	Rogers n=20	Tate n=18	Johnson n=16	Teacher 1 n=19
Criterion							
Holistic	.267	.250	.605	1.400	.917	1.281	.605
Content	.333	.395	.737	1.600	1.028	1.250	.737
Structure	.200	.278	.395	1.550	1.139	1.281	.395
Stance	.567	.444	.444	1.475	1.118	1.156	.444
Sentence Fluency	.633	.447	.639	1.175	.941	1.150	.639
Diction	.400	.556	.778	1.450	1.278	1.125	.778
Conventions	.333	.395	.774	1.275	.889	1.219	.974

Table 5: Mean Scores for All Criteria, by Teacher, All Sections

	Mean Scores								
	Rogers n=20			Tate n=45			Johnson n=36		
Criterion	Pre	Post	Mean Improvement	Pre	Post	Mean Improvement	Pre	Post	Mean Improvement
Holistic	2.45	3.85	1.400	3.306	4.333	1.028	3.292	4.014	.722
Content	2.475	3.975	1.600	3.250	4.231	1.981	3.361	3.972	.611
Structure	2.275	3.825	1.550	3.000	4.065	1.065	2.958	3.708	.750
Stance	2.4	3.875	1.475	3.278	4.333	1.056	3.278	4.000	.722
Sentence Fluency	2.475	3.65	1.175	3.258	4.370	1.111	3.364	4.139	.775
Diction	2.475	3.925	1.450	3.278	4.463	1.185	3.403	3.972	.569
Conventions	2.55	3.825	1.275	3.306	4.315	1.009	3.319	4.000	.681

When compared to teachers who chose not to adopt the strategies modeled in the year-long PD or adopted fewer of the strategies, the high-adopting teachers in this study emerged as having a unique combination of dispositions. Although there were low-adopting teachers who valued student engagement in writing instruction, these teachers did not also demonstrate the habits of thoughtful practitioners, possess positive attitudes toward PD, and demonstrate a willingness to change their instructional practices. It was these four dispositions in combination that high-adopters shared; while other participants in the study may have exhibited one or more of these dispositions, only the high-adopters exhibited all four in combination.

For Mrs. Rogers, her desire to engage her students led her to implement a more student-focused approach to instruction through the writer's workshop. Mrs. Rogers was also ready for change; as a writing teacher, she was apprehensive and felt she lacked the knowledge and skills she needed to teach effectively, describing herself as "hoping for the best" each year when it came to writing instruction. The PD seemed to offer her a structure, model, and the vocabulary she needed to teach writing and effectively communicate with her students. She demonstrated, according to her instructional coach and principal, the greatest shift in her practices in the school and also had the greatest gains in student improvement between her pre- and post-prompted student writing samples.

For other teachers, like Ms. Tate and Mrs. Johnson, elements of a workshop approach to writing were evident through their initial surveys and/or taped lessons, but they had not fully implemented this approach in their classrooms. Each teacher expressed her desire to improve her students' writing and expressed an openness to modify her approach to instruction at the start of the year; these dispositions were followed by shifts in instructional practices. Unlike Mrs. Rogers, who was unfamiliar with a workshop approach to instruction and started the year with a teacher-centered instructional model, Ms. Tate and Mrs. Johnson likely experienced less shift in their approach to teaching writing, but rather experienced a shift in practices that allowed them to better enact that approach in the writing classroom. Each moved to focused, brief mini-lessons, in which students were taught a writing strategy and asked to directly apply the strategy to their writing. Like Mrs. Rogers, both teachers noted that this structure and the use of common vocabulary to discuss writing facilitated instruction.

This case study does not provide causal evidence linking specific practices with improved student outcomes, but it does lay the groundwork for further study of the effects of practices common in a writing workshop on student writing. A limitation of this study is the limited number of data points for student writing. With only two samples from each student (pre- and post-prompted writing scores) and the limited number of students in the study (n=275 school-wide, n=101 for case study teachers), these outcomes cannot be generalized. When studied in conjunction with previous work citing effective teaching practices on student writing (e.g., Langer, 2000; Applebee & Langer, 2011), this study may offer further empirical support for identified instructional practices that are clearly tied to improved student writing.

Although we cannot assert causality, we saw connections between students' writing improvement scores and the structure within the high-adopters classrooms. We defined structure as having a consistent approach to writing instruction with a predictable daily structure. For example, Mrs. Rogers, the most structured of the three high-adopters, described running her classroom as a daily workshop during her 60 minutes of writing time. She consistently began with a mini-lesson incorporating a read aloud, followed by time for students to write, peer conference, and/or teacher conference, and concluded with time to share. This structure was in place and evident in her spring tape. Mrs. Rogers' students demonstrated the greatest gains. Ms. Tate's class was also a structured environment, with a typical writing block starting with a mini-lesson, incorporating literature as a model in some way, modeling for the students, giving the students time to write and peer conference, conferencing with students, and offering time to share. Mrs. Johnson offered the most variety in how her class was structured on a daily basis, sometimes skipping a mini-lesson in favor of having students immediately write. It appears having a predictable structure within the workshop may affect student improvement. Skipping the mini-lesson from time-to-time may also have resulted in students receiving less explicit writing strategy instruction in Mrs. Johnson's class, which could have affected the results given the importance of writing strategy instruction on student writing (Graham & Perin, 2007). Further research is needed to begin to examine the impact of structure on student writers.

This study represents the experiences of three teachers in a particular yearlong PD program and the findings here are not intended to be generalizable to other populations. Our intention is to offer a more complete picture of the dispositions shared by teachers who adopted practices demonstrated through a yearlong PD program in writing, as well as the practices they chose to implement.

This research also further demonstrates the complexity of delivering successful PD to teachers within a school, as evidenced by change in teacher practice and philosophy. Earlier research suggests that authentic PD is both voluntary and based on teachers' self-identified needs and interests (Avalos, 2011; Doolittle, Sudeck, & Rattigan, 2008; Flint, Zisook, & Fisher, 2011; Swars, Meyers, Mays, & Lack, 2009). Although teachers throughout the school embraced the PD offered, it is clear that for the high-adopting teachers, improvement in writing instruction was a compelling concern in their classrooms. Examining teachers who have demonstrated shifts in their practice, choosing to incorporate the workshop model in their classrooms, offers insights into possible factors that influence implementation of PD in writing. Finally, our research suggests that a workshop approach may be an effective way to prepare students for high-stakes testing, as evidenced by the improvement in students' prompted writing scores. Students in the high-adopting teachers' classrooms outperformed their peers within their school, suggesting that the practices modeled in the PD program and adopted by the teachers influenced student writing achievement. Again, this study suggests future research examining the relationship between writing strategies employed in classrooms and student writing achievement, to look for possible relationships between the types of strategies incorporated and student achievement in writing.

REFERENCES

Applebee, A. N., & Langer, J. A. (2011). A snapshot of writing instruction in middle schools and high schools. *English Journal, 100,* 14-17.

Atwell, N. (1987). *In the middle: Writers reading and learning with adolescents.* Portsmouth, NH: Boynton-Cook.

Avalos, B. (2011). Teacher PD in teaching and teacher education over ten years. *Teaching and Teacher Education, 27,* 10-20. doi:10.1016/j.tate.2010.08.007

Blau, S., Cabe, R. H., & Whitney, A. (2006). *Evaluating IIMPaC: Teacher and student outcomes through a PD program in the teaching of writing.* Retrieved from http://www.nwp.org/cs/public/print/resource/2599

Calkins, L. (1994). *The art of teaching writing.* Portsmouth, NH: Heinemann.

Calkins, L., Ehrenworth, M, & Lehman, C. (2012). *Pathways to the Common Core: Accelerating achievement.* Portsmouth, NH: Heinemann.

Campos, A. & Peach, R. (2006). *The impact of the New York City Writing Project: Teacher and student outcomes of a PD model for improving the teaching of writing.* Retrieved from http://www.nwp.org/cs/public/print/resource/2596

Darling-Hammond, L., & McLaughlin, M. W. (1995). Policies that support PD in an era of reform. *Phi Delta Kappan, 76,* 597-604.

Darling-Hammond, L., & Richardson, N. (2009). Teacher learning: What matters? *Educational Leadership, 66,* 46-53.

Desimone, L.M. (2009). Improving impact studies of teachers' PD: Toward better conceptualizations and measures. *Educational Researcher, 38,* 181-199. doi:10.3102/0013189X08331140

Desimone, L. M. (2011). A primer on effective PD. *Phi Delta Kappan, 92,* 68-71.

Doolittle, G., Sudeck, M., & Rattigan, P. (2008). Creating professional learning communities: The work of PD schools. *Theory Into Practice, 47,* 303-310. doi:10.1080/00405840802329276

Ellis, L., & Marsh, J. (2007). *Getting started: The reading-writing workshop, grades 4-8.* Portsmouth, NH: Heinemann.

Flint, A., Zisook, K., & Fisher, T. R. (2011). Not a one-shot deal: Generative PD among experienced teachers. *Teaching and Teacher Education: An International Journal Of Research and Studies, 27,* 1163-1169.

Flower, L., & Hayes, J. R. (1981). A cognitive process theory of writing. *College Composition and Communication, 32,* 365-387.

Garet, M. S., Porter, A. C., Desimone, L., Birman, B. F., & Yoon, K. S. (2001). What makes PD effective? Results from a national sample of teachers. *American Educational Research Journal, 38,* 915-945.

Graham, S. (2006). Strategy instruction and the teaching of writing: A meta-analysis. In C.A. MacArthur, S. Graham, & J. Fitzgerald (Eds.) *Handbook of writing research* (pp. 187–207). New York, NY: Guilford.

Graham, S., & Perin, D. (2007). *Writing next: Effective strategies to improve writing of adolescents in middle and high schools – A report to Carnegie Corporation of New York.* Washington, DC: Alliance for Excellent Education.

Langer, J. A. (2000). Beating the odds: Teaching middle and high school students to read and write well. *National Research Center on English Learning and Achievement.* Retrieved from http://cela.Albany.edu/eie2/index.html

Lave, J., & Wenger, W. (1991). *Situated learning: Legitimate peripheral participation.* Cambridge, MA: Cambridge University Press.

Lieberman, A. (1996). Creating intentional learning communities. *Educational Leadership, 54,* 51–55.

National Commission on Writing (2005, July). *Writing: A powerful message from state government.* Retrieved from http://www.collegeboard.com/prod_downloads/writingcom/powerful-message-from-state.pdf

National Governors Association Center for Best Practices and Council of Chief State School Offices (2010). *Common Core State Standards English Language Arts.* National Governors Association Center for Best Practices and Council of Chief State School Offices: Washington DC.

National Writing Project (2010). *About NWP.* Retrieved from http://www.nwp.org/cs/public/print/doc/about.csp

Rogoff, B. (1990). *Apprenticeship in thinking: Cognitive development in social context.* New York, NY: Oxford University Press.

Scott, C., & Sutton, R. E. (2009). Emotions and change during PD for teachers: A mixed methods study. *Journal of Mixed Methods Research, 3,* 151-171.

Singer, N. R., & Scollay, D. (2006). *Increasing student achievement in writing through teacher inquiry: An evaluation of PD impact.* Retrieved from http://www.nwp.org/cs/public/print/resource/2583

Strauss, J., & Corbin, A. C. (1990). *Basics of qualitative research: Grounded theory procedures and techniques.* Thousand Oaks, CA: Sage.

Swain, S. S., Graves, R. L., & Morse, D. (2006). *The effect of Mississippi Writing/ Thinking Institute PD on the writing achievement of ninth graders.* Retrieved from http://www.nwp.org/cs/public/print/resource/2597

Swars, S. L., Meyers, B., Mays, L. C., & Lack, B. (2009). A two-dimensional model of teacher retention and mobility: Classroom teachers and their university partners take a closer look at a vexing problem. *Journal of Teacher Education, 60,* 168-183.

Tashakkori, A., & Teddlie, C. (2003). *Mixed methods in social and behavioral research.* Thousand Oaks, CA: Sage.

Troia, G. A., Lin, S., Cohen, S., & Monroe, B. W. (2011). A year in the writing workshop. *The Elementary School Journal, 112,* 155-182.

Yin, R. K. (2009). *Case study research, design and methods* (4th ed.). Thousand Oaks, CA: Sage.

Professional Development as the Study of Self: Using Self-Knowledge to Mediate the Act of Teaching

Deborah MacPhee
Illinois State University

"The majority of the conversations that you and I have had are so deep rooted now that they're meaningful and I don't think that I will ever forget them. They have been life changing. They have been professionally defining for me."

The preceding remark was made during a final reflective interview by a teacher who participated in a year-long multiple case study that examined relationships between teachers' identities, beliefs, and practices. I had been a literacy coach for five years. Through systematic reflection on my experiences, I theorized that to be an effective coach, I needed to focus not on teachers' practices, but on their beliefs. Across a year, I engaged three teachers in life history interviews. I conducted classroom tours, classroom observations, and debriefing interviews with each teacher. I systematically analyzed all of the data and returned to each teacher for a final reflective interview.

Each teacher, during her final reflective interview, acknowledged that the process of considering teaching practices through a lens of self-knowledge was a powerful form of professional development. I was intrigued. The goal of the study was not to engage teachers in professional development, but because each teacher acknowledged that her participation in the study, specifically the final reflective interviews, challenged her professionally, it made sense to take a closer look at the interviews in this new light. To do this, I systematically examined the final reflective interviews from the original study asking: How does the process of using self-knowledge to mediate the act of teaching support teachers in their personal and professional development?

Through my analysis, I identified patterns across the participants' interviews that suggested there were specific ways of thinking about identity and teaching that lead to deep personal and professional reflection, and that these common ways of thinking support individual growth trajectories. In this article, I explain the theoretical frame from which I approached the data, describe the methods I used to analyze the final reflective interviews, and share findings that I argue have implications for teacher professional development.

LITERATURE REVIEW

Parker Palmer (1998) argues:

> Teaching, like any truly human activity, emerges from one's inwardness, for better or worse. As I teach, I project the condition of my soul onto my students, my subject, and our way of being together. The entanglements I experience in the classroom are often no more or less than the convolutions of my inner life. Viewed from this angle, teaching holds a mirror to the soul. If I am willing to look in that mirror and not run from what I see, I have a chance to gain self-knowledge – and knowing myself is as crucial to good teaching as knowing my students and my subject. (p. 2)

Palmer captures the meaning of identity in relation to teaching. He acknowledges that we are our identities and that "we teach who we are" (p. 2). Yet, relatively little time is spent examining how teaching influences identity development and how identities shape teaching practices. Overwhelmingly, identity research in the field of education focuses on the tensions faced by pre-service and early career teachers as they move from being students to becoming teachers. Largely, these studies are situated in pre-service teacher education programs and explore methods such as narrative inquiry and the use of metaphor to bring awareness of existing identities and construct new identities.

Richie and Wilson (2000), for example, used Bruner's (1986) idea that narrative is a way of knowing as a strategy for developing pre-service English teachers' awareness of their identities. They engaged their students in narrative inquiry over multiple semesters of their undergraduate teacher education program. The researchers believed that through narrative, students could reconsider and reconstruct their experiences in ways that would allow them to take a critical stance toward teaching. Ritchie and Wilson (2000) concluded that the pre-service teachers uncovered their unspoken assumptions, examined contradictions between pedagogies and experiences, integrated examined experiences into working conceptions of literacy and learning, and complicated their understandings of teaching.

Alsup (2006) also used narrative as a strategy for developing identity awareness and constructing new identities. She engaged six pre-service English education students in a two-year study of their evolving identities. The study was designed to investigate Alsup's hypothesis that constructing a professional identity was central in the process of becoming an effective teacher. She engaged participants in multiple discourses and identified five types of narratives that described the students' initial attempts at connecting multiple subjectivities to gain self-knowledge: narratives of tension, narratives of experience, narratives of the embodiment of teacher identity, narratives about family and friends, and borderland narratives. Alsup described borderland discourse as a complex, rich, context-specific discourse. Alsup (2006) argued that:

> ...within borderland discourse there is evidence of contact between disparate personal and professional subjectivities, which can lead to the eventual integration of these multiple subject positions. Such integration through discourse is vital for the developing teacher who must negotiate conflicting subject positions and ideologies while creating a professional self. (p. 6)

Much less frequently, and typically in the context of graduate coursework, researchers have engaged practicing teachers in exploring their identities through the use of metaphor. Tobin (1990), for example, conducted two case studies in which he used metaphor with practicing teachers to help them make sense of their roles, understand how belief sets were associated with specific roles and metaphors, and how new metaphors could be constructed to help reconceptualize roles and instructional practices. Tobin found that, by acknowledging conflicting metaphors, teachers were able to construct new metaphors that supported the rejection of previously held beliefs.

Although using identity to mediate learning has become more prevalent in pre-service teacher education, professional development for teachers rarely includes models of self-study. In fact, even though it is widely accepted that professional development should be anchored in teachers' reality, sustained over time, and collaborative (Chan & Pang, 2006; Richardson, 2003), the short-term transmission model is still acknowledged as the dominant approach to in-service professional development for teachers (Richardson, 2003). Musanti & Pence (2010) argue that more research is needed on professional development contexts that reflect what is already widely accepted, but rarely implemented. This study of self as a context for teacher learning and growth responds to this need for more research.

THEORETICAL FRAME

I understand identity as a socially constructed view of self and world that is enacted through social positioning (Davies and Harré, 1990; Gee, 1996) and influenced by issues of power that are constructed through discourse in social contexts (Lewis, Enciso & Moje, 2007). I distinguish between an internal, or conceptual identity, and an external, or enacted identity, in order to acknowledge both the personal and social nature of identity development (MacPhee, 2008). In my own theory of identity, I define conceptual identities as the patterns of interpreting self and world that are grounded in one's life experiences and enacted identities as the language and actions used by individuals in social contexts. Hence, individuals enact contextually mediated identities that are available within a continuously evolving view of self and world (conceptual identity).

The relationship between conceptual and enacted identities is dynamic, which is sustained by the processes of recognition and interpretation (Gee, 2000; MacPhee, 2008). As individuals participate in social contexts, they are recognized by others, as certain kinds of people. These recognitions are interpreted by individuals and become part of their view of self and world. Through these processes of recognition and interpretation, an individual can take up or reject any number of identities available within a fluid view of self and world.

METHODS

Participants

The participants in this study were three elementary school teachers from two Southeastern school districts. The teachers were selected using purposeful sampling (Merriam, 2009). The selection criteria included teachers' willingness to participate in the study and diversity among the participants with regard to teaching position and background. Carla, Mary, and Sarah (All names are pseudonyms.) accepted my invitation to participate in the study. I had established coaching relationships with each teacher prior to their participation in the research study. Carla was a self-contained second grade teacher. At the time of the study, Carla was in her eighth year of teaching in a rural elementary school. Prior to becoming a classroom teacher, Carla was a guidance counselor in the same elementary school. Mary, the youngest participant in the study, was a self-contained fourth grade teacher. She was in her sixth year of teaching, but unlike Carla, whose experience was all in the same school, Mary had taught second through sixth grades in low income and affluent school districts in both western and eastern regions of the United States. Sarah, the oldest participant in the study, was a K-5 resource teacher. At the time of the study, she had taught for eight years, although not consecutively. In a span of more than thirty years, Sarah earned multiple degrees and tried out numerous professions including speech pathologist, Title I reading teacher, lawyer, and special education/resource teacher.

I positioned myself within the study as a participant researcher. Because of my relationship with the participants, I believed it would be impossible to separate my roles as coach and researcher. As I collected data through life history, debriefing, and reflective interviews, I was at the same time engaging the participants in coaching conversations. Throughout the study, I recognized how my role as a researcher/coach who was positioning the teachers to consider their conceptual and enacted identities within their individual teaching contexts might influence their responses. To minimize a sense on the teachers' part that they needed to respond in a certain way, I discussed issues of power and positioning with each participant during the consent process and prior to each interview session. As part of the consent process, I articulated my view of a literacy coach as someone who engages with teachers to consider the relationship between their beliefs and practices as opposed to someone who makes judgments and recommends changes. Before each interview, as a form of member-checking, I encouraged the participants to make me aware when/if they felt I was making judgments during the research process. I remained open to additional discussion of my roles during the interviews and, as these discussions occurred, they became part of the data. I used open ended questions in all interviews and conducted all interviews in a location chosen by the teacher.

Data Sources

Data sources for this analysis center on the recorded and transcribed final reflective interviews from the larger study. During the final reflective interviews, I invited the teachers to respond to and discuss artifacts related to their conceptual identities and teaching practices. Conceptual identity models and teaching vignettes were the artifacts used to guide the interviews. I constructed a conceptual identity model for each participant in the larger study. I began with open coding on all data sources for each participant. I organized each participant's data in a separate spreadsheet that included columns for codes, participant number, data file, data sample, and line references. I conducted two peer debriefing sessions during the open coding phase of the analysis as to not limit the scope of the data and to remain open to multiple perspectives. The open coding produced an extensive number of data samples, as shown in Table 1, from which clear patterns that represented the participants' views of self and world emerged.

Next, I began a cross case analysis through which I identified psychological, social, and cognitive themes across participants. These themes were incorporated into each participant's unique conceptual identity model (see Appendix A). Because, by definition, a conceptual identity is ever-evolving, it is impossible to construct a complete representation of one's conceptual identity. The models I constructed, therefore, were grounded in the data collected during a ten-month data collection period.

Table 1: Summary of Open Coding

	Data Samples	Codes	Patterns
Participant 1	389	88	13
Participant 2	225	65	11
Participant 3	209	41	16

Table 2: Summary of Cross Case Analysis

Patterns	References in the Data	P1	P2	P3
Articulating explicit and tacit beliefs	12	5	4	3
Making connections between conceptual and enacted identities	42	13	15	14
Recognizing Conflicts	16	2	3	11
Questioning beliefs and practice	12	4	5	3

I crafted teaching vignettes from field notes taken during classroom observations and debriefing interviews that were conducted immediately following observations. There were two parts to the final reflective interview. In the first part I shared with the teachers what I had constructed as their conceptual identity and asked for their response. In the second part, I invited the teachers to read the teaching vignettes. I asked them if they felt the vignettes accurately captured instructional events and if they would talk to me about the relationship they saw (or did not see) between their acknowledged conceptual identities and their confirmed enacted identities.

Data Analysis

To make sense of how the process of examining conceptual and enacted identities supported the teachers' professional development, I listened to and transcribed the recorded interviews and wrote analytical memos about the participants' personal and professional growth. When I approached the transcripts to begin a more formal analysis using QSR International's NVivo 9 software (2010), I asked: What happened during the final reflective interviews that positioned the teachers to view the experience as powerful professional development? I performed an open coding with this question in mind. As I coded the data, patterns related to my question began to emerge. Some patterns that emerged from the initial open coding were *questioning practice, acknowledging conflicts, exploring possibilities, resisting an ascribed identity*, and *bringing tacit beliefs to the surface*. After the initial open coding, I read within each code and wrote memos about how the codes related to one another. Through this process I collapsed, renamed, deleted, and added codes to acknowledge patterns and relationships in the data. For example, the codes *negotiating practice* and *acknowledging conflicts* were collapsed into a new code—*recognizing conflicts*. Through the within code work, I created a new coding scheme that consisted of twelve codes (see Appendix B). I returned to the interviews to recode the data using the new coding scheme. Finally, I looked across the participants to identify the patterns that were present for all three participants, as shown in Table 2.

FINDINGS: FROM ONE PROCESS TO THREE PERSONALLY RELEVANT OUTCOMES

The findings revealed four ways of thinking about identity and teaching that were common across participants in the process of examining conceptual and enacted identities. All three teachers articulated explicit and tacit beliefs, made connections between conceptual and enacted identities, recognized conflicts, and questioned beliefs and practices. Although the participants shared common ways of thinking during their final reflective interviews, the personal nature of the experience positioned them to follow their own unique professional development trajectories.

SELF-KNOWLEDGE AS A MEDIATING FACTOR IN TEACHING

Through the process of examining conceptual and enacted identities, the teachers came to know and see themselves and their contexts in new ways. They articulated beliefs that, in some cases, they had not explicitly acknowledged before. The act of making beliefs explicit compelled the teachers to make connections and notice conflicts between their conceptual and enacted identities. These connections allowed them to see themselves in new ways, thus positioning them to take up new identities. Moreover, recognizing conflicts brought about cognitive dissonance, which created space for new learning and further personal and professional development.

Articulating explicit and tacit beliefs. As the teachers used the patterns from their conceptual identity models to reflect on their teaching vignettes, they named some of their beliefs about teaching and learning. The manner in which they articulated beliefs varied and impacted the participants in different ways. For example, Carla discussed a classroom vignette in which she, upon returning from spring break, decided to let students choose where they wanted to sit in the classroom. She stated, "I was doing that based on my belief and knowledge that learning is social and if they chose to sit with people they believed would make for better conversation with each other, then I wanted them to do that." In this quotation, Carla articulated a belief that explicitly guided her practice. She was making an intentional decision based on an explicit belief, positioning herself as one who aligns beliefs and practices and solidifying that view of self within the context of her classroom.

In contrast, after reading a vignette in which she created space in a read aloud discussion for a quiet student, Mary, more tentatively stated:

> I guess that ties into that same child because I think of Micah, who I have in my classroom this year, who has really great comments, but sometimes can't speak up over the louder ones. So I do think that that's my responsibility to notice when he's trying to say something and bring that up.

Mary was making connections between past and present classroom experiences to begin to see herself as the kind of person who advocated for her students, so their voices could be heard. She used the language, "So, I do think," which indicates that she has not fully recognized herself as this person yet.

Sarah, in reviewing the patterns in her conceptual identity model, came across the pattern *Holds a deficit model for students*. She stared at the paper for several seconds, and then said, "I do hold a deficit model given my role. That's true." Although Sarah emphatically stated that she did indeed hold a deficit view, she contextualized it by associating that belief with her role as a special education resource teacher. In this moment, she seemed to recognize herself as someone who holds a deficit view, but only within the context of her teaching position.

Making connections between conceptual and enacted identities. By presenting teachers with conceptual identity models and teaching vignettes, I challenged them to confront possible views of themselves and their worlds and to consider how these views influenced their teaching practices. As the teachers reflected on the patterns in their conceptual identity models and read their teaching vignettes, they made connections that deepened their understandings of themselves in their teaching contexts. For example, Carla read a vignette about the way she angrily confronted her colleagues during a grade-level professional development session in which only she and one other teacher came prepared to discuss the agreed upon reading. She initially thought that her angry response did not match her view of herself in that context. However, when she considered her conceptual identity model, she was able to explore why she may have responded angrily:

> At that point, I didn't want to be the teacher. I wanted more of a community. I just wasn't thinking about - well, I guess part of me, now that I'm thinking deeper, that *people deserve and can thrive in a safe environment*, because I can't, or don't, choose to invest any more of my energy if I'm not recognizing investment from other people, because it's not fair. That reciprocity is very important to me at this time because I feel like I've been burned too many times. I feel like I've been the one to stick my neck out and propose and initiate and there has not been reciprocity at the same level.

Carla used a pattern from her conceptual identity model to make sense of her enacted identity in the context of a grade-level professional development session. By drawing connections between her conceptual and enacted identities, Carla positioned herself to construct new, or different, views of herself and/or her world.

Mary also made connections between her conceptual and enacted identities. After reading a vignette in which she stopped multiple times during a read aloud to discuss parts of the text with her class, Mary acknowledged an ongoing struggle with whether she should stop and talk with her students during the read aloud or wait until after the read aloud to talk. She began to make sense of her struggle when she connected to a pattern from her conceptual identity model—*values thoughts, ideas, and feelings of others*:

> I guess I'm wondering now if the reason I struggle with that entire idea of stopping during the text or waiting, maybe that's because I'm afraid I'm not valuing the thoughts, ideas and feelings during the read aloud. Maybe that's why I struggle so much waiting until the end with that idea. So, I wait to the end to talk about it, because, like, what I said here, they have the look of engagement, but maybe the reason I have such a hard time waiting until the end, and I go back and forth on that idea, is because I'm afraid I'm not valuing their ideas and their thoughts by addressing them during the read aloud.

By using her conceptual identity model to mediate her teaching practice, Mary saw herself in new ways, and thus, created space to enact new identities during read aloud time in her classroom. In addition to deepening self-understanding, the process of making explicit connections between conceptual and enacted identities simultaneously brought forth conflicts that could be recognized and questioned.

Recognizing conflicts. Initially, Carla connected her actions during the grade level professional development session with the internal belief reflected in her conceptual identity model that people *deserve and can thrive in a safe environment*. As she continued to think through and talk about her actions in that situation, she began to see her actions as more in conflict with her belief than aligned with it:

> I wasn't feeling safe because I believe that we should have a safe environment, but I wasn't creating that for myself. It's all about taking risk. I was afraid when I was talking to them like this because I was facing rejection, and I was showing them that I was upset. And normally, I'm the person that wants to work well with everybody and smooth things over.

By recognizing this conflict, Carla was able to see herself as a risk taker in the professional development event. Historically, she perceived herself as a person who goes along with the group in order to create a sense of safety. Through this reflective interview, Carla constructed a new view of herself as a risk-taker, adding to the possible identities she could enact in future situations.

Mary continued to explore her belief in *valuing the thoughts, ideas, and feelings of others* as she considered additional teaching vignettes. With the following vignette, I led Mary to see some of her practices as conflicting with her acknowledged view of self:

> *After a lesson that was planned to help students understand writing prompts, Mrs. Johnson reflected with her students. She asked, "What might you think about now that maybe you hadn't thought about before?" As the students shared, Mrs. Johnson recorded their reflections on a chart. Later, Mrs. Johnson talked about her struggle during this reflection. "While I was scribing, not really scribing but kind of, I struggled with do I put exactly what they say word for word, or do I try and make it concise? But then by trying to make it concise for the purpose of making it real visible for them, I felt like when I was making it concise, I was putting, I don't want to put words in their mouth. Like, I wanted to value what they said as they said it."*

When Mary reflected on this vignette, she recognized that representing her students' ideas authentically during class engagements was an ongoing and unresolved struggle for her. After reading this vignette, Mary said, "This year…I've started to handle this more by having children scribe, more so, trying different things there, but I'm still struggling with it." Making connections between conceptual and enacted identities enabled Mary to recognize a conflict that potentially explained why she continued to struggle with specific classroom practices.

Of the three participants, Sarah recognized the most conflict between her conceptual and enacted identities. Sarah was a special education teacher working within a highly structured curricular model. She articulated, during the interview, that she often felt pressure to enact a specific identity in her classroom that conflicted with who she viewed herself to be. She acknowledged this conflict when reflecting on a teaching vignette in which she was implementing a program that was mandated by the school district.

> Oh, this is really dealing with my conflict. I think, again, with Lana, I really struggled with an approach with Lana. I have, we have to do progress monitoring in special ed., and we have to show the kids are making progress, and we have to show that they're going through a certain number of written mastery lessons. So I always feel like I have to do that because that is my job, and that is contextual. I didn't feel like it really worked for Lana.

Here, Sarah recognized conflict on multiple levels. She recognized that the mandated program did not seem to match the needs of the student, but at the same time, it was her job to implement the mandated program. The conflicts that the participants recognized during their interviews opened the door for more intentional questioning of beliefs and practices.

Questioning beliefs and practice.

Returning to the teaching vignette in which Carla considered allowing her students to choose their own seats in the classroom (as opposed to the common practice of assigning seats), she discussed her process of questioning a practice based on an acknowledged belief:

> I was questioning that and open to, is this going to work? And I was doing this based on my belief and knowledge that learning is social. If they chose to sit with people they believed would make for better conversation with each other, then I wanted them to do that...I was going to be observing the learners.

Describing this process supported Carla in seeing herself as someone who could make changes that might better facilitate learning for her students. Seeing herself in this way may make future change easier.

Sarah, in recognizing and acknowledging fundamental conflicts between her views of self and the expectations of the mandated program she implemented, seemed to begin questioning whether she had been positioned to take up an identity more in line with her special education teaching position than with her view of self. In the following excerpt, Sarah questioned the programmatic requirements for one of her students. She juxtaposed what she believed the student needed with what the program required and acknowledged her frustration with having no control. She said:

> I don't have control over the amount of time kids spend doing reading activities. You know? The team does. And a lot of times, the child can only attend for 10 minutes, but I have them for 50 minutes. So part of it is keeping her focused on something...it goes back to, when I think deep about it, the best thing for Lana would have been for somebody every hour asking her to read, instead of asking her to read for an hour. Does that make sense? If I could have designed a plan for Lana, it would be 5 minutes, 10 minutes every hour to work on a book, or every half-hour. Does that make sense?

The process of examining conceptual and enacted identities was professionally defining for the participants, not because they shared common ways of thinking, although I would argue that the thinking they engaged in is indicative of powerful and effective professional development, but because the experience was meaningful and relevant. Each participant was immersed in an exploration of self and professional context.

PERSONALLY MEANINGFUL PROFESSIONAL DEVELOPMENT

Although the ways of thinking the participants engaged in as they examined their conceptual and enacted identities were common, an analysis of individual participant data revealed that the process as a whole was unique for each participant. Carla used the process to make explicit and address some tacit conflicts between her conceptual and enacted identities to more deeply connect core beliefs with classroom practices. She described the process as a difficult, but worthy, one. She explained:

It wasn't until you challenged me on, you know, what I'm operating from and what my conceptual framework was that started to really – there were a couple of days that I was like, uh, this is hard…This is hard. It wasn't so hard that I ever thought I don't want to keep doing this, but it's, ooh, there's some work to be done here. If I'm going to get better, I need to face this because resistance is not productive. I felt like I met a resistance, but I decided to face it. And that's where I've grown more this year than any other place.

Mary used the process to contextually situate practices in order to be more flexible in her teaching. She used patterns from her conceptually identity model to broaden her way of thinking about her classroom practice. This process came across most clearly when she connected her value for others' thoughts, ideas, and feelings with her read aloud practice. She reflected:

But I never would have thought about that before, why I struggled with that particular battle that's always been. And I don't think there's a right or a wrong way, but that balance of wanting to keep them in that engaged zone, but yet not wanting to make them feel frustrated by having their ideas and thoughts ignored in the midst of a book.

With respect to discussing a text during or after reading it aloud, Mary recognized that it didn't have to be one way or the other, and she could make that decision based on the purpose for the read aloud and her students' level of engagement. Mary was coming to understand her enacted identity as mediated by the context, which would allow her more flexibility in her teaching decisions.

Sarah began to recognize a splintered internal identity as I engaged her in the process of examining conceptual and enacted identities. She brought forth multiple conflicting identities between who she viewed herself to be in the world and who she was expected to be in her position as a special education resource teacher. At the end of the interview, she shared:

Now that I'm talking about, at the time you were asking about it, it wasn't real clear that I had such conflict about what the team was doing. Do you know what I'm saying? I mean, I sort of talked about it, but I didn't have it. And I didn't even have it very clear when I walked in here what my conflict was with these kids, but that was, that is a huge conflict. These meetings do not necessarily reflect what, in my opinion, is in the best interest of the child.

Sarah's new understanding left her in a difficult position. She later confided in me that, as a result of what she had learned about herself, she had decided to apply for a new position in the school district as a reading interventionist.

DISCUSSION

The findings from this analysis extend our knowledge about the study of self as a model for teacher development. By examining artifacts that represented internal and external identities, three teachers recognized conflicts that positioned them to construct new views of themselves and their worlds. Such views expanded the potential for the teachers to consider and enact new identities in their classrooms. As I guided the teachers in working through the process of aligning their conceptual and enacted identities, they engaged in deep personal and professional reflection and learned to see themselves in ways that created space for developing new beliefs and practices.

The use of artifacts in this study was intentional. Bartlett (2005) argues that "the ongoing process of learning and employing literacies and responding to social positioning requires critical identity work that is accomplished through engagement with cultural artefacts" (pp. 1-2). The teachers' supported engagement with the conceptual identity models and the teaching vignettes guided the critical identity work that occurred in the final reflective interviews. As the teachers examined the representations of their conceptual and enacted identities, they engaged in ways of thinking that positioned them to develop their personal and professional selves. The artifacts were a valuable part of the process of examining conceptual and enacted identities. Holland, Lachicotte, Skinner and Cain (1998) argue that individuals are "always engaged in forming identities, in producing objectifications of self-understandings that may guide subsequent behavior" (p. 4). These authors acknowledge the role of cultural artifacts in identity formation as they study identity development in culturally constructed "worlds." I have expanded on their ideas by constructing and intentionally using artifacts to support professional development in the cultural world of teaching. More research is needed to explore artifacts that will support the process of examining conceptual and enacted identities.

The findings of this study have implications for professional development, and literacy coaching. The unique process that developed for each participant in this study suggests that professional development is a personal growth experience and should be structured in ways that acknowledge and extend teachers' personal beliefs and professional knowledge. Although identity work seems to be happening in schools of education with pre-service teachers (Alsup, 2006; Ritchie & Wilson, 2000), there is little evidence that this work is happening with practicing teachers. This dearth is likely because critical identity work, like the work that was done in this study, requires a knowledgeable and supportive other (Vygotsky, 1978), which, until recently, has not been a common structure for professional development in schools. Literacy coaching, however, has great potential for supporting critical identity work, but may require a reconceptualization of the work of a coach. Because professional development is a personal growth experience, a coach's work with individual teachers must begin by supporting them in accessing their beliefs as they relate to their practices, thus creating the potential for teachers to see themselves in new ways. These new views of self will make changes in classroom practice possible. Therefore, the goals of a literacy coach must shift from supporting teachers in implementing specific practices and programs to guiding teachers through a process of acknowledging and aligning conceptual and enacted identities.

Although the data from this study represent only three teachers' experiences, the findings raise important questions about the overall goals, structures, and content of professional development for teachers. For example, how might more intentional integration of personal and professional reflection in professional development practices improve teaching and learning? While this study suggests that examining conceptual and enacted identities contributes to the personal and professional growth of teachers, further research is needed to explore relationships between personal and professional identities and their influence on teaching practices.

Finally, understanding that the process of examining conceptual and enacted identities supports the recognition of tensions between internal and external aspects of identity and creates space for developing new views of self and world has significant implications in a time of educational reform. As professional educators are faced with new curriculum standards, instructional programs, and expectations from policy makers, a professional development process that initiates new ways of thinking and acting with regard to learning and teaching has the potential to positively impact reform efforts.

REFERENCES

Alsup, J. (2006). *Teacher identity discourses: Negotiating personal and professional spaces.* Urbana, IL: National Council of Teachers of English.

Bartlett, L. (2005). Identity work and cultural artefacts in literacy learning in use: A sociocultural analysis. *Language and Education, 19,* 1-9.

Bruner, J. (1986). *Actual minds, possible worlds.* Cambridge, MA: Harvard University Press.

Chan, C.K., & Pang, M.F. (2006). Teacher collaboration in learning communities. *Teaching Education, 17,* 1-5.

Davies, B., & Harré, R. (1990). Positioning: The discursive production of selves. *Journal for the Theory of Social Behavior, 20,* 43-63.

Gee, J. P. (1996). *Social linguistics and literacies: Ideology in discourses (2nd ed.).* Philadelphia, PA: Routledge/Falmer.

Gee, J. P. (2000). Identity as an analytic lens for research in education. *Review of Research in Education, 25,* 99-125.

Holland, D., Lachicotte, W., Skinner, D., & Cain, C. (1998). *Identity and agency in cultural worlds.* Cambridge, MA: Harvard University Press.

Lewis, C., Enciso, P., & Moje, E.B. (2007). *Reframing sociocultural research on literacy: Identity, agency, and power.* New York, NY: Routledge.

MacPhee (2008). *The identities we teach: An ethnographic study of three teachers' conceptual and enacted identities* (Unpublished doctoral dissertation, University of South Carolina, Columbia, SC).

Merriam, S.B. (2009). *Qualitative research: A guide to design and implementation.* San Francisco, CA: Jossey-Bass.

Musanti, S.I., & Pence, L. (2010). Collaboration and teacher development: Unpacking resistance, constructing knowledge, and navigating identities. *Teacher Education Quarterly, 37,* 73-89.

Palmer, P. J. (1998). *The courage to teach: Exploring the inner landscape of a teacher's life.* San Francisco, CA: Jossey-Bass.

QSR International. (2010). NVivo 9 [Computer software]. Available from http://www.qsrinternational.com.

Richardson, V. (2003). The dilemmas of professional development. *Phi Delta Kappan, 84,* 401-406.

Ritchie, J. S., & Wilson, D. E. (2000). *Teacher narrative as critical inquiry: Rewriting the script.* New York, NY: Teachers College Press.

Tobin, K. (1990). Changing metaphors and beliefs: A master switch for teaching? *Theory into Practice, 29,* 122-127.

Vygotsky, L. S. (1978). *Mind in society: The development of higher psychological processes.* Cambridge, MA: Harvard University Press.

Appendix A: Conceptual Identity Model

Aspect	Participant Pattern	% of Coded Data
Psychological	Believes people deserve and can thrive in a safe environment Believes in a rule governed world in which authority exists as a hierarchy Strives to please others Values others' perspectives Engages in reflective thought to make things better	51%
Social	Values relationships Believes when all members in a community act responsibly there is a greater sense of democracy Values language/talk	28%
Cognitive	Observes people and situations Envisions action as part of planning Questions practice/Open to new ideas Identifies priorities in organizing the physical environment and determining learning goals Makes decisions based on observations, beliefs, and knowledge base	21%

Appendix B: Summary of First and Second Cycle Coding

	Initial Codes	New Coding Scheme
1	Acknowledging the mediating process	Acknowledging the mediating process
2	Acknowledging conflicts	Recognizing conflicts
3	Negotiating practice	
4	Bringing tacit beliefs to the surface	Making connections between conceptual and enacted identities
5	Moving beliefs/practices from unconscious to conscious	
6	Clarifying an assumption	----------
7	Confirming previously stated beliefs	Confirming previously stated beliefs
8	Engaging in meta-reflection	----------
9	Exploring possibilities	Considering new ideas
10	Getting back to a moment in time	Connecting past to present
11	Issues of power	Issues of power
12	Negotiating belief/identity	Connecting actions to identity/belief
13	Questioning practice	Questioning beliefs and practice
14	Recognizing practice	----------
15	Resisting an ascribed identity	Resisting an ascribed identity
16	Stating a belief	Articulating explicit and tacit beliefs

Creating Praxis: Determining Teacher Perceptions of Struggling Readers and Their Impact on Instruction

Meghan Liebfreund
Amy Mattingly
North Carolina State University

Teacher perceptions of readers are essential to the process of identifying students as struggling readers and determining the actions that occur after students are identified as struggling (Pemberton & Miller, in press). When a teacher perceives a child as a struggling reader, a process begins that affects instruction, interventions, and/or special programs (Vaughn, Gersten, & Chard, 2000). Because teacher perceptions influence the learning contexts of struggling readers, they must be investigated.

Efforts to change teacher practices often first take teacher perceptions into account (e.g., Cochran-Smith & Lytle, 2001; Harwood, Hansen, & Lotter, 2006). In a review of literature focused on teacher education, Wideen, Mayer-Smith, and Moon (1998) acknowledged the pervasiveness in teacher education programs of the belief that programs should be designed to build upon perceptions of teachers. Frequently, the first step in educating teachers and changing teacher beliefs—the filter of experiences and foundation of new knowledge and practices—is to make implicit beliefs explicit. Only then can beliefs be examined and sometimes challenged for the successful integration of new information and practices (Kagan, 1992).

A multitude of issues complicate the study of teacher perceptions. Not only are perceptions often unconscious, rendering direct questioning ineffective (Pajares, 1992), but teacher perceptions and practices often fail to align, making observational study ineffective (Kagan, 1992). Furthermore, teachers are often unaware of their own perceptions and may not possess the language to describe and label their views (Cooney, 1985; Kagan, 1992).

The current study addressed the following questions: (a) What factors do teachers perceive as representative of struggling readers and how do they cluster to form dominant viewpoints within a school? (b) How do these perceptions influence instruction? (c) Where do teachers' perceptions come from? and (d) How can teachers reflect on their perceptions to create praxis? Additionally, the current study employed Q-methodology to determine and make teacher perceptions of struggling readers explicit, and to our knowledge is the first to use Q-methodology in this way. Through Q-methodology the subjectivity of participants is systematically and objectively studied, bridging quantitative and qualitative traditions (Sexton, Snyder, Wadsworth, Jardine, & Ernest, 1998).

RELATED LITERATURE

Deficit Beliefs

Some teachers hold deficit beliefs regarding struggling readers and their environment. Teachers with these views often attributed reading difficulties to inherent traits within the reader that resulted in blaming the reader and feeling that the reader needed to be fixed (Alvarez, Armstrong, Elish-Piper, Matthews, & Risko, 2009). Teachers also linked readers' background including their family, socio-economic status, and culture to their reading difficulties (Ahram, Fergus, & Noguera,

325

2011). When deficits were situated within the readers' background, teachers perceived the home as having competing values and lacking responsibility (Ahram, et al., 2011). While teachers blamed student and background variables for reading difficulties, teachers were actually found to have unacknowledged beliefs and practices that likely contributed to the students' reading problems including: social class assumptions; a lack of knowledge of reading pedagogy; under-developed relationships with students; and curricular decisions determined by accountability instead of student needs (Triplett, 2007).

Perceptions and Instruction

Teacher perceptions often act as a lens used for the identification of struggling readers, and this can be problematic when there is discordance between teacher perceptions and student assessment data (Bailey & Drummond, 2006). Notably, teacher perceptions were more accurate in identifying the reading performance of more-skilled than less-skilled students (Begeny, Eckert, Montarello, & Storie, 2008). Furthermore, teachers perceived higher achieving students as intrinsically motivated and lower achieving students as extrinsically motivated (Sweet, Guthrie, & Ng, 1998), however, awareness of instructional practices that benefit extrinsically motivated students did not consistently translate into practice. Teachers also relied on their perceptions of children's behavior to predict reading ability (Brown & Sherbenou, 1981).

In addition to perceptions of students, teachers also hold views about their own knowledge. Teachers overestimated their understanding of reading-related subject matter, lacking awareness of their areas of expertise and those in which they needed more professional development (Cunningham, Perry, Stanovich, & Stanovich, 2004).

Teacher Perceptions in a School Context

In addition to individual teacher beliefs, the school context—including its norms and policies—can reinforce teachers' deficit views and prevent teachers from drawing upon strengths of students and families to enhance achievement (McKenzie & Scheurich, 2004; Weiner, 2006). Therefore, the norms of the particular school must be investigated and made conscious in order for systematic change at the school level to take place (Kennedy & Kennedy, 1996; McKenzie & Scheurich, 2004; Richardson, 1990).

To determine school norms of how struggling readers are identified and supported, the term *teacher* must be expanded to include all who deliver reading instruction, which differs depending on the practices at individual schools. Given paraeducators are often included in the instruction of struggling readers (e.g., Allington, 2011; Caustin-Theoharris, Giangreco, Doyle & Vadasy, 2007), it becomes important to look beyond classroom teachers alone when considering teacher perceptions about struggling readers.

Changing Teacher Perceptions

Determining and changing teacher perceptions must include avenues that involve teachers in the process, while also introducing teachers to ways of thinking that differ from their personal experiences (Richardson, 1990). Bailey and Drummond (2006) found teachers had vague and undocumented reasons for reader difficulties that prevented them from determining appropriate instruction. However, when given a checklist of reading skills, initial teacher perceptions were altered, resulting in the identification of student needs more aligned with assessment data.

The school culture influences teacher perceptions and practices, resulting in the need for school-based solutions to alter school-wide deficit beliefs and practices (McKenzie & Scheurich, 2004). Suggestions to erase deficit views and enhance instruction include: three way conferencing (parent, teacher, and student), community walks, family or community history studies, diverse book studies for faculty, and collaboration among stakeholders (McKenzie & Scheurich, 2004).

The current study was an investigation into teacher perspectives and the extent that child, home environment, and school factors contributed to student difficulties in reading. In addition to establishing dominant viewpoints and school norms, this study also provided an examination of how teachers reflect on their perspectives and create plans of action to support struggling readers.

THEORETICAL FRAMEWORK

Sociocultural theory supports the purpose and design of this study. The social, cultural, and historical environment in schools contribute to reading failure (Clay, 1987). Therefore, in order to fully understand reading failure, we must investigate the complex school environment.

In addition, through social interactions and experiences, knowledge is constructed. Vygotsky (1978) described a person's cultural development as appearing twice. It occurs first between people on the social level and then inside the person on the individual level. An individual's beliefs therefore become a socially constructed lens that shapes and is shaped by lived experiences.

One strategy for emerging from and turning away from potentially oppressive beliefs is to develop *praxis*. Maxine Greene (1978) defined praxis as a social process for transformation:

> [P]raxis involves critical reflection—and action upon—a situation to some degree shared by persons with common interests and common needs. Of equal moment is the fact that praxis involves a transformation of the situation to the end of overcoming oppressiveness and domination. There must be collective self-reflection. (p. 100)

Through collectively reflecting on beliefs, one can determine an appropriate course of action to transform reality.

This study determined teachers' beliefs of the struggling reader using Q-methodology. Once beliefs were identified, teachers were invited to critically reflect both individually and as a social group, to create praxis with the goal of transforming the reality of the classroom for struggling readers at their school.

METHODOLOGY

Overview of Q

Q-methodology, developed by William Stephenson in 1936 (Watts & Stenner, 2012), can be utilized to study the subjectivity of people in a given situation (Brown, 1996). The participants in the study are known as the P-sample, while statements of belief are known as the Q-sample.

Participants are purposefully chosen because they have certain characteristics that warrant investigation into their beliefs or perceptions (Sexton, Snyder, Wadsworth, Jardine, & Ernest, 1998). Researchers create a Q-sample that participants rank based on their agreement with each statement on a continuum. This ranking is called the Q-sort. Participants give weight to their agreement with each statement in relation to the other statements, differing from a survey in which participants weigh agreement with each statement independently from one other. Scores for each person are standardized by utilizing by-person factor analysis that clusters participants with similar perceptions (Watts & Stenner, 2012). In the current study, factors were rotated using a Varimax rotation to create a factor array that represented the perceptions of each group (Sexton et al., 1998).

Q-set Design and Content

In the present study, we created a Q-sample with 25 statements, each containing possible explanations for why students might struggle with reading. Each statement was printed on an individual card and randomly assigned a number (see Table 1). To ensure a "balanced Q-set" that

Table 1: Q-set of Factors Influencing Struggling Readers		
Gender Struggling readers are predominately one sex (Usually male or usually female)	Classroom Instruction Struggling readers need instruction on phonics, phonemic awareness, fluency, vocabulary, comprehension	School Mandates The reading program at the school is not meeting struggling readers' needs
Disability There is a cognitive reason why the child struggles	Education Families of struggling readers have limited schooling	Intervention Intervention was too late or not enough
Behavior Struggling readers have behaviors that interfere with reading	Home Environment Struggling readers lack stimulation and interaction at home	Assessment Time for testing takes away from time for instruction
ELL Struggling readers are language learners	Teacher Quality Struggling readers' past instruction was ineffective	Standards State standards are above struggling readers' instructional level
Reading Strategies Struggling readers do not apply appropriate reading strategies	Home/School Disconnect Education is not valued outside of school	Family Structure Struggling readers come from a nontraditional home
Motivation Struggling readers do not enjoy reading	Structure How struggling readers speak is different from book talk	Pull-out Services Pull-out services are ineffective for struggling readers
Focus Struggling readers cannot attend to the text	Socioeconomic Status Income level of family	Background Knowledge Struggling readers have limited experiences
Professional Development Teachers need more training using assessments to drive instruction	Scheduling Classroom and intervention schedule conflict	Age Struggling readers are not mature enough for grade level concepts
Involvement Parents/guardians do not engage in their child's education		

Figure 1. Forced Frequency Distribution for Q-sort.

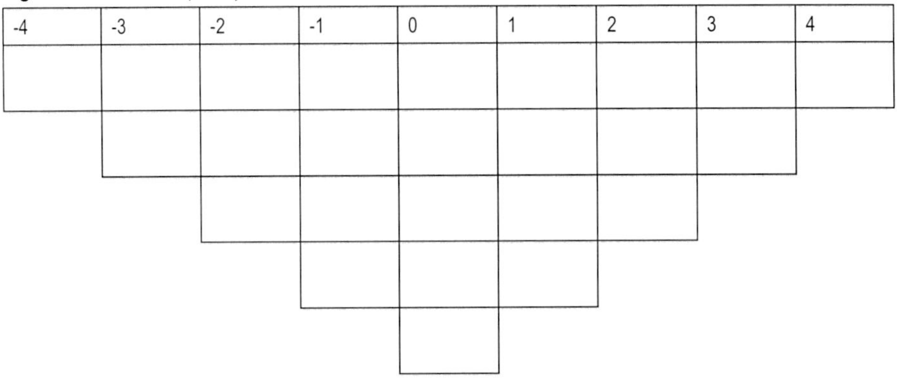

-4	-3	-2	-1	0	1	2	3	4

"came very close to capturing the full gamut of possible opinion and perspective" (Watts & Stenner, 2012, p. 58), statements were obtained from three sources. First, we conducted interviews with K-2 teachers at an elementary school in a different school from the participants in this study and explored their perceptions of struggling readers. Next, we conducted a literature review to determine characteristics associated with struggling readers. Then, after developing an initial list of statements, we piloted the items with a team of reading specialists. The pilot group made suggestions for the Q-sample that were incorporated into the design of this study. Changes included the addition of a statement to address scheduling and a clarification of the family structure statement.

During teachers' actual sorting, the researchers disseminated a prearranged frequency distribution, also known as the Q-sort (Watts & Stenner, 2012). The distribution ranged from -4 to +4. The statements in the plus (+) columns represented statements having more influence on struggling readers, while negative statements (-) represented less influence. Zero was a neutral or in-the-middle rating. See Figure 1 for the Q-sort distribution.

Participants

This study took place in a kindergarten through fifth grade elementary school in a small Southeastern city. Brighton Elementary, a pseudonym, was selected because it experienced two transitions with student assignment in the past five years, causing the demographics of the school population to be more diverse. According to school testing data and the School Improvement Plan, reading was an area that needed improvement. The school served approximately 450 students with 67% receiving free or reduced lunch. The student body was 63% African American, 28% Caucasian, 4% Hispanic, 3% Multiracial, and 2% Asian/Pacific Islander based on data from the 2010-2011 school year (National Center for Educational Statistics, 2012).

Any adult in the school who taught reading to students was eligible to participate. The responsibility of teaching reading engaged many members of the school (e.g., paraeducators, specialists, PE teacher) in providing intervention, so they were included as participants.

Thirty members (60%) of the faculty and staff participated in the study. The sample included 14 general education classroom teachers, six paraeducators, five teachers of exceptional children in self-contained classrooms, three specialists (physical education teacher, art teacher, library/media specialist), one intern, and one reading specialist. Participants were 90% female with an average of 11 years teaching experience. They worked in classrooms ranging from kindergarten through fifth grade, with six participants serving multiple grades. Sixty percent of the participants held a bachelors degree, 30% held a masters degree, and 10% held an associates degree. On average, each participant served 10 struggling readers.

Administering the Q-sort

All participants received written and verbal directions before receiving the Q-sample of 25 individual cards with statements regarding struggling readers (see Table 1 for Q-sample). Table 1 includes all cards with a label and a corresponding statement of belief to assist participants with interpreting each card. Because the term *struggling reader* implies a deficit, statements were phrased to either illustrate a deficit with the child, home, or school environment to explain its impact on struggling readers. Next, participants were asked to sort each statement on the continuum based on its perceived impact on struggling readers. After the sorting exercise, participants reflected on their individual sort and completed a post-sort questionnaire to explain the rationale behind card placement and cards they felt were left out. Participants also shared what influenced their perceptions and the impact of their perceptions on instruction.

Data Analysis

We performed individual by-person factor analysis using principal components analysis and Varimax rotation, which resulted in three model factor arrays. Z-scores for each statement were used to establish emergent factor arrays. Significance was determined by using the number of statements and the standard error. The significance level for this study was $p < .01$, factor loading > 0.52. The three factors accounted for 58% of the total variance and met the Kaiser-Guttman criterion of possessing an eigenvalue above 1.0 (Watts & Stenner, 2012).

After analyzing the Q-sort data, we returned to the school and placed participants into one of the three groups based on how their responses associated with a factor. The groups reflected on the Q-sorts and discussed open-ended questions designed to provide rich qualitative data to support each factor's distinct perspective. Then, groups discussed how they could use the information regarding their sort to create a plan to support struggling readers. Lastly, participants chose a partner from a different factor sort to discuss a varying perspective using open-ended questions to guide discussion and explain their thinking about struggling readers while individually recording responses. The post-sort discussion groups were designed to allow time for praxis and to create a plan to bring about action to assist struggling readers at Brighton Elementary.

Qualitative data including the individual and group reflection and post-sort questionnaires were analyzed. First reflection and post-sort data were compiled based on the factor analysis results so we could look within and across the three factors for comparison. Then, we used this data to provide insight to the underlying beliefs of the three factors to address our research questions.

FINDINGS

Q-methodology utilizes factor analysis to group participants with similar viewpoints using the card sort data. PQ Method, a statistical software program, was used to analyze the card sort data (Schmolk & Atkinson, 1997). Twenty-six of the 30 participants (87%) loaded on one of the

Table 2: Factor Loadings for Q Sort Data

Participant (n=30)	Factor 1	Factor 2	Factor 3
4	0.56*	0.47	0.36
5	0.56*	0.19	0.09
8	0.74*	0.03	-0.05
15	0.72*	0.16	0.40
19	0.83*	0.24	-0.10
21	0.55*	0.08	0.08
22	0.56*	0.23	0.39
29	0.78*	-0.06	0.41
30	0.69*	-0.30	0.18
1	0.43	0.66*	0.12
6	-0.02	0.68*	0.20
11	0.11	0.81*	0.09
12	0.14	0.68*	0.22
16	0.48	0.54*	0.13
18	-0.17	0.60*	-0.17
20	-0.20	0.55*	0.34
27	0.10	0.65*	0.15
28	0.36	0.54*	0.15
3	0.20	0.17	0.68*
10	0.37	0.12	0.72*
13	0.38	0.12	0.69*
14	0.42	0.21	0.62*
17	-0.05	0.18	0.78*
23	0.17	0.23	0.82*
26	-0.31	0.03	0.84*
2	0.51	0.34	0.54*
7	0.60*	-0.27	0.62*
9	0.36	0.32	0.45
24	0.49	0.12	0.45
25	0.29	0.51	0.49
Variance explained (%)	21	16	20
Cumulative variance explained (%)	21	37	58
Number of defining variables	9	9	8

Note: *p<.01 at factor loadings >0.52

Table 3: Distinguishing Statements for Factor 1

-4 Least representative	-3	-2	+2	+3	+4 Most representative
School Mandates	Gender	ELL	Reading Strategies	Intervention	Home Environment
	Family Structure	Pull-out Services	Home/School Disconnect	Classroom Instruction	
		SES	Involvement		

three factors indicating their Q-sort fit one of the three distinct viewpoints. One participant had a confounding sort that loaded on two factors and was placed in the group with the strongest association according to the Z-score. (Sorts greater than 0.52 are considered significant on a factor at $p < .01$). Three participants had non-significant sorts. See Table 2 for the factor loadings of all participants. Participants with confounding and non-significant sorts were included in the reflection groups to contribute to the discussion and encourage feelings of inclusion (Watts & Stenner, 2012).

Q-methodology data were paired with qualitative data from the questionnaires completed by each participant. Qualitative data were analyzed to identify themes by each factor and for triangulation of the data. The three different perspectives, or factors, are presented in the next section using factor analysis results in conjunction with participants' own words to describe the viewpoints of each Factor.

Factor 1: Teacher as an Island

The nine participants in Factor 1 emphasized a desire for more support from the Home Environment and School Interventions, but relied on Classroom Instruction to overcome these deficits according to the statements placed in +3 and +4 on the continuum. This "island" mentality was not desired by teachers, but because partnerships were lacking, teachers felt classroom instruction was their major support in teaching students how to read. This group desired strong partnerships as illustrated in one teacher's reflection that for struggling readers to be successful there should be "perfect partnerships between home and school. We've got to find the way to bridge that" (Participant 4). See Table 3 for Factor 1 distinguishing statements and rankings.

School Mandates, Gender, and Family Structure were seen as having the least impact on struggling readers according to the statements placed in -3 and -4 on the continuum. With respect to Gender, Participant 4 responded, "I try to teach individuals. Gender does not affect my expectations regarding a student's ability to read." Another teacher wrote School Mandates do not affect struggling readers because "reading programs at schools *do* work with most students. However, struggling readers without home support lack additional practice" (Participant 2). Non-traditional Family Structure was not seen as impacting struggling readers because "as long as a child is in a stable, nurturing environment or has their own intrinsic motivators they will succeed as a

Table 4: Distinguishing Statements for Factor 2

-4 Least representative	-3	-2	+2	+3	+4 Most representative
Gender	ELL	Teacher Quality	Intervention	Home Environment	Standards
	Professional Development	Behavior	Classroom Instruction	Home-School Disconnect	
		School Mandates	Involvement		

reader" (Participant 5). In addition, this group was surprised that motivation and focus were not ranked higher in their factor sort.

Participants reflected on the impact of their views on their instruction. One teacher shared she had "daily struggles to balance and make up for the gaps these factors create" (Participant 5). Background Knowledge also influenced instruction, which resulted in Participant 21 using an "intensive vocabulary program and SMART Board to enrich curriculum." Participant 29 focused on "motivation and finding ways to make reading fun."

Educators in Factor 1 gained their perspectives from their daily experiences as both teachers and parents. Teachers believed "experience tells all" (Participant 15), relying on their years of experience to label readers. When teachers were paired with a colleague they expanded on this notion of experience to include seeing "first-hand how uninvolved families influence readers" (Participant 2), "see[ing] the effect parents have on their students when they are uneducated" (Participant 24), and their "own experience as a learner/values/*culture*" (Participant 5). Participant 5 also felt so strongly about teachers' experience that she thought a card should be added to the Q-sort.

Factor 2: The Great "Barrier" Reefs

The nine participants in Factor 2 emphasized Home Environment and State Standards as the most influential reasons students struggle in reading according to statements in +3 and +4 on the continuum. Home and State Standards were seen as uncontrollable barriers limiting the impact of teachers' instruction. This Factor illustrated a home and political or institutional deficit view. See Table 4 for Factor 2 distinguishing statements and their rankings. Teachers reflected on how state standards impacted instruction in that "the state mandates too much of the instruction" (Participant 11) and noted that "students who struggle get more and more behind each year as the standards increase" (Participant 12). In addition, the participants saw a Home-School Disconnect in that school was not valued at home. One teacher felt "the majority of students who struggle with reading come from families who appear to be uneducated and are very disconnected from the school system" (Participant 20). The home was viewed as unsupportive and education not valued when papers were not signed or returned, homework was incomplete, and reading strategies were not practiced at home. Teachers felt "unable to change these things" (Participant 12).

Gender, Students' Language Status (ELL), and Professional Development were seen as having the least impact on struggling readers according to the statements placed in -3 and -4 on the continuum. Like Factor 1, Factor 2 participants did not believe that "a person's gender directly affects a person's reading ability" (Participant 1). With regards to Professional Development, Participant 12 summed it up saying, "Teachers have received training. We need time to put the training into practice." Participant 16 shared that ELL and SES were cards most difficult to place because she had "too many past experiences that don't fit this statement." In addition, this group was also surprised that motivation and teacher quality were not ranked higher in their sort.

Participants in Factor 2 viewed their perceptions as having an instructional impact. One teacher thought that "early intervention is very essential, along with family involvement" (Participant 1). Another sought to "compensate for these areas" she saw lacking with reading instruction (Participant 16). According to Participant 28 "limited experiences, speak[ing] different from book talk, [and] education is not valued outside of school" had a negative impact on instruction. Overall teachers felt they tried "to build vocabulary and provide background knowledge for students who are not from environments where they have been exposed to different experiences" (Participant 25).

Perceptions in Factor 2 came from experiences working with struggling readers. When this group elaborated with a colleague on what "experiences" meant to them, the responses included "the classroom we teach," seeing "parents who are nonreaders which often produces non-reading children or struggling readers," "students seem limited on background knowledge," and "experience dealing with students who have families not involved in their education" (Participants 11, 20, 16, and 12, respectively).

Factor 3: Students Don't Have Their Sea Legs Yet

The seven participants in Factor 3 emphasized that limited Background Knowledge had the greatest impact on struggling readers according to the statement placed in +4 on the continuum followed by Behavior and Involvement in +3. Teachers saw the home as the foundation of reading and struggling readers lacked this early supportive environment that provided experiences needed to thrive. Overall, teachers viewed their students as unaccustomed to the school culture and its expectations. This led to a child deficit view when students lacked the knowledge, behavior, and focus valued at school and a family deficit view when parents did not get involved to assist teachers in desired ways. See Table 5 for Factor 3 distinguishing statements and their rankings. During

Table 5: Distinguishing Statements for Factor 3

-4 Least representative	-3	-2	+2	+3	+4 Most representative
Gender	Professional Development	Teacher Quality	Home Environment	Behavior	Background Knowledge
	Scheduling	School Mandates	Reading Strategies	Involvement	
		Pull-out Services	Focus		

group reflection, all participants shared the view that the "formative years or experiences have a *big* impact on school successes or lack of" it (Participant 7). One participant illustrated this perspective in stating, "Students who have little or no life experiences outside of school and home struggle with reading. Students who come to school in kindergarten with lots of experiences turn out to be good readers" (Participant 17).

Like Factors 1 and 2, Gender was viewed as having little impact on struggling readers according to the statement placed in -4 on the continuum. Like Factor 2, Professional Development (placed in -3 on the continuum) was also seen as having little impact on struggling readers. Participant 17 believed "training - piling on more - is not at the root of the problem. When discussing the card that was most difficult to place, Participant 14 stated, "Teachers need more training? I think they get lots. Maybe it changes too often." Unlike the other groups, scheduling was seen as having little impact on struggling readers. Overall, this group was surprised by the diversity of their group in that it consisted of various grade levels and content areas.

Participants felt Homework and Class Size should be added to the Q-sort. Participant 17 suggested the addition of two cards and placement in the +3 column. These included "students who struggle do not have books in their home" and "students who struggle have never been to the library." Participant 2 felt genetics was also a factor that should be added.

Teachers believed the factors influencing struggling readers also impacted their classroom instruction. Teachers tried "to work with the students and provide assistance and encouragement" and teach "reading strategies" (Participants 13 and 14 respectively). Participant 17 tried to "expose my students to a wide range of texts, and hope that my passion for reading and literature shines through in my instruction, attitude towards reading, and daily read-alouds." Classroom instruction was also planned to "give direct instruction (120+ min) daily" (Participant 7). Motivation and Behavior influenced classroom instruction "in that disruptions often interfere with lessons" (Participant 2). In order to support the home environment teachers sent home nightly reading and invited parents to conferences and activities. The limited background experiences provided in the home made instruction less effective because "it is difficult to 'close gaps' that existed when the child entered school. Students cannot make valuable connections to the text (any genre) if there is nothing to connect to!" (Participant 17). Student deficits were also a factor in reading struggles due to behaviors that interfered with reading instruction, a lack of focus and inattention to texts, and not applying appropriate reading strategies.

The views and perceptions of this group came from a variety of sources. When meeting as a group, the teachers in this Factor did not initially cite experience like the other two Factors. Instead, teachers shared that school data showed "the same groups still struggling" and that every year it is the Black male population who have the biggest 'gap' in reading achievement (Participant 9 and 17). In addition to assessment data, experiences with the student population, including talking with them about their home life, parental involvement and conferences, seeing a lack of literacy in the families and parents, and being raised in the schools in the district shaped teachers' perceptions. When speaking with a colleague outside of the group context, teachers continued to share that the home and students were the source of their knowledge about struggling readers. In addition teachers had "classroom experiences with students who have background knowledge and a home environment that supports reading verses experiences with students who *do not* have a home environment that supports reading" (Participant 3). Other sources of teacher perceptions include personal values and expectations as well as fellow employees, friends, and parents.

Creating Praxis

After teachers reflected in groups with their sorts, they determined if and how their group with similar perceptions could work together at the school to address the perceived deficit area. The "Island" group representing Factor 1 focused on a plan to work together to reach out to parents to form partnerships and cultivate involvement. They suggested getting more involved in the local community as well as having workshops for parents to help motivate and "train" them to help and engage their children with reading at home. The "Barriers" group representing Factor 2 planned to reach into their school to form Professional Learning Communities to increase communication between teachers about student progress. This addressed their perceived deficit of high state standards impeding struggling readers' progress. The "Sea Legs" group representing Factor 3 planned to give students more life experiences both inside and outside of the school that built background knowledge through reading more nonfiction, advocating for more field trips, offering show and tell opportunities, and engaging in additional read-alouds. This addressed their perceived deficit in background knowledge.

Teachers also reflected on any changes they desired to make in their own teaching practice as a result of the Q-sort and reflection. Desired changes for all three Factors revolved around parents, professional development, and field trips. When reflecting on parents, Participant 4 stated, "I want to be more intentional and frequent in my communication with parents." Another teacher wanted to "find new ways to interact with parents" (Participant 25). There was a longing to "make parents more accountable" and be more "aware of the (lack of) knowledge that students come in with" (Participant 16). Several teachers desired more professional development to "educate myself further on better methods to help my struggling students" (Participant 13). In addition, they felt there was a "need to push at the county level for more field trips. Teachers need to seek out or write grants that would fund field trips" (Participant 17).

Participants felt they learned a great deal from this time for personal and group reflection. The reflection process "emphasized the need for creating strong working relationships with parents" and provided the opportunity to see that "closing the gap between home and school would help in this issue [struggling readers]" (Participant 5 and 8). Other teachers felt that reflection increased their awareness. Participant 11 stated, "Reading is so important to a child's development. I feel reflecting on this data has influenced me to be more aware of struggling readers and search out ways to help them." Three teachers learned more about their colleagues in that "other teachers see a deficit in children's background." Teachers also felt that their reflection experience "lets me take time to see where I can change my teaching to benefit my students" (Participant 13). Participant 2 noted that the reflection time was "too brief."

DISCUSSION

The three dominant viewpoints of teachers determined utilizing Q-methodology considered circumstances outside of the school, specifically the home, as most influential for struggling readers. In addition, Factor 1 viewed classroom instruction as the vehicle to make up for these gaps. Factor

2 viewed rising state standards as an institutional control limiting instruction. Factor 3 regarded the lack of background knowledge, behavior, and focus of struggling readers as problematic for effective instruction. Similar to Alvarez et al. (2009), the term *struggling reader* was differentially defined even within the same school, indicating no universal definition exists, specifically one that is skill- or data-driven.

Teacher perceptions originated from experiences, not research or school and classroom data. While some teachers initially cited data as a means to identify struggling readers, in group discussions they referred heavily to their experience, both in years teaching and interactions with students and families, to support their reasoning for why students struggle with reading. This is supported by the finding of Ahram et al. (2011) that teachers hold cultural deficit beliefs and these beliefs form personalized pedagogies that constrain "the teacher's perception, judgment, and behavior" (Kagan, 1992, p. 74).

To facilitate praxis, first we empowered teachers to make their beliefs explicit and public. Then, teachers were positioned to hear the views of others that could challenge their views and create change. During reflection, teachers focused on the similarities between their perceptions and those of other teachers. As a result, the different perspectives were unable to disrupt current views and create substantive changes. Instead, discussions mostly reinforced already formed perceptions. Action plans were created addressing each factor's perceived deficit area. Through creating action plans, Groups 2 and 3 moved from blame toward enhancing instruction to support students.

Similar to Ahram et al. (2011), teachers viewed the sources of students' struggles as outside of the school, and the teachers' immediate sphere of influence. As a result, the home was viewed as holding competing values and the focus of action was centered on ways to impact the home so it was more in line with teachers' views or enhancing classroom instruction to make up for perceived deficits with the home environment.

Limitations

Q-methodology is sometimes criticized for the use of a forced-choice format that ranks items dependently along a continuum that may have different standard deviations across participants. Teachers indicated they had a hard time with the forced-choice format because there were so many factors in the Q-sample they felt strongly about. Because Q-sample statements were phrased to indicate a deficit instead of a strength in the reader, home, or school, participant discussions and action plans may have been influenced. Also, due to constraints, only two days were devoted to reflection and there was no follow-up to determine if teachers implemented the action plans.

Implications

Creating praxis to challenge existing paradigms will require more than just exposure to varying viewpoints within the same school. In order to instigate deeper reflection and action, a more disruptive or divergent viewpoint should be included in the P-sample and reflection. Parental or student voice in the process may disrupt teacher perceptions and challenge the school culture. Also, because there is a discordance between teacher perceptions and student data (Bailey & Drummond, 2006), framing discussion and reflection with student data may challenge perceptions and enhance praxis.

Because *struggling reader* is a socially constructed label determined by teachers and the school context, researchers who desire to impact teachers with reading research and provide professional development should investigate how teachers define struggling readers and where the definition originated. Such investigations help in understanding the beliefs teachers use as a lens when internalizing reading research and professional development.

Despite research and literature attempting to remove the deficit view of students and families, it is still prominent in schools. There is a need for additional critical reflection that leads to action. The results of this study are compatible with those from researchers who have argued that efforts to change teacher practices must first take teachers' perceptions and opinions into account (Cochran-Smith & Lytle, 2001; Harwood, et al., 2006). By making teachers' perceptions explicit, a dialogue can begin to bring about change for struggling students.

Teachers in this study did not see professional development as impacting their struggling readers. Teachers may have viewed professional development as unnecessary because it was not aligned with their underlying beliefs or teachers overestimated their current knowledge (Cunningham et al., 2004).

Finally, this study gave teachers the opportunity to communicate perceptions of what impacts their struggling readers most and reflect on how they could be called to action to meet the needs of all students. The findings suggest that understanding the dominant viewpoints in a school will reflect the school norms and culture that defines who is considered a struggling reader. This information can offer insight into how *struggling reader* is defined at the school. Once this term is defined, teachers can then begin to challenge it, truly creating praxis that leads to action that advocates for the most marginalized students.

Authors' Note: *Both authors contributed equally and are presented in alphabetical order. We are grateful to Steve Amendm, Matt Militello, and Samuel Miller for their support and guidance throughout this research process.*

REFERENCES

Ahram, R., Fergus, E., & Noguera, P. (2011). Addressing racial/ethnic disproportionality in special education: Case studies of suburban school districts. *Teachers College Record*, 113, 2233-2266.

Allington, R. (2011). What at-risk readers need. *Educational Leadership*, 68, 40-45.

Alvarez, M., Armstrong, S., Elish-Piper, L., Matthews, M., Risko, V. (2009). Deconstructing the construct of 'struggling reader': Standing still or transforming expectations and instruction? *American Reading Forum Annual Yearbook* [online], 29.

Bailey, A. L., & Drummond, K. V. (2006). Who is at risk and why? Teachers' reasons for concern and their understanding and assessment of early literacy. *Educational Assessment*, 11, 149-178.

Begeny J., Eckert, T., Montarello, S., & Storie, M. (2008). Teachers' perceptions of students' reading abilities: An examination of the relationship between teachers' judgments and students' performance across a continuum of rating methods. *School Psychology Quarterly*, 23, 43-55.

Brown, L., & Sherbenou, R. (1981). A comparison of teacher perceptions of student reading ability, reading performance, and classroom behavior. *The Reading Teacher*, 34, 557-560.

Brown, S. R. (1996). Q methodology and qualitative research. *Qualitative Health Research*, 6, 561-567.

Caustin-Theoharris, J., Giangreco, M., Doyle, M., & Vadasy, P. (2007). The "sous-chefs" of literacy instruction. *TEACHING Exceptional Children*, 40, 56-62.

Clay, M. M. (1987). Learning to be learning disabled. *New Zealand Journal of Educational Studies*, 22, 155-173.

Cochran-Smith, M., & Lytle, A. L. (2001). Beyond certainty: Taking an inquiry stance on practice. In A. Lieberman & L. Miller (Eds.), *Teachers caught in the action: Professional development that matters* (pp. 45–58). New York: Teachers College Press.

Cooney, T. J. (1985), A beginning teacher's view of problem solving. *Journal for Research in Mathematics Education*, 16, 324-336.

Cunningham, A. E., Perry, K. E., Stanovich, K. E., & Stanovich, P. J. (2004). Disciplinary knowledge of K-3 teachers and their knowledge calibration in the domain of early literacy. *Annals of Dyslexia*, 54, 139-167.

Greene, M. (1978). *Landscapes of learning.* New York: Teachers College Press.

Harwood, W. S., Hansen, J., & Lotter, C. (2006). Measuring teacher beliefs about inquiry: The development of a blended qualitative/quantitative instrument. *Journal of Science Education and Technology,* 15, 69–79.

Kagan, D. M. (1992). Implication of research on teacher belief. *Educational Psychologist*, 27, 65-90.

Kennedy, C., & Kennedy, K. (1996). Teachers' attitudes and change implementation. *System,* 24, 351-360.

McKenzie, K. B., & Scheurich, J. J. (2004). Equity traps: A useful construct for preparing principals to lead schools that are successful with racially diverse students. *Educational Administration Quarterly*, 40, 601-632.

National Center for Educational Statistics. (2012). *CCD public school data 2010-2011 school year.* Retrieved from http://nces.ed.gov/ccd/schoolsearch/school_detail.asp?Search=1&InstName=wahl+coates&State=37&DistrictName=pitt&SchoolType=1&SchoolType=2&SchoolType=3&SchoolType=4&SpecificSchlTypes=all&IncGrade=-1&LoGrade=-1&HiGrade=-1&ID=370001202147.

Pajares, M. F. (1992). Teachers' beliefs and educational research: Cleaning up a messy construct. *Review of Educational Research,* 62, 307–332.

Pemberton, K., & Miller, S. (in press). Building home-school relationships to enhance reading achievement for students from families with limited financial resources. *Education and Urban Society.*

Richardson, V. (1990). Significant and worthwhile change in teaching practice. *Educational Researcher,* 19, 10-18.

Sexton, D., Snyder, P., Wadsworth, D., Jardine, A., & Ernest, J. (1998). Applying Q methodology to/ investigations of subjective judgments of early intervention effectiveness. *Topics in Early Childhood Special Education,* 18, 95–108.

Schmolck, P., & Atkinson, J. (1997). *PQMethod* (2.11). Retrieved from http://www.lrz.de/~schmolck/qmethod/

Sweet, A., Guthrie, J., & Ng, M. (1998). Teacher perceptions and student reading motivation. *Journal of Educational Psychology,* 90, 210-233.

Triplett, C. F. (2007). The social construction of "struggle": Influences of school literacy contexts, curriculum, and relationships. *Journal of Literacy Research*, 39, 95-126.

Vaughn, S., Gersten, R., & Chard, D. J. (2000). The underlying message in LD intervention research: Findings from research syntheses. *Exceptional Children,* 67, 99-114.

Vygotsky, L. S. (1978). *Mind in society: The development of higher psychological processes.* Cambridge, MA: Harvard University Press

Watts, S., & Stenner, P. (2012*). Doing Q methodological research theory.* Los Angeles, CA: Sage.

Weiner, L. (2006). Challenging deficit thinking. *Educational Leadership*, 64, 42-45.

Wideen, M., Mayer-Smith, J., & Moon, B. (1998). A critical analysis of the research on learning to teach: Making the case for an ecological perspective on inquiry. *Review of Educational Research*, 68, 130-178.

Douglas Fisher, Ph.D.
San Diego State University

Section V:
Writing

James Flood, former president of the National Reading Conference (now LRA), was the first person who told me that I could write. Actually, he said, "I bet no one has told you that you're a good writer." He was right. I had complied with a lot of teachers who had assigned writing tasks but I did not think of myself as a strong writer. Of course, I received feedback on my writing, but it was mostly corrections. This is not uncommon; teachers tend to focus on corrective feedback of student writing. As Fong, Williams, Schallert, and Warner (this volume) note, there is a "high prevalence of task-focused feedback" when teachers evaluate student writing and less focus on providing students with feedback about their processing of the task, self-regulation, or themselves as writers. I know that I needed feedback that was corrective in nature, but it sure would have been good to know that my processing of the task was resulting in effective papers before I was in graduate school.

In addition to the lack of robust types of feedback, one of the problems with writing instruction is teachers *cause* or *assign* writing rather than teach it. Although there have been a number of attempts to improve writing instruction (e.g., Fisher & Frey, 2007), many of them end up being formulaic, robotic, and artificial. I remember being taught to think of my writing as a hamburger. Topic sentence = top bun. Then include the lettuce sentence, the pickle sentence, the cheese sentence, and the meat sentence, all of which were details. Of course, our teacher would say, your hamburger will fall apart without the bottom bun, the concluding sentence. In too many classes, students are taught THE writing process, as if every writer, in every situation follows the same process. Writing teacher and researcher Donald Graves wrote:

> The writing process is anything a writer does for the time the idea came until the piece is completed or abandoned. There is no particular order. So it's not effective to teach writing process in a lock-step, rigid manner. What a good writing teacher does is help students see where writing comes from; in a chance remark or an article that really burns you up. I still hold by my original statement: if kids don't write more than three days a week they're dead, and it's very hard to become a writer. If you provide frequent occasions for writing then the students start to think about writing when they're not doing it. I call it a constant state of composition. (Graves, quoted in Nagin, 2003, p. 23)

In other words, there are writing processes that writers used that are dependent on a number of factors, including audience, purpose, and format. Of course, literacy researches know this but history is likely to repeat itself. The Common Core State Standards shift focus away from persuasion to argument writing, which is probably a good thing given the type of writing most college graduates will need to do in their professional lives. The problem is that we are already seeing a formulaic approach to argument writing. As Olsen, Ryu, and Bloome (this volume) note, "it is not atypical for argumentative writing to become a formulaic structure for students to implement" and that formula is most commonly the Toulmin approach. In their article, Olsen, Ryu, and Bloome profile teachers who are using multiple rationalities that "allow for divergent student perspectives and uptake of argumentative writing." That's what is really needed, if the outcomes outlined in the Common Core State Standards are to be realized. But even more importantly, the type of thinking described by Olsen, Ryu, and Bloome is important as teachers facilitate, and actually teach, students to write.

As I am composing this, I'm reminded of a favorite phrase of one of my colleagues, long-time LRA/NRC member Leif Fearn. He often says, "Every writer can read, but not every reader can write." If that is true, which I suspect it is, then shouldn't more instructional time be devoted to writing? Or do we have lower expectations for writing than for reading? We certainly assess reading way more often than writing, so that may be the case. But I was reminded of this statement, not because of the newish attention to writing (after all we changed our organization's name, in part, to include writing and other aspects of literacy), but rather because of the attention that has been placed on teachers' proficiency with writing. As Woodard (this volume) notes, there has been significant attention to the maxim that "writing teachers must write." It seems reasonable to suggest that it's hard to teach something you don't do, but is that the case? The question Woodard asks is this: What tensions exist between teachers' writing and instructional practices? Her answer suggests that this is much to be done if teachers are going to rely on their own practices to inform their writing instruction.

Actually, there is much to be done in the area of writing research and instruction. We have only scratched the surface in our understanding of this aspect of literacy. We understand the composing process of adolescents, thanks to Janet Emig (1971), and some fairly effective instructional approaches (e.g., Graham & Perin, 2007), but there is much to do and learn if we are to provide students an opportunity to share their thinking with the world. I hope that the articles in this section spur additional investigations, instructional interventions, and ideas. Who knows, our research might help a teacher guide the next Daniel Pink or Maya Angelou. Our students have so many ideas, desperate to get out. Let's help them become both consumers and producers of ideas, as James Flood did for me so many years ago.

REFERENCES

Emig, J. (1971). *The composing process of twelfth graders.* NCTE Research Report No. 13. Urbana, IL: National Council of Teachers of English.

Fisher, D., & Frey, N. (2007). *Scaffolding writing instruction: A gradual release model.* New York: Scholastic.

Graham, S., & Perin, D. (2007). *Writing Next: Effective strategies to improve writing of adolescents in middle and high schools—A report to Carnegie Corporation of New York.* Washington, DC: Alliance for Excellent Education. www.all4ed.org/files/WritingNext.pdf

Nagin, C. (2003). *Because writing matters: Improving student writing in our schools.* San Francisco: Jossey-Bass.

"Without Adding These Details, Your Writing is Meaningless": Evaluating Preservice Teachers' Constructive Feedback on a Writing Assignment

Carlton J. Fong
Kyle M. Williams
Diane L. Schallert
Jayce R. Warner
The University of Texas at Austin

The importance of feedback in educational settings has long been accepted by scholars and educators alike. Ilgen and Davis (2000) argued that "few beliefs are more widely accepted by psychologists, managers, educators, and others concerned with human performance than the belief that people need to receive feedback about how well they are performing their tasks/jobs" (p. 550-551). Research has overwhelmingly supported that providing feedback is one of the most powerful influences on learning and achievement and an integral part of the teaching process (Bangert-Drowns, Kulik, Kulik, & Morgan, 1991; Butler & Winne, 1995; Hattie & Timperley, 2007).

One aspect of feedback that has been a particularly salient research topic has to do with its positive-negative dichotomy. Because it has received less attention than positive feedback, negative feedback, in particular, raises special concerns. Ilgen and Davis (2000) have called negative feedback the "conundrum" of feedback. Van-Dijk and Kluger (2004) echoed this sentiment and labeled criticism a "dilemma." Giving information that highlights mistakes or shortcomings in a student's work can simultaneously support the student to make gains in learning and undermine the student's motivation and self-confidence (Cohen, Steele, & Ross, 1999). Giving constructive feedback, or feedback that encourages improvement, has been described as a sensitive and difficult art in teaching (Kilbourne, 1990). These delicate aspects of giving feedback become particularly important during writing instruction, where feedback on student writing is an integral part of the composition process. For these reasons, more research is needed to provide clear direction to teachers and writing tutors when evaluating writing tasks as to what might or might not constitute constructive feedback (Sansone, Sachau, & Weir, 1989). The current study seeks to contribute to this area of research by examining the constructive nature of feedback on student writing. In the sections that follow, we first review past research efforts on feedback in general and then turn to research that has focused specifically on feedback in writing.

FEEDBACK

A classic definition of instructional feedback is Winne and Butler's (1994) characterization of feedback as "information with which a learner can confirm, add to, overwrite, tune, or restructure information in memory, whether that information is domain knowledge, meta-cognitive knowledge, beliefs about self and tasks, or cognitive tactics and strategies" (p. 5740). Feedback can be corrective and provide direction specifically related to the task or process of learning, filling a gap between what is understood and what is aimed to be understood (Sadler, 1989). Kulhavy and Stock

(1989) outlined feedback components as primarily concerned with two dimensions: verification and elaboration. *Verification* refers to the dichotomous decision that a response is right or wrong, and is the first element of information required in instructional feedback. Verification can occur through a simple "yes" or "no," mapping directly to the performance, or, in the case of a more complex evaluation, the degree of feedback is matched to the learner's performance. In contrast, *elaboration* is any other content beyond a "right/wrong" or "yes/no." Kulhavy and Stock (1989) further described three classifications of elaboration: (a) task-specific, with its focus on restating the correct answer or falsifying incorrect responses; (b) instruction-based, which provides explanations of the correct answer or reiterates the source of the correct answer; and (c) extra-instructional, with examples, analogies, or new information introduced to clarify the feedback. Kulhavy and Wager (1993) proposed three broad purposes of feedback: (a) feedback as a motivator that increases a general commitment to a task; (b) feedback as a reward or punishment for particular prior behaviors; and (c) feedback as information used by a learner to change performance in a particular instance.

In a related approach, Hattie and Timperley (2007) reviewed the literature on the connection between feedback and learning, using the lens of three formative assessment questions that often guide the feedback-learning process: (a) Where am I going? (b) How am I going? and (c) Where to next? Following a goal control perspective (see Locke & Latham, 1990), they argued that feedback should reduce the discrepancy between one's goal and one's perception of current status. Feedback can be the information that drives the process of reducing this discrepancy, or it can be a stumbling block that derails it.

Hattie and Timperley (2007) argued that these feedback questions are linked to the type of focus for the feedback, what they called the *level* of feedback. First, *task-focused feedback* indicates whether work has correctly or incorrectly met the requirements of an assignment, and may provide guidance as to how to "correct" the missing components of an assignment, such as "You need to include more details on this topic." This is also known as corrective feedback or knowledge of results. Second, *process-focused feedback* refers to feedback on the process required to complete the task or to achieve greater understanding. For example, "Write some descriptor words that you might use for each event, and try to incorporate these in your paper." Third, *self-regulation feedback* targets greater skill in self-evaluation or self-efficacy to persist in a task, such as "Now, on your own, check to see if you have enough details through your paper." This type of feedback can also draw attention to other self-regulatory processes such as the effort or time needed in performing the task. Lastly, *self-focused feedback* informs a personal sense of value, such as "You are such a good writer."

Hattie and Timperley (2007) also argued that process feedback and self-regulation feedback are the most important for formative assessment and deeper learning, whereas self-focused feedback is least effective. As for the fourth category of feedback, task-focused feedback is similar to corrective feedback or verification of results and is only effective when leading to improved process or self-regulation. Moreover, research has indicated a high prevalence of task-related feedback (e.g., Dysthe, 2011), despite its lack of effectiveness if divorced from information related to process or self-regulation.

WRITING AND FEEDBACK

Instructor feedback on student writing is generally believed to be a supportive educational means for enhancing performance (Bruning & Horn, 2000; Duijnhouwer, Prins, & Stokking, 2010). However, despite the fact that teachers provide substantial amounts of feedback on student writing (Stern & Solomon, 2006), surprisingly little research has been done on the effectiveness of such feedback (Duijnhouwer, Prins, & Stokking, 2012; Graham & Perin, 2007).

Researchers have addressed one worry writing teachers have, which is that all their efforts spent in providing feedback to student writing may be for naught. Research findings have confirmed that teacher commenting on student writing is not a futile endeavor, but rather that students use this feedback to improve their writing and develop as writers (Beason, 1993; Lees, 1979; Straub, 1996). Studies in this area over the past 30 years have yielded a list of "best practices" to be used by teachers when providing comments on students' writing (Straub, 2000). Although the numerous practices can differentially influence students according to context and student characteristics, attempts to distinguish particular practices that are appropriate in all contexts have identified a few candidates: specificity and elaboration, limited scope and number of comments, and frequent use of praise. Research has shown that feedback in line with these practices tends to be viewed more favorably by students than negative or nonspecific comments (Straub, 2000).

In general, studies have found that students often prefer feedback that offers explanations for the feedback given, strategies for improvement, and clarity, and that does not appear controlling or judgmental (Kim, 2004; Straub, 2000). According to Straub (2000), comments should be written to foster a conversational tone and avoid "controlling" language that students interpret as criticism of ideas. A study by Straub (1996) looking at student perceptions of different feedback types found that although focus of comments was somewhat important to students, specificity and form of comments tended to be rated most favorably by students. In other words, students preferred feedback that specifically identified the problem and elaborated on ways to improve, and they preferred this feedback in the form of advice, questions, or praise.

In reviewing studies of writing feedback, Zellermayer (1989) noted that research has typically examined the issue through various characteristics or dimensions of teachers' comments, such as positive versus negative, specific versus vague, clarifying versus directing, and macro versus micro. Among these, studies that have looked at feedback as being either positive or negative are by far the most copious (Hillocks, 1982; Straub, 1996). For example, Gee (1972) noted that students who received praise on their writing held more positive attitudes and tended to write more than students receiving either criticism or no feedback. Straub (1997) noted that students responded favorably to praise statements, particularly when those statements were followed by explanations for the praise. However, Straub (1997) also cited evidence that although students may appreciate praise, they do not always see it as useful in improving their writing.

Some studies have made attempts at more systematic classifications of writing feedback (Barnes & Shemilt, 1974; Purves, 1984), but these have principally done so through grouping feedback according to the aspects of the composition process on which they were focused (e.g., planning, drafting, revising). Furthermore, the aim of these studies has tended toward either establishing a criterion scheme for grading (Purves, 1984) or analyzing teachers' perceptions of such (Barnes & Shemilt, 1974).

THE CURRENT STUDY

Hattie and Timperley's (2007) review of the research on the power of feedback is currently one of the most read articles from the *Review of Educational Research* (as indicated by the "most read rankings" provided by Sage Publications as of April 2013). As we mentioned earlier, Hattie and Timperley (2007) proposed that feedback can occur on four *levels* (we use the term *foci* instead of *levels*): feedback about task, process, self-regulation, and self. We chose the term *foci* or *focus* for two reasons: (a) to reflect that a feedback statement can include multiple of Hattie and Timperley's (2007) levels, and (b) because the authors do not present the four categories as representing a hierarchy, yet the term *levels* implies such a hierarchy. However, despite the popularity of their ideas, there seems to be little empirical work that relates Hattie and Timperley's (2007) model to real feedback from teachers, especially for writing tasks. One study examined teachers' self-reported usage of feedback on the four foci (Brown, Harris, & Harnett, 2012); however, our study applied their scheme to evaluate feedback provided by preservice teachers who had been asked to write a statement of constructive criticism to a hypothetical elementary school student's autobiographical essay. We hoped to see how well the model applied, as well as relate it to ratings of effectiveness of the statements.

In sum, although there has been a great deal of research examining feedback and writing, little research has focused exclusively on constructive feedback (see Shute, 2008), and despite Hattie and Timperley's (2007) highly read and impactful review and model of feedback, sparse empirical work has examined applications of their model and the validity of its conceptualization, either for research purposes and theoretical development or for practice. Therefore, our research questions were the following: (a) Which of Hattie and Timperley's (2007) four foci figured more prominently in preservice teachers' feedback statements on a writing assignment? (b) How are the four categories related to ratings of how effective each feedback statement would be in helping a student rewrite the essay? We followed answers to these questions with an examination of several illustrative statements with the purpose of exploring how teachers-in-training were or were not expressing each focus in their feedback statements.

METHOD

Data Sources, Setting, and Procedures

We obtained our data in two phases. In Phase 1, we collected feedback statements on a hypothetical writing assignment from preservice teachers. In Phase 2, we gathered ratings on the feedback statements from Phase 1 on how effective the feedback was for improved learning.

Phase 1: Obtaining feedback statements. The purpose of the first phase of our study was to generate feedback statements that would then be used in the next phase. For this first phase, participants were the 20 elementary school preservice teachers (18 women, 2 men) enrolled in a college-level learning foundations course at a large southwestern university. Just prior to the study, the preservice teachers had learned about effective classroom assessment and feedback practices; the timing of our study was meant to coincide with the instruction they had received. One week after the feedback lesson, they were given a scenario in which "Mary," an elementary level student, was struggling to write an autobiography with sufficient details about her life:

> Mary is continuing her autobiography assignment for English class. She has difficulty with providing vivid details in her paper, and consistently just lists events, like in a chronology. You have encouraged her to include more description before she turns it in, but she tends to rush through her work instead of spending time to add the required details. She hands you her autobiography, and after quickly glancing through the paper, you notice the same issue.

They were asked to imagine themselves as a teacher who wants to give constructive criticism to "Mary" in response to the prompt, "As a teacher, I would say …" We chose to provide a hypothetical situation instead of an authentic writing sample for two reasons: (a) given our goal to understand broadly the nature of constructive criticism, we wanted the feedback to be free of details not pertinent to the focus of our study (e.g., handwriting, spelling errors); and (b) providing a hypothetical situation allowed the preservice teachers to reflect on their own varied experiences, and an authentic writing sample may have reduced the variability of their feedback statements.

Taking no more than 10 minutes for the task, the students wrote statements that ranged in length from 35 to 107 words. The handwritten responses of the students were typed and made ready for Phase 2. Because our concerns were to keep the task manageable for the students in Phase 2 and also to remove any statement that seemed extremely similar to others already in the pool, we reduced the set of 20 statements to 14.

Phase 2: Rating the statements for degree of learning effectiveness. In the second phase, participants were 11 female students enrolled in a different class in the same teacher preparation program. These preservice teachers were asked to provide several ratings to the feedback statements the Phase 1 participants had generated: how constructive, supportive of motivation, and effective for learning each feedback statement seemed. Because these three ratings were highly correlated (bivariate correlations were all .97), we chose to use only the rating of effectiveness for learning.

Directions asked the preservice teachers to rate feedback statements for effectiveness for Mary's subsequent learning, using a 1 to 7 scale, in which "7" = "extremely effective feedback" and "1" = "extremely ineffective feedback." To check for how robust the ratings were, we first examined how students distributed their ratings across feedback statements. The full range of the scale seemed to have been considered as shown by the fact that nine students used five or more different points as they rated the 14 feedback statements, and the other two students used four of the scale points. We next assessed how consistent were the ratings for any one feedback statement by examining the standard deviation and distribution of ratings for each feedback statement. The mean of the standard deviations of the ratings was 1.01, and they ranged from .54 to 1.34, showing a relatively low to moderate amount of dispersion. Ten of the feedback statements showed dispersion across fewer than four scale points.

Data Coding and Analysis

To explore the validity of Hattie and Timperley's (2007) four foci of feedback in regard to constructive criticism, we coded each of the feedback statements in terms of the degree to which the statement reflected each focus. Although not a central point they made, Hattie and Timperley (2007) had noted that teachers possibly mix different foci of their feedback together. Therefore,

Table 1: Examples of Feedback Foci and Rating Level

Focus	"0" Rating (Absence)	"1" Rating (Low)	"2" Rating (Moderate)	"3" Rating (High)
Task	Mary, would you like some more time to work on your paper? I think that if you sit down and really put some time and thought into it like we've been talking about with your work then you could do an A+ job.	Let's go over the first few sentences in your paper to see if we can add a little more description.	These are all some great things you have written about, and I would love to hear more about each thing.	I noticed that you did not add in the required details that I asked for.
Process	Mary, you need to go back and give more detail about these events. Without adding these details, the assignment is meaningless. The more effort you put into the assignment, the more you will learn.	It is very important to take time on your work and include more descriptions. Would you mind taking some more time to add in these details to your autobiography?	How about I provide some examples of my biography and we can work together to see if we can make this paper even better than it is?	Why don't you try something different? Write the list events across a sheet of paper. Under each column, write what exactly happened. You can write who was there with you at the event, what exactly happened, when it happened, where did this happen, and why did it happen.
Self Regulation	Your autobiography tells me about you but I would like you to describe to meå the events. I would like it if you would add three descriptive sentences to each event you have in you autobiography. I want to feel like I am there with you experiencing the event."	Go back to [your] seat and try to correct the second half of [your] paper.	Tell me about what happened, who was there, where it was, and when it was. Try and tell it as a story." *(After she told me, I would then ask her to add the details she told me into her autobiography. Also I would remind her to write as a story).* "Do this with every event. Remember it is hard for someone to learn about you if you don't give details. Make it enjoyable to read.	Would you like to look over your autobiography one more time to make sure it has descriptions of your story?
Self	Let's go over the first few sentences in your paper to see if we can add a little more description.	You did a nice job, but I believe that you can add some more details to make it even better!	I really like the events that you've listed, but now I challenge you to bring them to life, but you're on a good start.	Job well done on putting the effort into providing more details. You have really used your brain.

we developed a four-point scale to allow us to rate each statement on each feedback focus (task, process, self-regulation, and self), using 0 to indicate the absence of a focus and 3 to indicate the full incorporation of a feedback focus in the statement. Note that our rating reflected the level to which a focus of feedback was present, not our evaluation of whether the focus had been necessarily expressed so as to be effective in improving the student's work. For these ratings, three of the authors coded each statement independently and then met to reach consensus on our ratings. When initial codings did not match, nearly always they were off by only one scale point. For these ratings, we used all 20 feedback statements, even though we only had 14 statements with ratings on the effectiveness for learning variable.

In Table 1, we list each of the four foci and provide examples of statements from our data for each scale point from 0 to 3. Note that because feedback statements often reflected multiple foci (at multiple levels), it was difficult to provide examples that strictly reflected one focus at one level. Thus, the examples chosen might include other foci along with the target focus/level. This was particularly true for those examples rated "0" as representing the absence of a particular focus.

The data were analyzed using quantitative approaches, followed up by examining selected feedback statements that illustrated each focus. For the quantitative analyses, we calculated means of the Hattie and Timperley (2007) ratings for each of the four foci and subjected them to one-way ANOVAs and Pearson product-moment correlation analysis. To locate illustrative examples, we examined particular feedback statements to see how they reflected different degrees of each focus. The purpose of examining statements was to explore how preservice teachers enacted what, to them, was constructive criticism.

RESULTS

We present our results in two main sections, first addressing the two research questions with quantitative analyses of the ratings obtained on each statement before moving to a section in which we examine selected statements for how they display the four foci.

Addressing Research Questions

The first question of the study asked which of Hattie and Timperley's (2007) four foci figured more prominently in preservice teachers' feedback statements on a writing assignment. We first calculated means across statements for each focus category and subjected these to a one-way analysis of variance (ANOVA) with statement as the replication factor to assess if there were any significant differences between preservice teachers' use of one or another of the foci (see Table 2). Results indicated that feedback statements received the highest ratings on task, mean = 2.38, followed by process = 1.95, self = 1.70, and self-regulation = 1.42. Planned comparisons revealed that only the contrast between the highest and lowest means was significant, with scores on task ratings significantly higher than scores on self-regulation ratings.

Thus, task-focused feedback was most prevalent in the feedback these preservice teachers gave on a writing assignment, indicating that they were mainly addressing whether Mary had correctly fulfilled the task assignment when evaluating her writing. Process-focused feedback was also prominent, suggesting that preservice teachers were providing directions for specific writing strategies and self-detection of errors in writing. Lastly, self-regulation feedback and self-focused

Table 2: Means and Standard Deviations of the Study Variables

Variable	n	M	SD
Foci of feedback[1]			
Task	20	2.38[a]	1.01
Process	20	1.95	1.09
Self-Regulation	20	1.42[a]	1.07
Self	20	1.70	1.03
Outcome[2]			
Effectiveness for Learning	14	5.15	0.67

Notes: [1] Scales for these foci ran from 0 (absence) to 3 (full reflection of the focus).
[2] This scale was a 7-point scale, with 1 = not effective at all and 7 = very effective.
[a] Denotes means that differed significantly at the $p < .05$ level. We calculated a Cohen's d (J. Cohen, 1988), a standardized mean difference, as a measure of effect size: task versus self-regulation ($d = .923$; a large effect size). Effect sizes for nonsignificant comparisons ranged from .236 (process versus self) to .667 (task versus self), which are considered small to moderate.

feedback were present to a low to moderate degree, indicating that some preservice teachers were encouraging metacognitive strategies, self-assessment, and autonomy when writing as well as providing some positive feedback about Mary's self-concept as a writer.

We next addressed our second question: how were the four categories related to ratings of how effective each feedback statement would be in helping Mary re-\write the essay? As a first step, we correlated the ratings of each focus with each other to produce an intercorrelation matrix of the ratings (see Table 3, upper part). That correlations were low and nonsignificant points to the fact that each feedback focus seems concerned with a different aspect of feedback, confirming Hattie and Timperley's (2007) categorization scheme as differentiating among dimensions of feedback.

Next, we correlated each focus rating with the ratings of effectiveness for learning. Keeping in mind that the number of statements, and therefore our n, is relatively low, we were nevertheless able to establish a significant and moderate positive correlation of .58 ($p < .05$) between process focus and effectiveness for learning. The low and negative correlation between task and effectiveness of -.21 was not significant and can be explained by the low variance on the task-focused scores and the fact that the two statements receiving a 0 on task received higher ratings on other foci (and thus, may have garnered some degree of effectiveness). In the next section, we analyze these very two statements along with other examples to provide case examples at how feedback foci were deployed by preservice teachers.

Table 3: Correlations Among Feedback Foci and Ratings of Effectiveness for Learning

Variable	1	2	3	4
Foci				
1 Task				
2 Process	-0.03			
3 Self-Regulation	0.05	-0.17		
4 Self	-0.27	-0.04	0.00	
Outcome				
5 Learning Effectiveness Rating	-0.21	0.58*	0.21	0.36

Illustrating Feedback Foci by Deconstructing Example Feedback Statements

Because we were interested in understanding, in a more holistic way, how the preservice teachers had expressed feedback to the fictional Mary scenario, we looked for particular examples that illustrated different degrees of each focus in constructive criticism. We began by looking at one statement that had received high scores (ratings of 3) on all four foci, addressing aspects of the task (adding more details), process (how to add more details), self-regulation (checking and monitoring the writing process), and the self (personal value as a writer):

> *Mary, I noticed when you re-submitted your essay, it looks a lot like it did before I asked you to include more description. Let's look at this section together and decide where more descriptions can be added. Your work is good, but I know you can make it excellent. Now, where in this section could you use more descriptions?...*[Ellipses in the original] *Great job, now take your paper a section at a time and do exactly what we did together before submitting it again. Thank you for hard work and patience.*

In this statement, *task focus* was reflected in the discussion of how the essay looked "a lot like it did before," implying a need for further description, as well as an invitation to find out where more description should be added. Second, a strong *process focus* was demonstrated in words encouraging Mary to revisit a particular section to decide where to add more descriptions. Third, asking where more description can be added in a section of Mary's paper and giving direction to go through the remaining sections on her own conveys a high level of focus on *self-regulation*. In particular, the questioning supports a metacognitive strategy to encourage Mary to check whether she has fulfilled the assignment's requirements in her writing, and the directive to transfer what she has learned to other sections of the essay suggests how she can self-regulate her writing process. Last, we assigned a high rating for *self focus* because of the compliments about Mary's writing ("Your work is good," "Great job") and about aspects of her effort and character ("Thank you for [your] hard work and patience").

We next examined feedback statements representative of different degrees of each focus. For task focus, the high overall mean rating indicated that nearly all statements were seen as giving feedback that highlighted how well Mary had fulfilled the assignment. One possible explanation for

Figure 1. Number of Feedback Statements at Each Rating (0-3) for the Four Feedback Foci

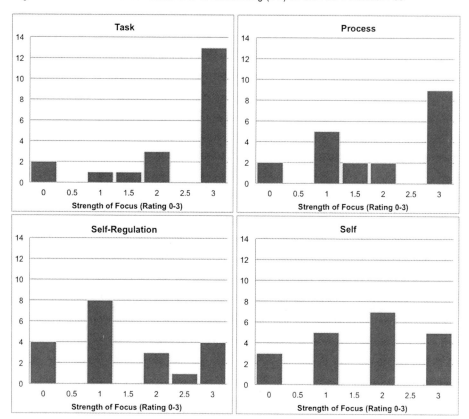

such a high mean rating may lie in the prompt the preservice teachers were given, in which lack of details in the autobiography was particularly emphasized. This may have led the preservice teachers to provide extra focus on the task level and to criticize elements of the writing that needed to be corrected. Alternatively, there simply may be a greater propensity for task-level feedback on writing (Dysthe, 2011; Shute, 2008).

Of the 20 feedback statements, 16 had a task level score of either a 2 or 3 (see Figure 1 for histograms showing the frequency of each rating). In light of such a high propensity for receiving task-focused feedback, we were particularly interested in the two statements that had received scores of 0, representing an atypical absence of task-level comments. The first of these two follows:

> *Mary, I can see that you are very good at remembering details of how things happened. What I want you to do now is go back and share your story with a friend, then listen to theirs. Come up with 3 things you liked about their story, and 3 things that you didn't understand or want to hear more about and ask them to do the same for your story. Then come back to me with your revisions and we'll go over it together.*

In this example, the teacher is not evaluating the task performance or describing aspects that are missing or incorrect, but praising Mary's memory capacity and providing a specific process for how to revise her paper. Interestingly, the preservice teacher giving the feedback never explicitly indicated that something was missing or wrong from the paper. One of the main purposes of task-focused feedback is to evaluate how well the assignment was completed, and perhaps the absence of such focus and a high degree of process focus makes the statement too indirect in guiding Mary in how she can improve her essay.

Another example of an absence of task focus coupled with a low score on process focus follows:

> *Mary, would you like some more time to work on your paper? I think that if you sit down and really put some time and thought into it like we've been talking about with your work then you could do an A+ job.*

Here, the preservice teacher omitted reference to elements of the task that are not only correct or incorrect but also neglected to provide any specific direction on how to improve the paper. Instead, there is an emphasis on how Mary can regulate her effort and time to improve her paper (self-regulation focus), and the statement provides praise regarding her potential to produce a superior paper.

Given the significant relationship between process-focus feedback and ratings on feedback effectiveness for subsequent learning, we also analyzed feedback statements that received a "0" rating on process focus. Interestingly, these statements also had the two lowest overall teacher ratings of effectiveness for learning.

For example, the following statement received a score of 3.7 out of 7 on effectiveness for learning, more than two standard deviations below the mean:

> *Let's think of more detailed descriptions. You would have a great fact base and a lot of information, but this is more like an outline of your life than a story. Do you know what I mean by 'story'? I want to get to know you through this paper. That means I need descriptive words, detail, and color. Can you add more to your paper? (I would also complement [sic] some element of her existing paper).*

This statement describes to Mary, with some degree of detail, what she needs to add to her paper, but there is no specific direction or method on how to supply the missing details. There is criticism that her autobiography is like an outline of events, but also praise for "a great fact base" and "a lot of information." However, without a clear direction but simply the directive to add what is still missing, this feedback statement seems to lack potency in affecting subsequent changes in learning, and this is reflected in the effectiveness rating provided by the preservice teachers in Phase 2.

Similarly, the statement with the second lowest rating of effectiveness for learning, a score of 4.2, also lacked process-focused feedback:

> *Mary, you need to go back and give more detail about these events. Without adding these details, the assignment is meaningless. The more effort you put into the assignment, the more you will learn.*

Although there is good degree of task focus in the feedback with the mention of missing elements of the paper as well as feedback about self-regulation of effort, the example clearly lacks process-focused feedback, providing virtually no direction on how to add the "meaning" or details to the paper. Moreover, the threat that Mary's paper may be meaningless would likely act as a blow to her self-efficacy and sense of value toward the task.

DISCUSSION

The purpose of this study was to understand how feedback on writing assignments would reflect the underlying dimensions or foci identified by Hattie and Timperley (2007). Because we generated the feedback statements by asking preservice teachers to respond to a hypothetical elementary school student's writing, our data are also interesting for what they say about what teachers in training focus on when providing constructive feedback. One of our initial observations of the preservice teachers' feedback when trying to categorize their statements into the four theorized foci was the lack of clarity regarding which of the foci was being addressed. Although Hattie and Timperley (2007) briefly mentioned the possibility of two foci being present within a single instance of feedback, our data pointed to the real complexities represented in authentic feedback. Nearly all the feedback statements included three of the four foci to some degree, with many of the feedback statements evaluating Mary's writing on all four foci.

Therefore, our choice of rating feedback statements in terms of the degree to which each focus seemed represented provided a more nuanced approach to understanding the complex nature of constructive feedback and the propensity teachers have of addressing multiple foci in one instance of feedback.

One notable result was the high prevalence of task-focused feedback from these preservice teachers when asked to give constructive feedback to a student's writing. This is consistent with previous research that has indicated that about 90% of teachers' questions and feedback to students is task-focused (Hattie & Timperley, 2007). Although other empirical research has supported this finding (Dysthe, 2011), the high degree of task-focused comments, to the point of almost no variance, implies that it is almost axiomatic practice to include some mention of what was inadequate in a student's response to an assignment. Perhaps by training, teachers are inclined, when giving feedback to identify, first and foremost, the problem, which in this case, was a lack of autobiographical details.

The lack of variance meant that ratings on the task focus variable could not show correlations with the ratings of effectiveness. And yet, we do not want to dismiss the importance of task-focused feedback to offer a proper diagnosis of a student's progress on an assignment or to lay the groundwork for process- or self-regulation-focused feedback. However, the nonsignificant correlation with effectiveness for learning may also reflect an underlying weak effect that task-focused feedback can have on improving performance when it occurs without concomitant process- or self-regulation-focused feedback (Dysthe, 2011). Although not explicitly substantiated in our data, previous research suggested that overusing task-focused feedback may encourage less cognitive effort invested by students in forming their own understanding of the feedback and planning for modifications in their approach to the task (Hattie & Timperley, 2007).

Perhaps not surprisingly, the relationship between process-focused feedback and ratings of effectiveness in our data was significant. This association suggests that feedback with comments directed at specific ways to improve the writing are perceived as effective for learning, which has been strongly supported by previous research (see Shute, 2008). For example, in a study by Schunk and Swartz (1993), fifth-grade students were provided with different types of feedback on how to write paragraphs. Results indicated that providing strategy goals or the steps involved in writing paragraphs caused the greatest gains in writing performance and self-efficacy compared to product (task) feedback or general goal feedback (e.g., "try to do your best"). Schunk and Swartz (1993) argued that specific strategies about the learning process provide students a useful means of improving their writing as well as motivation and efficacy to apply a new strategy. In our study, although the process focus variable only assessed the prevalence of process related comments and not necessarily the pedagogical effectiveness of the process feedback, we found it interesting that ratings of effectiveness for learning provided by a different set of raters showed a high correlation with prevalence of process focus. Another explanation is that process-focused feedback has been found to be more motivationally supportive, an important aspect of constructive criticism (Fong & Schallert, 2012), compared to feedback directed at the self (Kamins & Dweck, 1999).

The lack of focus on self-regulation throughout most of the feedback statements is worth noting. The importance of self-regulation to writing has been well-established (Graham & Harris, 1994; Zimmerman & Risemberg, 1997). Bereiter and Scardamalia (1987) described the writing process as a recursive problem that involves rhetorical and self-regulatory strategies. Whereas rhetorical strategies deal with actual wording solutions to make one's writing effective, self-regulatory strategies include managing one's thinking during writing. Despite the importance of addressing self-regulation in writing, our finding of little self-regulation feedback is consistent with previous research (Blote, 1995). One explanation is that novices seldom set writing goals, monitor their writing, and revise in an organized manner (Scardamalia & Bereiter, 1983). Given that the preservice teachers in our study were preparing to teach elementary school students, and an autobiographical essay might be perceived as an assignment for a younger student, the preservice teachers may have been tailoring their feedback for a novice and therefore included less feedback focused on self-regulation. Moreover, improved self-regulation for younger writers seems to require contextual support (Marcus, 1988) and help in recording their progress or managing their time (Van Houten, 1979). Feedback for self-regulation can promote self-assessment, self-efficacy, and commitment to writing, but more attention on how teachers can foster such focus is needed (Dysthe, 2011).

Self-focused feedback was fairly prominent in our data; however, it was not significantly related to how effective the feedback was for learning. This lack of relationship between effectiveness and prevalence of self-focused feedback has been reported previously in the literature (Hattie & Timperley, 2007). Self-focused feedback is unlikely to foster greater learning due to how little information it carries about how to improve writing performance. Moreover, it deflects attention from the task, focusing more on the student's self-concept. To be effective, self-focused feedback should lead to changes in student engagement and effort to use strategies or better understand the writing assignment (Hattie & Timperley, 2007). In addition, the prevalence of self-focused feedback (in this case, mostly praise) may have been heightened in our data as our scenario involves personally providing Mary constructive feedback, as opposed to, for example, addressing the entire class. Positive evaluations aimed toward the self often accompany one-on-one feedback, more so than when evaluating a group (Brophy, 1981).

LIMITATIONS

Our study is limited in its generalizability and by several features of the design. First, we only looked at feedback to a writing assignment. Second, the small number of feedback statements on just one scenario restricts our findings from a broader understanding of how preservice teachers provide feedback on writing. Third, the feedback statements were constructed from a hypothetical situation of a struggling writer and were not captured *in situ* through actual applied instruction; however, we did attempt to present a realistic setting and situation for the teachers to respond. Fourth, our effectiveness outcome measure was rated by a group of preservice teachers as to the degree they perceived each statement might lead to an improvement in learning and did not include students' actual improved performance on a writing assignment. Future research in this area may include analyzing feedback in a more realistic longitudinal study to link constructive feedback with actual student writing performance.

CONCLUSION

Overall, our findings contribute to the literature on theoretical models of feedback, in particular, Hattie and Timperley's (2007) four types of feedback. Understanding the focus of constructive feedback regarding writing and the writing process is important for teachers engaged in literacy and language instruction. In 2000, the National Reading Panel (National Institute of Child Health and Human Development, 2000) described writing as an essential component of literacy, a strong contributor to the development of reading skills and vocabulary. As a reciprocal element to reading, writing and writing education are in need of improvement (Duijnhouwer, Prins, & Stokking, 2012). Our results point to the need for professional development for teachers to provide different types of feedback aimed at promoting deeper learning and writing strategies. For theoretical and practical reasons, this study highlights a critical issue in furthering understanding of feedback practices in writing instruction.

REFERENCES

Bangert-Drowns, R. L., Kulik, C. C., Kulik, J. A., & Morgan, M. T. (1991). The instructional effect of feedback in test-like events. *Review of Educational Research, 61*, 213–238.

Barnes, D., & Shemilt, D. (1974). Transmission and interpretation. *Educational Review, 26*, 213-228.

Beason, L. (1993). Feedback and revision in writing across the curriculum classes. *Research in the Teaching of English, 27*, 395-422.

Bereiter, C., & Scardamalia, M. (1987). *The psychology of written composition.* Hillsdale, NJ: Erlbaum.

Blote, A. W. (1995). Students' self-concept in relation to perceived differential teacher treatment. *Learning & Instruction, 5*, 221–236.

Brophy, J. (1981). Teacher praise: A functional analysis. *Review of Educational Research, 51*, 5-32.

Brown, G. T. L., Harris, L. R., & Harnett, J. (2012). Teacher beliefs about feedback within an assessment for learning environment: Endorsement of improved learning over student well-being. *Teaching and Teacher Education, 28*, 968-978.

Bruning, R., & Horn, C. (2000). Developing motivation to write. *Educational Psychologist, 35*, 25-37.

Butler, D. L., & Winne, P. H. (1995). Feedback and self-regulated learning: A theoretical synthesis. *Review of Educational Research, 65*, 245-281.

Cohen, J. (1988). *Statistical power analysis for the behavioral sciences.* Hillsdale, NJ: Erlbaum.

Cohen, G. L., Steele, C. M., & Ross, L. D. (1999). The mentor's dilemma: Providing critical feedback across the racial divide. *Personality and Social Psychology Bulletin, 25*, 1302-1318.

Duijnhouwer, H., Prins, F. J., & Stokking, K. M. (2010). Progress feedback effects on students' writing mastery goal, self-efficacy beliefs, and performance. *Educational Research and Evaluation, 16*, 53-74.

Duijnhouwer, H., Prins, F. J., & Stokking, K. M. (2012). Feedback providing improvement strategies and reflection on feedback use: Effects on students' writing motivation, process, and performance. *Learning and Instruction, 22,* 171-184.

Dysthe, O. (2011). What is the purpose of feedback when revision is not expected?: A case study of feedback quality and study design in a first year master's programme. *Journal of Academic Writing, 1,* 135-142.

Fong, C. J., & Schallert, D. L. (2012, April). *What the filling in the "compliment sandwich" entails: Preservice teachers' views of constructive criticism.* Paper presented at the Annual Meeting of the American Educational Research Association, Vancouver, BC.

Gee, T. C. (1972). Students' responses to teacher comments. *Research in the Teaching of English, 6,* 212-221.

Graham, S., & Harris, K. R. (1994). The role and development of self-regulation in the writing process. In D. H. Schunk & B. J. Zimmerman (Eds.), *Self-regulation of learning and performance: Issues and educational applications* (pp. 203-228). Hillsdale, NJ: Erlbaum.

Graham, S., & Perin, D. (2007). A meta-analysis of writing instruction for adolescent students. *Journal of Educational Psychology, 99,* 445-476.

Hattie, J., & Timperley, H. (2007). The power of feedback. *Review of Educational Research, 77,* 81-112.

Hillocks, G. (1982). The interaction of instruction, teacher comment and revision in teaching the composing process. *Research in the Teaching of English, 6,* 261-278.

Ilgen, D. R., & Davis, C. A. (2000). Bearing bad news: Reaction to negative performance feedback. *Applied Psychology: International Review, 49,* 550–565.

Kamins, M. L., & Dweck, C. S. (1999). Person versus process praise and criticism: Implications for contingent self-worth and coping. *Developmental Psychology, 35,* 835-847.

Kilbourne, B. (1990). *Constructive feedback: Learning the art: The story of Oliver and Taylor.* Cambridge, UK: Ontario Institute for Studies in Education Press & Brookline Books.

Kim, L. (2004). Online technologies for teaching writing: Students react to teacher response in voice and written modalities. *Research in the Teaching of English, 38,* 304-337.

Kulhavy, R. W., & Stock, W. A. (1989). Feedback in written instruction: The place of response certitude. *Educational Psychology Review, 1,* 279–308.

Kulhavy, R. W., & Wager, W. (1993). Feedback in programmed instruction: Historical context and implications for practice. In J. V. Dempsey & G. C. Sales (Eds.), *Interactive instruction and feedback* (pp. 3-20). Englewood Cliffs, NJ: Educational Technology.

Lees, E. O. (1979). Evaluating student writing. *College Composition and Communication, 30,* 370-374.

Locke, E. A., & Latham, G. P. (1990). *A theory of goal setting and task performance.* Englewood Cliffs, NJ: Prentice Hall.

Marcus, M. (1988). *Self-regulation in expository writing.* (Unpublished doctoral dissertation). City University of New York, New York.

National Institute of Child Health and Human Development (2000). *Report of the National Reading Panel. Teaching children to read: An evidence-based assessment of the scientific research literature on reading and its implications for reading instruction: Reports of the subgroups* (NIH Publication No. 00-4754). Washington, DC: Government Printing Office.

Purves, A. C. (1984). The teacher as reader: An anatomy. *College English, 46,* 259-265.

Sadler, D. R. (1989). Formative assessment and the design of instructional systems. *Instructional Science, 18, 119-144.*

Sansone, C., Sachau, D. A., & Weir, C. (1989). Effects of instruction on intrinsic interest: The importance of context. *Journal of Personality and Social Psychology, 57,* 819-829.

Scardamalia, M., & Bereiter, C. (1983). The development of evaluative, diagnostic, and remedial capabilities in children's composing. In M. Martlew (Ed.), *The psychology of written language: Developmental and educational perspectives* (pp. 67-95). London, England: Wiley.

Schunk, D. H., & Swartz, C. W. (1993). Goals and progress feedback: Effects on self-efficacy and writing achievement. *Contemporary Educational Psychology, 18,* 337-354.

Shute, V. J. (2008). Focus on formative feedback. *Review of Educational Research, 78,* 153-189.

Stern, L. A., & Solomon, A. (2006). Effective faculty feedback: The road less traveled. *Assessing Writing, 11,* 22-41.

Straub, R. (1996). The concept of control in teacher response: Defining the varieties of "directive" and "facilitative" commentary. *College Composition and Communication, 47,* 223-251.

Straub, R. (1997). Students' reactions to teacher comments: An exploratory study. *Research in the Teaching of English, 31,* 91-119.

Straub, R. (2000). The student, the text, and the classroom context: A case study of teacher response. *Assessing Writing, 7,* 23-25.

Van-Dijk, D., & Kluger, A. N. (2004). Feedback sign effect on motivation: Is it moderated by regulatory focus? *Applied Psychology: International Review, 53,* 113-135.

Van Houten, R. (1979). The performance feedback system: Generalization of effects across time. *Child Behavior Therapy, 1,* 219–236.

Winne, P. H., & Butler, D. L. (1994). Student cognition in learning from teaching. In T. Husen & T. Postlewaite (Eds.), *International encyclopaedia of education* (2nd ed., pp. 5738-5745). Oxford, UK: Pergamon.

Zellermayer, M. (1989). The study of teachers' written feedback to students' writing: Changes in theoretical considerations and the expansion of research contexts. *Instructional Science, 18,* 145-165.

Zimmerman, B. J., & Risemberg, R. (1997). Becoming a self-regulated writer: A social cognitive perspective. *Contemporary Educational Psychology, 22,* 73-101.

(Re)Constructing Rationality and Social Relations in the Teaching and Learning of Argumentative Writing in Two High School English Language Arts Classrooms

Allison Wynhoff Olsen
Montana State University

SangHee Ryu
David Bloome
The Ohio State University

INTRODUCTION

Recently, there has been much interest in educational research in the teaching of argumentation and argumentative writing (see Newell, Beach, Smith, & VanDerHeide, 2011 for a review of related research). In part, this reflects the Common Core State Standards' (CCSS) emphasis on argumentative writing as critical to college and career readiness (Graff, 2000; Hillocks, 2011) and according to the CCSS what should be taught across disciplines and grade levels (National Governors Association for Best Practices, 2010).

To date, most studies of the teaching and learning of argumentative writing center on the questions, "Can students in grades K-12 be taught to effectively engage in argumentative writing? And if so, how?" Studies, such as those by Anderson, Chinn, Chang, Waggoner, & Yi (1997), Reznitskaya, Anderson & Kuo (2007), and McCann (2010) have shown that direct teaching methods and the use of what is called argument stratagems can be an effective approach to engaging even elementary and middle school students in argumentation. This parallels what we have observed in numerous high school classrooms, particularly when teachers offer argumentative writing as a new genre for students to learn. Although important, in our view the teaching of argumentative writing involves more than effectively teaching a written genre or acquiring argument schema or strategies. Our research on the teaching of argumentative writing in secondary classrooms shows teachers and students struggling with the complexities of argumentation including: what counts as knowledge, reconciling contraries, diverse perspectives, shifting social identities, and underlying rationality (e.g., what counts as reasonable). Here, we discuss the teaching and learning of argumentative writing focusing on rationality.

Argumentation, including argumentative writing, is built upon definitions of rationality, often defined as logic or reasoning. Although teachers and students may not directly consider the underlying rationality of their argumentation, their teaching and learning of argumentative writing nonetheless is both framed by a definition of rationality while simultaneously promulgating a definition of rationality (Bloome & Ryu, 2012). Building on discussions of rationality by Habermas (1984/1990), Foucault (1991), Flyvbjerg (2000), Searle (2001), and Walkerdine (1988), which suggest that rationality is not monolithic, we take a look at the teaching of argumentative writing in two high school English language arts (ELA) classrooms. In both classrooms there was an explicit emphasis on argumentative writing. The first classroom was an urban 9th grade ELA class embedded in a humanities course; the second a suburban Advanced Placement composition 12th grade class.

The purpose of this paper is to explore how the teaching of argumentative writing both reflects and constitutes different types of rationality and how diverse views are expressed, contrasted, and constructed within classrooms. We begin by briefly discussing our view of multiple rationalities. We then describe the broader study and our methodological perspective. Next, we offer our analysis of instructional conversations from each classroom, looking in depth at the promulgation of particular definitions of rationality. We also examine teachers' and students' interview data to triangulate and enrich findings from our analysis of conversations. Finally, we offer concluding remarks on how constructions of rationality(ies) may challenge and enrich dominant practices within the teaching and learning of argumentative writing.

VIEWS OF RATIONALITY

For heuristic purposes, we divide definitions of rationality into context-independent and context-embedded definitions. Context-independent definitions of rationality are often associated with Aristotle (1976), Hume (1748/2007), and Kant (1781/1965). From a context-independent perspective, rationality is defined as a set of logical propositions whose integrity is not violated by the social contexts or social situations within which it is employed. This is sometimes referred to as universal logic. If A is equal to B, and B is equal to C, then A is equal to C; and this is so regardless of who says it, how it is said, or where, when, and why it is said. Given this definition of rationality, rationality can be contrasted with irrationality as well as arguments motivated by feelings and unconscious and psychoanalytic drives. Philosophers, social theorists, linguists, and other scholars as diverse as Buber (1976), Freud (1923), Foucault (1984), Searle (2001), Walkerdine (1988), and Wittgenstein (1969) have suggested that what constitutes rationality both defines and is defined by definitions of personhood and is more so a function of social and cultural ideologies than abstracted, decontextualized, and universal logic. More simply stated, what constitutes rationality is a social and cultural construction; and as such, there is no separation between rationality and the people and social contexts and situations in which they find themselves. Rationality is context-embedded. From this perspective, a dichotomy between rationality and irrationality is a nonsequitur. Rather, the questions to ask are what rationalities are being employed? What is the nature of these rationalities? Who benefits from the particular definition(s) of rationality employed? How do definitions of rationality "govern" what people do?

We begin by exploring the underlying rationality in Toulmin's (1958) model of argumentation given its wide spread use in classrooms. We continue by discussing three context-embedded views of rationality, in particular those of Habermas (1984/1990), Foucault (1984), and Gilligan (1982). As themes emerged from our two focal classrooms, these different views of context-embedded rationality were helpful heuristics to understand how diverse underlying views of rationality were constructed and what they afforded teachers and students who wrote argumentative essays.

The Toulmin Model for Argumentation

Based on our observations[1], one of the models of argumentation that is widely employed in high schools is Toulmin's (1958) model. In this paper, we discuss this model based on its general usage in classrooms, rather than how it is actually described in Toulmin's scholarship. For instance, our reading of Toulmin's ideas suggests that his perspective on rationality is more complex and diverse than what we see teachers employ in classrooms. Toulmin (1958) recognized that disciplines maintain similar argumentative structures, yet vary in purpose and use of argument (Miller & Charney, 2008; Yeh, 1998); however, in our observations and study of the teaching of argumentative writing, it is common practice for teachers to base their argumentative writing curriculum on the Toulmin components: claim, data, warrant, qualifier, rebuttal, and backing (Toulmin, 1958; Toulmin, Rieke, & Janik, 1984) and use these as a decontextualized structure to explain how to do/write argumentation. As observed, the claim is presented as the conclusion to be argued for and data is evidence for the claim. A warrant then indicates the connection between the data and claim, showing how data provides support. A qualifier is a word such as "possibly," "probably," or "certainly," that indicates how strong a claim can be made based on the data and the warrant. Rebuttal is the consideration of counter arguments. Backing is the set of conditions where the warrant is applicable.

By stripping out these components and teaching them as *a priori* elements to reproduce, in our observations it is not atypical for argumentative writing to become a formulaic structure for students to implement. As such, when teachers enact a Toulmin approach, they employ an underlying context-independent model of rationality. Thus, related key questions for our study include, (a) Based on this approach to the teaching of argumentative writing, what kind of a person can be regarded as rational? and (b) What affordances and limitations are placed upon students when they reproduce the Toulmin components as their written structure?

Communicative Rationality

Habermas provides a different view of rationality, called 'communicative rationality': "This concept of 'communicative rationality' carries with it connotations based ultimately on the central experience of the unconstrained, unifying consensus-bringing force of argumentative speech, in which different participants overcome their merely subjective views" (Habermas, 1984, p. 10). Habermas emphasizes that argumentative speech acts as a force that brings consensus. Habermas contextualizes rationality within a democratic society and emphasizes being open to argument: all should have voice and numerous perspectives (not just polarizing positions) need to be considered. Unlike the Toulmin rationality—where claims, evidence, and warrant work together to create logic—we interpret communicative rationality to suggest that if a person has a clear position, appropriate reasons, and sound logic, but is lacking an attitude of being open to argument and working toward consensus, he/she should not be regarded as a "rational person." Rationality from a Habermasian view assumes that there are potentially diverse approaches to a problem and that the rational action is to engage in consensus building rather than taking polarizing and competitive positions. From this perspective, argumentative writing is framed as revealing diverse and creative approaches to issues. Further, argumentative writing is viewed as helping people to understand the diverse aspects of the issues and to consider the strong points and weak points of each approach. Critically, there is an effort by all parties to work toward consensus, not as political compromise, but rather as construction of an intersubjective understanding of the issue(s).

Although Habermas does not view knowledge and logic as existing apart from people's interactions, he believes that there could be universal principles for better argumentation. For better argumentation and communicative rationality, Habermas (1990) emphasized the universalization principle of discourse ethics. Habermas explained that discourse ethics "establishes a *procedure*...

to guarantee the impartiality of the process of judging" (Habermas, 1990, p. 122) and provided procedural requirements. The most important requirements were "ideal role taking" (Habermas, 1990, p. 198) and power neutrality in discussions.

Power and Rationality

Foucault offers a critique of Habermas's universalization principle of discourse ethics through an emphasis on power issues: power may not be neutralized. To be rational in a Foucauldian sense, one recognizes power issues in a context and adequately considers them in arguments. It is this perspective of rationality that we have observed the least in classrooms.

Foucault emphasizes that universals must always be questioned and argues for situational (contextually grounded) ethics. Foucault's contextuality questions laws, institutions, and history, particularly historical changes in rationality. As Flyvbjerg (2000) noted, "Foucault's emphasis on marginality and domination makes this thinking sensitive to difference, diversity, and the politics of identity, something which today is crucial for understanding power and affecting social and political change" (p. 12). Foucault (1984) also criticized Habermas' concept of concensus. According to Foucault, consensus within power neutrality is impossible and Habermas's approach to rationality was too idealistic.

Relational Aspects of Rationality

Gilligan (1982) drew on feminist theory and located rationality as context-embedded. While Gilligan distinguishes between masculine and feminine tendencies, this is not foregrounded in our conception. Rather, we focus on the relational aspects Gilligan offers for rationality. Gilligan frames rationality within an "ethic of care"—locating a "disparity between power and care" (Gilligan, 1982, p. 79) and problematizing an inability to merge the two. An ethics of care suggests that morality depends both on "specific projected consequences of actions" and on "friendship and kinship relations among the individuals involved" (Simson, 2005, p. 9). Who we interact with impacts our actions and intentions: all is relational. An attempt to separate logic from emotion is limiting, as interactions are infused with emotion.

While seeking for justice and care in relationships, Gilligan aligns herself with taking care of others so that "everyone will be responded to and included, that no one will be left alone or hurt" (1982, p. 63). It is this notion of respect and attention across and among students that we see enacted in our focal classrooms. Based on Gilligan's view of rationality, we can regard a person as rational if he/she considers human relationships and caring issues in a given specific context. Paying attention to how one's ideas situate within greater contexts matters. Argumentative writing with Gilligan's rationality then becomes a way to nuance interpretations of issues as writers consider how to build relationships within ideas.

Rationality(ies) as an Analytical Frame

Reflections and analyses of the instructional conversations in our focal classrooms extend our notions of argumentation and underlying rationalities. While each of the teachers made use of the Toulmin model, neither used it in isolation nor as an *a priori* structure; rather, various perspectives and layers surfaced as teachers and students acted and reacted to one another and played with argumentation. We use the three context-embedded perspectives of rationality—Habermas,

Foucault, and Gilligan—as well as the context-independent Toulmin method as heuristics to explore how the two classrooms were distinctive from others in our broad study.

METHODOLOGY

Our data is situated within a larger project (Newell, Bloome, Hirvela, & Marks, 2009) studying the teaching and learning of argumentative writing. Over the past two years we have been researching the teaching and learning of argumentative writing in high school ELA classrooms in urban and suburban districts that vary in economic, racial, and cultural demographics. Teachers were selected because they had local reputations of excellence. Case study students were selected on recommendations from their teachers as typically responsive students. Four case study students were selected per classroom in effort to represent variations in academic performance. We have video recorded daily one-, two-, and three-week units of instruction on argumentative writing in thirty-three high school ELA classrooms, interviewed teachers and students, collected student writing, pre-tested and post-tested student argumentative writing, and collected other data on student achievement.

Argumentation and Rationality(ies) in Two Classrooms

Here, we offer portraits from two high school ELA classrooms: a 9th grade ELA class situated within a humanities course and a 12th grade AP language class. We selected these particular classrooms out of our data corpus for a range of reasons. First, both teachers explicitly taught Toulmin structures, yet in neither classroom was the use of an *a priori* structure viewed as enough for a quality essay, nor for an understanding of argumentation. Instead, students had to exemplify creative and developed thinking beyond form. This shift immediately set our focal teachers apart from the majority of teachers observed in our study. Second, both teachers taught argumentation across the school year, rather than in discreet, short units, as was often the case in other observed classrooms. Finally, looking across grade levels allows us to consider how notions of rationality may be sequenced or layered over time.

While our project's broad corpus of data help contextualize and warrant our analyses, the focus for this article is one telling case (cf., Mitchell, 1984) per classroom. To arrive at the telling cases, we reviewed the instructional moves and student participation in both classrooms, noting patterns and how verbal repairs made visible the expectations within the classroom and the nuances for argumentation that were being taken up and applied. Employing a micro-ethnographic approach to discourse analysis (cf., Bloome, Carter, Christian, Otto, & Shuart-Faris, 2005), we transcribed key events from video recordings, organizing the discourse into message units (cf., Green and Wallat, 1981). We analyzed the message units with careful considerations of pronominalization, references to previous and future events, and references to argumentative elements. We noted the overall sequencing across speakers and their patterns and uptake, specifically recycling of and layering of ideas, shifts between the substance of an argument (the content) and the structure of an argument (its form), opportunities for engagement with others, and implications of rationalities. We also indexed teachers' and students' interview data and used the data to triangulate and enrich understanding of how teachers and students consider and discuss their experiences with argumentation.

9th grade ELA within Humanities. Data were collected in the English language arts section of a 9th grade humanities class at Center High School (a pseudonym, as are all names and places in this article). Ms. Cook, a White, female teacher with thirteen years' experience, taught 43 students: 63% females and 37% males; 51% White students and 49% students of color. The observed instructional unit occurred December 2010 through January 2011 and culminated in the first major essay (2-3 pages) of the school year.

12th grade AP Language. Data were collected in the 12th grade AP Language class at Sunshine High School. Ms. Jones, a White, female teacher with 12 years experience, taught 32 students: 63% females and 37% males; 72% White students and 28% students of color. The observed instructional unit occurred February 13 through April 4, 2012.

FINDINGS

As an exploratory idea, we suggest that a hidden curriculum of the teaching and learning of argumentative writing involves the promulgation of definitions of rationality. That is, diverse approaches to argumentative writing imply diverse rationalities. Of course, in the "real world" of classrooms, issues are usually complex and thus in some cases diverse rationalities may appear in the same lesson, as indicated in our upcoming findings.

Focal Lesson Analysis: 9th grade ELA within Humanities

Ms. Cook began the focal unit with non-print text, a study of two paintings: Ford Maddox Brown's *Work* and Diego Rivera's *Detroit Industry: Man and Machine*. For the summative essays, Ms. Cook assigned students to argue a claim interpreting one of the artist's purpose, supported with evidence from the painting and one of two paired written texts: *Bartleby the Scrivener* or an excerpt from *The Communist Manifesto*. Taking up Lunsford's belief, "Everything's an argument" (Lunsford, Ruszkiewicz, & Walters, 2010), Ms. Cook used the notion of argumentation as "an umbrella to which everything really does fit" and explicitly taught students argumentative elements (i.e., claim, evidence, counterclaim) as a linguistic structure and an entrance into the discourse of argumentation (Wynhoff Olsen & Bloome, in review). In particular, Ms. Cook offered the ABCD claim as a scaffold into how one writes a claim statement: "A = author's name and title of the work; B = abstract concept (themes) that you are analyzing; C = commentary on B; D = analysis of the devices used to analyze B." Though Ms. Cook stated—verbally and on teacher-created worksheets—that claim, evidence, and warrant help make arguments stronger, Ms. Cook did not limit her students' experiences to a context-independent rationality; rather, she moved across rationalities, offering various entry points for her students.

In transcript 1, Ms. Cook set the agenda (lines 34-41) to transition students from evidence construction (the focus of three previous instructional days) to claim construction (a new concept). While the selected bits of conversation do not explicitly mark the ABCD components, we can see Ms. Cook help reshape students' basic claim statements into claim statements with a more complex linguistic structure, one she deemed appropriate for argumentative essays. In the process, Ms. Cook makes clear that students are active agents, "coming up with" (line 44) their own claim around which to center their arguments.

The focus of our analysis is on the exchanges between Ms. Cook and Steve (lines 43-61) and how their conversation reveals their underlying rationalities. As noted in line 43, Steve's

Transcript 1

#	SPKR	Message Unit
34	Ms. Cook	alright ▲
35		shhhhhhhhhhhh
36		so you've got your basic thing
37		I'm going to analyze blah blah blah whatever
38		okay so let me call on you um just a couple of people want to volunteer
39		what their basic claim is gonna be
40		okay ahhhhh, let's see ||||
41		who shall I pick on T dramatizes picking
42	Megan	Me+gan
43	Steve	wait what is our claim have to be about
44	Ms. Cook	well that's your that's what you come up with
45		like ah
46		the painting one of the two paintings
47	Steve	oh okay
48	Steve	can I be like "Work is a representation of the class system"
49	Ms. Cook	ah, Work is the representation of what ki
50		what about the class system
51	Steve	of | how it works
52	Ms. Cook	um okay
53		(laughter across the classroom)
54		so you're saying that that's just you're not saying it's representation of good or bad that's just the basic ⌐
55	Steve	∟yea
56	Ms. Cook	it's representing the basic class structure of England ⌐
57	Steve	∟ yea
58	Ms. Cook	at the time
59	Steve	and how people are accepting it
60	Ms. Cook	ah, and peop, there's your argument right there
61		okay good

first bid for the floor is an interjection requiring clarification on claim statements. Ms. Cook's explanation (lines 44-46), albeit vague and without an elemental definition, assured Steve (line 47) and allowed him to enter the conversation with his ideas (lines 48 & 51). Steve offered a fact, "*Work* is a representation of the class system" (line 48) and Ms. Cook helped him offer an opinion about that fact (line 59), prodding Steve to critique the power dynamic within the class system (line 54). In this part Ms. Cook's underlying rationality hints at a Foucauldian rationality, but Steve did not take that up, nor did Ms. Cook explore it fully with the students. Rather, Steve acknowledged the power discrepancy [rather than critique it] and set his claim: people are accepting it. In turn, Ms. Cook evaluated Steve's claim as an appropriate argument.

In Transcript 2, Ms. Cook used Steve's ideas to help student Laura build her claim. Both Laura and Steve began creating their claim statements with careful attention to the text, implying an enactment of Toulmin's underlying rationality that one's claim needs to be carefully linked with

Transcript 2

#	SPKR	MESSAGE UNIT
116	Ms. Cook	alright Laura
117	Laura	I chose *Work* and like
118		(laughter across the classroom)
119		um like you can see how clearly divided the class systems are
120	Ms. Cook	okay
121	Laura	and so you can
122	Ms. Cook	so what what would be your claim about that
123		you know Steve's like oh well that's the way it was and they're not unhappy with it
124		or at least they're they're they're earning a living through that class system
125	Steve	yea they don't have to be happy about it they're just like that's the way it is
126	Ms. Cook	yea, it's just the way it is and that's okay with them

the evidence. As Ms. Cook pressed Laura for more (line 122), she revoiced Steve's claim (lines 123-4): a critical moment. First, it acknowledged that Steve's idea was valid yet not the only option: students were expected to have their own claims and offer varying perspectives on the same text. Second, it prompted Steve to reenter the conversation (line 125), reiterating his focus on the logic of the facts given in the text. Though Ms. Cook offered a consideration of emotion (line 123) and contextualization (line 124), Steve's response (line 125) indicates that for him, neither critique nor consideration of emotion (i.e., happiness) is needed to be rational. Steve appears to be taking up a context-independent rationality.

Laura, on the other hand, begins to show her construction of a new view of rationality.

Actively taking the floor, Ms. Cook prodded Laura to think beyond Steve's claim, offering

Transcript 3

#	SPKR	MESSAGE UNIT
127	Ms. Cook	soooo what's your, are you saying that the class system is <u>what</u>	
128		in *Work*
129			what do you think
130		is it a celebration of the worker
131		is it a critique of the class system where they're like
132		*oh look they're stratified and that's bad* *T uses a dramatized voice*
133		you know where they had the
134		(laughter across the classroom)
135	Ms. Cook	you know where Marie drew that
136	Laura	yea, that's what
137	Ms. Cook	okay
138		so you want to say that the the the+ levels of the class system
139		are you gonna say they're unfair
140	Laura	ye:a
141	Ms. Cook	okay ↑
142		that's that's an argument
143		because I can say *nuh-uh they are too fair*	*T uses a dramatized voice, hands on hips*
144	S?	Miss Cook *researchers cannot discern which student spoke*
145	Ms. Cook	*we must have our workers somebody's got to work at McDonald's* *T uses a dramatized voice*
146		haven't you ever heard people say that before
147		(laughter across the classroom)
148		*somebody's gotta work at McDonald's* *T uses a dramatized voice*
149		um well how come you're not ⌐
150	Steve	└yes
151	Ms. Cook	okay that kind of thing
152		(laughter across the classroom)
153		okay

critiques of power within the class systems (lines 130-131). Ms. Cook dramatized the power critique by shifting her register (line 132) and referenced a diagram that student Marie drew on the board a previous day (line 135). Though Laura's responses were brief, her tone and quick replies showed that she accepted the contextualized considerations of the textual evidence: the class systems were unfair. Laura took up a Foucauldian power critique. Though Laura's critique of power issues differs from Steve's acknowledgement of power, Ms. Cook acknowledged both as reasonable, an indication that Ms. Cook made space for multiple rationalities in her classroom.

As she did with Steve's claim, Ms. Cook confirmed her acceptance of Laura's claim by stating, "that's an argument" (line 142), yet took this evaluation further. Ms. Cook made public a counter-argument to Laura's claim (lines 143-148), again reminding students that various perspectives exist. Ms. Cook's extended performance (lines 143-148) also indicated that her students could relate to the topic of fairness and that she was revoicing with a register and message students may recognize. We find indications that Ms. Cook encouraged students to use their experiences and backgrounds when writing argumentative essays. As a result, argumentation is contextualized and relational; however, as indicated by Steve's conversations across the class period, not all students took up context-embedded notions of rationality.

Transcript 4 offers one more example of how Steve is working to understand claim and use the structure, the context-independent rationality. Again interrupting to clarify (line 157), Steve is still processing how to use his claim to write his essay. Steve's question in lines 158 through 161 reveals that though he had solidified his claim, he was considering how to structure his essay and wondered if he could use facts from the painting to support his claim. Steve's various entry points into the conversation help make visible his underlying view of a Toulmin rationality and the support he needed to understand how to enact it in his writing with a careful attention to claim and textual evidence.

Transcript 4

#	SPKR	MESSAGE UNIT
154	Ms. Cook	yea
155	S(?)	Miss Cook *researchers cannot discern which student spoke*
156	Ms. Cook	yea
157	Steve	um wait	
158		so like if I was going to do my argument about like that
159		*Work* is a representation of the class system and how people are accepting it

Interviews with Ms. Cook also indicate considerations of multiple rationalities. When asked the main take-away for this first argumentative writing unit, Ms. Cook explained:

> I wanted them to be able to understand that yes this is what I think and here's evidence to support that. I really want them to understand how to argue reasonably and rationally. And also to interpret other people's arguments and things like that. It's a give and take give and take.

In this small bit of interview data, Ms. Cook moved across rationalities. She began with a reference to Toulmin's rationality: the link between claim and evidence. *Understanding how* indicates a process, something more complex than a set of structural elements to be applied. Her further explanation (the next two sentences) adds contextual layers and suggests a desire for students to consider more than how to attend to a context-independent rationality while constructing their essays. Her use of *reasonably and rationally* (joined with coordinating conjunction *and*) is relational. For someone to be considered reasonable or rationale, there is at least one speaker and one interlocutor acting and reacting to one another, considering one another's ideas. Such a move makes us consider relational and caring issues, suggestive of Gilligan's rationality. This is supported by how Ms. Cook talked with her students during class, telling them to think about their ideas and consider how someone else will hear them, take them up, or reject them. This need indicates that who students are writing for matters; their ideas are relational. This notion was extended in Ms. Cook's desire for students to "interpret other people's argument," suggesting a connection with others, contextualizing through social relationships. Also, both verbs (*understanding and interpreting*) situate students as active agents. Finally, Ms. Cook named argumentative writing as a *give and take*. As we discussed previously, Habermas emphasizes overcoming our merely subjective views and moving toward a construction of intersubjective views. Here, the teacher highlighted the importance of having intersubjective (giving and taking) views as students construct their essays. While Ms. Cook did not insist her students achieve consensus, she expected her students to dialogue with their peers and consider this dialogue when writing.

Focal Lesson Analysis: 12th grade AP Language

During preparation for the AP exam, Ms. Jones assigned students a practice exam: write a response to Peter Singer's essay "Solutions for Poverty." The focus of our analysis is on one day's instruction (in March 2012). Students had written their responses and Ms. Jones was displeased with their work. The night before this focal day of instruction, female student Hannah sent Ms. Jones an email. It was typical for students in this class to email and Facebook Ms. Jones; however, this particular email seethed with anger. In the message, Hannah expressed irritation that she did not know how to write a better essay in the third quarter of her senior year. Instead of keep the email a personal matter; Ms. Jones used this real-life tension to teach her students how to use tension to deepen their argumentative essays.

Ms. Jones wrote three questions on the white board before class started:

(1) What does it mean to think critically?

(2) How will you further your point?

(3) How will you engage (text, audience, etc...) in a meaningful conversation?

On the white board was also a statement that argumentative writing is not a formula. Focusing this lesson on questions 1 and 2, Ms. Jones insisted that students reach for a higher level of complexity. Ms. Jones asked, "What does it mean to think critically? How do we get you to think critically? How do you think critically about this?" and then called on Amy:

T: Amy, how do you think critically about this?

A: Well I go through and examine all the different perspectives people take.

T: You examine them. What do you do?

A: You see how far you can take each point, like all the different possibilities for each

From their responses, we can see that Amy's and Ms. Jones's ideas are aligned. When one thinks critically, one examines different perspectives and shifts into more complex, more thoughtful essays. As the conversation continued, Ms. Jones explained that a reader does not have to agree with the author or the argument; however, s/he must be able to follow its construction.

Using the three questions and the tense email as springboards, Ms. Jones directed her students to consider past practices of essay writing. She then took them through an exercise of generating a list of pros and cons regarding Singer's "Solutions for Poverty."

Upon finishing the list of pros and cons, a familiar practice to students, the teacher informed the students that doing so was no longer enough.

Figure 1. The List of Pros and Cons Written on the Whiteboard

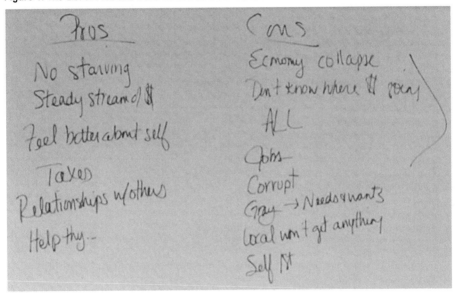

Figure 1, Pros: No starving, Steady stream of $, Feel better about self, Taxes, Relationships w/others, Help thy...
Cons: Economy collapse, Don't know where $ goes, All, Jobs, Corrupt, Gray—needs & wants, Local won't get anything, Self 1st

Lines 1 through 16 are based on the metaphor of movement, of having gone so far but not far enough, of the students "getting to" higher "levels" as if climbing. In lines 14 and 15, Ms. Jones

Transcript 5

#	SPKR	Message Unit
1	T	alright ↓ *T closes the cover of the pen used for writing on the board the list of pros and cons based on what the students are saying*
2		xxxxx stop there
3		we can go on+ ‖
4		alright now|
5		it is <u>not enough</u> to do this ‖ *T indicates the lists of pros and cons on the board with her hand*
6		this is not <u>all</u> the thinking you need to do
7		what I am seeing	is
8		a lot of your stuff and your thinking process <u>there</u>
9		and you're try to write this *T indicates the lists of pros and cons on the board*
10		with <u>just</u>	<u>this</u>	*T indicates the lists of pros and cons on the board*
11		okay ↑
12		<u>this</u>+	to create two lists
13		as I was looking through the work you did *T makes a motion that represents turning over students' writing papers*
14		to create two lists	<u>does</u>	<u>not</u>+| get you to the level of complexities|
15		the level of thinking that you need to be at ‖
16		why ↓‖| *T looks around the classroom waiting for students' responses*

points out the problems of argumentation and writing based only on polarizing positions in terms of "the level of complexities" of the argumentations. She then challenges by asking (line 26 below), "how do we go further?" Such a metaphor places argumentative writing practices in a continuum of less complex to more complex with the more complex preferred. What is not clear is what the goal of "climbing" is – to score well on the AP examination or to deepen one's understanding or both?

It is significant to note that when these 12th grade students were 9th grade students, some had Ms. Jones as their teacher. At that time, they read and studied Toulmin's elements of argumentation. During 12th grade AP, Ms. Jones referenced Toulmin's elements and argument structure, yet she did not reify it; rather, she used it as a beginning and then challenged her students to create and think across ideas. Ms. Jones focused on critical examinations across perspectives with her 12th grade students.

Ms. Jones then talked about her experiences reading the students' argumentative essays, pointing out that many students' essays were just based on the pro and con positions. As transcript 6 shows, Ms. Jones regards finding tensions in arguments as important to thinking critically and pushing the argument further.

Visible in lines 25-26 is the combination of modeling and articulating underlying principles (creating tensions as a way to reach a higher level of complexity). The writer brings the tensions to

Transcript 6

#	SPKR	Message Unit
25	T	In	argument			
26		how	do	we || go	further↓	
27		well+| let me show you↓
28		ok	so+		I do this
29		I look at my list
30		then, I am gonna think|
31		where	are	the	tensions↓||
32		what does that mean+||
33		when there is some tension	in something
34		when there is tension in a relationship
35		like in Hannah and my relationship evidently on Thursday night *T repeatedly moves her right hands to indicate the student, Hannah, in the classroom and herself*
36		where was there tension↓

the writing. In the classroom, the teacher often emphasized that different students might construct different sets of tensions and as such, argue differently, but not necessarily one better than the other. Indeed, they could all be "reasonable." The important thing the teacher highlighted is that they should be open to others' different perspectives. With this move, Ms. Jones makes visible a Habermasian approach to (communicative) rationality.

Ted, one of the students identified as a superior writer, suggested that Ms. Jones's philosophy and the underlying view of rationality was being taken up by at least some of the students. When asked what he had been learning about argumentative writing, Ted replied:

> Like not just learning how to argue but argue in a way that's open minded to multiple ideas and multiple perspectives. That way, 'cause that's how we kind of define mature reasoning is being able to be open minded because you can't really make a really accurate decision if you aren't able to fully consider all the options and really weigh them all without allowing preconceived bias in our decisions.

The need to consider multiple perspectives is evident, and Ted linked that with mature reasoning and being open minded. Such a connection suggests that this class is working toward a more complex understanding of argument. Later, as Ted explained his process as a writer, he stated, "Instead of you coming up with your claim and then trying to prove it, it's more like you figure out what all the information is and then you figure out what you're going to make as a claim of that." Ted's description that one needs to consider "all the information" is another indicator that he is taking up and revealing a Habermasian approach to (communicative) rationality.

CONCLUDING REMARKS

The illustrations above argue that there are diverse views on how to define and use rationality within the teaching and learning of argumentative writing and not all views are consistent within a shared classroom space. We believe that rationality is a hidden curriculum, evident within conversation and constructed in classroom contexts. In secondary schools, although teachers and students may not directly consider the underlying rationality(ies), their teaching and learning of argumentative writing nonetheless promulgates a definition of rationality; thereby, what students implicitly acquire through instruction might be called "rationality practices." We offer our concluding remarks in three categories: context-independent rationality as an entry point, the timing of/for multiple rationalities, and the affordances of multiple rationalities.

First, from what we observed in these two classrooms (and others from our broader study), a context-independent rationality may serve as an entry point for students who are learning to produce the discourse of argumentative writing, yet it need not be constraining or taught in isolation. It is possible that Toulmin's structure offers students a first step and that subsequently, teachers can layer and complexify argumentation via rationalities. There was up-take to this in Ms. Cook's classroom as she offered a linguistic structure for claim statements and then prodded students to think further. We argue that teaching only a context-independent rationality is not enough because it provides an *a priori*, fixed understanding that may lock students into a structure rather than asking them to create and be agentive.

A consideration of multiple rationalities takes time. In both classrooms, the teachers taught argumentative writing throughout the academic calendar and across school years. Ms. Cook's students began their work in the focal unit, but worked with argumentation and Ms. Cook across grades 9 and 10. Ms. Jones's students began their study in 9th grade and were deepening their understanding as 12th grade students. While this article does not focus on either teacher's full curricular sequences, both teachers offered students time to enter the discourse (i.e., learn argumentative elements and language), to play with ideas, to receive feedback, and to recontextualize understanding (Van Leeuwen, 2008).

Finally, we argue the affordances of multiple rationalities. Challenging a strict, context-independent rationality with context-embedded rationalities may expand notions of argumentation. When striving for a context-embedded approach, students and teachers may enrich thinking on multiple topics and create space to work together in ways that allows for listening (Schultz, 2003) and dialogism (Fecho, 2011). There was up-take to this in Ms. Jones's class as she encouraged students to think deeply and respect one another's ideas. Teaching context-embedded rationalities allows students to engage with argumentative writing and connect with what they live (ie. relationships, experiences, and varied backgrounds). We argue that the underlying rationality(ies) impacts how students understand and take up argumentation and is impacted by and affects the social relationships in the classroom space.

Multiple rationalities allow for divergent student perspectives and uptake of argumentative writing. In both classrooms, multiple rationalities were simultaneously at play. It is possible that Ms. Cook and Ms. Jones made this choice as they navigated various contexts (i.e., curricular standards, the AP exam, relationships with students) or perhaps it was because such "parallel play" helps develop strong argumentative writers (Bloome, Wynhoff Olsen, & Ryu, 2012). Making multiple rationalities explicit during the teaching and learning of argumentation, as well as during argumentative writing, contextualizes its use and broadens its impact. Multiple students can be considered rational. Making argumentation social (Bloome et al., 2005; Bloome, Carter, Christian, Otto, Shuart-Faris, Smith, & Madrid, 2008) and relational (Gilligan, 1982; Noddings, 2005) moves away from argumentation as a mere structure to imitate and moves toward ideas of creation and humanity (Kinloch & San Pedro, 2014) as teachers make space for students to interact and dialogue. Additionally, the capacity for students to move knowledge across disciplines as well as outside of school tasks is enhanced when there are varying contextualized and relational uses for and within argumentative writing.

REFERENCES

Anderson, R. C., Chinn, C., Chang, J., Waggoner, M., & Yi, H. (1997). On the logical integrity of children's arguments. *Cognition and Instruction, 15,* 135-167.

Aristotle, (1976). *The nicomachean ethics.* J. A. K. & H. Tredennick (Eds.). (J. A. K. Thomson, Trans.). New York, NY: Penguin.

Bloome, D., Carter, S., Christian, B., Otto, S., & Shuart-Faris, N. (2005). *Discourse analysis and the study of classroom language and literacy events.* Mahwah, NJ: Erlbaum.

Bloome, D., Carter, S., Christian, B., Otto, S., Shuart-Faris, N., Smith, M., & Madrid, S. (2008). *On discourse analysis: Approaches to language and literacy research.* New York, NY: Teachers College Press.

Bloome, D. & Ryu, S. (2012). *The social construction of rationality and the teaching and learning of argumentative writing.* Paper presented at the NCTEAR annual convention in Tuscaloosa, AL.

Bloome, D., Wynhoff Olsen, A., & Ryu, S. (2012). *(Re)constructing social relations and rationality in the teaching and learning of argumentative writing in one suburban advanced placement high school English language arts classroom.* Paper presented at the annual meeting of the American Educational Research Association, Vancouver, BC.

Buber, M. (1976). *I and thou* (2nd ed.). New York, NY: Charles Scribner's Sons.

Fecho, B. (2011). *Teaching for the students: Habits of heart, mind, and practice in the engaged classroom.* New York, NY: Teachers College.

Flyvbjerg, B. (2000, April). *Ideal theory, real rationality: Habermas versus Foucault and Nietzsche.* Paper for the Political Studies Association's 50th Annual Conference, The Challenges for Democracy in the 21st Century, London School of Economics and Political Science, London, England.

Foucault, M. (1984). *The Foucault Reader.* New York, NY: Random House.

Foucault, M. (1991). Governmentality. In G. Burchell, C. Gordon & P. Miller (Eds.). *The Foucault Effect* (pp. 87-104). Chicago, IL: The University of Chicago Press.

Freud, S. (1923). *The ego and the id.* J. Strachey (Ed.). New York, NY: W.W. Norton & Company.

Gilligan, C. (1982). *In a different voice: Psychological theory and women's development.* Cambridge, MA: Harvard University.

Graff, G. (2000). Two cheers for the argument culture. *The Hedgehog Review,* 2, 242-254.

Green, J. L., & Wallat, C. (1981). Mapping instructional conversations. In J. Green & C. Wallat (Ed.) Ethnography and language in educational contexts. Norwood, NJ: Ablex.

Habermas, J. (1984). *The theory of communicative action: Vol. 1. Reason and the rationalization of society.* (T. McCarthy, Trans.). Boston, MA: Beacon Press. (Original work published in 1981*).*

Habermas, J. (1990). *Moral consciousness and communicative action.* (C. Lenhardt & S. W. Nicholsen, Trans.). Cambridge, MA: The MIT Press. (Original work published in 1983).

Hillocks, G. (2011). *Teaching argument writing, grades 6-12: Supporting claims with relevant evidence and clear reasoning.* Portsmouth, NH: Heinemann.

Hume, D. (2007). *An enquiry concerning human understanding and other writings.* S. Buckle (Ed.). New York, NY: Cambridge University Press. (Original work published in 1748).

Kant, I. (1965). *The Critique of Pure Reason.* (K. S. Norman, Trans.). New York, NY: St. Martin's Press. (Original work published in 1781).

Kinloch, V., & San Pedro, T. (2014). *The Space Between Listening and Story-ing: Foundations for Projects in Humanization (PiH).* In D. Paris and M. Winn (Eds.) Humanizing research: Decolonizing qualitative inquiry with youth and communities (pp. 20-39), Los Angeles, CA: Sage.

Lunsford, A. A., Ruszkiewicz, J. J., & Walters, K. (2010). *Everything's an argument* (5th ed.). Boston, MA: Bedford/St. Martin's.

McCann, T. M. (2010). Gateways to writing logical arguments. *English Journal,* 99, 33-39.

Miller, C. R., & Charney, D. (2008). Persuasion, audience, and argument. In Bazerman, C. (Ed.), *Handbook of research on writing: History, society, school, individual, text,* (pp. 583-598). New York, NY: Lawrence Erlbaum Associates.

Mitchell, J. C. (1984). Typicality and the case study. In R. Ellen (Ed.) *Ethnographic research: A guide to general conduct* (pp. 238-241). New York, NY: Academic Press.

National Governors Association Center for Best Practices & Council of Chief State School Officers (2010). *Common Core State Standards* (English Language Arts). Washington DC: National Governors Association Center for Best Practices, Council of Chief State School Officers.

Newell, G.E., Bloome, D., Hirvela, A. & Marks, H. (2009). *Teaching and Learning Argumentative Writing in High School English Language Arts Classrooms.* Research supported by the Institute of Education Sciences, U.S. Department of Education, (Grant No. 305A100786). The Ohio State University.

Newell, G., Beach, R., Smith, J., & VanDerHeide, J. (2011). Teaching and learning argumentative reading and writing: A review of the research. *Reading Research Quarterly,* 46, 273-304.

Noddings, N. (2005). The challenge to care in schools: An alternative approach to education (2nd ed.). New York, NY: Teachers College Press.

Reznitskaya, A., Anderson, R. C., & Kuo, L. J. (2007). Teaching and learning argumentation. *The Elementary School Journal,* 107, 449-472.

Schultz, K. (2003). *Listening.* New York, NY: Teachers College Press.

Searle, J. (2001). *Rationality in action.* Cambridge, MA: MIT Press.

Simson, R. S. (2005). Feminine thinking. *Social theory and practice,* 31, 1-26.

Toulmin, S. E. (1958). *The uses of argument.* Cambridge: UK: Cambridge University Press.

Toulmin, S., Rieke, R., Janik, A. (1984). *An introduction to reasoning* (2nd ed.). New York, NY: Macmillan Publishing.

Van Leeuwen, T. (2008). *Discourse and practice: New tools for critical discourse analysis.* New York, NY: Oxford University Press.

Walkerdine, V. (1988). *The mastery of reason: Cognitive development and the production of rationality.* New York, NY: Routledge.

Wittgenstein, L. (1969). *On Certainty.* G. E. M. Anscombe and G. H. von Wright (Eds.). (Denis Paul & G. E. M. Anscombe Basil, Trans.). Oxford: Blackwell.

Wynhoff Olsen, A., & Bloome, D. (2013). *Language and Learning: A Classroom Microethnographic Discourse Analytic View.* Manuscript submitted for publication.

Yeh, S. S. (1998). Empowering education: Teaching argumentative writing to cultural minority middle-school students. *Research in the Teaching of English,* 33, 49-83.

[i] Data collected for this article are located within a larger dataset: a collaborative research project on argumentative writing in high school English language arts (ELA) classrooms, supported by the Institute of Education Sciences, U.S. Department of Education, through Grant 305A100786 The Ohio State University (George Newell, principal investigator). The opinions expressed within this article are those of the authors and do not represent views of the Institute or the U.S. Department of Education. We also gratefully acknowledge the support of CVEDA (The Center for Video, Ethnography, and Discourse Analysis) housed at The Ohio State University, within the School of Teaching and Learning. Part of the work in this manuscript was reported in papers presented at the AERA 2012 annual meeting and the 2012 LRA annual meeting.

Key to Message Unit Symbols (Bloome et al., 2008, p. 75)

↑ = rising intonation at end of utterance	⌐ line 1
↓ = falling intonation	⌐ line 1 = overlap
XXXX = unintelligible	∟ line 2
<u>stress</u>	
"reading from written text"	vowel+ = elongated vowel
▼ = less volume	* = voice, pitch or style change
▲ = more volume	*words* = boundaries of a voice, pitch or style change
▲ ▲ = greatly increased volume	*Nonverbal behavior or transcriber comments for*
| = short pause |||| = long pause	*clarification purpose in italics*
⌐ = interrupted by the next line	
∟	

Complicating 'Writing Teachers Must Write': Tensions Between Teachers' Literate and Instructional Practices

Rebecca Woodard

University of Illinois at Chicago

(Data collected at University of Illinois at Urbana-Champaign)

For over forty years, calls have been made to help teachers develop as writers in order to "enrich and inform their teaching of writing, to [encourage them to] participate in and shape public discussions about teaching, and to enrich their own lives" (Dawson, 2011, p. 11). Teacher writing has been advocated by proponents of the writing process (Calkins, 1994; Kittle, 2008), the National Writing Project (NWP & Nagin, 2006; Whitney, 2006), teacher research (Bissex & Bullock, 1987; Cochran-Smith & Lytle, 1993), and even policy makers (National Commission on Writing, 2003). Although the notion that "writing teachers must write" (NWP & Nagin, 2006) assumes that writing enriches instruction, the few studies of teacher writing that also focus on instruction document many tensions (Brooks, 2007; Gleeson & Prain, 1996; Robbins, 1996). For example, in Robbins' (1990) case studies of 12 high school English teachers, he found that most teachers who engaged in personally meaningful writing considered themselves non-writers, and their writing rarely informed their instruction.

Taking the perspective that such tensions are underexplored and that tension can serve as a site of learning and transformation for teachers (Alsup, 2006; Britzman, 1991), this study explores specific ways that teachers' personal literacies conflict with their teaching. This study is situated within sociocultural work that recognizes literacy and teaching as social practices and builds on research of students' out-of-school literacies by adding a focus on teachers. Case study methods are used to trace the participation of two teacher writers across settings, and the findings highlight tensions between their in- and out-of-school writing purposes, identities, and authority.

A SOCIAL PRACTICE PERSPECTIVE

Practice theories attend to the "milieu of social action" (Scollon, 2001, p. 7) and tend to trace back to Bourdieu (1977), who focused on the concrete actions of individuals and groups to understand how they functioned in the social world. He argued that we cannot understand human action as cognitive and voluntary, or as simple reactions to a stimulus (e.g., his notion of *habitus*). Both literacy and teaching, however, are sometimes viewed as an autonomous set of skills rather than complex social practices. This study takes a social practice perspective:

> Practice actually refers to the complicated pattern of behavior that emerges from people's actions with each other and with their social situation over time (Bourdieu, 1981)…The key to understanding practice is to understand how it arises from people's ongoing attempts to negotiate their relationship with their situation—social, material, cultural, and historical. (Spillane & Miele, 2007, pp. 58-59)

Similar dialogic understandings of practice exist in cultural psychology and sociolinguistics (Bakhtin, 1986; Freire, 1970). A social practice perspective is critical because autonomous understandings oversimplify complicated meaning-making endeavors.

Literacy Practice

Our field has taken up practice theories in situated studies of the social work involved in literacy (see Heath, 1983; Scribner & Cole, 1981; Street, 1984) and shifted from autonomous views of literacy with behaviorist orientations towards a view of literacy as a social practice (Street, 2000). Researchers have challenged decontextualized notions of literacy as functional skills primarily learned in schools and examined literacy as a "set of social practices deeply associated with identity and social position" (Street, 2000, p. 23) learned in situated contexts (Lave & Wenger, 1991; Street, 1984; Wertsch, 1998). In particular, researchers have highlighted how students' diverse home literacy practices and identities contest the authority of schools (Hull & Schultz, 2002; McCarthey, 1997; Moll, Amanti, Neff, & Gonzalez, 1992). Many literacy studies explore youths' unofficial literacies and celebrate their communicative competence, particularly outside of schools' institutional settings (Finders, 1997; Hymes, 1972; Lankshear & Knobel, 2006). Although such research has highlighted the diverse literacy practices of students, it has sometimes simplified the practices of teachers. By adding a focus on teachers' out-of-school literacies and the tensions they experience related to teaching, this study highlights the complexities of teacher practice.

Teacher Practice

Some teacher researchers also conceptualize teaching as social practice. Britzman (1991) writes that within a dialogic understanding of teaching, "the tensions among what has preceded, what is confronted, and what one desires shape the contradictory realities of learning to teach. Learning to teach is a social process of negotiation..." (p. 8). Prior (2008) similarly documents how Vygotsky, Luria, and Latour all "settled on genesis and disruption as key for researchers and participants to become aware of how things come together" (pp. 4-5). Studies of disrupted teaching are particularly important because of the opportunities for negotiation and learning through tension in the development of practices (Stolle, 2008; Whitney, 2009).

Alsup (2006) also advocates for the study of how teachers negotiate conflicting discourses to construct identities. Identities, like practices, are constructed through trajectories of participation across complex social practices (Dreier, 1999; Scollon, 2001; Wenger, 1998). When McKinney and Giorgis (2009) focused explicitly on how teachers construct and negotiate their identities as writers and teachers of writing, they found that there were discontinuities between writer identities and ways of teaching writing, and highlighted how "the ways we see ourselves as writers impact the way we teach writing" (p. 108). This study adds to their narrative inquiry with observations that provide insight into teachers' enactments of identity in practice.

TEACHERS AS WRITERS

As a social practice advocated by writing-focused teacher professional development movements like the National Writing Project (NWP) and Writing Across the Curriculum (WAC), teacher writing has the potential to bring together conversations about literacy and teacher practice.

The notion that "writing teachers must write" (NWP & Nagin, 2006) has been a cornerstone of the writing process movement for over forty years (Elbow, 1998; Emig, 1971; Murray, 1968); this philosophy simultaneously acknowledges that teachers' out-of-school literacy practices and identities matter and assumes that teachers' writing automatically or easily enriches instruction.

In fact, the instructional benefits of teacher writing have only been the topic of a few empirical studies (Brooks, 2007; Gleeson & Prain, 1996; Robbins, 1990; Thornton, 2010). In this study I present two cases to suggest the importance of studying teachers as participants across in- and out-of-school contexts. Beyond recognizing such participation, I suggest that, much as building explicit links to students' lives and attending to the tensions they experience can enrich their educations, encouraging such work for teachers can productively enrich (and potentially transform) teachers' pedagogical practices. My analysis aims to make visible the tensions one middle school English Language Arts teacher and one college composition instructor experience as they weave together everyday and professional worlds and identities. The major research question was: What tensions exist between teachers' writing and instructional practices?

METHODS

Because I sought to understand teachers' participation across complex structures of social practice (Dreier, 1999), qualitative inquiry, which focuses on the situated meaning perspectives of actors in particular contexts (Erikson, 1986), was an appropriate choice for this study. Specifically, I engaged in multiple case study research of two teachers and used qualitative observational and interview methods with goals of testing theories related to teacher writing and building theories related to literate and instructional practice (Yin, 2009).

Sites and Participants

Two teachers were invited to participate in this study because they wrote extensively outside of school, worked in very different settings, and allowed me extensive access to their classrooms and writing contexts. Lisa, the first focal teacher, was a seventh-year urban public school eighth grade literacy teacher in a major metropolitan area. Alice, the second focal teacher, was a second-year freshman composition instructor and third-year doctoral student in an English program at a large midwestern university.

I observed Lisa during the spring 2010 semester teaching historical fiction and poetry writing units to one of her eighth grade English Language Arts classes, and meeting with her personal writing instructor and creative writing group in coffee shops. She worked at an expanding small public school serving 424 students, with class sizes that averaged about 25 students. The student ethnicity breakdown was 88% Hispanic, 10% Black, 1% White, and 1% Asian. 92% of students received free or reduced lunch, and 36% were classified Limited English Proficient. Lisa served as the lead teacher on the school's Writing Curriculum Committee, which was developing a new writing curriculum to supplement Calkins' (2006) *Units of Study*. At the time of the study, Lisa was implementing historical fiction and poetry units based on the workshop-style curriculum. Throughout her career at the school, she participated in extensive school-sponsored professional development for her literacy curriculum. Lisa also took a creative writing class in 2008, and afterwards continued meeting with her instructor, Will, and started her own creative writing group.

Lisa expressed interests in eventually applying to MFA programs in creative writing and teaching writing at the college level.

I observed the second focal teacher, Alice, during the fall 2011 semester across multiple sites as well—teaching composition in her Rhetoric (Rhet) 105 classroom, meeting with students one-on-one during office hours, practicing for her special fields exam with fellow graduate students, and meeting with her academic writing group at the public library or local coffee shops. Alice was a third-year doctoral student in a Writing Studies program at a large Midwestern university. She was starting her second year as a Rhet 105 instructor, and implementing Wardle and Down's (2011) *Writing About Writing* curriculum for the first time. For the entering 2011 freshman class, the group Alice taught in her Rhet 105 class, students self-identified as 5.5% African American, 15.3% Asian, 7.4% Hispanic, 55% White, 13.2% Foreign, and 3.4% Other/Unknown.

Data Collection

Over a one-month period with Lisa and a two-month period with Alice, I collected over 255 minutes of interviews with the participants about their writing life histories and teaching experiences, 1500 minutes of classroom and out-of-school observations, and 89 artifacts created by teachers and participants they interacted with around writing and teaching writing, including students and writing group members (see Table 1 for an overview). In turn, I created over 120 pages of transcripts and 430 pages of field notes and reflections.

Table 1. Overview of Data Sources

	Lisa	Alice
Interviews	4 30-minute interviews	3 45-minute interviews
Classroom Observations	16 observations of 45- minute writing classes	6 observations of 75-minute writing classes
Out-of-school Observations	1 meeting with writing instructor, 1 meeting with writing group	2 meetings with writing group, 1 meeting with colleagues for mock fields exam, 1 1:1 meeting with a student for office hours
Artifacts	47 artifacts	42 artifacts

I focused my observations on easily observable writing activities—writing instruction and out-of-school writing groups. Recognizing that this focus limited my understanding of the teachers' full range of literate practices, I used supplementary interviews. I began with semi-structured questions about their life histories with literacy (Brandt, 2001), which included questions ranging from demographics to early childhood memories of writing, and added open questions about instruction and writing. I also collected any writing and materials referenced during lessons and writing group meetings to provide context for field notes and observations.

Data Analysis

Consistent with qualitative inquiry, data analysis was inductive, reflexive, and guided by my research questions (Dyson & Genishi, 2005). This process involved closely reading and rereading through all the data in chronological order. First, I identified the typical structures and practices that characterized the teachers' activities. I identified each teacher's participation in school events versus writing events, and created tables where I broke down each event into activities, or segments distinguished by different actions and goals (e.g., direct instruction, writing, talking about texts). Then, I noted approximately how much time was spent on each activity and what the teacher and other participants were doing. For example, in Lisa's first teaching event, there were three activities—first, students listened while Lisa taught a strategy and modeled (3 minutes); then, students edited independently while Lisa conducted conferences (20 minutes); finally, students wrote independently while Lisa managed the classroom (13 minutes). As I reread field notes and transcripts, I developed analytic codes to name links across and tensions between events. Initial codes included links in talk, actions, and goals/purposes, as well as tensions in actions, goals/purposes, identities, and authority. After selecting events for careful study that exhibited such links and tensions and seeking examples to confirm and disconfirm my preliminary analysis (Erickson, 1986), I refined the codes to focus on similar tensions for both teachers, and used these tensions to organize and analyze their experiences.

Limitations

Lisa's study was conducted over a short time period of intensive observations. Longitudinal studies could help develop more historical understandings of teachers' multiple trajectories of practice over time. A broader sample of teachers from K-college would also elucidate some of the findings more clearly. Both Lisa and Alice were actively involved with personally meaningful writing projects and groups outside of school; studies of teachers less motivated to write would also be of interest.

FINDINGS

In my analysis, I identified three tensions similarly identified or enacted by Lisa and Alice in writing purposes, identities, and authority, pointing towards broad underlying complexities in the teaching of writing.

Tension: Purposes

Over the course of the fall semester, Alice engaged in a variety of personally meaningful writing tasks, including required academic projects (e.g., her special fields qualifying exam), additional academic projects (i.e., two journal submissions), and reflective writing (i.e., teaching notebooks, daily personal journal, and qualifying exams reflection). She pursued writing to advance knowledge in her field, complete her Ph.D. program requirements, strengthen her future job applications, and to be a better teacher. Alice discussed how difficult it initially was for her to maintain personal writing when she entered academia:

> I've kept a journal since kindergarten. But a lot of time, especially during my Masters and the last 2 years [during my doctoral program], it's been a place to kind of rant and make to-do lists....[Recently, I've been] trying to make writing in my journal an almost daily practice, and I've been trying to force myself not to make lists. I really like that. I feel like I'm back to meaningful journal writing.

Overall, however, there was a remarkable fluidity between her personal and professional writing, and Alice had extensive support to pursue personally meaningful writing. At different points during the semester, Alice had in-person meetings and conversations about writing with her advisor, supervisors, program peers, and academic writing group. She also capitalized on both her in-person and virtual relationships to gather materials (e.g., sample mentor texts and readings), collaborate on writing, and get feedback. To prepare for her fields exam, for example, she shared her questions and preparatory documents with her writing group, advisor, and mock exam group (composed of peers in the program); went to dinner with her fellow graduate students to "talk about questions over fried chicken"; and looked at documents prepared by former students where they described their exam preparations and experiences. Alice described to me a time when she read a fellow student's account of how "spending time at a bar talking to...[her partner] was helpful," and this conversation gave her the idea to talk about her exam responses with her own partner. When Alice completed her exam, she prepared a similar document for future students, called "Alice's Special Fields Process in Micro-Detail," in which she gave an overview of the five month timeline for her preparation, overall tips (e.g., "Decide on your exam date and time with your committee members as soon as you have finished your rationale and list. It may scare you to lock yourself in, but you will be grateful!"), and advice for creating a reading list and keeping track of what you read.

The default syllabus for the rhetoric course Alice taught asked students to engage in writing that is fairly similar to the writing graduate students practice. Throughout the semester, students were supposed to develop a personally meaningful research question and explore it. Alice, though, decided to use a different textbook and assignment sequence because during her first year teaching the course she thought her students struggled:

> [They are supposed to] know what they are passionate about and develop a research question about it, but sometimes as freshman you don't always know, which is fine. Sometimes it generated stuff...that was more report-like. I felt frustrated with my own ability to help them figure out research questions that were arguable, that were answering something new and different, that were asking questions they genuinely puzzled about. Some students did really well, but other students struggled a lot, and I just got frustrated with what was happening especially with the weaker students. Also, compared to other writing courses I'd heard about, I felt like we weren't reflecting very much, and we weren't talking about issues related to writing, like issues with Standard English and controversies like that...we weren't talking about the writing process. So I felt like all the cool stuff I was learning about in Writing Studies and was passionate about we weren't getting to that.

Like many content teachers, then, Alice thought that one purpose of her course should be to teach students about the major topics and controversies in her field. She additionally wanted to teach students how to do research and write effective arguments. Missing from her description of writing purposes for her students, though, was the pursuit of personally meaningful topics—the guiding force in her own writing.

Unlike Alice, Lisa primarily engaged in creative writing and her personally meaningful writing was neither sponsored nor rewarded by her institution (Brandt, 2001). Lisa's beliefs that writers write professionally, for specific purposes, and take steps to "do it well and do it right," led her to join a creative writing class. She located and paid for this class herself. She met weekly with her creative writing group or instructor, and intended to work towards a degree in creative writing at some point in the future. She pursued writing to tell truths about the world, to master particular skills, to "professionalize," and to be a better teacher. For example, when I asked her to describe how her interests in writing manifested at different points in her life, she said:

> I've always loved to tell stories to people. But really in high school and college I didn't consider studying writing professionally, it was more just that I loved to read, and I hoped that some day I could write stories as good as the stories I read. And then when I started teaching writing I realized that I had to become a better writer on my own.

When I asked Lisa about what she believed the purposes of reading and writing were overall, it became clear that she saw creative writing as an opportunity to explore truth. She said, "I mean, I think that's probably the biggest purpose for my own life that reading and writing takes is to help explore truths about the world...and the different ways that human nature can be pushed and explored." In fact, she recently began writing a novel after she saw a program on the Food Network about factories and wondered about the kind of person who would work at a factory job her entire life, saying "and so I'm writing to find the answer [to] that question, I guess." She also believed that her own writing needed a purpose:

> I think unless you have a genuine purpose behind it [writing]—like I would like to write because I want to get published, or I want to write for a friend of mine, or because I want to submit it for an award ceremony or something—I think that unless you have a really true purpose, I don't know that you're actually going to push yourself to learn to do it well and to do it right.

Lisa felt torn about whether traditional writing instruction with a focus on grammar, skill mastery, and structure (like she learned in school growing up) or process writing instruction with a focus on meaning-making and interaction (like she practiced in her writing group, and was advocated in her curriculum and professional development) was best for her students. She said:

> To be quite honest, I feel like I did learn a lot about writing growing up.... I often wonder if that [her traditional, skill-driven instruction] actually has led to better creative writing than if I'd written and written and written creative writing growing up without first learning the structures and mechanics...I feel like there needs to be more balance than there currently is- and that's coming from someone who loves creative writing...they've shifted so far in the opposite [direction], and I just feel like our kids are so far off the mark in so many ways when it comes to academic-type writing.

While Lisa clearly valued her own experiences writing fiction and interacting with colleagues, she was unsure about whether similar experiences best served her students. Her own writing was purpose-driven, explored the "pursuit of truth," and focused almost exclusively on realistic fiction. Her values for her students' writing were less clear, but included a desire to work on meaningful peer review, structure and mechanics with them, and to expose them to a variety of text types. These latter values, in many ways, reflect her grade-level state standards and standardized tests, particularly powerful guiding forces in writing instruction in many K-12 public schools serving primarily low-income students (McCarthey, 2008).

Tension: Identities

Although Alice was a confident writer who shared her own research interests and personal writing with her students, she was "constantly grappling with feelings of insecurity as a [writing] teacher." During her second year teaching Rhet 105, she wanted to develop a syllabus that capitalized on her expertise, and felt some freedom to do that. She said:

> I felt like all the cool stuff I was learning about in Writing Studies and was passionate about we weren't getting to that [in the syllabus required for first year Rhet teachers], there wasn't time for that. And I wanted to make more time for that. Sort of like I wanted to feel like more of an expert in my course. I had heard about the *Writing about Writing* idea, maybe in journal articles written by the editors, and saw the book at…[a] conference and ordered it, and decided that I was going to try it…. I am really glad I'm teaching this new textbook.

However, she frequently "stressed out" about the ways she taught the course (e.g., the assignments she selected, how she connected the readings and assignments). Alice thought that she was "over resourced" but had too little time to improve her teaching. Similarly, she felt pulls on her time to engage in research and to teach. She said:

> [Time] is so connected to identity as a grad student. I think of [a fellow graduate student], who always says that the students at a Research I institution, their problem is that their TAs have priorities other than teaching…I actually love doing course planning…and reading blogs about teaching and talking to other people and reflecting on my own teaching. I really value it and find it so rewarding. I really want to be a teacher-scholar, and for teaching to be as important as research, but it can so easily consume so much time that I feel like I'm falling behind.

This sentiment, which was expressed at multiple points over the course of the study, reflects the ways that Alice's institutional rewards (i.e., a job in academia) informed the ways she distributed her labor—at times focusing more on her own research and writing than her teaching, and making it somewhat difficult for her to consistently identify as a confident writing teacher. However, the high alignment between the subject matter she taught and her personal writing interests allowed her to frequently capitalize on her writing experiences in her instruction.

Unlike Alice, Lisa spoke much less about her personal insecurities as a teacher and time conflicts. Lisa's curricular materials and extensive professional development espoused a writer's workshop approach to writing instruction, encouraged her to engage in the writing process, and helped inform her identity as a confident writing teacher. In the three years before this study occurred, Lisa attended a week-long Summer Institute, participated in a year-long professional development group focused on advanced readers and writers, and attended multiple one-day workshops related to upcoming *Units of Study* genres as well as school-based lab-sites facilitated by a staff developer about how to best implement the curricula in her classroom. She even credited the curriculum and professional development for helping her learn to write, saying "I think through them [the professional development staff] always forcing us to go through the process, I think I have learned a lot about what I like and don't like about writing."

However, Lisa had a more difficult time than Alice consistently identifying herself as a writer. Although Lisa engaged extensively with creative writing and was able to clearly articulate her reasons for pursuing such writing, she said, "I'm pretty hesitant to call myself a writer. I call myself someone who is interested in writing. I'm someone who writes, but I think a writer is someone who like, publishes things…for the most part, I'd say I'm a teacher who also is working towards becoming a writer." In observations, Lisa frequently modeled writing for assigned tasks, but rarely discussed her own out-of-school writing with her students.

She did, however, make some important moves with students based on her own writing experiences that may have reinforced her writing identity—she frequently praised them for taking risks and being "brave" writers, encouraged them to make "significant" revisions and cuts, and spent time teaching them how to give peer feedback. For example, after giving a lesson on peer critique in their poetry unit, she said "This [peer critique] comes straight from understanding the value of getting feedback…We used to be like 'it's too hard' or 'it's too much work' [to engage students in peer critique], but you can't do this work [writing] by yourself." In an earlier interview, she confirmed that this focus originated with her own experiences writing, saying, "something new we've been doing this year that I really liked, is this idea of teaching students how to make thoughtful comments to each other about their stories. This came about from this summer when I was doing workshopping [of my own pieces] more and I was realizing just how valuable and important it is to have people make thoughtful comments on your paper." However, although she and some fellow teachers spent time at the beginning of the year modeling peer critique, it took place infrequently over the course of observation for this study. Instead, Lisa spent more time having one-on-one instructional conferences with students.

Tension: Authority

Both Alice and Lisa sometimes enacted complicated understandings of writing authority, as shown in the following interaction between Alice and her students. Alice was teaching a lesson on the differences between scholarly and popular publications and asked the class if anyone knew what peer review meant. Wade volunteered and said that peer review meant it was "reviewed by someone at the same level as you, like writing level." Alice agreed with him, and explained that academic writers, like professors, often had their writing reviewed by other professors with disciplinary expertise, whereas magazine and newspaper writers usually only had their writing edited by someone who works for the publication and may know very little about the topic. Then Alice told students that when reviewers for scholarly journals receive articles to review, the author's name and institution are not listed with it. Alice asked the students, "What is the purpose of it [a review] being blind and anonymous?" A boy in the class said that blind reviews can probably be more sincere and straightforward. Alice agreed, and said, "so you might be an expert, but your writing can still be crap."

On the board, Alice pulled up a revise and resubmit letter from a journal that she had just received yesterday and showed students the reviews. As she scrolled through the reviews she told students, "You can see that it's honest. The reviewers tell you the truth." She mentioned that out of the three reviews given, the first and third ones were pretty helpful, but the second one, which read, "*An excellent article, I really enjoyed the article and learned from it,*" was "really crap" because it was so short and generic. When Alice asked students if they had any questions about the peer review process, a girl asked her if she had ever done a peer review. Alice responded, yes: "My advisor asked me too. But it's kind of crazy because I'm just a graduate student, and I'm probably reviewing something for a professor."

In this instance, Alice simultaneously challenged the idea that experts automatically had writing authority and reinforced the notion that novices had less authority to review texts. While she knew to tell students that expertise was not synonymous with authority, she did not necessarily apply this advice to herself and confirmed to me later that she was not even aware that she presented a vacillating stance to her students. Such conflicted framing (i.e., We are all writers with authority. But not really.), however, may work against sincere efforts to engage students as writers.

Lisa similarly framed writing authority in complicated ways. In an early interview, when asked about her interests in writing, she said: "When I had to start teaching writing I realized, you know, that I had to become a better writer on my own. Which is when I [also] realized again how much I really love writing and love telling stories. And from there I guess that pushed me into learning how to actually write like an adult instead of just writing like a teacher." This dichotomy between "writing for teaching" and "writing for myself" was reinforced in her classroom, where she modeled writing for students based on the curriculum-specific genres, but did not share any of her personal fiction writing.

She did not tend to consider herself a writer because she saw writers as published, sometimes paid, professionals. When discussing why she joined a writing group, she said, "I realized that I really do want to try to do this professionally on a greater level was what led me to try to take it seriously enough to learn more about it and to push myself to really doing it. Because I think people say all the time 'oh, I would like to be a writer'." Part of taking writing seriously, for Lisa, involved intentionally practicing particular writing strategies, which sometimes crossed from her own writing to her teaching. For example, when discussing her own writing, she described how she was working on "cutting out entire giant sections of stories that I was in love with but realized either wasn't moving the story forward or I needed to take the story in a different direction." In a meeting with her own writing instructor, Will, they discussed a similar strategy of making her creative writing piece more subtle by "burying it" and removing sections of text that were too obvious. Informed by her own writing work, Lisa had her students make "radical revisions" to their historical fiction stories by cutting out entire characters or rewriting them from a different perspective. She said that making big revisions, especially before a project was due, "used to scare me, but now I think they [students] are better for it."

A few weeks after Lisa told me she did not consider herself to be a writer, I asked her what she thought about students as writers. She replied, "I think they can call themselves *student* writers. I'm not a big label believer, so you know, if they want to call themselves writers fine. *Some*times I do talk about myself and say I'm a writer because of this, that, and the other…It's one component of who I am, but it wouldn't be the one fixed title I would claim." Lisa drew distinctions between being a published writer (professionals), "just" writing like a teacher (doing your job), writing like an adult (real writing with purpose), and student writing (writing for school). The notion of writer, for her, was related to authority, publication, and purpose. As with Alice, although Lisa knew to tell students that expertise was not synonymous with authority (e.g., "if they want to call themselves writers fine"), she did not necessarily apply this advice to herself ("I'm pretty hesitant to call myself a writer"), and was not attuned to how her conflicted stance on writing authority might be read by her students

DISCUSSION AND IMPLICATIONS

Teachers, like students, have rich out-of-school literacy experiences. However, Alice and Lisa's cases highlight why we cannot make assumptions about the ways teachers' everyday literacy practices inform their writing instruction. Tensions must be considered in order to develop understandings about how to help teachers intentionally capitalize on their out-of-school practices to enrich and transform their writing instruction. Whitney (2009) writes that the ways "tensions are taken up, talked about, attended to, and remedied by teachers…can produce development that crosses both personal and professional domains" (p. 2387; see also Alsup, 2006). Although this study only focused on two cases, the consistencies across cases and with the literature indicate some warranted conclusions and implications about teacher writing and instruction. Most importantly, teacher educators and professional developers need to do more than provide opportunities for teachers to experience the writing process. We need to help teachers figure out how to draw from such experiences in their instruction. Specifically, we need to address complexities of teaching writing in school, such as the conflicting purposes of writing in- and out-of-school, and tensions in writing identities and authority.

Writing In-school vs. Out-of-school: Writing for What and for Whom?

One significant way that Alice and Lisa's literacy practices diverged from their students was in their purposes for writing. They were both highly motivated to write for varied purposes and audiences, but tended to align their students' writing assignments to their curricula. For students, this meant that their purposes and audiences were typically limited to their classroom spaces. In Lisa's case this conflict was manifested in the types of writing she did with students—she wrote alongside them related to her assignments, but did not share any of her personal writing with students. This seemed to create a dichotomy between school as a place for "artificial" writing to assignments, and out-of-school for "real" motivated writing on topics of choice. Although Alice *did* share her authentic peer review experiences for journal submissions, her students' subsequent peer reviews were similarly related to the class assignments, not writing on topics and with audiences of choice. For teacher educators and professional developers, implications include exploring choice, purpose, and audience in our own writing versus our students' writing, and to critically examine the types of writing we share with our students.

Further exploration of the alignment of personal writing practices to curricula, particularly across K-16 contexts and accounting for increasingly mandated curricula, is also needed. Although Alice had a high alignment between her writing and curriculum, as a college instructor she had more freedom to control her curriculum than Lisa. She also had more support than Lisa to pursue authentic, personally meaningful writing within her institutional context. For professional developers, in particular, challenges include regularly providing support for such ongoing opportunities for elementary and middle school teachers, and helping them incorporate their own writing experiences into their instruction when working with mandated curricula.

Teachers' Writing Identities: Who is Authorized to be a Writer?

These cases reinforce research on the complex identity work engaged in by writing teachers at a time when our understandings of writing and writers are rapidly changing (Cremin & Baker, 2010; McKinney & Giorgis, 2009; Thornton, 2010). Although narrow ideas about writing as formal work and writers as published authors, espoused by practitioners and researchers alike, are common, conceptions are evolving to include informal and digital writing because "in the 21st century people write as never before—in print and online" (Yancey, 2009, p. 1). Although we are expanding our ideas of writing, deeply rooted ideas remain about writing as an official task that only some people have the authority to undertake. In Lisa's case, this meant that she drew distinctions between writing like an adult, a teacher, a student, or a professional. In Alice's case, it meant that she did not feel authorized to engage in high stakes scholarly peer review. However, she did provide low-stakes opportunities for peer review in her own classroom. For teacher educators and professional developers, implications include further exploring teachers' writing identities, and how our writing identities position students and can support more effective instructional practices.

Transformation of Instructional Practices

These cases point to multiple tensions across teacher writers' trajectories of practices, and a focus on tension is a prerequisite for transforming instructional practices. Whitney (2009), drawing on the work of Kegan (2000) and Mezirow (1991), explained how "transformational learning can be looked at as a process of gaining agency or control over one's processes of interpretation" (p. 147). In teacher education and professional development ranging from the NWP to WAC seminars, explicit discussions about in-school versus out-of-school writing, what writing means and who writers are, as well as the ways our personal writing experiences diverge from our students', are warranted. As a field, we need to continue exploring how, particularly in a highly regulated era of standardization (McCarthey, 2008), we can provide opportunities for our students to experience the most transformative, impactful aspects of our own writing practices.

AUTHOR'S NOTE

Many thanks to the anonymous reviewers whose feedback helped me improve this paper. Thanks also to Lisa and Alice for their generous participation and thoughtful inquiry into the teaching of writing.

REFERENCES

Alsup, J. (2006). *Teacher identity discourses: Negotiating personal and professional spaces.* Mahwah, NJ: Lawrence Erlbaum and the National Council of Teachers of English.

Bakhtin, M. M. (1986). *Speech genres and other late essays.* Austin, TX: University of Texas Press.

Bissex, G. L., & Bullock, R. H. (Eds.). (1987). *Seeing for ourselves: Case-study research by teachers of writing* (1st ed.). Portsmouth, NH: Heinemann.

Bourdieu, P. (1977). *Outline of a theory of practice.* Cambridge, UK: Cambridge University Press.

Bourdieu, P. (1981). Men and machines: In K. Knorr-Cetina & A. V. Cicourel (Eds.), *Advances in social theory and methodology* (pp. 304-317). London: Routledge.

Brandt, D. (2001). *Literacy in American lives.* New York, NY: Cambridge University Press.

Britzman, D. P. (1991). *Practice makes practice: A critical study of learning to teach.* Albany: State University of New York Press.

Brooks, G. W. (2007). Teachers as readers and writers and as teachers of reading and writing. *The Journal of Educational Research*, 100, 177-191.

Calkins, L. M. (1994). *The Art of Teaching Writing*. Portsmouth, NH: Heinemann.

Calkins, L. M. (2006). *The units of study for teaching writing, grades 3-5*. Portsmouth, NH: Heinemann.

Cochran-Smith, M., & Lytle, S. L. (1993). *Inside/outside: Teacher research and knowledge*. New York, NY: Teachers College Press.

Cremin, T., & Baker, S. (2010). Exploring teacher-writer identities in the classroom: Conceptualising the struggle. *English Teaching: Practice and Critique*, 9, 8-24.

Dawson, C. (2011). *Inventing teacher-writers* (Doctoral dissertation, Michigan State University).

Dreier, O. (1999). Personal trajectories of participation across contexts of social practice. *Outlines*, 1, 5-32.

Dyson, A. H., & Genishi, C. (2005). *On the case: Approaches to language and literacy research*. New York: Teachers College Press.

Elbow, P. (1998). *Writing without teachers* (2nd ed.). Oxford University Press, USA.

Emig, J. (1971). *The composing processes of twelfth graders*. Urbana, IL: The National Council of Teachers of English.

Erikson, F. (1986). Qualitative methods in research on teaching. In M. Wittrock (Ed.) *Handbook of research on teaching* (3rd ed., pp. 119-161). New York, NY: Macmillan.

Finders, M. (1997). *Just girls: Hidden lives and literacies in junior high*. New York, NY: Teachers College Press.

Freire, P. (1970). *Pedagogy of the oppressed*. New York, NY: Continuum.

Gleeson, A., & Prain, V. (1996). Should teachers of writing write themselves? An Australian contribution to the debate. *English Journal*, 85, 42-49.

Heath, S. B. (1983). *Ways with words: Language, life, and work in communities and classrooms*. Cambridge: Cambridge University Press.

Hull, G. A., & Schultz, K. (2002). *School's out: Bridging out-of-school literacies with classroom practice*. New York, NY: Teachers College Press.

Hymes, D.H. (1972). On communicative competence. In J.B. Pride & J. Holmes (Eds.). *Sociolinguistics: Selected readings*. Harmondsworth: Penguin, 269-293.

Kegan, R. (2000). What "form" transforms? A constructive-developmental approach to transformative learning. In J. Mezirow (Ed.), *Learning as transformation: Critical perspectives on a theory in progress* (pp. 35-69). San Francisco: Jossey-Bass.

Kittle, P. (2008). *Write beside them: Risk, voice, and clarity in high school writing*. Portsmouth, NH: Heinemann.

Lankshear, C., & Knobel, M. (2006). *New literacies: Everyday practices and classroom learning*. New York, NY: McGraw-Hill Open University Press.

Lave, J., & Wenger, E. (1991). *Situated learning: Legitimate peripheral participation*. Cambridge, UK: Cambridge University Press.

McCarthey, S. (2008). The impact of No Child Left Behind on teachers' writing instruction. *Written Communication*, 25, 462-505.

McCarthey, S. J. (1997). Connecting home and school literacy practices in classrooms with diverse populations. *Journal of Literacy Research*, 29, 145-182.

McKinney, M., & Giorgis, C. (2009). Narrating and performing identity: Literacy specialists' writing identities. *Journal of Literacy Research*, 41, 104-149. doi:10.1080/10862960802637604

Mezirow, J. (1991). *Transformative dimensions of adult learning*. San Francisco: Jossey-Bass.

Moll, L. C., Amanti, C., Neff, D., & Gonzalez, N. (1992). Funds of knowledge for teaching: Using a qualitative approach to connect homes and classrooms. *Theory Into Practice*, 31, 132-141.

Murray, D. M. (1968). *A writer teaches writing: A practical method of teaching composition*. Houghton Mifflin.

National Commission on Writing for America's Families, Schools, and Colleges. (2003). *The neglected "R": The need for a writing revolution*. New York: College Board.

National Writing Project & Nagin, C. (2006). Because writing matters: Improving student writing in our schools. San Francisco, CA: Jossey-Bass.

Prior, P. (2008). *Flat CHAT? Reassembling literate activity*. Invited paper presented at the Writing Research Across Borders Conference. Santa Barbara, CA.

Robbins, B. W. (1990). *Teachers as writers: Relationships between English teachers' own writing and instruction.* (Doctoral dissertation, Indiana University).

Robbins, B. W. (1996). Teachers as writers: Tensions between theory and practice. *Journal of Teaching Writing*, 15, 107-128.

Scollon, R. (2001). *Mediated discourse: The nexus of practice.* London: Routledge.

Scribner, S., & Cole, M. (1981*). The psychology of literacy.* Cambridge, MA: Harvard University Press.

Spillane, J. P., & Miele, D. S. (2007). Evidence in practice: A framing of the terrain. In P. A. Moss (Ed.), *106th Yearbooks of the National Society for the Study of Education,* pp. 46-73.

Stolle, E. (2008). Teachers, literacy, & technology: Tensions, complexities, conceptualizations & practice. In Y. Kim, V. Risko, D. Compton, D. Dickinson, M. Hundley, R. Jimenez, K. Leander, & D. Wells Rowe (Eds.), *57th Yearbook of the National Reading Conference* (pp. 56–69). Oak Creek, WI: National Reading Conference.

Street, B. V. (1984). *Literacy in theory and practice.* Cambridge, UK: Cambridge University Press.

Street, B. (2000). Literacy events and literacy practices: Theory and practice in the New Literacy Studies. In M. Martin-Jones, & K. Jones (Eds.), *Multilingual Literacies: Comparative Perspectives on Research and Practice* (pp. 17-30). Philadelphia, PA: John Benjamin's.

Thornton, A. (2010). *Teachers' self-perception of their writing and their teaching of writing.* (Doctoral dissertation, Indiana University).

Wardle, E., & Down, D. (2011). *Writing about writing: A college reader.* Boston: Bedford/St. Martin's.

Wenger, E. (1998). *Communities of practice: Learning, meaning, and identity.* Cambridge: Cambridge University Press.

Wertsch, J. V. (1998). *Mind as action.* New York: Oxford University Press.

Whitney, A. (2006). *The transformative power of writing: Teachers writing in a National Writing Project Summer Institute.* (Doctoral dissertation, University of California, Santa Barbara).

Whitney, A. (2009). Writer, teacher, person: Tensions between personal and professional writing in a National Writing Project Summer Institute. *English Education,* 41, 24.

Yancey, K. B. (2009). *Writing in the 21st century: A report from the National Council of Teachers of English.* Urbana, IL: National Council of Teachers of English.

Yin, R. K. (2009*). Case study research: Design and methods, Applied Social Research Methods* (4th ed.). Thousand Oaks, CA: Sage Publications.